How has missile defense
survived as the
foreign policy of
successive Administrations?
Read on.

Merry Christmas!
Martha + Simeon
2000

Also by Frances FitzGerald

Cities on a Hill: A Journey Through Contemporary American Cultures

America Revised: History Schoolbooks in the Twentieth Century

Fire in the Lake: The Vietnamese and the Americans in Vietnam

WAY OUT

REAGAN, STAR WARS AND THE END OF THE COLD WAR

SIMON & SCHUSTER
NEW YORK LONDON TORONTO SYDNEY SINGAPORE

THERE IN THE BLUE

FRANCES FITZGERALD

SIMON & SCHUSTER
Rockefeller Center
1230 Avenue of the Americas
New York, NY 10020

Designed by Edith Fowler
Manufactured in the United States of America

10 9 8 7 6 5 4 3 2 1

Library of Congress Cataloging-in-Publication Data

FitzGerald, Frances, date.
Way out there in the blue : Reagan, Star Wars and the end of the Cold War / Frances FitzGerald.
p. cm.
Includes bibliographical references (p.) and index.
1. Reagan, Ronald. 2. United States—Politics and government—1981–1989. 3. United States—Foreign relations—1981–1989. 4. United States—Foreign relations—Soviet Union. 5. Soviet Union—Foreign relations—United States. 6. Strategic Defense Initiative. 7. Nuclear arms control—United States—History. 8. Cold War. I. Title.

E876.F58 2000
973.927'092—dc21 *99-059913*
ISBN 0-684-84416-8

To Jim

"Nobody dast blame this man. You don't understand: Willy was a salesman. And for a salesman there is no rock bottom to the life. He don't put a bolt to a nut, he don't tell you the law or give you medicine. He's a man way out there in the blue, riding on a smile and a shoeshine. And when they start not smiling back—that's an earthquake. And then you get yourself a couple of spots on your hat, and you're finished. Nobody dast blame this man. A salesman is got to dream, boy. It comes with the territory."

—From Arthur Miller's *Death of a Salesman*

Contents

WAY OUT THERE IN THE BLUE

Author's Note

THIS BOOK BEGAN with my interest in the appeal Reagan had for the American public and the direct connection he made to the national imagination. Demonstrably Reagan did much to restore the national morale even while the achievements of his administration seemed elusive to many. To study his rhetoric and political persona is to learn much about this country, and in particular about the myths, traditions and stories that sustain us and color our thinking about the world. Star Wars, or the promise of a space-shield to protect the country against destruction by Soviet nuclear missiles, seemed to me to be the place to begin since it was surely his greatest rhetorical triumph. What other President, after all, could persuade the country of something that did not, and could not for the forseeable future, exist?

Reagan was an unusual politician and a most unusual chief executive. In the "kiss and tell" books of the late 1980s and early 1990s former officials told stories about Reagan's ignorance of policy issues, his disengagement from the work of the government, his distance from other people and so forth. These books, coming on top of the revelations of the Iran-contra affair, led many Americans to conclude that Reagan was an aging simpleton with a few strongly held ideas. But this is not what those books say, nor is it a conclusion that can be drawn from his life and career. Reagan puzzled me for a long time. A number of his close associates described him as living in a world of rhetoric, performance and perceptions. But it was years before I understood the extent to which this was the case.

The book opens with a chapter about Reagan's success in tapping into the mother lode of the American civil religion, with its substrata in nineteenth-century American evangelical Protestantism. As Reagan demonstrated, the national mythology is no dull centrist amalgam but rather a sparkling collection of elements, which, if arrayed on a spectrum, could appeal to the political right, center or left. His range and suppleness as a politician came from his ability to move through that spectrum, combining and recombining the elements at will.

Still, the Star Wars phenomenon was clearly not just of his making, but a collective enterprise.

Reagan's 1983 Star Wars speech surprised everyone in his administration except for a few White House aides. His call for an initiative to make ballistic missiles "impotent and obsolete" was initially ridiculed in Washington and apparently dismissed. Two years later, however, the administration launched a major research program in anti-missile technologies, the Strategic Defense Initiative. In congressional hearings senior Defense Department officials, distinguished scientists and strategic policy analysts argued about laser weapons and boost-phase defenses as if these weapons were about to jump off the assembly line. Television news programs showed animated renderings of space-weaponry destroying the entire Soviet ICBM fleet. In Geneva, U.S. arms control negotiators called upon the Soviets to agree to the deployment of anti-missile defenses and to the radical reduction, and eventual elimination, of nuclear arms.

How could this happen? How did Reagan's unworldly idea get through the gauntlet of technical experts in the Pentagon, the administration and Congress? What did administration officials hope to achieve in the arms talks? And what of the Soviet reaction? Was it true, as some said, that the idea of Star Wars frightened the Soviets into ending the Cold War?

How the rhetoric of Star Wars came into being and how it played out in Washington and in U.S.–Soviet negotiations as the Cold War came to an end is the main subject of this book. The quest for anti-missile weapons, however, continued after Reagan left office, and because in 1999 both the Clinton administration and Congress resolved to deploy a national missile defense system, I bring the quest up to date in an afterword.

Americans have always been skeptical of politicians and experts, but during the Cold War they trusted their government with national life and death. When it came to the Soviet Union, nuclear weapons and the balance of terror, they assumed their officials knew what they were doing and told them the truth. Yet to look back over the public record of the late 1970s and 1980s is to be struck by how little of what was said about these subjects had anything to do with reality. It is to enter a world of phantoms and mirages.

Reagan and his foreign policy advisers came into office on a wave of hyperbole about the Soviet threat designed to rally the American public to support a major military build-up. A number of Reagan's advisers belonged to an ideological faction whose views had not been substantially represented in Washington since the 1950s. Like their counterparts in the domestic arena who proudly proclaimed that they had come to create a "revolution" in government, they were radicals, in the sense of going back to the roots, and their ambitions were high. Like their forebears in the Eisenhower years, they wanted to roll back the Soviet empire and win the Cold War. When they came into office, they conditioned their public statements, and often the official estimates, in regard to Soviet intentions and capabilities upon these ambitions. Essentially they were not much interested in the ins and outs of what was happening in Moscow.

By 1983 the newly empowered enthusiasts—dominant in the administration—had managed to upset the elaborate system of conventions developed over two decades by the U.S., its NATO allies and the Soviet Union. The conventions on arms control were never well understood by the public because they involved a set of abstractions and conditionals which few but the experts could keep any account of, and because they did not stop the arms race but permitted both sides to develop prodigious numbers of nuclear weapons and preposterous strategies to go with them. Reagan was at one with the public on this score. The conventions nonetheless served to allay tensions and keep the risk of a nuclear war at bay. In flouting them the enthusiasts managed to create the worst period of friction in U.S.–Soviet relations since the Cuban missile crisis of 1962.

The public reaction to this friction permitted those within the administration who believed in reinstating the conventions to come to the fore. The "pragmatists" were, however, in the minority, and for most of the years of the two Reagan administrations U.S. policies toward the Soviet Union reflected results of every skirmish in the long and inconclusive struggle between the two camps. Both sides claimed Reagan as their own, but he never decided between them. In fact the president played almost no role in working out the policies of his administration.

When the SDI program got underway, discourse about strategic issues lifted off from reality altogether.

Behind Reagan and his "dream" of a shield against missiles and a non-nuclear world, the two warring factions within the administration pursued separate and contradictory agendas and fought for control over policy. With both sides vowing allegiance to the "dream," the battles within the administration became a shadow play in which maneuvers were hidden under layers of official deception and deceit. Washington journalists had great difficulty identifying the goals on each side, much less totting up the gains and the losses. In the U.S.–Soviet negotiations the administration's positions were rarely what they seemed, and from time to time, the levels of deception went so deep that even the most astute defense experts in Congress failed to penetrate them. At the Reykjavik summit, for example, Reagan and Gorbachev seemed to be gambling with their entire arsenals of nuclear arms.

Meanwhile Gorbachev launched a political revolution in the Soviet Union. Few in Washington understood what he was doing or where he was going, and the Cold War was over long before the American foreign policy establishment knew it.

To study this period is to reflect upon the extent to which our national discourse about foreign and defense policy is not about reality—or the best intelligence estimates about it—but instead a matter of domestic politics, history and mythology.

CHAPTER ONE

The American Everyman

On March 23, 1983, President Reagan announced that after consultations with the Joint Chiefs of Staff he had decided to embark on a long-range research-and-development effort to counter the threat of Soviet ballistic missiles and to make these nuclear weapons "impotent and obsolete." The announcement, made in an insert into a routine defense speech, came as a surprise to everyone in Washington except for a handful of White House aides. The insert had not been cleared with the Pentagon, and although Reagan was proposing to overturn the doctrine which had ruled U.S. nuclear strategy for more than three decades, the secretary of defense and the secretary of state were informed only a day or so before the speech was broadcast.

In background briefings White House aides explained that the research effort would be directed towards producing space-borne laser and particle-beam weapons with the potential to provide a reliable defense for the entire United States. Most of the scientists and defense experts invited to the White House for dinner that evening expressed incredulity: the technologies were so futuristic they would not be ready for decades, if then, and the cost of an all-out development effort would be staggering. Some further objected that any effort to develop an anti-ballistic missile capability would lead to a new and more dangerous form of arms race with the Soviet Union.

Reagan's proposal was so vague and so speculative that it was not taken altogether seriously at the time. Press attention soon shifted away from it and did not fully return until March 1985, when the administration launched the Strategic Defense Initiative with fanfare and asked the Congress to appropriate twenty-six billion dollars for it over the next five years.

At this point the debate over anti-missile defenses began in earnest, and journalists for the first time inquired about the origins of the proposal that Reagan had made so abruptly two years before. The President maintained that the idea was his to begin with, but said nothing more about it. However,

Martin Anderson, an economist at the Hoover Institution and a former Reagan aide for domestic policy, told journalists that the idea had first come to Reagan during a visit to the North American Aerospace Defense Command (NORAD) that he had made at the beginning of his presidential campaign in July 1979. In his book *Revolution,* published in 1988, Anderson described that visit at some length. His account subsequently became embedded in the history of the Strategic Defense Initiative. Journalists, academics and official SDI historians have all quoted it in more or less detail—and small wonder, for it is a marvelous story. To paraphrase Anderson's text, it is this:

On July 31, 1979, Anderson accompanied Reagan from Los Angeles to the NORAD base in Cheyenne Mountain, Colorado. The visit had been arranged by a Hollywood screenwriter and producer, Douglas Morrow, whom Reagan had known for some years, and Morrow came along on the trip. NORAD, Anderson explains, "is the nerve center of a far-flung, world-wide network of radar detectors that alerts us to any surprise attack." Its computers, he writes, would track a Soviet missile from its launch pad and give the President the facts he would have to rely on in deciding whether to launch a retaliatory strike. As for the command post, it is "a vast underground city, a multi-level maze of rooms and corridors carved deep into the solid granite core of Cheyenne Mountain," with "a massive steel door several feet thick." Once inside these portals, the visitors spent most of the day in a series of windowless conference rooms listening to briefings on the nuclear capabilities of the U.S. and the Soviet Union and on the means for detecting a nuclear attack. Towards the end of the day they were ushered into the command center, "a very large room several stories high," which looked "just like such command centers do in the movies." A huge display screen with an outline map of the United States covered one end of the room, and in front of it, facing video display screens with dozens of switches and lights, were "the young men and women who constantly monitor these displays for the first sign of a nuclear attack." Later the visitors talked with the base commander, General James Hill, and the discussion turned to the issue of what could be done if the Soviets fired just one missile at an American city. Hill replied that they could track the missile but that nothing could be done to stop it.

On the flight home to Los Angeles, Reagan, according to Anderson, seemed deeply concerned about what he had heard. "He couldn't believe the United States had no defense against Soviet missiles. He slowly shook his head and said, 'We have spent all that money and have all that equipment, and there is nothing we can do to prevent a nuclear missile from hitting us.' " Towards the end of the flight he reflected on the terrible dilemma that would face a U.S. president if, for whatever reason, nuclear missiles were fired at the United States and concluded, "We should have some way of defending ourselves against nuclear missiles."

Anderson then reminded Reagan of "the ABM debate that occurred early in President Nixon's first term of office, of how we pursued the idea of missile defense and then, inexplicably, abandoned it." He suggested that they look at "what technological advances had developed" and reexamine the idea. Reagan agreed, and a few days later Anderson, with the permission of the campaign manager, John Sears, wrote a memo on the broad issues of defense and foreign policy. In it he included a section proposing the development of a "protective missile system," arguing that "the idea is probably fundamentally far more appealing to the American people than the questionable satisfaction of knowing that those who initiated an attack against us were also blown away," and that "there have apparently been striking advances in missile technology during the past decade or so that would make such a system technically possible."

According to Anderson, Reagan embraced the idea wholeheartedly, and so did a number of his key campaign advisers. However, Reagan's political advisers vetoed the proposal on the grounds that "there was no way Reagan could discuss radical changes in traditional nuclear weapons policy without leaving himself wide open to demagogic attacks from his Democratic opponent." The idea was then shelved, but, as Anderson tells us, only temporarily.[1]

This story of Reagan's epiphany on Cheyenne Mountain is perfectly good history: General James Hill has confirmed the basic facts, and Reagan himself referred to his NORAD visit in an interview six months later when talking about the need for a defense against nuclear missiles. At the same time it must be regarded as something more than history. There is, after all, a high narrative gloss to the story, and in confirming it General Hill suggested that it had been somewhat dramatized.[2] Though life may well have been imitating art, the story sounds very much like the allegorical stories Reagan habitually told to illustrate the meaning and moral of an action. Because it first appeared in public long after Reagan's 1983 speech, it has always been understood in light of that speech, and as a reflection upon his exhortation to the scientific community to make "nuclear weapons impotent and obsolete." In a sense it is a myth of origins.

Of course, looked at in a certain way, the story is pure comedy. To read it literally, Reagan did not understand that the U.S. relied on deterrence until eighteen months before becoming President of the United States. Taken to NORAD by a Hollywood screenwriter, he discovered to his amazement that ballistic missiles could not be stopped in mid-flight. While in the grip of this revelation, he was told by an economist from the Hoover Institution—and one of the architects of Reaganomics—that there might be a way to stop them. Then the economist, who apparently did not know why Nixon and his successors failed to pursue the idea of missile defenses, went off and wrote a memo proposing that the candidate call for a change in the entire strategic posture of the United States. Reagan was thrilled, and had it not been for his political advisers, he might have gone along with the idea—and possibly lost the election.

Though the story would seem to show that a supply-side economist was the brains behind SDI, there is another possible author of SDI in the story: the Hollywood screenwriter, whom Anderson inexplicably abandons as a character early on in the narrative. Could the screenwriter have orchestrated the whole drama of Reagan's conversion and suggested the solution without Anderson's actually knowing it? Doubtless not. All the same, his presence in the narrative, and Anderson's observation that the NORAD command center looked like a movie set, seemed to lend credence to the theory held by a number of journalists and academics that Reagan took his missile-defense idea from a science-fiction film.

When Reagan announced his initiative in March 1983, the project was immediately dubbed "Star Wars" in the press. The title was a reflection not merely on the improbability of making nuclear missiles "impotent and obsolete," but on the fact that Reagan in a speech just two weeks before had spoken of the Soviet Union as "the evil empire," and commentators were still joking about "the Darth Vader speech." Yet those who later maintained that Reagan took his inspiration for SDI from the movies were not joking at all.

In the mid-eighties Dr. Michael Rogin, a political scientist at the University of California at Berkeley, published a series of scholarly papers making a case that Reagan's thinking was profoundly influenced by the movies he had starred in. The thesis seemed plausible to journalists covering Reagan, for by then many of them had noticed that Reagan took some of his best material from the screen. For one thing, he had a habit of quoting lines from the movies without attribution. For example, his famous retort to George Bush during the primary debate in Nashua, New Hampshire, "I'm paying for this microphone," came from a film called *State of the Union.* For another thing, he sometimes described movie scenes as if they had happened in real life. Speaking to the Congressional Medal of Honor Society in December 1983, he told a World War II story of a B-17 captain whose plane had been hit and who was unable to drag his wounded young ball-turret gunner out of the turret; instead of parachuting to safety with the rest of the crew, the captain took the frightened boy's hand and said, "Never mind, son, we'll ride it down together." Reagan concluded by telling the society that the captain had been posthumously awarded the Medal of Honor. But no such person existed: the story came from the 1946 movie *A Wing and a Prayer.*[3] Within a month of this event Reagan told the Israeli Prime Minister Yitzhak Shamir that the roots of his concern for Israel could be traced back to World War II, when he, as a Signal Corps photographer, had filmed the horrors of the Nazi death camps. Reagan, however, did not leave California during World War II; he had apparently seen a documentary about the camps.[4]

While screening some of Reagan's own films one day, Dr. Rogin came across a 1940 Warner Brothers spy movie called *Murder in the Air* in which Reagan had played an American secret agent charged with protecting a newly invented superweapon, the "Inertia Projector," capable of paralyzing electrical currents and destroying all enemy planes in the air. In the film a Navy admiral claims that the weapon "not only makes the United States invincible in war, but, in doing so, promises to become the greatest force for world peace ever discovered."[5] Rogin thought it obvious that this film had influenced Reagan's thinking about missile defenses. But there was another candidate: Alfred Hitchcock's *Torn Curtain,* a 1966 film which revolves around an attempt to develop an anti-missile missile. In it an American agent played by Paul Newman declares, "We will produce a defensive weapon that will make all nuclear weapons obsolete, and thereby abolish the terror of nuclear warfare." Reagan's own aides were struck by the similarity of the language to that of Reagan's speech.[6]

Historians of SDI have referred to these films as possible sources of Reagan's inspiration. Yet in retelling the Anderson story they pass over the movie references in it, and they pay small attention to the role of Anderson himself. The story as they tell it focuses on Reagan's epiphany about ballistic missiles and his resolve to end the existential tragedy of the balance of terror. This is, of course, the dramatic centerpiece of Anderson's narrative, and, read with or without irony, it is a great story in itself. It is in fact the perfect complement to the SDI speech, and to read it without irony, as most SDI historians have, is to see that it has a very rich symbolic content. But, then, the same is certainly true of the speech.

A year or so after Dr. Rogin discovered "the Inertia Projector," Professor G. Simon Harak of Fairfield University in Connecticut examined the SDI speech from a theological point of view. In an article published in the *Journal of the American Academy of Religion,* he asked why it was that Americans had become so enthralled with Reagan's vision of SDI in spite of all the evidence that a perfect defensive shield was currently beyond the reach of science. The answer, he maintained, lay in the way in which Reagan had laid claim to the soteriology, or the salvation doctrine, of the American civil religion.

In his speech Reagan had said, "I call upon the scientific community in our country, those who gave us nuclear weapons, to turn their great talents now to the cause of mankind and world peace, to give us the means of rendering these nuclear weapons impotent and obsolete." With this sentence, Harak writes, Reagan assumed the role of a prophet: he implicitly reproved the scientists for creating the Bomb in the first place and called upon them to redo their work. In reproving them thus he seemed to be identifying them—as they sometimes did themselves—with the "smiths" of mythology. Not only in the Norse myths but in other mythological traditions the "smiths" were at once feared and venerated because of their mastery over fire and metal; further, they were often portrayed as having their own agenda—as opposed to the master plan of the gods—and in a very human fashion creating mischief, or loosing disorder upon the world. Thus, in calling upon the "smiths" to redo their work, Reagan was asking for an act of redemptive reconstruction: the scientists were to restore the time of harmony and innocence before they had interfered with the God-given order of the world.

In the American context, Harak continues, the "smiths" are not just being asked to make up for their mischief in creating the Bomb; they are being asked to restore America to the time before it became vulnerable to nuclear annihilation: the time before the Bomb. In the American civil religion, he writes, America is seen as "the virgin land," protected by two oceans and innocent of the corruptions of the Old World; it is also seen as a nation guided by divine Providence with the mission of bringing light to the world. That foreigners had the ability to attack America from the skies was in itself a pollution of this Eden. By calling for a defense that would make nuclear weapons "impotent and obsolete," Reagan was, Harak writes, holding out the promise that America might once again become an invulnerable sanctuary, its sacred soil inviolate, as it was in the mythic past; then the nation, unsullied, could once again undertake its divinely ordained mission to the world. "My fellow Americans," Reagan said in peroration, "tonight we are launching an effort which holds the promise of changing the course of human history."[7]

Harak's analysis may seem a bit farfetched, drawn as it is from two sentences in the SDI speech. Yet Reagan later spoke quite often of his desire to create a "space shield" or a "roof" over the United States, and his speeches were often filled with the rhetoric of American exceptionalism. As President he repeatedly affirmed that a "divine plan" put the American continent between two oceans, where people who "had a special love of freedom" could come and create "something new in the history of mankind." Americans were God's chosen people, and, according to Reagan, they had a purpose. Celebrating the anniversary of the Constitution in 1987, Reagan said: "The guiding hand of providence did not create this new nation of America for ourselves alone, but for a higher cause: the preservation and extension of the sacred fire of human liberty. This is America's solemn duty."

The nation, Reagan insisted, had to be a model to mankind, "a beacon of hope, a shining city," with "a creed, a cause, a vision." On dozens of occasions Reagan concluded speeches with John Winthrop's image of the country as a "city on a hill" (or a "shining city," as Reagan preferred it) and with Tom Paine's words, "We have it within our power to begin the world all over again." But Reagan, unlike Paine, was not calling for something new under the sun; rather, he was asking for a "spiritual revival" or a "moral renewal" or a "rebuilding" of America, "the land of our dreams and mankind's great hope." Our need, he declared in his 1981 inaugural address, was "to renew ourselves here in our own land" so that we would again "be the exemplar of freedom and a beacon of hope for those who do not now have freedom." This was much the same message Harak drew from the SDI speech: at once nostalgic and forward-looking, at once isolationist and internationalist.[8]

Of course, many of those who listened to Reagan's patriotic pieties did not actually hear them, so perfectly liturgical were they. American exceptionalism had Puritan roots—in the conception of the country as a covenanted New Israel—but it was in its complete form a secularized, or, rather, a deicized version of nineteenth-century Protestant beliefs about spiritual rebirth, reform and evangelism. Since the mid-nineteenth century these pieties had been a staple of American civic rhetoric, not only in the political arena but in every setting where patriotism might be invoked. The admiral in *Murder in the Air* and the American agent played by Paul Newman in *Torn Curtain* delivered the message of American exceptionalism as well as any Rotary Club chairman in speaking of the purpose of their superweapons. Yet in the 1960s and '70s there had been some faltering in the incantation of this national mythology. American exceptionalism was challenged from the left, and, in the wake of the Vietnam debacle, domestic unrest and Watergate, Presidents Nixon and Ford found it difficult to use the rhetoric in any convincing fashion. Henry Kissinger did not believe in it, and Jimmy Carter, possibly because he was a devout Southern Baptist, tended to speak of what required redemption and renewal rather than of renewal, period. By the late 1970s many Americans seemed actively to crave such rhetoric—a surge in the membership of conservative evangelical churches was one evidence of this—and Reagan, who had never stopped speaking of American goodness, gave it to them like a diligent pastor. For the country Reagan's rhetoric was a ceremony that recalled the golden age of economic prosperity and military success before Vietnam, Watergate, civil disturbances, the oil shock, the hostage crisis and other disorders.

Though some associated him only with Hollywood, Reagan was in fact supremely well equipped to preach this national revival. His mother, Nelle, became a convert to born-again Christianity at the turn of the century, and until he left college he was thoroughly immersed in his mother's evangelical church. In later life he was far from a consistent churchgoer, but that in a sense was an advantage: the civil religion cannot be confused with any particular religion or it ceases to be national, and, as Jimmy Carter discovered to his dismay, it does not include all aspects of the Christian message in secular form. Yet it includes more than one, and Reagan had a range of expression quite exceptional among politicians of the 1980s.

In all the levity about Star Wars that followed a speech he gave on March 8, 1983, when he called the Soviet Union the "evil empire," it was generally forgotten that Reagan was talking to the National Association of Evangelicals, and that, as the clergymen understood him, he was speaking about *evil.* This was not the first time he had applied the word to the Soviet Union. In a speech at West Point in May 1981, for example, he had referred to the assembled cadets as a "chain holding back an evil force."[9] Yet the phrase "evil empire" had a much more precise theological significance. To conservative evangelicals, such as those in his audience, the phrase would trip-wire the whole eschatology of Armageddon. According to fundamentalist doctrine, derived from the Book of Ezekiel, the Book of Revelations and other sources, the evil empire will appear in the end-times under the leadership of the Anti-Christ; after a seven-year period of tribulations, Christ and his saints will fight the evil empire and confederated nations in a great battle on the field of Armageddon in Israel, and their victory will usher in the thousand-year reign of Christ on earth. The evangelical clergymen would not have been surprised that Reagan identified the Soviet Union as that empire, for ever since the Bolshevik revolution, fundamentalists had identified Russia as the Biblical "Ros," where the Beast would appear.[10]

To look at the Anderson story about Reagan on Cheyenne Mountain in the light of Harak's analysis of the SDI speech is to see a story that resonates with Biblical and mythological overtones. In that story Reagan can be seen as the innocent, the American Everyman who on the eve of his election must undergo initiation into the terrible secrets of power. Led into the "granite core" of a mountain—into the innermost sanctum of esoteric knowledge—he looks for the first time upon the horror that scientists and their masters have created for the country and for humankind. But then, rather than to accept initiation into the guardianship of this horror, as his predecessors have done, Reagan cuts through the arcane and dangerous knowledge with pure common sense and vows to deliver his people from impending doom. Anderson, his guide—his guardian angel or his Merlin—then shows him the road he must travel.

The Anderson story—or perhaps it is the Reagan story in that Reagan performed it for him—recalls a host of other stories, including some of the most powerful ones in the culture. It recalls, for example, "The Emperor's New Clothes," in which the adults are so blinded by deference to authority and their own hypocrisy that only the child, the innocent, can see the truth. The NORAD command center in the core of the mountain recalls the caves of the Nibelungen in Wagner's *Ring* and the caves of Norse mythology, where the dwarves, the "smiths," forge magical weapons: swords and spears which can never be broken and never miss their mark. In this setting the story is clearly that of the birth of the hero, or the moment when the pure youth receives his mission and sets forth on the difficult and dangerous quest. Here Reagan becomes Siegfried setting out to end the reign of the mischief-making dwarves and to restore the gods to their rightful place, bringing order once again to the world. Then, too, the story recalls a number of Biblical narratives about prophetic epiphanies and the banishment of scholastics and apostates, among them the story of Moses going up on a mountain to receive the tablets and descending to destroy the golden idol. It recalls Jesus's simple response when the Scribes and the Pharisees spoke to him of tradition; and it suggests the story of the temptation of Christ, in which the devil takes Jesus up on a mountain and offers him all the kingdoms of the world in return for the acknowledgment of his authority.

Of all these stories, the New Testament narratives may be the most relevant, in that they have some very specific reverberations in the American tradition.

At least until the twentieth century, most American Protestants, from the Puritans on down, saw the Roman Catholic church as a vast, sinister institution, whose rites were conducted in an arcane language and whose priestly hierarchy interposed papal authority and scholastic tradition between the believer and his God. Identifying themselves with the early Christians, they called for the restoration of a simple, democratic church, whose sole authority was the Biblical word of God, and whose Scriptures were an open book, available to all. Evangelical Protestantism, which sprang out of the Second Great Awakening of the 1820s and '30s, went a good deal further than Calvinism down this egalitarian, anti-institutional and anti-intellectual track. For evangelicals the emphasis was—and is—on the direct experience of Christ rather than on knowledge of doctrine or ritual practice, and on the individual rather than on the body of the church. Whether the evolution of American democracy in the nineteenth century created this particular form of Protestantism or vice versa, the same basic attitudes existed in the popular political movements of the period. The Populists, to pick just one example, tended to regard the financial centers of the Eastern Seaboard in much the same way that evangelicals regarded the Roman Catholic church. In secular as well as sacred contexts the primary conflict of American society was understood to be that of Christ versus the Scribes and the Pharisees, the pure and the innocent versus the worldly and corrupt, the plain people versus the cosmopolitan elite with its esoteric knowledge. Of course, by the early twentieth century urbanites regarded the Populists and fundamentalist evangelicals—the two united in the person of William Jennings Bryan—as provincial and backward-looking, as people left behind by the complex transactions of an industrializing society. Yet these "provincials" stood for the virtues still generally thought to be most quintessentially American: anti-elitism, distrust of the experts, a belief in democratic values, in plain speaking and common sense. It was they who created the American Everyman—or the part Reagan played in the Anderson story.

What all of this suggests is that the Martin Anderson story could stand as a synecdoche not merely for the appeal of SDI but for the appeal of Reagan himself. Certainly it is difficult to think of another politician who could have fit the role assigned to him so well. Anderson, an ardent supporter, spoke of Reagan as clear-sighted and steadfast—as a leader who could cut through the thickets of conventional wisdom with a simple truth. Tip O'Neill, the Speaker of the House and Reagan's favorite antagonist, saw him, by contrast, as stubborn, simple-minded and ignorant of the world. Yet the difference between the two perspectives was merely the difference between the two paradigmatic views of American populism. Supporters and critics alike would agree on the character he projected, both as an actor and as a president. In his fine book on the Reagan presidency, Lou Cannon, the journalist who knew Reagan the best, described it thus:

> Reagan was Illinois come to California. He was the wholesome citizen-hero who inhabits our democratic imaginations, an Everyman who was slow to anger but willing to fight for the right and correct wrongdoing when aroused. It was a role in a movie—personified by Reagan's friend Jimmy Stewart in *Mr. Smith Goes to Washington*—in which homespun American virtue prevails over the wily and devious "special interests" that rule that nation's capital.[11]

Throughout his political career, Reagan presented himself as a citizen-politician: an amateur who ran for office to restore common sense and common decency to a government which had grown too big, too complex and too far removed from the concerns of average Americans. There was always a populist and anti-intellectual theme to his rhetoric. The solution to the crime problem, he once said, "will not be found in the social worker's files, the psychiatrist's notes or the bureaucrat's budget. It is a problem of the human heart. . . ."[12] And, as Cannon writes, Reagan evoked the image of Cincinnatus, the Roman general who left his farm to lead the besieged armies of his nation to victory and then returned to the plow.

Of course, as Tip O'Neill might have pointed out, Reagan and the role he played were not always the same thing. This "Mr. Smith" had, after all, spent half of his working life as an actor-celebrity and the other half as a professional politician. This "populist" often suggested that, with all the employment ads he saw in the newspapers, there was no reason for anyone to be unemployed or poor. This "Cincinnatus" did not go home for twenty-two years after first taking office, and when he did, it was not to a farm but to a three-million-dollar house in Bel Air. But, then, the Anderson story had a certain theatrical quality to it.

The drama of the story resides in the notion that Reagan had never actually contemplated the fact of American vulnerability to nuclear weapons before his visit to Cheyenne Mountain. This was plausible enough. Both those who saw him as Mr. Smith and those who thought of him as a bubble-headed actor could imagine that he never really had grasped this fact of life before. In actuality Reagan had been preaching the horrors of deterrence for some years before he visited the NORAD base. Addressing the Republican National Convention in 1976, he told the delegates: "We live in a world in which the great powers have poised and aimed at each other horrible missiles of destruction, that can, in a matter of minutes, arrive in each other's country and destroy virtually the civilized world we live in."[13]

During his 1976 campaign for the Republican nomination Reagan often made the point that nuclear deterrence was like "two men pointing cocked and loaded pistols at each other's heads." Then, in a 1978 radio broadcast, he said, "If the Soviets push the button, there is no defense against them, no way to prevent the nuclear destruction of their targets in the United States."[14]

Even Mr. Smith could not have forgotten so basic a truth from one year to the next, and Reagan had, as it happened, a very good memory for the anecdotes and striking phrases that he himself had used before. Therefore, either Reagan reenacted the drama of his epiphany for Anderson, or Anderson, who certainly knew what Reagan felt about deterrence, used a bit more poetic license than historians generally consider legitimate.

Remarkably, however, the SDI historians who retell the story do not, with one exception, comment upon this piece of theatrics, even though several of them, including Anderson himself, also quote Reagan's previous remarks about the threat of nuclear weapons. But, then, no one ever took Reagan to task for being a professional politician rather than the amateur he played.

The explanation surely has to do with the power of a good story and the power of Reagan as an actor-narrator. Reagan was a simple person in the sense that he believed in simple ideas ("There are simple answers, just not easy ones," he liked to say), but he was not simple in the sense of being transparent. Reagan was not Mr. Smith. Yet he played Mr. Smith rather better than a real Mr. Smith might have played himself in front of cameras and a national audience. "Be yourself" is after all a command that only actors can respond to—and they do it by impersonating themselves. As Laurence Olivier has said, the art of mimesis consists in seizing upon certain recognizable characteristics and exaggerating them slightly, as opposed to copying all the overtones and subtle shadings that actually exist in life. Truth to an audience lies in some slight degree of caricature.[15]

All actors and all stories leave something to the imagination and lend themselves to more than one interpretation. In the Anderson story Reagan was playing a scene, not explaining precisely what was going through his mind. Left to the imagination is how Reagan conceived of a defense against nuclear missiles in July 1979. In light of the SDI speech, the account of Reagan's epiphany with all of its mythical and Biblical overtones would seem to suggest that Reagan always thought of an ABM defense as a way to rid the world of the threat of nuclear weapons. Yet this cannot be established as a fact from the story, nor can it be established from Reagan's speeches attacking deterrence. When Reagan compared the U.S. and the Soviet Union to two men with pistols pointed at each other's heads, he never proffered an alternative. In an ideal world, would both men be disarmed—or only one of them? Reagan's conservative supporters thought they knew what the answer was. Certainly they never thought of Reagan as a nuclear abolitionist or a closet one-worlder. Indeed, when during his second term as president he proposed the elimination of all nuclear weapons and embraced Gorbachev in Moscow, they claimed that he had changed, that he had abandoned all of his old principles. Possibly they were right, for Reagan did assume different roles. He did not always play Mr. Smith, the part was scripted for him when he began his political career in the 1966 campaign for the governorship of California. Before that he played a somewhat different character.

In 1954, with his movie career almost at an end, Reagan signed on with General Electric to be the host of a GE-sponsored television series and to make appearances around the country on behalf of the company. He stayed with the job for eight years. For the first couple of years, he spoke at GE plants, entertaining workers with stories of his experiences in Hollywood. Proving a popular speaker, he was sent out to Chambers of Commerce and other civic groups, and as time went on, his speeches grew more substantive. They also grew more and more right-wing. By the late fifties, he was denouncing all the New Deal measures still extant, from rural electrification to Social Security, and warning of the imminent demise of the free-market system. The Eisenhower administrations were hardly unfriendly to business, and yet Reagan grew more and more alarmist about the threat of creeping socialism. He took to calling the graduated income tax "this progressive system spawned by Karl Marx and declared by him to be the prime essential of a socialist state."[16] In his 1965 memoir Reagan explained that his speeches "underwent a kind of evolution, reflecting not only my changing philosophy but also the swiftly rising tide of collectivism that threatens to inundate what remains of our free economy."[17]

At the time, Reagan was not generally thought of as an expert on the political economy, so to give authority to his argument he studded his speeches with statistics and scraps of information gleaned from newspapers, right-wing periodicals, conversations and fan mail. According to Reagan, the Federal Power Commission once handed natural-gas producers a 428-page questionnaire that would require seventy thousand accountant man-hours to fill out; U.S. foreign aid paid for the construction of a model stock farm in Lebanon with nine stalls for each bull; a Washington bureaucrat, whose job was to initial documents and pass them on to the proper agency, once initialed a document he wasn't supposed to have read and twenty-four hours later was made to erase the initials and initial the erasure.[18] When Reagan spoke about Communism, he would begin by describing his efforts to defeat a vast Communist conspiracy to take over Hollywood when he was on the board of the Screen Actors Guild in the late forties. With his credentials thus established, he would go on to speak in apocalyptic terms about the global Communist threat. Addressing the Phoenix Chamber of Commerce in 1961, Reagan declared, "Wars end in victory or defeat. One of the foremost authorities on communism in the world today has said we have ten years. Not ten years to make up our minds, but ten years to win or lose—by 1970 the world will be all slave or all free."[19]

The version of the standard speech he included in his 1965 memoir is perhaps the most eloquent. In the introduction, Reagan struck the theme that would unify the long address. Americans, he said, were faced with the choice of going up towards freedom or down into "the ant heap of totalitarianism," and he warned: "Already the hour is late. Government has laid its hand on health, housing, farming, industry, commerce, education, and to an ever-increasing degree interferes with the people's right to know." Reagan then made his way through a mass of statistics on wasteful federal spending on farm subsidies, urban renewal, welfare, youth programs, and Social Security, stopping from time to time to tell anecdotes about bumbling bureaucrats.

Towards the end of the speech he turned to the subject of international Communism. "We are faced," he said, "with the most evil enemy mankind has known in his long climb from the swamp to the stars." Having figured Communism as the devil (though in the context of Darwinian evolution), he went on to suggest that American liberals were making a pact with him because of their policy of accommodation, which was appeasement. And he said: "We are being asked to buy our safety from the threat of the Bomb by selling into permanent slavery our fellow human beings enslaved behind the Iron Curtain. To tell them to give up their hope of freedom because we are ready to make a deal with their slave masters."

Though Reagan did not actually counsel an attack on the Soviet Union, he asked whether those Americans who believed it was better to be red than dead thought there was anything worth dying for: "Should Moses have told the children of Israel to live in slavery rather than dare the wilderness? Should Christ have refused the Cross? Should the patriots at Concord bridge have refused to fire the shot heard round the world?"

Americans, he concluded, had the choice of preserving "the last best hope of man on earth" or of sentencing their children to take the first step "into a thousand years of darkness."[20]

The year after Reagan published this speech in his memoir, he was running for the governorship of California with the backing of a number of wealthy Los Angeles businessmen anxious to unify the California Republican Party after the Goldwater-Rockefeller split of 1964. Under the tutelage of Stuart Spencer and Bill Roberts, the political consultants who had worked for Rockefeller, Reagan ran a mainstream campaign. Early on, Spencer and Roberts confronted Reagan with the fact that he was facing Governor Edmund G. "Pat" Brown, one of the most experienced and knowledgeable politicians in the state. It would therefore be unwise for Reagan to claim authority via his usual array of factoids and unsourced statistics. Reagan, they said, should play to his strength and campaign as a "citizen politician," as a "Joe Doakes running for office," as someone who shared the average voter's sense of alienation from professional politicians.[21] And Reagan did just that. The right-winger metamorphosed into the bland Mr. Smith.

The transformation was achieved more easily than might be imagined. On the one hand, Reagan took direction very well; on the other, there was far less distance between the American Everyman—particularly in the form of Jimmy Stewart's Mr. Smith—and the quintessential fluoride-in-the-water right-wing crackpot than most Americans have ever wanted to admit.

In the late fifties and early sixties a group of distinguished American scholars, including Richard Hofstadter and Daniel Bell, wrote a series of ground-breaking studies on the radical right of the period: the McCarthyites, the John Birch Society, the Ku Klux Klan and other groups. One of Hofstadter's contributions was his marvelous essay "The Paranoid Style in American Politics."

In the essay Hofstadter begins by explaining that he is using the term "paranoid style" in much the same way that an art historian would speak of mannerism or the baroque. He goes on to describe the salient characteristics of the style—and much of his description would loosely apply to Reagan's rhetoric of the early sixties. The central image, he writes, is that of a vast, sinister conspiracy, a gigantic yet subtle machinery of influence set in motion by forces of almost demonic power. The paranoid spokesman claims to know what others do not yet know, and sees himself as the center of an apocalyptic drama. "He is," Hofstadter writes, "always manning the barricades of civilization. He constantly lives at a turning point. Time is forever just running out. Like religious millenarians, he expresses the anxiety of those who are living through the last days."[22]

Though these apocalyptic warnings run close to hopeless pessimism, Hofstadter continues, they usually stop just short of it, their function being much the same as the description of the consequences of sin in a revivalist sermon. The paranoid spokesman sees the world as a conflict between absolute good and absolute evil; thus social conflict is not something to be mediated or compromised; only total victory will do. He is obsessed by one subject. His particular enemy is the cause of all evil—not just some of the evils of the world, but every one of them. The enemy is the perfect model of malign intent, and yet, possibly because the enemy is a projection of self, the paranoid spokesman tends to imitate its ways. If the enemy is Communism, his organization sets up secret cells; if the enemy is the cosmopolitan intellectual, he outdoes him in claims to elite knowledge and in the apparatus of scholarship.

The paranoid style, Hofstadter pointed out, was not confined to the American radical right of the 1950s and '60s. It was an international phenomenon, and examples of it could be found in many periods of history. In American history small explosions of it occurred in every decade from the founding of the Republic on. At the end of the eighteenth century, for example, at the time of the rise of Jeffersonian democracy, conservative Congregationalist divines, including the geographer Jedidiah Morse and Timothy Dwight, the president of Yale, announced that the United States had become the object of a Jacobinical plot conceived by the Bavarian Illuminati, and that this anti-clerical conspiracy would soon overwhelm the forces of religion and order across the country if Americans were not roused. In the 1820s Protestants in rural upstate New York attacked the Masonic Order—at that time a citadel of Enlightenment ideas—as a sinister elite conspiracy against Christianity and republicanism, some identifying it as an engine of Satan and one of the confederate powers that would fight against Christ in the battle of Armageddon. During the 1830s and '40s nativist and anti-Catholic spokesmen spun fanciful tales of Jesuit priests, financed by the Catholic powers of Europe, infiltrating the country in deep disguise to subvert American freedom. There were a few paranoid spokesmen among the abolitionists and, later in the century, among Populist leaders, the latter imagining that an international cabal of gold traders was secretly plotting to undermine the economy and pauperize American farmers. The paranoid style, in other words, appeared within both reformist and reactionary movements of the nineteenth century and within groups that would be difficult to place on the spectrum of right to left.

Hofstadter finds important differences between nineteenth-century conspiracy theorists and those of the radical right in the 1960s, but his own account shows a relationship between them: a line of succession. What the nineteenth-century groups had in common was their close association with evangelical Protestantism. Most of them sprang from revival movements, and their "paranoid" rhetoric appeared side-by-side with new Adventist doctrines and new social- or moral-reform agendas. Many of the twentieth-century groups Hofstadter discusses, including the Ku Klux Klan and the John Birch Society, were closely associated with Protestant fundamentalism, and, like some of their nineteenth-century counterparts, were nativist and anti-Catholic. Senator Joseph McCarthy, a Catholic, was an exception to this rule, and yet, elected in Protestant Wisconsin, he created a new and ecumenical form of nativism by labeling his opponents "un-American." To him, as to others of the radical right, Communism appeared in exactly the same dress as Catholicism had appeared to nineteenth-century nativist Protestants: as a vast international conspiracy with secret agents financed by foreign powers to subvert the Republic.

Like most nineteenth-century conspiracy theorists, the radical right-wingers of the fifties and early sixties were virulently anti-establishment and anti-intellectual. Though their economic program was far from egalitarian, they were engaged in a struggle against the cosmopolitan elite of the Eastern Seaboard, which, as they saw it, controlled Wall Street, the universities and the federal government. In this sense they could be called populists—though theirs was a form of populism that would make itself right at home in Scottsdale or Palm Springs.

Given this genealogy, the connection between the radical right-winger and the mythic American Everyman with his homespun virtues becomes easier to see. Related by their common origins in evangelical Protestantism and nineteenth-century populism, they shared certain salient characteristics. Anti-intellectual and anti-elitist, they both saw themselves as representing the plain folk, the real Americans, whom they picture as rugged individualists standing up to corporatism and collectivism. Both thought themselves commonsensical, and their enemies caught up in esoteric, irrational systems of thought. The radical right-wing movements of the 1950s and '60s were distinguished by the ugliness of their temper. But if you took away their hostility and their elaborate, quasi-metaphysical theories, they might look very much like the party of Mr. Smith.

What most people seem to remember about Frank Capra's *Mr. Smith Goes to Washington* is that it is the story of an endearingly naïve young man who, appointed to fill a vacant seat in the Senate, runs afoul of corrupt special interests, stands up for principle and eventually wins. Those who remember a bit more about the movie remember that Mr. Smith, who comes from some unidentified Western state, is bewildered by the ways of the capital and horrified when he discovers that his fellow senator, Joseph Paine, has sold out to the political boss of the state for the sake of his own presidential aspirations. Paine, Smith discovers, has sponsored a bill providing for the construction of a dam that the boss will profit from through kickbacks. Smith knows this because he has just written a bill that would establish a national boys' camp on the proposed site of the dam. He objects. Paine, who has previously befriended Smith, takes his junior senator before the Senate Ethics Committee, claiming that Smith owns the land around the dam. The Ethics Committee, whose members have interests as murky as Paine's, charges Smith with conflict of interest and calls for his removal from the Senate. Smith asks the people of his state to support him and filibusters on the floor of the Senate for twenty-four hours until the letters of support can arrive. However, since the political boss owns all the newspapers and radio stations in the state, the journalists report that Smith is guilty of conflict of interest. Therefore, all the letters that come in condemn Smith. But then, just as Smith is about to collapse from fatigue and disappointment, Paine rushes onto the floor of the Senate and confesses that he, not Smith, is the guilty one.

Mr. Smith is about the virtuous individual versus the corrupt system, but there are a number of overlapping themes.

To begin with, Capra creates what must be the apotheosis of the American civil religion in film. The score is a medley of patriotic tunes—"My Country 'Tis of Thee," "Yankee Doodle," "Taps," and the "Battle Hymn of the Republic," among others—plus a few sentimental favorites, such as "Jeanie with the Light Brown Hair" and "Auld Lang Syne." In his unidentified Western state, Mr. Jefferson Smith is said by the governor's children to be "the greatest hero . . . the greatest American we've ever had," though for reasons the film quickly passes over. Arriving in Washington, Smith neglects pressing business to tour the national shrines—the Washington Monument, the Lincoln Memorial, Mount Vernon and so forth. The camera dwells on the statue of Lincoln, presenting him to Smith's eyes, and to ours, not as the great debater, politician and statesman, but as an icon, the graven image of a martyr or a god. In his filibuster Smith reads all the national scriptures—the Declaration of Independence, the Constitution and the Gettysburg Address—apparently for the edification of the other senators. Smith thus emerges with the mantle of pure patriotism swung about him, representing all that is good in the nation. In the end Senator Paine, abandoning his own selfish interests, rushes down the aisle of the Senate and flings himself on the low wooden railing in front of the dais. "I am not fit for office," he cries. Clearly he is making an act of contrition, or having a born-again experience, on the altar rail of the national church.

What is disturbing about this theme is the suggestion of Caesarism or Bonapartism, if not something worse, for in the course of the film it becomes clear that the problem is not simply that there is corruption in Smith's own state, but that *all* congressional politics are corrupt. Under the glorious capitol dome that Smith so venerates, there are a lot of cynical, small-minded men who, in corrupt solidarity with Paine, unjustly condemn the innocent Smith. However bumbling Smith is, and however much of an underdog, he is still in his own way a Siegfried among the scheming, deal-making dwarves. Charged with graft, he defends himself not by the legal route of proving that he does not own the land around the disputed site but by the demagogic tactic of calling upon the people of the state to attest to his virtue. This tactic does not succeed, because the boss and the political "machine" of the state tell the journalists what to write, and the people believe what they are told. Clearly the people are not responsible citizens, but a mob.

In addition there is the theme of nostalgia for a purer, more idealistic past. Senator Paine and Jefferson's father, Clayton Smith, had been friends in the old days, when Smith had run a crusading four-page newspaper and before Paine had sold out to the bosses (also, presumably, before he had acquired his transatlantic accent). Clayton Smith, who is said to be "the patron saint of lost causes," had taken up the case of a single miner against a mining syndicate and had paid for bucking the system with his life. Paine had found Smith slumped over a rolltop desk with a bullet in his head and his soft-brimmed hat still on him.

The third, and connecting, theme concerns the difference between boys and men: the boys are pure and idealistic and the men are cynical, powerful and corrupt. Smith, played by a very young Jimmy Stewart, is a hero to the children of his state because he is the head of an organization called "The Boy Rangers" and because he has helped put out a forest fire. When he gets to Washington—arriving with a basket of white pigeons—he behaves like a child, playing hooky amid the national monuments, and then like a shy adolescent in the face of Paine's sophisticated, conniving daughter. The only possible love interest for Smith in the film is his worldly, somewhat older, secretary, who teaches him the ways of the Senate and says she loves him "like a mother." The only friend Smith has in the Senate is a pageboy, and his only supporters are the boys of his state and, in the galleries of the Senate, a troop of boy scouts, or "Boy Rangers," who come to listen to his maiden speech proposing a national boys' camp. Childishly, Smith never asks himself whether the camp is a workable idea—or whether the dam might not actually help the people of the state in spite of the graft. No, he is right and the men are wrong. "Either I'm right, or I'm crazy," he says. Confronting him with the political facts of life, Paine tells Smith, "You live in a boys' world. This is a world of men, and it's a brutal one." Later Smith, in defending his proposal for the camp, counters, "Men all start life being boys." In the end, when justice triumphs, it is the man, the surrogate father, Paine, who prostrates himself before the pure, innocent boy.

This last theme seems to beg for psychological interpretation, but, looking past that to the politics of the movie, Mr. Smith is clearly not the pragmatic republican that liberal historians have conjured up as the American Everyman. Indeed, given a different temperament, Mr. Smith might take his sense of victimization and create an explanatory structure around it having to do with the near-victory of demonic forces over the America he knows and loves. As it is, Smith sees himself as a lonely prophet, and the key figure in a national struggle of good versus evil. Like Hofstadter's paranoid spokesman, he believes that individuals, and indeed whole societies, can be transformed overnight from one to the other. Because he believes himself to be without self-interest, he cannot imagine that politics might be a negotiation between legitimate interest groups; and no matter how much he reads the Constitution, he cannot understand that human societies require checks and balances. He is a believer in natural harmony. He is, of course, an optimist, but so, too, in the final analysis, is the paranoid spokesman. In a sense the two are alter egos; there is something quite childish about both of them. The difference is that the first Mr. Smith remains wide-eyed and extroverted, whereas the second one retreats into the solitude of his own imagination and creates the model of a hostile world in which trains will crash and armies will be swept from the board—unless he at the last moment intervenes to save them. Yet for both Smiths the world is controlled by powerful adults with whom it is impossible to negotiate.

Historically speaking, the connection between the two Mr. Smiths is nineteenth-century evangelical Protestantism. Indeed, its two major eschatologies—post-millennialism, or the belief that as a result of Christian zeal society will soon grow to such a state of perfection that Christ will return, and pre-millennialism, or the belief that society is falling into such sin and apostasy that Armageddon is nigh—more or less mirror their contrasting temperaments.

What made Ronald Reagan exceptional as a politician in the 1980s is that he could speak the language of both the post- and the pre-millennial Mr. Smith. As if in homage to Capra, he often told stories about unsung American heroes—ordinary people who by their moral courage and persistence had triumphed against all odds. He also liked to picture his antagonists, whether bureaucrats, liberals or professors, as a collection of faceless little men. Reagan always looked and sounded like the first Mr. Smith. Even in his seventies he had pink cheeks and a boyish charm about him that suggested modesty and goodness, and he was unfailingly optimistic. Yet sometimes, in a sweet and slightly bumbling manner, he would deliver the lines of the other Mr. Smith. He never stopped telling people that he knew the purposes of the Kremlin from his reading of Karl Marx, and like some earlier Cold War leaders, he sometimes came quite close to the paranoid style. For example, describing the purpose of American military aid to El Salvador in 1981, he said:

> What we're doing . . . is [to] try to halt the infiltration into the Americas by terrorists, by outside interference and those who aren't just aiming at El Salvador but, I think, are aiming at the whole of Central and possibly later South America—and, I'm sure, eventually North America. But this is what we're doing, is trying to stop this destabilizing force of terrorism and guerrilla warfare and revolution from being exported in here, backed by the Soviet Union and Cuba and those others that we've named.[23]

Two years later the President revealed to a joint session of Congress the probable consequence of inaction in Central America: "If we cannot defend ourselves there, we cannot expect to prevail elsewhere. Our credibility would collapse, our alliances would crumble, and the safety of our homeland would be put in jeopardy."[24]

In the course of his career, Reagan veered back and forth several times between the two rhetorical styles, but at no time was his oscillation more abrupt or more radical than at the time of his SDI speech.

Reagan's March 23, 1983, speech is now generally thought of as his SDI speech, though only the last few paragraphs concern the initiative. The rest is what Washington journalists at the time called "the standard threat speech." In it Reagan painted an alarming picture of the Soviet military buildup, called for a sizable increase in spending for offensive weapons and in peroration asked Americans to choose wisely between the "hard but necessary task of preserving peace and freedom and the temptation to ignore our duty and blindly hope for the best while the enemies of freedom grow stronger every day." This mini-jeremiad echoed the "evil-empire" speech he had made just two weeks before. Reagan then changed gears. He had, he said, been talking with the Joint Chiefs of Staff about the need "to break out of a future" that relied solely on nuclear retaliation. "Over the course of these discussions," he said, "I've become more and more deeply convinced that the human spirit must be capable of rising above dealing with other nations and human beings by threatening their existence. . . . Wouldn't it be better to save lives than to avenge them?"

With hardly a paragraph of transition, Reagan had leapt from one form of millennial prophecy to another. No longer was the Beast slouching towards Armageddon, but the human spirit was rising towards heaven, and the enemy had disappeared. "We seek," he continued, "neither military superiority nor political advantage. Our only purpose—one all people share—is to search for ways to reduce the danger of nuclear war." In closing he declared, "My fellow Americans, tonight we're launching an effort which holds the promise of changing the course of human history." Here the innocent, optimistic Mr. Smith was asking his countrymen to undertake their time-honored task of making the world all over again.[25]

Still, Reagan's call for a defensive shield could be seen to complement his earlier call for more offensive weaponry. Both proposals, after all, offered technological rather than political solutions to the problem of the Cold War. Further, a shield can be used for offensive as well as defensive purposes. Reagan acknowledged this objection in his speech and answered it by promising to share SDI technology with the Soviet Union as well as with America's allies. The proposal was never taken seriously in Washington, much less Moscow, yet that was precisely what the American admiral in *Murder in the Air* and the Paul Newman character in *Torn Curtain* had proposed: their superweapons were going to make the United States invincible in war and then the great force for world peace. Movie audiences suspended disbelief, for to Americans it seemed perfectly plausible that the United States would disarm its enemy and then seek no advantage for itself.

The promise of an anti-missile shield was surely Reagan's most characteristic idea, for, being perfectly ambiguous, it had appeal for both Mr. Smiths: for the pre-millennialist who saw enemies advancing from all quarters and for the post-millennialist who believed that the human spirit could rise to an almost godlike state of disinterestedness. It was the ambiguity inherent in the idea which allowed Reagan to make the transition between a vision of the Soviet Union as the "evil empire," and a vision of world peace and disarmament. These perceptions seemed contradictory to many in his administration, but in the national liturgy they were merely a harmonic interval apart.

Though a defense shield might have been the conception of either the pre-millennial of the post-millennial Reagan, it was certainly that of Reagan the actor and storyteller. A perfect anti-ballistic missile defense was beyond the reach of technology. It was just a story, and yet to trust the polls, the idea had great popular appeal in the mid-eighties, and many Americans believed such a thing could be built. In that sense the Strategic Defense Initiative was Reagan's greatest triumph as an actor-storyteller. The fact that the program did not produce a single weapon only helped Reagan, for had it produced some sort of ABM system, the story with all of its mythic overtones would have given place to a piece of technology with a lot of practical difficulties attached. Politically at least, anti-missile defenses were better air than metal.

According to Cannon, President Reagan used to bridle when his movie career was mentioned in the press, for so often in the past his opponents had joked about his old movies and tried to dismiss him as "just an actor." (It was only in the last month of his presidency that he spoke of the link between his two careers, telling David Brinkley that he sometimes wondered how anyone could do the job who hadn't been an actor.)[26] Similarly, Reagan was annoyed when his defense initiative was dubbed "Star Wars." Richard Perle, however, his brilliant young assistant secretary of defense, told colleagues that he thought the name wasn't so bad. "Why not?" he said. "It's a good movie. Besides, the good guys won."[27] What Perle meant, of course, was that the George Lucas movie—which was far better known than the initiative at this point—had good associations for people that might rub off on the program. Perle might have said much the same thing about Reagan's movie roles, for the aura of the decent all-American hero he had so often played hung about Reagan in his political career. And Reagan surely knew this. In a commencement address at Notre Dame in 1981 he described how the role of the Gipper came his way and then made the film *Knute Rockne—All American* into an allegory of American patriotism. As Paul Erickson has pointed out in his marvelous analysis of Reagan's rhetoric, Reagan managed to read himself into both the role of Rockne and that of the Gipper, and, by moving back and forth between fiction and the real world, to associate Rockne and his team with the Founding Fathers.[28] He also managed to move American history and the American future into the safe space of a movie in which the good guys won.

Still, an actor's roles and his persona are two different things. Those who associated Reagan with the roles he played were in some degree suspending disbelief, just as people do in the movies. On the other hand, those who pointed to the President as a former actor or "just an actor" were focusing attention on the possibility of deception or inauthenticity. This was, of course, what worried Reagan, both in regard to himself and in regard to the name "Star Wars." Yet some movie actors are not just actors but celebrities—stars—who inhabit a magical realm somewhere between the real world and fiction. They are a kind of royalty, not just because they light up rooms with their entrances but because, unlike partisan politicians, they belong to all of us equally. What is more, even the aura of inauthenticity—or unreality—they bring along with them has its attractions. Anderson's story of Reagan's epiphany on Cheyenne Mountain suggests the purposes the aura might serve.

Reagan surely would have disliked the movie references in the story of his conversion to anti-ballistic missile systems. Certainly, when he spoke of the NORAD visit, he did not say that it had been arranged by a screenwriter. And yet these references do a great deal for the story. Because movies are the common currency of American life, Anderson was describing the NORAD command center in the most efficient manner possible when he said that it looked just the way such command centers do in movies. He was also triggering that slight sense of unreality that most people feel when contemplating the possibility of a nuclear war. His own discussion of Soviet first strikes is far less alarming than it otherwise would have been, and, given the light touch, neither he nor Reagan has to play the heavy: both are at one remove from actually thinking about weapons systems and nuclear war. Of course, to look at the symbolic content of the story, the Hollywood set makes a bizarre backdrop for the epiphany scene with all of its mythic and Biblical implications; it gives the whole story an uncomfortable post-modern quality. But there is a strategy to post-modern design: with a hint of play, or self-conscious levity, the liturgical repetition of classical forms cannot be dismissed as trite or impossibly earnest. In the case of the Anderson narrative, the movie references provide a bubble-gum-pink coating for an extremely heavy dose of symbolism. Readers may think they have just seen Reagan wandering about a movie set dreaming of an Inertia Projector, whereas in fact they have swallowed the whole epiphany, complete with Siegfried, and Christ among the Pharisees.

In the same way, those who sneered that Reagan was "just an actor" were not necessarily producing the effect they intended. According to the polls, large numbers of Americans voted for Reagan who did not agree with many of the conservative positions he took. Many of these liked the character Reagan projected, but some of them must have told themselves that Reagan was, after all, only an actor, so there was no need to take his rhetoric too seriously: perhaps he did not really think the Soviet Union was "evil," and even if he did, responsible people in his administration would surely prevail. By 1983 a fair number of Republicans who thought they had voted for a good-natured actor had unhappily concluded that they had elected an ideologue. Conversely, by 1988 conservative spokesmen in Washington were complaining that the man they had thought a true conservative had turned out to be a man without substance or principles, particularly when it came to his dealings with the Soviet Union. These spokesmen, however, represented only a small fraction of the public. Most Americans did not want a continuing state of conflict with the Soviet Union, and had never been ready to send American boys to fight Communism in Central America—and they were extremely happy when Reagan turned out to be less than serious about either enterprise.

In fact, it could be argued that what Americans really wanted in the 1980s was an actor for President. Many, after all, were able to persuade themselves that America was "back" and "standing tall" when American troops managed to occupy the island of Grenada. And many thought the handsome front-man, Colonel Oliver North, a red-blooded American hero. Even at the time, the 1980s was not thought of as a period of national dedication and sacrifice, but rather as a time of false prosperity, indulgence and speculation, when even the most solid middle-class citizens dreamed of getting something for nothing. Most Americans wanted military spending and a tax cut; they wanted a tax cut and Social Security with cost-of-living increases; they bought junk bonds and forgot the risk associated with them. They went to visit theme parks rather than real places, and they seemed to want a President who could speak all the lines of FDR and Churchill and Tom Paine without seriously threatening to act upon them. Certainly they did not seem to mind that the President who spoke of homespun virtues and old-fashioned family values was a divorcé who rarely saw his children or went to church and whose wife shopped on Rodeo Drive. In the days of Jim and Tammy Bakker, when Pentecostalists prayed for the miracle of a Cadillac, who wanted the innocent, self-righteous Mr. Smith? Who wanted a real populist, anyway? Better an actor who could play Mr. Smith but who, reassuringly, spent the Christmas season in Palm Springs. Better a President who would promise the miracle of a perfect defense and world peace without preaching the need for struggle or compromise. Reagan, the actor and politician, may have understood this.

CHAPTER TWO

The Making of an Orator

> "The motion picture business presents right and wrong as the Bible does. By showing both right and wrong we teach the right."
>
> —Harry Warner[1]

Ronald Reagan always associated his childhood with Dixon, Illinois, a small town on the banks of the Rock River surrounded by dairy farms and open country. And the people of Dixon claimed him as their own. When he became a famous actor, and later in his life, they always spoke of him as he was at age seventeen or eighteen, when he was a hometown celebrity. In his last year of high school Reagan was nearly six feet tall, handsome, and muscled in the way that swimmers are. He was class president and the star of the drama club, and a tackle on the varsity football team. Every summer he worked as a lifeguard at Lowell Park, on a part of the river where dangerous currents swept along the forested bluffs of the far shore. In seven summers on the river he saved seventy-seven people from drowning. Dixon people remembered him as poised, self-possessed and nice to everyone. He taught Sunday school, dated Margaret Cleaver, the pretty, intelligent daughter of the pastor in his mother's church, and saved up money for college. He was, people said, an all-American boy with a good sense of humor.[2]

As a politician Reagan associated himself with Dixon and with the stability, neighborliness and rock-solid middle-class values of a small Midwestern town. But he spent most of his childhood living out of a suitcase in less-than-middle-class circumstances, his parents at odds with each other and constantly on the move.

Both of Reagan's parents had grown up on farms and had no more than primary educations, but they were urban people—people of the air, as opposed to the earth—who worked, as might be said today, in communications. His father, John Edward Reagan, whom everyone called "Jack," was of Irish Catholic stock. Dark, muscular and good-looking, he was a salesman and a dashing dresser with the gift of gab. "No one I ever met," Reagan wrote in a memoir, "could tell a story better than he could."[3] His mother, Nelle Clyde

Wilson, was of Scots-English extraction; blue-eyed, auburn-haired and energetic, she taught herself elocution, became a lay evangelist for her church and star performer in a group that gave dramatic readings of passages from plays, speeches and books. "Nelle really threw herself into a part," Reagan wrote. "She loved it. Performing, I think, was her first love."[4] Married in 1904, the two had their first child, Neil, nicknamed "Moon," four years later. Ronald, called "Dutch" because his father said he looked like "a fat little Dutchman," was born in Tampico, Illinois, on February 6, 1911.

Restless and ambitious, Jack took the family from Tampico to Chicago, then to Galesburg, Monmouth and Tampico again before settling in Dixon in 1920. Working as a clerk, and always at the largest and best-stocked emporium in town, he dreamed of success as a manager or an owner of a first-class store.[5] His opportunity seemed to come when a former employer gave him the financial backing to open a shoe shop in Dixon, but the Fashion Boot Shop never did enough business for him to buy into it, and his earnings were often small. Reagan wrote that his life in Dixon was "sweet and idyllic as it could be,"[6] but in the ten years he lived there, the family moved five times, always renting, and always to smaller quarters than before. Nelle took in sewing and, when she had a house, she took in boarders to make ends meet. Dutch slept with his brother in one small bed and wore hand-me-down clothes; there was always food on the table, but the main meal, at noon, often consisted of hamburger meat mixed with a batch of oatmeal.[7] A committed Christian, Nelle always looked on the bright side and insisted that there were people much worse off than they. Quietly she pushed her sons towards education and a better life, taking them with her to lectures, readings and plays. According to Reagan, she always saw the best in people, whereas Jack was a cynic with a mordant wit. Jack was also an alcoholic, a binge drinker who would go on sprees lasting days.[8]

Jack was sober for long stretches of time, but, in Reagan's memory at least, the threat of his binges always hung over the family, particularly on holidays and family celebrations, when Jack was most likely to go on a bender. According to Reagan, Nelle never blamed Jack for his bouts with the bottle and told the boys that alcoholism was a sickness over which he had no control.[9] Perhaps she told the boys that, but if so, it was surely just for their sake.

Born a Methodist, Nelle did not take religion very seriously while growing up: she married a Catholic and promised to have her children reared as Catholics. But in the sixth year of her marriage, the year before Dutch was born, she was baptized by immersion into the Disciples of Christ Christian Church. An evangelical offshoot of Presbyterianism, the church had a literalist interpretation of the Bible and an optimistic post-millennial theology, which placed emphasis on individual responsibility and social reform. Champions of the work ethic, the Disciples were strongly pro-temperance—they regarded drinking as a sin—and they were militantly anti-Catholic. Nelle threw herself into church activities. She went to prayer meetings two nights a week as well as Sunday services, and on settling in Dixon she became the leader of a women's Bible group, a Sunday-school teacher and a local missionary, making regular visits to prisoners and patients in state mental hospitals. She also ministered to friends and acquaintances in distress and developed a reputation for healing by prayer.[10]

The Disciples of Christ clearly suited Nelle's optimistic and activist temperament, and she became a much-respected member of the community. All the same, it is difficult not to see her conversion to that church as a reproach to her husband, and her constant round of church activities as escape, or, more positively, an attempt to make a more satisfactory life for herself apart from him. In later life the two Reagan boys never complained about her absences, but they described them, and by other accounts she spent a great deal of time in the service of others and away from home.[11] Then, as so often happens in unhappy marriages, the two boys took sides. Moon took his father's part, Dutch his mother's, and the two boys developed according to their allegiances.

An extrovert and an athlete, Moon rebelled at his mother's strictures and went off with rowdy friends; brash and articulate in the way his father was, he became a cutup and spent time at the forbidden pool hall. Nelle had both boys baptized into her church, but at the age of eighteen Moon converted to Catholicism.[12]

Dutch by contrast was a quiet child, obedient and withdrawn. "As a kid I lived in a world of pretend," he once said. "I had a great imagination. . . . I used to love to make up plays and act in them myself. . . . But by the time I was [eight or nine] I felt self-conscious about it. People made fun of me. . . . 'What are you doing, kid? Talking to yourself?' Enough people make cracks like that, and a sensitive boy . . . begins to feel a little silly. . . . So from then on he doesn't pretend openly."[13]

Small as a boy, Dutch was acutely shortsighted—though neither he nor his parents realized it until he happened to look through his mother's glasses at the age of thirteen. He learned to read at an early age, and since he could not see the blackboard, he developed an almost photographic memory for words on the page. He had playmates, he remembered, but he spent a good deal of time alone. He wandered the countryside, dreamed of being a trapper and at the age of ten began to check books—mostly boys' adventure stories—out of the library every weekend.[14] "I was a little introverted and probably a little slow in making really close friends," he wrote of his first years in Dixon. "In some ways I think this reluctance to get close to people never left me completely."[15]

Reagan's myopia prevented him from playing baseball, but it did not stop him from playing football. He was never a very good football player, but he made the high-school varsity by sheer scrappiness and determination. Lou Cannon wrote that football seemed to fill some deep need in Reagan. In

1981 Reagan told an interviewer that football "is the last thing left in civilization where two men can literally fling themselves bodily at one another and not be at war. It's a kind of clean hatred. . . . I know of no other game that gave me the same feeling football did."[16]

It was a side of Reagan that showed up in few other ways. As far as Dixon people were concerned, Dutch at the age of seventeen had no darkness in his nature.[17]

In the fall of 1928 Reagan entered Eureka College, a Disciples of Christ liberal-arts college eighty miles south of Dixon, with twenty in faculty and just under two hundred students. Margaret Cleaver entered the same class, and Moon, who initially refused to go to college, followed a year later. The college found enough work for the two boys to pay their tuition and board. Dutch majored in sociology and economics, but he was an indifferent student; he relied on his photographic memory to get him through with passing grades. His interests lay in sports and drama. He made the football team, coached swimming, starred in college productions and won a national award for acting. He also became class president, and on one celebrated occasion he made a speech in support of a student-faculty protest against a highly unpopular college president. "I discovered that night," he later wrote, "that an audience has a feel to it, and in the parlance of the theater, that audience and I were together. . . . It was heady wine."[18]

While Reagan was in college, the Depression hit, the Fashion Boot Shop folded and his father took to the road, first as a traveling salesman and then as the manager of a small, cheap shoe store in Springfield, Illinois. Nelle went to work in a dress shop, and the marriage faltered. Friends and neighbors suggested she get a divorce; she told them her religious principles would not allow it.[19] On Christmas Eve, 1931, when Dutch and Moon were home from college, a special-delivery notice arrived for Jack telling him he was fired from his Springfield job. He and Nelle had to move into a one-room apartment, and Dutch sent money home.[20] The following year, Jack's life took a turn for the better. A lifelong Democrat, Jack worked hard for Franklin Roosevelt, and when his man was elected, he was rewarded with a job as district manager for the New Deal emergency-relief programs. He found the job fulfilling, and his drinking problem subsided. But in 1934 he suffered a severe heart attack and thereafter could not work at all. Dutch, who had by then found a well-paying job, supported his parents for the rest of their lives.

In his high-school years Dutch began to find mentors among the older men he admired: the Christian Church minister, his drama teacher and successful businessmen who brought their children to Lowell Park. This practice, which continued throughout the first half of his life, was surely a healthy way of compensating for his father's emotional absence, and often it had more than psychological rewards. In his last year in college he was taken up by Sid Altschuler, a wealthy Kansas City businessman with ties to Dixon, and when he graduated, he asked Altschuler's advice about getting a job. Dutch loved acting, but the idea of becoming an actor seemed so impractical he didn't even bring it up. Instead he spoke tentatively about going into radio broadcasting. Altschuler told him radio was a growth industry and one that had many opportunities to offer if he could get in on the ground floor.[21]

On the strength of the endorsement, Dutch hitchhiked to Chicago and then to Davenport, Iowa, where he found a job as a sportscaster at a local station. He was an immediate success. Articulate and imaginative, he had a talent for giving vivid descriptions of the crowds, the players and the dramas of the game. He covered the nearby sports events in person, but he narrated the baseball games in Chicago from the telegraphed codes sent into the station after each play. Though he had never seen a major-league baseball game, he described the games as if he were there, making up accounts of the action on the field, the changing weather conditions, the mood of the spectators and so forth from his own imagination. On one occasion the wire went dead just as the game was tied up in the ninth inning, and for six minutes Reagan described foul ball after foul ball until the wire came back again. The batter had popped out on the first pitch.[22]

In 1933 Reagan moved to Des Moines, Iowa, with the station and, thanks to a new and more powerful transmitter, his mellow voice became well known throughout the Midwest. Moon followed him and found a job which eventually led him into network production and from there into a successful career in advertising. Margaret Cleaver, however, went to Europe and a year later wrote Dutch that she was going to marry a young foreign-service officer. Reagan was shocked. He had been engaged to Margaret for years and always assumed he would marry her. But she thought he lacked ambition, a sense of adventure and cultural curiosity. "He was always a leader," she later said. "Still, I didn't think he'd end up accomplishing anything."[23]

In Des Moines, Reagan, now financially secure, began to expand his horizons. He joined a cavalry regiment as a reserve officer and learned to ride; he dated a number of attractive women, interviewed sports stars and other visiting celebrities and got to know the politicians in town. He took all of this in his stride, and four years later his dream of becoming an actor no longer seemed impossible. In February 1937 he went to Los Angeles on a spring-training trip with the Chicago Cubs. Through an actress friend he found an agent, and, exaggerating his acting experience and his salary at the radio station, he got a screen test at Warner Bros. The studio liked his clean good looks, his natural manner in front of the camera. Jack Warner gave him a contract and shortly afterwards the lead in a B-picture about a Midwestern sportscaster.[24]

In the thirties the Hollywood studios, each with its stable of contract actors, were making enormous numbers of films a year, most of them low-budget pictures that could be shot in a matter of weeks. For an actor, and particularly for an actor like Reagan, it was a great time to come to town. Reagan made eight pictures in 1938, eight in 1939 and seven in 1940. Disciplined and aided by his photographic memory, he always showed up on the set with his lines perfectly memorized and his character well thought out. He took direction well, and he did everything the publicity department asked of him. Jack Warner, the tyrannical head of the studio, liked him. Reagan—now Ronald not Dutch—played leading roles in the B-pictures and supporting roles in the major features. Often he played stock figures: a wisecracking reporter; an earnest, idealistic young man. In three films he played a comic-strip action hero, Lieutenant "Brass" Bancroft of the Secret Service. His idols were Spencer Tracy, Gary Cooper and Jimmy Stewart, and he watched many of their pictures, including *Mr. Deeds Goes to Town, Meet John Doe,* and *Mr. Smith Goes to Washington,* over and over again. In the judgment of the Hollywood biographer Anne Edwards, his own acting lacked passion and friction, but he was good at light, romantic comedy: he read lines well, and his timing was perfect.[25]

In 1940 Reagan married Jane Wyman. Louella Parsons, the powerful Hollywood gossip columnist, who also came from Dixon, Illinois, virtually arranged the marriage. The fan magazines immediately cast Ronnie and Jane as the Perfect All-American Couple, two innocent young sweethearts in love for the first time—though in fact Wyman had been married before. That same year Reagan made a breakthrough as an actor in *Knute Rockne,* playing the talented Notre Dame football player George Gipp, who died of pneumonia in his senior year. His success led to parts in other A-pictures, an official studio designation as a star and a salary of a thousand dollars a week. In 1941 he joined the board of the Screen Actors Guild.[26] He also made *King's Row,* a melodrama in which he played Drake McHugh, a rake who has his legs amputated by a mad surgeon. He later considered *King's Row* his best film, but, as Garry Wills points out in *Reagan's America,* Reagan is for most of his time on the screen the light, witty fellow of his earlier films. As for the scene in which Drake McHugh comes to consciousness after the operation and cries, "Where's the rest of me?" McHugh is off camera for much of the time. The scene belongs to Ann Sheridan as Randy, not to Reagan.[27]

In 1942 Reagan went into active service in the Army. Still entranced with the image of the Perfect Couple—now one with a baby girl, Maureen—the fan magazines pictured him as going "away" or "off to war" while Jane bravely endured the anguish of a separation.[28] In fact, Reagan, far too myopic to be sent into combat, spent most of the next three years at the First Motion Picture Unit of the Army Air Corps at the old Hal Roach Studios in Culver City. He saw his family regularly and even acted in a Warner Bros. film, *This Is the Army,* a musical adapted from Irving Berlin's Broadway hit. Otherwise, he made Air Corps training films, often with footage of real combat wrapped around his scenes.[29] In his 1965 memoir Reagan tells us that he was driving over to the Disney Studios when the explosion of the atomic bomb was announced. But he also tells us, "By the time I got out of the Army Air Corps, all I wanted to do—in common with several million other veterans—was to rest up awhile, make love to my wife, and come up refreshed to do a better job in an ideal world." As if he had actually been away.[30]

The immediate post-war world was far from ideal for Reagan. For one thing, his career went into a stall. Reagan supposed that *King's Row* would propel him into stardom, and he had a million-dollar contract with Warner Bros., which his agent Lew Wasserman of MCA got him while he was in the Army. But for months no scripts came his way, and in 1947 he made two films that flopped. At bottom the issue was what kind of an actor he was, or could be, and Reagan and the studio did not see eye-to-eye on the question. Wyman, who had always been typecast as a dizzy blonde, was turning into a serious actress. She worked hard at her acting and took unglamorous roles—an alcoholic's fiancée, a sternly tried mother—and in 1948 she won an Oscar for playing a deaf-mute teenager. Reagan had no such ambitions. For him the movies were entertainment, and he wanted to be a star. He never took drama lessons or worked in small theaters, as many contract players did, and he never sought roles that would deliver him from typecasting or challenge him to plumb any emotional depths. He wanted to be typecast. The problem was that he wanted to be another John Wayne or Errol Flynn—a hero in action-adventure movies. "I was the Errol Flynn of the B-movies," he often joked later on. But, as Garry Wills points out, he had badly miscast himself. To the studios, and to his audiences, he was not a tough guy but, rather, the nice Ronald Reagan, who could deliver a quip—and he was always more popular with women than men. He continued to do well in light, romantic comedies, but he wanted heavier parts, and when he got them, he could not sustain them.[31]

His marriage, as it turned out, was not well cast either. In 1948 Wyman sued for divorce. It was a case of mistaken identities all around. Initially it was Jane who had the romance with Ronald, whom she found not only attractive but overwhelmingly kind and good. Reagan for his part treated Jane rather casually at first.[32] Once married, he came to believe the fan-magazine story about the two nice, ordinary kids who fall in love and have an ideal marriage. He never had much idea what Margaret Cleaver was like, and he did not understand Jane any better. He treated her as if she were as cute and flighty as she appeared in her films, and he was amazed when she claimed that he paid no attention to her needs and her views.[33] Afterwards he could never explain what had happened. "I suppose there had been warning signs, if only I hadn't been so busy," he wrote, "but small-town boys grow up thinking only other people get divorced. The plain truth is that such a thing was so far from being even imagined by me that I had no resources to call upon."[34]

• • •

On leaving the service in 1945, Reagan began to devote more of his energies to the Screen Actors Guild and to politics. Reagan had always taken a lively interest in politics and government. A Democrat and staunch Roosevelt supporter, he had argued politics incessantly with the Republican news manager of the station in Des Moines. In Hollywood he filled the idle hours on movie sets reading newspapers and talking politics. At dinner parties in the early forties he would often dominate the conversation with talk of world events. At the time Wyman found him impressive—she once said he might be President one day—but in 1948 she sued him for divorce on the grounds of the mental cruelty associated with such evenings. What she disliked, she said, was that discussions would either turn argumentative or end with Reagan on a soapbox lecturing.[35]

In 1945 Reagan joined a series of pro-Roosevelt organizations, including the American Veterans Committee and the Americans for Democratic Action, and gave speeches opposing atomic weapons and the Ku Klux Klan. He became a board member of the Hollywood Independent Citizens Committee of the Arts, Sciences and Professions (HICCASP), an organization which included many Hollywood notables and the President's son Jimmy Roosevelt. "I was a near-hopeless hemophiliac liberal," Reagan later wrote.[36] Possibly he was, but if so, it was not for very long.

In 1946 the post–World War II Red Scare hit Hollywood. Following Roosevelt's death and the beginning of the Cold War, right-wingers began a domestic crusade against Communist infiltrators and saboteurs, using this popular cause to attack the New Deal, discredit the radical, or simply activist, unions and tar liberal Democrats with being "soft on Communism." Witch hunts for Communists and Communist sympathizers began with the House Un-American Activities Committee and J. Edgar Hoover's FBI in the lead. Hollywood was an important target because of its visibility. Sensitive as always to the mood in the country, the studio producers veered sharply to the right, and many movie people active in liberal organizations began to think differently about the minority of Communists in their ranks, and to worry about their associations.

For Reagan there was nothing at all abstract about the Red Scare. His brother, Neil, who had become a right-wing Republican and, secretly, an FBI informant, warned him that some of his associates in HICCASP were under government surveillance. Then, in the summer of 1946, three FBI agents came to see him to ask for information about fellow members of the organization. "You served with the Air Corps. You know what spies and saboteurs are," they said. Reagan, who had played Brass Bancroft, Secret Service, gave them the information they wanted. What they did not tell him, but what he might well have suspected, was that, because of his membership in liberal organizations, the FBI considered him a Communist sympathizer.[37]

In that same summer of 1946, Reagan quit HICCASP, along with

Jimmy Roosevelt, Dore Schary, Olivia de Havilland and most of those on its right and center, leaving the organization to the left-wingers and the FBI. That fall he, as a member of SAG's Emergency Committee, played an important role in deciding the future of unionism in Hollywood.

In the early forties a new alliance of Hollywood craft unions, the Conference of Studio Unions (CSU), under the leadership of Herb Sorrell of the Painters' Union, had mounted a challenge to the International Alliance of Theatrical Stage Employees (IATSE), the dominant union in Hollywood. Because some of IATSE's leaders had been found to be mobsters, the challenge was successful, and by 1946 IATSE, one of the oldest unions in the American Federation of Labor, was fighting for its life. The studio executives sided with IATSE because, among other things, the alliance included the projectionists' union, and thus had the power to shut all the exhibitors down. With IATSE they maneuvered the CSU into going out on strike, and violence ensued. In the course of the struggle Roy Brewer, the new head of IATSE, made unsubstantiated charges that Herb Sorrell was a Communist and that Communists under the direction of Moscow were attempting to take over the motion-picture industry through the CSU.

SAG was officially neutral in the conflict, but the actors had to decide whether or not to cross the picket lines, and since the studios could not make movies without them, SAG's decision was crucial. At some point in the summer of 1946, Reagan decided that Sorrell was a Communist, and afterwards paid no attention to bread-and-butter issues or to the merits of the CSU case. He led the fight to have SAG declare the dispute jurisdictional, so that under AFL rules the actors could cross the picket lines. On October 20, after a sharp conflict, SAG members supported Reagan's position. The strike collapsed, and the weakened CSU folded.

Both at the time and subsequently, many outside observers concluded that IATSE and the studio executives had ganged up to defeat an aggressive, independent union.[38] But Reagan drew a different conclusion. In his 1965 memoir he wrote:

> The Communist plan for Hollywood was remarkably simple. It was merely to take over the motion picture business. Not only for profit, as the hoodlums had tried—but also for a grand worldwide propaganda base. In those days before television and massive foreign film production, American films dominated 95 per cent of the world's movie screens. We had a weekly audience of 500,000,000 souls. Takeover of this enormous plant and its gradual transformation into a Communist gristmill was a grandiose idea. It would have been a magnificent coup for our enemies.[39]

In this, his first brush with real politics, Reagan had become a hero in his own drama, the fate of the free world in his hands. "The Russians," he told a conservative audience in 1951, "sent their first team, their ace string, here to take us over. . . . We were up against hard-core organizers."[40]

In October 1947 the House Un-American Activities Committee held hearings on the Communist menace to Hollywood. Reagan, now the president of SAG, testified as a friendly witness. He confirmed that there had been a "small clique" within SAG that had generally followed the Communist line, but named no names and assured the committee that the film community had confronted the problem and turned back the threat. He said that it was up to Congress to decide whether to outlaw the Communist Party as a subversive organization, but that as a citizen he would not like to see any party outlawed on the grounds of its political ideology. Democracy, he said, "is strong enough to stand up and fight against the inroads of any ideology. . . . I believe that, as Thomas Jefferson put it, if all the American people know all of the facts, they will never make a mistake."[41]

At the time even liberals considered Reagan's testimony sensible and restrained, and largely on the strength of it Reagan maintained the reputation of a moderate throughout the 1940s and '50s.[42] But Reagan acted differently behind the scenes.

Reagan's FBI files, released under the Freedom of Information Act in 1985, show that in April 1947 he had a second interview with FBI agents, this one at his own request, in which he gave them the names of six SAG members he thought were following the Communist Party line and stated his firm conviction that the Communist Party was a foreign-inspired conspiracy and should be outlawed by Congress. Subsequently he became an FBI informant with the code name T-10. This was not just patriotic enthusiasm. The motion-picture executives had decided to try to preempt any special legislation involving the industry by blacklisting all those suspected of having ties to the Communist Party, and Reagan, according to agents, told the FBI that he had been made a member of a committee headed by Louis B. Mayer, the purpose of which was to "purge" the industry of party members. At the HUAC hearing he was supporting the studio executives' position that Hollywood was policing itself well enough and that no special legislation was required.[43]

Between 1947 and 1960 the studios black- and gray-listed over two thousand people, ruining their careers. Reagan repeatedly denied the existence of a blacklist and repeatedly said that SAG would never be a party to any such thing. But Reagan knew about the list, and the guild under his regime banned suspected Communists and those who refused to cooperate with congressional investigations.[44] When Gale Sondergaard, an Academy Award–winning actress, wrote the SAG board that she was going to take the Fifth Amendment at a HUAC hearing and asked that SAG oppose the blacklist, the board responded with a letter, drafted by a small group that included Reagan, saying that "all participants in the international Communist Party conspiracy against our nation should be exposed for what they are," and that the guild would not defend any actor who by his own actions "so offended American public opinion that he has made himself unsalable at the box office."[45]

In truth Reagan's claim to have been a "near-hemophiliac liberal" was probably an exaggeration of the sort that conversion stories seem to require. He had been brought up a Democrat in a Republican town, and after he left home his mentors and best friends were all Republicans. In Hollywood he and his wife had lived in a world of successful, conservative actors and businessmen. Dick Powell and George Murphy were friends, so was Justin Dart, a tough, shrewd drugstore tycoon and one of the top fund-raisers for the Republican Party in California.[46] Reagan supported the New Deal, but his enthusiasm had centered on Roosevelt the man rather than on his institutional reforms. According to Jack Dales, the executive secretary of SAG, Reagan "idolized [Roosevelt] as some people would idolize a film star—he thought he was an almost godlike man."[47] FDR was, after all, a strong, popular president and a war leader, the kind of man Reagan admired.

After 1946 Reagan grew increasingly conservative. He did not change his voting registration until 1962, but he left the Democratic Party well before that. He did not much like Truman, though he voted for him in 1948, and, understandably, he did not like the high post-war taxes that took a huge bite out of his salary. In 1952 he chaired a Democrats for Eisenhower committee, and for the next decade he was always a Democrat for Republicans.[48] Most biographers report that he backed Helen Gahagan Douglas against Nixon in the 1950 senatorial campaign. Helen and her husband, Melvyn Douglas, were friends of his, he pledged her his support and his name appears in her campaign literature. But Anne Edwards offers evidence that he secretly raised money for Nixon's red-baiting campaign against her.[49]

Reagan served as SAG president from 1947 to 1952 and returned for another year in 1959–60. In those years he negotiated a number of important agreements for screen actors, including one that changed the face of the industry and put his own career in jeopardy.

In 1952, when television was still in its infancy, the Music Corporation of America, the powerful talent agency built by Jules Stein, asked for an unprecedented blanket waiver from the SAG rules that would allow it to go into television production. MCA executives promised that they could bring a great deal of work to Hollywood actors and, unlike the studio heads, they promised TV residuals to SAG members. Reagan might have recused himself from the decision since it involved his own agency, but instead he pushed the deal through, and in 1954 the SAG board, on which he still sat, renewed it. No other talent agency ever got such a waiver from SAG, and by the early 1960s MCA controlled some 60 percent of the entertainment industry.[50]

In 1961 the Justice Department initiated a grand-jury investigation to discover whether MCA had violated the anti-trust laws. Reagan was called as a witness. By that time MCA was not only his agent but his employer in a television series. On the stand in February 1962 Reagan could recall little for the jurors about the waivers except for two things: one, that other agencies had been given the same kind of waiver, and two, that no arrangements about the residuals had been made in the course of the negotiations. When evidence was produced to show that both contentions were untrue, he retreated further into forgetfulness and contradicted himself on the reason for his memory lapses.

The Justice Department brought a civil suit against MCA for conspiracy in restraint of trade, naming SAG as a co-conspirator. MCA decided to settle out of court and to divest itself of its talent agency, thereby avoiding a trial that would have been embarrassing to the company. Had the Justice Department brought criminal charges against MCA, or had the company not decided to settle, Reagan would have been seriously embarrassed as well.[51]

In the fall of 1949, Reagan met Nancy Davis, an aspiring young actress who had just arrived in Hollywood and had a small part in a film directed by Mervyn LeRoy. Her mother, Edith Luckett, was a stage actress who had worked with Walter Huston, Spencer Tracy and George M. Cohan and knew many of the major figures of the entertainment world. Edith's first marriage, to Kenneth Robbins, had failed soon after Nancy was born, and Nancy changed her name to Davis after her mother married the eminent Chicago neurosurgeon Loyal Davis in 1929. Having grown up without a father—and with her mother often away on the road—Nancy formed a deep attachment to her forbidding and profoundly conservative stepfather, and her devotion was reciprocated. Educated at private schools and at Smith College, she went into summer stock; later, and with the help of her mother's friend ZaSu Pitts, she got small parts in stage plays and did some work in television. Spencer Tracy and Benjamin Thau, the powerful MGM executive, arranged for her to go to Hollywood for a screen test at MGM with George Cukor. She was not star material by the studio's estimation, but she was good enough to get a contract. In filling out the MGM publicity form, she wrote that outside of her career her greatest ambition was "to have a successful marriage."[52]

By most accounts Ronald and Nancy had what screenwriters call a "cute" meeting. In his 1965 memoir Reagan wrote that Mervyn LeRoy called him on behalf of a young actress, who was very distressed because her name kept showing up on rosters of Communist-front organizations. After doing some checking, he found that there was another Nancy Davis, and this one was "in the clear." As a courtesy, he took her out to dinner and, though he planned to make it an early evening, he was so entranced with her that they talked until three-thirty in the morning.[53]

This story, which has Reagan rescuing a damsel in political distress and falling for Nancy at first sight, was often repeated, and it appears in both their autobiographies. But in her book *Early Reagan,* Anne Edwards presents much evidence to show that the confusion with the other Nancy Davis occurred many years later. By Edwards's account the two met at a small dinner party that Dore Schary's wife, Miriam, arranged to bring Nancy together with the man who topped her list of eligible bachelors in Hollywood. The Scharys were liberal Democrats, and to their dismay Reagan talked about his anti-Communist activities all evening and left early without offering to take Nancy home. Shortly afterwards Nancy called him at the guild office and, according to the guild minutes, said she was interested in joining the SAG board. Reagan then took her to dinner, and a couple of months later, when she joined the board as a temporary member, they began to meet regularly and often went out together.[54]

Nancy decided rather quickly that she had found the man she wanted to marry, but Reagan, recently divorced, proved reluctant. He dated many other women, haunted the nightclubs and, in his newfound celebrity as an anti-Communist hero, traveled a great deal making speeches. "I did everything wrong," he later wrote, "dating her on and off . . . doing everything which could have lost her."[55] Nancy, however, persevered. Ignoring the other women, she sat through SAG meetings, painted fences on his ranch and spent countless evenings at home with him watching TV. Two and a half years later he proposed. They were married on March 4, 1952, and their first child, Patti, was born seven and a half months later.[56]

Nancy devoted herself to her husband—she rarely left his side—and the marriage became an extremely happy one. Temperamentally the two were as different as people could be. He was optimistic and confident, she high-strung and insecure. He sailed through life while she worried, fretted and feared the worst. He trusted those around him; she suspected people's motives and stood watchful guard against the slightest sign of disloyalty to her husband. Many people found her trying, but Reagan, unfailingly upbeat, sunny-tempered and distant, did not seem to notice how "difficult" she was.

It was Nancy who put all the energy into the marriage, for, although Reagan charmed audiences and acquaintances, he had no intimate relationships—indeed, he seemed to live on a different planet from everyone else. This distance of his was not generally known about until the "kiss-and-tell" books appeared late in his presidency, but afterwards everyone who knew him well remarked upon it. Lyn Nofziger, who once spent nine months campaigning with him, said that there was "a veil between Ronald Reagan and the rest of the world."[57] Helene von Damm, his assistant in Sacramento and Washington, wrote, "There was a wall beyond which you could not penetrate. . . . He was a fundamentally difficult man to know."[58] Forced to deal with the issue in her 1989 autobiography, Nancy wrote: "Although he loves people, he often seems remote, and he doesn't let anybody get too close.

There's a wall around him. He lets me come closer than anyone else, but there are times when even I feel that barrier."[59] People simply supposed that there was something behind the wall.

Nancy put up with his remoteness. As is clear from her autobiography, she felt she had found her cause and her career as his protector. He for his part came to depend on her. Possibly her grating nervous energy helped to connect him to the world. Possibly it did the opposite, for, as time went on, she increasingly assumed the tasks he did not want to perform himself. Michael Deaver in his memoir wrote: "At times Ronald Reagan has been very much a puzzle to me. I had never known anyone so unable to deal with close personal conflict. When problems arose related to the family, or with the personnel in his office, Nancy had to carry the load."[60]

Nancy felt the burden. Over the years, she writes, "I think I've come to worry even more than I used to because Ronnie doesn't worry at all. I seem to do the worrying for both of us." She continues, "Every marriage finds its own balance. It's part of Ronnie's character not to confront certain problems, so I'm usually the one who brings up the tough subjects—which often makes me seem like the bad guy."[61] Possibly Nancy, in addition to compensating for her husband's inability to deal with personal problems and conflicts, became a conduit for the negative emotions he could not, or did not want to, express himself. Certainly after many years of marriage they seemed, like Aristophanes' lovers, to be two half-creatures who had found their other half.

What was missing from this ensemble was much concern for anyone else, including the children—not only Reagan's children with Wyman, Maureen and Michael, but his children with Nancy as well. Patti described her parents as two halves of a circle, and Ron, the youngest, and the child who seemed to suffer the least, told a television interviewer that he never had a real conversation with his father.[62]

Reagan made twenty-two films after the war, but by 1953 his career had again stalled: though he was still getting movie offers, they were not for parts he wanted, and, while rich in real estate, he was cash-poor. At this juncture Taft Schreiber at MCA's Revue Productions brought him the *General Electric Theater* and a whole new career. Reagan had always said that he would not work in television, but the deal was too good to turn down: at a starting salary of $125,000 a year he would host a weekly dramatic program featuring guest stars and would act in a few of the plays each season; in addition he would spend several weeks a year touring GE plants around the country as a part of their "employee and community relations program." In his memoir Reagan writes that Revue Productions had conceived the package with him in mind, and that it was the idea of making appearances all over the country that intrigued him.[63] In reality GE had offered the package to several other actors ahead of him, and it seems unlikely that he actually wanted to visit GE plants all over the country, particularly since he was afraid of flying. But Reagan made the best of it.

In the eight years the *General Electric Theater* lasted, Reagan visited all, or most, of the 139 GE plants scattered over thirty-nine states. On arriving at a plant, he would meet the managers, talk with groups of workers and walk the assembly line signing autographs, telling stories and joking. In the evening he would address a civic group in the community. According to Edward Langley, a GE public-relations man who traveled with him, Reagan made thousands of speeches in the course of eight years. "We drove him to the utmost limits," he said.[64] The trips, usually made by train, were doubtless grueling, but surely not as grueling as Reagan remembered them. In his 1965 memoir Reagan claimed that he had performed the Bunyonesque feats of shaking two thousand hands in one day, signing ten thousand autographs in two days, walking forty-six miles of an assembly line in one day—and another forty-six miles that evening for the night shift.[65]

Paul Gavaghan, a GE public-relations man who accompanied Reagan on one trip, remembered that the pace was rather less hectic and that Reagan was always in control. "He was very different in private from his public personality, so outgoing. In private he was more restrained, disciplined, careful. He knew what he was doing all the time. He conserved his time and energy. As he said, 'We sell the difference,' and for him the difference was appearance. He took very good care of himself. He was not a nine-to-five man. He needed time off to rest and exercise and keep himself in shape. He was a professional."[66]

On that particular trip, Gavaghan remembered: "His speech was always the same, he had it polished to perfection. It was old American values—the ones I believe in, but it was like the Boy Scout code, you know, not very informative. But always lively with entertaining stories. . . . He promoted anti-Communism and the free enterprise system."[67]

In the course of the 1950s, however, Reagan's speech changed considerably. By the late fifties he was denouncing Medicare as "a foot in the door of a government take-over of all medicine," urging that Social Security be made voluntary and questioning every social program enacted since 1932. In 1961 he made the surprising announcement that "the Communist party has ordered once again the infiltration of the picture business as well as the theater and television. They are crawling out from under the rocks. . . ."[68]

Why Reagan moved so far to the right in this period has been variously explained. Langley later opined that it was because of his exposure to Middle America. Edwards by contrast suggests that it was the influence of his right-wing GE handlers.[69] But neither explanation will do, for Middle America had not turned against the New Deal, and Reagan's handlers, though very conservative, had no interest in stirring up political controversy around the company. Reagan doubtless picked up ideas from his audiences, his associates and his friends. His attacks on "socialized medicine," for example, surely owed much to his father-in-law. Still, he seems to have generated much of the heat on his own, and, as Garry Wills proposes, it seems to have been a matter of his rhetoric's running away with him. "I did it with my own speeches," Reagan later said. And he wrote, "I wasn't just making speeches—I was preaching a sermon."[70]

The process by which Reagan composed the Speech is in any case of some interest, for his method of composition never changed. It was the way his mind worked.

Throughout his life Reagan collected stories and anecdotes. He also collected bits of information. Lawrence Williams, an actor who worked with Reagan on five pre-war films, told Edwards:

> Statistical information of all sorts was a commodity Ronnie always had in extraordinary supplies, carried either in his pockets or in his head. Not only was this information abundant, it was stunning in its catholicity. There seemed to be absolutely no subject, however recondite, without its immediately accessible file. Ron had the dope on just about everything: this quarter's up—or down—figure on GNP growth, V. I. Lenin's grandfather's occupation, all history's baseball pitchers' ERAs, the optimistic outlook for California sugar-beet production in the year 2000, the recent diminution of the rainfall level causing everything to go to hell in summer [in] Kansas and so on.[71]

At the time some of Reagan's colleagues thought the young actor a naïve and a memory bank without a purpose.[72] But as Reagan's political views took shape, he began looking for statistics and anecdotes to deploy about his new certainties. He called this "research," but, as his campaign managers later discovered, he picked up pieces of information like a magpie without concern for the provenance. He valued every piece equally, and there was no piece that could be not replaced by another that would illustrate his point just as well.

At Hollywood dinner parties, where he practiced his speeches, some found his performances amusing and informative, others not. "I just thought he was stupid," said an art dealer who met him at a dinner at Edward G. Robinson's house. "He gave this speech, and you felt that if he stopped giving it he would fall off the edge. There wouldn't be anything there to hold on to."

The underpinnings Reagan's speeches lacked—and the art dealer found sorely missing—were the classical modes of argument. The method Reagan used was not deductive; it was not inductive either, for the conclusion came before the evidence. Rather, it was agglutinative. That is, his assumptions and moral precepts served as aggregation devices for anecdotes and bits of information that he would store away for future use—and anything that did not adhere to them would simply pass him by. Just as in a sermon, Reagan began with a lesson and then worked to present it as convincingly as possible.

As a Sunday-school teacher in Dixon, Reagan had illustrated his lessons with tales of courage and individual initiative shown by young men lost in the jungle, battling flood-swollen rivers or facing moments of truth on schoolboy fields of honor. Many of these stories were doubtless taken from the boys' adventure books he checked out of the library.[73] In his speeches Reagan told countless stories of individual heroism and, occasionally, villainy, some of them from the movies, some of them apocryphal. In the 1980s commentators politely assumed that he believed these stories to be true—and possibly he did by then. But in the fifties he narrated movie plots as true stories not so long after the movies came out. For example, he used the story about the heroic B-17 captain from the 1946 movie *A Wing and a Prayer* in a commencement address he made in 1952.[74] Since he had an excellent memory, it is reasonable to assume that he knew the story was a fiction but just did not care—accuracy being unimportant where moral certainty and the Truth were concerned.[75]

The Speech was always a work in progress. Reagan would add new examples, try out new anecdotes and drop lines for more felicitous phrases. His basic precepts never changed after the 1950s. What changed was the amount of stress he put on them. For example, he always complained that government was too big, but sometimes he figured the problem as minor—a matter of waste and fraud in the bureaucracy—sometimes as major and sometimes as a dire threat to American freedom. In general, the further away from power he was, the more alarmist his rhetoric. In office he often sounded like a complacent pastor; out of it he became a tent revivalist. In the early sixties he was a voice crying in the wilderness, and his rhetoric, unchecked by political necessity, slid over to the extreme end of the spectrum.

The *General Electric Theater* went off the air in 1962.[76] By that time Reagan was financially secure and much in demand as a speaker. In the next four years he made one film and did some television work, principally in a series called *Death Valley Days,* which his brother, Neil, now a vice-president in the advertising firm of McCann, Erickson, brought to him. But in those years he spent most of his time, and earned most of his living, on what he called "the mashed potato circuit." Naturally he was in demand with right-wing groups, and in southern California, where a new right-wing movement was taking shape, he spoke to a rally of Dr. Fred Schwartz's Christian Anti-Communism Crusade and at a fund-raising dinner for Representative John Rousselot, a self-acknowledged member of the John Birch Society.[77] After he changed his party registration in 1962, a number of wealthy California conservatives tried to persuade him to run for office.[78] Reagan kept turning them down, but he was clearly preparing for a political career. In 1964 he wrote a memoir with Richard Hubler, devoting much of the book to his work as a SAG negotiator and as leader in the anti-Communist struggle. The title of his book, *Where's the Rest of Me?,* came from his favorite film, *King's Row,* and the answer to the question, implicit in the book, was that there was much more to Reagan than what he called "the colored shadow" that appeared on the screen.

That same year Reagan served as co-chair of the California Citizens for Goldwater-Miller.[79] Goldwater was an old friend of his—he saw the senator frequently when he stayed at the Loyal Davises' house in Phoenix. Pleading other commitments, he did not spend much time on the campaign, but he did agree to tape a version of the Speech for national broadcast as a paid political advertisement for the campaign.

When Goldwater's advisers saw the text of the speech, they asked that the broadcast be canceled because they feared it would push their candidate even further into the right-wing corner he had painted himself into. But the California committee insisted it be aired, and Goldwater eventually let the Californians have their way. The speech, called "A Time for Choosing," was a huge success. Reagan, with his low-key manner and easy charm, made even attacks on the social-security net sound reassuring, and since he confined himself to generalized warnings about the Soviet threat, he seemed altogether more reasonable than Goldwater.[80] The speech raised a great deal of money for the campaign and received a very favorable comment from pundits and political handicappers. David Broder called it "the most successful national political debut since William Jennings Bryan electrified the 1896 convention with the 'Cross of Gold' speech."[81] Just as Goldwater was going down to defeat, Reagan became the new face in Republican politics.

Even before the 1964 election results were in, Goldwater's principal financial backers in California—among them Holmes Tuttle, a successful auto dealer; Henry Salvatori, an oil developer; and Cy Rubel, the chairman of the board of Union Oil—realized that they had been backing not only a loser but a losing strategy. These men had put up the money to broadcast Reagan's speech, and the success of it persuaded them that they had a far better candidate. Reagan, Salvatori said, "has a great image, a way to get through to people. . . . [Goldwater's] philosophy was sound, but he didn't articulate it moderately."[82] Justin Dart, another supporter, later said, "I don't think he's the most brilliant man I ever met, but I always knew Ron was a real leader—he's got credibility. He can get on his feet and influence people."[83] But before Reagan could run for President, he would, they determined, have to run for governor in 1966, and to do this successfully he would have to unite the Republican Party in California.

This time Reagan was easily persuaded to run. He did not declare his candidacy until 1966, but the strategy—one which he duplicated in other campaigns—was to let "Friends of Reagan" committees get out in front, drum up support and appear to be courting him. He was also persuaded of the need to appeal to moderate Republicans in the state. This was not his original intention. Shortly after the 1964 election he had told a meeting of the Los Angeles Young Republicans that Goldwater's defeat did not mean that the voters had repudiated conservatism or conservatives. "We don't," he said, "intend to turn the Republican party over to the traitors in the battle just ended. The conservative philosophy was not repudiated.... We will have no more of those candidates who are pledged to the same socialist philosophy of our opposition."[84]

Reagan was referring to the liberal Republican Senator Thomas Kuchel, who had refused to support Goldwater. Not long afterwards he abandoned this line and actively supported Salvatori's effort to bring in Stuart Spencer and William Roberts, who had managed the Rockefeller campaign.[85] His eagerness to run was such that he agreed to travel the state by airplane.

Having decided that Reagan should run as a "citizen politician," "a Joe Doakes," Spencer and Roberts hired BASICO, the Behavioral Science Corporation of Reseda, California, established by Dr. Stanley Plog and Dr. Kenneth Holden, to help retool their candidate for the campaign. Behavioral psychologists who taught at universities in southern California and advised businesses on human-relations issues, Plog and Holden had decided to look at the campaign as a complex problem in human behavior. But on meeting Reagan, Plog discovered that the candidate knew "zero about California . . . I mean zero." The psychologists therefore had to go back to the basics. Though no experts on state affairs themselves, they researched the issues and presented Reagan with position papers and eight books of five-by-eight cards that gave him the essential facts about the state. On the campaign trail they followed him everywhere and kept vigilant watch over him to see that he used their facts and not the ones he picked up for himself. They also changed his message. "We made certain that Reagan came across as a reasonable guy, not as a fanatic," Holden said. "One of the first things I got Ron to do was to stop using that terrible phrase 'totalitarian ant heap.' His basic speech was too negative, so we provided him with creative alternatives to combat that Far Right image with constructive proposals."[86] They also encouraged him to have a "total concept" of himself as candidate. Reagan, they discovered, was happy to be coached and happy to be spoon-fed answers to questions.[87] Under their guidance, he came out for unemployment benefits and Social Security, and he campaigned on high taxes, the growing cost of welfare, the unrest on California's campuses and the unpopular decisions Governor Brown had made in the course of his two terms.

The campaign was extremely well financed. Reagan's supporters included Alfred Bloomingdale, Jack Warner, Lew Wasserman of MCA and a roster of Hollywood stars, Jimmy Stewart and John Wayne among them. Henry Salvatori, Holmes Tuttle, Taft Schreiber of MCA, Reagan's lawyer William French Smith, Leonard Firestone (president of the tire company), Jaquelin Hume, president of Basic Vegetable Products, Inc., and others formed an executive committee to raise funds and otherwise assist the candidate.[88]

In spite of this muscle, Pat Brown thought Reagan would be easy to beat. "We rubbed our hands in gleeful anticipation of beating this politically inexperienced, right-wing extremist and aging actor," he wrote.[89] Brown had badly miscalculated. In the first place, Californians, who had just elected George Murphy to the Senate, had no aversion to actors; and in the second, Reagan had made many more speeches than Brown had in the course of his career. In the care of his handlers Reagan proved a fine campaigner. Given a light schedule with plenty of rest and the comforts of a star on location, he was always up, always impeccable, always charming. He was quick on his feet and always ready with a quip. Journalists despaired of his habit of repeating the same answers over and over again, as if someone had hit the "play" button, but few others cared, and it kept him from making mistakes.[90] Brown did his best to pin Reagan as a right-winger, but he never succeeded, for Spencer and Roberts kept all right-wingers out of the campaign, and Reagan did not sound or act like one. He spoke about the brilliant future of California. "Our problems are many but our capacity for solving them limitless," he proclaimed.[91] He made self-deprecating jokes, and he seemed to have no hostility to anyone—not even to members of the press. As for the charge that he lacked experience, Reagan turned the barb back on itself by saying, "The man who has the job has more experience than anybody. That's why I'm running."[92]

Nineteen-sixty-six was a good year for the Republicans nationally. In California, Reagan was helped by the Watts riots, by the behavior of student radicals on University of California campuses and by the fact that for many people Brown had been around too long. In November, Reagan won by almost a million votes.

During the campaign, Bill Roberts had paused for a moment to consider the possible result of his efforts. "What will the poor soul do if he's ever elected governor!" he said of Reagan.[93] Lyn Nofziger, a reporter for the Copely Newspapers, who had become Reagan's press secretary, later remembered having had sinking feeling after the victory. Reagan had "materialized out of thin air with no political background, no political cronies and no political machine. He didn't even run his own campaign. His campaign was run by hired people who then walked away and left it. Therefore, when he was elected, the big question was, 'My God, what do we do now?' "[94]

Reagan was almost fifty-six years old when he took office. He knew nothing about government—how budgets were made, how bills were passed—and he had no organizational experience outside of SAG. His Los Angeles executive committee, later known as the Kitchen Cabinet, helped with appointments and offered advice. But in the beginning Reagan had only the staff which remained with him from the campaign. Because Spencer and Roberts had chosen people who did not have political loyalties to one side or the other of the California Republican Party, most of them were young and inexperienced. Philip M. Battaglia, a brilliant and ambitious thirty-one-year-old attorney, who had chaired the campaign, became his executive secretary, or chief of staff. Thomas C. Reed, a thirty-year-old engineer, who headed the campaign in northern California, became his first appointments secretary.[95]

In line with his campaign rhetoric, Reagan proclaimed himself a citizen governor, a Mr. Smith, who would sweep the capitol with a new broom. Reagan spoke of the career civil servants as "them," and vowed there would be no more political horse-trading with the legislators.[96] "For many years now," he said in his inaugural address, "you and I have been shushed like children and told there are no simple answers to the complex problems which are beyond our comprehension. Well, the truth is, there are simple answers—there just are not easy ones."[97] In his first year, simplicity, or pure simple-mindedness, prevailed.

Reagan had run against high taxes, but on arriving in Sacramento he discovered that Brown had left the state with a deficit for the coming year and that he had a constitutional duty to close it. His first remedy was to order the state budget cut by 10 percent across the board. The order could not be universally obeyed, because many programs were legally mandated or pegged to particular revenue streams, but to the extent that it was, it cut into all programs indiscriminately, causing costly disruptions and delays. Other impractical schemes followed. State employees were asked to work voluntarily on Lincoln's and Washington's birthdays and were virtually barred from travel out of state; twenty-eight hundred mental-hospital workers were laid off; there was a freeze on the purchase of state automobiles; construction work was canceled and maintenance deferred. It was as if the Red Queen had gone after the California state budget, chopping off bits of the bureaucracy here and there. At the same time, the citizen governor had an acrimonious and highly publicized series of fights with the University of California Board of Regents in which he reduced its funding request by 15 percent and insisted that the students pay some tuition.

But none of these economies could save Reagan from the need to raise taxes. Anxious to blame his predecessor for the levy, he and his aides wrote a tax bill in great haste and made numerous political deals with Republican legislators in order to get it passed. The bill gave California the steepest tax increase in its history; it produced revenues far in excess of what was needed to cover the deficit, and since Jesse Unruh, the powerful Democratic Speaker of the Assembly, knew far more about the tax system than they did, it mandated a highly progressive tax.

Lou Cannon describes these measures as mistakes made by the novice governor and his novice staff; Wills, however, points out that dramatic budget cuts played well in the press, and the tax increase was blamed on Brown.[98]

After the first year or so, Reagan's California administration settled down and began to behave in a much more orthodox fashion. The ideological fervor diminished, and so did the quest for dramatic, short-term results. By the end of four years, Reagan could point to few legislative successes and, as Lou Cannon writes, his achievements were by any standards modest. On the other hand, his administration was considered by many to be moderate and responsible. Its top appointees, among them Caspar Weinberger, a San Francisco attorney who replaced Reagan's first finance director, were generally given high marks for competence.[99]

The turn-about coincided with a change in Reagan's staff.

In the spring of 1967 Lyn Nofziger heard rumors of what came to be called "a homosexual ring" operating out of the governor's office. Alarmed that a scandal might break out, and knowing full well that the political consequences would be severe if it did, Nofziger launched an investigation and after some months amassed evidence that the rumors had foundation. On September 7, Nofziger, Reed and several other staff members took the report to the governor, who was then recuperating from a prostate operation in San Diego. Reagan read the report and with a stricken look said, "My God, has government failed?"[100]

Reagan's chief of staff resigned, and a paralysis descended upon the governor's office. Rather than taking charge himself, Reagan drifted away, and his staff virtually stopped functioning. "The governorship went into receivership," one staff member later said.[101] Eventually William P. Clark, his Cabinet secretary, and a few other top aides drew together and formed a leadership team. A trial lawyer with considerable management skills, Clark created an organizational structure that lasted for the rest of Reagan's governorship. His deputy, and his replacement after Reagan appointed him to the California bench in 1971, Edwin Meese III, was another important member of the team. A graduate of Yale and the University of California at Berkeley law school, Meese had served for six years as deputy district attorney of Alameda County before becoming Reagan's legal secretary. He had made his reputation by supervising the police crackdown on the Free Speech movement at Berkeley, arresting some seven hundred students. When anti-war demonstrations and other civil disturbances erupted in the late sixties, he directed Governor Reagan's hard-line response.[102] Meese's deputy, Michael Deaver, became another key member of the team. A graduate of San Jose State, a piano player and sometime IBM salesman, he had joined Reagan's gubernatorial campaign at the age of twenty-eight and later went to work for Clark.[103] Deaver had no background in administration or policy-making, but, equipped with excellent political antennae, he eventually carved out a role for himself as Reagan's scheduler, troubleshooter and public-relations specialist. He also took on the job that no one else wanted: that of making Mrs. Reagan feel comfortable and secure. Over the years he grew close to Mrs. Reagan, and, partly as a result, came to have a good deal of influence over her husband.

Clark and Meese restored order and momentum to the governor's office. They created a working governor's Cabinet and acted as honest brokers for contending views. In addition they established a routine that suited Reagan and permitted him to function as chief executive of the state.

In his eight years in Sacramento, Reagan never worked long hours or spent evenings drinking with legislators: he left the office every afternoon at five, went home to a quiet dinner with Nancy and was usually in bed by ten. He worked hard on his speeches and on certain major issues, but the day-to-day work of governance did not interest him, and he left a great deal of it to Clark and Meese. As a result, he remained ignorant of much that went on in the governor's office. In the midst of an interview two and a half months after his inauguration, he turned to his aides and said, "I could take some coaching from the sidelines, if anyone can recall my legislative program."[104] Clark dealt with the selectivity of his attention by giving him mini-memos that summarized issues and recommended solutions.[105] He also provided Reagan with the kind of direction he seemed to require. "For eight years," Reagan later said, "somebody handed me a piece of paper every night that told me what I was going to be doing the next day."[106]

In Sacramento, Reagan's aides often described their boss's management style as being much like President Eisenhower's. The governor, they said, believed in a Cabinet government and had a relaxed, corporate approach; he believed in choosing good people and allowing them to run their departments while he acted as a kind of chairman of the board. Reagan may well have believed that this was how he governed, but the description was only half true. Reagan did have a relaxed approach, and he did delegate a good deal of authority to his department heads. But he never hired or fired anybody. According to Nofziger, his first staff members had to hire themselves and then hire everyone else. "Reagan was a macro-manager and sometimes no manager at all," Nofziger wrote. Further, Reagan depended so heavily on his staff that he sometimes appeared to be presiding over his government rather than running it.[107]

At a Cabinet meeting in the spring of 1967, Reagan and his advisers discussed a proposal from the state utility to build a nuclear-power plant in Diablo Canyon and a counter-proposal from conservationists to have the canyon set aside as a park. Reagan, who had read an article on the subject, remarked that the canyon sounded very beautiful and asked whether it wouldn't be best suited to private development, if not a park. His advisers, however, favored the nuclear plant. At the end of the meeting Reagan apologized for taking so long on the subject of the canyon and said, "I was really hoping that someone would say the canyon is just too beautiful for a plant. It sounds like a great place for a ranch." Cannon, who obtained the minutes to the meeting, points out that it did not seem to occur to Reagan that the "someone" who might have insisted on an alternative was himself.[108]

Reagan made decisions easily when his close aides were united and when issues fit into his ideological framework. Otherwise he made them hesitantly and unhappily. This was the case when a bill to liberalize abortions in California came up in 1967, five years before the *Roe* v. *Wade* decision and the political controversies it generated. Francis Cardinal McIntyre of California opposed the bill, Loyal Davis was for it and the governor's aides and friends were all over the map. Reagan waffled for weeks. He finally signed the bill, but, when confronted with the fact that it effectively legalized abortion, he complained that there were "loopholes" in it he had not understood.[109]

"Reagan is drawn to decisive types who are very positive in their recommendations," a former political consultant of his observed. "He accepts uncritically the theories of men of action who manage to speak in unqualified terms about getting things done. When Reagan handles a problem with clear-cut alternatives of good or bad, he can be effective, as in the campaign. But government contains so many options it frustrates anyone who tries to think in absolutes. Reagan doesn't have the knack for weighing alternatives."[110]

A few days after Reagan's election as governor, eight or ten of his supporters convened at his house on Pacific Palisades. Lyn Nofziger opened the meeting. "OK, now, you've been elected governor," he said, "let's look and see what we can do about electing you President in 1968."[111] The group, which included Tuttle and Salvatori, agreed that Tom Reed would mount an independent Reagan-for-President campaign, and that Reagan would cooperate by speaking widely and keeping his options open. Salvatori and Tuttle raised $440,000 for the effort, and as soon as the governor's office was staffed, Reed took off around the country booking speeches for the governor and talking with Republican leaders. Catching wind of this activity, the press naturally took to speculating that Reagan would run in 1968. Reagan issued firm denials.[112]

In July 1967 Reagan and Nixon met at the Bohemian Grove. Reagan said that he would not enter the primaries and, Nixon recalled, he said he was "surprised, flattered and somewhat concerned about all the presidential speculation surrounding him." A month later, however, Reagan put out word to conservative leaders, asking them to "wait and see" rather than announcing for Nixon.[113] That fall he went on the road and made speeches across the South and the West. Nixon had him outflanked in both regions, but his enthusiastic audiences so encouraged him and his political managers that he paid no attention when Goldwater and others told him that the best he could do was to split the conservative vote and hand the nomination to Nelson Rockefeller.[114] Still publicly insisting that he was not a candidate, he broke his promise to Nixon, entered the favorite-son primary in California and easily won. In July 1968 he assured Rockefeller's confidant, Emmett John Hughes, that he was in the race for keeps, and that, if they could stop Nixon, he and Rockefeller would battle it out for the nomination.[115] At the Miami convention he and his people had such high expectations of an upwelling of support that he declared himself a candidate just hours before Nixon won on the first ballot.[116]

Nixon, however, bore no obvious grudge, and once in office, he took pains to cultivate the popular California governor, inviting him often to White House dinners and giving him direct access to the Oval Office. He also gave him his first exposure to international affairs.

When Reagan took office as governor at the age of fifty-five, he had been abroad only once in his life, and that was in 1947, when he made a film called *The Hasty Heart* in England. Possibly he realized his need for more foreign experience in the 1968 campaign, for, after Nixon was elected, he asked the White House to send him abroad on official missions. Nixon's aides advised against sending this foreign-policy novice as an emissary, but Nixon overruled them. In the course of six years Nixon dispatched the Reagans on four official trips, one of them an extensive tour of East Asia, another a three-week trip to Europe.[117] The missions were largely ceremonial, but the Reagans traveled on White House planes and met with heads of state.* In addition, Nixon himself gave Reagan lessons in foreign policy. When he made his opening to China and broke with other traditional Republican policies, he carefully explained his actions to the governor. His solicitude paid off, for Reagan supported him on China and on the withdrawal from Vietnam and told his conservative supporters they could trust Nixon to respond to international challenges without appeasing the Communists.[119]

In 1970 Reagan ran for reelection against Jesse Unruh, the Speaker of the California Assembly. During the campaign he reverted to his citizen-politician rhetoric and ran against government, campaigning as if he had not been a part of the government for four years. He won by a half a million votes. Even Deaver could not understand how he managed to do this. "I can't explain it," Deaver wrote. "He touched feelings in people about the bureaucracy, and about the size and the role and cost of government. And very effectively he would lay that beast at the feet of someone else." Stuart Spencer, who managed his campaign, could not get over it. "He ran against . . . the government he was running. I mean he believes he's above it all. He believes it. That's why [the voters] believe it. I can't believe it. But they do."[120] Possibly, however, the voters understood better than Spencer how abstracted Reagan was from his own government.

In the view of journalists and public-policy experts in California the second Reagan administration was a major improvement over the first.

* What Reagan learned on these trips is not entirely clear. In Paris he and Mrs. Reagan refused the entire program the embassy planned for them and announced they wanted to meet counts and countesses. (This was surely her idea.) Still, the Reagans came back with photographs of themselves with foreign heads of state, notably one with Ferdinand and Imelda Marcos, which they put, silver-framed, on their piano, next to the silver-framed photographs of Nixon and Eisenhower.[118]

Reagan's biggest achievement was passing a welfare-reform bill, negotiated with the Democratic leadership, which tightened up administration and accountability and raised benefits for the truly needy. The bill became a model for welfare reform in other states. In addition, Reagan made solid contributions in areas where he might least have been expected to make them. For example, he substantially increased funding for the public schools and the state universities, and he warmly supported Wilson Riles, the Democratic reformer who was elected superintendent of public instruction. He provided new money for community mental-health programs, and he established an environmental record that pleasantly surprised liberals.[121]

In the areas of finance and administration, Reagan did his part for what he had previously figured as creeping socialism. By the end of his second term the state budget had more than doubled, going from $4.6 to $10.2 billion. Much of the increase owed to inflation, but not by any means all of it. Reagan did slow the growth in the number of state employees and lowered property taxes, but over eight years income taxes rose substantially. In his first term he had strongly opposed a withholding system on the grounds that citizens ought to feel the pain of taxes, but when Verne Orr, who succeeded Weinberger as finance director, explained the benefits it would have for the state, Reagan changed his mind and adopted a withholding system. In the view of at least some public-policy analysts, this and other managerial reforms adopted by the Reagan administration made the government run better and permitted it to deliver services more efficiently.[122]

In his second term Reagan spoke with pride about the achievements of his administration. Later, however, he claimed that he had cut spending in California and ran against big government all over again.[123]

In his last year or so in office Reagan seemed to Cannon to be drifting and uncertain of what to do next. Urged to run for a third term, he decided against it. He was tired of being governor, Cannon reports.[124] His backers had long supposed that he would run for President after Nixon completed his second term, but Watergate and the related scandals clouded his prospects. As the scandals unfolded, Reagan defended Nixon and his associates doggedly and without reservation. In May 1973 he said that the Watergate conspirators "are not criminals at heart." Later he maintained that Nixon was doing a good job of governing, and in private spoke of a "lynch mob" forming to get the President.[125] In private he also defended Spiro Agnew. Even after the vice-president had resigned, pleading no contest to charges of bribery, Reagan maintained that Agnew was a decent man who had been treated unfairly.[126] Issues of ethics and legality seemed to pass over his head. Also, he was slow to realize the consequences of the scandals for Nixon and the Republican Party. This obtuseness may well have owed to wishful thinking. In the opinion of many around him, his run for president depended on Nixon surviving in office and serving out his second term.[127] The week before Nixon resigned and long after the congressional hearings had exposed the Watergate cover-up, Reagan bewilderingly said, "Now, for the first time, it has been revealed that neither the Congress nor the American people had been told the entire truth about Watergate."[128] What could no longer be denied was that Nixon had badly hurt the Republican Party and that Gerald Ford would be running for President as an incumbent in 1976.

In May 1974, when it still looked as if Nixon might weather the scandals, Reagan met with a group that included two of his backers, Holmes Tuttle and Justin Dart, plus several of his close aides and a few outside political strategists, among them John P. Sears. A thirty-four-year-old attorney, Sears had worked for Nixon's firm, Mudge, Rose, and Guthrie, and had won his political spurs directing Nixon's delegate search in 1968. He had acted as Nixon's political adviser until he fell afoul of Attorney General John Mitchell in 1969. During the meeting Sears caught Reagan's attention by predicting that Nixon would not survive and that Gerald Ford would not be able to lead the country after he was gone. Whatever happened, Sears was suggesting, Reagan should run in 1976.[129]

Reagan and his advisers were not yet ready to accept such a proposition, but after Nixon resigned, the idea began to take hold. Conservatives across the country objected mightily when Ford made Nelson Rockefeller his vice-president. Reagan, according to Cannon, was disappointed that he himself did not get the job.[130] In the wake of the appointment, Reagan differed publicly with Ford on several policy issues, and when the new President offered him a Cabinet post, he turned the job down. In the fall of 1974 he told Cannon, "Now, I hope and pray that this administration is successful. And that would take care of '76. Because it's never—in my book—it's never been important who's in the White House, it's what's done.... Whatever may happen, I would like to feel that I can continue to be a voice in the Republican Party insuring that the party pursues the philosophy that I believe should be the Republican philosophy."[131] Clearly Reagan was beginning to position himself as the conservative champion and the alternative to Ford.

On leaving office in January 1975, Reagan returned to the "mashed potato circuit." With Michael Deaver and Peter Hannaford from his Sacramento staff acting as his agents and researchers, he was soon making eight to ten speeches a month for handsome sums; he also wrote a syndicated column that appeared in 174 newspapers and did regular radio commentaries for more than two hundred radio stations.[132] Speaking at conservative banquets and otherwise preaching to the faithful, Reagan reverted to the ideological simplicities of "A Time for Choosing" and to his former habit of gleaning statistics and anecdotes from such periodicals as *Reader's Digest* and *Human Events.* Caught up in this activity, he flirted with the idea of a third-party candidacy, but Holmes Tuttle and other big contributors refused to hear of it.[133] In July a "Citizens for Reagan" committee materialized. Reagan said nothing and kept on making money from his lectures, but the appearance of the committee signaled that he had decided to take on Ford in the

Republican primaries. The decision did not sit well with all of his backers. Some, Henry Salvatori among them, thought it disloyal of him to run against a Republican incumbent—and particularly one who was no Eastern liberal. Others, however, thought he had a better chance than Ford to win the presidential election.[134] John Sears, who in other meetings had consistently displayed political acumen, became his campaign chief of staff.[135]

Sears's strategy was for Reagan to run hard in the first few primaries, win in Michigan, Illinois and Wisconsin and then coast to victory in the South and the West. When the campaign season opened, Reagan's chances of taking an early lead looked pretty good. Ford had alienated many voters by pardoning Nixon; his détente policy was under siege from the right, and Reagan's polls showed that the fall of Saigon the previous spring had created a backlash in the country.[136] Then, too, Reagan was a better campaigner than the former Michigan congressman, and many thought him a more inspiring candidate. But the Sears plan fell apart in New Hampshire.

The previous September, Reagan had given a speech in Chicago written by Jeffrey Bell, a young right-winger who had picked up some notions about tax-cutting from Jude Wanniski of *The Wall Street Journal,* and who thought the candidate needed new ideas. In the speech Reagan, after an introduction about "the crushing weight of the central government . . . threatening the freedom of individuals and families," proposed a program of "creative federalism" that would transfer "authority and resources" from the federal government to the states, and in doing so cut the federal budget by ninety billion dollars and reduce the citizen's tax burden by an average of 23 percent. The background material specified that the federal government would maintain responsibility for such things as the space program and the national defense, but that most social-welfare programs would devolve upon the states and that many government services would be cut or privatized, among them the U.S. mail.[137] At the time the press virtually ignored this inventive proposal, but Stu Spencer, who had left Reagan to become Ford's campaign director, gave it his full attention, and in New Hampshire Reagan faced a barrage of questions from journalists that he could not answer without making matters worse. Sears called in Martin Anderson, an economics professor who had worked with him in the Nixon White House, to do what Nofziger describes as double-talking the proposal into innocuousness.[138] Anderson succeeded admirably, but the specifics of the original background material continued to haunt the candidate, and Reagan lost New Hampshire by just a few votes.

Sears had planned for Reagan to win by steering a fairly moderate course and observing what in California was known as the Eleventh Commandment: never speak ill of another Republican. But immediately after New Hampshire he and Reagan's pollster, Richard Wirthlin, realized that this strategy would no longer do: Reagan would have to go after Ford directly and hit him hard on defense and foreign policy, where he was weakest with the conservative primary voters.

Reagan adopted the new strategy with enthusiasm, and although he had supported the Nixon-Kissinger policies, he waged a hard-hitting campaign against the Ford-Kissinger policies for the rest of the primary season. Barnstorming through the South, he made an issue of the forthcoming Panama Canal treaties, charging that Ford was planning to "give away" the Canal to a tinhorn dictator. "We bought it, we paid for it, it's ours and we're going to keep it!" he declared triumphantly. He also accused Ford of not being tough enough on Cuba. His main theme, however, was American weakness in the face of the Soviet threat. Asserting that the Soviet Union had achieved military supremacy, he charged that Secretary of State Kissinger had presided over the loss of American power and that President Ford had shown "neither the vision nor the leadership necessary to halt and reverse the diplomatic and military decline of the United States." Specifically, he maintained that under Kissinger's stewardship the Soviet Union had gained nuclear superiority over the United States. Militarily, he said, we have become "Number Two in a world where it is dangerous, if not fatal, to be second best." Détente, he insisted, was a one-way street of benefit only to the Soviet Union.[139]

The crudeness of Reagan's attack on détente alarmed many liberal Republicans and caused party organizers in the Northeast to mutter that the Californian was "another Goldwater."[140] Ford's political advisers were alarmed as well. Ford wanted to counter-attack, but they argued that defense and foreign policy had become dangerous ground and succeeded in convincing him to back away and back down. As Reagan, with the help of Jesse Helms and George Wallace organizers, racked up primary victories in North Carolina, Texas and the Deep South, Ford expunged the word "détente" from the administration's vocabulary and substituted "peace through strength." He also decided against attempting to conclude the SALT II arms treaty before the election.[141] These tactics may have calmed conservative ire, or they may simply have helped to make Reagan's point that Ford lacked leadership qualities. In any case, Reagan made a strong showing in the South and the West, and Ford just managed to pick up enough delegates in the East and Midwest to fend off his bid for the presidential nomination.

At the Republican convention of 1976, Reagan was, to say the least, a controversial figure. He had divided the party; he had weakened Ford as the Republican contender; he had attacked détente and arms control; he had gone a long way towards undermining the treaties that most congressional Republicans, including Barry Goldwater, thought the only way to deal with the future of the Panama Canal. Therefore, when Ford, after his acceptance speech, called Reagan up to the podium to make a few remarks, Reagan, not surprisingly, called for party unity and made appeals to both sides. In a six-minute speech he praised the party's platform—always the preserve of the right; then, picturing himself driving down the beautiful Pacific highway composing a letter for a hundred-year time capsule, he proposed that there were two major challenges for the future: stemming "the erosion of freedom that has taken place under Democrat* rule in this country" and averting nuclear war in a world where "the great powers have poised and aimed at each other horrible missiles of destruction." If the task Reagan had set himself was to rouse his supporters and to reassure Republican moderates that he was not "another Goldwater," then he accomplished it nicely. The convention went wild with applause.[142]

In retrospect, the nomination of Ford was a boon to Reagan. In the wake of Watergate it would have been difficult for any Republican to have won in 1976. Also, Reagan had positioned himself so far to the right he would have had a hard time moving to the center, particularly with his Republican rival in the White House. As it was, Ford went down to defeat, and four years later Reagan was back on the campaign trail, the front-runner for the Republican nomination with the political winds behind him.

Reagan spent the intervening years giving speeches for other Republicans, doing a once-a-week radio show and chairing a political-action committee that funded Republican candidates. In the process he put a number of party leaders in his debt, just as Nixon had between 1962 and 1968. In those years he kept on speaking about the need to cut taxes, the need to increase the military budget and the need to reassert American strength in the world.

Reagan's basic message did not change, but circumstances did. By 1979 the country was suffering from a combination of recession and inflation; the Carter administration was smarting under a series of foreign-policy reverses; high oil prices and the growing public realization that Japan and Germany had grown into economic superpowers convinced many Americans that the United States had not only lost its preeminent position in the world but was fast losing control of its destiny. In addition, the social and cultural innovations of the sixties and seventies, and the domestic turmoil that accompanied them, had given rise to a powerful conservative reaction. Americans, President Carter said in July 1979, were suffering from "a crisis of confidence . . . that strikes at the very heart and soul and spirit of our national will."[143] It remained for Reagan to tell the country that the problem lay not with the American people but in Washington.

* Reagan normally used the adjective "Democratic," as all Democrats did, but he made an exception in this case.

CHAPTER THREE

Doubling the Volume

RUNNING AGAINST FORD IN 1976, Reagan had of necessity run on the right of the Republican Party and looked for the support of the conservatives in the South. But in the 1980 primaries he faced a field of little-known candidates. As the front-runner he might have been expected to moderate his rhetoric and move towards the center in preparation for the presidential campaign. Instead he ran and won the nomination on defense and foreign-policy positions that were at least as hard-line as those he took in the previous campaign.

In the space of four years, the American political landscape had changed. Not only had a conservative mood swept over the country, but the Republican Party had for structural reasons moved to the right. By 1980 Nixon's Southern strategy, and Reagan's, had come to fruition: conservative white Southerners had left the Democratic Party and the George Wallace party, breaking up the New Deal coalition and moving the South into the Republican column. The result was that both the Republican and the Democratic parties had become far more ideologically coherent than before. Then, in part because of this realignment, the right wing of the Republican Party, based in the South, the Southwest and the Rocky Mountain states, had grown to a strength it had not had since the 1964 Goldwater campaign. The New Right, as the movement came to be known, made a dramatic appearance in 1980 with fundamentalist televangelists exhorting the faithful to join a Christian political crusade, and a host of new political-action committees in Washington raising money and mobilizing voters with computerized databases and direct mail. In addition, the foreign-policy establishment had split apart, and by 1980 the conservative wing of it, which included a number of former Democrats, had gained ascendancy and was calling for an end to détente and a renewal of the Cold War.

The Republican right, which Reagan had cultivated ever since Goldwater's defeat, naturally fell in behind Reagan; somewhat more surprisingly, so, too, did the conservative wing of the foreign-policy community. In terms of foreign and defense policy, the combination proved an ideologically potent brew. Out of it came the most anti-Soviet rhetoric that the country had heard in two decades and Reagan's idea for a shield against nuclear weapons.

Journalists covering the 1980 campaign sometimes had difficulty interpreting what Reagan said about foreign policy. Generally Reagan spoke in a familiar Cold War idiom, but there were times when the language of the Republican right broke through, and what it signified had been largely forgotten. After all, no post-war President had belonged to that wing of the party, and since 1964 those who remained faithful to Goldwater's views of the time had been wandering in the wilderness, far from the centers of power.

Journalists, among others, tended to think of Republican right-wingers as being at the extreme end of the Republican political spectrum—the unexamined assumption being that the difference between the views of right-wingers and moderates was simply one of degree. In reality the difference was qualitative. That is, right-wingers had a set of concerns and enthusiasms which other Republicans lacked, some of which ill-accorded with the priorities of the Cold War establishment. They had, for example, little interest in Europe, but an almost obsessive concern with Central America and the Caribbean—thus the success of Reagan's assault on the Panama Canal treaties in 1976. They were fascinated by guerrillas and terrorists. Also, they did not see American vulnerability to Soviet nuclear weapons as ineluctable, and those who took an interest in military matters longed for weapons in space. These concerns were not ad hoc, nor were they simply an agglomeration of single issues: rather, they belonged to a coherent world-view encoded in a distinct political tradition that went back to the nineteenth century.

The New Right activists in Washington—the "movement conservatives," as they sometimes called themselves—never spoke of the sources of their conservatism. While calling for the restoration of "traditional values," they also called for a "revolution" in government and talked with excitement about all the new ideas for policies and programs pouring out of the new right-wing think-tanks and foundations. But, then, rather than revolution, their project was the restoration of a world so antique that they themselves did not know what they were trying to restore.

Reagan, for his part, never spoke of the political tradition from which his own views came. A Democrat until after World War II, he took small interest in the history of the Republican Party, and as governor he disassociated himself from the tattered remnants of the Goldwater party. Yet it was that tradition that permitted him to tell stories that resonated deeply in the American political unconscious, and it was his rhetoric that provided a connection to the lost world.

In the 1980 campaign Reagan spoke for the first time at length about foreign policy in the hearing of national political reporters. In an essay on his campaign published the following year, Hedrick Smith of the *New York Times* wrote that Reagan approached the world with "a basic philosophical outlook which is a throwback to the 1950s when American power was paramount." The global power rivalry with Moscow, Smith wrote, not only animated his thinking but was the prism through which he viewed the entire world. In Asia, Africa and Central America, Smith wrote, Reagan saw the Soviets at work behind all the ferment of change. "Let us not delude ourselves," Reagan told *The Wall Street Journal*. "The Soviet Union underlies all the unrest that is going on. If they weren't engaged in this game of dominoes, there wouldn't be any hot spots in the world." On another occasion he lamented, "All over the world, we can see that in the face of declining American power, the Soviets and their friends are advancing." Sometimes Reagan spoke as if the Sino-Soviet split had never happened and seemed to ignore the purpose of Nixon's opening to China. In the midst of the campaign he called the whole U.S.-China relationship into question by promising to establish an official relationship with Taiwan. "There is a Communist plan for world conquest," he maintained. Similarly, Reagan seemed to imagine that if the U.S. showed firm leadership its allies in Europe would fall into line like so many soldiers on parade. Then, too, though Reagan pictured the Soviets as implacable foes bent on world domination, he seemed at the same time confident that, if challenged, they would back away from confrontation with the United States. At one point in the primary season he proposed a blockade of Cuba as a means of getting the Soviets to withdraw from Afghanistan. When George Bush, his leading opponent in the primaries, protested that a blockade might result in a clash with the Soviet Union, Reagan insisted that he was "not talking about war" and that in his opinion "a little call on the hotline with this kind of threat might get the withdrawal of troops from Afghanistan."[1]

During the campaign John Sears told Smith, "There's a generation gap between what Reagan thinks he knows about the world and the reality. His is a kind of 1952 world. He sees the world in black and white terms."[2] Indeed, much of what Reagan said about foreign policy in 1980 sounded not very far removed from the Speech.

Still, Reagan sometimes offered views strikingly at odds with his rhetoric about U.S. leadership in the global contest with Communism. During the campaign, Smith reports, Reagan told a journalist that one of his fondest memories was of watching a newsreel in which an American naval company marched "through the streets at double-time" to an American legation in a Spanish coastal city to rescue American citizens trapped by the fighting during the Spanish Civil War. "You couldn't help but thrill with pride at that," he said. Smith quotes this story as evidence of Reagan's nostalgia for the days of Pax Americana and his view that America must act more forcefully to protect its interests around the world. But the interpretation is anachronistic. The incident, after all, took place in the 1930s, and the U.S.

naval intervention had nothing to do with the Spanish Civil War as such, but merely with the rescue of American citizens from a foreign conflict.[3]

In a book of interviews with Reagan produced for the 1976 campaign, a conservative supporter, Charles Hobbs, asked Reagan what his philosophy of foreign policy was. "Our foreign policy," Reagan replied, "should be based on the principle that we will go anywhere and do anything that has to be done to protect our citizens from unjust treatment. Our national defense policy should back that up with force." Rather than citing any other principles, Reagan went on to illustrate this one with a very long story about an American naval captain who rescued a resident of the United States from an Austrian ship in the Turkish harbor of Smyrna in 1853. Only under prodding from Hobbs did he take up the theme of anti-Communism.[4]

These stories are startling, yet they fit very well with the world Reagan often conjured up when speaking of domestic affairs: an earlier America of small towns and face-to-face relationships, a world of hard work, self-reliance and individual acts of charity.

Sears was, of course, right: Reagan had learned his politics in the fifties. But he had learned them not from the party of Adlai Stevenson or that of Dwight Eisenhower but, rather, from the Republican right, then a party of the Midwestern heartland and still dominated by the starchy figure of Senator Robert A. Taft.

Born in 1889, Senator Taft was the son of William Howard Taft, the twenty-seventh President, and the grandson of Alphonso Taft, who served as secretary of war and attorney general under Ulysses S. Grant. The careers of the three Tafts spanned the period of the Republican Ascendancy, the seventy years between the beginning of the Civil War and the Depression, during which the Republican Party dominated American politics. The great achievement of that period was the creation of a nation from the two halves of the old union and the territories of the frontier. In that period the Republican Midwest was the source of the integrating myths of the new nation: rugged individualism, Manifest Destiny and the idea of America as a land of small communities and a sober, cloth-coated middle class. Elected to the U.S. Senate in 1938, Robert Taft, in his staunch conservatism, was a link to the nineteenth-century GOP.

In *The Odyssey of the American Right,* Michael Miles tells us that even in the 1930s Midwestern Republicans had a provincial and quasi-Jeffersonian view of the country.[5] Gentry-folk representing rural areas, small cities and towns, they envisioned America as made up of their own kind: small businessmen and well-to-do farmers of North European extraction. Liberals in the nineteenth-century sense of that word, they believed in individual liberty, small business and local government control. In their view the concentration of economic power on Wall Street and in the big corporations with their large labor forces threatened the true America—and their whole way of life. Midwesterners, the Progressives as well as the Republicans, thought of Europe as Jefferson sometimes did, as the Old World: decadent, feudalistic, corrupt and the very antithesis of the American Republic with its solid, independent, God-fearing citizenry. In the Midwestern view extremes of wealth and poverty and feckless aristocracies had made Europe a cauldron of radical ideas that boiled over into revolution and tyranny.

In terms of foreign policy, Republicans and Progressives endlessly repeated President Washington's warning about the danger of "entangling alliances" with European powers and called for high tariff barriers. For them Europe was remote—but not remote enough. In their view European trade and investment only enriched Wall Street, promoted big business and created outposts of Europe in the cities of the Eastern Seaboard: not only a mass of immigrants but an Anglophile elite that aped European fashions and imported its decadent art. Midwesterners had no particular favorite among the European powers, or among what Taft called Europe's "welter of races" with their ancient, incomprehensible quarrels.[6] Woodrow Wilson's call for intervention to help Britain against Germany in World War I met with flinty opposition in the Midwest. In the inter-war years Midwesterners denounced the League of Nations as a Great Power scheme for world domination. Senator William Borah of Idaho, a Republican and the chair of the Senate Foreign Relations Committee, maintained on one occasion that the league was a bankers' plot and on another that it smelled to him of Bolshevism.[7]

Evangelical Protestantism was the dominant religious stream in the provincial Midwest, and its radical individualism, its rejection of the hierarchical institutions of the Catholic church ran in the same current with Republican political ideology. In the nineteenth and early twentieth centuries, when the boundary between religious and secular discourse was far more permeable than it later became, politicians sometimes described Wall Street, or alternatively Bolshevism, as a vast, insidious conspiracy with demonic powers. Midwestern Republicans possessed a completely coherent economic and social theory—it was Marxism in reverse—but as conservative evangelicals they believed that God and the devil were at work in the world.

During the inter-war years the "internationalists" of the East branded all those who opposed the league and the American entry into the war against Hitler as "isolationists." The term was a misnomer. Since the Civil War, the Republican Party had presided over the American continental expansion and the drive into Central America and the Pacific. Manifest Destiny and the notion of ever-expanding frontiers played an important role in the mythology of the Midwest, and in the early years of the century Midwestern Republicans rivaled Theodore Roosevelt in their enthusiasm for American imperial adventures to the south and the west. William Howard Taft had served as the first civil governor of the Philippines, and as President sent the Marines to Nicaragua and attempted to extend U.S. hegemony over the Caribbean and Latin America with "dollar diplomacy." In 1917 Albert Beveridge, a former senator from Indiana and one of the leading crusaders against Wilsonian internationalism, went so far as to urge that the U.S. invade and occupy Mexico.[8] In the inter-war years General Douglas MacArthur served several tours of duty in the Philippines and became the symbol of the American imperial mission in the Pacific. Midwestern Progressives actually were "isolationists" in that they disliked American imperialism as much as they did "entangling alliances" in Europe, but Midwestern Republicans simply preferred military action on the opposite side of the continent to the Eastern "internationalists."

American imperialism was an attenuated enterprise by the 1930s, but it left Midwestern Republicans with a very different image of the world from the one Easterners had. Looking across the Atlantic, Easterners, both Republicans and Democrats, saw a continent of heavily armed nations with strong economies and strong cultural ties to the United States: Europe might be decadent, but it represented civilization, and beside it the United States had long been a "developing country" and not a little provincial. Oriented towards the Caribbean and the Pacific, Midwestern Republicans on the other hand looked out upon countries inhabited by peoples of alien cultures, all of them technologically and militarily inferior to the United States. To most of them these countries were pure abstractions—mere objects of American nationalist pride, commercial activity and the American civilizing mission. "With God's help, we will lift Shanghai up and up until it is just like Kansas City," declared Senator Keith Wherry of Nebraska, one of Taft's closest allies. Under the circumstances Midwestern Republicans saw no need for alliances and almost no need for diplomacy. "It is in the pattern of the Oriental psychology to respect and follow aggressive, resolute and dynamic leadership," General MacArthur averred as he disregarded Chou Enlai's warning that China would enter the Korean War if the UN forces crossed the 38th parallel.[9] A resolute attitude and a whiff of grapeshot would surely do.

In the late 1930s the historians Charles and Mary Beard identified Midwestern Republicans as "imperial isolationists," as opposed to the "collective internationalists" of the East Coast. These two positions carried with them different military strategies.

In the late nineteenth century Midwestern Republicans—and Republicans generally—became advocates of a powerful navy, for the Navy could be used to defend American shores against the European powers, to enforce the Monroe Doctrine in the Caribbean and to extend the American reach into the Pacific. In the 1890s the American naval historian Alfred Thayer Mahan taught them that the great European empires had been founded upon their conquest of the oceans. Later Midwestern Republicans came to look with suspicion upon any plan for enlarging the U.S. Army, for in their view the only conceivable function of a large army was to intervene in European wars, as the Democrats wished. In addition, the maintenance of a large standing army was extremely expensive, and, consistent to a fault, they believed that all public expenditure should be restricted. With the advent of airplanes, they backed the development of an air force as a cheap substitute.

Midwestern Republicans preferred sea and air power for practical reasons, yet there was also surely some magical, or symbolic, thinking involved. The idea of exerting power at a distance—or exerting power while remaining isolated—was, after all, the whole project of "imperial isolationism." In the 1940s and '50s Taft objected to the stationing of American troops abroad on the grounds that it would entail direct American involvement with everlasting quarrels of foreigners. The Navy and the Air Force would transcend foreign politics; they would allow America both to pursue its God-given mission abroad and to remain the virgin land, uncorrupted by the selfish interests of others or foreign doctrines. Thus, while the Democrats, the party of the immigrants, fought land wars, compromised and negotiated, true Republicans would preach to the benighted foreigners and command the world from the heights of the air and the great distances of the sea.

In 1940 Taft opposed the American entry into the war against Hitler, but after Pearl Harbor he supported Roosevelt's military buildup, stressing the importance of air power, on the grounds that the United States had to remain militarily invulnerable. "My whole idea of foreign policy," he said, "is based largely on the position that America can successfully defend itself against the rest of the world."[10]

After the war Taft remained faithful to his views, but many of his Midwestern colleagues broke with the tradition he represented in two important respects. In the first place, convinced that the New Deal was plunging the country into socialism, many of them made common cause with big business. The alliance made sense as a practical, but not a philosophical, matter, and thereafter the Republican right existed in a state of tension between laissez-faire economics and social conservatism. The contradiction was never resolved but merely papered over by spokesmen such as Reagan, who championed both forty-six-mile-long assembly lines and the values of small, face-to-face communities in the name of freedom. Then, in the area of foreign policy, most Midwestern conservatives broke with Taft to the extent of voting for the initiatives the Truman administration took to protect Western Europe against the spread of Communism and the possibility of Soviet aggression. They could hardly do otherwise, given their fierce anti-Communism; all the same, the decision caused them some anguish, and it was only the Truman Doctrine with its promise of support for "free peoples" everywhere—including, presumably, China—that brought them around.

By the 1950s Republican conservatives supported NATO and most of the other American efforts to defend Western Europe. Still, they remained Asia-firsters, protectionists and unilateralists. And, true to their evangelical tradition, they pictured the world as a single battlefield between the forces of good and evil: one in which compromise meant surrender and there could be no agreement to disagree. They never accepted the containment policy to the extent that it meant coexistence with the Soviet Union but, decade after decade, called for a "rollback" of Soviet power. Preaching anti-Communism would help, they believed. The dilemma of how to extend the U.S. military reach while keeping the federal budget in check was one they resolved by calling for a heavy reliance on the Navy, on the Air Force and on atomic, and later nuclear, weapons. This was the strategy adopted by the Eisenhower administration, only they, unlike Eisenhower, saw it as a winning strategy even after the Soviets acquired nuclear weapons.[11] In the early 1960s their hero, General Curtis Le May, the head of the Strategic Air Command, still believed that the Air Force could beat the Soviets to the draw, take out their bomber and missile bases in a preemptive strike and win a nuclear war with acceptable casualties.[12]

By the mid-sixties conservative politicians, among them Goldwater, accepted the fact of American vulnerability to nuclear weapons and joined the debates about how deterrence was to be maintained and how much was enough. Yet in groups such as those Reagan spoke to on the mashed-potato circuit and on the campaign trail in the late sixties and seventies there remained a great deal of frustration. Those who saw the Soviet Union as evil incarnate had no hope that war could be averted by arms-control treaties or summit meetings: only ideological victory or a war-winning military capability would do. In this period Phyllis Schlafly, who had made her national political debut in the 1964 campaign with a pamphlet entitled *A Choice Not an Echo,* proclaiming Barry Goldwater the heir to Senator Taft, co-authored five books on strategic nuclear policy in which she charged that Robert McNamara, Henry Kissinger, Paul Nitze and their colleagues had deliberately chosen to prevent the U.S. from obtaining "a decisive war-winning response to any attack."[13] Schlafly went on to other issues, but she, and the sense of frustration that she expressed so vividly in her books, reappeared in the Reagan campaign.

> "... the creation of a vast armament in itself calls for a condition midway between war and peace. Mass emotion on a substantial scale is prerequisite. The willingness to sacrifice must be engendered. A sense of peril from abroad must be cultivated."
>
> —John Foster Dulles, 1939[14]

In 1976 Reagan had no full-time defense or foreign-policy adviser. The campaign did not really require one, and no prestigious foreign-policy expert sprang forward to offer his services. The right wing of the Republican

Party was understandably short on people with such expertise. The federal bureaucracy in general, and the foreign service in particular, were not major career destinations for those in the Goldwater camp. Moreover, the foreign-policy community in Washington tended to reject right-wingers, as it rejected those on the left of the political spectrum. Reagan's outside advisers included a few members of Congress, a few military officers and a few academics: the Republican right had little more to give him.

Yet by 1979 the permanent Reagan campaign had attracted a host of defense and foreign-policy experts, a number of them lifelong Democrats, and some of them, such as Paul Nitze and Eugene Rostow, charter members of the establishment which had guided American foreign policy since World War II. These people gave the campaign credibility it might otherwise have lacked and later provided the administration with a cadre of experienced policy-makers to fill its national-security posts. The experts had, as it happened, developed a rhetoric about the military contest with the Soviet Union that was hugely influential in the world from which they came. Because it meshed with Reagan's own, that rhetoric set the course of the Reagan administration for the first three years.

Historically speaking, the alliance was a strange one: never before had the heirs to Truman and Acheson made common cause with an heir to Taft and Goldwater. But since 1968 the foreign-policy establishment had gone through a traumatic upheaval, and in the mid-seventies it split into two warring factions. The split did not occur all at once but, rather, like the political shifts in the country at large during that period, there was a movement to the left, then a movement to the right, and many within the establishment and its penumbra among policy analysts, journalists and others went along with the tide.

The breakup of the establishment and the bipartisan coalition that supported it began with the opposition to the Vietnam War led by Eugene McCarthy and Robert Kennedy in the 1968 election; it proceeded apace during the Nixon administrations as Nixon and Kissinger slowly withdrew American troops from Vietnam, established a détente with the Soviet Union and opened relations with the People's Republic of China. Nixon's continuing prosecution of the war provoked a full-scale revolt among liberals in Congress, leading them to question the whole set of ideas and practices on which the war was based, even as détente and the opening to China undermined a good many other Cold War orthodoxies. Then, when the Vietnam War ended in 1975 with a victory for the Communists and détente did not persuade the Soviets to abandon their ambitions with regard to the Third World, many in the American foreign-policy establishment went into reaction. By the time Jimmy Carter took office in 1977, liberals and conservatives were producing descriptions of the world that differed so fundamentally that historians of the future may wonder whether they lived on the same planet.

By the early seventies the emerging consensus among Democrats in the foreign-policy community was that the U.S.-Soviet conflict was not as central to international relations and to American interests as it had been understood to be. While American attention was riveted to the Cold War, much else had happened. The world of the 1970s was quite different from that of the immediate post-war period—and from that spelled out in Cold War doctrines. For one thing, it was far more complex. New centers of economic power were challenging U.S. and Soviet hegemony, and so, too, was nationalism in the Third World. In addition, there were new problems, from unruly global financial flows to global environmental degradation, which could not be addressed within the narrow framework of the Cold War. The academic shorthand for all of this was "global interdependence" and a "multi-polar world." In the view of most within this emerging consensus, the Soviet Union remained a formidable military power, but, because of the nature of its system, it was fast losing ground as an economic power and losing the ideological struggle as well. Further, the nuclear arms race was not as important a determinant of power and influence as had been supposed. Rather the U.S. and the Soviet Union were, as the defense expert Paul Warnke put it, like "apes on a treadmill," wasting their strength on an activity that was virtually meaningless given the thousands of deployed nuclear weapons.[15] What was required, it seemed to many, was a new form of internationalism.

In response to these perceptions, David Rockefeller and others created the Trilateral Commission, an organization of businessmen, academics and former senior foreign-policy–makers from the United States, Europe and Japan. The commission set itself to work on three major tasks: managing the world economy, satisfying basic human needs in the developing world and keeping the peace with the Soviet Union.

While this new internationalism was under construction, some members of the foreign-policy community moved sharply to the right and developed a neo-orthodox position. The movement included a small but articulate group of intellectuals headquartered in New York around *Commentary* magazine, who called themselves "neo-conservatives." Former liberal Democrats, a number of whom had been Trotskyites in their youth, the "neo-conservatives" had concerns that went far beyond foreign policy. Having viewed the various disturbances of the sixties, from inner-city rioting to student activism to gay liberation, as attacks on legitimate social and cultural authority—if not on civilization itself—they were calling for a general counter-offensive. Most of them had opposed the Vietnam War, but all of them feared that the reaction to it would lead to the decline of American power and of American willingness to maintain its Cold War commitments. The larger group in the neo-orthodox movement consisted of members of the foreign-policy establishment whose views had not changed at all. Less ideological than the neo-conservatives, these people were more or less strictly concerned with what they saw as the decline of U.S. military power and prestige in the wake of Vietnam and signs of a dangerous slackening in the permanent exertion required to sustain the Cold War.[16]

In the fall of 1975 Eugene V. Rostow, a law professor and former dean of the Yale Law School, who had served as undersecretary of state in the Johnson administration, wrote to Nitze and a number of other, like-minded citizens, proposing that they form a committee to alert the nation to what Rostow described as the growing Soviet threat to the United States, and to call for a military buildup. In March 1976 Nitze, Rostow and others held an organizing meeting and named their group the Committee on the Present Danger, after a similar group formed in the early 1950s.[17] The CPD was to be bipartisan, so it was decided that the formal inauguration should wait until after the 1976 presidential election, but by the fall it had an impressive list of board members that included Douglas Dillon, Treasury secretary under Eisenhower; retired generals Matthew Ridgeway, Lyman Lemnitzer and Maxwell Taylor; Dean Rusk, Kennedy's secretary of state; and David Packard, Nixon's deputy secretary of defense. The work of the committee was, however, done by Rostow, Nitze, Richard Pipes, a professor of Russian history at Harvard, and an enthusiastic corps of younger members, many of them neo-conservatives. The CPD focused on the strategic nuclear threat, and Nitze, who took the position of chairman of policy studies, did most of the analytical work on the subject for the Committee.[18]

Nitze was a legend in Washington. A Wall Street banker who went to Washington at the outbreak of World War II, he had served five presidents and had played a role in most of the major events of the Cold War: the development of the Marshall Plan, the military containment of the Soviet Union, the Korean War, the Berlin and Cuban missile crises, the Vietnam War and the SALT negotiations. Over the years he had held numerous government posts, among them chief of the State Department's policy-planning staff, secretary of the Navy and deputy secretary of defense. But his influence was far greater than the sum of his government positions, and in the area of strategic-weapons policy and arms control, he was perhaps the most influential figure in the post-war period. Certainly no one could match the length and breadth of his experience with these issues. His involvement had begun in 1945–46, when, as vice-chair of the Strategic Bombing Survey, he had studied the effects of the atom bomb on Hiroshima and Nagasaki, and it had continued ever since, whether he was in or out of government. Serving under Acheson in the early fifties, he had played a key role in the decision to develop the H-bomb and later participated in studies that had an important influence on the design of U.S. nuclear forces. In the early sixties he worked on the first arms-control agreement with the Soviet Union, the partial test-ban treaty of 1961, and helped lay the intellectual foundations for the rest. A senior negotiator in the Strategic Arms Limitation Talks from 1969 to 1974, he had been one of the principal negotiators of the ABM Treaty. Though an *éminence grise,* he was a superb technician whose detailed knowledge of the nuclear calculus could hardly be matched. He was also a cat who walked by himself and, though universally respected, he inspired less affection than admiration and fear.

Nitze left the Nixon administration in May 1974, citing differences with the administration's approach to SALT II and the deleterious effects of Watergate on the negotiations. A month later he told a congressional subcommittee that the Soviet Union was well on its way to achieving usable strategic superiority over the United States and the administration was doing nothing about it.[19] In January 1976 he spelled out this contention in an article in *Foreign Affairs* magazine entitled "Assuring Strategic Stability in an Era of Detente." That spring, while helping to organize the Committee on the Present Danger, he served as an adviser to the Carter campaign. In perennial fashion, he was under consideration for a top post in the administration. When he did not get a job—he antagonized Carter with his dogmatic insistence on the perilous condition of the U.S. nuclear deterrent—he threw himself into the work of the CPD and that fall participated in an exercise known as Team B.[20]

One of the more noteworthy products of the ideological divide, Team B had its origins in efforts by the hawkish members of Gerald Ford's Foreign Intelligence Advisory Board to show that the CIA had been underestimating the Soviet strategic threat. Anxious to protect Ford from the right, George Bush, the director of the CIA in 1976, agreed to appoint a panel of outsiders to review the agency's estimates, and he approved the selection of a group of well-known hard-liners, including Richard Pipes, who chaired the group; Lieutenant General Daniel O. Graham, who had headed the Defense Intelligence Agency; and William Van Cleave, a professor of international relations and strategic studies at the University of Southern California and a member of the CPD. Team B was given unprecedented access to the CIA's raw intelligence files, and after studying them for three months, it delivered a report in December 1976. The report was highly classified, but its conclusions were soon leaked to the press: Team B had castigated the CIA for underestimating Soviet strategic capabilities and the malevolence of Soviet intentions; it had found that the Soviets were striving for, and gaining, a nuclear-war–winning capability. Later General Graham told journalists that one of the "catalytic" factors which caused Team B to reevaluate Soviet intentions was the "discovery of a very important [Soviet] civil defense effort."[21]

The Committee on the Present Danger was inaugurated while the panel was at work, and in its initial statement of purpose the Committee warned: "Our country is in a period of danger, and the danger is increasing. Unless decisive steps are taken to alert the nation, and to change the course of its policy, our economic and military capacity will become inadequate to assure peace with security." This was so, the committee argued, because the Soviets, in their "drive for dominance" and for a "Communist world order," had undertaken an "unparalleled military build-up" which was "in part reminiscent of Nazi Germany's rearmament in the 1930s." If past trends continued, it asserted, the Soviets would "within several years achieve strategic superiority over the United States." The Soviet Union, it continued, "does not subscribe to American notions of nuclear sufficiency and mutually assured deterrence"; rather, "Soviet nuclear offensive and defensive forces are designed to enable the USSR to fight, survive and win a nuclear war."[22]

Before the election CPD members had some hope that Jimmy Carter, a Southern governor, would take their counsel, but, not entirely to their surprise, Carter, whose only real exposure to foreign affairs had been as a member of the Trilateral Commission, recruited people with a wide range of views, but none of their number and a good many new internationalists. Thereafter the CPD became the scourge of his defense and foreign policies.

In regard to foreign policy, one of the main tasks Carter faced was rhetorical. Many of his appointees had a new vision of the world and a new agenda, but since the election had been fought on other grounds, their view had yet to be translated into the American political discourse. In effect Carter had to come up with a new definition of national security and persuade the public to adopt it. The task was not at all easy, for, among other things, it involved displacing the rhetoric dominant for the past thirty years. Carter's policy appointees were not much help: their rebellion was precisely against the ideological simplifications of the past. As Leslie Gelb, Carter's assistant secretary of state for politico-military affairs, put it, "The environment we are looking at is far too complex to be reduced to a doctrine in the tradition of post–World War II American foreign policy."[23] As for Carter's political advisers, they did not grasp the importance of the task. Carter's advocacy of human rights struck a chord with the public, but otherwise his efforts were not so successful.

Carter had appointed a liberal, Cyrus Vance, as secretary of state, and a conservative, Zbigniew Brzezinski, to head his National Security Council staff. Without a clear view of his own on many issues, he shifted back and forth between them and developed a reputation for indecisiveness. A devout Southern Baptist, he had a strong sense of rectitude and of personal mission. In his view, Nixon and Kissinger were cynics who had neglected the moral dimension of American foreign policy. The difficulty was that, like many Americans, he also considered politics—in the sense of the manipulation of interests and of power—morally suspect. This combination of moral clarity and political opacity was nowhere more pronounced than in the area of strategic policy and U.S.-Soviet relations.

In his inaugural address President Carter spoke of the need to rid the planet of nuclear weapons. This was no empty remark: Carter was serious about disarmament. Just a few days before taking office he had shocked the Joint Chiefs of Staff by telling them that he could envision a world in which the U.S. and the Soviet Union had only a minimum deterrent of two hundred submarine-based missiles apiece.[24] As he later pointed out, there were enough warheads on one Polaris submarine to destroy every large and medium-sized city in the Soviet Union.[25] Carter, who had served as an officer on a nuclear submarine, knew more about the technology of nuclear weapons than any of his predecessors, and he was not naïve enough to imagine that nuclear disarmament would happen overnight. But he did believe that he could negotiate arms reductions, as opposed to the constraints on future deployments then under discussion in the SALT talks. And, naïvely, he thought that such an approach would pacify Senator Henry Jackson and other conservatives on the Armed Services Committee, who had complained that the SALT I treaty did not reduce the Soviet arsenal. Shortly after his inauguration Carter told the State Department to ignore the complex negotiating formula that had been worked out by Kissinger and to come up with a proposal for deep cuts in the strategic arsenals. But he failed to take the Soviet perspective and the technical difficulty of the arms-control process into account. SALT I, which included the ABM Treaty and an agreement freezing ballistic missile launchers, had taken almost three years to complete. During the Ford administration U.S. and Soviet negotiators had come close to concluding a SALT II agreement, and the Soviets—always impatient with the changes that came with every new American administration—wanted a treaty signed and sealed so that the two sides could move on. Not knowing Carter, they understandably interpreted his proposal for deep cuts as pure propaganda—and a means of scotching the deal they had spent so much time negotiating. Angrily they rejected the proposal, and Carter officials retreated to cobble together a less ambitious strategy.[26]

In the meantime Carter, who hoped to hold down the military budget after the vast expense of the Vietnam War, had to make decisions about the procurement of new strategic weapons. As it happened, his first major decision was to cancel the B-1 bomber in favor of an expanded cruise-missile program. The determination was made on technical and military grounds (Carter listed the merits and demerits of the B-1 on a yellow legal pad), and it was a political disaster.[27] The Air Force had not had a new strategic bomber since the early sixties, and the cancellation of such a long-heralded and politically visible system allowed Air Force supporters in Congress to label Carter weak on defense and to make new demands. In addition, it permitted conservatives to pursue a line of argument they had advanced after the conclusion of SALT I accords.

During the 1970s the principal concern of U.S. strategic planners, and all those who followed strategic issues closely, was the growing Soviet capability in land-based ICBMs. The U.S. held the lead in most technologies, including that of missile launchers, and it had a quantitative as well as a qualitative advantage in submarine-launched ballistic missiles and cruise-missiles. The U.S. was also years ahead in the technology of multiple independently targeted reentry vehicles (MIRVs). Nonetheless, the number and size of Soviet ICBMs struck some analysts as ominous. Land-based missiles were faster than bombers and more accurate than submarine-based missiles. In theory they could destroy the enemy's land-based nuclear forces if fired first. In the analysts' jargon, they were "counter-force" weapons, and they were thought to create instability, for in a crisis the temptation would be to use them first or risk losing them to the attacker. The Soviets understood this logic, but because they were far behind in other technologies, they had produced quantities of them in order to compensate. Then, too, Soviet ICBMs were much larger than their American counterparts, the Minuteman missiles. This was so because of their technological inferiority, but the fact remained that they had greater "throw-weight"—or the capacity to loft more payload over intercontinental distances.*

The issue of throw-weight had been a matter of concern to American negotiators during the SALT I talks, but it became a matter of intense concern in the mid-seventies, when the Soviets began testing MIRVs, for the heaviest Soviet ICBM, the SS-18, could carry up to ten independently targeted warheads, whereas the U.S. Minuteman carried only three. In theory, therefore, the Soviets could destroy all one thousand U.S. Minutemen with only a couple of hundred heavy missiles. Whether they could actually do this was another matter, but the theoretical capability was a concern to strategic planners. In retrospect, many U.S. analysts thought that the Nixon administration should have negotiated a ban on MIRVs in the SALT I process, before the Soviets had mastered the technology. But now it was too late for that. In SALT II, U.S. negotiators had to attempt to limit the number of warheads as well as the number of launchers—and their efforts were never good enough as far as defense hawks were concerned.

In the wake of Carter's decision to cancel the B-1 bomber, the Air Force began to push for the development of the MX missile. This ICBM, a seventy-ton behemoth capable of carrying ten independently targeted warheads, had been put into development by Nixon's defense secretary, James Schlesinger, as a counter to the Soviet heavy missiles. After Schlesinger left office in 1976, the program was cut back on the grounds that it would not only fail to solve the problem of the Minutemen's vulnerability but that it would itself be a tempting target and would aggravate the problem of crisis instability.

Predictably, the Air Force advocacy of the MX touched off long and acrimonious debate in Congress. In the midst of it, U.S. intelligence analysts discovered that the Soviets were testing a new guidance package for their MIRVed SS-18s, and the test results suggested that the U.S. Minutemen would become vulnerable in four or five years, as opposed to ten or fifteen years, as had been previously assumed. These test results later turned out to

* Most Soviet boosters used liquid fuel; U.S. rockets used solid fuel, which was more compact, and which permitted them to rise out of the atmosphere faster.

be misleading, but alarm bells went off in the Pentagon, and Pentagon officials began to speak of a "window of vulnerability." The phrase, as they used it, meant the interval between the Soviet deployment of the SS-18s with their new guidance systems and the American deployment of an accurate new ICBM which could survive their attack. This "window" was a chessboard abstraction signifying the theoretical vulnerability of one leg of the strategic triad, but the phrase had an ominous ring to it. Then, though the MX did not fit the bill of a missile that was, in the analysts' jargon, "survivable," the phrase was transmuted into an argument for the MX.[28]

Under pressure from the Pentagon and other quarters Carter eventually adopted an extremely orthodox set of strategic policies—ones difficult to distinguish from those of James Schlesinger in the last Nixon administration. He increased defense spending each year, and the increases permitted Harold Brown, a physicist and the most technically qualified secretary of defense since the job was created after World War II, to carry out a program of force modernization that included building the Trident submarine, upgrading ICBM warheads, developing new cruise missiles and beginning work on a "stealth" bomber, known as the B-2. In June 1979 Carter concluded a SALT II treaty, which the chairman of the Joint Chiefs called a "modest but useful step" that would add a measure of "predictability" to Soviet programs.[29] Advised that the MX would be the price for getting the treaty ratified, he came out for the big missile a week before the concluding summit with Brezhnev—leaving Harold Brown with the task of figuring out some way of making it survivable.[30]

None of this was of any help politically. The conservatives had already pinned Carter as weak on defense. What was more, events abroad seemed to conspire to demonstrate that the nation was weak and had lost its credibility in the world. In 1978 the Shah of Iran, a long-term American ally, was deposed in a revolution headed by the Ayatollah Khomeini and other fundamentalist Muslim clerics; the Soviets were contesting the U.S. position in the Horn of Africa, and Cuban troops were sent to support Marxist regimes in Ethiopia and South Yemen, as well as in Angola. In 1979 the Sandinista revolution triumphed in Nicaragua. In November of that year the Ayatollah's Revolutionary Guard seized the U.S. Embassy in Teheran and took its staff hostage. A month later the Soviets invaded Afghanistan to prop up the regime they had installed the year before. To many Americans Vietnam seemed to be only the first in a series of humiliations and reverses; and to many the United States seemed to have become the "pitiful helpless giant" Nixon had spoken of. Americans did not want U.S. troops sent into any of these conflicts, but—somewhat paradoxically—they wanted a military buildup.

In the mid- to late seventies fierce battles raged in such gentlemanly fora as the Council on Foreign Relations. Now on the offensive, foreign-policy hawks attacked former friends and allies with a ferocity unknown since the height of the Vietnam War and in rhetoric as fraught as that of student demonstrators. At one conference, for example, Eugene Rostow charged, "Since the final bitter phases of the Vietnam War, our governments have been reacting with the same fear, passivity, and inadequacy which characterized British and American policy so fatally in the thirties and British policy before 1914."[31] Rostow named no names, but the only possible candidates he could have had in mind for the role of Neville Chamberlain were Kissinger and Vance—both former colleagues of his. Neo-conservatives for their part claimed that a "liberal elite" had taken control of the American establishment and that there was a clear and present danger that under the sway of this elite the country would retreat into isolationism, fail to honor its commitments, abandon its allies and allow the Soviet Union to pull ahead both politically and militarily. The United States, they argued, had all the resources necessary to continue the global struggle as it had in the past; the impediment was merely a "failure of nerve" within the establishment, brought on by the Vietnam War.

In 1979 the Committee on the Present Danger launched a full-scale attack on the SALT II treaty. It sent speakers to hundreds of public events, produced reports and distributed maps showing the American cities that could be destroyed by a single Soviet SS-18. Nitze led the campaign. He wrote articles, made speeches around the country, gave radio and television interviews; when the treaty came up for ratification, he testified before the Senate twice, making headlines on both occasions.[32]

On the face of it the SALT II treaty seemed a strange target for Nitze to attack. Carter-administration officials had consulted Nitze frequently during the negotiations and had resolved many of his initial objections before the treaty was signed. Its final version contained some features that would limit ballistic-missile throw-weights as well as the number of warheads the Soviets could deploy. And, as Nitze himself later wrote in his memoirs, it did not prevent the U.S. from deploying any of the weaponry it planned to field before the expiration date at the end of 1985. Furthermore, Nitze's behavior at the time was puzzling. Testifying before the Senate Foreign Relations Committee in July 1979, Nitze criticized almost every aspect of the treaty, yet, when asked point-blank whether the U.S. would be better or worse off with the treaty as it stood, he avoided answering the question. His main objection to the treaty seemed to be that it would not produce the kind of shift in the strategic balance he thought was required. In testimony both he and Rostow went on and on about the "horrible prospect" of a Soviet war-winning capability and called for a major military buildup.[33] Apparently they had decided that a U.S.-Soviet treaty signed at this juncture would lull the public and the Congress into complacency about the need for a buildup. SALT II, "with all its fallacies and implausibilities," Nitze told the Senate Foreign Relations Committee, "can only incapacitate our minds and wills."[34]

In the battle against SALT II and for a major strategic buildup, the

CPD's main weapon was a scenario, outlined in its initial statement of purpose, whereby the Soviet Union might force the United States into an irreversible, worldwide retreat through its ability "to fight, survive and win a nuclear war." In a series of position papers and signed essays issued between 1976 and 1980 the CPD spelled out this scenario in greater detail. Some of the papers contained graphs illustrating trend lines in megatonnages and throw-weights, some were less technical, but all of them pointed to a rapid growth of Soviet forces and insisted upon the difference between U.S. and Soviet intentions.[35] "Soviet literature," the Committee maintained in one essay,

> tells us that the Soviets do not agree with the Americans that nuclear war is unthinkable and unwinnable and that the only objective of strategic doctrine must be mutual deterrence. On the contrary, it tells us that they look at the world differently; that war is an extension of diplomacy; that nuclear superiority is politically usable and that the Soviets must prepare for war-fighting, war-surviving and war-winning.[36]

The Soviets, the committee wrote, give emphasis to counter-force weapons: that is, to heavy, accurate land-based missiles which, if used in a first strike, could destroy a high percentage of U.S. ICBMs and "could reduce significantly the effectiveness of residual U.S. strategic forces."[37] In addition, it continued, the Soviets have put a great deal of effort into building defenses, including air defenses, ballistic-missile defenses and civil defenses for the purpose of surviving an American counter-attack. Their "massive" civil defense program involved evacuation programs for the urban population and the dispersal and hardening of industrial facilities. "There is no equivalent U.S. counterpart of these programs, the CPD wrote,

> and perhaps there cannot be, given the unattractiveness of civil defense to an open society. But the potential effect of such a war-survival program on our deterrent could be so great as to nearly nullify it—some calculations indicate that the Soviet civil defense and industrial dispersal programs would reduce Soviet casualties during a full nuclear exchange to *one-tenth* those of the United States.[38]

In other words, the Soviet civil-defense program was as dangerous to the United States as any weapons system, for with it the Soviets could hope to survive a nuclear war.

Of course, the committee's argument continued, the Soviets' goal "is not to wage a nuclear war but to win political predominance without having to fight."[39] If allowed to achieve strategic superiority, they could in a crisis threaten to raise the stakes and force the U.S. to back down. If they could attack our ICBMs and other military installations and still have greater numbers of more powerful weapons left than the U.S., an American president would be faced with the choice of attacking Soviet cities and industries, knowing that they could do the same with greater force, or seeking a political settlement on their terms. Thus the committee concluded in its statement of purpose:

> If we continue to drift, we shall become second best to the Soviet Union in overall military strength; our alliances will weaken; our promising rapprochement with China could be reversed. Then we could find ourselves isolated in a hostile world, facing the unremitting pressures of Soviet policy backed by an overwhelming preponderance of power. Our national survival would be in peril, and we should face, one after another, bitter choices between war and acquiescence under pressure.[40]

In the face of this horrible prospect, the committee in 1978 proposed a major military buildup that included the rehabilitation of air-defense programs, a reexamination of U.S. civil-defense programs and a reinvigoration of ABM research-and-development programs.[41] In May 1980 it proposed a buildup that it estimated would cost an additional $260 billion over the next five years. In the strategic realm it called for the development of two additional Trident submarines, one hundred B-1 bombers, additional cruise missiles and three hundred more of the latest model Minuteman ICBMs. On the defense side it recommended "expanded civil defense planning and preparations" but made no mention of air defenses or ABM systems.[42]

Because three of the most active CPD members—Nitze, Pipes and Van Cleave—had served on Team B, it was generally assumed that the CPD had gathered its intelligence on the dire threat of a Soviet victory from the CIA files. However, Nitze had anticipated all of Team B's reported conclusions, including its "discovery" of a massive Soviet civil-defense effort, in his *Foreign Affairs* piece of January 1976. In fact, he had anticipated the entire CPD scenario in that article.

To many in the foreign-policy community the scenario sounded familiar.

As chief of the Foreign Policy Planning Staff under Acheson in 1950, Nitze had drafted an interagency document known as NSC-68, one of the most influential policy statements of the early Cold War. A wide-ranging analysis of the U.S.-Soviet conflict, the document provided the intellectual underpinnings for the first peacetime military buildup in American history and established the proposition that defense spending should have an overriding claim on U.S. economic resources for as long as the Soviet Union should last. NSC-68, since declassified, characterized the Soviet Union as "inescapably militant," "animated by a fanatic faith, antithetical to our own," and seeking to "impose its absolute authority over the rest of the world."[43] According to its authors, the military trends were all adverse: Soviets were developing the capability to fulfill their grand design while the relative strength of the free world was declining. If war were to break out now, its authors wrote, the Soviets could overrun most of Western Europe and attack selected targets in the United States with atomic weapons. In 1954, when they would have an estimated two hundred atomic bombs and the bombers to deliver them, they could, by striking "swiftly and with stealth," deal a devastating blow to "the vital centers of the United States."[44] Already, the authors wrote, the Soviet Union "possesses armed forces far in excess of those necessary to defend its national territory," and this "excessive strength, coupled now with an atomic capability," provided it "with great coercive power for use in time of peace in furtherance of its aims." Already, they wrote, the Soviets were gaining ground by infiltration and subversion backed by the threat of force; morale was declining in Europe, and if present trends continued, our allies "may drift off into a course of neutrality eventually leading to Soviet domination."[45]

NSC-68 maintained that there would never be an "absolute defense" against atomic weapons,[46] but it proposed to check the Kremlin's designs with a major U.S. military buildup—one its authors informally estimated would cost about three times the current defense budget. According to NSC-68, the U.S. could easily support this burden, since its economy was far larger than that of the Soviet Union, and it was allocating a much smaller proportion of its GNP to the military budget. The only question was whether Americans would decide to make the necessary sacrifices to defend their freedom. The authors did not ask this question lightly: "Our fundamental purpose is more likely to be defeated from lack of will to maintain it, than from any mistakes we may make or assault we may undergo because of asserting that will."[47]

When NSC-68 was declassified in the early sixties, scholars discovered that its authors had written it without the benefit of much evidence about Soviet capabilities and in the face of protests from the leading U.S. Soviet-experts about their depiction of Soviet intentions.[48] Acheson, under whose watchful eye Nitze had drafted the document, later admitted that precision was not what the authors were after. In his 1969 memoir he wrote, "The purpose of NSC-68 was to so bludgeon the mass mind of 'top government' that not only could the President make a decision but that the decision could be carried out." He also admitted that as he went around the country that year "preaching" the premise of NSC-68 he had, for the purposes of communication, to make points that were "clearer than the truth."[49]

NSC-68 was later characterized as an early example of "threat inflation." But it was not only that. To look at it from a rhetorical point of view, it, like Reagan's Speech of the early sixties, had the form of a revivalist sermon, or an Old Testament jeremiad. That Acheson and Nitze would preach in this fashion seems extraordinary, but they did so by conscious decision—and because of one of the most interesting bargains in American history.

In his memoir Acheson describes the famous meeting of February 27, 1947, in which President Truman, Secretary of State George Marshall and he, then an undersecretary of state, asked the congressional leadership to make the first Cold War commitment: a grant of four hundred million dollars to the non-Communist governments of Greece and Turkey. Acheson and his superiors believed that if those governments did not hold firm, the Soviet Union would extend its influence into the Eastern Mediterranean and undermine the fragile non-Communist consensus in war-torn Western Europe. The problem lay in convincing the Republican leaders, and in particular the Midwestern conservatives, that the U.S. had vital interests in a region that lay completely outside their ken.

"I knew we were met at Armageddon," Acheson later wrote of the meeting. "These congressmen had no conception of what challenged them." After Marshall tried and failed to convince them with a geopolitical argument, Acheson took the floor and launched into a highly charged speech, calling Greece and Turkey the key to the worldwide ideological struggle between good and evil, freedom and dictatorship. "Like apples in a barrel infected by one rotten one," he said, "the corruption of Greece would infect Iran and all to the east. It would also carry infection through Asia Minor, and to Europe through Italy and France . . ." and if this happened, America itself could not be secure.[50]

Realizing that the conservatives across the table could not be persuaded by geopolitical calculations, Acheson had adopted their own quasi-religious language. Apparently he had not thought his speech out in advance, but since he was the son of a clergyman and well versed in the Bible, the language came naturally to him.

A long silence followed. Then Republican Senator Arthur Vandenburg of Michigan said that he had been greatly impressed, even shaken, by what he had heard, and declared that, if the President would say the same thing to the Congress and the country, the Congress would surely support him.[51]

Three weeks later the President announced what became known as the Truman Doctrine, promising to support "free peoples" everywhere in their struggle against Communist subversion. The speech not only persuaded the Congress to vote for aid to Greece and Turkey, but ushered in a two-year period of bipartisan cooperation in which the Congress funded all the elements of the Marshall Plan.[52]

Acheson surely learned something from this success. In any case, NSC-68 followed the form of a revivalist sermon even more closely than his impromptu speech. Its authors not only posed a choice between absolute good and absolute evil but, based on esoteric information, prophesied that doomsday would come at a specific date unless Americans made the decision for national salvation. Whether the American people were willing to make the necessary sacrifices to resist evil was the central question the authors posed.

During the 1950s such doomsday scenarios, in which Soviet thermonuclear weapons stood in for the fires of hell, became a more or less ordinary means of communicating a sense of urgency about military preparedness. Nitze wrote several of them himself, the most notable of them the report of the Gaither Committee, a blue ribbon commission, named for its chairman, H. Rowan Gaither, studying civil defense and strategic weapons for the Eisenhower administration in 1957. The Gaither report maintained that the Soviet Union had made "spectacular progress" in increasing its military might, including its air force and its air-defense systems, and was now in the process of developing intercontinental ballistic missiles capable of a "disarming counter-force attack" on the United States. It recommended that the U.S. accelerate its ICBM program and spend thirty billion dollars on fallout shelters before "the year of maximum danger," in 1959.

News of the report was leaked to the press, and in the 1960 campaign Senator John F. Kennedy, among others, charged that the Republicans had created a dangerous "missile gap." However, a month after Kennedy's inauguration, photographs from the first American spy satellites showed that, though there was a "missile gap," it was one that greatly favored the United States.[53]

As common as these doomsday scenarios had been in the fifties, the appearance of the CPD scenario took Carter-administration officials by surprise. For a decade or more it had been quite generally assumed that nuclear war was unwinnable and that deterrence had been achieved.

In the early sixties Defense Secretary Robert McNamara had for a short time focused strategic planning on the destruction of Soviet nuclear forces in the hopes of preventing a holocaust. He soon came to the conclusion that no attainable level of force was sufficient to destroy a satisfactory percentage of the Soviet military forces—and never would be as long as the Soviets kept building more weapons. In consequence the U.S. could merely hope to deter the Soviets from nuclear war. In an attempt to answer the question of how much force was enough to ensure deterrence, he came up with a new standard for procurement. The U.S., he said in 1968, must maintain an ability to inflict "unacceptable damage" upon an aggressor "at any time during the course of a strategic nuclear exchange, even after absorbing a surprise first strike." Deterrence, he said, "means the certainty of suicide to the aggressor, not merely to his military forces, but to his society as a whole." He called this capability "assured destruction" and defined it as the capability to destroy half of the enemy's industrial capacity and a fifth to a fourth of his population.[54] To maintain the survivability of U.S. nuclear forces, he created a force structure composed of land-based missiles, nuclear bombers and submarine-based missiles: the strategic triad. By the late sixties, when the Soviets began to turn out ICBMs "like sausages," as Khrushchev had promised, even Curtis Le May's successors acknowledged that nuclear war could have no winners, and that mutual deterrence, or "mutual assured destruction," was a fact of life.[55]

From that time on most Americans, including many who considered themselves knowledgeable about the subject, assumed that the U.S., and presumably the Soviet Union as well, had some large, but nonetheless limited, number of nuclear weapons targeted on each other's cities. That, in the view of most, was the definition of nuclear deterrence—or "mutual assured destruction." Those who paid serious attention to the subject knew this was not the case. In part because of pressures from the Air Force, and in part because of political pressures to maintain U.S. nuclear superiority, McNamara and his successors did not limit U.S. strategic procurements to the standard of "assured destruction." And rather than to adopt a purely "city-busting" strategy, they continued to target Soviet nuclear facilities in the hopes of limiting the damage to the American population and their own facilities.[56] The Soviets did likewise, and since no "damage limitation" could ever be enough, the strategic arsenals grew apace and were continually "modernized"—or technically improved. Eventually the technical improvements led to greater accuracy, which in turn led planners on both sides to worry about the vulnerability of their own strategic forces—thus the "window of vulnerability." All the same, in a world where both sides had weapons based in survivable modes on submarines and alert bombers, the balance of terror did not appear all that fragile. Given that a single Polaris submarine carried enough missiles to destroy every large and medium-sized city in the Soviet Union, it was very difficult to imagine how the Soviets would propose to win a nuclear war.

In fact, the doomsday scenario Nitze proffered in his *Foreign Affairs* article and in the CPD papers was a good deal more complicated than his earlier efforts. When spelled out in technical terms, it involved three propositions and a set of underlying assumptions. The first proposition was that trend lines in U.S. and Soviet procurements showed the Soviets gaining a large advantage in throw-weights over the next few years. The second was that these excessive throw-weights posed a dire threat to the United States. To show why this might be, Nitze laid out a scenario for nuclear war involving three exchanges, beginning with a Soviet first strike. In the first exchange Nitze assumed that the Soviets would destroy some significant percentage of U.S. counter-force weapons, and that the U.S. would retaliate with what remained of these weapons to reduce Soviet throw-weight to the greatest extent possible. By 1977, he calculated, the Soviets would have a huge advantage in residual forces after this first exchange.[57] After the second exchange they would by his calculations have a clearly war-winning advantage. As one CPD paper put it, "A clearly superior Soviet *third*-strike capability . . . would undermine the credibility of our second-strike capacity, and could lead us, either to accommodation without fighting or to the acceptance of unmanageable risks.[58]

But that was not all there was to the scenario. To the obvious question of why the Soviets would initiate a war when they knew the U.S. could retaliate not once but twice, his answer—and his third proposition—was that the Soviet civil-defense effort might be so effective that it would protect their industries and keep their civilian casualties down to an acceptable level.

Wherever Nitze got this unusual idea, it was certainly not from the CIA, for, two years after he had surfaced it, CIA analysts made a study of Soviet civil-defense measures and concluded that, though the Soviets had made a sustained effort to provide blast shelters for their leaders, they had not implemented any program to protect their industry and could have no confidence of protecting their population in a nuclear exchange.[59]

On top of all this Nitze argued that if the Soviets gained the strategic superiority he described, they could—as NSC-68 had proposed—use it in peacetime to produce dramatic shifts in the overall balance of power. In his current scenario a future American president and future allied leaders would count up the throw-weights on both sides and surrender in advance when they found the Soviets would have the advantage after one or two nuclear exchanges.

This tower of conditionals resting upon a hypothetical "window of vulnerability" struck some defense experts as a Rube Goldberg contraption. Lawrence Freedman, the British historian of nuclear strategy, wrote that the methodology involved reminded him of Stephen Potter's advice to the chess player in *Gamesmanship:* if you want to one-up a more experienced opponent, make three moves at random and then concede defeat, explaining that your situation is hopeless given the brilliant checkmate he will make twenty moves hence.[60]

In fact, some of the methods used in the CPD papers were a good deal more underhanded than anything Stephen Potter would have recommended. For example, in his *Foreign Affairs* article Nitze defined "assured destruction" as "massive urban/industrial retaliation"—when he certainly knew that was not McNamara's definition or U.S. policy. But it was this definition which allowed him and the CPD to claim that the Soviets did not believe in "mutual assured destruction," thereby implying that the Soviets did not believe in the condition of mutual deterrence, and that only the Soviets engaged in counter-force targeting.[61] The CPD authors often used "mutual assured destruction" in this fashion, but on occasion they gave it another meaning, one even more removed from reality. In one paper the committee wrote:

> The Soviets believe in the importance of air defense of their homeland, whereas the United States has abandoned air defense on the premise that it is not useful in the absence of ballistic mis-

> sile defense. The Soviets also believe in ballistic missile defense. They signed the ABM Treaty in 1972 because the United States had a long technological lead, not because we had converted them to the concept of Mutual Assured Destruction (MAD), the mutual-hostage theory.
>
> While we have deactivated and partially dismantled our sole permitted ABM site, and have cut back our ABM research and development program, the Soviets have maintained their Moscow site and are vigorously pursuing ABM research and development. . . .[62]

To a layman this passage would surely suggest that Soviet air and anti-missile defenses had some significant military utility—though it does not actually say so. In practice the advent of ICBMs had made anti-aircraft weaponry almost irrelevant to the strategic balance. The Soviets had maintained their air defenses largely because they had armed neighbors they did not trust. As for anti-ballistic missile defenses, they had been deemed ineffective for reasons that were not so much technical as conceptual: hitting a missile in flight was almost by definition more difficult than launching one on another country, and therefore, whatever number of ABMs were built by one side, the other side could defeat them much more cheaply by building additional missiles or warheads. This logic was better known to the CPD's chairman of policy studies than to almost anyone else.

American experts had conceived the unhappy idea that there might be no effective defense against missiles when the Germans began experimenting with rockets near the end of World War II. The authors of NSC-68 went as far as to say that, given the trends in weapons development, there would "never" be an "absolute defense" of the United States. Eisenhower made the same judgment. The U.S. and the U.S.S.R. nonetheless went ahead with an attempt to develop ABM systems with the idea of gaining some form of comparative advantage. The systems they developed were disappointing, and in 1967 McNamara proposed that the first step towards limiting the arms race should be a ban on ABM systems, because negotiators would never be able to agree on a trade-off between offensive and defensive arms. The idea did not originate with him. In 1963 Paul Nitze, then secretary of the Navy, and Admiral Elmo Zumwalt proposed that an agreement to limit offensive weapons would be possible only if there were "measures prohibiting the deployment of ABM systems."[63] It took some time to convince the Soviets of this. At the Glassboro summit in 1967 President Kosygin objected heatedly to the idea of banning ABMs. "Defense is moral, offense is immoral!" he exclaimed.[64] It took even more time to convince skeptics in Washington, but eventually the negotiations began, and Nitze and his colleagues worked out an agreement with the Soviets, the ABM Treaty of 1972, permitting ABM research but limiting deployments to two sites (later reduced to one) in each country.

In the passage about ABM systems the CPD authors again implied that "mutual assured destruction"—"the mutual hostage theory"—was a choice rather than an ineluctable fact. The rhetorical sleight-of-hand in this context also had a history well known to them.

After the ABM Treaty was ratified by the U.S. Senate, Donald Brennan, an analyst at the Hudson Institute, who had been working on missile defense issues, published an article in the *National Review* in which he bitterly attacked what he called "the concept of mutual assured destruction" and argued that a strategy that left millions of innocent civilians defenseless was immoral. "As a goal," he wrote, that concept was, as its acronym suggested, "mad, MAD." Disingenuously Brennan ignored the logic that lay behind the treaty and offered no alternative to offensive deterrence, but he had invented a powerful acronym.[65]

Serious defense experts knew exactly what the CPD was up to, and still Nitze's doomsday scenario had a forceful effect on Washington.

In 1979 Leslie Gelb, who had recently resigned as assistant secretary of state for politico-military affairs in the Carter administration, attempted to put together a bipartisan group to contradict the CPD implicitly by laying out the facts of the strategic balance, but he could find very few volunteers.[66] For those who made their careers as defense experts it was never totally safe to be on the left of a strategic debate, and in a time when the country was in a conservative mood, it was downright dangerous.

Just before leaving office in January 1977, Henry Kissinger had said that he did not believe that the Soviets were achieving strategic superiority over the United States. He added: "Military superiority has no practical significance . . . under circumstances in which both sides have the capability to annihilate one another. . . . Those who are still talking about superiority are not doing the American people a service."[67] But in testifying before the Senate on SALT II in 1979, he warned that the Soviets were gaining strategic superiority and said that, because of the vulnerability of U.S. land-based missiles, Soviet willingness to run risks "must exponentially increase." There would, he said, be a "period of maximum danger" in the coming five years.[68]

For defense experts Nitze's doomsday scenario appeared as the gorgeous displays of plumage in a war dance, its very extravagance flaunting the political might of the CPD.

By October the SALT II treaty was stalled in the Senate, and in December, when the Soviets invaded Afghanistan, the Carter administration withdrew it from the ratification process. By that time Rostow, Nitze and forty-four of their CPD colleagues, including William Casey, Richard Pipes, Jeane Kirkpatrick, William Van Cleave, Richard Perle and Kenneth Adelman had joined the Reagan campaign.

Along with Rostow and Nitze, one of the founding members of the Committee on the Present Danger was Richard V. Allen. An economist by training, Allen had been Nixon's foreign-policy adviser in the 1968 campaign and had worked in the Nixon White House, briefly on Kissinger's staff, and then as deputy assistant to the President on international economic affairs. To the right of many in the Nixon administration, and no admirer of Kissinger's, he opposed détente and was never entirely at home with the new China policy.[69] On leaving the administration, Allen, who had known Martin Anderson since the '68 campaign, joined him as fellow of the Hoover Institution, and in 1976 he was one of the people the Reagan campaign called upon for expert advice. In 1977 he met with Reagan again and threw in his lot with the former governor for the next campaign.[70]

Allen, who made his living as an international business consultant, quickly made himself useful. In 1978 he accompanied Reagan on a trip to Europe and a trip to East Asia to prepare him for the campaign. He, along with Peter Hannaford, Deaver's partner in the PR firm that handled Reagan, wrote much of the foreign-policy material Reagan used in speeches and radio broadcasts. "I tried to fill the lacunae in his knowledge," Allen later said. "I was trying to crowd out what he learned from *Human Events!*"[71] He also provided Reagan with a bridge to the conservative Democrats of the CPD.

In 1978–79 Reagan devoted a series of six radio broadcasts to Eugene Rostow's critique of SALT II, and quoted Richard Pipes's views on the Soviet Union at length.[72] On trips to Washington to raise support for his new presidential campaign he met with a number of CPD members, including Jeane Kirkpatrick, a professor at Georgetown University and a leading neoconservative, whose paper on the virtues of authoritarian, as opposed to totalitarian, regimes appealed to Reagan. In January 1979 Reagan became a member of the CPD executive board, and Nitze invited him to dine at his house with a small group that included Meese, Deaver and Rostow. "As I remember it," Nitze said, "Gene and I were in pretty good voice; we rather dominated the conversation. Mr. Reagan was impressed because he really didn't know much about the national security situation at that time, he really didn't."[73]

By the time Reagan's 1980 campaign was fully under way Richard Allen had become his in-house foreign-policy adviser; William Van Cleave, another CPD member, had become his defense adviser; and forty-six members of the CPD executive board had joined his advisory task force.[74] In effect the CPD had become the Reagan campaign's brain trust for defense and foreign policy.

In the summer of 1979, when Reagan paid his famous visit to NORAD, he was, as it happened, thoroughly immersed in the CPD's arguments about strategic nuclear policy. What these experts were saying about the weakness of American leadership and the apocalyptic Soviet threat accorded perfectly with what he had been saying off and on since the early 1950s. That the eminences of the CPD were now using his story doubtless did not surprise Reagan, but historically speaking it was a conjunction of the stars. Acheson had, after all, adopted this rhetoric from Reagan's political forebears at the beginning of the Cold War, and now, more than thirty years later, his heirs were bringing it back to Reagan.

By July 1979 John Sears had returned to direct the 1980 campaign, and Martin Anderson, who had taken a leave of absence from the Hoover Institution earlier that year, had returned as director of policy development. Allen had not yet joined the campaign full-time, so when Douglas Morrow, the screenwriter, arranged for Reagan to visit NORAD, it was Anderson who accompanied him.[75]

NORAD had been created in the 1950s, as the North American Air Defense Command to coordinate U.S. and Canadian defenses against Soviet bombers. As such it had for many years had operational control over an extensive network of interceptor squadrons and anti-aircraft missile batteries. In the sixties, as the threat of Soviet missiles superseded that of Soviet bombers, NORAD's elaborate sensing and communications equipment were redesigned to provide an early-warning system for a ballistic-missile attack and to keep track of the U.S. and Soviet space programs. Then, when the Soviet missile forces grew to the point where air defenses seemed almost irrelevant to stopping a Soviet attack, NORAD's obsolete anti-aircraft batteries were dismantled, and the interceptor squadrons turned over to the Coast Guard and the Air National Guard and redeployed on other missions. By the mid-seventies NORAD, now known as the North American Aerospace Defense Command, had become simply an early-warning system, plus a tracking station for objects in space and for unidentified aircraft coming over the U.S. borders. It had lost its operational capabilities, and since this is a sorry state for any command, NORAD commanders had long been engaged in an effort to restore them. In the spirit of this endeavor, General James Hill opened up the Cheyenne Mountain base to visitors, offered tours to its impressive facilities and allowed Hollywood filmmakers to shoot scenes in its command center. (Scenes from *War Games* were shot there.) Thousands of people visited NORAD, and as each tour group went through, one of the visitors would inevitably ask what the United States would do when all this expensive and sophisticated equipment warned that a Soviet attack was coming. The answer, carefully prepared and endlessly repeated, was "Nothing." And the visitors would go away shaken, as was intended.[76]

Reagan had, in other words, participated in a public-relations enterprise—though, of course, the answer was no news to him.

Around the time of the NORAD visit, Anderson, by his account, found that John Sears was becoming nervous about Reagan's political vulnerability on the foreign-policy side. Anderson had thus far devised an economic program and an energy policy for the candidate, but, as he saw it, the campaign was not yet covered on foreign or defense policy, and Sears, according to Anderson, was particularly worried about Reagan's position on nuclear weapons and arms control.[77] Sears by his own account had some reason for concern.

It was John Sears's experience that candidates go through phases of interest in different issues, and in the summer of 1979 Reagan was, Sears remembered years later, going through a period of fascination with nuclear weapons and nuclear strategy. He was learning all he could about the new weapons technologies and the scenarios of nuclear conflict, and he was anxious to put what he had learned into his speeches. Sears, however, kept heading him off. For the 1980 campaign Sears believed that Reagan should position himself as the Republican unity candidate. On foreign and defense issues what this meant was that Reagan should make it clear that he would stand up to the Russians and that he would build up the American military arsenal. Reagan had always stood for a more assertive America, and now, in Sears's view, the country was ready for his message. Yet, given Reagan's well-known hawkishness, Sears felt it important that the candidate run on broad principles and avoid the details, particularly where nuclear weapons were concerned. "If we talked too much about defense," he said, "we'd get into this other world of stuff about how, if they do this, we shoot off that, and the computers will handle it all. All that scary stuff."[78]

Anderson agreed. A few days after the NORAD visit he wrote a memorandum for the campaign in which he posed the basic problem. "Until fairly recently," he wrote, Reagan was perceived "as being somewhat inexperienced in foreign affairs, and perhaps prone to follow policies that could conceivably plunge this country into Vietnam-like wars.... He was not perceived as someone to whom world peace was a top priority...." However, Anderson continued, events of recent years had shown that Reagan was right in 1976 when he said we had become number two to the Soviet Union in military power. "The informed judgment of military experts is now virtually unanimous: the United States is in a time of peril, and is in danger of becoming gravely so during the next four or five years." The problem, he wrote, "is how to take advantage of the public's rapidly changing concern about our national security, capitalizing on Reagan's strong leadership record in this area, while avoiding an overly aggressive stance that would be counterproductive."

In case any reader might have missed the point, Anderson added: "There has to be a switch from the false perception that Reagan sees complex foreign policy issues in black and white, that he favors repressive regimes, that he is itching to send in the Marines to resolve disputes, that he is only concerned with relatively narrow foreign and defense policy issues such as the Panama Canal, buying chrome from Rhodesia, SALT II, propping up the white government in South Africa, and stockpiling nuclear weapons to blast the Soviet Union."

In other words, the question was how the candidate should respond to the "time of peril" without coming across as a right-wing ideologue.

The answer Anderson proposed was that Reagan should come up with an overall foreign-policy plan, spelling out basic goals and strategies. One basic goal, he wrote, "should be to attain and maintain *world peace.* In fact, if properly formulated, the policy should become known in the press as 'Reagan's Peace Plan' or some such nomenclature."

In regard to national defense, Anderson maintained that there were three options, the first two of which were: (1) to rely on Soviet good intentions and (2) to match the Soviet buildup. The first option he naturally dismissed out of hand. But he dismissed the second as well, this one on the grounds that "a lengthy public debate on the virtues of quantum leaps in the levels of assured nuclear destruction is apt to frighten as many people as it consoles," and "substantial increases in the attack missile capability of the United States would be a powerful, emotional issue to deal with politically—especially by Reagan."

Option 3 was "Develop a Protective Missile System." Of this option Anderson wrote:

> During the early 1970s there was a great debate about whether or not this country should build an anti-ballistic missile system. The ABM lost, and is now prohibited by SALT agreements. But perhaps it is now time to seriously reconsider the concept.
>
> To begin with, such a system concentrates on defense, on making sure that enemy missiles never strike U.S. soil. And that idea is probably fundamentally far more appealing to the American people than the questionable satisfaction of knowing that those who initiated an attack against us were also blown away. Moreover, the installation of an effective protective missile system would also prevent even an accidental missile from landing. Of course, there is the question of feasibility . . . but there have apparently been striking advances in missile technology during the past decade or so that would make such a system technically possible.
>
> If it could be done, it would be a major step toward redressing the balance of power, and it would be a purely defensive step.
>
> Taken in conjunction with a reasonable buildup in our conventional forces, and an acceleration in the development of cruise missiles, laser beam technology, and conventional nuclear missiles like the MX, the development of an effective protective missile system might go a long way toward establishing the kind of national security that will be necessary in the 1980s.[79]

Anderson was, of course, no military expert, and his list, with its peculiar terminology ("conventional nuclear missiles") and its juxtaposition of futuristic laser weapons with missiles then under development, shows that he was talking through his hat where weapons systems were concerned. But, then, his memo was not about weapons. It was about what Reagan should say. In this context his proposal was clearly that Reagan should continue to call for a major buildup of "attack missiles" but should subsume this project within talk of "world peace" and a "protective missile shield." The "shield" would be advertised as purely defensive, but it would be a weapon and a part of the buildup.

In his book Anderson tells us that on reading the memo Reagan embraced the principle of missile defense wholeheartedly, asking only, "Can we do it? Is the technology available?" and later, "How soon can we do it? How much would it cost?"[80]

Sears did not go on the NORAD trip, and ten years later he did not remember that Anderson had accompanied Reagan—nor did he remember Anderson's memo. What he did remember distinctly was that after the trip Reagan himself spoke enthusiastically about the idea of an anti-ballistic missile system and wanted to put it in his speeches. Sears supposed that some military officer had promoted ABM systems in a briefing. In any case, Reagan's enthusiasm seemed to be "just another instance of his wanting to talk about how terrible the Soviet Union was and how we needed more machinery."

Asked if Reagan ever waxed philosophical about the existential horror of nuclear deterrence or mused about an ideal world without nuclear weapons, Sears said, "Well, there were a lot of ideal worlds in Reagan's mind, and sometimes he lived in them. But this one he'd argue himself out of quite quickly. He'd quickly come back to reality. . . . Of course, he was never for deterrence in the sense of two men with pistols pointed at each other's heads. It was simply his instinct that we should get the edge in all places, and the idea of a missile defense appealed to him along these lines. . . . He thought of it as a piece of military weaponry he was interested in developing."

Sears, as he remembered it, told Reagan that it might be better to have the ABM question looked into before they raised the issue in the campaign, and, as was his habit in such cases, he shunted the matter aside. Later, when others pressed the idea of missile defenses, he found new reasons why the issue should not be raised. "This hadn't anything to do with the substance of the issue," he said. "I didn't know about that. I hadn't looked into it. It was just a matter of what was politically good for him to be talking about, given his conservatism and his anti-Soviet posture." Also, Sears added, "Such a plan would obviously have been challenged quickly, and, given Reagan's background and his not necessarily knowing what he was talking about to the eighth level, such challenges were to be avoided."

That Reagan had expressed an enthusiasm for missile defenses did not concern Sears as much as it might have had it come from another candidate, for over the years Sears had learned that Reagan had a degree of detachment from policy issues that was unique among politicians he had known. When he was governor of California, Reagan had been accused of lacking interest in the day-to-day management of government, but that, Sears had come to understand, was the least of it. The fact was that Reagan lacked interest in many forms of reality. He had his views about the way the world worked, and he had his solutions—lower taxes, less government and a stronger America. But he had small interest in the application of his ideas. When he was first elected governor, Sears recalled, he found that he had to raise taxes rather than lowering them as he had promised. "He explained this," Sears said, "by saying he had no idea how bad the situation was. And he hadn't. He hadn't looked into it."

Reagan was well known for being a man of firm principles, and in office he had gained a helpful reputation for pragmatism, but in some sense, as Sears explained it, neither reputation was deserved. Reagan's detachment gave his staff enormous powers. "You could do almost anything you wanted," Sears said, "and you didn't have to check with anybody. You could do all these amazing things. . . . Reagan wasn't involved. . . . He let everybody—as long as they stayed within a little bit of a framework—do anything they wanted. . . . What he was doing in his speeches was stating limits in the form of principles. He didn't like to retreat from those, but in the application of them he was ready for anybody around him to tell him, 'Well, this is an exception.' Or 'This is a little different application.' And he'd say, 'OK, fine!' As long as you stayed within certain limits—and there were limits—he was malleable, very malleable."

This was not because Reagan was unsure of himself. In Sears's view Reagan was very secure as a person. It was just that he had a certain view of the division of labor which came from his days as an actor and a spokesman for GE: he gave the speeches and made the appearances—and the rest was the work of his staff. There was no need to ask Reagan about policy implementation or to persuade him of the ins and outs of a position the staff had worked out for him, Sears said. "He'd say, 'That's your business. I'm out here selling it. You tell me.' Well, he used to say sometimes that he was a salesman, and he was!"

Sears had a theory about Reagan's detachment. There were, he said, two kinds of actors: the great ones, who were often messy and troublesome, and the good ones, who made it by sheer discipline—by getting up at ungodly hours in the morning, going into Makeup, learning their lines and saying them as the director wanted them said. An actor of this kind would never question the scriptwriter; he would never complain about the lighting or argue with the direction. Such an actor wouldn't involve himself. If the producer and the director fought, he'd say to himself, "Too bad, but it's their problem. It hasn't got anything to do with me. The worst thing I can do is get involved or I won't get another job." Then, when the picture came out, it would be the actor, the star, who would get most of the credit or blame. But he wouldn't take it personally, because he'd know that in reality he didn't have as much to do with the product as everybody thought. Reagan, Sears said, was an actor of this kind, and since he'd had great success behaving in this way, so as a politician he followed the same pattern. "In many ways he was a very disciplined man. He was not a stupid man. It's just that he had gotten on in his life by not using the substantive part of his brain. Everything he had done, even before he became an actor, was a matter of perception."

In Sears's view Reagan made an excellent candidate, and in part just because he did not try to be his own campaign manager. Reagan, in great contrast to Nixon, was happy to do his own job and let his staff members do theirs. Sears, for example, never worried that Reagan would seize on a proposal that someone walked through the door with, as many politicians did in the midst of campaigns. "He wouldn't do anything unless those in charge of the area said it should be done. With Reagan you never had to waste any time on that kind of thing. He had no ego that way." In fact, he continued, Reagan normally did only what his inner staff had already agreed upon. But there were exceptions. "Sometimes he'd say things.... This would be when he was answering questions, not making speeches. This was the worst time, because he'd repeat something he'd just read, and it might have been in some strange letter he got. I mean, you couldn't tell where he got the idea [he once expressed] that Alaska had more oil than in Saudi Arabia. You know, he read his mail!" But generally, Sears added, Reagan's discipline was such that when on unfamiliar terrain he would confine himself to the material his staff had prepared for him. "He was very good about that. So there was no problem letting anyone in to see him. Letting people in gave the impression of openness." His outside advisers—the economists, foreign-policy experts and the like—would usually deal with his inner staff, but when they got in to see Reagan, he would already have been briefed on what they were going to tell him. "He wanted the stuff screened—so [these sessions] were more for their benefit than his. He would play his role and ask the questions his staff had given him, and they would go away thinking he was smart, which was a part of this, too. But he never thought he was going to decide. Someone closer to him was going to tell him what to do."[81]

Reagan formally announced his candidacy in November 1979. For a week he kept up a brisk schedule but stumbled repeatedly in his answers to questions from local reporters. Sears then slowed down the pace and had Reagan conduct the campaign from airplanes and speakers' rostrums, avoiding debates with the other Republican candidates and avoiding the informal contacts that primary contenders usually have with audiences and the press. Sears overdid this regal, front-runner strategy, for Reagan lost the Iowa caucuses to Bush—Reagan had hardly spent any time in the state—and the campaign was so expensive that by February 1980 it had bumped up against the federal spending limits. Immediately Sears turned the campaign around. In New Hampshire, Reagan traveled by bus with reporters, put in long days and took on Bush in two debates. Running against six other Republican candidates, he won the primary with 51 percent of the vote. But in previous months Sears had angered the conservatives; he had also alienated the Californians around Reagan by forcing Lyn Nofziger and Michael Deaver out of the campaign. The Iowa defeat gave his rivals the opportunity to strike back. On the eve of the New Hampshire primary, he and his associates were summarily dismissed. A new team headed by Edwin Meese and William Casey, a New York lawyer and financier, took over, and the exiled California aides returned. The new team, however, believed in "letting Reagan be Reagan," and the system Sears had set up to protect the candidate broke down.[82]

As Reagan racked up primary victories in March, Robert Scheer of the *Los Angeles Times* interviewed the candidate over a period of several days, spending much time on defense and foreign policy. A patient interviewer, Scheer repeatedly asked Reagan to explain what seemed to him the inconsistencies in the candidate's views about Communism and the Soviet threat. If the Communists wanted world revolution, why had the Chinese turned against the Soviets? If we could get along with the Chinese, why couldn't we get along with the Russians? Were the Soviets really more powerful now than before the Sino-Soviet split? And so forth. Scheer also questioned Reagan closely about his views on nuclear weapons, and for the first time in the campaign, and perhaps the last time in his political career, Reagan spoke informally and at length to a journalist about the nuclear balance and strategic policy. In one of these conversations Reagan brought up the idea of a defense against ballistic missiles.[83]

At the start of one interview session Scheer asked Reagan about a report he had mentioned in a recent primary debate concerning the number of bombers that would get through U.S. defenses in the case of a Soviet attack. Reagan replied that "a very high ranking—extremely high-ranking—Air Force officer" had told him that 87 to 96 percent of the Soviet bombers would get through, depending on the route they took. Was this based on a study, Scheer asked, or was this his own judgment? "This is based on what they know at NORAD," Reagan replied. "You know, we can track the missiles if they were fired, we can track them all the way from firing to know their time of arrival and their targets, and we couldn't do anything to stop the missiles."

The non-sequitur—the shift from bombers to missiles—was startling, but since Scheer did not interrupt, Reagan went on: "NORAD is an amazing place—that's out in Colorado, you know, under the mountain there. They are actually tracking several thousand objects in space, meaning satellites of ours and everyone else's, even down to the point that they actually are tracking a glove lost by an astronaut that is still circling the earth up there." What struck him, he said, was "the irony that here, with this great technology of ours, we can do all of this yet we cannot stop any of the weapons that are coming at us." And he continued, "I don't think there's been a time in history when there wasn't a defense against some kind of thrust, even back in the old-fashioned days when we had coast artillery that would stop invading ships if they came."

Scheer asked if the Soviets had a defense against the U.S., and Reagan replied: "Yes, they have gone very largely into a great civil defense program, providing shelters, some of their industry is underground, and all of it hardened to the point of being able to withstand a nuclear blast." He also claimed that the Soviets had practiced evacuation procedures and that "in one summer alone they took over 20 million young people out of the cities into the country to give them training in just living off the countryside."

Scheer asked whether the U.S. should do the same kind of thing.

"I think we're going to have to start a civil defense program," Reagan replied. "I think—see, they violated and we kept to the promise that McNamara, in the original getting-together and what resulted in doing away with our antiballistic missile system, at a time when we were ahead of them in technology on that. The idea was the Mutual Assured Destruction plan—MAD, the MAD policy, it was called—and what this policy said was that if neither country defended its citizenry, then neither country could afford to push the button, because they would know that in an exchange of weapons, both countries' populations would be decimated. And they didn't hold to that. . . . We paid no attention to the fact that the Soviet Union had put a high-ranking general, who was on the Politburo, in a high command, in charge of civil defense. And they had come to the conclusion that there could be a nuclear war and it could be winnable—by them."

Scheer ignored the McNamara story and persisted: should the U.S. build underground shelters and evacuate the young to the countryside?

"I don't know whether we should be doing the same things of that kind," Reagan replied, "but I do think that it is time to turn the expertise that we have in that field . . . loose on what do we need in the line of defense against their weaponry and defend our population, because we can't be sitting here—this could become the vulnerable point for us in the event of an ultimatum."

When Scheer asked if Americans should really build backyard shelters, Reagan continued: "I don't know about the backyard shelters with today's technology or not, but as I say, one of the first things I would do would be to turn to those who are knowledgeable in military affairs, knowledgeable in the weaponry that would be coming at us, and so forth, to find out what we could do. Now, it could well be that maybe there is another defense, maybe there is a defense through having superior offensive ability to keep them from doing this. See, what they have built their nuclear strength to is based on being able to knock out our missiles in their silos, and then still have enough nuclear power left that if we, with say some remaining submarines or something, attack their cities, that they could wipe out our population, our industry, and our cities."

"But they can't touch our submarines and our bombers and all that stuff, can they?" Scheer demurred.

"Yes, they can," Reagan said. "The only bombers that we have are the aging B-52s and . . ."

"What about the nuclear subs, and all that?"

"All right, we have some but we can't match them in number, speed, diving depth, or range of missiles."

In the interview Reagan's train of thought is sometimes difficult to follow, but clearly the candidate was giving Scheer his own version of the CPD doomsday scenario. His version had some elements that did not exist in the original—or anywhere else, for that matter. Scheer, who later interviewed most of the new civil-defense enthusiasts, could find no source for the assertion that all Soviet industry was hardened sufficiently to withstand a nuclear blast, or for the report that twenty million Soviet young people had practiced evacuation to the countryside.[84] As for Reagan's claim that American nuclear submarines were inferior to their Soviet counterparts, the reverse was the case. Apparently the complex and improbable narrative about the importance of residual throw-weight ratios after a third strike had befuddled Reagan as much as it did most other people, so, to bridge the gap it left in the story, he had simply declared all three legs of the U.S. strategic triad vulnerable.

Still, Reagan had gotten the gist of the scenario. He had understood that civil-defense measures were the key to it. He had also grasped the idea that the danger lay in a Soviet capability for nuclear blackmail at some point in the future—and the logical corollary that did not appear in the CPD papers: if the Soviets could use nuclear superiority for geopolitical ends, the U.S. could, too. Speaking of the Soviet troops in Afghanistan, he told Scheer, "We have been sending the kind of signals that made that possible, and what we need to do is send them [the Soviets] some signals that let them know there is a point beyond which they cannot go in the world without risking a direct confrontation with us. Now I say that because I don't believe the Soviet Union at this time wants a direct confrontation with us. They're not—they don't want that until they have such an edge that they could realize their dream of perhaps taking us by telephone . . . that we would have no choice left except surrender or die."[85]

Reagan had no trouble reproducing this part of the scenario. It was, after all, the same story he had told in the days of General Electric and the Goldwater campaign. The difference was that in those days he had suggested that the U.S. should use the Bomb, and now he maintained that it could not because of McNamara's MAD policy. When Scheer took the point of his statement about sending signals to the Soviets and asked if the U.S. needed to think about a "nuclear option," Reagan said no and repeated his argument: McNamara had seen to it that the U.S. had no defense. He added: "The difficulty with that was that the Soviet Union decided some time ago that nuclear war was possible and was winnable, and they have proceeded with an elaborate and extensive civil protection program. We do not have anything of the kind because we went along with what the policy was supposed to be."[86]

In answer to Scheer's questions about what he would do to avert the approaching crisis, Reagan spoke tentatively about an offensive buildup and civil-defense measures, but, as Scheer observed at the time, he seemed to be "longing for the ultimate anti-ballistic missile weapon."[87]

Literalists were always inclined to believe that Reagan was a fantasist dreaming of science-fiction weapons. But this interview shows quite clearly the context in which he conceived of an anti-missile shield.

Reagan's eminent defense experts had handed him a doomsday scenario, and he was following it fairly closely. He did not get it exactly right—and he never did. (A year after his election he had forgotten that the Soviet advantage lay in land-based missiles. Asked what the "window of vulnerability" was, he spoke of "the imbalance of forces" in Europe and then said that the Soviets had superiority at sea.)[88] But, then, he surely did not take the story of fast-approaching nuclear peril literally: he had, after all, been telling the same story himself for at least twenty years. He was simply following a narrative and giving it an appropriate ending. Jeremiads always end with the promise of salvation, but the CPD was offering merely to keep evil at bay with more ships, more planes and more missiles. The solution was unsatisfactory; it was also beside the point if, as the CPD said, the Soviets were about to win because they were building defenses.

Reagan knew perfectly well that Americans were not going to dig backyard shelters—but why not an anti-missile shield? The committee had, after all, written, "The Soviets believe . . . in ballistic missile defense. They signed the ABM treaty in 1972 because the United States had a long technological lead, not because we had converted them to the concept of Mutual Assured Destruction (MAD), the mutual hostage theory. . . ."

In thinking about an ABM weapon, Reagan was being altogether more logical than the committee, for if MAD was a "plan" or a "policy," it followed that the plan could be changed and the policy reversed, and an anti-missile shield might materialize once the experts put their minds to it. The solution satisfied every instinct of the Republican right: the desire for superior military technology, for an impregnable defense of the country and for a means of taking the offense again. Further, it was a logical extension of the historical progression from ships to airplanes and from the seas to the air.

Obediently Reagan did not insist on his own solution, but clearly a "protective missile shield" fit into the doomsday scenario like the missing piece of a puzzle. Of course, the solution did not exist, but, then, the problem did not either, so in that sense it was the perfect solution.*

REAGAN DID NOT MENTION his missile-shield idea again that season, for his top advisers, including Allen, judged that it would be impolitic. Instead, as he coasted through the primaries and fought the presidential campaign, he spoke of the Soviet threat and called for a military buildup. On these issues the CPD rhetoric and his own coincided, creating a harmonic and an extraordinary amplification of the message.

In his essay on the campaign Hedrick Smith wrote that not since the early days of the Cold War had a successful presidential candidate sounded the alarm about the Soviet Union the way Reagan did in 1980. His vision of American and of Western peril was, Smith wrote, apocalyptic. "We now enter one of the most dangerous decades of Western civilization," Reagan warned in January 1980. The Soviets, he claimed in subsequent speeches, were menacing Iran and the whole Middle East; Hanoi had "annexed" Indochina; Castro, as an agent of the Kremlin, was trying to turn the Caribbean into a "red sea" that would engulf Mexico. As for the United States, the country, he said, had been through an era of "vacillation, appeasement and aimlessness," and the result was that "we find ourselves increasingly in a position of dangerous isolation. Our allies are losing confidence in us, and our adversaries no longer respect us." On more than one occasion Reagan compared American policy towards the Soviet Union to the Allied appeasement of Hitler in the late 1930s. "I believe we are seeing the same situation as when Mr. Chamberlain was tapping the cobblestones of Munich," he said.[90]

On the subject of defense in general and strategic weapons in particular, Reagan was far more alarmist than he had been in 1976. Carter, he said, had made a "shambles" of defense; indeed, "totally oblivious to the Soviet drive for world domination," he had tried "systematically to diminish and dismantle the great arsenal of democracy."[91] As a result, the Soviets had pulled way ahead. In one speech Reagan estimated that the Soviets had spent

* In the interview sessions Reagan was inconsistent in his prescription for what it would take to catch up with the Soviets. In some contrast to what he had said in 1976, he did not charge Ford with delinquency on defense. Ford, he said, had started building the B-1 bomber, the neutron bomb and the cruise missile, but the Democratic Congress had cut the defense budget and Carter had "stopped the military buildup." This led him to a fairly optimistic conclusion: "I think if we instantly reverse our own course and set out to rebuild, reinstitute the program of building that we had before Carter became President, in which he canceled virtually every weapon system that we were developing, I think that it's possible to keep the Soviets from getting the kind of edge that would lead them to go adventuring against us." On the other hand, in the context of the doomsday scenario, he figured the United States as undefended except by some inferior submarines and a few "aging B-52s."[89]

$240 billion more than the U.S. on defense over the past decade and were now outspending America by fifty billion dollars a year. In another speech he maintained that the Soviets "lead us in all but six or eight of the forty strategic military categories and may well surpass us in those if present trends continue." We were, he said repeatedly, in an arms race, "but only one side is racing." Arms control in his view was not the answer, since the Soviets would never agree to slow their military buildup while the United States was "unilaterally disarming" and while the Soviets remained confident that their lead would keep on increasing. The solution, he said, was to spend "whatever is necessary" to match the Soviet buildup, for, if Moscow's drive for strategic superiority went unchecked, the West could be threatened with the alternative of war or surrender. "The Soviets want peace and victory," Reagan told the Veterans of Foreign Wars in August 1980. "They seek a superiority in military strength that, in the event of a confrontation, would leave us with an unacceptable choice between submission and conflict." The country, he warned on another occasion, "is in greater danger today than it was on the day of Pearl Harbor."[92] On the other hand, Reagan seemed to be promising that the U.S. would regain military superiority over the Soviets. "Since when has it been wrong for America to be first in military strength?" he asked in a speech to the American Legion. "How is military superiority dangerous?"[93]

Reagan did not himself enumerate the weapons systems he would acquire, or put a price tag on the military buildup, but his defense advisers, William Van Cleave and Edward Rowney, called for such an array of weaponry that Leonard Silk, the economic columnist of the *New York Times*, estimated that the buildup would demand a 7- to 9-percent increase in the defense budget each year, excluding inflation, and that, assuming an inflation rate of 10 percent a year, the defense budget would double between 1981 and 1985. Reagan's economic advisers, such as William Simon and Caspar Weinberger, however, refused to endorse these estimates, so the issue remained moot.[94]

On arms control Reagan was somewhat more specific: he said he would shelve the SALT II treaty, restore U.S. defenses in order to negotiate from strength and then seek deep reductions in the nuclear arsenals.[95]

In mid-August the Reagan campaign hit a rough patch. At the Democratic convention Jimmy Carter called the election "a choice between two futures," one of "security, justice and peace," the other of economic injustice and risk: "the risk of international confrontation; the risk of an uncontrollable, unaffordable, and unwinnable nuclear arms race."[96] Because political analysts had discovered that many voters did not take Reagan seriously—one of Reagan's aides called the phenomenon "Reagan's secret weapon"—Carter set out to convince voters that Reagan was a serious right-winger who represented a threat to world peace. The strategy succeeded for a while, and the President, who had been way behind in the polls, began to pull up to his opponent. At the same time, with Sears gone and Meese at the controls, Reagan made a series of political blunders and, reverting to his habit of picking up material from dubious sources, made so many errors of fact that he came close to making his own competence, as opposed to Jimmy Carter's record, the main issue of the campaign.[97]

In early September, at the behest of Nancy Reagan, Stu Spencer, who had managed Reagan's gubernatorial campaigns, was called in to perform damage control. Spencer, who, according to Cannon, called Reagan "old foot-in-the-mouth," kept the candidate away from reporters for a period and impressed him with the fact that he was talking to the whole nation every time he made a statement, not just to the audience at hand. Spencer stuck close by the candidate for the rest of the campaign, with the result that Reagan made far fewer errors and no more political gaffes. In answer to Carter's increasingly strident attacks, Reagan adopted an attitude of injured innocence, and the closer election day came, the more the deep coloring of his rhetoric washed out into acceptable shades of pale.[98] In the presidential debate on October 28 Reagan talked about his devotion to "world peace," and when Carter said, quite accurately, that his opponent had begun his political career campaigning against Medicare, Reagan clinched the debate, as far as many were concerned, by shrugging his shoulders, looking over at his opponent forlornly and saying, "There you go again."[99]

Stu Spencer had banished the right-winger and re-created the American Everyman.

Reagan's performance in the last few weeks of the campaign reassured voters and turned the election back into a referendum on Carter's record and the dismal state of current affairs: economic stagnation, inflation running at 18 percent, the Soviets in Afghanistan, the U.S. Embassy hostages still in Teheran and so on. According to the pollster Daniel Yankelovich, the public mood was characterized by injured national pride, unqualified support for increasing the defense budget and a general desire to see American power become more assertive. The election was for Reagan to lose; as it was, he won by a landslide, taking an absolute majority of the vote, carrying all but six states and helping to boost the Republicans to a majority in the Senate.[100]

Whatever voters thought of Reagan after all the ups and downs of the campaign, the candidate's performance in the last few weeks persuaded many journalists that Reagan was not the threat to peace and stability that Carter had made him out to be. Hedrick Smith, for one, wrote that Reagan had two sides to him: the rhetorical right-winger and the pragmatic practitioner of power. Reagan, he observed, had always run highly ideological campaigns, but as governor of California he had proved to be quite flexible and pragmatic: he struck deals, made compromises and even swallowed campaign slogans when the need arose. In Smith's view this affable politician was likely to emerge as a counterpart to Leonid Brezhnev, a man who had formed his views long ago and spoke like a true believer, but who acted in cautious, conservative fashion and preferred to avoid confrontation with the United States.[101]

Other reporters put the matter less vividly, but the conventional wisdom of the time was that Reagan would prove to be much more moderate as a president than he sometimes sounded on the campaign trail.[102]

The Reagan transition took place without much public ado.

Long before the election Reagan's staff members had let it be known that, like Eisenhower, Reagan had a corporate management style and preferred a Cabinet government. This sounded plausible, so press attention naturally focused on his nominee for secretary of state, Alexander Haig, and on his secretary of defense–designate, Caspar Weinberger. Not until later did enough attention go to the important question of who would staff his White House.[103]

Throughout the campaign it had been generally assumed that Edwin Meese would become Reagan's chief of staff. Meese had, after all, worked for Reagan off and on since 1967 and had headed Reagan's staff during the governor's successful second term. But Stu Spencer and Michael Deaver thought he would be a disaster in the job. He was too right-wing for their tastes; beyond that, he knew nothing about Washington and was a poor administrator. He was forever making lists and drawing up charts, but this was merely a form of dyslexic compensation: he was hopelessly disorganized.[104] Spencer's candidate for the post was James A. Baker III, the sophisticated Ivy League Houston lawyer who had managed George Bush's primary campaign. Baker had never been on Reagan's side of the Republican Party—in 1976 he had directed Ford's successful delegate-hunt and managed his presidential campaign—but he was a great political tactician and administrator with a thorough knowledge of Republican politics and Washington. Deaver was enthusiastic, and so was Nancy Reagan. The President-elect eventually came around to their view, but made it clear he wanted Meese in the White House as well.[105]

A virtual stranger to Reagan and his entourage, Baker made Deaver his deputy chief of staff and on paper worked out an elaborate agreement with Meese on the division of their powers: Meese would have Cabinet rank, the title of chief counselor to the President and authority over the Domestic Council and National Security Council staff, while Baker would have control over the paper flow, the President's schedule and the rest of the White House staff functions. The official announcement of the arrangement left the clear impression that Meese would have the responsibility for policy formulation and Baker would cope with the administrative details. Later it occurred to reporters that Baker had control of all the lines of communication in and out of the White House—and thus control over policy issues as well.[106] Still, the arrangement was far from ideal as far as Baker's interests were concerned, and its most serious flaw was Meese's jurisdiction over the

NSC staff. But Baker could do little about that, since the subordination of the NSC adviser had already been decided upon.

Two weeks before the election Reagan had announced that he would make "structural changes" to ensure that his secretary of state would be his foreign-policy principal and that his national-security adviser would play the modest role of coordinator. What these changes would be Reagan did not specify, but the announcement went down well in Washington. It seemed to follow from Reagan's oft-stated views about the virtue of Cabinet government; it accorded with the conservative view that NSC advisers tended to be fancy East Coast establishment academics, and that the very last thing Reagan needed was another Kissinger. Furthermore, to those who had watched the destructive struggle between Brzezinski and Vance that had culminated in Vance's resignation, the idea of reducing the power of the NSC adviser relative to the secretary of state seemed a pretty good one. The notion thus became doctrine in the Reagan camp; it solved a personnel problem as well.

Meese, who had taken charge of the transition, had long planned to make Richard Allen NSC adviser, but newspaper reports appearing over the summer and fall had put his candidate under a cloud. In his career as an international business consultant, Allen had, it appeared, taken on a number of questionable clients, among them the notorious stock swindler Robert Vesco, who became a fugitive from justice; one of Vesco's rivals, a Denver financier who subsequently served a prison term; and a Portuguese business consortium that was trying to sell Washington on continued white rule in Angola and Mozambique.[107] When, a few days before the election, *The Wall Street Journal* ran a piece showing that Allen had tried to profit from a business arrangement he had promoted while in the Nixon administration, Allen resigned from the campaign.[108] Meese brought him back shortly after the election, however, and Allen was made Reagan's NSC adviser. Journalists were then told that the appointment was a sop to the right, and a relatively modest one in that the position of NSC adviser had been downgraded. Interest in Allen and his background gradually faded away.[109]

Possibly Baker and Deaver thought they could make do with Allen and with a system that returned his office to the obscurity from which it had come in the Eisenhower administration. But the 1950s was a simpler time, and Eisenhower had no need for anything but a coordinator, since he was the foremost national-security expert in his administration. Reagan, by contrast, knew virtually nothing about foreign or defense policy, and Baker, Meese and Deaver had no experience in these areas. Thus, when Reagan took office, he had no source of advice on national-security policy in the White House except for Allen, who was not in a position to give it.

Allen was, as it happened, an advocate of strategic defenses, and so, too, was Meese. Appointed NSC adviser, Allen looked forward to pressing the issue from within the Reagan White House.

CHAPTER FOUR

Space Defense Enthusiasts

IN 1980, THE IDEA of building strategic defenses had virtually no constituency in the Pentagon, or indeed almost anywhere in the defense community. By that time U.S. military planners had more than thirty years of experience with the subject, none of it very encouraging.

The quest for an anti-ballistic missile system had begun shortly after World War II, when analyses of the German guided-missile program indicated that the development of an intercontinental ballistic missile was only a matter of time. Intercepting a missile traveling at thousands of miles per hour was, of course, a formidable task, but since an ICBM armed with an atomic bomb would pose a new order of threat to the United States, technical studies on the problem began immediately. By the mid-1950s the Army was developing a surface-to-air guided missile equipped with a nuclear warhead. Based on a former air-defense system, it was designed to shoot down incoming missiles in the last few minutes of their flight and to provide a "point defense" for military targets, or even cities. Meanwhile, the Pentagon's Defense Advanced Research Projects Agency (DARPA) explored futuristic technologies and concepts for attacking missiles in their boost phase—or as they rose through the atmosphere just after their launch—that might defend the country as a whole. Its Project BAMBI (ballistic-missile boost intercept) came up with a number of concepts for defenses in space, one of which involved tracking satellites and interceptor missiles housed in larger vehicles that would be stationed in orbit over the ICBM sites.[1] In the course of these explorations DARPA farmed its work out to a variety of contractors, from the national laboratories to private think-tanks, and in doing so created a community of scientists, technologists and strategists well versed in the issues of strategic defenses: not only how they might be built, but how they might be penetrated and the relative costs of each.[2]

By 1965 the Joint Chiefs and their allies in Congress were pressing hard for the deployment of the Army's ABM system. In 1962 the Army had fired a radar-guided ZEUS missile with a dummy nuclear warhead from the Kwajalein atoll, and the missile passed within two kilometers of the reentry vehicle of an Atlas missile launched from Vandenberg Air Force Base in California—or close enough to destroy it with a nuclear blast. Other successful tests followed. The system, however, proved incapable of discriminating between warheads and other metal objects, so a short-range interceptor was added as a backup to attack warheads after the atmosphere had burned away the chaff and any potential decoys. A good many technical uncertainties remained, however, among them the distinct possibility that the explosion of the interceptor's nuclear warhead would blow out the delicate radars and blind the system. In addition, the ABM warhead could be a threat to those in the area the system was designed to protect. In the view of the Army, the system could be upgraded as time went on, and fallout shelters could be built around ABM deployments.[3]

McNamara and his civilian advisers, however, opposed a deployment on military grounds. The current system was, as the Army admitted, more complex, less reliable and vastly more expensive than the missiles it was designed to defeat, and if it was deployed to defend a city or a missile field, the Soviets could overwhelm it by adding more ICBMs to the target, or simply adding decoys. The system could be upgraded, but the problem was that any improvement in it could much more easily and cheaply be countered by adding offensive weapons, or by improving their speed and elusiveness. In addition, because the offense consisted of nuclear warheads, the defense faced a very different test from, say, the anti-aircraft batteries around London in World War II, for an entire city could be destroyed if only one warhead got through. In a 1962 article in *Scientific American* Herbert York, a former director of DARPA, and Jerome Wiesner, Kennedy's science adviser, argued that developing defenses would merely spur the Soviets on to a new cycle of building, which the U.S. would then have to match, confronting both sides with the "dilemma of steadily increasing military power and steadily decreasing national security." They added, "It is our considered professional judgment that this dilemma has no technical solution."[4]

The Joint Chiefs, however, thought little of these arguments. The Army had long argued that its system could at the very least be used to protect vital military assets and to complicate plans for a Soviet counter-force attack, and to military men, whose job was to defend the country, refusing to deploy defenses seemed perverse. The logic of cost-effectiveness did not impress the Army brass, nor did that of what the analysts called "the responsive threat." Besides, the Soviets were beginning to deploy their own ABM system around Moscow.[5]

The solution McNamara proposed in 1966 was to negotiate a ban on anti-missile systems with the Soviets, and in 1972 the Nixon administration did virtually that. In the meantime, the Johnson and Nixon administrations pressed forward with the development of the nuclear-armed ABM system.

Funding was, however, difficult to come by, for, as the system moved towards deployment, public opposition to it grew. In congressional hearings each year, scientists and public activists testified against the ABM, exposing the technical flaws in the system, its enormous expense and its limited capabilities. People who lived around the proposed ABM sites protested that it would make their cities and towns a prime target for attack and might itself destroy them. In August 1969 the authorization bill for the first phase of the deployments squeaked through the Senate, but only because the SALT I talks were already under way, and the senators did not want to deprive the administration of a bargaining chip in the negotiations. By the time the ABM Treaty was signed in 1972 the Senate had already voted to restrict the deployments to two sites—the number specified in the treaty—and the treaty was ratified with only two senators voting against it.[6]

In the two years that followed, the U.S. completed the construction of one ABM site at Grand Forks, North Dakota, and planned for the deployment of a hundred ABM weapons, as permitted by the treaty. But in a world of MIRVed nuclear weapons, one hundred ABMs were clearly of no military significance, and in 1975, a year after the site became operational, the Congress cut off funding for its upkeep, and the site, which had thus far cost six billion dollars, was dismantled. The Soviets maintained the site they had built near Moscow, equipped with sixty-four GALOSH missiles, but since these missiles were inferior to the American ABM system and since U.S. military planners had long ago retargeted, rendering them militarily irrelevant, there was no anxiety about this in Washington.[7]

Within the terms of the ABM Treaty the Defense Department continued to support research on missile defenses, not only for the purpose of exploring potential opportunities but also to provide an incentive for the Soviets to comply with the treaty and to enable the U.S. to respond quickly if the Soviets broke out of the accord. The research effort was not trivial. During the late 1970s the Pentagon spent about a billion dollars a year for dedicated ballistic-missile defense research. It also funded technologies which, though advanced for other purposes, would be relevant to missile defenses, such as computer software and satellite-borne surveillance systems. The long fight over the ABM deployments had largely discredited nuclear-armed defensive weapons; all the same, the Army continued to research systems that could be used to defend ICBMs. Efforts also went into research on non-nuclear systems. Working on ground-based defenses, the Army attempted to develop an interceptor so accurate it would hit its target and destroy it by the force of impact. The Air Force, for its part, continued to develop concepts for space-based defenses using hit-to-kill, or kinetic-energy, technologies. In addition, all three military services and DARPA spent between one and two hundred million dollars a year on high-energy lasers and other directed-energy technologies in the hopes of creating revolutionary new weapons with beams that traveled at the speed of light.[8] Yet by the fall of 1980 Pentagon program managers had found no technology, or system of technologies, which in their view offered the promise of a countrywide defense, or even a cost-effective defense for ICBMs.

All the same, there was a groundswell of interest in strategic defenses around the Reagan campaign. Not just Martin Anderson but a number of people brought the subject up, and the candidate's close advisers had to keep on explaining that it would be bad for Reagan to talk about ABMs during the campaign. These people fell into two fairly distinct camps.

The first camp was that of mainstream Republican defense experts, such as former Defense Secretary Melvin Laird. These experts had questions, not answers, and their interest in the subject, roughly paralleling that within the Pentagon, revolved around the problem of how to base the MX missile when it came on line in the mid-eighties.[9]

The MX (or the Missile Experimental) had been developed as a match for the new heavy Soviet ICBMs and had been designed for counter-force accuracy. The difficulty was that, if based in a silo, it would, Pentagon experts feared, be vulnerable to a Soviet attack, and with its ten warheads it would be a key target. The problem was, then, how to make the seventy-foot-long one-hundred-ton missile "survivable" without reducing its accuracy. Under the Carter administration the Pentagon had struggled with this problem for two years and had considered some twenty-seven possible basing modes. One of them involved an Army concept for a low-altitude nuclear-armed ABM interceptor, but the Carter-administration officials eventually rejected it for familiar reasons, one of which was that the Soviets could easily overwhelm it.[10]

In September 1979 Defense Secretary Harold Brown announced his solution to the MX basing issue: two hundred MXs would be built, and each one would be deployed on its own loop of roadway and shuttled about between twenty-three shelters spaced over a mile apart. Because the missiles would be moved about at random on their loops, Soviet attack planners could not predict where any one of them would be in the event of a crisis, so that instead of two hundred targets they would have forty-six hundred—or more than they could cover with their most accurate ICBMs. In order to permit verification of the SALT II treaty—or any future treaty—each shelter was to have a port on its roof that could be opened on request, so that the Soviets could see that there was only one missile on each loop of road.

The shell-game solution was an ingenious one from a military point of view. It had, however, a few drawbacks. As some in Congress protested, each loop or "racetrack" would circumscribe an area of some thirty square miles, and all of it together would ring six thousand square miles. The following spring Brown, in response to such objections, modified the plan by straightening out the loops and shortening the distance between shelters, thus reducing the area enclosed. The "racetrack" was no more. All the same, the modified plan, now known as MX/MPS—the acronym standing for MX/Multiple Protective Shelter—would clearly require an enormous amount of land. It would require the construction of forty-six hundred shelters and support facilities plus thousands of miles of roads built solidly enough to bear the weight of the missile and its transporter. The Air Force and critics of the program differed widely in their estimates of the requirements and the costs, but even by Air Force estimates it would cost over thirty-three billion dollars. By some estimates it would be the largest public-works program ever undertaken by the United States, not excepting the Panama Canal.[11]

MX/MPS was an incipient nightmare, but the consternation about it in Congress was far greater among Republicans than among Democrats. Many Democrats, after all, opposed building the MX, and among those who voted for it, many regarded it as a bargaining chip to be traded away for Soviet missiles, not built or deployed. In the main it was the Republicans who wanted to deploy the MX, and if Reagan won, they would have to construct the basing system—and this meant a host of political problems.

Since McNamara had built the Minuteman missile fields, attitudes about the environment, not to mention the desirability of nearby missiles—or "bombs in the backyard"—had changed. The only plausible place to put the MXs was in the Great Basin, a vast tract of scrubland and mountains, much of it owned by the Bureau of Land and Management, which ran through the center of Utah and Nevada. But even the Great Basin was not a wilderness: it had cattle ranches and recreational areas, and some thirty-five thousand people lived there. Environmental groups opposed the project, but so, too, did the Mormon church and a great many of the citizens of Utah and Nevada, many of whom, as it happened, voted Republican. In the Senate, Jake Garn and Orrin Hatch of Utah and Paul Laxalt of Nevada led the opposition to the project. All three were deep-dyed conservatives with close ties to Reagan, and though the Air Force appealed to their patriotism, they would not be moved. As a result, Reagan spoke out against the MX/MPS several times during the campaign. The candidate proposed no alternative, but if elected he would surely have to come up with one—particularly because he had insisted that the "window" was not just a theoretical vulnerability but one which might permit the Soviets to "take us with a phone call." It therefore occurred to a number of his establishment defense advisers that, with all of its concern for arms control, the Carter administration might not have looked hard enough at the option of ABM technologies to protect the MX.[12]

The second group of missile-defense advocates around the Reagan campaign were the ideological purists of the Republican right. Few of these people were technical or military experts; they simply believed that the U.S. should pursue the arms race in every area of military technology. For purists the whole arms-control process was a dangerous trap, and the ABM Treaty the worst of all agreements, precisely because it was the foundation of all the rest. Some of them had hopes for effective defenses; others accepted the fact that offensive strategic weapons were more cost-effective than any ABM system on the horizon but nonetheless longed for the day when the public would support defensive as well as offensive weaponry. And by 1980 they had some reason to hope that the day would soon come.

The views of this group were expressed in the defense plank of the Republican platform. The plank called for the U.S. "to achieve overall military and technical superiority over the Soviet Union" and "to create a strategic and civil defense which would protect the American people against nuclear war at least as well as the Soviet population is protected." Further, it called quite specifically for "a vigorous research and development of an effective anti-ballistic missile system, such as is already at hand in the Soviet Union, as well as more modern ABM technologies."[13] At the time journalists paid little attention to this rhetoric. Party platforms are normally the preserves of the extreme wings of the parties, and their planks often have no bearing on what a candidate will do if elected. But in this case the platform was the work of Reagan loyalists, and the ABM section was largely written by a group which included Representative Jack Kemp; his defense analyst, William Schneider, Jr., soon to be chief of the national-security section of the Office of Management and the Budget; and Richard V. Allen. "We were all against the ABM Treaty," Allen later said.[14]

A confidential policy paper prepared for Allen later in the campaign proposed that the United States should explore the possibility of defending against a nuclear attack by heavily investing in civil defense and reviving a program for building anti-ballistic missiles. "The United States will not accept permanent abstention from the right to protect its citizens from the effects of nuclear attack," it reported.[15]

On January 15, 1981, just a few days before Reagan took office, Secretary of Defense–designate Caspar Weinberger told Hedrick Smith of the *New York Times* that the administration would consider reviving plans for an ABM system to protect American ICBMs and that the extension of the ABM Treaty beyond 1982 was not a foregone conclusion.[16] During his confirmation hearing three weeks later, Weinberger, in answer to a question from Democratic Senator William Proxmire of Wisconsin, wrote: "I think we must look very hard at ABM technology. . . . If we were to achieve a significant breakthrough in the ABM area, we might—after extensive study—be able to deploy MX in fixed silos protected by ABM."[17] A newcomer to technical issues, Weinberger was an agnostic on the subject of ABMs. His comments reflected not his own preferences but administration policy developed during the transition by Allen and William Van Cleave, who ran the Defense Department transition team.

In his memoir Weinberger tells us that shortly after the inauguration he asked for a briefing on the status of ABM work and discussed the makeup of a possible commission to look at whether effective defense systems could be developed.[18] He does not tell us the outcome of this activity, but in the general review of military programs conducted over the next six months Pentagon officials did study ballistic-missile defenses along with possible air and civil-defense measures, revisiting all the issues—technical, strategic and political—that had been debated many times before. A panel of the Defense Science Board also gave missile-defense technologies a thorough review.

By sheer coincidence the chair of the DSB panel was Thomas C. Reed, Reagan's campaign aide in both gubernatorial elections and in the 1968 presidential race. A former Air Force officer who had worked on nuclear-weapons design at the Lawrence Livermore National Laboratory, Reed had served as secretary of the Air Force in the Ford administration and had stayed over into the Carter administration. Harold Brown had appointed him to the DSB, and in 1981 the chair of the board had asked him to look into defensive technologies.

According to Reed, the panel looked at the whole defense menu from civil defenses to directed-energy technologies and had considered even the most "out of the box" solutions. After weeks of study in the summer of 1981 it came to the same conclusion DSB panels had reached in the past: on the whole the best defense was an offense; space-based defenses were not going to work; there were no laser or particle-beam technologies on the horizon; as for the available technologies to defend missile fields, they were not going to get through the Congress, because no one wanted nuclear-tipped ABMs going off in the atmosphere.[19]

At the conclusion of these studies, Pentagon officials came up with programs for air and civil defenses and they proposed a heavy increase in funding for work on the low-altitude interceptor. But they did not recommend an ABM deployment. Weinberger's hard-line deputies for policy made no attempt to alter this verdict, for in their view pressing the Congress to support an ABM system would endanger the administration's drive to build offensive strategic weapons. Thus, when the President and the secretary of defense unveiled the administration's strategic modernization plan in October 1981, there was no provision for an ABM. The White House background statement reported that the administration would pursue research and development on ground- and space-based defenses, "but today ballistic missile defense technology is not at the stage where it could provide an adequate defense against Soviet missiles."[20] Weinberger then dropped the issue, and as far as he and his deputies were concerned, the case was essentially closed.[21]

But the case was not closed as far as Allen was concerned, and in the first year of the Reagan administration he, with the help of Meese, brought people with proposals for Star Wars defenses directly to the White House.

When the administration formally presented the Strategic Defense Initiative program to Congress in 1985, journalists went looking for the source of the President's technological inspiration that had launched the program in March 1983. In their search they discovered that a number of people had proposed concepts for umbrella defenses to Reagan in the years before the speech. One of them was Senator Malcolm Wallop, a conservative Republican from Wyoming; another was retired Lieutenant General Daniel O. Graham, who had headed the Defense Intelligence Agency and had been a member of Team B; a third was the renowned scientist Edward Teller. In 1981 Graham and Teller plus a small group of Reagan's old California friends and political backers had urged the President to launch a major Strategic Defense Initiative and had, it was said, convinced him to go forward with a plan based on Teller's idea for a futuristic laser weapon.

That a small group of private individuals could persuade the President to revolutionize strategic doctrine and create a multi-billion-dollar research project seemed extraordinary, but the group, known as the High Frontier panel, had been mentioned in the background briefings to Reagan's speech, and Anderson, Teller and others maintained that they had influenced the President. This, then, became the legend—or yet another legend surrounding the origin of Star Wars.[22]

In reality, Wallop, Graham and Teller did not inspire Reagan with their technical enthusiasms or persuade him to make the 1983 speech, though they tried hard enough. But in other ways they played an important role in launching the SDI program. In the years before the speech they campaigned mightily for their own particular strategic-defense concepts, besieging the Congress and the Pentagon as well as the White House, and publicizing their concepts through the press. In the process they created a public stir around the idea of missile defenses and kept the issue alive throughout the days of apostasy in Weinberger's Pentagon. Then, too, partly as a result of their efforts, the particular technologies they espoused later became major elements of the SDI program.

Of the three strategic-defense advocates, it would be hard to say which was the most committed and the most persistent, but Senator Wallop was the first off the mark and the first to present his idea to Reagan.

In August 1979, just after Reagan's visit to NORAD, Senator Wallop sent Reagan the draft of an article he had written for a conservative journal, *Strategic Review,* in which he maintained that technology was rendering the balance of terror "obsolete" and was promising "a considerable measure of safety from the threat of ballistic missiles." Chemically powered lasers, he wrote, had clearly shown the potential for ballistic-missile defense; and if two dozen laser weapons were stationed in space, they "could conceivably destroy a whole fleet of ballistic missiles." This technology, he wrote, was now mature enough so that, if the U.S. were to make the decision, the first space-based battle stations incorporating laser weapons could be in orbit by the mid-1980s and a full-fledged defense could materialize well before the end of the decade.[23]

Wallop had come to this idea thanks to the work of Angelo Codevilla, a young staff assistant on the Senate Select Committee on Intelligence. A Rutgers graduate who had done his military service in naval intelligence, Codevilla had joined the staff of the Select Committee in 1975 and two years later attached himself to the newly elected senator from Wyoming. He was a member of the Madison Group, a circle of young New Right policy enthusiasts, and his special area of interest was nuclear strategy. Though entirely self-taught, he could have been said to belong to the Curtis Le May–Phyllis Schlafly school of strategy, for he maintained that there was no essential difference between nuclear and conventional weapons and that with enough counter-force weapons and civil-defense measures the U.S. could protect 90 percent of its population in a full-scale nuclear war. That the U.S. had not developed this capability—while the Soviets, he claimed, had—owed in his view to a combination of bureaucratic inertia and the waning of the belief that man was made in God's image. American policy-makers, he opined, were increasingly unable to distinguish good from evil, or to see that the moral difference between the U.S. and the Soviet Union was such as to justify nuclear war for the preservation of American society.[24]

While working for the Select Committee, Codevilla began to think about how the extraordinary pointing and tracking capabilities of the new U.S. intelligence satellites might be used in missile defenses. He had no technical background, yet, sure of his insight, he sought out experts in government and industry who might have information about new technologies being developed for anti-missile use. In the summer of 1978 he met Maxwell W. Hunter II, a senior aerospace engineer at Lockheed. Having worked on the design of missiles for the Army's ABM program in the 1950s, Hunter had an abiding interest in missile defenses, and was now circulating a paper, permitted but not promoted by the Lockheed management, in which he advocated taking a new look at space-based defenses using chemically powered lasers as the interceptors. "I suddenly realized that lasers are something we hadn't tried before," he later told the official historian of SDI, Donald R. Baucom. The best interceptors were the fastest ones, he said, and laser beams could travel through space at the speed of light, so, if you could build up their energy to the point where "they have enough pizzazz to hurt something," they might be used to destroy ICBMs in their boost phase. To Baucom, Hunter acknowledged that the idea was fairly speculative. "It may be decades before we understand the full implications of a speed-of-light interceptor," he said. At the time, however, Hunter maintained that laser weapons could be built fairly soon if only the U.S. put enough resources into developing them.[25]

Excited by Hunter's ideas, Codevilla introduced the Lockheed engineer to Wallop, and, acting on Hunter's advice, the senator and his aide visited the Army's Ballistic Missile Defense Advanced Technology Command in Huntsville, Alabama; they also met with Alan Pike, the deputy director of the directed-energy program at DARPA. Somewhere along the line Codevilla concluded that chemical lasers were the answer to the problem of U.S. national security; he embraced them, one analyst wrote, as if they were "the philosopher's stone."[26] By mid-1979 he thought he knew enough about the various technologies to propose a missile-defense system. The *Strategic Review* article, which he drafted for Wallop, reported that the main elements of the system would be the laser itself, a large mirror to focus the beam over distances, sensors that pick up the target and a mechanism to point it. Battle stations containing these elements could be put into orbit eight hundred miles above earth and have a range of three thousand miles. Two dozen such stations would cover every spot on the globe, and each could cope with "the theoretical contingency of a thousand missiles launched beneath it in almost simultaneous barrage." Such battle stations, the author wrote, would not be invulnerable to attack—technology would always find a chink in the armor—but they would be "a step in the evolution of warfare," and at least for the foreseeable future they would "command the portals of space." An all-out effort on the scale of the Manhattan Project, which developed the atom bomb, would permit the system to be deployed well before the close of the 1980s.[27]

In the fall of 1979 Wallop and Codevilla began an effort to persuade other senators to support work on a space-based laser system. One difficulty was that the senator had no committee position which would allow him to hold hearings on the subject. Another was that Alan Pike and the other laser experts at DARPA, though happy to testify to the need for more research, would not promise a missile-defense system on the schedule laid out in the *Strategic Review* article.[28] So Wallop and Codevilla decided to ask the aerospace companies working on elements of their proposed system to send them representatives to give informal briefings in the Senate. The executives of these companies initially turned them down, on the grounds that the Pentagon would regard briefings by defense contractors as lobbying and a violation of its rules on conflict of interest. However, they proved willing to allow employees recruited by Hunter to brief the senators as long as they identified themselves as private citizens. Under Wallop's auspices Hunter and three engineers—a group which became known as "the gang of four"—made several presentations to senators and Senate staff members, Hunter laying out a design for an anti-missile system and the other three describing the work that had to be done on the various components. According to

Codevilla, Hunter maintained that as few as twenty-four laser battle stations in space would probably be enough to destroy all the missiles that the Soviets might reasonably be expected to use in a counter-force attack. A workable system, he said, might be cobbled together in as little as four years if the Pentagon abandoned its normal acquisitions process and pushed the project forward as it would under wartime conditions.[29]

These briefings attracted a good deal of attention, much of it negative. Army and Air Force officers in charge of R&D complained that they violated the lobbying code and were also highly misleading. According to Codevilla, Seymour Zeiberg, the deputy undersecretary for research and engineering, expressed scorn at Wallop's proposal and made calls to key senators and staff aides to forewarn them. A study he commissioned on the *Strategic Review* piece concluded that, in the unlikely event laser battle stations could be built, some 1,444 of them would be required to do the job the senator had defined, and the cost would be $1.5 trillion. The briefings nonetheless put Wallop's project on the Senate agenda, and in 1979 the Armed Services Committee increased the funding available for work related to space-based lasers from forty-eight to sixty-eight million dollars.[30]

The following year Wallop introduced an amendment which called for an additional $160 million in funding and required that the Pentagon redirect its chemical-laser research program towards the development of a space-based weapon. His amendment was defeated, but it attracted other sponsors, and thirty-nine senators voted for it. Apparently a "laser lobby" had come into being in the Senate. In order to appease their Republican colleagues, Democrats on the Armed Services Committee asked the Pentagon for a study of space-based lasers. According to Codevilla, Defense Secretary Harold Brown then directed the military services to explore the uses of high-energy lasers in space; William Perry, the undersecretary for research and engineering, did not object, and DARPA reshaped its three principal programs involving chemical lasers in the direction Wallop had proposed.[31]

By the time of Reagan's inauguration Wallop and Codevilla had many reasons for optimism about their project. A number of senators supported research on space-based lasers; the secretary and an undersecretary of defense had given it their endorsement; Reagan himself seemed enthusiastic. After sending Reagan the draft of his *Strategic Review* article, Senator Wallop had the opportunity to talk with the candidate about it at a barbecue at Senator Laxalt's camp in the Sierra Nevadas, and Reagan had promised to make anti-missile defenses an issue in the campaign. Michael Deaver and John Sears vetoed the idea, but Reagan apparently remembered what Wallop said, for in the course of a conversation with Senator Harrison Schmitt a month before his inauguration he asked the former astronaut about the feasibility of modern anti-ballistic missile technologies, including lasers.[32]

In February 1980 Reagan heard from another advocate of missile defenses: Daniel O. Graham. A friend and neighbor of Richard Allen's in

Washington and a defense adviser in both Reagan campaigns, Graham had been called in by Allen a few days before the New Hampshire primary to brief Reagan on the findings of Team B before a debate with George Bush. Meeting with the candidate in Nashua, New Hampshire, Graham talked about Team B and then went on to propose the creation of a defense in space.[33] In Graham's recollection, Allen and William Casey were angry that he took the time out of an intelligence briefing to make the proposal, but Meese reacted positively. "Reagan," Graham said, "seemed very interested. He got out his three-by-five cards and started asking questions."[34]

At that point Graham, who had not much in the way of a technological background, would not have been prepared to answer many detailed questions about his concept, for he had just begun to develop his idea.

A West Point graduate, Graham had made his career in Army intelligence, much of it in the Soviet branch, and he had ended it as director of the Defense Intelligence Agency. Short, feisty and tenacious, he had been given the nickname "Little Dog" at West Point, his initials suggesting the appellation. In the intelligence community he was known for staking out extreme positions and defending them relentlessly—often in the face of the facts as his colleagues understood them. In Washington he generally took the position that the Soviet Union was far stronger and more aggressive than was the consensus within the intelligence community. In 1969, for example, he argued that the Soviets would soon conduct a surgical strike on the Chinese nuclear-weapons facilities. When he failed to convince his colleagues, he leaked his prediction to the columnist Joseph Alsop and created an uproar in Washington. Tactics like these made him enemies within the intelligence community, and by his own account he retired from the DIA in 1976 because Henry Kissinger was about to get rid of him. Before resigning, however, he went to see Reagan, and despite the sensitivity of his job and the security restrictions under which he operated, he served as an adviser to the Reagan campaign.[35]

Once out of office, Graham joined several groups lobbying for a military buildup and publicly argued that the Soviet buildup was far greater than the U.S. intelligence agencies judged it to be. After participating in Team B, he, like the CPD members, argued the efficacy of civil defenses, but, as usual, he went a bit further than anyone else. In a speech attacking SALT II in the late 1970s, he told an audience to stop worrying about nuclear war because there was already a defense against it: "your feet.... If you can run, you can get away and protect yourself."[36] He was not asked to join the Committee on the Present Danger.

In 1979 Graham published *Shall America Be Defended?*, a book written with the help of Angelo Codevilla, the main thesis of which was that the SALT agreements and the fact that U.S. officials had accepted "mutual assured destruction" had allowed the Soviets to gain such a degree of nuclear superiority as to permit them to win a nuclear war. Though he favored ABM weapons to protect the MX, he argued that the U.S. should defend itself primarily with counter-force weapons and with a civil-defense program.[37] Graham began working on strategic defenses only after the book was published, and from all indications in response to the talk coming out of the second Reagan campaign.

In 1980 Graham put together a small group of people to design a concept for missile defenses, and after Reagan's election he began to raise money for the project and, as he put it, "to put flesh on the bones" of his "basic idea."[38] In the spring of 1981 he put his concept on paper for the first time in an article for *Strategic Review.*

In the article, "Toward a New U.S. Strategy: Bold Strokes Rather Than Increments," Graham wrote that the victory of Ronald Reagan signified an end to the dangerous concept of "mutual assured destruction," and an end to détente, arms control and "graceful accommodation to the power of adversaries." However, he wrote, the administration's budget recommendations essentially called for incremental additions to existing programs, and this was a mistake: the Soviets would doubtless accelerate their own military programs, and though the U.S. might gain a qualitative edge, it would never win the race for quantity. Citing CPD estimates, he argued that the cost of such an approach would be staggering, and that, even after five or ten years of spending huge sums for additional weapons, the U.S. would probably find itself in a more precarious position than it was before. The only real hope for the U.S., he said, was to take a bold new approach and use its technological assets to create a space-borne defense against Soviet missiles.[39]

Graham went on to advance another argument for space weaponry. In the past, he wrote, those nations which first projected their military capabilities into new realms of human activity had reaped enormous advantages. The Phoenicians and the Vikings, for example, came to control large territories by sending their warships into the coastal seas. Spain, Portugal and later Britain built great empires on the strength of their oceangoing navies. After World War II the United States took dominion over the new medium of commerce and communication—the air—and established strategic superiority for three decades. In the last quarter of the twentieth century, he contended, space was the new frontier for exploration, for communication and for the exploitation of primary resources, such as energy. And because "inexorable pressures" were forcing the U.S. and the Soviet Union into competition for this domain, the U.S. had to take the strategic high ground with space-based missile defenses.

Like some new Alfred Thayer Mahan, Graham was offering the grand—and, indeed, imperial—vision of America ruling space as Britannia once ruled the waves. Surprisingly, however, his claims for the efficacy of space-based defenses were quite modest. In the history of warfare, he wrote, there has never been an impermeable defense, and there never will be. Space-based defenses would, however, introduce uncertainty into the mind of an attacker and make a Soviet first strike less likely. In other words, they would enhance deterrence, rather than lead to a basic change of strategy.

Graham's first choice for the technology of defenses in space was a small one-man space cruiser with high maneuverability. A fleet of these cruisers could, he wrote, be stationed in orbit, and on warning from intelligence satellites the cruisers could move into position to intercept and destroy Soviet ICBMs with projectile or laser weapons. His conception was, in other words, of lonesome astronaut-cowboys patrolling the boundaries of space and waiting, year in, year out, for the Soviets to start shooting. The concept did not, as he later put it, "stand up to doubt." A few months later Graham and his advisers changed their approach, proposing instead a series of unmanned battle stations armed with kinetic kill vehicles—or guided projectiles—which would destroy their targets by collision. Here they were on somewhat solider ground, for the Air Force and DARPA had been working on similar concepts for many years. In addition, they proposed the building of a space plane and a solar-power satellite to collect the sun's energy and transmit it to earth.[40]

While Graham was revising his proposals and preparing to take them to his contacts in the administration, Edward Teller appeared in Washington to report that an underground nuclear test had delivered the promise of a weapon that could protect America from ballistic missiles.

The founder of the Lawrence Livermore Laboratory and one of the most influential scientists of the nuclear era, Edward Teller was a visionary. He was also a hero to Republican right-wingers—the only major scientist who was. Not long after World War II, Teller had come to conceive of the Soviet Union as an implacable foe bent on world conquest, a foe that respected only superior force and superior military technology. In *The Legacy of Hiroshima,* published in 1962, Teller advocated "localized, limited nuclear war" as a response to Soviet aggression. Well aware of the deadly power of nuclear fission, he urged that the U.S. build both active and passive defenses against nuclear weapons, so that Washington would be free to initiate such an attack.[41] In the early sixties he campaigned for a plan to build a fifty-billion-dollar system of civil-defense shelters across the nation—shelters which would have to be dug deeper and deeper and at further cost as the Soviets acquired more capable weapons.[42] In the mid-sixties, he became a passionate advocate of anti-ballistic missile systems and planned to build a giant warhead for the ABM interceptor that would simplify the task of hitting enemy warheads in space. Later he reluctantly came out for the ABM Treaty because the Congress and the public clearly would not support a nationwide system of ABMs.[43]

In 1979 Teller had contributed an essay to a Hoover Institution publication, *The United States in the 1980s,* in which he expressed extreme pessimism about the course of the strategic-arms race. The time, he wrote, was approaching when our country "may find itself in the situation where it has to give in to Russian demands or face the end of the United States." Like Nitze and like Graham at that time, he maintained that this parlous situation had come to pass in large part because the Soviets had built a civil-defense system so effective that they would soon be able to launch a nuclear war without fear of U.S. retaliation.[44] Two years later, at a conference of strategic experts in Italy, Teller uttered the same dire warning but on completely new grounds. Russia, he said by way of introduction, had been expansionist for centuries; its desire for power was now so strong that its leaders were prepared to threaten nuclear war and quite possibly to carry out their threat. To achieve their ends, the Soviets required missile defenses based in space to protect their population from a U.S. retaliatory strike, and they were so far ahead in the development of these weapons that they might feel "very sure that we cannot retaliate." If the Soviets got this defense and the U.S. did not, there would, Teller said, be a nuclear war whose outcome was certain: "The United States will be wiped out by a fraction of the Soviet weapons, and the Soviets will then be able to impose their will on the rest of the world."[45]

Teller's new concern was curious in that there was no more evidence that the Soviets were building anti-missile space weaponry in 1981 than there had been in 1979. But what had happened in the meantime was that scientists from the Lawrence Livermore Laboratory had produced the first X-ray laser beam. The achievement was a triumph, and to Teller it held the promise of a revolutionary new weapons system.

Livermore scientists had struggled for almost a decade to create such a beam. The X-ray laser had a very short wavelength and a great deal of energy; if generated in a laboratory, it could in theory illuminate objects as small as molecules and lead to important breakthroughs in biology and medicine. In 1978, after many unsuccessful attempts to produce the laser in a lab, Livermore scientists turned to the idea of generating it by a nuclear explosion. A bomb-pumped laser would, of course, be useless for biological research, but it might have military applications, particularly in space. The earth's atmosphere quickly absorbed X-rays; a laser based in space, however, could flash its beam over thousands of miles at the speed of light, and with adequate power it could actually disintegrate its target. In November 1980 an experiment, code-named Dauphin, was carried out during one of the Pentagon's scheduled underground nuclear tests in the Nevada desert. The experiment was a crude one, and the beam it produced had only a small fraction of the energy required for a weapon. Nonetheless, the beam was very powerful, and the laser itself, built around a thick metallic rod, was small by comparison with other high-energy lasers. To Livermore scientists the success of the experiment conjured up the possibility of producing a weapon that would be light enough to lift easily into space and powerful enough to destroy targets, including missiles and warheads, outside the atmosphere. Creating such a device would take many years and many more nuclear tests—if in fact it could be done at all—but the possibility existed that the laser, which the Livermore team dubbed Excalibur, might become the ultimate anti-ballistic missile weapon.[46]

In February 1981 Teller and Lowell R. Wood, Jr., the head of the Excalibur project, went to Washington together to break the news of the successful experiment and to drum up support for the top-secret project from congressional leaders and the Pentagon. Because of the need for nuclear tests, the project would be expensive right from the start. Roy Woodruff, the associate director of Livermore for nuclear design, went along on the trip to see that the briefings stayed within the appropriate bounds. Teller's ideas were always big ideas, and he tended to proclaim each new Livermore project as the solution to one of the world's great problems. Recently, for example, he had conceived that the hydrogen bomb could be used to dig a sea-level waterway across Central America as an alternative to the Panama Canal.[47] Quite naturally, not all of his ideas seemed entirely sensible to others, and, just as naturally, not all of the projects Livermore undertook panned out in the way he advertised them. In relation to the Excalibur briefings, what worried Woodruff was the propensity of both Teller and Wood to overlook technological problems and describe hypothetical outcomes as if they were virtual accomplishments. This form of salesmanship did not ruffle the expert Pentagon technologists, but it sometimes created unfortunate mood swings in the Congress: excitement succeeded by a disillusionment that hurt the credibility of the Livermore Lab. Roy Woodruff was therefore pleased when under his watchful eye Teller and Wood gave properly qualified briefings to the congressional leaders, setting no unrealistic target dates. But then, at the end of February, an article appeared in *Aviation Week and Space Technology*, a trade publication, describing the highly classified Excalibur project and maintaining that "X-ray lasers based on the successful Dauphin test . . . are so small that a single payload bay on the space shuttle could carry to orbit a number sufficient to stop a Soviet nuclear weapons attack."[48]

While Teller and Wood lobbied for Excalibur, Wallop and Codevilla mounted a new effort on behalf of chemical lasers. In the last years of the Carter administration they had managed to shape an exotic research program into the first stage of a weapons-design project. With Reagan in the White House they meant to push the Pentagon into building chemical-laser weapons and stationing them in space to shoot down ICBMs. However, the advent of a Republican administration and a Republican-controlled Senate did not prove the boon to the project that they had expected. Indeed, the going was a good deal heavier than it had been before.

A month after Reagan's inauguration Codevilla went to William Schneider, Jack Kemp's defense analyst who had become chief of the national-security division of the Office of Management and the Budget, and asked for his help. Schneider formally suggested to the Pentagon that it be allocated $502.9 million for fiscal years 1981–83—over and above what it had applied for—to accelerate DARPA's space-laser program. To Codevilla's surprise, the Pentagon turned the offer down. Afterwards Wallop wrote to the President and the secretary of defense asking for their assistance on his project. The responses were negative. Then, in April, a panel of the Pentagon's Defense Science Board completed the study on space-based lasers (SBLs) previously requested by the Senate and concluded, "It's too soon to attempt to accelerate the SBL development toward integrated space demonstration for any mission, particularly for ballistic missile defense." The panel did recommend $50 million more for SBL research, but since the chair of the panel, John S. Foster, Jr., was a senior executive at TRW, a company with a substantial financial stake in space-based lasers, questions were raised about conflict of interest.[49]

Undeterred, Wallop and Codevilla offered a new amendment adding more funds for laser-related research and requiring the Air Force to proceed with the production of a prototype chemical laser, giving detailed instructions as to how this would be done. The amendment raised hackles not only in the Pentagon but on the Senate Armed Services Committee. Senators John Tower and John Warner, the ranking Republican members, asked Wallop to amend his bill in line with the DSB panel's conclusions. Wallop agreed to take out the detailed instructions, but the amendment, when it went to the floor, still contained a provision establishing a program office for space-laser work within the Air Force. Though the amendment passed on the floor, the staff of the Senate Armed Services Committee dropped it in conference with the House committee. Furious, Wallop sought the help of a senatorial ally on the Appropriations Committee and attached his amendment to another bill. Tower retaliated by calling the comptroller of the Pentagon and telling him that, if the Pentagon spent even a cent of the money appropriated under an amendment which had not been authorized by his committee, he would cut the Pentagon budget the following year. Wallop's funds were not released.[50]

In his book *While Others Build,* Codevilla expresses surprise at the treatment Wallop's project received in the hands of Republicans. But, then, Codevilla, who now thought of himself as a far greater authority on chemical lasers than Foster or any Pentagon technologist, did not perceive that from the point of view of the defense community the project had a lunatic tinge to it.[51] Wallop was not, after all, a member of the Armed Services Committee; neither he nor Codevilla had any technical or military expertise; yet the two of them were advocating a fundamental change in the U.S. strategic posture based on the potential of a single laser which the Pentagon experts considered blue-sky technology. In the view of the Pentagon, their harebrained scheme to build a prototype would not only be an enormous waste of resources but would signal a U.S. breakout from the ABM Treaty, thereby causing all kinds of havoc in U.S.-Soviet relations. In 1979 and 1980 the

Carter administration and the Democrats in the Senate had been on the run before the conservatives, and they had done what they could to pacify Wallop. But Reagan's appointees to the Defense Department and the Republican conservatives who now controlled the Armed Services Committee in the Senate had no reason to defer to the junior senator from Wyoming. Wallop had violated the protocol of the Senate by making an end-run on the committee, so Tower and Warner responded in kind.

In the late spring of 1981 Daniel O. Graham began shopping his idea for strategic defenses to friends and acquaintances in government, including Secretary of State Alexander Haig and the Army chief of staff, General Edward C. Meyer. The responses to his letters were polite but noncommittal. Graham also made speeches at defense-community gatherings, and after one of them he was introduced to Karl R. Bendetsen, the retired CEO of the Champion International Corporation, a forest-products company. Tall and patrician-looking, Bendetsen was well known on the West Coast both as a successful businessman and as a backer of conservative causes. Having served as an Army colonel during World War II and later as undersecretary of the Army in the Truman administration, he had maintained his interest in military affairs: he was a board member of the National Strategy Information Center and a founding member of the Committee on the Present Danger. Bendetsen expressed interest in Graham's proposal, and over dinner the two formed an alliance to bring the missile-defense concept to national attention and to see that it became policy. That summer the two set out to raise money and to bring in consultants for a technical study of the project; they also put together a panel to oversee the study and to ensure that it received a hearing in Washington. In order to obtain access to the White House, Bendetsen included three of Reagan's old friends and supporters: Joseph Coors, the doughty conservative brewer from Colorado; William A. Wilson, the oilman and rancher who was Reagan's neighbor in Santa Barbara and the trustee of his finances; and Jaquelin H. Hume, the grocery magnate, who had known Reagan since 1965 and was a close friend of Edwin Meese. Bendetsen also invited Edward Teller to join the panel. Teller was a natural addition to the group. Bendetsen had known him for many years, and Reagan was well acquainted with him. In 1967 Teller had given the new governor of California a tour of the Livermore Lab and talked to him about the work he was doing on a warhead for the ABM system then under development.[52]

In May, Bendetsen and Graham set up the non-profit group they called High Frontier, later moving it under the institutional umbrella of the Heritage Foundation, a conservative think-tank with close ties to the Reagan administration. The initial idea was to produce a study on anti-missile defenses and other space ventures for publication and dissemination to government agencies, the Congress and the public. But by July the panel had White House sponsorship and another agenda.

• • •

During the campaign Richard Allen had helped to keep the issue of missile defenses out of Reagan's speeches, but he believed strongly that defenses should be a part of the military buildup. In his view the ABM Treaty, like the rest of the SALT process, represented the defeatist, détente policies of the past. The U.S. had to regain strategic superiority and use it to develop momentum to roll back Soviet power. This meant an across-the-board buildup that included a heavy investment in civil defenses and a program for building anti-ballistic missiles.[53] In February, less than a month after the inauguration, Allen invited his friend Daniel Graham to the White House to talk with Meese about his idea for a space-based kinetic-energy anti-missile system. Following the meeting, Allen wrote a memorandum advocating a presidential initiative on strategic defenses, arguing that it would be immensely popular with the American people. Just think of how the crowds in football stadiums chant "Defense, defense," he wrote.[54]

Meese was interested, and so, too, was Martin Anderson, whom Meese had brought in to head his Office for Policy Development. After Graham linked up with Bendetsen, Meese agreed to help with the fund-raising for High Frontier by making calls to Reagan's old friends and contributors. On July 28 he met with Bendetsen, Graham and Teller to discuss the effort, and asked for a written statement of the purposes of the group. In a follow-up letter Bendetsen wrote him that the panel would be submitting recommendations for a "space-borne ballistic missile defense and other defense systems" to the White House and that these recommendations might "present an historic opportunity for the President to announce a bold new initiative." He added that the group would use due care to avoid publicity and would have a draft proposal of "the Reagan initiative" ready for Meese by November.[55]

That Allen, Meese and Anderson would ask a group of private citizens to design a presidential plan for a major change in strategic policy was, to say the least of it, unorthodox. In his book Anderson writes that the President favored missile defenses, so the only real issue, apart from the politics of the matter, was technical: was there a technical justification to revive the research and development that had been dormant since the early 1970s? The normal way to proceed, he writes, would have been to ask the Defense Department to study the issue, but this option was not even considered, because the group knew it would not work: all large bureaucracies resist new ideas, and besides, the Defense Department had been allergic to the ABM issue ever since the bruising battles of the late sixties.[56]

By the early fall of 1981 Bendetsen and Graham had succeeded in raising over a quarter of a million dollars from foundations and wealthy conservatives. With the money Graham hired a group of advisers to flesh out his proposals—a rather eclectic group, which included a consultant from Arthur D. Little and Company and a science-fiction writer. For his systems design

Graham seems to have relied principally on Fred W. Redding, Jr., an engineer from the Stanford Research Institute, one of the contractors for the Army's BMD program. During the fall these people elaborated a plan which included solar-energy satellites and an anti-missile system they called Global Ballistic Missile Defense, composed of space weapons undergirded by ground-based ABMs and civil-defense shelters. For the space system they envisaged a manned space plane plus 432 satellites or "trucks," each containing forty to forty-five miniature homing vehicles to intercept ballistic missiles in the first phases of their trajectory. The system, Graham acknowledged, would intercept only some proportion of the missiles in an all-out Soviet barrage, but the virtue of it, he maintained, was that it would use "off-the-shelf" technology and be ready in five or six years at a cost of less than fourteen billion dollars. With it, he wrote, the U.S. could, in infantry parlance, take and hold space, and then improve the system as technology advanced.[57]

Bendetsen's High Frontier panel met twice in early September and laid out a work plan and a schedule. Graham and his consultants were to draft a report by mid-November; the panel would then review the report, prepare a briefing and present the briefing to the President on November 30.[58]

On September 14 Bendetsen, Graham and Teller met in Meese's office with Meese, his administrative aide Edwin W. Thomas, Anderson and the President's science adviser, George Keyworth, who was made liaison to the panel. In his account of the meeting Anderson reports that as the discussion progressed he "felt a rising sense of excitement," for it became clear that "not only did everyone feel we should pursue the idea of missile defenses, but they also deeply believed it could be done." There was general agreement that U.S. nuclear strategy should move away from total reliance on offense to reliance on both offense and defense; there was also agreement that a major part of the defense system would be based in space and that an effective missile-defense effort "could defend not only our population and our cities but also our offensive nuclear missiles." His notes on the meeting suggest that some of the discussion revolved around the limited goal of defending the MX.[59]

On October 12 Bendetsen and Graham went to the White House again and spoke with Meese, Thomas and Anderson. According to Anderson, the two gave a glowing account of the status of their efforts and indicated that there was increasing support for their work among those they had talked with in Congress, the CIA, the Defense Department, the Air Force and NASA.[60]

Graham, who had many contacts in the national-security bureaucracy and among the top administration appointees, had in fact taken his proposal to several agencies for review. Possibly he believed there was growing support for it, but the internal reviews of his plan, released some years later, show that if he did he was sadly mistaken. In the first place, the ideas he presented were not new. The concept of a solar-power satellite which would beam the sun's energy to earth had been around for many years, but technology had not yet produced a means of making it even remotely cost-effective. As for the anti-missile plan, it was based on the BAMBI concept DARPA had developed in the 1950s. The concept had been revisited many times by the Air Force and its corporate contractors as technology progressed, but, as studies showed, there was still no solution to the numerous problems involved—one of which was the enormous weight of the system and the difficulty of getting it up into orbit. In the second place, according to the Defense Department analyst who looked at the anti-missile plan in September, Graham's designer, Fred Redding, had not only failed to solve the problems that had been previously identified, but had not even addressed most of them. The plan, the analyst concluded in his formal point paper, contained "major technical uncertainties" and was "too immature to assess feasibility."[61]

In his book Anderson speaks as if Bendetsen, Graham and Teller were of one mind, but in reality Graham was also having trouble with the Bendetsen group. The panel which had been formed to review and promote his proposal was pulling away from his project and heading off in another direction.[62]

Bendetsen and his colleagues did not, of course, know anything about the Defense Department's assessment of Graham's plan, but the panel members soon began to have doubts of their own about the Global Ballistic Missile Defense project. At the outset Jaquelin Hume, the eighty-year-old food magnate, asked a number of sensible questions. How would the Soviets react to the deployment of such a system? Could they not shoot down the "trucks" with anti-satellite weapons? What were the risks that such a system with all of its untried new elements, would fail in a crisis?[63] Apparently the answers were not all that reassuring, for some of the panel members began to worry about the very idea of deploying a system that would be susceptible to Soviet counter-measures and that would in any case provide only a partial defense. Edward Teller contributed mightily to their sense of unease. In meetings he attacked Graham's system as expensive, antiquated, impossibly heavy and incapable of stopping any significant proportion of the missiles in a Soviet barrage. In the course of the proceedings panel members came around to the view that Graham was too rigidly committed to a single system and that their job was to present the President with a general account of the technical options available. Teller, not surprisingly, supported this approach. But, then, he had an alternative for them.[64]

At the September 14 White House meeting Teller broke into discussion of how to defend the MX missile with a dramatic statement. The ultimate goal, he said, was not to defend missiles but to protect populations: the goal was "assured survival" as opposed to "assured destruction." Later, at meetings of the panel, Teller and Lowell Wood, whom he brought along with him, described the successful Dauphin experiment and spoke of the promise of Excalibur. The claims they made for Excalibur appear in an extraordinary letter Bendetsen sent Meese on October 20. In the letter Bendetsen made a direct request for fifty million dollars in additional funds for Excalibur and explained that the matter was so important to the national defense that it could not wait even the month until the report of the panel was due. The letter described the X-ray laser concept in some technical detail, speaking of a device which would focus the energy of a small hydrogen bomb into a beam with a million times the brightness of the bomb's undirected energy and would have a lethal range of thousands of miles. Of course, the Dauphin experiment had not demonstrated any of this: the "device" was a theoretical construct that might or might not become a reality after years of research. Yet Bendetsen's letter promised a "fully weaponized" X-ray laser "for ballistic missile defense on a five-year time scale." It concluded that "X-ray lasers may represent the largest advance in strategic warfare since the hydrogen bomb itself."[65]

Teller and Wood were selling the X-ray laser in exactly the manner Woodruff had feared they would—and the California conservatives had neither the background nor the inclination to doubt them. Only Graham was less than enthusiastic. Later he recalled the graphic description Teller and Wood gave of the X-ray laser weapon. "There were to be long rods sticking out of the satellite," he said. "We called it the space-based sea urchin." Graham, however, did not challenge Teller's timetable. He was in no position to do that. Instead he attacked the concept on political and tactical grounds. The American public, he said, would never stand for a nuclear weapon in space—and besides, this weapon had a fatal flaw. "It may be a technical marvel," he told Teller, "but it involves a military paradox. If somebody fires a weapon at this kind of satellite, its only reaction is to destroy itself or be destroyed. It can only protect itself by blowing itself up." His remark stumped Teller. Apparently the scientist had not thought of this problem before. But at the next meeting he and Wood came back with a solution: the X-ray laser weapons would be based in a survivable mode, perhaps on submarines, and at the signal of a nuclear attack, they would be "popped up" by a rocket into space. This plan for "pop-up" deployment became a permanent feature of the X-ray laser concept, and in retrospect Graham was triumphant. "I convinced Ed that putting that sucker up into space wasn't going to work. Any infantryman could tell you that." Yet Teller had won this round, for Graham had unwittingly reinforced the presumption that an X-ray laser weapon was a near-term reality.[66]

Graham was no match for Teller—certainly not in the eyes of the California conservatives. Furthermore, he was offering only a partial defense. His GBMD might, the panel recognized, prove to be as politically unattractive as the old ABM system, and it might actually be dangerous if deployed.

Teller, on the other hand, was offering an end to the threat of ballistic missiles, and perhaps an end to the threat of other weapons as well. In a meeting in early November, held in Keyworth's office at the White House, he told the panel that an entire new generation of weapons was coming along, a "third generation," to succeed the atomic and hydrogen bombs. Whereas the first two generations had radiated their energy spherically, the third generation would direct energy into beams. The X-ray laser was the most mature of these technologies, but behind it there were many others, including microwave and particle beams, that would provide the weapons of the future.[67]

The panel completed its report at the end of November, and in December the High Frontier panel split apart. The proximate cause of the rupture was Graham's insistence on publishing his own GBMD project in the face of Bendetsen's desire to keep the whole initiative confidential until the President could make his decision on the High Frontier report. Graham argued that he had a legal obligation to publish a report since he had accepted over a quarter-million dollars in tax-free donations. In this he was correct, but the fact was that he certainly knew that the report of the panel would contain Teller's recommendations, not his; though he agreed to wait until the President had a chance to respond, he decided to detach himself from the rest of the group and go it alone.[68]

On January 8, 1982, when Bendetsen and other members of his group were given their promised meeting with Reagan, the memorandum they handed the President rang with the rhetoric of Edward Teller. The threat of Soviet strategic weapons was growing, the memo reported, and the U.S. had no hope of matching it; further, there were strong indications that the Soviets were about to deploy "powerful directed energy weapons" that would allow them to "militarily dominate both space and the earth, conclusively altering the world balance of power." In response, it said, America must abandon the strategy of "mutual assured destruction" and move to a strategy of "assured survival." The report urged the President to appoint a task force to choose defensive systems for development, and it called for an intensification of the nation's directed-energy efforts but said nothing of Graham's kinetic-energy weapons. Warning that the nation could not survive the delays inherent in the Pentagon's normal acquisition process, it urged the President to mount an effort as great as that of the Manhattan Project.[69] According to Bendetsen, the discussion at the meeting focused on directed-energy weapons; there was talk of their potential as anti-aircraft as well as anti-missile weapons, and much talk of lasers. Members of the group actually lobbied for Teller's laser, as against Wallop's chemical lasers, for they told the President that the Pentagon was experimenting with lasers which would have only limited capacity because their wavelengths were too long.[70]

By Anderson's account the meeting in which Bendetsen and his colleagues presented their memo to Reagan was a critical turning point for the Strategic Defense Initiative. The discussion was lively and animated, and the meeting, which was scheduled for fifteen minutes, lasted an hour. The President, Anderson writes, did not have to be convinced that building a missile defense was the right thing to do. His questions were directed to the feasibility and cost of the proposal, and by the end of the meeting he seemed to be satisfied. "As I left the Roosevelt Room," Anderson writes, "I was personally convinced that President Reagan was going ahead with missile defense. How or when I did not know. But I did know that whenever he decided to move forward on such an important policy path he rarely looked back or changed his mind."[71]

Bendetsen and his colleagues, however, had a different impression: the President did express interest in their project, and the meeting made them optimistic, but otherwise the White House response to their work was distinctly and surprisingly cool. The panel had, after all, completed its report by the end of November. On White House instructions, Bendetsen had reduced the report to a page and a half for the President to read, but then he could not seem to set up a meeting with Reagan. In late December he told the other panel members that he was not sure the meeting would ever take place. In the first week in January, Jaquelin Hume and William Wilson, Reagan's two close friends on the panel, called the White House themselves. On January 7 Bendetsen, who was then in New York, received a call from Meese's office telling him that the President would meet with the panel for fifteen minutes the following day. The President's other California backers received the same call, but apparently Teller did not: though he was in Washington, he does not seem to have attended the meeting. Wilson could not attend the meeting—he was on his way to Europe—but Bendetsen, Hume and Coors arrived at the White House at 2:00 P.M. with their page-and-a-half report. Anderson believes the meeting lasted an hour, but according to Bendetsen's contemporary notes, it ran only five or ten minutes over time. This gave the panel members only twenty or twenty-five minutes to make their case for a revolutionary change in American strategic policy. According to one participant, the President, though showing interest, said that he would have to consult his secretary of defense, thereby indicating that he was not going to make the decision himself.[72]

After the meeting Bendetsen received a cordial letter from the President promising a rapid follow-up on the panel's report. But then silence followed. A month later he learned that the White House science adviser, George Keyworth, had been asked to set up a task force to study strategic defenses, and that the study was due to be completed at the end of the year. This was not at all what Bendetsen wanted. True, his memorandum had called for the creation of a presidential task force, but the agreement he had entered into with Meese back in July was that the report would lead to a major presidential initiative, and he was eager for action. In May he received a memorandum from Keyworth, who had just met with Graham, reporting that a panel of the White House Science Council was studying defensive technologies and a presidential decision was still months away. At that point Bendetsen began to believe that the issue was being studied to death and nothing would be done.[73]

The cooling of enthusiasm for missile defenses in the White House was mysterious to Bendetsen, but between October and January the White House staff was reshuffled, and the three leading advocates of missile defenses were shorn of their national-security roles.

Some six months after the inauguration Baker and Deaver had concluded that the system they had set up to deal with foreign and defense policy was not working. They had hoped to put foreign policy on the back burner while they concentrated on getting the President's economic program and defense budget through the Congress, but major issues kept cropping up, and decisions had to be made. Meese was theoretically in charge of the process, but, given his disorganization, decision memos and national-security documents would disappear into the piles of paper in his office, never to reemerge. Allen rarely saw the President, and since Meese knew little about the issues, Reagan was not properly briefed; many decisions remained pending, others were made by default, and Secretary of State Alexander Haig was raising Cain. Then, on August 19, an embarrassing incident occurred. Two U.S. Navy fighter planes shot down two attacking Libyan jets sixty miles off the Libyan coast. Allen informed Meese at 11:00 P.M., but Meese did not wake the President until four-thirty the next morning. The delay had no consequence, because there was no action to be taken, but since Reagan was already acquiring a reputation for idleness and for inattention to pressing matters of national security, the news of Meese's failure to wake him gave rise to innumerable jokes and editorial cartoons.[74]

After this incident Baker and Deaver decided that the role of the national-security adviser had to be upgraded and that Richard Allen would have to go. Meese naturally resisted having the NSC staff taken out from under his jurisdiction, and since Reagan disliked settling disputes among his advisers, it took Baker and Deaver some time, and the help of Nancy Reagan, to obtain the President's consent to the reorganization. To make the change more palatable to Reagan, they proposed that William Clark, his old friend from California, who had been brought into the administration as Haig's deputy secretary of state, be made NSC adviser. Then they held off replacing Allen because a feud had developed between Allen and Haig, and they did not want to leave the impression that Haig had triumphed over the White House staff. While they were waiting for the fuss to blow over, an NSC aide—Colonel Oliver North—found a thousand dollars in cash in Richard Allen's safe. It transpired that, back in January, Allen had obtained an interview with Nancy Reagan for a Japanese women's magazine as a favor to Japanese business friends. The journalist gave him an envelope with a wad of cash destined for Nancy Reagan, and, rather than turning it down, he had put it in his safe. Allen was investigated and it eventually emerged that he had asked his secretary to turn the cash over to the Treasury, and she had forgotten to do it. But, given the previous news stories about Allen's business dealings, the incident got a good deal of press attention, and Baker and Deaver took the opportunity to let Allen go.[75]

On taking office on January 1, Clark began reporting directly to the President, thus removing Meese and his policy staff from any line responsibility for national-security affairs. A neophyte in foreign and defense policy, Clark brought Robert McFarlane, a former Marine lieutenant colonel who had served on Kissinger's NSC staff, with him from the State Department to serve as his deputy and foreign-policy adviser. To help him with defense issues, he brought in Thomas C. Reed, an old friend of his from California. Reed, who had just reviewed strategic defenses for the Pentagon's Defense Science Board and concluded that none of them currently looked promising, had no interest in hearing from outside lobbyists.[76] Clark, who knew nothing about the subject, took the advice of his aides and paid no attention. The whole issue of missile defenses thus passed into the hands of the President's science adviser, George Keyworth.

At the time missile-defense advocates inside and outside the White House did not register any alarm about the changes in the staff. Clark, another California conservative, could be expected to share their views. Plus they thought Keyworth an advocate of defenses, and had some reason to think so.

In the spring of 1981 the search for a White House science adviser had fallen to Anderson's Office for Policy Development, and Anderson had looked for a very particular sort of person to fill the job. While working for the Nixon administration, Anderson had, so he tells us, observed that the role of the science adviser had changed: whereas the adviser had started as a representative of the President's, he had become a representative of the scientific community to the President, and, in Anderson's view, the representative of "just one more powerful special interest group whose eyes were fixed on the growing pots of money in Washington."[77] This was a fairly common view in the Reagan administration, and in the interests of cutting back the bureaucracy OMB officials had toyed with the idea of dispensing with a science adviser and with the White House Office of Science and Technology Policy altogether.[78] Anderson had favored reducing the OSTP staff, and he had looked for a science adviser who would support the administration's policies and otherwise do what he was told to do. Keyworth, a forty-one-year-old nuclear physicist from Los Alamos, seemed to fit his requirements perfectly. He was, Anderson observed, "a relatively unknown scientist" who "was not hostile to using science to help defend the country," and he had been recommended to the White House by Edward Teller.[79] Most of the scientific establishment had reacted with unease, or actual alarm, to his appointment, and once in the White House Keyworth had made it plain that he understood what was required of him. He had supported the administration's decisions to make drastic cuts in the funding of basic science research; he had supported all the administration's decisions on strategic-weapons procurement; he had told members of the OSTP staff that they should consider themselves "the President's slaves."[80]

As White House liaison to the High Frontier panel, Keyworth attended all of its meetings, and although he apparently did not say very much, he left the impression that he was sympathetic to the purposes of the group. He was solicitous of Teller, lending him his office to brief the panel, acknowledging that he owed his job to Teller, and saying on one occasion that the old man was like a father to him. In November he wrote Bendetsen a note praising the "collective skill and experience" of the group, adding, "I laud your efforts." Bendetsen, for one, believed that Keyworth approved of the report that the panel had prepared for the White House. On January 9, the day after the meeting with the President, he wrote his colleagues saying that he was "confident" that the science adviser "thinks well of our proposal."[81] But this was a misunderstanding.

Whatever Keyworth had said to Bendetsen—and doubtless he had been tactful—he was highly skeptical about the potential of exotic technologies for missile defenses. He was, after all, a physicist who had worked on lasers as well as nuclear weapons, and who had for years observed the struggles with ballistic-missile defense research at Los Alamos.[82] Even while attending the High Frontier meetings, he had been working to defeat Senator Wallop's campaign to develop chemical-laser weapons for missile defenses. In an interview in September he had said of congressional support for these weapons, "It's in an area, in my opinion, where there has been a definite lack of expert involvement, and, I would say, there have been a lot of unrealistic arguments made." He had added: "People don't realize that shooting down a satellite is not too tough. . . . But the really meaningful thing is to shoot down a missile in the boost phase. This is a formidable task and the technology is not in hand today. I would claim that self-pronounced laser experts who claim that it is something we are a few years away from doing are plain not supported by the scientific and engineering communities. . . ."[83]

In September, Keyworth hired Victor H. Reis, an MIT engineer and a well-known critic of Wallop's proposal, from the Pentagon's Office of Research and Engineering, to help him analyze weapons systems.[84] It was Reis who the previous year had written that, in the unlikely event that chemical-laser battle stations could be built, it would take 1,444 of them to do the job at the cost of $1.5 trillion. Keyworth and Reis worked so effectively together to stop Wallop's project that in November Wallop wrote James Baker a letter urging that Keyworth be fired.[85]

Anderson, and doubtless Bendetsen, assumed that because Keyworth was a protégé of Teller's he would back Teller's proposals for missile defenses. But, then, Anderson and the laymen on the High Frontier panel had no notion that Teller's claims for the X-ray laser went far beyond anything considered appropriate at the Livermore Lab. Keyworth supported research on the X-ray laser, but he did so with the explicit understanding that it was a basic research project and many years away from becoming a weapons program. At High Frontier meetings he apparently did not argue with Teller or try to temper the panel's enthusiasm for directed-energy weapons, but a few days after the Bendetsen group had met with the President, he said in a White House staff meeting that the plan the group presented had "very difficult technical aspects." A year later he broke the official silence on Excalibur in a public speech at the Livermore Lab. In the presence of Teller he called the X-ray laser "one of the most important programs that may seriously influence the nation's defense posture in the next decades." The statement may have sounded enthusiastic to reporters, but Keyworth had made no specific claim for the laser, and after the speech he told reporters that the laser was probably unsuited to missile defenses.[86]

At Meese's suggestion, Keyworth did follow up on the High Frontier report by setting up a special panel of the White House Science Council. The panel was to look at how new technologies, including lasers, might affect the administration's strategic-modernization program as well as strategic defense. Chaired by Dr. Edward A. Frieman, a physicist and the vice-president of Science Applications, Inc., it included a number of the leading authorities in the field, among them Dr. Harold M. Agnew, a former director of Los Alamos, and Charles Townes, one of the inventors of directed-energy devices, who was then chairing a Defense Department panel on the MX basing mode. Some of the members had institutional links to laser research projects, and none of them could have been considered remotely "hostile to using science help defend the country," as Anderson put it. Yet Teller, who was not made a member of the panel, worried from the beginning that their findings would not support his claims.[87] Under guidelines laid down by Reis, Frieman undertook a yearlong study of the new technologies and kept to his schedule. Keyworth did not intervene in the work, and there were no pressures on him from anywhere in the White House to speed the pace or to push for positive results.

The year 1982 was, as Anderson reports, a quiet one for missile defenses.[88]

In March, General Graham, now independent of the Bendetsen group, published his own High Frontier proposal in a glossy paperback volume with artists' renderings of his Global Ballistic Missile Defense concept. In the foreword he thanked Bendetsen for his help in raising money, but, by agreement with the panel members, made no mention of the panel or its White House interlocutors. Even before publication he sent the study to the Pentagon for review. Thanks to his high-level contacts and to the influence of the Heritage Foundation, the Army and the Air Force conducted full-dress evaluations of his missile-defense plan. The results were unambiguous. The evaluations included such comments as: "This concept is not new, nor did the proposal address the technical problems identified in prior studies. ... The technologies are not off-the-shelf.... It is the unanimous opinion of the Air Force technical community that the High Frontier proposals are unrealistic regarding state of technology, cost and schedule.... This evaluation concluded that the proposal has no technical merit and should be rejected."[89]

The previous September a Defense Department analyst had written a similar evaluation of Graham's proposal after listening to a briefing from its designer, Fred W. Redding, Jr. The cover memo he wrote to his superiors in the Office of the Undersecretary for Policy gives the flavor of the Graham enterprise in a way that the formal reviews could not. "Mr. Redding," the analyst wrote,

> describes himself as a concept development engineer. He seems very sincere in his attempts to uncover unique solutions to major defense problems. Unfortunately, his sincerity and enthusiasm are seldom tempered by practical engineering considerations. In addition, he appears to be a master of self-deception and is not averse to stretching the truth well beyond the breaking point. As a result, his credibility within the Defense community is very low.
>
> His attitude toward the military "with their institutional biases and automatic rejection of original thinking" is his explanation for the lack of enthusiasm and support from the DoD and his justification for "making an end run around the bureaucracy." According to Mr. Redding, most of the villains are in the DoD and he sees it as his duty to rescue us from ourselves.[90]

Graham was informed of the results of the Army and Air Force evaluations of his concept, but these in no way deterred him. Over the course of 1982 he established a new High Frontier organization, raised more money from conservative sources and besieged Secretary Weinberger with letters urging further consideration of his project. In these letters he claimed that there was growing support for the High Frontier concept within the national-security community and that "destroying Soviet ICBMs in the early stages of trajectory with non-nuclear projectiles ... is now widely accepted as practicable."[91] Apparently Graham had caught the Fred Redding virus.

On November 24 Caspar Weinberger wrote Graham in terms that seemed designed to put an end to the matter. Speaking for himself and for Richard DeLauer, the Pentagon's chief of research and engineering, he wrote: "He and I agree with you that a policy based on effective space defense would enhance national security. However, we differ with you on the availability of technology to support such a policy. Although we appreciate your optimism that technicians will find the way and quickly, we are unwilling to commit this nation to a course which calls for growing into a capability that does not currently exist."[92]

In 1982 Wallop and Codevilla became of necessity more inventive in their struggle for missile defenses. The Wallop amendment of that year did not propose any new funds for chemical lasers; it simply ordered the secretary of defense to build a chemical-laser weapon as quickly as possible and to present Congress with the bill. Possibly because the amendment had no funds attached to it, it escaped the immediate attention of the Senate Armed Services Committee and was passed by a voice vote on the Senate floor. The "laser lobby" seemed to be back in force. This was something of an illusion. Most of the senators who voted for Wallop's bill did not focus very clearly on it, or on what Wallop was trying to do, and years later Codevilla admitted, "There was no laser lobby. It was just me dragging the brush around as the Indians did when they wanted to pretend there was a crowd of them."[93] Nonetheless, Keyworth and the DARPA chief, Robert S. Cooper, were with some reason alarmed. In March, Keyworth went to see Wallop. According to Codevilla, he was polite to the senator but he pointed at Codevilla with a shaking finger and accused him of doing incalculable harm to the nation's security by campaigning for the development of a chemical-laser weapon. In their effort to stop the amendment, Keyworth and Cooper found an ally in Anthony Battista, a powerful staff member of the House Armed Services Committee who had run the R&D subcommittee for almost a decade. The three worked out a strategy whereby Battista would eliminate all funding for the chemical laser and invite Keyworth and Cooper to testify that lasers of shorter wavelengths, such as the X-ray laser, held much more promise for missile defenses—though of course they would not be ready for years. The maneuver allowed Senators Tower and Warner to go to the House-Senate conference and drop Wallop's amendment in exchange for a restoration of the previous year's chemical-laser research funds. Wallop and Codevilla now gave up all hope of using legislation to pressure the Pentagon into developing a chemical-laser weapon.[94]

In the fall, as something of a last-ditch effort, Wallop and Codevilla went to the President and the secretary of defense to plead their cause. According to Codevilla, Wallop talked with Reagan for an hour, and Reagan was wonderfully encouraging until Wallop asked for his help. "I'll ask Paul Thayer about it," Reagan said, referring to a defense aide. Wallop, knowing Thayer would do nothing, challenged Reagan to make the decision himself. But Reagan—rather helplessly, in Codevilla's view—just kept repeating that he would ask Thayer about it.[95]

The meeting with Weinberger was hardly more productive. Richard DeLauer and Alan Pike, the laser expert from DARPA, attended the meeting, and for nearly an hour Codevilla, Pike and DeLauer argued joules and megawatts in front of the senator and the secretary. At the end Wallop challenged Weinberger to make a judgment about who was right and who was wrong. According to Codevilla, Weinberger said that he was not qualified to make such a judgment. Wallop then asked him if he didn't agree that the Soviet ICBM force was the principal military threat to the United States and that the revolution in anti-missile technology was the most important strategic development since the atom bomb. Weinberger replied that these matters were essential but that others would have to make the technical judgments.[96]

Wallop was now completely blocked. The opposition to his project had become a solid wall that ran through the Senate and the House Armed Services Committees, the Army and the Air Force, the Pentagon's Office of Research and Engineering, DARPA, the White House and the Office of the Secretary of Defense. Only the defense contractors still favored the project—but they were not allowed to testify at the Armed Services Committee hearings. Towards the end of the year Cooper, with the consent of Congress, reduced DARPA's chemical-laser programs to a much smaller research activity. There was nothing Wallop could do about it.[97]

By the end of 1982 Edward Teller had also gotten nowhere with his project. Thanks in part to the administration's attempt to stop Wallop's campaign, the Livermore X-ray laser program was receiving an ample share of the laser research funds, but Teller had much larger ambitions for Excalibur: he wanted a program on the scale of the Manhattan Project. On trips to Washington he lobbied congressmen and administration officials indefatigably, and since he was a member of the White House Science Council, he lobbied the Frieman panel whenever he could.

In June the Frieman panel had held a review of the X-ray laser. Under the supervision of their director, Roy Woodruff, the Livermore scientists gave a far less optimistic account of its prospects than Teller had given the Bendetsen group. Asked for their scenario, they said that, if an additional $150–200 million were put into Excalibur for six years, they could complete all the nuclear tests required to bring the X-ray laser to the second phase of the development process: an assessment of its scientific feasibility. After that the lab would have to tackle all the work of making the laser into a weapon, plus all the difficult tasks involved with creating instruments to track enemy missiles and point the laser. Even if some of these tasks could be performed simultaneously, there could, according to the scientists, be no laser anti-missile weapon until the mid-1990s, and that at the earliest. In the late fall the Frieman panel reported that the X-ray laser could not yet be thought of as military technology.[98]

When Teller heard what the panel had concluded, he threw a fit and threatened to resign from the White House Science Council if the panel did not review the X-ray laser again. In order to avert the political storm his resignation would have caused, Frieman agreed to listen to a second Livermore briefing. Teller then went to work on Woodruff to change the Livermore report to reflect his own view that a "fully weaponized" laser could be built in five years. Aware that he, and not Teller, would be held responsible for promises that Livermore could not keep, Woodruff refused, and at the second review session, in February 1983, he gave an even more conservative schedule for the X-ray laser than had been given before.[99]

In the meantime, Teller made efforts to see the President. He pressed Keyworth to get him a private interview, but Keyworth, who did not share Teller's view of the laser, and who knew that Reagan's aides took pains to avoid exposing the President to special pleading, dodged his requests whenever they came up. In June, Teller tried another tack. During an appearance on William F. Buckley's television show, *Firing Line,* he warned that the Soviets were developing advanced anti-missile weapons and spoke of a dire threat to the United States. When Buckley asked why he did not take this important matter to the President, Teller said that he had not had a single opportunity to see Reagan since he was nominated. This public complaint galvanized the White House to grant Teller the audience he sought.[100]

The meeting took place on September 14, and, according to a National Security Council staff member who sat in on it, Teller made a powerful presentation on "third-generation" nuclear weapons and their potential to destroy enemy missiles and revolutionize American strategy. Reagan asked if an anti-missile system could be made to work, and Teller said that there was good evidence that it could. According to the NSC staff member, Reagan seemed to accept what Teller had told him, but William Clark expressed doubts and questioned Teller closely about third-generation weapons.[101] Later Keyworth called the meeting a "disaster"; Teller had baldly asked Reagan for a huge increase in funding for the X-ray laser, and Meese and Clark had had to cut the meeting short.[102]

Possibly Teller's talk of laser weapons made some impression on Reagan; possibly the President was simply listening politely to the eminent conservative. In any case, just as at the January 1982 meeting, he left the matter to his staff to resolve, and clearly his key advisers were not in the grip of any technological enthusiasm. Teller persistently lobbied the White House, but there was no follow-up to the meeting.

In October, Bendetsen, having come to the end of his patience, decided to reconvene his High Frontier panel to "prod" the White House into action. The group met on December 21 at the headquarters of the Northrop Corporation in Los Angeles and determined that it would provide the White House with draft remarks for an insert into the President's forthcoming State of the Union address. As composed by Bendetsen and amended by Teller, the draft called for a transition from the "anachronistic doctrine of MAD" to a doctrine of "assured survival." The nation, it said, was now ready to exploit the "new and revolutionary" ideas for defense and would start to do so immediately. The first goal would be to deploy an ABM system to defend the MX missiles, and after that the system would be expanded to protect the nation's population and its cities. Bendetsen sent the draft to Keyworth and to Anthony Dolan, Reagan's most conservative speechwriter, but no more was heard of it.[103]

Three months later White House officials pointed to the High Frontier panel as the source of the President's inspiration for a missile-defense initiative, suggesting that Teller and the members of his Kitchen Cabinet had infected him with their own enthusiasm for lasers and other "third-generation" technologies. Years later, however, the very same officials told historians that the High Frontier panel had had virtually nothing to do with the President's speech. Why they initially claimed it did is on the face of it puzzling, for to critics of the SDI program the claim seemed to demonstrate how shaky the technical basis for the program really was. The eminent physicist Herbert York, for example, wrote in 1985 that SDI was "an instance of exceedingly expensive technical exuberance sold privately to an uninformed leadership by a tiny in-group of especially privileged advisers."[104] But, then, explaining the initiative by some technical enthusiasm, however bizarre, was better than confessing that technology had nothing to do with it at all.

CHAPTER FIVE

To the Star Wars Speech

THE REAGAN ADMINISTRATION came into office in January 1981 with a great deal of martial music about the Soviet threat and the need for a military buildup. Experienced observers in Washington, Moscow and European capitals, however, discounted the campaign rhetoric. Other presidents, notably Kennedy and Nixon, had come to Washington charging that the U.S. was falling badly behind in the arms race, only to change their tune shortly after taking office. Of course the country was in a conservative mood; it had elected Reagan to rebuild American military power and to take a tougher line with the Russians and Third World troublemakers than the Carter administration had. But the change, it was thought, would be one of degree, for the Carter administration had already increased defense spending, détente was a dead letter and there were limits to the uses of American military power. In Moscow officials expressed hope that Reagan would be "another Nixon"—a conservative and a tough bargainer, but more consistent and pragmatic than Jimmy Carter.[1]

Reagan's Cabinet choices gave such observers no reason to doubt their initial view. Most of the domestic-policy posts went to moderate conservatives, such as Malcolm Baldridge, the secretary of commerce, and Drew Lewis, the secretary of transportation, or to men like Donald T. Regan, the Treasury secretary, who had no clear ideological position. In the national-security arena the two most important jobs went to men with long track records in Washington. Secretary of State Alexander Haig was a major figure in the foreign-policy establishment. An Army officer who had risen to the rank of four-star general, he had served for five years as Kissinger's military deputy on the NSC staff and later as Supreme Allied Commander in Europe. He was close to Richard Nixon, and his views were thought to be similar to those of the former President. Secretary of Defense Caspar Weinberger was one of Reagan's California associates and new to the defense arena, but between 1969 and 1975 he had served in four important posts in the Nixon and Ford administrations, the last with Cabinet rank. In those years he had built a reputation as an effective bureaucrat and was remembered as "Cap the Knife" for his dedicated efforts to cut federal spending as head of the Office of Management and the Budget.

Ronald Reagan himself was, of course, still something of an unknown quantity. At his first press conference, on January 29, he reported that the Soviets were continuing to promote world revolution and a one-world Communist state, and that they had publicly declared that "they reserve unto themselves the right to commit any crime, to lie, to cheat, in order to attain [their ends.]" The remark caused a stir in Washington. In a meeting with Haig that same day, the Soviet ambassador, Anatoly Dobrynin, said, "This will cause great puzzlement in Moscow. I hope it will not continue."[2] Haig told him that the President had called to say that statement was not meant to offend anyone in Moscow but was just an expression of his deepest convictions. Dobrynin replied that the clarification only made things worse.

Yet Dobrynin, who had been ambassador to the United States for almost twenty years, drew no conclusions about Reagan. A sophisticate with a puckish sense of humor, he contented himself with remarking that the administration was sounding as moralistic as the Carter administration—thereby managing, quite satisfactorily, to infuriate Haig.[3]

Like Dobrynin, most Washington observers did not ponder the presidential sally for long. Reagan, they had learned, had a trove of made-up Lenin quotations he had gleaned from obscure right-wing publications, but since he always delivered these lines with an air of childish wonderment, he seemed not to be entirely serious. On the whole it seemed difficult to believe that this genial, laid-back former actor would actually carry out the confrontational policies he had proposed during the campaign.

It was thus that the Reagan administration surprised diplomats and other knowledgeable observers. Within its first two years in office, the administration raised the fear of war in Moscow and in the West, fell out with its NATO allies and many of its supporters in Congress and engendered a major, broad-based anti-nuclear movement in Europe and the United States.

In May 1981 the KGB advised its stations in Western capitals that the United States might be preparing to attack the Soviet Union. Its stations were put on the alert and asked to provide Moscow with every scrap of information that might constitute a warning. Washington learned of this from the KGB chief of station in London, who defected to the West in 1985. Apparently what alarmed Moscow was exactly what alarmed the European and American publics: that is, not any one event but, rather, a pattern.[4]

On taking office the Reagan administration launched the largest peacetime military buildup in American history. Not long after the inauguration the Office of the Secretary of Defense proposed a $32.6-billion add-on to the defense budgets for 1981 and 1982. Because the Congress had previously enacted a 1981 budget with a 9-percent real increase built into it, this meant that defense spending would rise from $142 billion in 1980 to $222 billion in 1982. From 1982 on the Pentagon was asking for a yearly real increase of 7 percent. In all, the administration was planning to spend almost $1.5 trillion in five years and to create budgets larger in real dollars—or dollars adjusted for inflation—than those at the peak of the Vietnam and the Korean wars.[5] Of that sum, over two hundred billion dollars was to go for strategic forces. In October, after the first defense budget was passed, the administration presented a strategic-modernization package that included plans to develop a Stealth bomber (the B-2) and to build a hundred MX missiles, six new Trident submarines with accurate MIRVed D-5 missiles, three thousand air-launched cruise missiles and a hundred B-1 bombers. In addition, the package included an expansion of air and civil-defense systems, ABM research and an expensive investment in command, control and communications systems for U.S. nuclear forces.[6]

Weinberger, who sold the vast yearly budgets to Congress, adopted wartime rhetoric. The threat to the West, he told reporters, was much like that of the 1930s, when Hitler was building the German war machine and Churchill's was the lone voice calling for rearmament.[7] The Soviets, he said, "have out-invested us by eighty or ninety percent in the last few years." Weinberger often insisted that the Soviets had gained strategic superiority by mass-producing missiles and spoke of the "window of vulnerability" as if it meant U.S. strategic inferiority and the vulnerability of the entire deterrent. The U.S., he said, had to make it "eminently clear to [the Soviets] that if they should launch a first-strike, they would never be able to bear the retaliatory cost that we could inflict."[8] In conventional forces the U.S., he said, had fallen so far behind that it courted a global disaster. "We must," he warned, "be prepared for waging a conventional war that may extend to many parts of the globe if persistent local aggression by superior forces cannot be turned around."[9] In congressional hearings he would insist that if his budget was cut by a single penny the U.S. would have to write off the Middle East, Korea or the Caribbean. In hearing after hearing, he would come back with the same arguments, using the same phrases—"the threat we face" and "the decade of neglect." When members of Congress criticized Pentagon operations, he would respond that they were damaging national security and helping the Soviets.[10]

Secretary Haig in his first two months in office repeatedly accused the Soviets of backing all international terrorism; he also charged that the Soviets had a "hit list" for the "take-over of Central America" and threatened to go to "the source"—by which he seemed to mean taking military action against Cuba.[11]

Even more alarming, administration officials engaged in a great deal of talk about nuclear-war–fighting capabilities and limited war options. At his confirmation hearing Deputy Defense Secretary Frank Carlucci said, "I think the Soviets are developing a nuclear war–fighting capability, and we are going to have to do the same." Weinberger, in an early budget hearing, spoke of the need for force parity "across the full range of plausible nuclear war–fighting scenarios with the Soviet Union."[12] Haig and Weinberger argued in public about whether NATO's contingency plans included firing a nuclear demonstration shot, and in a press conference Reagan suggested that a tactical exchange of nuclear weapons in Europe would not necessarily entail a wider war.[13] During the campaign both Reagan and Bush had made statements suggesting that they did not regard nuclear war as catastrophic. Reagan had charged that the Soviets believed nuclear war was winnable, and Bush had told a reporter that nuclear superiority did not matter "if you believe that there is no such thing as a winner in a nuclear war. . . . And I don't believe that."[14] In August 1981 senior Pentagon officials told *New York Times* reporters that the plan was to enable the United States to regain nuclear superiority within the decade and to fight a nuclear war, from a limited strike to an all-out exchange.[15]

To defense sophisticates in Washington it seemed fairly clear that the most senior administration officials had small acquaintance with the world of nuclear weapons. Reagan, for example, once maintained that submarine-based missiles could be recalled, and Weinberger surprised everyone in the Pentagon by saying, "Soviet missiles are far more accurate than ours."[16] This naïveté was not reassuring, in that a number of the administration's strategic experts came from the right-wing fringes of their profession. At least one of them, Colin Gray, a consultant to the Arms Control and Disarmament Agency (ACDA), seemed to regard nuclear conflict as a plausible instrument of national policy. In 1980 he and a co-author, Keith Payne, had written an article in *Foreign Policy* in which they maintained: "The United States should plan to defeat the Soviet Union and to do so at a cost that would not prohibit U.S. recovery. Washington should identify war aims that in the last resort would contemplate the destruction of Soviet political authority and the emergence of a post-war world order compatible with Western values."[17] Other specialists held that the two societies could survive a nuclear war. Charles Kupperman, for example, a Reagan appointee to ACDA, told a reporter: "Nuclear war is a destructive thing, but it is still in large part a physics problem."[18] Then there was T. K. Jones, the deputy undersecretary of defense for research and engineering/strategic and theater nuclear forces, who had studied Soviet civil-defense measures for the Committee on the Present Danger, had become a convert to bomb shelters. In an interview with Robert Scheer in the fall of 1981, Jones said that the United States could recover from an all-out war with the Soviet Union in just two to four years. He explained that nuclear war was not so devastating as it had been portrayed, and that civil-defense measures would provide protection. "If there are enough shovels to go around, everybody's going to make it," he said. "It's the dirt that does it."[19]

When Jones's remark appeared in the *Los Angeles Times,* a furor broke out in the Congress. Jones was muzzled, and subsequently senior officials curbed their own talk of war-fighting. However, in May 1982, Richard Halloran of the *New York Times* reported that a five-year Defense Guidance, approved by Weinberger, contained plans for fighting a "protracted" nuclear war. According to Halloran, Defense Department planners had debated whether a protracted war was possible and had decided that it was. American nuclear forces, they said, "must prevail and be able to force the Soviet Union to seek earliest termination of hostilities on terms favorable to the United States." The new strategy called for American forces able to "render ineffective the total Soviet military and political power structure" and to maintain, "through a protracted conflict period and afterward, the capability to inflict very high levels of damage" on Soviet industry.[20]

Commentators in the American and European press expressed shock and outrage. Did administration officials actually believe that the U.S. could *win* a "protracted" nuclear war? Had they abandoned deterrence for the dangerous illusion that the U.S. could destroy the Soviet nuclear capability? Weinberger attempted to defend the policy and made matters worse. "We've stated many times that we don't think nuclear war is winnable," he told the *New York Times*. But then, asked how this jibed with the goal of "prevailing," he said, "We certainly are not planning to be defeated."[21]

Since 1960 every incoming administration had made the U.S.-Soviet relationship its first order of business and had set about putting its own stamp on the arms-control process. The Reagan administration was an exception. For the first two years it had virtually no dealings with the Soviet Union. Secretary Haig met with Dobrynin and with Soviet Foreign Minister Andrei Gromyko, but merely to register administration complaints about Soviet behavior and to reject Dobrynin's calls for a resumption of the SALT dialogue. The President for his part seemed not at all interested in summitry. Indeed, he sometimes suggested that the U.S. did not have to have a relationship with the Soviet Union. In November 1981, for example, he assured an audience at Notre Dame University, "The West won't contain Communism, it will transcend it. It won't bother to denounce it, will dismiss it as some sort of bizarre chapter in human history whose last pages are even now being written."[22]

During the campaign Reagan had said that he would not begin arms-control negotiations until the country undertook a military buildup. Most in Washington assumed that this meant, if anything, a few months' delay, but months passed and all the administration did was change the name of the strategic talks from SALT for Strategic Arms Limitation to START for Strategic Arms Reduction. Instead of making a proposal, administration officials, including Reagan himself, repeatedly charged the Soviets with cheating on past agreements, insisted that arms control would depend on a change in Soviet behavior in world affairs and questioned the value of existing treaties.

On March 3, 1981, Secretary of the Navy John Lehman announced that the U.S. should not comply with either the SALT I or SALT II constraints on offensive arms. The next day the State Department issued a statement, which originated with Haig, saying that Lehman's statement had not been authorized, and that the U.S. would "take no action that would undercut existing agreements so long as the Soviet Union exercises the same restraint." But Haig's statement had not been authorized by the White House either, and though his no-undercut policy remained in effect, other administration officials continued to maintain that the U.S. would be better off without the SALT treaties.[23]

In 1980 the Carter administration had begun talks with the Soviet Union on intermediate-range nuclear forces in Europe and the western part of the Soviet Union. It was generally expected that the Reagan administration would resume the negotiations immediately, since the matter was of great concern to the European allies. In the late 1970s the Soviets had begun to replace their obsolescent intermediate-range weapons, the SS-4s and SS-5s, with a powerful new missile, the SS-20, armed with three MIRVed warheads. With a range of three thousand miles, the SS-20 was capable of striking any city in Western Europe from bases on either side of the Ural Mountains. At the request of West German Chancellor Helmut Schmidt and the NATO defense ministers, the U.S. had committed itself to a two-track strategy: it had promised to deploy a new generation of intermediate-range weapons in Europe, and it had promised to negotiate with the Soviets for a reduction in the numbers of the proposed deployments on both sides. But the Reagan administration made no move to go back to the table.

Faced with the prospect of hundreds of powerful new nuclear weapons deployed in and around Europe, the West European governments pressed Washington to take up the negotiations, but to no avail. In March, Lawrence Eagleburger, Haig's deputy for West European affairs, told NATO officials that the U.S. was taking steps to begin the arms talks, but in April, on his first trip to Europe as secretary of defense, Weinberger told them that there would have to be many changes on the Soviet side before the talks could begin. "If the movement from the Cold War to détente is progress, then let me say we cannot afford much more progress," he declared. And he said, "What this alliance wants, or at least what it needs, is leadership, not compromise."[24]

In the late spring hundreds of thousands of Europeans took to the streets to call for an end to the arms race. There had always been small ban-the-bomb groups in Britain and other NATO countries, but in this case the demonstrations included huge numbers of ordinary middle-class people from provincial cities as well as capitals across Northern Europe. And although the Soviets had begun the buildup, the demonstrations had a distinctly anti-American tone.[25] Left-wingers charged that the U.S. was creating East-West tensions so that it could dominate Western Europe as it had in the early days of the Cold War; the far more widespread concern was that the saber-rattling in Washington would provoke war fears in Moscow and cause a serious international crisis. Thus the American missiles, which had once been seen as a counter to the Soviet missiles, were now seen as threats to peace.[26]

By the summer of 1981 the demonstrations, most of them in Northern Europe, built to the point where they split the social-democratic parties and threatened to bring down the very governments which had called for the American deployments. In October a quarter-million people attended an anti-nuclear rally in Bonn—the largest gathering of Germans since John F. Kennedy's visit to Berlin in 1963.[27] Finally, the administration acted.

In mid-November, President Reagan announced his negotiating proposal: the U.S. would cancel deployments of all its intermediate-range weapons if the Soviets would dismantle their SS-20s and the older systems they were replacing. The proposal, known as the "zero option," was praised in some quarters as bold and politically brilliant. Experienced diplomats, however, remained unimpressed, for, as they pointed out, the administration was asking the Soviets to dismantle hundreds of expensive new weapons in return for a U.S. agreement not to deploy a missile force that had not yet been built. The proposal did not appear to be negotiable.[28]

The Intermediate Nuclear Force (INF) talks began but went nowhere, and by the spring of 1982 anti-nuclear activism was spreading across the United States as fast as it had spread across Europe, and a resolution calling for a bilateral freeze on all nuclear weapons was gaining ground in the Congress. In mid-April peace groups collaborated on Ground Zero Week, a national campaign of teach-ins and demonstrations, which reached over a million Americans across the country. A nationwide poll taken that month indicated that 70 percent of all Americans wanted a negotiated freeze on nuclear weapons.[29]

On May 9, 1982, President Reagan made the first strategic-arms-control proposal of his presidency. In a speech at his alma mater, Eureka College in Illinois, he outlined what he called a "practical phased reduction plan" that would proceed in two stages. In the first phase strategic warheads would be cut by a third and there would be significant reductions in ballistic missiles; in the second phase the U.S. would seek to achieve a ceiling on ballistic missile throw-weights and on other elements of the strategic forces. All three networks headlined the speech, and the initial reaction from commentators was almost as enthusiastic as it had been to his INF proposal. But when the congressional defense analysts had a chance to examine the full text of the proposal, they realized that, just like the zero option, the START proposal was almost certainly not negotiable. In Phase I the administration was calling for ceilings on ballistic-missile launchers and warheads that would require the Soviets to get rid of most of their best strategic weapons—the SS-17s, -18s and -19s—while the U.S. would be able to keep most of its Minutemen and proceed with its planned deployment of a hundred MXs. In addition, the U.S. could go ahead with cruise-missile deployments and the modernization of its submarine and bomber fleets. Then, in Phase II, the U.S. would be asking the Soviets to reduce their aggregate throw-weight by almost two-thirds, while the U.S. made no cuts at all. In effect, the administration was proposing that the Soviets virtually disarm themselves until they could redesign their missiles and their force structure along American lines. A defense analyst for the Senate Intelligence Committee voiced a common view when he said that the START proposal was "so one-sided . . . it appears insincere."[30]

On June 12, three-quarters of a million people gathered in Central Park in New York City to protest the nuclear-arms race. The rally was larger than any of the anti–Vietnam War demonstrations that had taken place in the city.

That same month, President Reagan, in an address to the British Parliament, spoke of the "decay of the Soviet experiment" and "the great revolutionary crisis within the Soviet bloc." Playing on Khrushchev's taunt that socialism would bury the West, he said, "The march of freedom and democracy . . . will leave Marxism-Leninism on the ash heap of history as it has left other tyrannies which stifle the freedom and muzzle the self-expression of people." He spoke of the strength of the Solidarity labor movement in Poland and the desire for freedom and self-determination within the whole Communist world. He also observed that the rate of growth in the Soviet GNP had been falling since the fifties, that Soviet agriculture could no longer feed the population and that the growth of military production was putting a heavy strain on the Soviet people. "Now, I don't want to sound overly optimistic," he said, "yet the Soviet Union is not immune from the reality of what is going on in the world. It has happened in the past—a small ruling elite either mistakenly attempts to ease domestic unrest through greater repression and foreign adventure, or it chooses a wiser course. It begins to allow its people a voice in their own destiny." Reagan repeatedly quoted Winston Churchill and called for a "crusade for freedom."[31]

In some circles the speech was read as a masterful statement of the challenge of democracy and capitalism to Communist rule in the Soviet bloc. In others it was seen as ominous. Over the past year and a half a number of officials had indicated that the administration was determined to reverse the Brezhnev Doctrine—or Brezhnev's claim of 1968 that the Soviet Union had the right to intervene in any Soviet-bloc country where Communist rule was threatened.[32] Further, the Defense Guidance had called for the development of "more effective linkages with the peoples of East Europe so as to deny Soviet confidence in the reliability of its allies," and for trade policies that would put the maximum pressure on the Soviet economy.[33] It thus seemed possible that Reagan meant that the administration was preparing to take major risks to bring about a "rollback" of Soviet power.

Still, as the *New York Times* noted after the speech, there was not much connection between the administration's brave words and its deeds. The administration had not, for example, imposed trade sanctions on the Soviet Union; to the contrary, it had lifted the embargo on grain sales imposed by the Carter administration after the Soviet invasion of Afghanistan. Then, too, it had watched passively when, in December 1981, the Jaruzelski government in Poland declared martial law and cracked down on Solidarity, forcing the movement into the underground. Similarly, it had taken no military action against Cuba, and it had sent no American troops to fight Soviet-backed governments or insurgencies anywhere in the world. Moreover, what measures it had taken had shown no results. For example, the administration's refusal to engage in serious arms-control negotiations had not persuaded the Soviets to stop supporting their Third World allies and clients—and was not likely to, since the administration had offered no quid pro quo. In sum, the administration seemed to have no Soviet policy.

At the same time that the administration was running into trouble with the public over its lack of an arms-control policy, it was running into trouble with the Congress over its military buildup. Weinberger kept calling for higher defense budgets, but the deep tax cuts the administration had passed in 1981 had raised the specter of huge deficits in the years ahead, and in the view of the Armed Services Committees the buildup was directionless.

Under normal circumstances managing the Pentagon was a formidable task, and with the vastly increased military budgets it was a monumental one, but Weinberger showed no inclination for management or administration. His job, as he defined it, was in the public arena. Always available to journalists, he appeared often on the Sunday-morning talk shows and accepted speaking engagements across the country. In addition, he traveled abroad frequently, visiting thirty-five countries in his first two years in office. It was generally known that he had wanted to be secretary of state rather than secretary of defense, and he took an active role in foreign-policy–making. What he did not do was probe the service budgets or learn about weapons systems in any detail. In an attempt at systemic management reform, he and Carlucci gave the services far more control over procurement than they had had since Robert McNamara took office in 1961. Though there were some benefits to this approach, planning now came much more from the bottom up than from the top down, with the result that there were soon "requirements" for nine new types of fighter planes, seven air-defense weapons, two new aircraft carriers and three new strategic-bomber programs. And Weinberger did not veto any of them. "The generals are in Beulah Land," a former secretary of defense said. "Anything they want, he gives them."[34]

Furthermore, Weinberger seemed to have no discernible defense strategy, or at least none that bore any relationship to U.S. capabilities or procurements. Under the Nixon, Ford and Carter administrations military doctrine called for the capability to fight one and a half wars simultaneously, but Weinberger abandoned this standard. He spoke of fighting simultaneously in Europe, the Pacific and the Middle East; Secretary of the Navy John Lehman spoke of fighting on all seven seas at once. Weinberger maintained that the U.S. must be prepared to "meet any contingency," thus begging the perennial question of how much was enough.[35] Then, too, the Defense Guidance and other administration policy directives laid plans for the use of conventional forces so ambitious as to defy military logic. In the case of Soviet aggression in Western Europe, the Defense Guidance proposed that the U.S. and its allies should be able to put "at risk Soviet interests, including the Soviet homeland"—a strategy Napoleon had once attempted. Another plan was for "horizontal escalation." As Weinberger and William Clark explained it, the U.S. would not just respond to aggression in the region in which it occurred, but would launch conventional counter-offensives in other regions as well. According to the Defense Guidance, the potential targets, in case of a Soviet move into, say, the Persian Gulf, were Cuba, North Korea and Vietnam.[36] Then, though the Defense Guidance called for the capability to wage a protracted nuclear war with the Soviets, Weinberger had not yet found a survivable basing mode for the MX missile—or a way to close the "window of vulnerability."

By the end of December 1982 the administration had reached an impasse in regard to the buildup. The anti-nuclear movement was continuing to grow; public support for increased military spending had gone from 80 percent to 20 percent in the space of two years; the Congress had refused to appropriate further funds for the MX until the basing-mode issue was resolved; the House would be voting on a nuclear-freeze resolution again in the spring; and Reagan's approval rating had dropped sharply because of an economic recession and because of public anxieties about war.[37]

Under the circumstances Reagan and some of his aides began to think about a missile-defense initiative.

Why the administration had gone so far out on a limb and created such political trouble for itself puzzled many in the Congress. But then most expectations are based on past experience, and the Reagan administration was not like any of its predecessors in the post-war period.

For one thing, its national-security bureaucracy was far to the right of those in previous administrations. Rather than representing an intra-party coalition, its appointees belonged to an ideological right that included right-wing Republicans and neo-conservatives—among them some fifty members of the Committee on the Present Danger.

In the Office of the Secretary of Defense the key policy-making posts went to hard-line defense intellectuals. This was not Weinberger's doing. Shortly after his appointment Weinberger dismissed Van Cleave and the rest of the Defense Department's transition team with a flourish, but Weinberger had no experience in the defense arena and no network of contacts, so in practice the appointments process was dominated by Reagan's right-wing campaign defense advisers and conservative Republicans on the Senate Armed Services Committee.[38] In fact, Weinberger made only one appointment: that of his deputy, Frank Carlucci, an experienced civil servant, whom Van Cleave considered far too dovish for the job. In the area of international policy, the two top posts went to hard-line opponents of détente. Fred Iklé, the deputy secretary of defense for policy, a Swiss-born professor of political science and strategic studies, was known for his hostility to the SALT agreements and the complexity of his prose. Richard Perle, the assistant secretary of defense for international-security affairs, had worked for Senator Henry Jackson for almost a decade, opposing the arms-control initiatives of three administrations. In addition, there was John Lehman, Jr., the brash young secretary of the Navy, who was known as the *enfant terrible* of the defense community. Brought to Washington by Richard Allen in 1969, he had, as congressional liaison on Kissinger's NSC staff, provoked Senator William Fulbright to wrath by his persistent efforts to block congressional oversight of foreign policy. Iklé, Perle and Lehman had been allies in the seventies and had played leading roles in the Committee on the Present Danger.[39]

To head the CIA, Reagan had chosen William Casey, his finance chairman and campaign manager. During World War II, Casey had served in the OSS, organizing French resistance actions in support of the Normandy invasion. According to Robert Gates, the career CIA officer who became his executive assistant, Casey came to the CIA "primarily to wage war against the Soviet Union." He planned to fight the Soviets and their allies in much the same way as he had fought Hitler, through covert operations and the building of guerrilla insurgencies. His interest in intelligence was limited to that which informed or provoked action. He was focused and in a hurry. In April 1981 he began preparations to arm and train a guerrilla army to fight the Sandinista government in Nicaragua.[40]

For the State Department, Haig had chosen a number of moderate conservatives—or "pragmatists," as they came to be known—including a number who, like himself, had worked on Kissinger's staff. But as U.S. representative to the United Nations he had accepted Jeane J. Kirkpatrick, the neo-conservative political-science professor who had attracted Reagan's attention with her article on the virtues of authoritarian regimes. Then, too, the Arms Control and Disarmament Agency, normally to the left of the State Department, was in this case far to its right. Its director, Eugene Rostow, the former co-chair of the CPD, had compared the Soviet Union to Hitler's Germany, and liked to explain that arms control was a fruitless endeavor and had been one for the past two centuries. His second-in-command, and the head of the START negotiating team, was Edward Rowney, a former Army general and latterly an adviser to Senator Jesse Helms. A man with a profound distrust of diplomacy, Rowney maintained that arms control should be no more than a part of a strategy for winning the arms race and bringing the Soviets to heel.[41] It was a measure of ACDA that Paul Nitze, the chief delegate to the INF negotiations, was the least hawkish of the principals.

As for Richard Allen's NSC staff, it had no balance even of the traditional conservative sort. The senior Soviet specialist was Richard Pipes, the Harvard historian and CPD author, who in early 1981 declared that the Soviets would have to choose between changing their system and going to war.[42] William Clark, who replaced Allen at the end of 1981, was just as right-wing as his predecessor.

Given their density within the administration and their sense of triumph on taking power, the hard-liners were on a roll.

Still, at the level of the White House, the Reagan administration was far less determined and purposeful than it sometimes appeared. Certainly the President and his close aides never made a concerted decision to put $1.5 trillion into the arms race, to call a halt to arms control—or to strike the fear of war into the American public. That they managed to do these things owed in surprising measure to accident and blunder. In the first place, the two top Cabinet officers, Weinberger and Haig, turned out rather differently from what anyone had expected; in the second, the decision-making process left a good deal to be desired. But, then, Reagan did not operate like any other president.

How different Reagan was from his predecessors began to emerge only in the last years of his presidency, when his aides and Cabinet secretaries began to publish their memoirs. By the mid-1990s some fourteen former administration officials—including a secretary of defense, two secretaries of state, two national-security advisers, a chief of staff and a deputy chief of staff—had delivered themselves of books on the administration. One of the first of the memoirs to appear was David Stockman's *The Triumph of Politics,* published in 1986. In his book Stockman, who became Reagan's first director of the Office of Management and the Budget at the age of thirty-five, quite exceptionally acknowledges that he did not always serve Reagan well.[43]

According to Stockman, the administration's decision to spend $1.5 trillion on defense over five years owed in large part to his own mistake in arithmetic. Stockman, a two-term congressman, who had been a Marxist in college and later a divinity student, came into office with the mission of freeing the great productive engine of American capitalism from what he saw as the shackles big government had placed upon it for a half-century. His plan was to cut taxes drastically and to cut spending just as drastically, so that what remained was a "minimalist government . . . a spare and stingy creature, which offered even-handed justice, but no more."[44]

Stockman's enthusiasm for tax cuts came in part from his association with Arthur Laffer and other supply-side economists, who believed that tax cuts would immediately produce economic growth and enhance government revenues. But long before the inauguration Stockman had figured out that if there were a decline in the inflation rate, which had been high for some years, government revenues would decline anyway, and now, thanks to Paul Volcker, the chairman of the Federal Reserve Board, inflation was on the decline. However, after all the years of inflation and bracket-creep, the Congress favored a tax cut, and the administration was staking its reputation on the passage of a major across-the-board tax-cutting bill known as Kemp-Roth. Thus, in the three weeks following the inauguration, Stockman was working twelve-to-sixteen-hour days to make cuts of hundreds of billions of dollars in current and future budgets. Though the defense was exempt from these cuts, Stockman needed to know the general trajectory military spending would take over the next five years.

At seven-thirty in the evening on January 30, 1981, Stockman met with Weinberger in the secretary's office to decide on the annual rate of increase for the defense budget. The only two others present were Frank Carlucci and William Schneider, the conservative defense analyst, who had recently become the associate director of OMB for national-security affairs.[45] At the start of the meeting Carlucci proposed an increase of 8 or 9 percent a year in real dollars—or dollars adjusted for inflation. Stockman was not shocked by this figure. He supported a big defense buildup, and the Reagan campaign had been all over the lot on this issue. He suggested that they split the difference and go with a 7 percent yearly increase, and Weinberger agreed. Carlucci proposed they take 1982 as the base year for the increases, and Stockman said OK. The meeting then ended, and Stockman was grateful, for it had taken less than a half-hour, and his day had begun at four-thirty that morning.[46]

Some weeks later, when Stockman had a chance to examine the defense-budget projections in detail, he saw to his horror that the figures spiraled up from $142 billion in 1980 to $368 billion in 1986: he had agreed to $1.42 trillion in defense spending in just five years. Going back over the figures, he realized what he had done. The Reagan campaign proposals for budget increases had been predicated on Carter's 1980 defense budget, but he had agreed to begin the 7-percent yearly increases in 1982. What he had forgotten was that the Congress had raised the 1981 budget by 9 percent and the Reagan administration had already plugged in an additional $32.6-billion increase for 1981 and 1982, so the baseline for the 7-percent increases started at $222 billion—not $142 billion, as he had assumed. This meant a yearly increase of 10 percent between 1980 and 1986—or even more than had been estimated for the buildup Van Cleave had proposed during the campaign. It meant that the defense budget would grow by 160 percent in just six years. Stockman stormed about his office, but by that time the defense-budget figures were out and there was nothing he could immediately do.[47]

By August, Stockman realized that he had made one or two other mistakes as well. On the strength of optimistic economic forecasts the administration had forced the Kemp-Roth bill through the Congress and, in order to pass it, had agreed to two other tax-reduction measures favored by various members of Congress. But the forecasts had been far too optimistic; the economy was now headed into a recession, and huge deficits loomed. Stockman's proposed budget cuts had proved too radical for anyone in Washington to accept, and White House officials refused to take the political heat that would come from attempting to cut Social Security and the other entitlement programs that made up the bulk of domestic spending. Politics, Stockman mournfully concluded, had triumphed over "the Reagan revolution"—or, rather, the revolution he had wanted to make in Reagan's name.

On August 3, just as reporters and pundits were writing that the Reagan team had driven through the most radical change in national economic policy since the New Deal, Stockman, at a luncheon in the White House, gave Reagan and his advisers the bad news: the potential deficit numbers were so large that they threatened to wreck the President's entire economic program. One option, he said, was to abandon the 1984 balanced-budget target and just hope to get there by 1986. Some of the economists in the room strongly objected to the idea, and the President said, "No, we can't give up on the balanced budget. Deficit spending is how we got into this mess." The next option, Stockman said, was to slow the defense buildup. The President jumped in first. "There must be no perception by anyone in the world that we're backing down on the defense build-up," he said firmly. "When I was asked during the campaign about what I would do if it came to a choice between defense and deficits, I always said national security had to come first, and people applauded every time."[48]

Another option was to impose some new taxes—or to delay the Kemp-Roth tax cuts. But the President didn't want that either. "Delay would be a total retreat," he said when the subject came up at another meeting. "We would be admitting that we were wrong."[49] When Stockman raised the issue of deep cuts in domestic spending, including entitlements, the conversation, led by Counselor to the President Edwin Meese, veered off into a discussion about "bureaucratic waste" and cutting the "fat" out of the federal bureaucracy. Reagan happily took up this old theme of his, and the discussion never returned to the real issue of the major federal spending programs.[50]

Other meetings on fiscal policy followed with much the same results. Stockman would pose the choices open to the administration, the President would not agree to any of them and the discussion would float away into eddies of irrelevance and wishful thinking.

When it became obvious to the Congress that the President was not going to modify the tax cuts to fit the new economic environment, Democratic Senator Daniel Patrick Moynihan of New York, who had been Stockman's mentor at Harvard, maintained that Reagan was deliberately creating deficits in order to force the Congress to make deep cuts in entitlements and other domestic spending programs in the long run. Stockman disagreed. Having watched the President in action, he knew that Reagan simply refused to accept that there was a conflict between tax cuts and politically desirable spending programs. Reagan liked to tell the story about two boys, one an optimist, the other a pessimist, getting their Christmas presents. The pessimist finds a roomful of toys and is miserable because he is sure that there must be some catch involved. The optimist finds a roomful of horse manure and is delighted because he is sure that with all that manure there must be a pony. Reagan's optimism was, Stockman wrote, "terminal."[51]

Yet, focused as he was on the fiscal disaster, Stockman did not hear exactly what the President was saying to him.

During the campaign Reagan had promised tax cuts, higher defense spending, smaller government and balanced budgets. But, as Stockman had observed, he had had little or nothing to do with translating these goals into policies. In the strategy meetings before the inauguration he had sat passive and serene, giving no orders, asking no questions, just listening, nodding and smiling. "We have a great task ahead of us," he would say, and stop there. To his advisers he conveyed the impression that, since they knew what needed to be done, they should just get on with the job.[52] Reagan, Stockman wrote, seemed as far above the detail work of building the economic program as a ceremonial monarch is above politics.[53]

But what Reagan *had* done was to sell the tax cuts and the defense budget to the Congress with the rosy economic forecasts his advisers had provided. He had staked his reputation on the supply-side "Reagan revolution." At the August 3 luncheon meeting he was telling his advisers that to retreat from any one of the positions he had taken would be an admission of weakness and error. And he did not want to be perceived as weak. That was all he was saying. The real trouble was that, because of the complexity of the federal budget and the unpleasantness of the choices Stockman was offering, his aides and advisers had given in to the all-too-human urge to put the hard decisions off until another day.

Stockman, however, knew that something had to be done immediately or the administration would lose all control over economic planning. Among other things, the projected defense budgets had to be reduced, for the Congress would refuse to make further cuts in domestic spending if they were not. He knew this would be difficult, because the armed services had already figured out how to spend the full amount, and the secretary of defense had for months been publicly insisting on the inviolability of the budgets. Still, Weinberger, who had once been in Stockman's shoes, understood the fiscal equation, and surely "Cap the Knife" could figure out how to build the nation's defenses at a somewhat lower cost.[54]

In mid-August, Stockman went to the White House with a proposal for a slightly reduced rate of growth in the defense budget—a buildup that would cost $1.33 trillion instead of $1.46 trillion over five years. But he wanted thirty billion dollars out of the budgets for fiscal years 1982–84 to meet his deficit target and to permit spending to rise later on. At the time the President was taking a monthlong vacation on his ranch in Santa Barbara, so the first high-level meeting on the issue took place in Los Angeles. At the meeting Weinberger proved adamant: he would not come down a single dollar, and Stockman's projections of ballooning deficits left him wholly unmoved. Stockman tried to enlist the secretary of the Treasury, Donald Regan, but Regan, whose nose Stockman had put severely out of joint by making up the budget without him, refused to accept Stockman's deficit projections.

By this time Ed Meese and Reagan's chief of staff, Jim Baker, had begun to understand the implications of the tax cuts, so they called another meeting and another, but Weinberger refused to budge. During the third meeting Weinberger produced a series of charts depicting the enormity of the Soviet threat and a cartoon of a powerful American soldier reduced to Woody Allen size by Stockman's budget cuts. Taking one look at the charts, Stockman knew he was in deep trouble. The President had taken to saying, "Defense is not a budget issue. You spend what you need." It was beyond Stockman's power to make it clear to him that the Pentagon's "need" had been defined by a more or less arbitrary percentage of increase in the budget that he, Stockman, had mistakenly agreed to the previous January.[55]

By this point Stockman realized he could not convince the President by arguing with Cap in this fashion. He had learned that Reagan did not like to take sides when Cabinet members or his senior advisers disagreed. When there was an argument and a decision was due, Ed Meese habitually stepped in and suggested that the contenders take their dispute to some other forum, thus relieving the President of the unpleasant task of having to choose. Reagan would then smile and say contentedly, "OK, you fellas work it out."[56]

Still, Stockman was marginally optimistic, for, though still bemused by the complexity of the economic case he was making, Baker and Meese seemed prepared to help. In late August, Meese told Stockman that the President would like to see a compromise and that he, Meese, would work quietly with Weinberger to bring one about. Baker for his part told reporters on background that twenty or thirty billion would be cut over three years—or just about what OMB wanted.[57]

At the end of the third meeting the President in his own way called for a compromise. "Now," he said pleasantly to Weinberger and Stockman, "why don't you fellas get together and see if you can work it out in this area in between."[58]

Realizing full well that there was no "in between" and that Weinberger and Stockman were never going to agree, Baker and Meese ushered the group out and said that they would stay with the President and help him pick some numbers.

The three huddled in the Oval Office, and when they had finished, the President called Weinberger to inform him of the decision. Shortly afterwards Baker called Stockman and said jauntily, "The President came through for you. We've got $26 billion of your $30 billion." But when Baker read out the numbers, Stockman realized that Baker and Meese did not understand the intricacies of the defense budget and had made their calculations on the wrong set of figures—on the budget-authority numbers rather than on outlays—so that they had gotten only four billion dollars in cuts.[59]

According to Stockman, Baker was appalled. He understood that the administration was in deep budgetary trouble, and that he had just blown his opportunity to do something about it. The President was getting angry: he had made his decision and *still* the tedious matter wouldn't go away. As a last resort Baker got Deaver to give the President another memo from Stockman and to set up yet another meeting with Weinberger.[60]

The next morning Stockman went to the White House again. Ushered into the Oval Office, he found himself alone with Weinberger and the President. Baker, Meese and Deaver almost never allowed policy-makers to see the President alone, so their absence gave Stockman an uneasy feeling. It suggested that Reagan was so fed up with the dispute that they did not even want to be around. When he went in, the President was busy with correspondence, forwarded to him from the mail room, from American citizens who had written in with their concerns. Clearly loath to broach the subject at hand, he read Weinberger and Stockman heartwarming passages from the letters and from his own planned replies.

When the discussion finally began, Stockman proposed a compromise: a twenty five-billion-dollar cut over three years. He expected that Weinberger would counter with a smaller number and that he would split the difference with him. Instead Weinberger, who by now had grudgingly agreed to an eight-billion-dollar cut, gave a short speech about the vital need to restore the nation's defenses and refused to move off the mark. Even after Stockman had lowered his figure to twenty-three billion, he would not offer a single dollar more.

The meeting dragged on, and after an hour Stockman could see that the President was becoming uncomfortable, even desperate. Clearly Reagan did not want to overrule his secretary of defense, and yet he thought that the meeting should end with some kind of a compromise. Stockman gave in and split the difference himself, offering fifteen billion, as the halfway mark between twenty-three and eight. Looking relieved, Reagan asked Weinberger if he could live with that figure. Rather than agreeing, Weinberger made another little speech about vital defense needs and said he could cut eleven billion. After doing some arithmetic on a pad, Reagan, taking his first initiative of the meeting, suggested thirteen billion "in savings" over three years. "If that's your decision, sir," Weinberger said stiffly, "we'll find some way to manage." The meeting ended, and as Stockman walked out of the Oval Office in deep dejection, he saw the President, still smiling at the compromise he had arranged, return to his constituents' mail.[61]

Weinberger's intransigence over the defense budget had initially surprised Stockman—and it surprised most in Washington when the battle over defense spending moved to the Hill. When his appointment as defense secretary was announced, conservative columnists had protested vociferously: Weinberger had no defense background except for combat duty in the Pacific during World War II; he did not seem to be of their ideological persuasion, and he was known as one of the most dedicated cost-cutters ever to head the OMB. Before he took office, friends and former associates confidently predicted that he would run a tight ship at the Pentagon: he would get tough on cost overruns and flashy hardware and spend his time administering the vast bureaucracy. Even Reagan's close aides seem to have had their expectations confounded.[62]

A San Franciscan and a graduate of Harvard College and Harvard Law School, Weinberger had worked for a leading San Francisco law firm and gone into politics with a group of moderate Republicans dedicated to reforming the old California party machine. In 1964 he had worked for Rockefeller against Goldwater, and in 1966 he had backed George Christopher, a former mayor of San Francisco, and a moderate, against Ronald Reagan in the gubernatorial primaries. He later campaigned for Reagan and was invited to join the administration after the initial zealotry died away.

An effective finance director for Reagan—one reputed to know every line in the California budget—he had been recruited into the Nixon administration at its outset in 1969 as head of the Federal Trade Commission. Given the go-ahead by Nixon to reform the commission, he hired one of Ralph Nader's raiders, William Howard Taft IV, replaced almost two-thirds of its top-level staff and turned what had been a sleepy little backwater into an active anti-trust and regulatory agency.[63] Six months later he was appointed to the OMB. Serving first as deputy director to George Shultz, he became director in 1972, when Shultz was appointed secretary of the Treasury.

At the OMB, Weinberger made a zealous effort to cut federal spending, standing up to Cabinet members, lobbyists and powerful congressmen to hold the budget line. When the Congress refused to cut social spending as the administration asked, he resorted to the controversial technique of impounding appropriated funds. Past administrations had impounded small sums for specific reasons, but he used the technique across the board to reduce the overall budget, impounding $11.2 billion in just one year. Domestic programs suffered more than defense from his budgetary knife; nonetheless, he and Shultz fought the Pentagon over the B-1 bomber, and two of the three defense budgets he worked on showed modest decreases from previous years.[64]

In 1973 Weinberger was appointed secretary of health, education and welfare. In this job he provoked the wrath of liberals and civil-rights groups by attempting to curtail health and education programs, but on regulatory matters he took an activist role.[65] In 1975 he left Washington and joined the Bechtel Corporation of San Francisco, a large international engineering firm that had hired Shultz as its president. Given the title of special counsel, he was elected vice-president and director of the company. Back in California, he renewed his ties to Reagan.

In the 1980 campaign Weinberger headed Reagan's budget task force. Along with Martin Anderson and Reagan's other economic advisers, he supported a 5-percent increase in the defense budget—as opposed to the 9 percent Van Cleave wanted. In October, when campaign staffers were preparing Reagan for a debate with President Carter, Van Cleave, playing a reporter, asked Reagan by how much he would increase defense spending. Reagan answered 5 percent. No, that's wrong, Van Cleave said, we haven't committed to that. Oh, yes, we have, Weinberger countered quickly, 5 percent is definite, and we're not promising any more than that. Thus 5 percent was the figure Reagan used.[66]

Interviewed by the news magazines after the election but before his appointment as secretary of defense, Weinberger sounded very much like the OMB director he had once been, for he attacked Carter for deficit spending and stressed the need to reduce federal outlays and to balance the budget. Asked about defense, he said that there would be an increase in defense spending but that no section of the defense budget would be spared rigorous examination and that it was entirely possible that trims might be made in some sections. "There is fraud, waste and mismanagement everywhere, and that includes defense," he said. "Nothing can be untouchable. Nothing sacred."[67] Apparently Reagan, too, believed that he had hired "Cap the Knife," for in March 1981 he told reporters, "Cap Weinberger is anything but a big spender. . . . I can assure you that Cap is going to do a lot of trimming over there."[68]

When Washington journalists came around to remaking their portrait of Weinberger, Nicholas Lemann in a perceptive piece in *The Atlantic Monthly,* pointed out that it was not the positions Weinberger took in the Nixon administration that revealed the man but, rather, the way he went about his work. At bottom Weinberger was neither a liberal nor a conservative but a stubborn lawyer who did what his client wanted to the best of his abilities, no questions asked. Given a mission, he would pursue it with fierce, single-minded determination. Asked to clean up the FTC, he found his way around the civil-service rules to purge the agency; asked to cut government spending, he impounded billions of dollars, never asking what the consequences might be.[69] In personal relations Weinberger was courteous, unassuming and not at all opinionated, but in public life he was a fighter and something of a bore, for he argued without much concern for accuracy, or even reason. He prided himself on his stubbornness and his ability to take the pummeling. As Lemann pointed out, he would always describe the stands he took as "unpopular" and would use words like "facile" or "comfortable" to characterize his opponents' positions, and words like "difficult" or "disagreeable" to describe his own.[70] His allies found a heroic quality in his stubbornness, but his opponents thought him shallow—and for an intelligent man, exceptionally so.

Later it occurred to some that this small, rather shy man was quite insecure.[71]

In his hurried calculations on January 30, 1981, Stockman had made an error, but the defense-budget increases were not errors as far as anyone else in the meeting was concerned. The request for an immediate increase of $32.6 billion had been developed by his OMB subordinate William Schneider, William Van Cleave and other members of the defense transition team in consultation with Senator John Tower, the new chairman of the Senate Armed Services Committee. The intent was to take advantage of the administration's "honeymoon" with the Congress to establish a high baseline for further percentage increases. Weinberger simply accepted the figure. According to Tower, he accepted it because he "did not know defense and was willing to rely on people who did." Weinberger was in a strange environment; he was also in a difficult political position, because his reputation as a cost-cutter, his ejection of the defense transition team and his choice of Carlucci had put him in disfavor with the right—or with most of those he had to deal with from day to day.[72]

Having accepted the figure and the annual percentage increases, Weinberger asked the armed services to come up with the programs to match them. Stunned, the Chiefs went from their wish lists to their dream lists, pulling out proposals they never thought would see the light of day.[73] Then Weinberger, as the chief salesman for the programs in Congress, came up with the threat to justify them.

Weinberger had never held hard-line anti-Soviet views. As secretary of HEW, he had taken a sixteen-day trip to the Soviet Union and set up a direct-link cable between Washington and Moscow for the exchange of information on medical research. On his return he criticized the National Academy of Sciences for threatening to end its participation in joint research projects with the Soviets in protest against the treatment of the physicist and human-rights activist Andrei Sakharov.[74] Nevertheless, a month after he took office as secretary of defense, he became a passionate exponent of the notion that the Soviets posed the same threat to the United States as Hitler had posed to Britain. He attributed his conversion to the briefings he got on the Soviet threat when he took office. The briefers did paint a horrific picture of the threat, but apparently Weinberger did not press them too closely on how it was that Brezhnev could have turned into Hitler in the five years he had been out of Washington.[75] Thereafter Weinberger echoed the views of his hard-line policy advisers—Iklé, Perle and the rest—and adopted all the rhetoric of the Committee on the Present Danger.

In his memoir *Fighting for Peace,* Weinberger tells us that as a young man at Harvard in the 1930s he followed Churchill's long campaign to rearm Britain with "passionate intensity" and a "deep sense of almost personal involvement."[76] Weinberger quoted Churchill often, and over his desk there hung a framed quotation from Churchill: "Never give in, never, never, never, never: in nothing great or small, large or petty, never give in."[77] Churchill, of course, had more sense than to obey his own dictum, but Weinberger followed it to the letter.

In his memoir Weinberger tells us that the congressional hearings in which he testified on the budget were "adversarial" and "confrontational." He does not exaggerate. Support for a military buildup was strong in the Congress, and particularly in the Senate, where John Tower and Henry Jackson ruled the Armed Services Committee. Still, after the dimensions of the fiscal crisis became evident in September 1981, even Tower maintained that the defense budgets had to be scaled back a bit. Yet Weinberger would not give an inch. When Congress cut nineteen billion dollars from the defense budget for fiscal year 1983, he refused to provide any guidance about where the cuts should be made.[78] "I acquired a reputation of being stubborn, uncompromising, immoderate and unpragmatic," he writes. "Congressmen and Senators would regularly plead with me . . . to 'be more reasonable,' to 'give something,' to 'compromise.' " Yet Weinberger rebuffed their entreaties: "None of these congressional pleas or demands was based on military needs; they were all designed simply to reduce defense spending for *political* reasons."[79] Weinberger would never acknowledge that one of the "political" reasons was that the government did not have the money. And while he went about creating the maximum friction with Congress, he forgot that to Ronald Reagan politics mattered a great deal.

NOT ON THE DEFENSE BUDGET but on arms control and U.S.-Soviet relations, Weinberger's main opponent in the Cabinet was Alexander Haig. Reagan had only a passing acquaintance with Haig before December 1980. The only substantive conversation the two had ever had was at the beginning of the 1980 campaign, when Reagan had invited him to his California ranch. But the talk was incidental; Reagan's aides wanted to find out whether or not he would be running for President, and if not, whether he would support their boss.[80] According to Cannon, Reagan appointed Haig secretary of state largely on the recommendation of Richard Nixon, whose judgment he trusted, and whom he consulted somewhat surreptitiously during the campaign. In a memo to Reagan, Nixon wrote that Haig had a thorough understanding of foreign policy, and that he shared many of Reagan's long-stated views—a combination which, he wrote, not many people possessed.[81]

Haig's views cannot have come as much of a surprise to Reagan and his aides. The handsome four-star general had, after all, spent much of his long Army career in Washington. In the 1960s he had been the military assistant to Kennedy's secretary of the Army, Cyrus Vance, and then an aide to the defense secretary, Robert McNamara. In his five years as Kissinger's deputy on the NSC staff, Haig had never publicly differed with Kissinger, but he was reputed to be more of a Cold Warrior than his boss, and he had taken a very hard line on the Vietnam War, consistently arguing for more drastic military operations against North Vietnam and against Viet Cong sanctuaries in Cambodia. Haig had served with General Douglas MacArthur as a young man, and, as William Bundy wrote, he was a MacArthur man: a believer in the inherent weakness of Third World countries and the efficacy of air power.[82] Nonetheless, he agreed with the broad lines of Nixon's policies towards China and the Soviet Union, and as NATO commander he had become well versed in European politics and attuned to the sensitivities of his counterparts. Haig was a surprise of another kind.

In the Nixon White House, Haig had gained a reputation for being the perfect military staff man—hardworking, orderly, efficient and unflappable; not an original thinker but someone who knew how to get things done. Both Kissinger and Nixon had prized him for these qualities. Perhaps because he was a military man who had worked for other demanding bosses, he had put up with Kissinger's temper tantrums far better than most of the civilian intellectuals on the NSC staff. He had also been extremely loyal to Nixon. When the Watergate scandal forced Nixon to fire Haldeman and Erlichman, Nixon brought in Haig to run the White House while he dealt with the threat of impeachment. Haig repaid his trust by managing Nixon's resignation and the presidential transition in an orderly and dignified fashion. But now, just six years later, he seemed a different person. He was arrogant, impatient, irritable and bullying.[83]

On January 6, 1981, in his first discussion with the President-elect, Haig sought an assurance from Reagan that he would be the single manager and the single voice for foreign policy in the administration. His request was reasonable enough: he did not know Reagan, and he had seen what had happened to Nixon's first secretary of state, William Rogers, when foreign-policy–making was centralized in the White House. Reagan seemed to understand his position and nodded in agreement after every point he made. Haig then told the press in a rather grandiose fashion that he had been anointed "vicar" of foreign policy. On inauguration day he delivered the draft of a national-security "decision directive," NSDD-1, to Meese for the President to sign. The document, which he had cleared with Weinberger, Casey and Allen, laid out a structure for decision-making that gave him broad powers. But it disappeared into Meese's briefcase, and according to Allen, it could not be found.[84]

Instead of taking the hint, Haig pestered the President and his staff about the document and became touchy about every issue involving his authority. Each foreign-policy statement from the White House would call forth a bellow of protest and a charge that his authority was being undermined by the staff. So insistent were his demands for control over policy that White House officials, borrowing the military acronym for "commander-in-chief," took to calling him CINCWORLD.[85] In March, when the White House announced that Vice-President George Bush would head "a new structure for national security crisis management," Haig flew into a rage and called the White House to complain. Both Meese and the President assured him that this "structure" was no more than a formality, but after the announcement was repeated, Haig stormed into the Oval Office and threatened to resign. Again the President reassured him, but Haig refused to be mollified until the President made a public statement that Haig was his foreign-policy chief.[86]

Possibly it was the word "crisis" which set Haig off, for the new secretary of state saw crises everywhere and himself at the center of the storm—or, to use a phrase from his own particular lexicon, "the vortex of cruciality."[87] In his memoir *Caveat* he tells us that in 1981 the U.S. faced "a world-wide climate of uncertainty . . . dangerous in the extreme." The Soviet Union "had been seduced by the weakness of the American will and [had] extended itself beyond the natural limits of its own apparent interests and influence," to the point where "the whole balance of the world was disturbed." Crises, he writes, loomed everywhere: the Persian Gulf was threatened; Africa was threatened; the Chinese were wondering about the value of the U.S. relationship; propaganda against NATO was circulating in Europe; the "fires of insurrection," fed by the Soviets and the Cubans, were spreading unchecked in Central America. In Haig's opinion, strong signals were needed; lines had to be drawn; decisive actions had to be taken. Within the administration he proposed that the U.S. should blockade, or even attack, Cuba, if the Soviets and the Cubans did not withdraw their support for the leftists in Central America. He was quite serious about this. He asked his staff to draw up a feasibility study, and though his staff failed to come up with any plausible military solution, he took the idea to the President and his staff and told them that, if given the go-ahead, he would turn Cuba into "a fucking parking lot."[88]

Haig's vision of the world in the grip of crisis with the Soviets and Cubans on the march accorded perfectly with Reagan's campaign rhetoric, and his promise to make Cuba a "parking lot" echoed Reagan's call of October 1965 to declare war on Vietnam and "pave the whole country and put parking stripes on it."[89] Both were, after all, MacArthur fans. Haig, however, wanted to practice what he preached, and this was not what Baker, Meese and Deaver wanted to hear from the secretary of state. In the first place, bombing Cuba seemed to them a remarkably bad idea; in the second, they had decided that the administration could launch only one major initiative at a time, and 1981 was to be the year of Reagan's economic revolution, so foreign policy had to wait. Thereafter they became extremely wary of Haig and let him know through press leaks and other roundabout means that everything he did that caught press attention was a distraction from the White House agenda.[90]

What bothered the White House staffers about Haig became plain to the rest of the nation on March 30, when President Reagan was shot and badly wounded by John Hinckley, a mentally ill young man. About an hour after the shooting, with the President's survival still in doubt and Vice-President Bush on his way back from Texas, Haig rushed into the White House press room, breathing hard, to announce in a shaky voice, "As of now, I am in control here."

Haig had some reason for alarm on this occasion. He had been sitting downstairs in the Situation Room with other Cabinet officials and members of the White House staff when, about an hour after the shooting, Weinberger came in and, as if to apologize for his lateness, announced that he had raised the alert status of the American forces. "Cap, what do you mean?" Haig asked. "Have you changed the Defcon of our forces?" Haig was shocked. Any change in the U.S. defense condition would be picked up by the Soviets and might signal that the U.S. thought them responsible for the assassination attempt; they would raise their alert status, and the U.S. would respond in kind. The consequences, Haig thought, would be "incalculable."

Weinberger did not answer Haig directly, and after a confusing series of exchanges about what he had or had not done, Haig began to suspect that Cap did not know what the Defcon was, or whether or not he had raised it. Weinberger then went off to a telephone and came back ten minutes later saying that he had not formally raised the Defcon. At that moment Haig heard Larry Speakes, the White House press secretary, on television telling reporters that he did not have any information about how the government would operate while the President was out of commission and was not aware of any change in the alert status. Haig then raced upstairs to the briefing room, intending to reassure the press that the government was operating normally and everything was under control. But because of his breathlessness from the stairs, his state of emotion and his blunder in saying that he personally was in control, he sounded as though he were announcing a military coup.[91]

Haig never really recovered from this performance. Publicly Baker and Meese insisted on his "competence" and his "steadiness," but Haig felt that they overdid it and drew further attention to his blunder. Possibly he was right about this: in their effort to control him, Reagan's aides made his life very difficult indeed.

Around the time of the first Cabinet meeting, mysterious little obstacles began to spring up in Haig's path. His memos to the President were leaked to the press; White House staff members would issue foreign-policy statements without consulting him, and sometimes in direct contradiction to what he had said. On one occasion a White House spokesman countermanded a decision for which Haig had obtained the President's approval on the telephone. His request to meet with the President on a regular basis went unanswered, and his NSDD-1 went unsigned. To Haig the White House was "as mysterious as a ghost ship; you heard the creak of the rigging and the groan of the timbers and sometimes even glimpsed the crew on deck. But which of the crew had the helm? . . . It was impossible to know for sure."[92]

In his history of the Reagan administration, Lou Cannon faults Haig for not understanding Reagan's "delegative proclivities" and for not accepting the fact that Baker, Meese and Deaver spoke for the President.[93] Yet Reagan's proclivities would have been a mystery to someone who had worked for MacArthur, Vance, McNamara, Kissinger and Nixon. Indeed, to Haig the most enigmatic figure on this "ghost ship" was the President himself. On those occasions when he was allowed into the Oval Office, and when he spoke with the President on the phone, Reagan was invariably cordial and encouraging. He listened attentively to what Haig said and generally seemed to agree with him. Certainly he never raised an objection or gave Haig any reason to believe that he did not thoroughly approve of what he was doing. When Haig complained of the leaks and the contradictory statements coming out of the White House, Reagan would appear concerned and reassure him, "Al, I'm with you. Al, you're my man." But the leaks and the contradictions continued. At NSC meetings the President would rarely give an opinion on contentious matters, and decisions were often deferred to another day. On some issues State and Defense would battle for months on end without a decision from the President. When Haig talked with the President without another policy-maker present, he could often persuade him of his position, but he was rarely allowed in to see him alone. The threat of resignation often seemed the only way he could get the President's attention.[94]

Other Cabinet members put up with these arrangements, and some used them to their advantage. The secretary of education, Terrel Bell, for example, used them to defeat the purposes of those who wanted the Department of Education abolished. But Haig lived on a psychological edge. Eternally choleric, always on the verge of a tantrum, he raised tempers even when he was warning against overreaction and urging cautious diplomacy. At NSC meetings he would lecture, hector, pound his first on the table and contradict others flatly. To Reagan, who liked others to be as easygoing, unassuming and sanguine as he was, this behavior was like fingernails on a blackboard. Though a newcomer to Reagan's entourage, Haig never attempted to make allies in the Cabinet or among the White House staff. To the contrary, he made it plain that he thought himself the only competent professional in the group and contemptuously spoke of the staff as that "bunch of second-rate hambones in the White House."[95] Once the decision about the "crisis-management team" sent him clattering and snorting into the Oval Office like a bull after a matador's cape, the White House staff had his number. In June 1982, in the midst of the crisis over the Israeli invasion of Lebanon, he offered his resignation again, and it was accepted.

The irony was that in most matters, and certainly in terms of U.S. relations with Europe and the Soviet Union, Haig actually did serve as a steadying force on the administration and helped to get it through its first two years without a major international crisis. But his views were not always taken as seriously as they might have been.

In the spring of 1981 Haig in a series of speeches and statements laid out what he called the "four pillars" of the administration's foreign policy: building U.S. military strength, reinvigorating American alliances, assisting in the development of the Third World and developing U.S. relations with the Soviet Union on the basis of "restraint and reciprocity." On several occasions he made it clear that what he meant by the latter was greater Soviet restraint and reciprocity, and that the other three pillars would create the conditions that would lead the Soviets to the fourth. He indicated that containing and countering Soviet expansion beyond the Soviet bloc would be the main theme of U.S. policy, yet he added that there would be not only "penalties for aggression" but "incentives for restraint," and that the incentives would include political agreements to resolve outstanding regional conflicts, balanced and verifiable arms-control agreements and greater East-West trade. In other words, trade and arms control would be conditioned upon Soviet measures to withdraw from the Third World.

The policy was reminiscent of Nixon's largely unsuccessful attempt to link arms control to Soviet concessions on other issues. But, ambitious as it was, it was not ambitious enough for the hard-liners, and though it became official policy, Haig could not even attempt to implement it.[96]

During his year and a half in office Haig met fairly regularly with Ambassador Dobrynin, and on three occasions with the Soviet foreign minister, Andrei Gromyko. In these meetings he confined himself to protests about Soviet behavior in the Third World and to warnings against intervention in Poland. By his account, the Soviets showed "an interesting tendency to register flexibility on every subject except one: Poland." They made it clear that they had no interest in Libya, because they thought Colonel Muammar Qaddafi "a madman." They indicated that they were telling the Sandinista government in Nicaragua to mend its relations with the United States. Most interesting of all, Dobrynin in one meeting suggested that his government was considering a new direction in Afghanistan, perhaps even a withdrawal of Soviet forces and the establishment of an autonomous state. Haig, by his own account, did not follow up on any of these suggestions—he did not even ask Dobrynin what he meant by an "autonomous state"—but simply kept repeating that the administration had to see proof of Soviet restraint before it could think about a dialogue on arms control and trade.[97]

Haig had no authorization to do anything more. He did not even attempt to establish a formal charter for policy towards the Soviet Union, because the hard-liners who dominated the NSC staff, the Office of the Secretary of Defense and other centers of power in the national-security bureaucracy did not want to negotiate with the Soviets, and they had no intention of offering trade and arms control as rewards for good behavior.[98] Rather, they saw an expanded arms race and trade restrictions as a means to roll back the Soviet dominion over Eastern Europe and put an end to the Communist regime in Moscow.[99] Public talk about rollback was generally discouraged, for it put the wind up in the Congress and in European capitals, but within the administration there was a great deal of euphoria about reversing the Brezhnev Doctrine and bringing the Soviet Union "to its knees."[100]

How these high resolves might be translated into policy was, however, another issue, and as the Polish crisis unfolded, it became clear that this was one the hard-liners had not very well thought through.

In the spring of 1981 Poland was close to bankruptcy because of trade-union strikes. The Jaruzelski government, which had recognized Solidarity, was asking Western governments for a rescheduling of its debt. The specter of economic and political chaos loomed. In Haig's view all the U.S. could do was to help alleviate the economic crisis by contributing to the debt rescheduling while putting as much diplomatic pressure as it could upon Moscow to keep its troops out and let the Poles settle their own problems. The hard-liners, however, thought these policies insufficiently red-blooded. According to Haig, they regarded an anti-Communist uprising in Poland as "an opportunity to inflict mortal political, economic and propaganda damage on the USSR." Haig wondered what they were thinking. Moscow would not permit Solidarity to triumph: not only would its security arrangements be seriously threatened if Poland left the Warsaw Pact, but democratic reforms might spread through the whole of Eastern Europe. The Soviets had made it clear that they would regard an anti-Communist uprising as a *causus belli.* On the other hand, there was no willingness within the Reagan administration to shed American blood over Poland. Thus, if an uprising occurred, the U.S. would have to watch helplessly, just as it had during the Hungarian uprising of 1956, while Moscow crushed the opposition movement with tanks.[101]

The hard-liners contended that the U.S. could control Soviet behavior towards Poland through economic and trade sanctions. Haig thought the proposition ill-founded. Total U.S. trade with the Soviet Union amounted to less than 1 percent of the Soviet GNP, and in April, Reagan, over the objections of his NSC principals, had decided to lift the embargo on grain sales to the Soviet Union that Carter had imposed after the Soviet invasion of

Afghanistan. The decision was taken for domestic reasons. During the campaign Reagan had promised to lift the embargo on the grounds that it was an unfair burden on the farmers, and Meese, for one, believed it important for Reagan to keep his promises. Secretary of Agriculture John Block argued that the Soviets would soon be able to find all the grain they needed on the world market, and a U.S. embargo would only penalize American farmers. Haig thought that Block was right about this and that the embargo would eventually have to be lifted, but he objected to the timing, because it reduced the U.S. leverage. The day after the announcement, he told the press that if the Soviet Union invaded Poland the administration would impose a complete ban on exports to the Soviet Union. White House officials then said, on background, that his statement did not represent the President's views.[102]

Haig's arguments otherwise prevailed; the Polish debt was rescheduled, and the economic crisis in Poland eased. Then, in December 1981, General Jaruzelski declared martial law and arrested the leaders of Solidarity and other reformers.

The U.S. and its NATO allies responded by imposing some economic sanctions on Poland, and the U.S.—quite alone—imposed some sanctions on the Soviet Union as well. The anti-Soviet sanctions were largely toothless, for there was little to cut back on. They did, however, include a suspension of the sale of oil and gas technologies to the Soviet Union, and this infuriated the British, French and West German governments. A number of European companies, with the support of their governments, had just launched plans to help the Soviets build a natural-gas pipeline from Siberia to seven countries of Western Europe, and the suspension was a direct challenge to the project. The European governments refused to go along with the embargo, and when, six months later, the administration, over Haig's protests, extended the ban, they threatened to violate it and to find alternate sources of technology. In late 1982 the administration, in one of the more embarrassing chapters in the annals of American diplomacy, had to back down.[103]

Later the CIA sent covert financial assistance to the Solidarity underground, but, apparently chastened, the hard-liners did not advertise it, as they did "covert" operations elsewhere. The aid, sent through intermediaries, did not include lethal assistance and did not come with any call for action. In combination with aid from other sources, it simply helped the movement survive.[104]

In an article published in 1996, Richard V. Allen wrote that President Reagan entered office with a clear strategy in mind. Reagan "rejected the doctrine of 'containment.' . . . He believed in developing momentum through strength and applying that momentum to the Cold War equation. He knew that it would entail a risk, but in his view a worthwhile and manageable risk, one that stopped short of outright provocation or war in order to achieve victory. . . . The weakness and inflexibility of the Soviet command economy were key factors in the Reagan strategy. To the extent that the U.S. initiatives would place strains on that cumbersome machine, the Reagan administration sought to increase the pressures substantially. So, the screws were tightened, one turn at a time."[105]

This was certainly Allen's strategy—though the screws in it were extremely loose. That it was Reagan's own personal strategy is questionable.

In those years Henry Kissinger was occasionally invited to the White House to talk with the President about world affairs. James Baker and those other White House aides who worried that Reagan was too much identified with the right wing of the party thought it good public relations for the President to be seen consulting with the acknowledged master of geopolitics, whose policies had come under attack from the right. Kissinger was always happy to accept these invitations, though, after a few meetings with Reagan, he realized that they were essentially for show. In the course of their talks the President displayed little knowledge of world affairs and almost no curiosity about them. What was more, he seemed quite unconcerned with foreign policy. It was as if thinking about long-term strategies was something that other people were paid to do. When Kissinger talked about what the U.S. government ought to be doing in the coming years, Reagan often tuned out of the conversation altogether. "He would try to avoid policy discussions," Kissinger said. "If he couldn't, he'd resort to his cue cards. If he was alone, I knew that nothing would go on—he was just massaging me. Only if there was someone there would there be a discussion of substance."

After experimenting with a number of conversational gambits, Kissinger discovered that the best way to get Reagan's attention was to talk about what he ought to say publicly on an issue. If there was talk of a speech or a public statement, Reagan would sit up and his eyes would come back into focus. "He was an actor," Kissinger said, "the quintessential actor. What he said was what he believed. He didn't stand in front of his mirror in the morning while he shaved wondering whether that was the truth or not. If I told him Dobrynin had just told me that the Soviets couldn't stand it anymore and would be launching their missiles in forty-eight hours, Reagan would not call the JCS. He would talk from his cue cards, then he would tell some Hollywood stories, and when I left, he would not call someone and say, 'You know, Henry Kissinger has gone mad.' "

"It's very unusual," Kissinger said, "to have a president who is not interested in policy at all."[106]

On foreign-policy issues Haig could sometimes get his way, but when it came to arms control he had little leverage, because the Defense Department and ACDA were directly involved. He and his aides put up a major bureaucratic struggle over the Intermediate Nuclear Force negotiations. But on this matter the unworldliness of the hard-liners prevailed.

On the INF talks, as on all arms-control issues, policy for the Defense

Department was made largely by the thirty-nine-year-old assistant secretary for international-security affairs, Richard Perle. Perle was only a third-echelon official, but Weinberger had no competence in arms control, and Fred Iklé, his deputy for policy, was far more at home writing articles and lectures than operating in the rough-and-tumble world of bureaucratic politics. Perle by contrast was highly qualified and very experienced: he had spent his entire life in training for the work he did in the Reagan administration. As a high-school student in Los Angeles he had become a protégé of Albert Wohlstetter, the intellectual master of strategic analysis at the Rand Corporation. In 1969, after taking degrees in international relations at UCLA and Princeton, he went to Washington to work with Wohlstetter on the committee formed by Nitze and Acheson to lobby for the funding of the ABM. He then took a job with Senator Henry Jackson, a conservative Democrat and a major power on the Armed Services Committee.

A brilliant analyst and an equally brilliant political tactician, Perle became Jackson's alter ego on strategic-weapons policy and arms control. Throughout the seventies, Jackson and Perle scored impressive victories against arms control even when the political tide was running against them. They could not stop the SALT I accords, but they managed to pass a resolution restricting future agreements on offensive weapons and to persuade Nixon to purge the Arms Control and Disarmament Agency of all those who had negotiated it. Later they fought Kissinger's attempt to conclude a SALT II treaty, and during the Carter administration they played a major role in preventing the ratification of SALT II.

Perle was Henry Kissinger's *bête noire.* In his second volume of memoir, Kissinger paid him a tribute when he wrote that Jackson "was aided by one of the ablest—and the most ruthless—staffs that I have encountered in Washington."[107] Though in many ways a sophisticate, Perle had small experience of the world beyond Washington and a simple and unshakable conviction that the Soviet Union was a barbarian regime that would heed only the reason of superior force. He never said this in so many words, nor did he ever say flatly that he opposed arms control, but not long after joining the Reagan administration he told an interviewer, "It's not in our interests to sign agreements that do not entail a significant improvement in the strategic balance."[108] Perle did not, of course, imagine that the Soviets would voluntarily sign agreements that were contrary to their interests, so in practice this meant no agreement. A colleague in the Senate who had debated him for many years said, "He thinks that we should run an arms race with the Russians and win."[109]

The issue of what to do about the Soviet INF deployments surfaced shortly after the inauguration. According to Strobe Talbott's detailed account of the deliberations in *Deadly Gambits,* Perle initially counseled that the administration should do nothing at all. He argued that the 572 intermediate-range weapons (a combination of Pershing II ballistic missiles and Tomahawk ground-launched cruise missiles) that the Carter administration had proposed to deploy were no match for the Soviet SS-20s and that the costs of deployment were greater than the benefits of making a "marginal military fix."[110] Haig, however, believed that the administration had to stick with Carter's "dual track" approach for the sake of continuity in U.S. policy, to avoid a rift with the Allies and to avoid reinforcing the reputation Reagan had acquired during the campaign for hostility to arms control. Since the White House took no position on the matter, delegations from State and Defense went to Europe in the spring with contradictory messages.[111]

In early April, with the West European governments pressing hard for negotiations, Haig argued that the U.S. should commit itself to a timetable for beginning the talks. Weinberger, however, dug his heels in. Contending that U.S. policy should not be driven by solicitude for the Europeans, he, on Perle's advice, called for a comprehensive study of the Soviet threat to Europe that would take many months to complete. The discussion went on over a period of weeks, with Allen and his aides supporting Weinberger and complaining to reporters that the U.S. was sitting still for "blackmail" and "pressure tactics" from the Europeans and that Haig had gone over to the side of the "striped-pants set" and "the softies."[112]

Haig, however, was merely being realistic. In mid-April Chancellor Helmut Schmidt sent word to Washington that he had to have a starting date for the negotiations or he could not keep his government on the track towards the INF deployments. This put the administration in a bind, for if it decided not to deploy the missiles it would be seen as giving in to the Soviets, and if it decided to deploy them it might find that the European governments would refuse to accept them.

On April 30 Haig managed to obtain the President's authorization to commit the U.S. to negotiations by the end of the year. Perle then adopted delaying tactics, with the result that huge demonstrations erupted across Western Europe, the Soviets took and held the propaganda advantage and the strains on NATO were severe. When it became clear that the administration had to meet the deadline, Perle designed an unworkable negotiating position.

As far as Haig was concerned, the problem was to get the Soviets to agree to as low a level of missile deployments as possible—say six hundred warheads on each side. Members of the German Social Democratic Party had, however, proposed that both sides reduce their INF deployments to zero, and in order to quiet the anti-nuclear protests that threatened to split his party, Helmut Schmidt endorsed the proposal. During a visit to Bonn in September, Haig, as a gesture of support for Schmidt and as a means of taking the propaganda initiative from Moscow, added the word "zero" to his own preliminary position. The U.S., State Department memos reported, would seek "reductions to the lowest possible level, including, ideally, zero."[113] Perle then leaped on the "zero option." Give the Soviets an ultimatum, he reasoned, and if they accepted it they would have to dismantle all their offending weapons at no cost to the United States; on the other hand, if they refused it, as was highly probable, the U.S. would score a propaganda victory in Europe. In either case the administration would not have to engage in bean-counting negotiations.[114]

Faced with this maneuver, Haig and his aides argued in meeting after meeting that the Soviets would reject the zero option summarily, and that any propaganda advantage the U.S. gained by it would not last for very long. To maintain any semblance of credibility, the U.S. had to go to Geneva with something more than an ultimatum: its negotiators had to be able to negotiate. Weinberger, however, backed Perle's position, and since neither secretary was willing to give in, the argument over "zero only" versus what became known as "zero plus" went to the National Security Council; on November 12, and just days before the deadline, the President decided for "zero only."[115]

What prompted Reagan to adopt the zero option later became a matter for speculation in Washington. To supporters of the freeze movement in 1982–83 it seemed fairly clear that he had chosen it because he knew it was not negotiable. After all, Reagan had never in his entire political career supported an arms-control agreement: he had opposed the 1963 Limited Test Ban Treaty, the 1968 Non-Proliferation Treaty, the 1972 SALT I agreement and the ABM Treaty, the Peaceful Nuclear Explosions Treaty of 1976 and, of course, SALT II in 1979.[116] Years later, however, after the Reykjavik summit, journalists writing the first histories of the administration maintained that he had chosen it because he was a nuclear abolitionist and the zero option with all of its boldness and simplicity looked like real disarmament to him.[117] But there is not much evidence for either interpretation.

At the NSC meeting on November 12, Reagan, by Talbott's account, listened to Weinberger argue that the zero option was bold, simple and what the Allies wanted. And he listened to Haig insist that only "zero plus," with its inherent flexibility, could be negotiated. He did not pronounce a judgment, but he made it clear that he preferred the zero option because of its neatness and simplicity. At one point he said that "zero plus" would be a bit too much like playing a poker hand by laying all one's cards out on the table. This was an argument for the zero option, but the remark suggested he thought the U.S. ought to have more than "zero" in its hand. At another point, in answer to Haig's concern about negotiability, he told a story about the actor Paul Muni, who in a play about an idealistic union organizer spoke the organizer's lines so powerfully that the actor playing his adversary forgot his lines, and instead of saying, "I will give them *nothing*" said, "I will give them *everything!*" Apparently Reagan was suggesting that American negotiators could win over the Soviets to "zero" by sheer force of eloquence. Reagan sided with Haig on the details of the proposal and assured him that the intention was to negotiate in good faith. Later, when the time came to write the speech, he rejected the Defense Department's draft with its harsh language and chose the State Department's version, which made the zero option sound more like a genuine offer than an ultimatum.[118]

Reagan had often said that the SALT agreements were too complicated and that they did not reduce the size of the arsenals but—by setting high limits on future deployments—allowed them to grow much larger. Speaking of the INF proposal, he by one account told Richard Allen, "Give me a proposal that can be expressed in a single sentence and that sounds like real disarmament."[119] Reporters who paid attention to these remarks tended to assume that Reagan had a simple-minded view of arms control. But Reagan was not talking about his own preference for simplicity. Rather, he was saying that the SALT treaties did not appeal to the public because they were complicated and did not do what common sense demanded of arms control. In asking Allen for a proposal that could be expressed in a sentence and that sounded like disarmament, he was asking for a proposal he could sell in a speech.

In a nationally televised address on November 18 Reagan said, "The United States is prepared to cancel its deployment of Pershing II and ground-launched cruise missiles if the Soviets will dismantle their SS-20, SS-4 and SS-5 missiles."[120] There was the one-sentence proposal, and the speech was a huge success.

But the speech was successful in part because arms-control experts on both sides of the Atlantic assumed that the proposal was merely a going-in position for the negotiations.[121] In the months that followed, Haig attempted to get the administration to move off zero, but the hard-liners were too strong for him. When the Soviets presented a counter-proposal, the administration merely repeated itself, and the talks went nowhere.[122]

By the following spring it was clear to all those who followed arms-control issues that the administration was not negotiating. At that point the freeze movement took off.

> "Democracies will not sacrifice to protect their security in the absence of a sense of danger, and every time we create the impression that we and the Soviets are cooperating and moderating the competition, we diminish the sense of apprehension."
>
> —Richard Perle, *Newsweek*, February 18, 1983[123]

The emergence of the nuclear-freeze movement took the administration by surprise. Public concern about nuclear weapons had been growing since the late seventies, and even then figures as eminent as Reverend Theodore Hesburgh of Notre Dame University and Reverend Billy Graham had spoken out about the danger of nuclear war. But the concern had been eclipsed by the conservative, nationalist mood in the country, and because peace activists were Balkanized into a variety of different groups, some of them religious, others secular, each with its own immediate objectives—some opposed the B-1 bomber, and others the MX—and each with its own agenda for ending the arms race. In 1980, however, Randall Forsberg, a peace-movement defense analyst, drafted a resolution around which these groups could unite. An arms-control proposal rather than a disarmament plan, the resolution called upon both superpowers to halt the "testing, production and deployment of nuclear weapons" as a crucial first step towards "lessening the risk of nuclear war." Moderate, simple and symmetrical, the proposal was designed to appeal not just to peace activists but to ordinary people who were concerned about the arms race but did not want to risk harming the nation's defenses. The freeze proposal did just that. Grass-roots organizing began in 1980, and in the spring of 1981 the movement took off and, gaining support from churches, university groups and local politicians, spread through New England and then across the country. Sixty-nine Catholic bishops endorsed the freeze, as did several major Protestant denominations, including the United Presbyterian Church and the American Baptist Church. Thirty New England towns adopted freeze resolutions, and so did eight city councils and five state legislatures around the country. By the end of 1981 campaign leaders estimated that there were twenty thousand freeze activists organizing in forty-three states and two-thirds of the nation's congressional districts.[124]

In Washington freeze supporters spoke the language of arms control, debating their colleagues on the virtues of the freeze as opposed to other approaches to negotiations, such as limits on warheads and launchers. But outside Washington a new language emerged. The psychiatrist Robert Lifton argued that Americans suffered from "psychic numbing." He had used the same term in regard to the survivors of Hiroshima, but in this case what he meant was that Americans had grown so used to the idea of nuclear weapons that they had lost touch with the danger they represented. For anti-nuclear activists the lesson was that, if Americans were going to act against the threat, they had first to reimagine what these weapons could do. In his influential book *The Fate of the Earth,* published in 1982, Jonathan Schell prefaced his call for complete nuclear disarmament with a powerful description of what would happen to New York City after the explosion of one nuclear weapon, and to the country in the event of a full-scale nuclear war. Reasoning as Lifton did, he wrote, "It may only be by descending into this hell in imagination now that we can hope to escape descending into it in reality sometime later."[125] Books and films about nuclear war proliferated, and, inspired by this literature, anti-nuclear activists made graphic descriptions of nuclear holocaust a staple in university lectures, at peace rallies and on television. As one scholar put it, they went about the country "like religious revivalists of old," preaching the threat of nuclear damnation with vivid evocations of a hell on earth and calling upon Americans to act before it was too late.[126] The rhetoric was not unlike that of the Committee on the Present Danger, only the enemy was not the Soviet Union but nuclear war itself. Coming on top of all the administration's talk of war-fighting and the vulnerability of the American deterrent, it raised American anxieties about nuclear war to a level they had not reached since the Cuban missile crisis of 1962.

In March 1982 Democratic Representative Edward Markey of Massachusetts introduced a resolution into the House of Representatives with 115 co-sponsors calling upon the administration to negotiate a freeze upon the testing, production and deployment of nuclear weapons. Senators Edward Kennedy (Democrat of Massachusetts) and Mark Hatfield (Republican of Oregon) brought a similar resolution to the Senate. At the time Markey and his colleagues thought that the President could easily kill the freeze resolution by the simple stratagem of expressing his concern for the threat of nuclear war and promising to take the freeze proposal into account when the arms talks began. Given Reagan's political skills, they thought it likely that the President would do just that. Instead, the administration took the opposite tack and denounced the freeze as a threat to American security. Secretary Haig called it "bad defense and security policy"; Vice-President Bush maintained that it "would be harmful to our security and that of our allies"; Eugene Rostow, director of the Arms Control and Disarmament Agency, claimed that it would "play entirely into the hands of the Soviet Union." In a press conference Reagan said that a freeze on nuclear weapons would be disadvantageous to the U.S. and perhaps even dangerous, because "on balance the Soviet Union does have a definite measure of superiority."

Reagan had made claims about Soviet superiority during the campaign without much contradiction, but freeze advocates seized upon this remark and savaged it, producing statements from Secretary Haig and the Joint Chiefs of Staff in which these authorities said they would not trade the U.S. deterrent for the Soviet forces. The remark was brought up again and again on the news. "I just wish the President would stop bad-mouthing our nation's defenses," Markey said, and a conservative Democrat on the Senate Armed Services Committee confessed to being "astounded" by Reagan's statement.[127] What the debate showed was that in just two years the freeze had achieved rhetorical dominance over the administration.

For all of their public attacks on the freeze, some administration officials were concerned enough about the movement to urge another approach. In March, Eugene Rostow warned in a memo that the freeze was not just a movement of students and radicals; rather, he wrote, "there is participation on an increasing scale in the U.S., of three groups whose potential impact should be cause for concern. They are the churches, the 'loyal opposition' and, perhaps most important, the unpoliticized public." Rostow recommended that the administration gear a START proposal to the freeze movement and mount a major public-relations campaign to convince Americans that the President shared their interest in arms control.[128]

More important, James Baker and other White House "pragmatists" had begun to worry about the effect the anti-nuclear movement might have on the defense buildup and even on Reagan's chances for reelection. Baker, who, according to Talbott, saw himself as responsible for "domestic input where foreign policy is concerned," thought that the President needed to put a strategic-arms-control proposal on the table to compete with the freeze. Robert McFarlane, the deputy national-security adviser, agreed. The NSC bureaucracy had been working in desultory fashion on a negotiating strategy for START for some time, but at the end of February 1982 McFarlane, with Clark's approval, issued an NSC directive giving the executive branch a deadline of two months to come up with a unified proposal.[129] He later set up a working group to package and disseminate information on the administration's arms-control policies.[130]

What White House officials thought would happen as a result of the NSC directive on START is unclear. In the previous months Defense and State had developed two entirely incompatible approaches to the strategic-arms negotiations. For the Defense Department, Richard Perle was advocating a reduction in ballistic-missile throw-weights. The approach had never been tried before, because it was virtually unverifiable and because the Soviets, with their larger, more powerful rockets, would alone be penalized by it. The throw-weight ceiling Perle proposed would bring the Soviet strategic arsenal down by 60 percent while leaving the American arsenal untouched. For the State Department, Perle's opposite number, Richard Burt, the thirty-three-year-old assistant secretary of state for politico-military affairs, was advocating the traditional SALT approach of limiting warheads and launchers.[131]

Arms-control proposals had never been the stuff of drama for journalists, but in the fraught atmosphere of the time, START was a matter of intense interest in Washington, and journalists made much of the contest between the two young defense intellectuals. The casting was, after all, cinematic: Richard Perle, the dark-haired hard-liner from Defense, known as the Prince of Darkness because of his occasional black rages, versus Richard Burt, the fair-haired moderate from State, with his handsome, chiseled profile and his high-strung temperament. The "two Richards," as they were called, were not averse to media attention, and in the news magazines of the time, accounts of their disputes over megatonnages turned up in heroic tropes: the two young princes of nuclear strategy engaged in an epic contest for the soul of the administration.

In reality there was no contest—that is, no contest that could possibly end in a negotiable START proposal. Putting together an arms-control proposal agreeable to all the national-security agencies was an arduous task under any circumstances, and in this case the number of ranking administration officials who seriously wanted a strategic-arms agreement could probably have been counted on the fingers of one hand. Then, given the strictures already announced by Reagan, Burt had to come up with a proposal that addressed the Soviet advantage in land-based missiles, that mandated real reductions and that looked nothing like SALT II. Given the Soviet reaction to Carter's attempt to obtain real reductions, it seemed unlikely that any such proposal would be negotiable.

On the defensive from the beginning, Burt decided to propose a ceiling of twelve hundred on ballistic missile launchers and a ceiling of six thousand on ballistic-missile warheads. Then, so that the President could say that he was seeking a one-third reduction in warheads, he put the warhead ceiling at five thousand, a half of which could be on land-based missiles. He realized these numbers were not likely to be acceptable to the Soviets, since the launcher ceiling would require the Soviets to dismantle almost three times the number of launchers the U.S. did, and the sub-ceiling on ICBM warheads would allow the U.S. to increase its arsenal while forcing the Soviets to cut theirs by almost a half. But his object was to persuade the National Security Council to turn down Perle's throw-weight approach. According to Talbott, Burt and his administration ally, Robert McFarlane, were so intimidated by the hard-liners that in meetings they never dared use the word "negotiability," but instead spoke of "plausibility" or "credibility"—meaning that the proposal could not look as if it were designed to fail, even if it was.[132]

At the first NSC meeting on the subject, on April 21, Weinberger, by Talbott's account, put forth Perle's proposal for a throw-weight ceiling and exhorted his colleagues to offer the Soviets a "challenge." He repeated the word several times. What he seemed to be recommending was that the U.S. offer the Soviets an ultimatum: either they could decide to accept the U.S. terms for a stand-down, or they could look forward to an arms race that would make them tremble. Weinberger also reminded the President of the success of his speech presenting the INF proposal and urged him to choose an equally bold and simple plan for START. Rostow followed up with a ringing endorsement of Weinberger's call to get tough with the Russians. Then the President made his contribution to the proceedings. He said that START, unlike SALT II, should be based on deep reductions, and he told the group that he wanted to make a dramatic speech unveiling the proposal before leaving for Europe in June. He then went on to give a short but confusing discourse on the strategic triad. Missiles, he said, were the big problem. Bombers could be recalled when they were in the air, and they could be shot down; as for submarines, they could be "sunk."[133]

All around the room, people strove desperately to interpret what the President was saying. Some thought he was talking about the offsetting vulnerabilities of American bombers to Soviet air defenses and of Soviet submarines to U.S. anti-submarine warfare capabilities. Others, including Haig, thought that he was talking about an approach to START which would concentrate on reducing land-based missiles and worried that he favored the throw-weight proposal. In practice Reagan seems to have been giving a garbled version of the one lesson he had ever managed to retain about the strategic triad: that "fast-fliers" were bad because they were first-strike weapons and "slow-fliers" were good because they were not. But Haig, alarmed, warned him sternly that, if the U.S. presented a proposal that could be dismissed as implausible and cynical, it would lead to a military catastrophe when Congress and the NATO allies refused to support the administration's rearmament program.[134]

With only ten days remaining before the deadline, Burt went to the Joint Chiefs of Staff, who had thus far been silent on the issue, to ask for their support. The Chiefs, he knew, were in a difficult position. They were holdovers from the Carter administration; all of them had approved SALT II, and their chairman, General David C. Jones, due to retire soon, fought constantly with Weinberger and his aides on arms control and other issues. Because of the requirements of the 1982 Defense Guidance in regard to protracted nuclear war, the Chiefs were, as it turned out, even more keen on limiting ballistic-missile launchers than Burt was. The new targeting plan would require them to destroy a huge number of hardened targets—Soviet missile silos, command centers and so forth—in a "time-urgent" fashion: that is, with high-speed ballistic missiles rather than slow-flying cruise missiles and bombers. On the other hand, Burt's START proposal mandated deep cuts in ballistic-missile warheads, or the very weapons they would need to accomplish this task. They therefore favored the only logical way out of this predicament: a very low ceiling on launchers, so that they would have fewer "time-urgent" targets to hit. Specifically, they wanted a ceiling of 850 launchers to match the one-third cut in warheads, and, to gain them as allies, Burt agreed. Then, with the idea of presenting a "consensus approach" to the White House, he included Perle's throw-weight ceiling as a goal for "Phase II"—a phase which he assumed could be put off into the indefinite future. With the help of Baker and McFarlane, he managed to fend off Weinberger and to obtain the President's consent to the package.[135]

When the President presented the "consensus approach" to the nation a week later, in his Eureka College speech, Burt and his allies were, according to Talbott, elated. However, deciding not to gloat, they told the press modestly in background briefings that the proposal was a synthesis of the best ideas available in the government. In the thrill of victory Burt had clearly lost sight of what he had done. His initial proposal was, as he had realized at the time, not negotiable. But then, for the purposes of the President's speech, he had lowered the ballistic-missile warhead ceiling to five thousand, and in order to get the Joint Chiefs on board, he had reduced the launcher ceiling to 850. Not only were these numbers less negotiable than his first set, but they amounted to a textbook case of "crisis instability": if each side had five thousand warheads packed onto 850 missiles, both sides would be vulnerable to a first strike and in a crisis would be tempted to use their missiles first or risk losing them. The plan so contravened the logic of arms control that Paul Warnke, who had directed ACDA in the Carter administration, said, "If the Russians accept Mr. Reagan's proposal, he'll be forced to reject it himself."[136] On top of that, Burt had incorporated Perle's throw-weight ceiling into the proposal, and though he intended it as a dead letter, his intentions were quite invisible to the outside world, and in any case not official government policy. The "consensus" proposal was thus doubly non-negotiable, and so obviously so it appeared cynical.

Normally it would be politically dangerous for a congressman to attack a negotiating proposal before it reached the table in Geneva, but Markey and other freeze proponents in Congress blithely tore into the START proposal, telling audience after audience that it was not negotiable and nothing more than a maneuver to undercut the freeze. They were hardly gainsaid. Henry Kissinger, Senator Sam Nunn and other defense-establishment figures diplomatically avoided discussing the proposal and pressed for a ratification of the SALT II treaty instead. Even the administration experts did not defend it very vigorously, for most had reservations about one or another of the provisions. The proposal went to Geneva, and became the centerpiece of an acrimonious debate between Soviet and U.S. negotiators, but as a political initiative it disappeared. A few weeks later it was so completely forgotten it might never have existed.[137]

On May 30, just three weeks after Reagan's speech, much of Weinberger's five-year Defense Guidance was leaked to the press. Its call for strategic forces adequate to "prevail" in a "protracted" nuclear war created a storm of protest so great that three months later Weinberger complained that he had been forced to spend "a very large fraction" of his time defending the policy in speeches, press and television interviews, background briefings and letters to editors.[138]

Weinberger was naïve in such matters, but so, too, were some of his critics. Theodore Draper, among others, writing in *The New York Review of Books*, accused the administration of abandoning "mutual assured destruction" for the attempt to gain nuclear superiority and a war-fighting capability.[139] The assumption was that ever since the days of McNamara the U.S. had adhered to a policy of "assured destruction," or to what analysts called a secure second-strike capability. The assumption, however, owed to the amnesia that habitually settled over the public after every discussion of nuclear policy—and to the right-wing literature of the period, with its deceptive attacks on "MAD." Operational U.S. nuclear strategy had always included planning for counter-force strikes, or "war-fighting," on the principle that the U.S. should be able to limit the damage to itself if deterrence failed.[140] Then, too, since the Kennedy administration civilian planners had attempted to see to it that the SIOP, the Single Integrated Operational Plan, or the set of contingency plans for nuclear war, gave the President options for limited strikes and negotiating pauses. The President, officials argued, had to have options other than unleashing the holocaust if deterrence failed; further, they argued, he had to have some way to make the deterrent credible—and threat of all-out nuclear war in response to, say, a conventional Soviet attack into Western Europe was not, they felt, credible. The quest for a credible deterrent led to elaborate strategies for nuclear-war–fighting that involved ladders of escalation and requirements for superiority at every rung on the ladder. Most military men involved with targeting did not believe that nuclear war could be limited or controlled, and in twenty years of trying, civilian analysts never came up with a scenario that convinced them—with the result that the complex instructions civilians gave them for withholding nuclear forces rarely affected the targeting plans. Nonetheless, the civilian quest continued, along with the military quest for counter-force capabilities to "limit the damage" to the United States. In January 1974 Secretary of Defense James Schlesinger publicly announced a plan to develop a wide range of nuclear options to control escalation from a conventional to an all-out nuclear war. In June 1980 President Carter, at the urging of Zbigniew Brzezinski, issued PD 59, a presidential directive that called for enhancing deterrence by improving the U.S. capacity to wage a "protracted" nuclear war.

In regard to rhetoric, the only novelty of Weinberger's directive was the use of the word "prevail." In the past officials had always emphasized the defensive functions of their strategies. Defense Secretary Harold Brown, for example, had defused criticism of PD-59 by calling it a "countervailing" strategy and explaining that the U.S. ability to fight a "protracted" war was necessary simply in order to dispel any illusion the Soviets might have that a nuclear war was winnable. Brown was, as it happened, extremely skeptical about the possibility of controlling nuclear war. Still, any plan to wage nuclear war, defensive though it might be, was by definition a plan to prevail—since the alternative was to plan to lose.[141]

The Defense Guidance directive did not herald a major change in U.S. nuclear doctrines—nor was it quite as ominous a signal of the administration's intentions as it sounded to some. No senior Reagan-administration official believed the U.S. should fight an offensive nuclear war, and in a crisis would doubtless not have put any more faith in a limited nuclear war than Kennedy-administration officials had during the Berlin crisis of 1961. Certainly that was what their behavior in regard to Poland suggested. All the same, there was a good deal less skepticism about the notion of nuclear "strategy" in the Reagan administration than there had been in administrations past. For example, in the tradition of Wohlstetter and the Rand Corporation theoreticians, Richard Perle worried about "an American President feeling that he cannot afford to take action in a crisis because Soviet nuclear forces are such that, if escalation took place, they are better poised than we are to move up the escalation ladder."[142] What officials failed to focus upon was the possibility that their enthusiasms might create war fears in Moscow and thus increase the chances of an accidental nuclear war.[143] In this sense they trusted the Soviets more than any of their immediate predecessors had.

Then, too, the goals for war planning set out in the Defense Guidance were a good deal more ambitious than those in previous directives. PD-59 had called for forces sufficient to render the whole Soviet military and political power structure ineffective—a strategy known as "decapitation"—and forces capable of fighting a protracted conflict. The Defense Guidance did the same.[144] In addition, it called for the capability to fight a six-month nuclear war with pauses for reloading and refiring. Astonishingly, it also called for "a reserve of nuclear forces sufficient for trans- and post-attack protection and coercion"—or for enough nuclear weapons remaining after the conflict to see that the war stayed won.[145] The actual requirements for the administration's strategy were deeply classified, but it was later discovered that they included a wholly impractical program—on which eight billion dollars was spent—to remove U.S. leaders from Washington and to enable them to command U.S. strategic forces for the duration of a long war.[146]

The war plans so offended the outgoing chairman of the Joint Chiefs of Staff, General David C. Jones, that on leaving office in June he breached all protocol by saying that planning for a protracted war would be throwing money down a "bottomless pit," adding, "I don't see much of a chance of nuclear war being limited or protracted."[147]

Administration officials had their ambitions, but by the end of 1982 their ambitions seemed at particular odds with reality. For one thing, public support for increased defense spending had melted away. For another, Weinberger had failed to come up with an acceptable basing mode for the MX—with the result that the very missile required for the protracted-war strategy was in jeopardy in the Congress.

The quest to find a suitable home for the MX was a ludicrous enterprise, and its failure one of the reasons for Reagan's Star Wars speech.

From the beginning the administration had made the MX the centerpiece of its strategic buildup. It had ordered up another missile system, the D-5, for the Trident submarines, but the huge ten-warhead MX missile had long been advertised as the answer to the threat of the heavy, land-based Soviet ICBMs and the means of closing the "window of vulnerability." In addition, one hundred MXs would have one thousand warheads capable—at least in theory—of attacking Soviet missile silos in a "time-urgent" fashion. The difficulty was that the congressional Republicans from the Western states adamantly opposed Harold Brown's plan for basing it. The Multiple Protective Shelter, or MX/MPS, plan was less extensive than the former "racetrack" scheme, but it still involved building hundreds of protective shelters and hundreds of miles of roadway across the Great Basin, and Reagan had come out against it during the campaign.

Two months after the inauguration Weinberger created a panel under the leadership of the Nobel Prize–winning physicist Charles Townes to study the MX-basing issue, warning Townes at the outset that environmental lawsuits would delay the MX/MPS for years and might even doom it to oblivion. Weinberger could hardly have been clearer: come up with something other than MPS. The panel nonetheless recommended that the administration deploy a hundred MXs in a flexible, scaled-down version of the MPS.[148]

The Townes Committee report was almost a foregone conclusion. Weinberger later claimed that the Carter administration had examined no other options before proposing the MX/MPS, but this was far from the case. The Pentagon had been searching for an acceptable basing mode for the MX since the missile was first conceived in the early seventies, and when the Carter administration had decided to go ahead with it, the Pentagon had put on a full-scale two-year effort to solve the problem of making the missile survivable while retaining its accuracy. Technologists, both military and civilian, had come up with hundreds of ideas. Among those seriously considered, one, known as Orca, would have had the enormous MIRVed missile anchored offshore in a capsule until the launch order arrived, at which point the capsule would be released and would float to the surface so that the missile could be fired. Another idea was to have the missiles floating unattended in the ocean like so many beer bottles until the launch order came. Yet another was to have the missiles randomly shuttled between forty-six hundred opaque water pools distributed over an area of five thousand square miles. "Pools" was ruled out because the only empty five thousand square miles in the country was virtual desert with no water source. Dirigibles, sea planes, trucks and trains were all considered as vehicles for the missile, but all were eventually judged unsuitable. Pondered for some time was the idea of shuttling each of the missiles about in a fifty-mile-long trench. The idea was rejected not only because it would mean digging five thousand miles of trenches, but because, in the view of some, a trench would direct the incoming nuclear blast towards the missile. Various designs for ABM systems to protect the MX had been studied, but even the most promising one, the low-altitude system known as LoADs, was thought to have marginal utility even in conjunction with a mobile, deceptive basing mode. In the view of most, MX/MPS had its problems but it was the best that could be done.[149]

The Townes plan might, or might not, have proved politically acceptable, but Weinberger refused to consider it. To him any version of the MX/MPS was anathema—a holdover from the discredited Carter administration. In fact, all versions seemed to be the same to him, for he kept calling MX/MPS "the racetrack" and could never get the acronym right.[150] Other NSC principals, including Haig and Casey, favored some version of the MX/MPS. So, too, did Senator Tower and Representative William Dickson, the ranking Republican on the House Armed Services Committee. But Weinberger ignored all of them. According to Cannon, he thought Reagan was personally opposed to it, and this was enough for him. In any case, the MX/MPS was just one of those issues on which he dug in his heels and followed the dictum on the wall of his office, "Never give in, never, never, never . . ." and so on. By his order the Townes report was not circulated and was kept a secret even from the Air Force.[151]

Weinberger asked for new ideas, and under his prodding the Pentagon produced several more basing concepts. One of them, known as DUMB, for "deep underground missile basing," involved a corkscrew device that would burrow the missile into the earth and then screw it in the opposite direction for launching. Weinberger's own preferred solution was to build large transport planes to fly the MXs around on constant patrol, but "Big Bird," as this plan was known, involved a good many technical uncertainties, among them whether the wings would fall off when the missile was fired and what would happen if the plane crashed with the missile aboard.[152] The Townes Committee rejected the idea. When the deadline for a proposal arrived, Weinberger decided to accept the temporary measure suggested by his deputy for research and engineering, Richard DeLauer: a small number of MXs, perhaps forty, would be deployed as soon as possible in super-hardened Minuteman or Titan silos, and the search for an acceptable permanent basing mode would continue. The Joint Chiefs objected that no known method of hardening the silos would protect the missiles from an accurate nuclear strike, but Weinberger had made up his mind.[153]

On October 2, 1981, Reagan announced the MX deployment decision while unveiling the administration's entire strategic-modernization plan. He began by reading a statement drafted in Weinberger's office speaking of the "window of vulnerability" as if it meant the vulnerability of the entire deterrent.[154] When a reporter asked why he favored putting the MXs in vulnerable silos if this was the case, Reagan was stumped. But then he was stumped by the next question as well. Could a B-1 bomber penetrate Soviet defenses? Reagan did not know. After two more questions he turned over the podium to Weinberger. It was an embarrassing performance, and to many reporters in the room, it was clear that Reagan did not understand what he had signed on to.[155]

The MX decision was the first strategic initiative the administration had taken, but the reaction was hostile. In congressional hearings defense experts testified that the missile would be burned to cinders if the Soviets targeted it in a first strike. Critics argued that, given its vulnerability in a fixed silo, it could only be used as a first-strike or a launch-on-warning weapon. Pointing out that the decision did nothing to close the "window of vulnerability," a *Washington Post* reporter asked whether that "window" was going to disappear in the way that the "missile gap" disappeared after the Kennedy campaign in 1960. A *New York Times* editorial suggested that it might be better if the administration forgot the MX and simply drilled more holes in the missile fields to make the Russians think we had more missiles. In December the Congress passed legislation making it clear that the Weinberger solution was not acceptable and that the administration had to come up with a permanent basing mode.[156]

Pentagon planners returned to their task, and in the late spring of 1982, a new concept known as "Dense Pack" surfaced in the Office of the Secretary of Defense. Under this plan all one hundred missiles were to be based quite close together on a narrow strip of land and were to rely on a phenomenon called "fratricide" for their survival. The theory was that, because the incoming warheads would explode very close together, the first explosion would destroy the rest of the warheads and some of the MXs would survive. The concept could not be tested, for the Limited Test Ban Treaty of 1963 had banned nuclear explosions in the atmosphere, and many military experts were leery of it. Nonetheless, a second Townes Committee that was formed to review the idea gave it a cautious and qualified approval, and in November the administration announced that it would deploy the MXs in a Dense Pack configuration. But to many in Congress the plan sounded no more plausible than Orca or Big Bird, and some time after the announcement, General John W. Vessey, who had succeeded Jones as chairman of the Joint Chiefs, revealed in testimony to the Senate that the Chiefs themselves were divided over Dense Pack. Three out of five of them, it later appeared, wanted to delay the program until certain technical uncertainties could be resolved. The plan was now completely dead, and on December 7 the House voted 245 to 176 to eliminate the funds scheduled for the procurement of the MX.[157]

The House vote was the first major defeat for the administration's defense program, and to White House officials it seemed to bode very badly indeed for the future. The basing fiasco antagonized many Republican defense hawks and drove the new generation of Democratic leaders on the Armed Services Committees into open revolt against administration policies. Senator Sam Nunn (Democrat of Georgia), Senator Al Gore (Democrat of Tennessee) and Representative Les Aspin (Democrat of Wisconsin) began to design their own strategic-weapons policies with the support of moderate Republicans in Congress and with the approval of Henry Kissinger and other heavyweights in the defense community. Most of the moderates did not want to kill the MX at this late date, but they had come to the conclusion that MIRVed land-based missiles were inherently destabilizing and that the U.S. should place more emphasis on submarine-based forces and redesign its procurement and arms-control strategies so as to eliminate MIRVed weapons in the long run. To White House officials it seemed clear that the administration was losing control of its strategic-weapons policy.[158]

In the meantime, the anti-nuclear movement continued to gain ground. During the spring and summer of 1982 nationwide polls indicated that public support for the freeze had risen to more than 70 percent.[159] McFarlane geared up his Arms Control Information Working Group and, putting together a briefing book, he asked every official in the national-security bureaucracy from the level of deputy assistant secretary up to spend four days in one of fourteen major media markets explaining the administration's arms-control policies and attacking the freeze arguments. By his account high administration officials made more than six hundred appearances across the country in this pursuit.[160]

The results were not encouraging. In August the freeze resolution went to the floor of the House of Representatives, and although the Armed Services Committee opposed it, the resolution failed by only one vote. Reagan later suggested that the freeze was being manipulated by the Soviet Union, but the tactic backfired, and he was accused of red-baiting.[161] In October the National Council of Catholic Bishops released the draft of a proposed pastoral letter to be sent to the fifty-one million Catholics in the United States on the moral issues surrounding nuclear weapons. The product of long deliberations within the church, the letter condemned the arms race, war-fighting doctrines and first-strike weapons. Moreover, it came very close to declaring deterrence immoral by condemning the implied threat to use nuclear weapons.[162] By November seventeen state legislatures and over eight hundred city and county councils and town meetings had passed freeze referenda. In midterm elections eight states plus thirty-six cities and counties across the nation passed them as well. In addition, the Democrats picked up twenty-six seats in the House of Representatives, giving the freeze resolution an excellent chance of passing the House the following spring.[163]

By December, Reagan's approval rating had declined to 41 percent—an all-time low for an elected post-war president in his second year in office. The recession that had set in as a result of the Fed's attempt to stem inflation through high interest rates had much to do with the decline, but so did the administration's positions on defense and foreign policy. A Lou Harris poll released in January found that 66 percent of Americans believed that Reagan was doing an unsatisfactory job in arms control and 57 percent were worried that he might involve the U.S. in a nuclear war. The President was well aware of this sentiment, for he spoke to friends about the problem of his "hawkish image," and he told an outside adviser that something was wrong with his policy towards the Soviet Union, though he did not know where the fault lay.[164]

> "[The President] had a strong and persistent sense of responsibility to protect Americans against attack. He had mentioned it on occasion, whenever we would be discussing some military program or other—Tridents, or nuclear submarines, or ICBMs.—'You know,' he would say, 'I just wish we could deliver on these things and protect Americans from this scourge of nuclear annihilation.' He was convinced that we were in fact heading toward Armageddon, the final battle between good and evil. 'I'm telling you, it's coming,' he would say. 'Go read your Scripture.' "
>
> —Robert McFarlane[165]

In December 1982 Ronald Reagan and others in the White House realized that the strategic-nuclear-weapons policies the administration had been pursuing could no longer be sustained. Out of this understanding came two initiatives. One of them was the establishment of a blue-ribbon presidential commission on strategic forces. The other was what later became known as the Strategic Defense Initiative. The two efforts could hardly have been more different, and yet the prime mover in both of them was Robert McFarlane.

When William Clark brought McFarlane with him from the State Department to serve as deputy on the NSC staff, members of the Armed Services and Foreign Affairs Committees in Congress breathed a sigh of relief. Unlike some on the NSC staff, McFarlane was neither an ideologue nor a stranger to foreign policy. The son of a Texas congressman, he had served in the Marine Corps for twenty years and retired as a lieutenant colonel with a degree in international relations and many years of experience in Washington. He had worked on Kissinger's NSC staff and later, after leaving the Marines, as an aide to Senator Tower on the Armed Services Committee. Conscientious and well organized, he was a good staff man, and thoroughly at home with the abstractions of strategic policy. In this area, as in most, he held conventional conservative views. He believed that a military buildup was necessary to restore the strategic balance, and though he had helped Tower fight the SALT II treaty, he thought the administration should have a sensible arms-control policy to complement it.

To most people McFarlane seemed neither very supple nor very imaginative—there was a strange, wooden quality to his speech—but, rather, a good soldier, competent and reliable. Yet McFarlane had left the Marines because he was not given a major command, and, as it later turned out, his soldierly front concealed a great deal of inner turmoil.

A few days after the House vote on the MX, McFarlane, by his account, went to see Senator Nunn, Senator Tower and Senator William Cohen (Republican of Maine) and asked them how they thought the MX might be saved. All three said much the same thing: figuring out an adequate basing mode for the MX would be relatively easy; the real problem was that Weinberger had lost so much credibility on the Hill that any solution he proposed was bound to be rejected. Cohen advised McFarlane to take the issue out of Weinberger's hands and to put together a blue-ribbon panel of defense experts to study the issue and to come up with a solution before the deadline for the next vote, in April. McFarlane, who was by now fed up with Weinberger, thought this an excellent idea, and Clark, who had heard the same complaints from his own sources on the Hill, concurred.[166]

McFarlane and Thomas C. Reed, the other defense expert on the NSC staff, worked together on the project, and by the end of December they had established the President's Commission on Strategic Forces. The chair of the panel was Brent Scowcroft, a retired Air Force general who has served as NSC adviser to President Ford. With the assistance of Vice-President Bush, Scowcroft and the NSC staff assembled a group which included many of the leading lights of the old defense establishment. From the Nixon administration there was Henry Kissinger and former Defense Secretary James Schlesinger; from the Carter administration, Harold Brown and his former deputy, William Perry. Also invited was Alexander Haig—just six months after the administration had fired him as secretary of state. When completed, the panel included two former secretaries of state, Kissinger and Haig; two former CIA directors, Richard Helms and John McCone; four ex–secretaries of defense, Melvin Laird and Donald Rumsfeld as well as Schlesinger and Brown—plus assorted other luminaries. Reed served as a vice-chair and represented the White House. The panel, which became known as the Scowcroft Commission, was charged not only with settling the issue of the MX basing mode but with outlining long-term policies for strategic modernization and arms control. According to James Woolsey, a young Washington lawyer who served as Scowcroft's right-hand man on the panel, the task of the commission was to rebuild a bipartisan consensus on strategic issues in cooperation with key members of the congressional armed-services committees.[167]

In effect, without any fanfare and in the best establishment tradition, McFarlane and Reed had put the Office of the Secretary of Defense into receivership.

Three months later the Scowcroft Commission completed its report. The commissioners had conceived of their task politically, and had brokered a deal between Representative Les Aspin, a key Democrat on the House Armed Services Committee, Secretary Weinberger and others. Their report had something for everyone. For the administration it had a recommendation of one hundred MXs; for the Democrats in Congress, a suggestion that the MX might be traded away in the arms talks, and a proposal that in the future more emphasis should be put on survivable, submarine-based weapons. The commission approved the huge new Trident submarine but maintained that in the future the U.S. should build smaller subs and more of them; it also approved the MX and D-5 missiles while proposing that in the future the superpowers should move away from MIRVed weapons and the U.S. should build a single-warhead mobile missile to replace the MX. In other words, the Pentagon would get the weapons it had already developed, the administration would get its counter to the Soviet heavy missiles, and Senator Gore and the rest of the congressional moderates would get at least the satisfaction of being judged right about small mobile ICBMs. In addition, the commission, in a diplomatic but unmistakable fashion, warned that the administration would have to seek more realistic objectives in its arms-control proposals. The message was that arms control would be the quid pro quo for congressional cooperation on the strategic buildup.[168]

Under the terms of the report, one hundred MXs were to be based in fixed silos, just as Weinberger had recommended. There was no danger in doing this, the commission said, because for a number of years the Soviets would have difficulty destroying the ICBM and the strategic-bomber fleet simultaneously, as a result of the different flight-times of the different missiles that would be used in such an attack. In other words, the U.S. deterrent was not broken and did not need to be fixed. The administration could have its MXs, but the price was that it had to admit that the "window of vulnerability" was a theoretical problem of no real military significance.[169]

The Scowcroft Commission presented its report to the White House on April 6, 1983. Its conclusions came as no surprise to the NSC staff or the Joint Chiefs, for both had been consulted. Yet, two weeks before it presented its report, President Reagan made his speech calling upon scientists to render nuclear missiles "impotent and obsolete."

After the SDI program was formally launched in 1985, journalists put a great deal of effort into the attempt to discover how Ronald Reagan's SDI speech came into being. What they immediately discovered was that on the day of the speech White House officials said that the initiative was based on the plan known as High Frontier, which had been much discussed and advocated by prominent conservatives. Teller, who attended a dinner at the White House on the evening of the speech, had been mentioned in connection with the proposal and a week later wrote an Op Ed piece in the *New York Times* taking credit for having introduced the President to the defensive technologies being pioneered by "an ingenious group of young scientists."[170] With this lead, journalists unearthed the history of the Bendetsen group and Teller's attempt to persuade the President to support a strategic-defense project based on the X-ray laser. To journalists and others it seemed entirely plausible that Teller, given his stature in conservative circles and his entrée to the White House, had persuaded a gullible president and uninformed White House advisers of the efficacy of laser weapons. But Reagan's aides had laid down a false trail.

A few years later, just as the Reagan administration was leaving office, a new story about the origins of the initiative began to emerge—one that left Teller far in the background. The main source for it was McFarlane, then in disgrace for his role in the Iran-contra affair, but there were a number of other people happy to take credit for their part in launching SDI. The idea for the initiative, it now appeared, had originated with McFarlane and other members of the NSC staff, and with Admiral James Watkins, the chief of naval operations. None of these men had been involved with the High Frontier group, and none were uninformed about the technologies or the strategic issues involved with anti-missile defenses. McFarlane had specialized in strategic studies, and the staff members he brought into the project included Vice-Admiral John M. Poindexter, a nuclear physicist by training; General Richard Bovarie and Colonel Robert Linhard of the Air Force; Ray Pollock, a scientist-technocrat who had worked at Los Alamos; and Alton G. Keel, Jr., a former assistant secretary of the Air Force for research and development.

Admiral Watkins, an engineer by training, had commanded the Navy's first nuclear-powered cruiser, and he had the scientific and technical resources of the Navy at his disposal.[171] George Keyworth, it appeared, had helped to draft Reagan's speech.

The story, as it emerged in interviews, memoirs and journalistic and military histories, was an extremely curious one.[172] It had many versions, not all of which were perfectly consistent, but, broadly speaking, the story went something like this:

In December 1982 Robert McFarlane watched in dismay as Reagan's defense coalition crumbled. What concerned him was not just the fate of the MX but a larger strategic crisis: the Soviet Union had the capacity to turn out ICBMs and their warheads much faster than the United States, and the ability to deploy them at will. Already it had two new mobile land-based missiles under development; the U.S., by contrast, had none—and even if it had one, it probably could not field it. "The politics of deploying ICBMs in the United States was becoming too difficult," McFarlane said. In consequence, the U.S. was facing an emerging Soviet ability to launch a first strike and the possibility that the U.S. might never regain the strategic balance in counterforce weapons. "The traditional concept of offensive deterrence was becoming less stable," he said.[173] McFarlane, by his own account, came to believe that the solution was to stop competing with the Soviets on their terms and to move into the arena of high technology, where the U.S. had the comparative advantage. "I didn't care whether the investment was in the offense or the defense," he said, "but when I asked the experts in the Pentagon and elsewhere whether we should put more money into guidance systems, they said it wasn't necessary because we had as good a system as the Soviets did." McFarlane then began to consider an investment in defensive technologies.[174]

At the same time, Vice-Admiral Poindexter, Clark's military deputy, was having similar thoughts regarding the strategic crisis, and he, too, thought that the U.S. should investigate the possibility of developing an effective anti-missile system.[175] At McFarlane's request he queried experts on the NSC staff about the status of research into defensive technologies. He also queried Admiral Watkins and came back with a report that Watkins was highly optimistic that advances in directed-energy weapons and high-speed computers might in the long term offer the possibility of moving from an offensive to a defensive strategy.[176]

Encouraged, McFarlane decided to move ahead. Watkins had offered no certainties, but, then, as McFarlane saw it, a defense initiative would be valuable as a bargaining chip. If launched with great fanfare, a research effort could, he thought, be used to leverage Soviet behavior and might be traded for deep reductions in Soviet ICBMs. It would, he later said, "be the greatest sting operation in history."[177]

At the end of 1982—so the story continues—Watkins felt a sense of crisis akin to McFarlane's. Since taking office in June, he had given a great deal of time and attention to the issue of the MX basing mode and had finally concluded that there was no way to make the MX survivable, for the Soviets, with their superiority in heavy ICBMs, could destroy the MX in any basing mode the U.S. might select. In trying to compete with the Soviets where they were the strongest, the U.S., he told one interviewer, was "heading into a strategic valley of death." We were, he said, "reaching a point where we were losing our hat, ass and overcoat at Geneva. We had no bargaining chip, no strength with which to negotiate. The Soviets could just sit in Geneva and watch us throw away all of our chips right here in Washington."[178] At the same time, Watkins, a devout Catholic, was profoundly sensitive to the questions the Catholic bishops were raising about the morality of nuclear deterrence. While wrestling with the issue of vulnerability, he began to have doubts about the nation's absolute reliance on offensive deterrence. The country, he felt, might not support "mutual assured destruction" much longer. With some knowledge of the advances being made in computer technology and high-energy lasers and particle beams, he thought an effort to develop missile defenses might produce the solution to both problems. Why, he asked his staff, "don't we use our applied technological genius to achieve our deterrent instead of sticking with an offensive land-based rocket exchange which [the Soviets] will win every time?"[179]

In early January 1983 Watkins began to work on a strategic-defense proposal for the Chiefs to present at their next quarterly meeting with the President, scheduled for February 11. On January 20 he lunched with Edward Teller and listened to Teller speak with passionate enthusiasm of the Excalibur experiment and other potential defense technologies. Watkins did not favor the X-ray laser, for he felt that any defensive system that relied on nuclear explosions would prove politically unacceptable, but Teller made a deep impression on him, and the discussion, he later said, convinced him that "strategic defenses offered a way to use the resources of American technology to move beyond the sterile debate over MX basing modes in the short term" and to a more palatable form of deterrence in the long run.[180] A few days later he had two staff members write a brief presentation on strategic defenses for the Chiefs and had them write it over and over again until he was satisfied with the wording. On February 5 Watkins made his presentation to the Chiefs. Somewhat to his surprise, they unanimously adopted his proposal and voted to include it among the options that they would give the President the following week.[181]

By all accounts the Chiefs agreed to Watkins's proposal because they were at their wits' end. Since June they had had forty meetings on the issue of the MX basing mode and had found no acceptable solution. Their chairman, General Vessey, was embarrassed at having revealed their differences over Dense Pack before the House vote, and all of them were discouraged, for they could see no way to avert the demise of the MX when the Congress next took up the issue in March. In addition, they dreaded the prospect of another meeting with the President at which they would have to confess that they still had no acceptable way to base the MX. In preparation for the meeting, they had come up with other options, but only Watkins's idea was new. General Vessey later said that he had spent a lot of time keeping the Army's ballistic-missile defense program alive and that he shared some of Watkins's moral and military qualms about deterrence. "Relying totally on the idea that you would destroy the other side is not moral, and it's not very logical," he told Lou Cannon. "It leaves you with two unacceptable alternatives. Not only do you wipe out the population of the Soviet Union, but you have a fair chance of wiping out your own population as well."[182]

On February 11 there was a snowstorm in Washington, an unusually large one for the city, and the Chiefs had to make their way to the White House in four-wheel-drive vehicles. At the meeting General Vessey briefed the President about the strategic situation and laid out five options, the last of which was Watkins's proposal on missile defenses. Secretary Weinberger had opposed the inclusion of this option on the grounds that it had not yet been studied. "I don't agree with the chiefs," he told the President at the meeting, "but you should hear them out."[183] The last section of Vessey's briefing paper, which followed closely along the lines of Watkins's paper, said that "forward strategic defenses" would "move the battle from our shores and skies" and create a "middle ground" between the "dangerous extremes of (a) threatening a preemptive strike or (b) passively absorbing a Soviet first strike." The report also said that defenses were "more moral and therefore more palatable to the American people" than offenses, and that the aim of such a defense was to "protect the American people, not just avenge them."[184] When Vessey had finished, Watkins strongly supported the proposal. "You know, Mr. President," he said, "I think the time has come where we ought to [take] another look at defensive technologies. And it seems to me that it's possibly within reach that we could develop systems that would defeat a missile attack."[185]

McFarlane, who knew the proposal would be made, then picked up the cue and underlined what Watkins had said for the President's benefit. "I believe," he said, "that Jim is suggesting that new technologies may offer the possibility of enabling us to deal with a Soviet missile attack by defensive means."

"I understand," the President said; "that's what I've been hoping." He then asked the other Chiefs one by one what they thought of Watkins's proposal, and one by one they agreed that it was a good idea. At the conclusion of the meeting he asked them to report to him promptly on what steps should be taken to launch such an initiative.[186]

Two days later General Vessey called William Clark, who had been out of town the day of the meeting, and asked if he had heard what he thought he had. "You sure did," said Clark.[187]

After this meeting it was the President who pushed the idea forward. The Chiefs expected that their ill-defined proposal would be staffed out and studied. McFarlane thought the President would not expect a report until after the Scowcroft Commission completed its work in April. But in mid-March the President told him that he was ready to announce the Strategic Defense Initiative publicly. McFarlane argued that it would be better to forge support for the proposal in the bureaucracy, in the Congress and in the Scowcroft Commission before announcing it publicly, but the President disagreed: he thought the proposal would be argued to death before it ever saw the light of day. He and Clark urged McFarlane to develop the idea on a "close-hold" basis, telling no one outside the NSC staff.[188]

Initially the NSC staffers debated whether to recommend a broad research effort or one focused on a single program, such as the Army's ballistic-missile defense program, but the President soon let them know what he had in mind: he wanted to announce a program that would save Americans from nuclear war.[189] McFarlane, who thought of the initiative simply as a research effort and a bargaining chip, tried to talk the President out of this idea, but in vain. "I went all through this reasoning," McFarlane said, "but he did not understand my investment strategy. For him the idea of anti-missile defenses had an appeal in itself. My own concepts for leveraging Soviet behavior were lost on him."[190]

On Friday, March 18, Reagan and Clark, then at Camp David for the weekend, asked McFarlane to write up the idea as an insert to the speech Reagan was to give on March 23 in support of the 1984 defense budget.[191] On March 19 McFarlane recruited George Keyworth to help with the background briefings. McFarlane worried about the reaction from Congress and the NATO allies, and wanted to delay the speech until he could create bipartisan support for the idea. But, McFarlane told Cannon, "Reagan wanted it out as soon as possible. He was so swept away by his ability to stand up and announce a program that would defend Americans from nuclear war [that] he couldn't wait."[192]

Only a handful of people in the White House knew about the insert. The Joint Chiefs were shown a draft on March 20; Secretary of State George Shultz was informed the following day, and Secretary Weinberger, who was then in Portugal for a NATO meeting, did not receive a draft until midnight the day before the speech. Shultz made numerous objections to the draft; Weinberger's aides, Richard Perle and Ronald Lehman, spent the night calling around Washington and pleading with McFarlane to delay the announcement until the NATO allies could be informed; Keyworth and McFarlane tried to persuade the President to tone down the language of the insert.[193] But there was no stopping Reagan, and at 8:00 P.M. on March 23, the President launched his radical and utopian proposal upon a startled world.

In broad outline this is the account usually given of the origins of the SDI speech. Yet it is a very peculiar story. To read it in the histories of the period is to be struck by the unlikely poses adopted by the participants.

The cast of characters, after all, seems to include a deputy national-security adviser, one not known for his flights of the imagination, who, faced with one of the most serious strategic crises of the Cold War, conceives of "the greatest sting in history"—but somehow could not make the President understand his idea. Stranger still, the cast includes two members of the JCS who have moral qualms about deterrence, and one, the chief of naval operations, who describes the "strategic crisis" without ever mentioning a submarine. Only the President seems to be in character—or at least in the character ascribed to him by Martin Anderson: Ronald Reagan, the dreamer, the nuclear abolitionist, the naïve. The implausibilities do not stop there.

Years after the event McFarlane, Poindexter and Watkins portrayed the missile-defense initiative as a response to a grave strategic crisis. But what crisis? True, the administration could not come up with a survivable basing mode for the MX, but the Scowcroft Commission was already resolving the MX problem. Then, all three of them came to the conclusion that recent technological advances justified the launch of a major new research program in defensive technologies—though the Pentagon and the White House Science Council had been studying defensive technologies non-stop for the past two years without finding any justification for such an effort.[194] Neither McFarlane nor the Chiefs asked for another study: they simply told the President that "effective" defenses could be achieved. Watkins did meet with Teller, and later claimed to come away with greater certainty about strategic defenses. However, he rejected the only technology Teller was promoting for strategic defense. Then, at the February 11 meeting, Vessey told Reagan that defenses are "more moral" than offenses—though the Army's BMD program was at that point focused on defending ICBMs, not people.

To read all the versions of this story closely is, moreover, to find a good many inconsistencies among the accounts. In the first place, the participants did not always tell interviewers exactly the same thing, and when later asked to explain the discrepancies, some changed their testimony again. Second, there are pieces of evidence scattered about, particularly in the work of the official SDIO historian, Donald R. Baucom, and that of the Naval War College historian, Frederick H. Hartmann, that do not fit this story at all. Finally, except in interviews with Baucom, the participants fail to mention a phenomenon of great importance to them at the time. Once this element is introduced, the story begins to make sense—otherwise it is like the score of a piano concerto with the piano part missing. The phenomenon is, of course, the anti-nuclear movement: the freeze.

According to Donald Baucom, who sometimes elicited more candor from officials than journalists did, the strategic crisis McFarlane envisioned in December 1982 was not technical but political: on the one hand, there was the problem with Congress and the MX; on the other, there was the problem of the freeze.[195] That McFarlane had the freeze on his mind can hardly be doubted, since that summer and fall he had mounted a major public-relations campaign to combat it, with high officials making appearances in media markets across the country. According to Baucom, McFarlane first presented the idea to the President after Reagan made a campaign visit to New York—presumably before the November election—during which he spoke with local officials about the damage the freeze movement might do to the defense buildup. Sometime after the election—with its disappointing results—McFarlane informed Reagan that he was working on a concept that might "outflank the Freeze" while solving the problem of the nuclear imbalance. The President, McFarlane said, encouraged him to pursue his solution and report on his work in January.[196]

McFarlane's idea for a defense initiative was not quite as imaginative as he later made it sound. The idea was, after all, in the Republican platform, and in the past two years Wallop, Graham and Teller had given it a good deal of currency. Further, every major administration pronouncement on strategic policy, most recently the President's statement on Dense Pack of November 22, had promised that the administration would be pursuing research on ballistic missile defense technologies.[197] Then, too, among its many recommendations, the 1982 Defense Guidance called for the development of "weapons that are difficult for the Soviets to counter, impose disproportionate costs, open up new areas of major military competition and obsolesce previous Soviet investment." Specifically it called for "prototype development of space-based weapon systems," including anti-satellite weapons.[198]

McFarlane told some journalists that he conceived of an investment in defenses as a bargaining chip and tried unsuccessfully to convince the President to see it as such. He certainly made this argument to the President later on. But in December 1982 the administration was not in a negotiating mode—much less losing its hat and overcoat in Geneva, as Watkins told one interviewer. By other evidence McFarlane and Poindexter initially presented the idea of a defense initiative as Martin Anderson did in 1979: as a part of the strategic buildup and as a way to dispel Reagan's hawkish image. The initiative, Poindexter told Baucom, would be popular with the American people.[199]

McFarlane and Poindexter did not ask for a study of strategic defenses, but, according to Baucom, Poindexter invited Alton Keel and the two Air Force officers on the NSC staff to a "brainstorming" session on defensive technologies. Keel evinced skepticism, but the group apparently decided that developing these technologies was worth "a concerted effort."[200] Interestingly, McFarlane did not inform the real White House experts on this subject, Thomas C. Reed and George Keyworth, about the idea. But, then, both men had come out officially against putting more effort into defensive technologies, particularly lasers.[201]

By some accounts Watkins arrived at the idea for missile defenses independently. But the evidence is that he acted in response to a request from the NSC staff. According to McFarlane, Poindexter queried Watkins about defensive technologies in late 1982 and returned with a report that he was highly optimistic. Then, realizing he would have to get the Chiefs on board if the project were to succeed, McFarlane lunched with Watkins and Poindexter at Watkins's home in the Washington Navy Yard in early January. Thus Watkins certainly knew of the White House interest in defenses well before he presented the idea to the rest of the Chiefs.[202]

Among the Chiefs, Watkins had taken the lead in opposing Dense Pack. Theodore Postol, his science adviser from MIT, had made a convincing case against the implausible Air Force plan, and Watkins had brought along General Robert H. Barrow, the Marine commandant; and General Edward C. Meyer, the Army chief of staff.[203] In the end, only General Vessey, the chairman, supported the Air Force chief, Charles M. Gabriel. Vessey, an old-fashioned troop commander, had been loyal to the administration, but when asked in a congressional committee whether the Chiefs supported Dense Pack, he revealed the division among the Chiefs. Watkins and Vessey had the vote against the MX on their consciences.

Then, too, Watkins was very concerned about the anti-nuclear movement. By some accounts the admiral had moral qualms about nuclear deterrence.[204] But this is ridiculous. As a devout Catholic, Watkins was very sensitive to the moral objections the Catholic bishops were making—not because he personally had any qualms about deterrence, or, for that matter, war-fighting doctrines or "first-strike" weapons. He hardly would have become CNO if he had. What worried him, as Baucom points out, was that the bishops' statements were causing Catholics to quit the Navy and turning the American Catholic laity against the military buildup. In the summer of 1982 he gave a commencement address at Marymount College in Arlington—meant for wider distribution—defending deterrence on moral grounds and, implicitly at least, reproving anti-nuclear activism in the church.[205] In 1990 he clearly told Cannon that it was the anti-nuclear sentiment in the country which led him to the idea of a strategic defense initiative. The moral issue was important, he said, "in that the American people thought mutual assured destruction morally distasteful—and it was a political loser."[206]

On January 10, when Clark summoned the Chiefs to meet with the President on February 11, Watkins put his aide, Captain Linton Brooks, to work on a presentation to the Chiefs in preparation for the meeting. According to Hartmann, the naval historian, the presentation Watkins made on February 5 contained a number of key points: (1) that the Triad should be supported; (2) that the administration's strategic-modernization program had restored the credibility of American strategic forces, making the ICBM survivability issue less pressing; and (3) that the U.S. should for the present put forty MXs in existing silos—while pushing for a long-term strategy based on defenses.[207] In other words, just as the Scowcroft Commission was going to point out, there was no "window of vulnerability," and the MXs could be deployed as Weinberger had proposed in 1981. Years later, when asked about the capability of submarine-based missiles, Watkins called the Trident's D-5 missile the "ace in the hole . . . the last trump card." With it, he said, the Navy had "a war-terminating strategy—an ability to carry the last day and . . . maybe even win a nuclear exchange." In Watkins's revised view, it was not the U.S. but the Soviet Union which faced a strategic crisis.[208]

By several accounts Watkins was enthusiastic about the progress being made in directed-energy technologies and computational speeds. Still, Watkins did not believe that population defenses would materialize in the foreseeable future. Referring to himself and the other chiefs, he told Cannon, "We never believed in the umbrella. What we said is that if you could confuse the Soviets [with a defensive system that would stop some of the missiles] there would never be a first strike."[209] Watkins lunched with Edward Teller on January 20, but the luncheon seems to have been a formality, for he had already dismissed the X-ray laser as a candidate for an anti-missile defense. "I knew the wheat from the chaff," he said, referring to Excalibur and Teller's exaggerated claims for its application to strategic defense. He added, "The X-ray laser is an OK research program but for other reasons."[210]

Following the luncheon Watkins asked Rear Admiral W. J. Holland and his aide, Captain Brooks, to "develop on a close hold basis a very brief (five minute) presentation which would offer a vision of strategic defense as a way out of the MX debate."[211] There followed a series of meetings in which Watkins repeatedly rejected their formulations—without giving a specific reason for doing so. Apparently Brooks got the rhetoric right when he wrote that a defense was "more moral and therefore more palatable to the American people" than offensive weapons, and that the aim of such a defense was "to protect the American people, not just avenge them."[212]

What, then, did the Chiefs have in mind when they proposed a missile-defense initiative to the President on February 11? Asked that question years later, Admiral Watkins, General Vessey and General E. C. Meyer insisted that they didn't have very much in mind at all: putting money into missile-defense research was one of five options they gave the President, and their proposal was vague and general. "There was no program definition," Vessey told Hedrick Smith. "It was the idea that defenses might enter into the equation more than in the past." General Meyer said, "I don't think any of us had a clear vision of what form this strategic defense would take. The issue needed to be debated at the very highest level by people concerned with policy and people concerned with technology."[213] According to Hartmann, the Chiefs were not ready to make defense "the primary strategic response, let alone fund it on any substantial scale." Specifically they did not want anything that would interfere financially with their individual service programs.[214] General Vessey's briefing paper for the President said that the Chiefs supported the

Triad and the MX plus a continuing research-and-development effort—"on a wide range of alternatives with more focus on Small Land Mobiles and BMD . . . to facilitate future deployment options" if the Soviets failed to respond to U.S. arms-control initiatives. At the February 11 meeting, according to Hartmann, the Chiefs made the point that lately discussions of strategic issues had focused far too much on basing modes and they would have to "find a better way to present the case in a larger context."[215]

What this seems to indicate is that the Chiefs wanted to keep on doing exactly what they were already doing—that is, modernizing the Triad and funding BMD research—but they wanted their efforts put "in a larger context." Clearly the Chiefs did not see a "strategic crisis" on the horizon, and if more focus was to be put on anti-missile research, its main function would be to serve as a distraction from the whole mighty embarrassment of the MX. As for Brooks's rhetoric, which Watkins transmitted in the form of a question—"Wouldn't it be better to protect the American people rather than avenge them?"—it seems to have been a speech line for the President.

Brooks was triumphant when the President used his words. Theodore Postol by contrast was outraged. After the initiative was launched, he spoke to Watkins about some of the risks involved in an attempt to achieve population defenses with space-based weapons. The admiral, who had consulted with him regularly until then, never asked Postol back to his office again, and thereafter turned away from him when the two passed in the halls.[216]

When McFarlane met with Reagan and Clark in mid-March, the three discussed the speech Reagan was scheduled to give on March 23 in support of the defense budget for fiscal year 1984.[217] According to McFarlane, Reagan did not want to give the speech that had been drafted by the Defense Department.[218] On March 8 he had made a highly charged address to the National Association of Evangelicals calling the Soviet Union "the evil empire." Given the mood of the times, the speech had prompted a good deal of sarcasm and a rash of political cartoons featuring Darth Vader. Then, too, the second debate on the freeze was scheduled to begin soon in the House. For March 23 the Defense Department had served up a speech describing the Soviet threat and the need for a military buildup in the same rhetoric that Reagan and Weinberger had been using for years. "The enemies of freedom grow stronger every day . . . far more missiles than they need to deter an attack . . . the decade of neglect . . ." All the old chestnuts were there. In addition, the speech warned of the vulnerability of "all of our missiles on the ground" and contained an attack on the freeze.[219] McFarlane told Baucom that Reagan asked him to write up the strategic-defense idea because he wanted to "break something new" in the speech, and that he specifically wanted to provide the nation with something reassuring that might stem the growth of the freeze.[220] "Reagan's view of the political payoff was sufficient rationale as far as he was concerned," McFarlane told Hedrick Smith years later. "By that I mean providing the American people with an appealing answer to their fears—the intrinsic value of being able to tell Americans, 'For the first time in the nuclear age, I'm doing something to save your lives. I'm telling you that we can get rid of nuclear weapons.' "[221] By that time McFarlane had come to suspect that Reagan's political advisers were encouraging the President to take some action to outflank the freeze.[222]

As soon as the President said he wanted to announce the initiative, McFarlane got cold feet about the project. He argued that the idea should go through the bureaucratic process and be sold to the Scowcroft Commission and Congress before the President made his speech—though clearly this would have killed it.[223] The problem for McFarlane was not just what the President should say but what he, McFarlane, should say in background briefings to justify the initiative.

On Saturday, March 19, McFarlane called George Keyworth into his office. By Keyworth's account, McFarlane said that the President had asked a question: "Is now a good time to renew our efforts in strategic defense?" Keyworth was "surprised, shocked, even stunned" by the question. Just two months before, the Frieman panel had delivered its final report to the White House Science Council, with the results of its yearlong investigation into directed-energy weapons and other emerging technologies. The report had concluded that except in the area of adaptive optics—in which deformable mirrors are used to compensate for the distortion of light as it passes through the atmosphere—there had been little progress, and that the emerging technologies were not likely to have any military utility for the foreseeable future.[224] This judgment was fresh in Keyworth's mind, for, at the end of a White House Science Council meeting the day before, Keyworth had quite routinely asked whether any of the emerging technologies held military promise over the next five years, and the answer was the same categorical no. Yet, when McFarlane asked whether this was a good time to renew U.S. efforts on strategic defenses, Keyworth dodged the question.

Keyworth had been hired to support the President's policies, but over the past eighteen months he had opposed the administration on a number of issues, including its plan to build a huge space station and its dismissal of acid rain as a serious environmental threat. Mindful of the precariousness of his position, he had advocated Dense Pack so strongly that people took to calling him "Dr. Dense Pack."[225] In answer to McFarlane's question, he spoke about the one promising note in the Frieman report. When McFarlane assured him that only a research effort was envisioned, he agreed to help. But after reading McFarlane's draft of the insert for the President's speech, he had second thoughts, and that afternoon he returned to McFarlane's office to express concern about the magnitude and direction of the initiative. By Keyworth's account, McFarlane and Poindexter dispelled his doubts in an hour of intense discussion. Keyworth signed onto the project and never looked back.[226]

Later that day Keyworth tried to convince his deputy, Victor Reis, to support the initiative. According to Reis, Keyworth said, "This is a political decision, not a technical one, and in political things you and I are not experts." Reis, however, refused to cooperate. Relying on lasers to shoot down missiles was like relying on laetrile to cure cancer, he said. Years afterwards he told an interviewer that Keyworth "felt very strongly about the need to support the President on the things the President felt strongly about."[227]

Over the weekend Keyworth made frantic attempts to reconvene the White House Science Council to discuss strategic defense. Of those members who were able to come to his office and read the speech insert, none were inclined to support it and several expressed amazement at what the President was proposing. "I almost fell out of my chair when I saw it," Frieman said. But he, along with others, concluded that there were "forces at work" in the White House so major that "there was just no way any individual was going to stop this thing dead in its tracks."[228]

Keyworth helped with the drafting of the speech insert and took on the task of briefing Pentagon and State Department officials about it. Within the administration he took much of the blame for the speech.

Informed of the insert on the morning of March 21, Secretary of State George Shultz was aghast. The President had told him of his desire for a defense against nuclear weapons after the February 11 meeting with the Chiefs, but Shultz had, he later wrote," absolutely no idea that the views he was expressing had any near-term operational significance." Clearly he had thought he was listening to a presidential fantasy and had not bothered to argue. "We don't have the technology to say this," he told his aides. That afternoon he met with the President and objected forcefully to the wording of the insert, and in particular to one paragraph, which in his view, called for "a revolution in our strategic doctrine." But the President seemed reluctant to make any changes in the draft, and when he called Keyworth in to field Shultz's elementary questions about technology and strategy (Can you be sure of an impenetrable shield? What about cruise missiles and stealth bombers? What about the ABM Treaty? and so on), Keyworth had no satisfactory answers. Shultz left even more perturbed than he had come.

By the next morning the draft had been toned down, but Shultz still found it disturbing. In a telephone conversation with the President he warned that the Soviets might react badly if they thought the U.S. had made a major scientific breakthrough. The President interrupted to say that this was the part that would make a news item and attract the networks. "It's more than a news item. It's a sweeping proposal," Shultz objected.

With Reagan's permission, Shultz made another attempt to tone down the draft, telling McFarlane that he was doing so and that Clark should know it. "I feel you guys are leading the president out on a limb, and people will saw it off. The Chiefs should have their necks wrung," he said. When the draft came back to him little changed from the previous day, Shultz blamed Keyworth as well as McFarlane and Clark. "You are a lunatic," he bellowed at the President's science adviser.[229]

Secretary Weinberger, who was in Portugal, did not personally intervene, but his two aides Richard Perle and Ron Lehman, spent all night on the phone to Washington trying to get the announcement delayed, expressing extreme, and for them unusual, concern about the effect it would have on the NATO allies. The insert, Lehman said, will create "a furor from which we will never recover." Perle more characteristically objected that the initiative would provide ammunition to those in Congress who were trying to kill the President's defense and arms-control programs, and he called upon Keyworth to "fall on his sword."[230]

But the idea was not Keyworth's—nor was the rhetoric. "If there is one thing I do not mean by this, gentlemen," Reagan told the drafters of the insert on Monday, March 21, "it is some kind of a string of terminal defenses around this country." He also insisted the speech suggest that the initiative would render not just ballistic missiles but all nuclear weapons "obsolete."[231]

Years afterwards Keyworth said, "The fact is, I learned much more from the President than he learned from me in preparing that speech."[232]

In the 1985 account of the origins of the speech, the technological exuberance of Teller, Graham and others persuaded the President and his ill-informed staff to launch SDI. By McFarlane's account the President's own enthusiasm for defenses overcame the doubts and hesitations of his technically competent staff. On the strength of this account many reporters concluded that Ronald Reagan, a visionary and a romantic, simply believed that American technology could produce miracles and put an end to the threat of nuclear war. Lou Cannon, for one, wrote: "Reagan totally believed in the science-fiction solution he had proposed without consultation with his secretary of state or his secretary of defense. . . . Reagan was convinced that American ingenuity could find a way to protect the American people from the nightmare of Armageddon. As he saw it, the Strategic Defense Initiative was a dream come true."[233]

Perhaps. But the President surely saw what would have been obvious to anyone in his position: You can't tell the American people that you will make them half safe. You can't say that defenses are "more moral" than offenses if they are designed to protect ICBMs. And you can't promise "to protect American lives rather than to avenge them" unless you can propose to make nuclear weapons obsolete. Then, too, what Reagan wrote at the time about the initiative contains no suggestion of ardor.

Reagan's 1990 autobiography, *An American Life*, includes a number of excerpts from the diary Reagan dutifully kept throughout the years of his presidency. Given the importance he later ascribed to the SDI decision, he, or his ghost writer, included what seems to be every passage referring to the initiative on the days surrounding the March 23 speech.

For Tuesday, March 22, the single entry is this: "Another day that shouldn't happen. On my desk was a draft of the speech to be delivered tomorrow night on TV. This one was hassled over by NSC, State and Defense. Finally I had a crack at it. I did a lot of rewriting. Much of it was to change bureaucratese into people talk." Reagan then goes on to complain mildly of having had far too many meetings crowded into that day.[234]

The draft of the speech which turned up on Reagan's desk at 9:30 A.M. on March 22 was one that Keyworth had last worked on, and it contained a number of lines suggesting that the initiative was designed to replace offensive weapons with effective defenses: "Would it not be better to embark upon a path that will eventually let us and our allies use *defensive* measures—not the threat of retaliation—to deter aggression in the free world? . . . In short, how much better it would be if we could begin to shift from a strategy of deterrence with offensive weapons to a strategy of forward strategic defense. . . . But is it not worth every investment necessary to free the world from the threat of nuclear war? . . ." And so on in this vein. Scrawled across one line in what must be Keyworth's handwriting is the question Admiral Watkins had asked, "Wouldn't it be better to save lives than to avenge them?"[235] To examine these sentences is, however, to see that they are phrased in such a way as to avoid any actual claim that an umbrella defense could be built.

Reagan did a great deal of rewriting on the speech that day. The draft of 9:30 A.M. shows extensive changes made in his handwriting. A great many awkward or pretentious phrases—"shouldered this awesome responsibility," "accomplish this through the innovative use of," "no near-term panacea"—have been crossed out, and simpler, more graceful language has been substituted. Reagan crossed out the entire sentence "In short, how much better it would be if we could begin to shift from a strategy of deterrence with offensive weapons to a strategy of forward strategic defense." He also scratched out a lumpy piece of prose just before the peroration and substituted the beautiful sentence "I call upon the scientific community in this country, who gave us nuclear weapons, to turn their great talents to the cause of mankind and world peace; to give us the means of rendering these weapons impotent and obsolete."

Reagan's diary entry for March 23 reads: "The big thing today was the 8 p.m. TV speech on all networks about national security. We've been working on that speech for 72 hours and right down to the deadline. We had a group in for dinner at the White House. . . . I did the speech from the Oval Office at 8 and then joined the party for coffee. I guess it was OK, they all praised it to the sky and seemed to think it would be a source of debate for some time to come. I did the bulk of the speech on why the arms buildup was necessary and then finished with a call to the scientific community to join me in research starting now to develop defensive weapons that would render nuclear missiles obsolete. I made no optimistic forecasts—said it might take 20 years or more but we had to do it. I felt good."[236]

The group invited to the White House that evening included the secretary of state, the Joint Chiefs, Edward Teller and a number of other eminent scientists. Many of the guests were more or less appalled by the speech insert, but apparently none of them told the President that.[237]

On March 24 Reagan wrote in his diary: "The reports are in on last night's speech. The biggest return—phone calls, wires, etc., on any speech so far and running heavily in my favor . . ."[238]

On March 25 he wrote: "A poll taken before the speech shows I've gained on job approval with regard to the economy, but the drum beat of anti-defense propaganda has reduced my ratings on foreign affairs. I'd be interested to see how that holds for a poll after the speech."[239]

That is all Reagan's diary tells us about the speech, but on March 26 Michael Deaver told Ambassador Dobrynin at a reception that he saw the initiative as a campaign issue because it held out hope to the American voters that the nuclear threat would be neutralized, thus blunting Democratic attacks on Reagan as a warmonger.[240]

In question-and-answer sessions with reporters on March 25 and March 29 Reagan spoke at some length about the initiative, and his comments suggest how he conceived the speech.

Asked during the first session why he launched a strategic-defense initiative at this particular time, Reagan said that the idea had been "kicking around" in his mind "for some time here recently," and after discussing it with the Chiefs, he thought it was time to start, "since we don't know how long it will take or if—or ever, that we have to start—the quicker we start the better." In other words, now was a good time, since no one knew when, or even if, the initiative would produce results. "But it's inconceivable to me," he continued, "that we can go on thinking down the future, not only for ourselves and our lifetime but for other generations, that the great nations of the world will sit here, like people facing themselves across a table [sic], each with a cocked gun and no one knowing whether someone must tighten their finger on the trigger."[241]

Four days later Reagan returned to the same theme: "To look down to an endless future with both of us sitting here with these horrible missiles aimed at each other and the only thing preventing a holocaust is just so long as no one pulls the trigger—this is unthinkable."[242]

There were, he said, two possible solutions: "There is one way, and the way we're pursuing, which is to see if we can get mutual agreement to reduce these weapons and, hopefully, to eliminate them, as we're trying in INF. There is another way, and that is if we could, the same scientists who gave us this kind of destructive power, if they could turn their talent to the job of, perhaps, coming up with something that would render these weapons obsolete. And I don't know how long it's going to take, but we're going to start."[243]

In this explanation there is nothing of Edward Teller's rhetoric, and there is no technological enthusiasm: Reagan does not even hazard a guess as to what the scientists will come up with, much less talk of lasers and other Buck Rogers weaponry. No, the explanation is made up of lines from Reagan's previous speeches—from the speeches designed to show that he was not a nuclear warmonger. The metaphor of the two men with the cocked pistols he had used over and over again to describe the nuclear dilemma. The phrase "horrible missiles" and the notion of the judgment of future generations came from his much-applauded speech at the 1976 Republican convention. The idea of eliminating nuclear missiles came, as he here suggests, from his successful speech announcing the INF proposal. In addition, there is a part of a line from the movie *Torn Curtain* about making missiles "obsolete." What many inferred from the phrase was that Reagan believed what he had once seen in a science-fiction movie. But to look at the explanation as a whole is to see that he was following a train of thought—or simply a trail of applause lines—from one reassuring speech to another and then appropriating a dramatic phrase, whose origin he may or may not have remembered, for his peroration. The line was so beautiful that it is small wonder that Reagan refused to let Keyworth and McFarlane take it out.

CHAPTER SIX

Selling the Strategic Defense Initiative

NOT SURPRISINGLY, the President's call for a program to make ballistic missiles obsolete appalled defense experts in and out of the administration. The Joint Chiefs were stunned by the precipitous action and the sweeping language. The chief technical experts in the Pentagon were furious. According to witnesses, Richard DeLauer, the undersecretary of defense for research and engineering, "went ballistic" and asked how nuclear policy could be the subject of such a "half-baked political travesty."[1] The day before Reagan's speech, Major General Donald L. Lamberson, the director of the Pentagon's directed-energy programs, had told a Senate Armed Services subcommittee that space-based laser weapons were insufficiently promising to warrant additional funding; and on the day of the speech, Dr. Robert Cooper, the Defense Department's director of advanced research, told a House committee much the same thing. Warned in advance about the initiative, Brent Scowcroft urged McFarlane to put the speech on hold until the MX issue could be resolved. He thought it an attempt to steal the antinuclear movement's clothes. The report of his commission, which went to the White House on April 6, stated quite flatly that "applications of current technology offer no real promise of being able to defend the United States against massive nuclear attack in this century."[2]

Beyond that, the initiative was a political disaster. Calls and telegrams to the White House may have run in its favor, but the reaction was otherwise almost entirely negative. In the Congress only Malcolm Wallop and the few other missile-defense enthusiasts volunteered support. In the House, where a debate on the freeze resolution was proceeding, Democrats derided the idea mercilessly. "The only thing the President did not tell us last night," Representative Tom Downey (Democrat of New York) scoffed, "was that the Evil Empire was about to launch a Death Star against the United States." Referring to another current movie, Representative Edward Markey (Democrat of Massachusetts) called Edward Teller "the original E.T." and accused him of wanting to create a "pin-ball outer-space war between the Force of Evil and the Force of Good."[3] The Republicans did not know how to respond. What *was* the President talking about? Like the Democrats, most assimilated the initiative to the rest of the President's bellicose speech and assumed that, if anything, he was proposing some new kind of ABM system.[4] Since the House had just cut the administration's request for an increase in the military budget by more than half, this seemed political folly. Not wanting to criticize the President, however, most Republicans fell into a deep silence on the issue. Backed into a corner by journalists, the minority leader of the House, the mild-mannered Robert Michel of Illinois, said that the speech might be "a bit of overkill" and worried that people were getting "a general image of [Republicans] being rather macho on the defense budget."[5]

The initiative received a great deal of press attention and was generally treated as a scandal. The April 4 cover of *Newsweek* read: "Star Wars: Will Space Be the Next Battleground?" *Time* magazine, whose cover depicted Reagan against a backdrop of Buck Rogers weaponry, spoke of the President's "video-game vision" and speculated that, although it was "vintage Reagan" in its sweeping simplicity, it was also "partly a political ploy to change the context of the debate over defense spending."[6] Editorialists around the country were generally harsh in their judgments. The *New York Times* called Reagan's idea "a pipe dream, a projection of fantasy in policy." The *Chicago Sun Times* called the speech "an appalling disservice," and the *Atlanta Constitution* warned that the initiative might destabilize the already tenuous military balance between the U.S. and the Soviet Union.[7] Many editorialists seemed unable to decide whether the initiative was dangerous or a transparent hoax—or just a fantasy. In the *New York Times,* Leslie Gelb reported that some administration officials were speculating that Reagan had made the speech in order to divert attention from the freeze movement.[8]

A few days after the speech, White House and other administration officials began beating a public retreat from the President's dramatic announcement. Officials said that the initiative was an idea, not a program, and that it involved directed-energy weapons, which would not be ready for twenty years. They assured reporters that it entailed no more than a change in the emphasis of research, since the Pentagon was already spending a billion dollars a year on conventional and exotic missile-defense technologies. In any case, they said, the March 23 speech was only the first part of a "trilogy," which would include a speech on arms control and a report on the conclusions of the Scowcroft Commission.[9] On March 29 Reagan himself maintained that the initiative would not be a crash program, such as the one that had produced the atom bomb, but merely an extension of the research programs already under way. Asked if he would like to see the research funds doubled or tripled, he said, "I don't see any need for that, no."[10] The question was then: what had he been talking about?

The official backpedaling contributed mightily to the view that the initiative was a fraud and the speech a Wizard of Oz performance designed to distract the public from the administration's enormous military budget and the MX fiasco—and to undercut the freeze. It also made the initiative less newsworthy, so, a week after the speech, the *New York Times* and the *Washington Post* dropped the story and went back to matters generally considered more substantial, such as whether or not the administration was showing any flexibility on its zero-zero INF proposal. A few weeks later *The New Republic* predicted that the Star Wars initiative would be no more than a dim memory in six months' time.[11]

The New Republic was correct, and yet two years later the Strategic Defense Initiative, as Reagan's program was now officially known, was on its way to becoming the largest military-research program the U.S. had ever undertaken. Lieutenant General James A. Abrahamson, a former administrator at NASA who headed the program, was calling for an appropriation of twenty-six billion dollars over five years—or twice as much as the Manhattan Project had cost in current dollars.[12] In press briefings he and other administration experts spoke of the amazing scientific and technological progress that had been achieved since the demise of the old ABM system in the early seventies and described a dazzling array of new technologies, including lasers, particle beams and infrared sensors. The Strategic Defense Initiative was the talk of Washington. That spring the Congress held twenty-three separate hearings on the subject in which distinguished scientists, including Hans Bethe and Sidney Drell, argued with administration experts about the feasibility of population defenses, and prominent foreign-policy experts debated the impact of missile defenses on U.S. relations with the NATO allies and the Soviet Union. The discussion of SDI superseded all other strategic debates and was constantly in the news. Reagan's vision, the *New York Times* reported, had "assault[ed] the core of nuclear philosophy" and was "shaking the foundations of American military policy—strategic doctrine, the shape of military spending, alliance relations and arms control."[13]

How the initiative had managed to attain this importance after its unpromising beginnings was a question not well explained at the time. In 1985 many journalists put the phenomenon of SDI down to the President's long-standing aversion to developments in mutual assured destruction and technology, which had put the promise of exotic weaponry within reach. But there had been no technological breakthrough in the two years since the President's speech. What had happened was that U.S.-Soviet relations, having gone through a period of great tension, had markedly improved, Reagan had won reelection in a landslide and the President's advisers had found policy uses for SDI.

That there was an improvement in U.S.-Soviet relations by the spring of 1985 owed largely to the efforts of Secretary of State George P. Shultz. In

1983 and 1984 Shultz worked long and hard for a change in the administration policy. His efforts were often frustrated, but he kept working doggedly, taking advantage of the opportunities as they arose. Shultz in his own way was as stubborn as Weinberger.

When Haig resigned in June 1982 Reagan and his White House aides chose his successor immediately and with little discussion. In 1980 Shultz had been the first choice of Reagan's transition advisory committee for secretary of state. He was Deaver's candidate, and in the intervening years he had at Deaver's instigation visited the Oval Office several times. With his calm, low-key manner Shultz had impressed Reagan and his national-security adviser, William Clark, as being altogether preferable to the choleric and unpredictable Haig.[14]

Sixty-three years old when he took office, Shultz had had a broad-gauged career in academia, government and business. The son of a Columbia-trained historian who worked for the New York Stock Exchange, he had gone to Princeton, where he majored in economics and played varsity football. When World War II broke out, he joined the Marines and rose to the rank of captain fighting the bloody campaigns across the archipelagos of the Pacific. Afterwards he took a Ph.D. in industrial economics and taught at MIT and the University of Chicago while working as a labor-management mediator. For a period he served on the staff of Eisenhower's Council of Economic Advisers. In 1962 he was appointed dean of the business school of the University of Chicago. In 1968 Nixon made him secretary of labor at the recommendation of Arthur Burns, who had chaired Eisenhower's Council of Economic Advisers. Shultz spent the next six years in government, taking over the Office of Management and the Budget when it was created in 1970, and later moving on to become secretary of the Treasury. In 1974 he left Washington to become president of the Bechtel Corporation in San Francisco and a professor at the Stanford University business school.[15]

As secretary of the Treasury, Shultz was generally considered the most valuable member of the Nixon team next to Kissinger. By reputation he was an able negotiator, a consensus-builder and a firm and effective boss. A large man with a strong, expressionless face, he was known as "the Buddha" or "the Sphinx" for his imperturbability and his capacity for listening to others at length without revealing his position. Those close to him knew that his stone face concealed shrewd insights, a smoldering temper and some very definite views. Unlike Kissinger, he was not—nor did he fancy himself—an intellectual or a geopolitical strategist. He had a pragmatic problem-solving approach to policy, and in the Nixon administration he had become a formidable bureaucratic player.

Why Reagan passed over Shultz in 1980 puzzled many members of his transition team. The two had met in 1974, when Reagan, then in his last year as governor, called Shultz in to quiz him about Washington and the way the presidency worked. Shultz supported the incumbent Gerald Ford in 1976, but members of Reagan's staff, convinced that he would be valuable to Reagan, brought the two together again in 1978, and two years later Shultz chaired Reagan's campaign economic-advisory committee. At the time of the election Deaver was so certain that Shultz was Reagan's choice for secretary of state that he actually thought the President had called to ask him but had muffed the telephone call.[16] What Deaver did not know was that Reagan had acted on Nixon's advice in the matter, and Nixon had not only argued forcefully for Haig's appointment but had advised against choosing Shultz. "George Shultz has done a superb job in every government position to which I appointed him," Nixon wrote. "However, I do not believe that he has the depth of understanding of world issues generally and the Soviet Union in particular that is needed for this job."[17] Nixon may have been influenced by matters closer to home: Haig had served him in many ways, among them assisting with the wiretapping of reporters and NSC staff members, but Shultz had not been close to Nixon, and when Nixon asked him to order the IRS to harass those on the presidential-enemies list, Shultz refused.[18]

In *Turmoil and Triumph,* his memoir of his years as secretary of state, Shultz tells us that on taking office he thought U.S.-Soviet relations the most critical issue to be dealt with, and the one which would require the hardest work. "Relations between the two superpowers were not simply bad; they were virtually non-existent," he writes of mid-1982.[19] In Shultz's view the estrangement was imprudent given the existence of nuclear weapons, and it was self-defeating. Unlike his predecessor, Shultz did not believe that the U.S. could persuade the Soviets to get out of the Third World by holding out the carrot of arms control and trade. Rather, he thought that regional issues, arms control, human rights and other issues had to be addressed separately. In his view the problem that needed immediate attention was the INF talks. The U.S. medium-range missile deployments were scheduled for 1983; if the U.S. did not come off the zero option and begin negotiating, the NATO allies might refuse to accept the missiles, and the Atlantic alliance would break apart.[20] Yet it was six months before Shultz took the first step to change administration policy.

In the Nixon administrations Shultz had been a centrist. But in the Reagan administration there was no center, and in NSC meetings he confronted a phalanx of hard-liners: Weinberger, Casey, Meese, Clark and UN Ambassador Jeane Kirkpatrick. Among the Cabinet officers his main rival was Weinberger. The two men had a history that went back to 1970, when Shultz was made director and Weinberger deputy director of OMB. From the beginning the two had been at odds: Weinberger, the feisty litigator with his hard-edged positions and his lack of reflectiveness, had irritated Shultz, and Shultz, who could be imperious with subordinates, had not bothered to hide his annoyance. Weinberger for his part had chafed under Shultz's authority. The antagonism between them flared up again at Bechtel, where Shultz was the much-respected CEO and Weinberger the aggressive senior attorney. In 1980 Weinberger had lobbied to become secretary of state, and, according to some, he had played a role in persuading Reagan not to appoint Shultz. While Haig was in office, Weinberger had grown accustomed to playing a role in foreign policy, and he held a more powerful position in the administration than Shultz because of his many allies and in particular because of his old friend Bill Clark.[21]

The arrival of Clark as NSC adviser in January 1982 had changed the balance of power in the White House. Previously there had been a "troika" of Baker, Deaver and Meese; with the addition of Clark, there was a foursome and an ideological split down the middle: Baker and Deaver versus Meese and Clark. When Clark found his feet, he took charge of the foreign-policy process, putting some order in the system for the first time and seeing to it that the President was properly briefed. The conservatives loved Clark; they found him kind, considerate and totally loyal to the President's ideals. The pragmatists, on the other hand, thought him a caricature of Reagan—or rather of the image some had of the President. A rancher as well as judge, Clark seemed to see himself as a frontier lawman, for even in Washington he wore hand-tooled cowboy boots and a Stetson and had a U.S. marshall's badge and a Colt .45 on display in his office. His views on foreign policy accorded with this role, and he could not deal with the press.[22] When quizzed by the Senate for his first post as deputy secretary of state, he frankly admitted he didn't know anything about foreign affairs. He had not learned very much in the course of a year, but there were many on the NSC staff and elsewhere in the administration who shared his opinions and were quite willing to advise him. The immediate result was a series of national-security decision directives proposing the rollback of Communism in Eastern Europe and the Soviet Union through economic pressures, propaganda and a defense buildup.[23] Under his regime, Weinberger had unlimited access to the Oval Office, and Casey was frequently called in.

Given the lineup against him, Shultz believed that the only way he could bring about a change in U.S.-Soviet policy was by getting to the President. Not long after taking office, he told Donald Kendall, the powerful Pepsico chairman who favored détente, that the President was "not hopeless" but was stubborn and not ideologically prepared for agreements with the Russians. "We'll have to bide our time," he said.[24]

But the problem of getting to Reagan was not the same as that of getting to any other president, and Shultz, who had never worked with Reagan before, had a good deal to learn about his boss.

In the White House, Reagan had settled into an invariable routine. He and Mrs. Reagan woke at seven or seven-thirty; they breakfasted in bed and read the White House daily news summaries and glanced at the newspapers—the President always looking at the comics and the conservative columnists first. Reagan went to the Oval Office at nine on the dot and fed the squirrels on the terrace before getting down to work. At nine-thirty he had his national-security briefing; from ten to eleven he had "personal time" in which he read, wrote speeches or caught up with correspondence. Every week the White House mail room would give him letters from citizens who had moving stories to tell or who volunteered tokens of affection and support. Reagan would reply to all of them, occasionally writing a small personal check to those in need. At twelve he had a light lunch; and at five o'clock he left the office for the residential quarters in the White House, taking a pile of papers to work on. He exercised for an hour or so, and then, if there was no state dinner, he and Mrs. Reagan would be in their pajamas and robes by six, reading or watching TV, and in bed by ten-thirty or eleven. The Reagans spent most of their weekends by themselves at Camp David and their holidays by themselves at their ranch, north of Santa Barbara. By Lou Cannon's count, they spent 345 days at the ranch—or almost a year in the eight years of Reagan's presidency.[25]

This quiet life and restful routine were not dictated by the President's age. Rather, it was more or less the routine Reagan had followed at least since the 1950s. It was the life of a disciplined, old-fashioned movie star who answers his fan mail and conserves his energies to appear on the set gleaming.

Michael Deaver and his aides did everything possible to make life easy for the Reagans: they arranged the details of their lives, anticipating problems, creating a pleasant, upbeat atmosphere and generally insulating them from the hubbub of life.[26] Another of Deaver's jobs was the stage-managing of Reagan's public appearances—the daily photo opportunities; the two-minute spots for the evening news; the ceremonies in the Rose Garden or on the White House steps. Every word was scripted, and every place where Reagan would stand was chalked with toe marks. "You have to treat him as if you were the director and he was the actor, and you tell him what to say and what not to say," one White House aide explained.[27] Donald Regan, who became Reagan's chief of staff in 1985, was amazed at the time and energy that went into preparing the President's public appearances and the "practically superhuman good nature" with which Reagan performed his tasks. Eventually Regan realized that it was not good nature so much as second nature: Reagan had, after all, been "learning his lines, composing his facial expression, hitting his toe marks for half a century."[28]

Reagan put the same kind of effort into all of his performances. He always wore a coat and tie in the Oval Office, and his shoes, always brilliantly shined, never had crease marks across the instep.[29] Before he entered a room, he would pause at the entrance and prepare, drawing in his breath, squaring his shoulders, sucking in his stomach. Then he would bound into the room, acknowledging the faces turned towards him. He would greet his guests, tell a joke and make a short speech from his three-by-five cards. When he appeared at Cabinet meetings, White House aides were tempted to add directions: enter stage left, action, exit stage right. Often he would sit in silence for most of the meeting, but he would look around the room, making eye contact with everyone looking at him. If he saw a staff aide gazing at him rather than paying attention to whoever was talking, he might wink as though the two of them shared some secret understanding. "He was a compulsive entertainer," wrote Peggy Noonan, his celebrated speechwriter. "He had the American disease—he wanted to be loved."[30]

Every morning the chief of staff gave the President his daily schedule. Reagan followed it scrupulously. He was never late for an appointment; he never allowed any discussion to run beyond its allotted time; and when he was done, he would draw a line through the item to cross it off.[31]

Working for Reagan was a pleasure in that he never decided on the spur of the moment to cancel an appointment and rarely failed to complete what he called his "homework" in the evening. But once he completed an assignment, he seemed to lose interest in it.[32] "They tell me what to do," Reagan once said in the hearing of White House press spokesman Larry Speakes. "Each morning I get a piece of paper that tells me what I do all day long." Speakes thought that in saying this Reagan was belittling himself and his office. But Don Regan came to see that, given the habits of a lifetime, the President regarded the schedule as "something like a shooting script" in which characters came and went and the plot was advanced one day at a time, though not necessarily in chronological order. He came to believe that the very discipline with which Reagan followed the schedule "gave his life a regularity and tangible measure of accomplishment that evidently was deeply pleasing to him."[33]

On the other hand, the Oval Office was not the exciting place it had been in other administrations. The able and ambitious Helene von Damm, who had served as Reagan's secretary in Sacramento and later taken other posts, returned to be his secretary in the White House but quit after a few months out of boredom. "He was never the initiator," she wrote. "He never even asked me to get [Secretary of Commerce] Mac Baldridge or Bill Casey on the phone just because he hadn't heard from them in a while. He would make decisions as they were presented to him."[34] Senator Bob Dole (Republican of Kansas), the chair of the Finance Committee in Reagan's first term and the minority leader in his second, later said that he had never had a private meeting with Reagan. "He did invite a few of us up to the study, twice that I can recall, for Cokes. I don't think I talked to him on the phone about business more than two or three times."[35]

During the first term most of Washington was under the impression that Reagan was a successful executive because, like Eisenhower, he ran a Cabinet government and concentrated on the grand outlines of policy, rather than worrying about the details, as Nixon and Carter had done. This is what Reagan himself claimed to believe, and what Meese, Baker and Deaver told the press. "Surround yourself with the best people you can find, delegate authority and don't interfere as long as the policy you've decided upon is being carried out," Reagan told *Fortune* magazine in 1986, just two months before the disclosure of the Iran arms deals.[36] Yet everyone who worked closely with Reagan over the years knew that his "management style" was, as Martin Anderson put it, "highly unusual, perhaps unique." According to Anderson:

> He made no demands, and gave almost no instructions. Essentially, he just responded to whatever was brought to his attention and said yes or no, or I'll think about it. At times he would just change the subject, maybe tell a funny story, and you would not find out what he thought about it, one way or the other. . . . Rarely did he ask searching questions and demand to know why someone had or had not done something. He just sat back in a supremely calm, relaxed manner and waited until important things were brought to him.

Anderson adds that Reagan's way of operating, which he characterizes as like that of "an ancient king or a Turkish pasha," made him very dependent on his advisers.[37]

Newcomers to Reagan's inner staff always imagined that there would be a moment when the President sat down with them and talked about his objectives and what he expected of them. But that moment never seemed to come. During the transition, Jim Baker and his staff had drawn up a detailed plan for Reagan's first hundred days, and, worried about presuming to tell a man they hardly knew how to spend his first three months in office, they prepared for the presentation as for an exam, trying to anticipate the questions he would ask and working up background material in case he pressed them on any given point. But when they made the presentation, Reagan asked no questions at all. "Sounds great. Go to it," was all he said.[38]

Eventually Baker realized, as John Sears had in California, that Reagan expected his advisers to make the policies—generally consistent with his speeches—and that his job, as he saw it, was to sell the policies to the public.[39] Donald Regan came to much the same understanding. Reagan, he writes,

> chose his aides and then followed their advice almost without question. He trusted his lieutenants to act on his intentions, rather than on his spoken instructions . . .
>
> Never did he issue a direct order, although I, at least, sometimes devoutly wished that he would. He listened, acquiesced, played his role and waited for the next act to be written.[40]

Frank Carlucci, Reagan's NSC adviser in 1987, and his deputy, General Colin Powell, had to find this out for themselves. According to Powell, Reagan would say little at the morning NSC briefings until Carlucci had laid out the options and given his recommendation. "And then the President would merely acknowledge that he had heard him, without saying yes, no or maybe. Frank and I would walk down the hall afterward with Frank muttering, 'Was that a yes?' . . . One morning after we had gotten another decision by default on a key arms control issue, Frank moaned as we left, 'My God, we didn't sign on to run this country!' "[41]

All Reagan's inner-staff members knew how the President operated, but they rarely talked about it among themselves and never told outsiders—not even their subordinates on the White House staff. This discretion was not just a matter of loyalty, it was self-protection: the inner-staff members did not want to admit the extent to which they were making national policy themselves.

To most of his aides and advisers Reagan was an enigma. In meetings he would often keep silent while his advisers battled, then change the subject or tell a story when a decision was due. Cabinet officers and outer-staff members would strain to interpret what he was saying—or attempt to read his body language. According to Cannon, "An imperceptible bobbing of Reagan's head was supposed to mean that he was pleased with a point, while a slight tightening of the mouth was considered a sign of disapproval." The problem came when he did not make any physical movement, leaving staff members to guess "whether or not he had any opinion—or any thought—at all."[42] More often, administration officials simply read into his silence the message they wanted to hear. One NSC staff member told Cannon he was sure that the President favored a negotiated settlement with the Sandinista government in Nicaragua because, when he was given a paper advocating such a settlement, Reagan not only signed it but gave evidence that he had read it by correcting the spelling and punctuation errors.[43] It did not occur to the staff member that Reagan was just correcting the spelling and punctuation—and approving what the latest of his advisers had happened to advocate.

Reagan's passivity placed a tremendous burden on his close advisers. Even those who did not feel uneasy about making policy for Reagan soon realized the penalties they had to pay for it. In deciding any contentious issue, they created bureaucratic winners and losers, and without any clear statement from the President, the losers could claim that "the President's policy" had been subverted by disloyal minions. Guerrilla warfare would ensue, the losers sniping at the winners, leaking to the press and using cutthroat bureaucratic tactics to sabotage the policy. Or someone with access to the Oval Office would slip in and persuade the President to reverse the decision. "The timing of meetings with Reagan is very important," one high Pentagon official said, "because everybody knows that with people he likes, the last one to see him can usually carry the day." Reagan's close advisers therefore became extremely protective of the President. Standing guard over the Oval

Office, they tried to keep members of one or another faction out; failing that, they went in afterwards and had the last word. They felt they had to do this, or the policy would keep on changing, but in the view of outsiders, they isolated the President, kept him like a bird in a gilded cage.[44]

The new secretary of state was an outsider, and he proceeded cautiously.

In September Shultz had his first meeting with Gromyko, but he had nothing new to say, nor did the Soviet foreign minister. In mid-November he went to Moscow for the funeral of General Secretary Leonid Brezhnev. Brezhnev had been ailing for years, and in recent months he had seemed not to be in charge. His successor, Yuri Andropov, had taken office by the time Shultz arrived, and after the funeral Shultz and Vice-President Bush met with the new general secretary. Andropov, who had headed the KGB for many years and led the reformist faction within the Politburo, was himself in poor health. To Shultz he looked like a cadaver, but he projected intelligence and energy. His statement was concise, his manner direct, and he indicated a willingness to ignore the anti-Soviet rhetoric coming out of Washington in the interests of doing business.[45]

On December 6 Dobrynin proposed to Shultz that their governments begin discussions, potentially at all levels, starting with systematic conversations between the two of them. Shultz was keen to respond, but he knew that the hard-liners would oppose any discussions and that he could not move forward without the President.[46]

Shultz then prepared what amounted to the third initiative of December 1982—the first two being the Scowcroft Commission and the SDI speech.

Shultz's first opportunity to talk with the President about U.S.-Soviet relations came at Walter Annenberg's annual New Year's Eve party for the Reagans in Palm Springs. The President had asked Shultz to give him some advice on domestic economics, so, at a favorable moment on the afternoon of the party, Shultz took Reagan and Clark into Annenberg's study, and after discussing economic policy, changed the subject to arms control. Making the case that more attention had to be paid to the INF negotiations, he suggested opening a dialogue with Dobrynin. The President made no decision, but Shultz took encouragement from the fact that Reagan had heard him out.[47]

On January 19, 1983, he sent the President a formal memorandum proposing intensified contacts with the Soviets and a four-part agenda dealing with human rights, regional issues, bilateral economic issues and arms control. He suggested three levels of official contacts—between specialists, ambassadors and foreign ministers—and an eventual summit meeting if the results of the discussions warranted it. After a great deal of arguing with the NSC staff, he gained permission to talk with the Soviet ambassador—but without any authorized agenda. He met with Dobrynin and then made a long trip to the Far East, returning on February 10.[48]

On Saturday, February 12, the day after the Joint Chiefs proposed a missile-defense initiative to the President, Washington was still snowbound. The Reagans could not go to Camp David as they normally did, and that afternoon Nancy Reagan called and invited the Shultzes for dinner in the family quarters of the White House. At dinner Reagan told stories. ("If the president heard a story he liked, he never forgot it," Shultz writes. "And I would hear it again and again, further embellished and perfected with each telling.") Shultz then brought the conversation around to the Soviet Union and China. In the absence of Clark, the President expressed himself freely. Shultz gathered that he wanted to move the relationship with both powers forward, but recognized that it would be difficult given the attitude of his advisers and his own past rhetoric. Somewhat to Shultz's surprise, Reagan expressed a desire to travel to these countries, and he seemed to relish the idea of negotiating with the Communist leaders himself. He spoke of the experience he had had as a negotiator going back to his days as president of the Screen Actors Guild. Realizing that the President had never had a real conversation with a Soviet official, Shultz offered to bring Ambassador Dobrynin over to the White House for a private chat. "Great," the President said. But he added, "We have to keep this secret."[49]

The following Tuesday, when Dobrynin arrived at the State Department for a scheduled visit, Shultz invited the ambassador to go with him to see the President. Dobrynin was delighted, so Shultz bundled him into a limousine in the underground garage and by prearrangement with Deaver spirited him unnoticed through the east gate of the White House and into the family quarters. Shultz thought that Dobrynin, a gregarious man with a fund of amusing stories, would engage Reagan. He was nonetheless prepared for a brief meeting. But Reagan seemed to enjoy himself, and the three men talked for two hours.[50]

According to Shultz, Reagan had given a good deal of thought to the meeting and had serious issues of substance to talk about, from the INF negotiations to Afghanistan. He had, of course, been well briefed by Shultz. Following his script, the President raised the subject of the seven Pentecostal Christians who had taken refuge in the U.S. Embassy in Moscow five years before, and who wanted to emigrate but could not get visas. Shultz thought the issue would attract the President's attention, and he knew it was one which the Soviets could settle if they wanted to make a gesture of good will. Humanitarian ends would be served, and the embassy relieved of its burden. Most important, perhaps, the President could take pride in the success of his personal diplomacy, and, with concrete proof that the Soviets could be flexible, he might be tempted to make further efforts at diplomacy. As it was, Reagan told Dobrynin that the American public would welcome the Soviet move with more enthusiasm than any other bilateral agreement. Dobrynin thought that he was probably right, given the way Americans tended to focus on individual stories. According to Dobrynin, the President also went on at some length about the Marxist-Leninist teaching that the future belonged to Communism and asked how the Soviet Union could possibly feel threatened by U.S. nuclear weapons, given that America had not used them when it had a monopoly on them just after World War II. But he did deliver the message Shultz most wanted to get across: "If you are ready to move forward, so are we."[51]

William Clark was, Helene von Damm reported, "fit to be tied." Informed of the meeting in advance, he had tried and failed to argue the President out of it. Years later he blamed Nancy Reagan and Michael Deaver. "Mike and Nancy were anxious for an outbreak of world peace," he told Lou Cannon sourly. "They thought that by getting Dobrynin into the East Wing, peace would prevail."[52]

Reflecting on the meeting, Shultz told aides that the President wanted to get involved but did not quite know how to do it. His NSC staff had cut him off. Clark, he writes, did not want to let the President move in a new direction, for he feared that, if given his head, the President would make mistakes. Clark and his aides had a good deal of leverage, because the President did not like to act in isolation. Haig, Shultz ruminated, had gotten into trouble because he had tried to get the President to make decisions on his own, or to let Haig make them, when Reagan needed his staff and wanted general agreement before he would act. "The president is not a loner," he told his undersecretary of state, Lawrence Eagleburger. "He does not want to be the subject of an end run. In this instance, he end ran his own staff."[53]

Shultz had, however, noticed that the President had not gone around all of his staff: rather, he had bypassed his NSC adviser in order to do what Michael Deaver and Nancy Reagan urged. Shultz could have kicked himself for not having realized what was happening sooner. The two-week trip he had just taken to the Far East, he writes, had caused him to lose "the taste and feel of the White House"; had he stayed in Washington, he would have been "more attuned to the growing friction between Clark and Deaver." This time, he thought, he had simply been lucky: if it hadn't snowed in Washington, the President would have gone to Camp David; Shultz would not have been invited to dinner with the Reagans, and he would not have had the chance "to gain the insight and opportunity to help him engage directly with the Soviets." In the future, he concluded, he would have to insist on dealing directly with the President.[54]

On February 28 Dobrynin called to say that he had a message from the Soviet government, and that because he was ill he would send it over with his deputy. Shultz, who had been waiting for the message, breached State Department protocol and received the deputy ambassador himself. The news was good: the Soviets were responding positively to the President's intervention on behalf of the Pentecostals. There was more negotiating to be done to resolve the problem, but Shultz felt that his gamble would pay off.[55]

In early March Shultz presented the President with a detailed memorandum entitled "U.S.-Soviet Relations: Where Do We Want to Be and How Do We Get There?" Shultz framed the proposal in rhetoric about the importance of rebuilding U.S. military strength and the need to make it clear that the U.S. would not permit the Soviets to resume their geopolitical expansion. But he reported that the Soviets had showed signs of willingness to move forward on specific issues, such as the Pentecostals and consular affairs, and that there was a chance to go beyond these matters to negotiations on key regional issues, such as Afghanistan and southern Africa, and to make progress towards "a more stable and constructive U.S.-Soviet relationship over the next two years or so."[56]

On March 10 Shultz went to the White House for a meeting that Clark had scheduled for him to discuss the memorandum. The auspices were not good. Two days before, Reagan had delivered his "evil-empire" speech to the National Association of Evangelicals. The speech, Shultz writes, had not undergone any bureaucratic vetting. "No doubt Soviet leaders were offended, and many of our friends were alarmed. How conscious of the implications of their words the President and his speech-writers were, I do not know."[57]

Before the meeting McFarlane gave Shultz a memo "to read and destroy." It urged that the President make a positive response to Shultz's proposal. Clark, he said, had rejected it.

As Shultz walked into the Oval Office, the President took him aside and said, "I don't want all these people to know about Dobrynin"—meaning the ambassador's visit to the White House. The secretary of state was taken aback.

Shultz had expected a more or less private meeting, but, to his discomfiture, the room was filled with people: Clark, McFarlane, Baker, Meese and a number of people he did not recognize. He began by saying that he wanted to speak candidly but that he didn't even know who all these people were.

"This is Richard Pipes," Clark said, gesturing towards the man Shultz happened to be looking at. "He's an NSC member. He's on the payroll."

Shultz, of course, knew of Pipes by reputation, but Clark seemed to be suggesting that he was ill-informed about Soviet affairs and administration personnel if he did not know every face in the room.

Shultz made his case to the President, and afterwards Clark called on Pipes and then on Leslie Lenkowsky, also of the NSC staff, whom Clark described as a "Soviet expert."* Their attitude, Shultz wrote, "was that *after* the Soviets had changed, *then* maybe we can do something with them."

* Lenkowsky later became quite well known. Appointed deputy director of USIA in September 1983, he was never confirmed because he was so insistent that only ideological hard-liners speak for the U.S. abroad that his staff prepared a blacklist of ninety-five people who would not be permitted to go on USIA trips. The list included such people as Walter Cronkite, Paul Samuelson, Senator Gary Hart and Coretta Scott King. When news of the list leaked out,

Shultz was in a temper and didn't bother concealing it. He gathered, he said, that the view of the staff people was that he should stop seeing Dobrynin and should leave things as they were. Many in the room protested that this was not the opinion of the group, and the meeting broke up.[59]

Reflecting on this encounter, Shultz concluded that Reagan wanted to pursue Shultz's agenda but was a prisoner of his own staff. "The president was posturing in front of those guys," he told Larry Eagleburger. "That's why he told me he didn't want to talk about Dobrynin."

Shultz realized that he faced a practical problem. It was not enough for the President to encourage Shultz's plans in private: he would have to say openly and publicly that he wanted a change. "If he doesn't express himself," Shultz told Eagleburger, "the bureaucracy won't react."[60]

That evening Clark called and, speaking as if nothing unusual had happened, said that the President would let Shultz know his decision the following day. The next day, March 11, Shultz had a private conversation with the President, and after he had laid out his agenda again, the President said, "Go ahead." But he said it in such a way that Shultz thought that he, along with Clark, worried that Shultz would go off and make changes in U.S.-Soviet relations that they did not approve. Shultz then knew that he faced "a steep, uphill battle." He would have to keep talking with the President privately, getting his assent to each step proposed, and then seeking ways to get him to "make his own administration *follow through* on his decisions."[61]

The day afterwards Mike Deaver telephoned to say that the President thought there had been too many people in the March 10 meeting, and he wanted Shultz to know that. Deaver added that, whenever Shultz wanted to see the President alone, he should call. Deaver was obviously inviting him to go around Clark. Shultz debated the matter with himself. An end-run around Clark could cause real problems, and he needed a working relationship with the NSC adviser. On the other hand, he had to have regular access to the President, and Clark would not set regular meetings, so the only way was through Deaver. He had decided to take Deaver up on his offer when, on March 24, Clark called and asked him to come and discuss foreign policy with the President in much smaller gatherings a couple of times a week. Shultz laughed when he hung up the phone, wondering whether his office was bugged by the NSC.[62] There was a simpler explanation: March 24 was the day after Reagan's Star Wars speech, and the White House was in turmoil over the disaster.

The following afternoon Shultz had a private meeting with the President. That morning Reagan had heard from his pollster Richard Wirthlin on his standing with the public on foreign policy, and the results were not good.

Lenkowsky lied about his involvement and then blamed it on career USIA officials. When challenged in the Senate Foreign Relations Committee, he uttered the memorable line "I'm prepared to stand by what I meant to say."[58]

Shultz found the President and his NSC adviser far more receptive to his proposals than they had previously been. Reagan said he was "open to a summit meeting" with Andropov and gave Shultz the go-ahead to talk about arms control with Dobrynin between sessions in Geneva. Clark proposed that Shultz put arms-control matters directly to the President without the intervention of the NSC staff.[63]

Clark, however, did not keep his word. Shultz did not get regular private meetings with the President; Clark continued to block even the smallest steps Shultz wanted to take to improve U.S.-Soviet relations and, according to Vice-President Bush, the NSC staff gave the President "absolutely vicious" memos about Shultz's papers for Reagan. When Shultz did meet with the President, he would remind him what he had agreed to in principle the time before and present him with a specific proposal—such as an exchange of consulates. The President would agree, but there would be no follow-through. In interagency meetings, Shultz writes, the topic would not be consular exchanges but, rather, "the same old fundamental question: should the United States have *any* contacts with the Soviet Union. The NSC staff answer was, as ever, a resounding no."[64]

On May 4 the freeze resolution passed the House of Representatives. Two weeks later Reagan said publicly that he was ready to meet with Andropov if he came to the U.S. for the opening of the UN General Assembly session in September. Shultz, who was not consulted on the statement, tells us that he was glad the President knew the direction he was headed in, but that between Clark, who wanted no U.S.-Soviet contacts, and Deaver, who thought that a summit would have political value even if the NSC staff had drained all substance from it, they were headed for disaster. Shultz, however, did not have to worry, for the Soviets did not respond. According to Dobrynin, Andropov dismissed the offer because nothing had been said about it in diplomatic channels and because the American side seemed to have nothing to discuss.[65]

In June, Shultz took what he considered an important initiative. In testimony to the Senate Foreign Relations Committee he made a statement which he said the President had read and approved. Following his text, Shultz pointed up the differences between the U.S. and Soviet systems, argued that the restoration of American military power had restrained the Soviets more effectively than détente and said, "Having begun to rebuild our strength, we now seek to engage the Soviet leaders in constructive dialogue." Shultz's intention was to signal a change in U.S.-Soviet policy, but the statement was as carefully worded and finely balanced as any Politburo utterance, so the message escaped some. The *New York Times* reporter thought it conciliatory, the *Washington Post* reporter found it confrontational.[66]

After his testimony and a long battle with the NSC staff, Shultz was finally given the authority he had been seeking since January to start negotiations on cultural exchanges and the opening of consulates. In July the Soviets agreed to begin these talks, and they concluded a long-term agreement to purchase grain from the United States. In addition, there were U.S.-Soviet talks on improving the hot line between Washington and Moscow and on keeping nuclear weapons out of terrorists' hands.[67] By then Shultz's attempt to get the Pentecostals out of the Soviet Union had succeeded, and the last of the families was allowed to emigrate. Also in July, Andropov wrote Reagan a personal letter expressing a wish for arms reductions. Reagan composed a short, handwritten reply and sent it off without telling anyone except Clark. He assured Andropov that the American people were dedicated to the cause of peace and the elimination of the nuclear threat and called for a "more active level of exchange." Historically, he wrote, "our predecessors have made better progress when communicating has been private and candid. If you wish to engage in such communication, you will find me ready."[68]

In his memoirs Shultz maintains that by August U.S.-Soviet relations had improved to such a degree that "we were witnessing a 'mini-thaw' in the cold war."[69] He might more accurately have said that he had made a very small chip in the glacier of the current relationship. After a year of hard work he had made some progress on a few peripheral issues, but on the central issue of arms control there was no movement at all.

The deal the Scowcroft Commission had brokered between Weinberger and the moderates on the Armed Services Committees was that the administration could have its MX in unprotected silos so long as it made its START proposal more negotiable and less likely to confer a first-strike capability on either side. On May 24 Les Aspin and his Democratic colleagues in the House fulfilled their part of the bargain by approving resolutions to release funding for the MX. The next day the Republican-controlled Senate did the same.[70] But the administration reneged on its part of the deal. After the Scowcroft report appeared, Richard Perle claimed in testimony to the Congress that it endorsed his original view that START should reduce missile throw-weights. Scowcroft was astonished. In a conversation with McFarlane he warned that the commission would not allow the Pentagon to misuse its report. "We think," he said, "that a punitive attempt through arms control to force the Soviets into unilateral throw-weight reductions is not the way to go. Any revision of START in that direction would be counter-productive; it would be disastrous."[71] Perle nonetheless made throw-weight reduction the main subject of interagency discussions, and this time around the Chiefs supported him. Burt objected, but Shultz, who was new to the issue, could not see what was wrong with it. The upshot was a State Department "compromise" plan that gave the Soviets the choice of limiting throw-weights or limiting the number of their heavy, land-based missiles. It was not much of a choice.

Like the first START proposal, it was a call for unilateral Soviet disarmament—until the Soviets could redesign their forces along American lines.[72]

When the proposal came under attack in Congress that fall, the President told a group of congressmen that when he made the first START proposal, the year before, he had no idea that the Soviet strategic forces were concentrated in land-based missiles and thus no idea that his proposal might be interpreted as being one-sided. Asked how he remained innocent of this central fact about the Soviet arsenal, he said, "I never heard any one of our negotiators or any of our military people or anyone else bring up that particular point."[73] Possibly none of them had.

As far as Shultz was concerned, the pressing arms-control issue was that of Intermediate Nuclear Forces. Since the early spring Margaret Thatcher, Helmut Kohl (the new chancellor of West Germany) and other European leaders had clamored for the U.S. to show some flexibility on the INF talks. The deadline for the American missile deployments was in November, and if there was no INF agreement, public protests against the deployments might, they feared, be strong enough to topple West European governments and shake the foundations of NATO. Besides, without an agreement the Soviets would be free to deploy as many SS-20s as they pleased—or enough to overwhelm the American missiles. The entreaties of Thatcher and Kohl were sufficient to prompt a new administration review of the zero-zero proposal and a decision to fashion an "interim agreement" on the way to zero. The position developed by the State Department was that the U.S. should offer to limit its deployments to three hundred warheads if the Soviets would agree to build down to that level. Shultz presented the position at a National Security Council meeting on March 18, arguing that it was necessary to propose a specific number in order to advance the negotiations and to satisfy the needs of the Allies, particularly the British, for a concrete interim proposal. Weinberger, however, argued that the U.S. should not propose a specific number and that there should be no interim agreement unless the Soviets accepted an "eventual zero outcome" in advance of it. The meeting ended in a deadlock.

On March 30 Reagan called for an interim agreement reducing U.S. and Soviet intermediate-range forces to an equal level but without specifying any particular level. This solution was Clark's, and it was a compromise in the sense that the President had rejected Weinberger's insistence that the Soviets accept zero-zero in principle and Shultz's demand for a number. However, it was not a compromise in that, a year and a half into the INF negotiations, it did not constitute an actual arms-control proposal. On April 2 Soviet Foreign Minister Andrei Gromyko rejected the initiative flatly, pointing out that the President had taken no account of the Soviet position at all.[74]

There matters rested until late August, when Reagan, anxious to show flexibility, adopted a proposal fashioned by Richard Burt that was so complicated that even Allied diplomats could not understand it.[75] By that time it was in any case too late: the Soviets had repeatedly said that if there was to be an agreement it would have to come before the U.S. deployments began; the administration refused to delay the deployments or move towards the Soviet position, and an agreement on entirely new terms could not be negotiated in three months.

That fall the tensions between the U.S. and the Soviet Union reached a near-crisis point.

On September 1 a Soviet fighter plane shot down a Korean Air Lines jumbo jet that had wandered a hundred miles into Soviet airspace north of Japan; all 269 people on board, including a U.S. congressman and sixty other American citizens, were killed. Shultz, the only high-ranking official in Washington at the time, called a press conference and, without waiting for any explanation from the Soviets, denounced the attack as appalling and inexcusable. The Soviets expressed indignation that the plane had violated their airspace; they did not admit to having shot the plane down but claimed that it was on a U.S. intelligence mission. On the basis of electronic intercepts, CIA analysts in Washington reported that the Soviets had mistaken the airliner for a spy plane. Shultz did not believe them, and in a speech on September 5 Reagan called the shoot-down a "massacre" and a "crime against humanity." He also said that there was no way that the Soviets could have taken the plane for anything other than a civilian airliner.[76] But the pilot had made a mistake, and since KAL flight 007 had somehow wandered into a gap in the Soviet radar defenses, the local Soviet military commanders had jumped to the conclusion that the U.S. was probing the gap. Their superiors believed them, and, given the rigidities of their system and the state of Cold War tensions, it took a month for Moscow to discover, and to admit, that the pilot had mistakenly shot down a passenger plane.[77] In the meantime, the exchanges between Washington and Moscow were so acrimonious that a war scare developed in Europe. Pope John Paul II warned that the world might be moving from the post-war era to "a new prewar phase," and French President François Mitterrand said that the situation was comparable in its seriousness to the Cuban missile crisis of 1962. But on Shultz's advice the administration took no serious retaliatory action. In his speech of September 5 Reagan said that the U.S. would not call off the arms talks: precisely because of dangerous crises like this one, he said, it was essential to keep on searching for a way to curb the most dangerous weapons of all. Yet he continued to denounce the Soviet action, and the atmosphere remained poisonous.[78]

On September 28 Andropov made a statement unprecedented in the annals of Soviet diplomacy in which he essentially wrote off any improvement in U.S.-Soviet relations for as long as Ronald Reagan remained in office. All the administration was doing in the INF talks, he said, was to "prattle about some sort of flexibility." The new U.S. position was much like the old one: the U.S. was still asking the Soviet Union to dismantle some number of its medium-range missiles in exchange for an increase in NATO missiles. "Even if someone had any illusions about the possible evolution for the better in the policy of the present U.S. administration, the latest developments have finally dispelled them," he said.[79]

On October 25, U.S. forces invaded the tiny island of Grenada, where a left-wing regime that Reagan had long figured a Communist threat to the Caribbean, fell apart, leaving the island in a state of anarchy and a number of American medical-school students stranded. The invasion was very popular in the United States, but the Soviets saw it as an earnest of the administration's willingness to use military power in the Third World.

In early November the U.S. and its NATO allies conducted an exercise to test command-and-control procedures for the use of nuclear weapons in the case of war. Such exercises were fairly routine, but this one, known as Able Archer 83, was more extensive than those in the past, and it involved the participation of higher-level officials, including defense ministers. The KGB had always suspected that if the U.S. were going to launch a nuclear strike it would do so under the cover of a military exercise, and when Able Archer 83 began, some in the KGB headquarters in Moscow warned that the U.S. was preparing to launch a nuclear war. At the time U.S. intelligence had a report of this war scare from a KGB double agent in London, but U.S. officials did not take it very seriously until early 1984, when the CIA reviewed the whole range of intelligence data collected at the time of Able Archer.[80]

The war scare in the Kremlin was not public knowledge, yet the state of tension between Washington and Moscow following the KAL shoot-down was obvious to all. On October 22 and 23 two million Europeans had demonstrated against the impending deployment of the American medium-range missiles. In the United States talk of nuclear weapons dominated the news. In November a group of scientists convened in Washington to consider the question of whether a "nuclear winter" might result from even a small-scale nuclear exchange. That same month ABC Television aired *The Day After*, a two-hour drama about the effects of a nuclear war on Lawrence, Kansas, showing horrifying scenes of death and destruction resulting from firestorms, radiation and the lack of food, water and medical supplies. George Shultz was so disturbed by the film that he appeared on an ABC news show just after the broadcast to reassure its one hundred million viewers that nuclear war was not imminent and to defend the administration's arms-control policies.[81] Unfortunately, the appearance of the real-life secretary of state talking somberly about nuclear weapons gave the movie even more verisimilitude.

In mid-November the Italian and West German parliaments voted to approve the American missile deployment, and on November 23 the first Pershing II missiles arrived in West Germany. That same day the Soviet negotiators walked out of the INF talks in Geneva. When the START negotiations recessed for the holidays on December 8, the Soviet delegation left without setting a date for their resumption. On December 15 Soviet diplomats left the conventional-weapons talks in Vienna, also without setting a resumption date. The Soviet leadership launched a propaganda campaign to persuade Europeans that the American missiles raised the level of the nuclear threat, and Soviet officials castigated the Reagan administration, often in the same terms U.S. officials had used about them, charging that the administration was "bent on world domination" and wanted to "launch a decapitating nuclear first strike."[82]

In mid-December Shultz returned from a NATO foreign ministers' meeting to find that the President wanted to give a major speech calling for the elimination of nuclear weapons.

In his discussions of U.S.-Soviet relations in his memoir, Shultz passes fairly quickly over the year from the fall of 1983 to the fall of 1984. Yet during this period he worked extremely hard to reestablish the relationship, and for the first time he had full cooperation from the White House and a minimum of interference from the rest of the bureaucracy. In other words, just as the doors in Moscow clanged shut, the doors in Washington sprang open to him.

One reason for this change of direction was the departure of William Clark and the resolution of the power struggle that had been going on in the White House for the past two years. The dénouement of the conflict was pure theater. It was also an important turning point for the Reagan presidency.

The beginning of the end came in late July 1983, when William Clark appeared on the cover of *Time* magazine with a story describing him as the new power in the administration's foreign policy. As *Time* reporters pointed out, Clark, with the backing of the hard-liners, had taken control of Central American policy some months before and with his "big stick approach" had managed to create a major confrontation with the Congress.[83]

Official U.S. policy in Central America—and the only one the Congress would support—was to bolster the anti-Communist forces and to use the military pressure to bring about a negotiated settlement in the region. In the settlement envisaged by the State Department, the left-wing Sandinista government of Nicaragua would agree to dismiss its Cuban advisers, stop interfering with its neighbors and open up its political process. Hard-liners in the administration, however, saw negotiations as a disguise for surrender: they wanted to bring the Sandinista government down. How they would do this was not obvious even to themselves, for the contras, the anti-Sandinista guerrillas supported by the CIA, had small hope of defeating the Sandinistas on their own, and the Pentagon—as well as the Congress and the public—opposed sending American troops into combat in Central America. Nonetheless, they sabotaged the State Department's somewhat feeble attempts to create a negotiating track and planned a series of military and paramilitary operations.

In May an interagency committee headed by Clark authorized the CIA to mine Nicaragua's harbors and to attack its port facilities with high-speed patrol boats—using its own agents. Shultz managed to persuade the President to derail the plan. Then, in July, the Pentagon, with Clark's approval, launched a six-month-long military exercise, Big Pine II, that included naval maneuvers around Nicaragua and U.S. troop deployments in Honduras. Shultz was not given advance notice of the exercise, and had to read about it in the newspapers.[84]

A few days after the launching of Big Pine II, Shultz discovered that Clark had sent McFarlane on a secret mission to the Middle East. Furious, he went to see the President and threatened to resign. In front of Bush, Baker, Meese and Clark, whose presence he had requested, Shultz complained of the decisions that had been made behind his back and in strong language took the President to task for undercutting him and making it impossible for him to do his job. "You can conduct foreign policy out of the White House, but you don't need me under those circumstances," he said. If Reagan wanted an errand boy, he could get someone else. Shultz went on to suggest some names the President might consider in choosing his successor. "Bill Clark seems to want the job," he said, "because he is trying to run everything. There is also Jeane Kirkpatrick. Or Henry Kissinger. You can get lots of good people."

The President, Shultz writes, was visibly shaken. He told Shultz that he had no idea how these things happened but could understand how they affected him, and urged Shultz to stay on. Shultz agreed, though he didn't believe the President would make any changes.[85]

Big Pine II, however, raised fears in the United States that the administration was going to send American troops into combat in Central America. On July 28 the House of Representatives voted 228 to 195 to shut off aid to the contras, handing the administration the worst legislative defeat it had yet sustained. The following day the *Time* cover story on Clark appeared. That day Nancy Reagan called Shultz in a fury and said that Clark ought to be fired. Shultz then assumed it was only a matter of time.[86]

In mid-September, Clark made one more mistake. With Meese's approval he had the President sign a letter asking the attorney general to conduct an FBI investigation into a news leak from the White House. This was far from the first of such orders, for, given their dislike of journalists and their ineptitude at dealing with them, Meese and Clark lived in a constant state of frustration about leaks, most of which they assumed emanated from Baker and his staff. But this was the first order specifically authorizing polygraph testing as a part of a criminal investigation.[87]

Baker found out about the letter the same morning and, certain that the investigation was aimed at him, barged into the private dining room, where Reagan was lunching with Vice-President Bush and Shultz, and told the President that the order would have dire consequences. It would mean that even the vice-president and the secretary of state could be given lie-detector tests—and did the President really want that? Shultz said that if anyone tried to polygraph him they would do it only once. Bush agreed that the order was a bad idea. Upset by the ruckus, Reagan said, "Bill shouldn't have done that"—though, of course, he had signed the letter himself.[88]

Thereafter the President treated Clark coolly, and Mrs. Reagan wouldn't speak to him. Clark began to look for a way to leave the White House. When James G. Watt, the secretary of the interior, was forced to resign in early October, Clark volunteered to take his place, and the President happily agreed.*[89]

With the NSC job open, Baker and Deaver took matters into their own hands. They decided that Baker should succeed Clark and that Deaver should become chief of staff. They discussed the idea with Nancy Reagan, Bush and Shultz, all of whom approved it enthusiastically. They then informed the President, who approved the appointments, but otherwise they kept the plan a secret, for they knew the conservatives would block it unless it were a fait accompli.

On Friday, October 14, White House reporters were told to be in the briefing at 4:00 P.M. for an announcement. The President lunched with Shultz. He was then scheduled to attend a National Security Planning Group meeting, where he would make the announcement. But he lingered in Deaver's office, and Clark, who was extremely punctual, came up the stairs to find him and bring him down to the Situation Room. On the way down Reagan casually told Clark that he was going to appoint Baker as his successor. Clark asked him to delay the announcement until after the meeting.

During the meeting Clark passed notes to Weinberger, Casey and Meese, and afterwards the four gathered in Clark's office with the President. All four objected vehemently to Baker's appointment, arguing that this would send the wrong signal to the Soviets and that it would be dangerous to have a leaker like Baker as head of the NSC staff.

* Praising a commission that was reviewing the Interior Department's coal-leasing program on September 21, Watt said, "We have every kind of mix you can have. I have a black, I have a woman, two Jews and a cripple. And we have talent." A former New Right activist, Watt was not known for his political sensitivities, but this was too much. Senator Paul Laxalt, who paid much attention to the Interior Department, advised Watt to resign and started looking for a replacement.[90]

On his return to the Oval Office, Reagan buzzed for Baker and Deaver. "The fellas have a real problem with this," he told them. "I want to think about it over the weekend."[91]

In his diary for that day Reagan wrote, "Jim took it well, but Mike was pretty upset.... Not a pleasant evening what with all the hassle over the NSC spot."[92]

On Monday, after a weekend of taking calls from conservatives, Reagan decided against Baker. He also decided against Jeane Kirkpatrick, the conservatives' candidate for the NSC job. Choosing the line of least resistance, he picked the distant second choice of both factions: Robert McFarlane.

The decision was a blow to Baker and Deaver—and particularly to Deaver, who had served Reagan for sixteen years. Exhausted by the constant battling with the conservatives, and disappointed with Reagan, they decided they would not stay on in their positions for a second term. Baker thought about leaving to become commissioner of baseball but was persuaded to remain at his job through the presidential campaign the following year.[93]

In his memoir Reagan wrote, "I had no idea at the time how significant ... my decision not to appoint Jim Baker as national security adviser ... would prove to be."[94] The implication was that Baker would have saved him from the Iran-contra affair.

Still, for the present, the replacement of Clark by McFarlane was a boon to the President. McFarlane was not a hard-liner, and he did not object when Deaver gave Shultz complete access to the Oval Office. On U.S.-Soviet relations he tended to take Shultz's side, and he was supported by Jack Matlock, an experienced foreign service officer who had succeeded Richard Pipes as the Soviet specialist on the NSC staff.[95] McFarlane's appointment shifted the balance of forces in the White House to "the pragmatists"—and it permitted Reagan to run an almost perfect campaign.

To reporters and pundits the 1984 campaign was one of the least exciting and least illuminating on record. In a memo Baker's aide Richard Darman wrote, "Paint Reagan as the personification of all that is right with, or heroized by, America. Leave [former Vice-President Walter] Mondale in a position where an attack on Reagan is tantamount to an attack on America's idealized image of itself—where a vote against Reagan is, in some subliminal sense, a vote against a mythic AMERICA."[96] And that was exactly what was done. President Reagan, who was judged by much of the press to be the "inevitable" victor from the beginning, conducted his campaign as if it were a royal progress, rarely joining the political fray and rarely holding press conferences or speaking to reporters. His campaign was dominated by commercials proclaiming that "America Is Back" and that it was "Morning Again in America"—commercials with soft, stirring music, and with images of farm families raising the American flag and Olympic athletes passing the torch. "Reagan is rebuilding the American dream," a voice-over intoned. Even at the Republican convention the star was not so much Reagan himself as the filmed tribute to Reagan showing him performing the ceremonial roles of his office with charming naturalness. In his speeches Reagan celebrated the country's economic rebound and its spiritual recovery from a sense of impotence and injured pride. Reporters waited for some new idea, some new program or even some sense of the direction he would take in his second term. None came.[97] But the Reagan campaign was more carefully calibrated than most understood at the time.

In calculating Reagan's chances for reelection at the beginning of 1984, Republican strategists noted that of the two major issues in any presidential campaign—peace and prosperity—Reagan had high marks on the second. He had taken office in a period of double-digit inflation, high unemployment and economic stagnation. Since then the Federal Reserve's tight money policy had wrung the inflation out of the economy. It had also created a deep recession. But thanks in part to Reagan's tax cuts and deficit spending, the economy had quickly rebounded, creating a record number of jobs. Business investment was up, unemployment down and the stock market bullish. As a result, Reagan's overall job-approval rating had climbed from a low of 35 percent in the depths of the recession to a healthy 53 percent in January 1984. On economic issues Reagan was the clear winner—all the more so because Mondale, his opponent, could be tagged with the horrendous stagflation of the Carter years. But on war-peace issues Reagan had serious vulnerabilities. On the one hand, Americans considered him a strong leader who had rebuilt the nation's defenses and restored a sense of national pride. On the other hand, they were nervous about him. Wirthlin's polls of early September 1983 showed that only 41 percent of Americans approved of Reagan's handling of foreign policy. Nicaragua was, Wirthlin said, "pure poison" in the polls; the U.S. involvement in a peacemaking mission in Lebanon was unpopular as well, and particularly so after October 23, when a terrorist bomb killed 241 U.S. Marines in their barracks. The public was evenly split on whether Reagan's handling of the Soviet Union was increasing or decreasing the chances of war.[98] After the Soviets walked out of the arms talks in December, the President's ratings sank lower still. At the beginning of 1984 Gallup polls showed that the public rated the threat of war and international tensions as by far the most important problems facing the country. In addition, most Americans believed that Reagan had not done enough to bring about disarmament and thought the Democrats more likely to keep the country out of war.[99]

Accordingly, the Reagan campaign took two different approaches. On domestic issues the strategy was simplicity itself. Reagan framed the election as a choice between the bad old days of "Carter-Mondale," with their high "misery index," and the prosperity of the present. Though calling the campaign a contest between "two visions of America," Reagan avoided the social issues of the religious right and, in sharp contrast to 1980, he said nothing about cutting social spending. In sum, he stood squarely on the status quo. But on foreign and defense issues there was a great deal to be done.

Between November 1983 and June 1984 Reagan traveled to Japan, Korea, China, Ireland, Britain and France. In none of these countries did he have any substantive task to accomplish, but foreign travel normally gives presidents the aura of statesmanship—and Reagan had not traveled overseas very much until then. On his visit to China, his first to a Communist country, he signed agreements on investments and cultural exchanges which had already been negotiated, and he gave speeches extolling faith in God, the power of freedom and the magic of the marketplace.[100] In Tokyo he made a speech in the Japanese Diet calling for the elimination of nuclear weapons, and in South Korea he addressed the American forces and was photographed looking out from a bunker across the DMZ. In France he spoke at Pointe du Hoc and Omaha Beach on the anniversary of D-Day, celebrating the heroism of the American troops who fought there and recalling the glory days of World War II. Meanwhile, to the intense dismay of administration hard-liners, he allowed the Congress to cut all aid to the contras with hardly a word of protest.[101]

Conspicuously missing from Reagan's repertoire that year was the "standard-threat speech" with its strident rhetoric about the Soviet military buildup and its pitch for more defense spending. Gone were warnings about the vulnerability of the American deterrent. The U.S., Reagan said in January, was "in its strongest position in years": its economy was recovering, its defenses were being rebuilt and "restored deterrence" was making the world a safer place.[102] In his acceptance speech at the Republican convention, Reagan spoke as if America's defenses had already been rebuilt; later he asserted that the United States was no longer "inferior" in military power to the Soviet Union.[103]

That Reagan had so sharply revised his estimates was curious in that the military balance had hardly changed at all in the course of four years. True, the Pentagon was spending a great deal of money developing new strategic weapons, but in terms of deployed weapons, the U.S. had fallen slightly behind where it was in 1980, for it had retired some of its older Titan missiles and had not yet deployed the MX. Reagan, however, was perfectly safe in making these statements, for there was a rough parity between the U.S. and the Soviet Union, just as there had been in 1980. The Democrats were not about to attack him for acknowledging it; the public assumed that more defense spending must mean more defense; and the Republicans were happy to take credit for solving a problem that did not exist. When Senator Steve Symms, a conservative Republican from Idaho, was asked how he calculated that the military gap had closed, he said, ". . . just Ronald Reagan's election made us stronger. . . . It's a state of mind."[104]

• • •

In his campaign plan of September 1983, Richard Wirthlin wrote that "a year from now the claim that the Reagan administration has maintained the peace would be fortified if we could show some progress in negotiating an arms settlement."[105] The following year the President's position on U.S.-Soviet relations softened appreciably.

On January 16 Reagan made a major speech in which he admitted, "Our working relations with the Soviets are not what they might be," and vowed to engage the Soviets in a dialogue to promote peace in the Third World, to reduce the level of arms and to build a "constructive" relationship. He made no specific proposal, but his remarks contrasted sharply with the official rhetoric of the past three years. As if speaking to members of his own administration, he said, "Neither we nor the Soviet Union can wish away the differences between our two societies and our philosophies. But we should always remember that we have common interests. And foremost among them is to avoid war and reduce the level of arms." In the past Reagan had claimed that the Soviets were the cause of all the trouble in the world, but in this speech he said that most of the conflicts going on in the world "have their origins in local problems," and he expressed the hope that actions might be taken to reduce the risk of a superpower confrontation arising out of them. There was, he said, "no rational alternative" to steering a course of "credible deterrence and peaceful competition" in the hopes of finding areas of "constructive cooperation." Having explored the alternative, he had apparently thought better of it. "Nineteen eighty-four," he said, "is the year of opportunities for peace."[106]

In the same speech Reagan said that he favored "a zero option on all nuclear arms" and declared that his "dream" was to "see the day when nuclear weapons will be banished from the earth." Because the Soviets had ritualistically been calling for the abolition of nuclear weapons for about forty years, and because the President otherwise endorsed deterrence, reporters paid no attention to these remarks.[107]

Two days after the speech Shultz met with Gromyko at a conference in Stockholm. The President had authorized him to offer greater flexibility in the U.S. approach to the START talks, including a recognition of "the different structures of our respective strategic systems."[108] This meant that the administration would no longer be asking the Soviets to redesign their forces along American lines. In Stockholm, Shultz listened to Gromyko give a "brutal" speech, accusing the U.S. of a variety of crimes against humanity, but their private meeting went well. Shultz thought that Gromyko was looking for a formula that would allow the Soviets to return to the arms talks without losing face. However, Gromyko refused to mention the discussion in public, and later Andropov wrote the President a letter criticizing the INF deployments in Europe and saying, "There is no way of making things look as if nothing had happened. . . . A heavy blow has been dealt to the very process of nuclear arms limitations."[109] Having just walked out of the arms talks, the Soviets were not ready to walk right back in.

On February 9 Andropov died and was replaced by Konstantin Chernenko, an aging party boss and former crony of Brezhnev's with an advanced case of emphysema. Chosen by the Politburo as a transitional figure, Chernenko, according to Dobrynin, looked to Gromyko for his direction in foreign affairs.[110]

According to Shultz, a number of political people urged Reagan to attend Andropov's funeral, but after a brief debate it was decided that he should not go. Reagan wrote a letter of condolence, and Vice-President Bush led the delegation to Moscow.

Bush cabled back that Chernenko "looks almost as young as Reagan, ruddy, almost tanned in appearance . . . not polemical, more relaxing to be with than Andropov. Twinkle in his eye, speech quick and precise. Fellow you feel you could talk to, no impression that he is slow of mind." The report was puzzling in that journalists on the trip portrayed Chernenko as sickly, gasping from emphysema and too weak to salute all the Soviet troops marching by Lenin's tomb.[111]

On February 23 Chernenko replied to Reagan with a letter that, according to Shultz, was relatively warm in tone.

Shultz took the occasion to develop a framework for U.S.-Soviet relations, including a checklist of some thirty-nine items for discussion and a timetable of meetings between the ambassadors, and between himself and Gromyko. As a first step he drafted a reply from Reagan to Chernenko on the strategic-arms talks, declaring that the administration intended not to "attempt to restructure your forces without any attendant change in our forces" but to achieve "significant reductions in the strategic systems of both sides." On March 7 he discussed the letter with Dobrynin and suggested ways in which it might be followed up.[112]

According to Shultz, Dobrynin called the exchange "a good effort," but soon afterwards the tone shifted, and Chernenko in his next letter complained about the "strategic threat" of the INF deployments in Europe, and in addition about the "development of large-scale ABM systems"—a reference to talk in Washington about a prospective strategic-defense program.[113] By May, Reagan had written Chernenko five letters and received as many replies. But their letters were no longer warm, and though Shultz continued to talk with Dobrynin, making proposals "on a wide range of issues," he received no positive response.

Also in May the Soviets announced that they would not participate in the Olympic Games to be held in Los Angeles that July, because of inadequate security arrangements for their athletes. After the invasion of Afghanistan the Carter administration had instructed American athletes to boycott the 1980 Olympics in Moscow. Four years later the Soviets had decided to retaliate with another political boycott. In late July the Soviets publicly proposed talks on preventing the "militarization of outer space," but when Shultz accepted on condition that the talks be expanded to include offensive strategic weapons, they turned the counter-offer down.[114] Meanwhile, the Soviet press denounced Ronald Reagan in virulent terms. The Soviets, Shultz later wrote, seemed to be combining delaying tactics in private with propaganda in public. Clearly they hoped to turn the Europeans against the INF deployments, and the American voters against Ronald Reagan, but they did not want to burn their bridges, for they were not sure they would succeed.[115]

This is Shultz's version of what happened that spring. But to read Reagan's memoir is to see that Shultz is not being entirely candid about the reason for his strenuous diplomatic efforts and the flurry of letters between Reagan and Chernenko. Shultz wanted to restore the relationship on general principles, but Reagan had something quite specific in mind, and far higher hopes for what Shultz called "realistic reengagement" than the press or the public knew at the time.

In his three years in Washington, Reagan writes, he had learned something surprising about the Russians: many people at the top of the Soviet hierarchy were "genuinely afraid of America and Americans." To his amazement he found that Soviet officials "feared us not only as adversaries but as potential aggressors who might hurl nuclear weapons at them in a first strike." Well, if that was the case, he writes, "I was anxious to get a top Soviet leader in a room alone and try to convince him that we had no designs on the Soviet Union and Russians had nothing to fear from us." In something of a non-sequitur, he adds that the balance in the arms race had changed in favor of the United States, and that was sure to get the Russians' attention.[116]

Reagan quotes his January 16 speech at length and goes on to observe that Andropov criticized it harshly not long before he died. George Bush, he writes, led the delegation to the funeral and came back with the report that Chernenko was "less hard-nosed and abrasive" than his predecessor. Here Reagan includes an excerpt from his diary of that date: "I have a gut feeling I'd like to talk to him [Chernenko] about our problems man to man. . . . I have our team considering an invitation to him to be my guest at the opening of the Olympics, July in L.A. Then he and I could have a session together in which we could start the ball rolling for an outright summit on arms reductions, human rights, etc. We'll see."[117]

Here Reagan is giving a fine performance as Ronald Reagan writing his diary. Chernenko was not the man to inspire a "gut feeling" in anybody. But Reagan wanted a meeting with him—no matter how unpropitious the circumstances—and Bush's unlikely description of the new general secretary was surely designed to egg the President on.

Chernenko's first letter was not encouraging, but Reagan remained optimistic. "Despite the rebuff from Moscow," he writes, "I still felt that the time had come to explore holding a summit conference with Chernenko."

His feeling, he now explains, had nothing to do with the man he would be having the man-to-man talk with. "Chernenko," he writes, "was cut from the same cloth as Brezhnev and Andropov—a tough, old-line Communist addicted to Lenin's secular religion of expansionism and world domination. . . ." Rather, it came from another gut instinct: "I felt we could now go to the summit from a position of strength."[118]

In his diary Reagan wrote of the "exciting hours" he spent at a JCS briefing on the achievements of the Pentagon in the past three years. Then, on March 2, he wrote: "I'm convinced the time has come for me to meet with Chernenko about July 1. We're going to start with some ministerial-level meetings on a number of substantive matters that have been on ice since the KAL 007 shoot-down." By his account only Bush, Shultz, Weinberger and McFarlane were involved in the planning.[119]

On March 5 he writes: "Helmut Kohl, West German chancellor, arrived. We had a good meeting and lunch. . . . He too thinks I should meet Chernenko."

And on March 7: "George Shultz and I met. Our plans about the Soviet Union are going forward. He is giving Ambassador Dobrynin my letter for delivery to Chernenko."[120]

Dobrynin, however, told Shultz that the Soviet leadership was not interested in a summit, and Chernenko in his reply stated that he had no interest in pursuing a dialogue without "acts of concrete, weighty substance" on the part of the United States—by which he meant removing the INF missiles from Europe. But Reagan would not take no for an answer. Even after the Soviets announced they were not coming to the Olympics, he continued to pester Shultz to keep probing for a summit. "I had a gut feeling we should do this," he wrote in his diary, and Shultz obediently "worked hard in meetings with Dobrynin and other Soviet officials through the spring and summer of 1984 to reopen a U.S.-Soviet dialogue, but without much success."[121]

Unable to get a summit, Reagan made do with reassuring speeches. Throughout that election year he continued to insist that the U.S. and the Soviet Union had common interests, and the first among them was reducing the danger of nuclear war. "A nuclear war can never be won and must never be fought" was a line he used often that year.[122] He called for arms reductions and for a "better understanding" with the Soviets, and spoke of his fervent desire to see the elimination of all nuclear weapons. He made no specific proposals, but his peace rhetoric was so consistent that, in the foreign-policy debate between the two candidates in October, Mondale felt it necessary to say, "Mr. President, I accept your commitment to peace, but I want you to accept my commitment to a strong national defense."

In his closing statement in that debate Reagan described himself driving along the Pacific-coast highway wondering what he was going to say in a letter that was to be placed in a time capsule. What, he asked, would those who dug the capsule up a hundred years hence think of how we dealt with our problems of living in a world of "nuclear weapons of terrible destructive power aimed at each other, capable of crossing the ocean in a matter of minutes and destroying civilization as we knew it"? He did not say how the catastrophe would be averted, but it was a beautiful speech, and reporters did not remember that he had made the same one at the Republican convention of 1976.* [123]

In late August the White House issued an invitation to Gromyko to meet with the President when he came to the United States to attend the opening of the UN General Assembly session in late September. In the past the Soviet foreign minister had visited the White House every year on this occasion, but after the Soviets invaded Afghanistan, President Carter withheld the invitation, and Reagan did not renew it. Shultz asked Reagan whether he would be willing to reinstate the invitation without a change in Afghanistan, proposing that he think the matter over. Reagan replied that he didn't need to think about it. It was the right thing to do.[125]

Reagan, Shultz writes, regarded the meeting with Gromyko as "one of critical importance." He prepared for it intensively, and consulted with former President Nixon and with Henry Kissinger. He even rewrote the talking points Shultz gave him to set the tone and to make it clear to Gromyko that the United States wanted peace. "This was vintage Ronald Reagan," Shultz comments; "it came from the inside out." On September 24 Reagan gave a conciliatory speech at the UN in which he uttered not a word of criticism about the Soviet Union and made an almost maudlin plea that the superpowers "approach each other with ten-fold trust and thousand-fold affection" for the sake of world peace.[126] Gromyko did not return the favor; his speech was a barrage of accusations and recriminations so vitriolic that Shultz felt obliged to respond. Nonetheless, the treatment he received at the White House was, Shultz noted, "of a magnitude greater than anything given to any other foreign minister and was on a scale with the visit of a head of government." [127]

In the morning meeting Reagan and Gromyko made formal speeches, and when it broke up, the President asked the foreign minister to stay behind in the Oval Office for a private discussion. He had previously told his aides that he wanted a face-to-face conversation with Gromyko, but he did not tell them what it would be about.

The door of the Oval Office was left ajar so that the duty officer could

* Reagan almost undid all of this work on August 11, when, during a microphone check for his weekly Saturday radio speech, he joked, "My fellow Americans, I am pleased to tell you today that I've signed legislation that will outlaw Russia forever. We begin bombing in five minutes." The remark was dismissed by officials as harmless clowning, but after it Wirthlin's polls showed a significant increase in the percentage of Americans who thought Reagan might get the country into a war.[124]

peep in, in case the President summoned him. The President and the foreign minister exchanged a few words—Gromyko speaking English. Then the President retired to his private bathroom, emerged and asked Gromyko if he wanted to use it. Gromyko did. The duty officer did not hear what was said, so Reagan's aides, inflamed with curiosity, were not sure whether the President had forgotten his intention to talk with Gromyko in private, changed his mind or what.

Gromyko later told Dobrynin that he didn't know what all the excitement was about. The President, he said, had told him, as if this were a big secret, that his personal dream was a "world without nuclear arms." He replied that nuclear disarmament was the "question of questions," and both agreed that the eventual goal should be the complete elimination of nuclear weapons. And that was that.[128]

The meeting, the first President Reagan had had with a member of the Soviet leadership, was a huge press event. An immense throng of reporters and photographers turned out for it and went through the Oval Office in waves taking pictures and shouting questions.[129] But by that time the publicity was no longer crucial, for the game that the Politburo and the administration had been playing for a year was almost at an end. Reagan was way ahead of Mondale in the polls, and Gromyko knew it.

On November 6 Ronald Reagan was reelected in a landslide, carrying forty-nine states and receiving the largest electoral vote in U.S. history. In an election-day interview with Lou Cannon he spoke of his desire for a line item veto and balanced-budget amendment to the Constitution—two chimerical solutions to the problem of reducing the deficits. He also said that his first priority was "peace, disarmament," and that a defense against missiles would be the greatest incentive for the Soviets to reduce or eliminate their missiles.[130] On November 15 he sent Chernenko a letter drafted by Shultz proposing umbrella talks on space weapons and offensive arms, including strategic and INF systems. Chernenko accepted, and a meeting between Gromyko and Shultz was set for early January 1985.[131]

BY THE FALL OF 1984 the proposal Reagan had made in his March 1983 speech materialized into a major research program, the Strategic Defense Initiative.

Reagan said almost nothing about the program during the campaign—he had hardly mentioned anti-missile defenses since the spring of 1983—and the initial funding request for the program was fairly low. "There was a conscious decision not to invest more in it this year, because it's an election year," one official told the *Washington Post*. "He's low-keyed the program."[132] Conservatives urged the President to press the issue, but many Republicans in Congress looked askance at SDI, and Reagan's political advisers wouldn't hear of it. "Everyone knew Reagan was for defense," Reagan's pollster Richard Wirthlin explained succinctly.[133] When Senator Wallop and others on the Republican platform committee drafted a call to build an anti-missile system—as opposed to researching defensive technologies—McFarlane sent his deputy to the convention to try to stop them. Senator John Warner (Republican of Virginia), speaking, he said, with the authority of the President, the secretary of defense and the nation's military leaders, told the committee that the attempt to develop an anti-missile defense would be premature and subversive of the nation's military structure. The plank passed nonetheless, and that evening the President himself called Representative Marjorie Holt, the co-chair of the platform committee, to ask that as a personal favor she delete the passage about the party's commitment to building an anti-missile device. Holt replied that the favor was not hers to give, but the word "build" was changed to "achieve."[134]

During the campaign Walter Mondale condemned Star Wars as a dangerous hoax that would cost untold billions, speed up the arms race and fail to provide any real protection.[135] Reagan responded only when he had to, and then vaguely. In the foreign-policy debate with Mondale he called SDI a research program to see if there wasn't "a defensive weapon to defend against incoming missiles," and offered to share the technology with the Soviets and "free mankind" from the threat of nuclear weapons.[136]

Yet in mid-June a high administration official had told a reporter that President Reagan would redouble his efforts on behalf of the program if he were returned to office. The President, the official said, had an abiding interest in SDI and believed it a moral imperative.[137] Sure enough, just as soon as the election results were in, the President said that SDI would be the greatest incentive to the Soviets to reduce or eliminate their missiles, adding, "since we've proven that it's possible to be invulnerable to such an attack."[138] The statement struck reporters as significant, because Reagan had proposed little else for his second term.

In the months after Reagan's reelection administration officials, including those most disturbed by Reagan's 1983 speech, publicly professed faith in SDI in a manner that reminded former Deputy Secretary of State George Ball of the mass conversion decreed by King Ethelbert of Kent in the sixth century.[139] High officials spoke of "the President's vision" and vowed fealty to Reagan's "ultimate goal." Secretary Weinberger went as far as to say that SDI was "the only thing that offers any real hope to the world."[140]

In early 1985 Secretaries Weinberger and Shultz announced that SDI would play a central role in U.S. policy and that it was crucial to the stability of the strategic relationship with the Soviet Union and to hopes for reducing the threat of nuclear war. Quoting from the Defense Department posture statement for 1985, Undersecretary of Defense Fred Iklé told the Senate Armed Services Committee, "The Strategic Defense Initiative is not an optional program, at the margin of the defense effort. It's central, at the very core of our long-term policy for reducing the risk of nuclear war."[141] The President highlighted the program in his second inaugural address and thereafter devoted numerous speeches and press interviews to it, claiming on one occasion that "it could save millions of lives, indeed humanity itself."[142]

In March, when the administration's first major funding request for SDI went to Congress, journalists from the major news organizations took the opportunity to review the development of the program, the claims made for it and the controversies that had surrounded it since its inception. The task was not easy, for the subject was arcane and the research largely classified.

Two days after the speech Clark and McFarlane had issued a national-security decision directive (NSDD-85) calling for a long-term research-and-development plan to achieve the President's goal of the "elimination of the threat of ballistic missile attack." Three weeks later they produced a national-security study directive (NSSD 6-83) asking the Department of Defense to study and report on how a research-and-development program might be shaped "to achieve our ultimate goal of eliminating the threat posed by strategic nuclear missiles."[143] Caspar Weinberger had by then embraced the initiative. Appearing on NBC's *Meet the Press* on March 27, 1983, he had vowed fealty to the President's goal of developing "technologies that can insure that we would have an ability to protect people from Soviet missiles falling on this soil." The defense systems, he said, "are not designed to be partial. What we want to try to get is a system which will develop a defense that is thoroughly reliable and total." He added, "I don't see any reason why that can't be done."[144]

Under Weinberger's direction the Pentagon proceeded to establish three study groups: the Defense Technologies Study Team, chaired by Dr. James C. Fletcher, a former NASA director; the Future Security Strategy Study group, chaired by Fred S. Hoffman, the president of a defense consulting firm; and an interagency working group on strategy, chaired by Franklin C. Miller, the director of the Office of Strategic Forces Policy at the Pentagon. By March 1984 the Fletcher and Hoffman panels had delivered reports recommending that the Pentagon undertake a major research program in anti-ballistic missile technologies. The Fletcher panel, composed of fifty prominent scientists and engineers, mainly from private industry, universities and the national weapons labs, produced a seven-volume study laying out the requirements for a countrywide defense against ballistic missiles and creating a five-year research-and-development plan. The report was highly classified, but the executive summary released to Congress concluded: "Powerful new technologies are becoming available that justify a major technological development effort offering future technical options to implement a defense strategy." Quoting the President, the unclassified summary reported, "The scientific community may indeed give the United States 'the means of rendering' the ballistic missile threat 'impotent and obsolete.' "[145]

In early 1984 the Pentagon created the Strategic Defense Initiative Organization (SDIO) as an independent entity, responsible only to the secretary of defense, and named Lieutenant General James A. Abrahamson, Jr., its director. A former fighter pilot and astronaut, Abrahamson had served as program manager for the F-16 jet fighter, and most recently as director of NASA's space-shuttle program. That spring Abrahamson asked Congress for two billion dollars for the new program—or about double the amount expended the previous year for research in these technologies. That summer he invited bids from defense contractors and went with the White House science adviser, George Keyworth, on a speaking tour across the country to publicize the new initiative. He then launched the program recommended by the Fletcher report with a four-billion-dollar request for fiscal year 1986 and budgets that ramped sharply upwards for the years ahead.[146]

Before the program was inaugurated many in the Pentagon, and in particular the R&D chiefs, had voiced considerable skepticism about the President's project. Richard DeLauer, the undersecretary of defense for research and engineering and the Pentagon's chief scientist, virtually called the whole idea nonsense. In May 1983 he told reporters, "With unconstrained proliferation, no defensive system will work."[147] And in November 1984 he had told a congressional committee that each of the eight technology areas that had to be addressed would require an effort greater than the Manhattan Project.[148] But when the program began, DeLauer—along with Robert S. Cooper, director of the Defense Advanced Research Projects Agency (DARPA), and the rest of the R&D chiefs—joined the procession of administration officials going up to the Hill to testify on behalf of the research program. Asked about DeLauer's initial assessment, Keyworth said, "I totally disagree [with it], and I think Dick would disagree now. That comment was made a very very short time after the president's speech on March 23rd 1983, before he had become fully aware of all the technological advances that led to the president's speech."[149]

In congressional hearings and press interviews General Abrahamson, slight, boyish-looking and articulate, would speak of the tremendous progress made since the late sixties, and of a bewildering array of new technologies: miniature homing projectiles known as "smart rocks," precision sensors, directed-energy weapons such as lasers and particle beams. To help make his case, SDIO officials unveiled a number of highly classified weapons projects and authorized press visits to the national weapons labs and defense-industry plants where scientists were working on such exotics as the X-ray laser, the Sigma Tau chemical laser, a "space-fed" radar and an electromagnetic rail gun that would shoot homing projectiles through space.[150] In addition, the SDIO announced the results of two spectacular tests. In June

1984, in a project known as the Homing Overlay Experiment (HOE), the Army succeeded in destroying a dummy reentry vehicle in space with a non-nuclear homing projectile fired into space by an Atlas rocket. The test, officials said, showed that with the new heat-seeking sensors and guidance rockets it was now finally possible to "hit a bullet with a bullet." The following year the Pentagon released a videotape showing a blue-green laser knifing up into space and bouncing off a mirror on the space shuttle *Discovery* traveling at seventeen thousand miles an hour overhead. According to SDIO officials, the test demonstrated that ground-based lasers could be used to destroy warheads in space. "In the directed energy field," Abrahamson told a House committee on science and technology, "work with atmospheric compensation technologies has progressed to the point where it appears that the potential for large, effective ground-based lasers is very real." Newspaper headlines hailed the demonstration as a success and a "first for Star Wars."[151]

Asked how a Star Wars defense might work, SDIO officials explained that, in line with previous studies, the Fletcher team had assumed that an anti-missile defense would not be a single weapons system but, rather, a multi-tiered system with layers that would attack the ballistic missile in each stage of its trajectory: the boost phase, during "bus," with its warheads is shot up through the atmosphere by first- and second-stage rockets; the post-boost phase in which the "bus" maneuvers and flings its warheads, and perhaps decoys, into space; the mid-course phase, during which the warheads fly from continent to continent; and the reentry, or terminal, phase in which the independently targeted warheads and the heavier decoys descend through the atmosphere to earth. For the purposes of responding to a full-fledged Soviet attack, the boost phase was crucial, for then an interceptor could destroy the missile with all of its warheads in a single blow. Moreover, because missiles emitted a strong heat signal during the boost phase, it was easier to detect them at that point. Candidates for the boost-phase interceptor included kinetic- and directed-energy weapons. These weapons could be based in orbiting battle stations or—in the case of lasers—could be beamed up from earth and redirected by orbiting mirrors to their targets or "popped up" into space by rockets at the first sign of an attack. The warhead-laden buses which survived the boost phase could be tracked, targeted and attacked by the same weapons, as could the warheads in their mid-course flight; then those warheads which "leaked" through the first two layers of defense could be attacked from the ground. The multi-tiered system would require space-based radars and sensors for surveillance and tracking and for discriminating between warheads and decoys, plus a computerized battle-management system to provide the necessary command and control. According to the unclassified executive summary of the Fletcher report, technological advances made it likely that these capabilities could be achieved.[152]

The unveiling of these new technologies and the design for a Star Wars defense quite naturally received a good deal of attention from the news media. *Aviation Week and Space Technology* was the first off the mark—but the major newspapers and news magazines were not far behind it, with sketches of a ballistic missile's trajectory and laser battle stations in space. In the summer of 1984 two of the three television networks aired documentaries on the initiative, filming scientists working in their labs and showing artists' animated renderings of how the anti-missile system would work. Still, journalists reviewing the initiative in the spring of 1985 realized that there was a great deal more to be said about it.

In March the *New York Times* ran a five-part series on the technological and strategic issues posed by the initiative; the *Washington Post* ran a similar series. Writers for journals of opinion offered their views, and newspapers around the country ran SDI stories every few days. Not only Congress but the public at large became quite familiar with talk of laser weapons and concepts such as "boost-phase intercept." Journalists for the major news organizations routinely warned that the exotic weapons might take years to develop. They also noted that a number of distinguished scientists and defense experts maintained that a Star Wars defense might cost a trillion dollars and still not provide protection from Soviet ICBMs.

In fact, the Fletcher report and the SDI program had given rise to a number of technical controversies and to a series of exchanges among scientists that were so intemperate they were known as "the science wars." In the fall of 1983 the Congress had asked its own Office of Technology Assessment (OTA) to study directed-energy weapons and missile defenses in space. Dr. Ashton Carter, a Harvard professor and a former systems analyst for the Defense Department, directed the study. With full access to classified information, Carter explored the range of technologies under consideration by the SDIO and found every one of them inadequate to serve as the basis for a major change in American strategy. The prospect for a perfect, or near-perfect, defense was, his report concluded, "so remote that it should not serve as the basis of public expectations of national policy on ballistic missile defense."[153] A few weeks later the SDIO counter-attacked. In a paper written largely by a Los Alamos physicist, Gregory Canavan, the SDIO charged that the OTA report was full of "technical errors, unsubstantiated assumptions, and conclusions that are inconsistent with the body of the report." The paper also attacked Carter personally, charging that he was politically biased and that he had revealed national-security information in his report.[154]

During the same period the Union of Concerned Scientists, a group which included Hans Bethe and a number of other prestigious nuclear physicists, made its own study of directed-energy weapons and strategic defenses. Its report, written largely by Richard Garwin, who had worked on the MX basing mode for the Pentagon, also concluded that there was little prospect for a perfect or near-perfect defense. One of the observations the report made was that an effective defense using chemical lasers would require a globe-girdling network of twenty-four hundred battle stations, each weighing fifty to a hundred tons and each costing about a billion dollars. SDI scientists from the national laboratories objected that ninety battle stations were enough, and that the UCS analysts were either bad mathematicians or had set out to kill SDI. UCS then discovered that it had made an error, or errors, and lowered its estimates to eight hundred, and then to three hundred battle stations—though only temporarily. In an article in *Commentary* magazine, "The War Against Star Wars," Robert Jastrow, a former NASA astrophysicist teaching at Dartmouth, publicized the SDIO responses to the Carter and the Garwin studies, charging UCS with "shoddy work" and numerous errors and pessimistic performance estimates, all of which went "in one direction only—toward making the president's plan seem impractical, costly and ineffective."[155] In a second piece, "Reagan vs. the Scientists: Why the President Is Right About Missile Defenses," he wrote that among the experts working on laser defense "the consensus is that no basic scientific obstacles stand in the way of success." Garwin responded that the UCS study was based on the improbable assumption that the complex battle stations would work flawlessly, and that if allowances were made for minute imperfections—say, in the speed with which the mirror swiveled from target to target—a Star Wars defense would require 2,263 battle stations. He also wrote that Jastrow was not an expert on strategic defenses, that he had a habit of using other people's data and that he had made "a career of hyena-like behavior." Later the controversy erupted again in the editorial pages of *The Wall Street Journal*, with Jastrow, Lowell Wood of the Livermore Lab and two Los Alamos scientists attacking the UCS and the OTA studies, and the authors of those studies responding in kind.[156]

As time went on other scientists and defense experts, including Sidney Drell, Harold Brown, William Perry, James Schlesinger and Robert McNamara, weighed in on the debate. For the benefit of non-specialists, they described in laymen's terms some of the difficulties involved in mounting a defense against ballistic missiles. In their view, as in that of the Fletcher panel, an effective boost-phase interceptor was critical, for, once in space, a Soviet missile might release ten or more warheads together with hundreds of decoys and quantities of so-called penetration aids—such as chaff or clouds of infrared-emitting gases. Thus a thousand heavy Soviet ICBMs could present the defense with hundreds of thousands of potential targets. To find and destroy the ten thousand warheads within this "threat cloud" in the twenty minutes it took them to fly from continent to continent was too daunting a task. Among other things, the computer which could handle the battle management for so many simultaneous engagements did not exist. Thus the defense had to destroy most of the Soviet missiles before they could release their independently targeted warheads. Yet a boost-phase interceptor that could stop an all-out Soviet attack would have to destroy the two thousand–plus ICBMs and SLBMs the Soviets currently possessed in the three to five minutes it took them to get up out of the atmosphere.[157] Conceivably weapons could be built that would accomplish this task, but if they were, the Soviets could adopt counter-measures. For example, if the system was to react quickly enough, some, or all, of its components would have to be based in orbit over Soviet territory—in which case they would be easy targets. In launching an ICBM attack, the Soviets would simply have to begin by clearing away the satellites with space mines, anti-satellite weapons or nuclear bursts at high altitudes. Space-based battle stations could be equipped with defenses, but the fact remained that it was far easier to destroy the space-based components of a strategic-defense system than to destroy ballistic missiles in flight.[158]

Administration officials, however, simply brushed aside all of the negative assessments. "There is very little question that we can build a very highly effective defense against ballistic missiles someday," General Abrahamson said. "The question is how soon and how affordable and what degree of effectiveness can initial steps allow us."[159] On another occasion he said, "I am a little dismayed at some of the critics who keep saying that we can't do something. I don't think that the history of what we have done in this country technically is something that supports a lot of their pessimism."[160] Secretary Weinberger also dismissed the technical objections: "Many scientists said a few years ago that we couldn't ever reach the moon . . . many scientists have said a great many things that have proven to be wrong once the work has been done," he said on an NBC broadcast. The critics, he said, were "traditional thinkers" and people "congenitally opposed to new ideas."[161] He and other SDI supporters reminded critics of all the times that experts had wrongly predicted that some technical feat could not be accomplished, evoked the can-do spirit of America, and suggested that it was almost unpatriotic to doubt that the goal could be achieved. "I don't think anything in this country is technically impossible," Abrahamson said. "We have a nation which indeed can produce miracles."[162]

While the technical debates proceeded, administration officials and their critics argued about the strategic implications of deploying a Star Wars defense. According to the President, SDI offered "a way out of our nuclear dilemma, the one that has confounded mankind for four decades," and according to the secretary of defense, it was "one of history's best chances to end the shadow and fear of nuclear weapons."[163] Critics, however, pointed out that even a perfect ballistic-missile defense would not stop bombers, cruise missiles or short-range missiles launched from submarines—and thus would not end the threat of nuclear destruction. Furthermore, they charged, an anti-missile system would be dangerous. If the U.S. deployed such a system unilaterally, the Soviets would certainly see it as threatening, and since it could not be deployed all at once, they would take measures to defeat it, thus fueling the arms race and increasing the threat of nuclear war. Even if both sides could agree to substitute defenses for offensive weapons, it was difficult to see how the transition might be handled, for, at some point along the way, one side or the other might feel itself mortally threatened by a first strike and might calculate that a preemptive attack was its least bad option. Furthermore, a Star Wars defense might prove dangerous in and of itself. Hans Bethe, the Nobel physics laureate, concluded, "It's difficult to imagine a system more likely to induce catastrophe than one that requires critical decisions by the second, is itself untested and fragile and yet is threatening to the other side's retaliatory capability."[164] The administration, critics charged, had not begun to think these issues through.

In a hearing of the Senate Foreign Relations Committee in April 1984, administration officials, questioned closely about the Star Wars concept, acknowledged that a system capable of shooting down Soviet missiles in the boost phase would have to be triggered on such short notice that the command decision might have to be made by computer.

"Well, that would argue that in the 1990s we should run R2D2 for President," Senator Paul Tsongas (Democrat of Massachusetts) said, referring to the robot in the movie *Star Wars*. "[At least] he'd be on line all the time."

"Has the President been informed that he's out of the decision-making loop?" Tsongas continued.

"I most certainly have not [informed him]," George Keyworth replied.

Robert S. Cooper, director of DARPA, chimed in with the suggestion that the President could carry a strategic-defense trigger "even into the bathroom."

Senator Joseph Biden (Democrat of Delaware) then asked if the proposed defensive weapons might be fired accidentally—provoking the Soviets to launch an attack. "Now, let's assume that it was a mistaken judgment," he began.

"We're not ready to assume that," Dr. Cooper interrupted, "because we don't know but what in that time period we couldn't create technologies that would not make such a mistake possible."

"O.K.," Biden said. "You've convinced me that I don't want the program in the hands of a man like you."

Richard Perle came to Cooper's defense. "Frankly," he said, "I think the question of Presidential intervention or any other intervention is a minor, second-order issue when the real issue is whether you do or do not stop the destruction of the United States."

"How does the President feel about your viewing him as a minor, second-order level of decision-making?" Tsongas asked.

"I said the decision is a minor decision because it does no harm if it turns out there is not an attack, and if there is an attack . . ."

"Some of us believe that nuclear war is not a minor decision," Tsongas said.

The argument continued in this vein until Senator John Glenn (Democrat of Ohio), the former astronaut, broke in in exasperation. "I have," he said, "followed all the different types of lasers, high-velocity kinetic weapons, particles and such for fifteen or eighteen years now. . . . I have supported laser research and particle beam research. . . . But it seemed to me, and it seemed to me ever since the President talked about this, that what we are talking about is something that has not yet been invented. . . . I cannot believe we are discussing layers one through five and just assuming that the basic physics of this thing works."

When Cooper and other officials demurred, insisting that SDI was simply a research program, Glenn quoted Weinberger's statement: " 'What we want to try to get is a system that will develop a defense that is thoroughly reliable and total, I don't see any reason why it can't be done.' "

"Well, I do," Glenn said. "It hasn't been invented yet."[165]

To a non-expert diligently reading the press reports and the transcripts of congressional hearings on SDI in 1984–85, Senator Glenn's remarks would surely come as a shock. For months Pentagon officials, scientists, former defense secretaries and members of Congress had been arguing about an umbrella defense and the relative merits of lasers and kinetic-energy weapons, the required number of orbiting battle stations, the problems of battle management, possible Soviet counter-measures and so forth. True, many scientists and defense experts were arguing that perfect defenses could not be achieved—but they, too, were apparently assuming that the technologies had been invented and that the deployment of space weaponry was on the horizon.

In practice, defense experts were making no such assumption. After all, in 1983 the consensus among Pentagon experts had been that the U.S. could not effectively defend the MX missile, much less anything else. There had been no major technological breakthrough since then, and the SDIO had not yet proposed a system, or weapons of any sort, to be developed for a Star Wars defense. Rather, for lack of any such proposal, the critics were talking about the concept of space-based defenses, and they were making an essential point—and one that was not rocket science.

In the Senate Foreign Relations Committee hearing, General Abrahamson said that the Fletcher report outlined a strategic-defense concept with five layers that would be 99.9-percent effective. Though he did not explain why he used this figure, the reason for it was simple enough: if the Soviets launched an ICBM attack with, say, ten thousand warheads, a missile defense that was 99-percent effective would permit a hundred warheads to get through. But a system which permitted the destruction of a hundred American cities clearly did not constitute a "population defense." Only a 99.9-percent-effective system could be called that. But if 99.9-percent effectiveness was beyond the realm of possibility, then the American population could not be defended, and even the longest-term goal of SDI could only be to protect American missiles—and thereby gain a theoretical strategic advantage. As Harold Brown put it, anything less than a perfect defense would serve merely to permit more efficient counter-force targeting.[166] Or as former President Richard Nixon put it, "With 10,000 of those damn things [nuclear warheads] there is no defense."[167]

In fact, Harold Brown and other experts were arguing about perfect, or near-perfect, defenses for the sake of non-specialists. Among experts the logic was so well understood as to require no argument. Administration experts might seem to be arguing the feasibility of population defenses, but in reality they were doing no such thing—at least not in the company of knowledgeable people.

In March and April 1984, or just around the time of the R2D2 discussion in the Foreign Relations Committee, the Senate Armed Services Committee held a full-dress hearing on SDI, bringing in the whole roster of officials concerned with the initiative to testify: Fred Iklé, General Abrahamson, James Fletcher, Richard DeLauer, Robert Cooper, Franklin C. Miller and General Robert R. Rankine, the chief of the Pentagon's directed-energy programs. On the first day of the hearing Senator Sam Nunn (Democrat of Georgia), the ranking minority member and an acknowledged military expert, introduced a short prepared statement. "The American people," he said, "have been led to believe that we are working to eliminate the need for offensive retaliatory capabilities by providing invulnerable defenses." However, he said, "there are indications in news reports, and in some of the prepared statements presented here today, that this is not the ultimate objective of the SDI program, that the technologists have already conceded that the objective of highly reliable population defense is unattainable." The committee, he continued, should clarify the issue, for, if the latter were the case, the debate would not be about ending the balance of terror but about "adding a defensive arms race to our present, substantial, costly strategic offensive modernization." Such an objective, he added, probably lacked "the general public enthusiasm of the President's initiative and would not be able to justify a five-year program of the magnitude requested."[168]

In the three days of hearings, the administration officials did not dispute the point Nunn was making; rather, in more or less elliptical language, they acknowledged that a countrywide defense was not the goal of SDI. In an opening statement on the first day of the hearing, Dr. Fletcher maintained that there were two rationales for proceeding with SDI: the pessimistic one, that the Soviets would get a ballistic-missile defense before the U.S., and the optimistic one, that "strategic relations based on a balance of offensive and defensive forces is not only morally correct, but can lead to a safer world." Dr. DeLauer for his part agreed that one goal of the program was to protect the nation's retaliatory capability. Under questioning from Nunn, both DeLauer and Iklé admitted that they could not envision a system that would obviate the need for offensive forces. Dr. Cooper went further. "I think," he said, "it is fair to say that there is no combination of gold or platinum bullets that we see in our technological arsenal and that we are pursuing in this program that would make it possible to do away with our strategic offensive ICBM forces."

Nunn then noted that the President had said the goal was to render missiles "impotent and obsolete." But, he said, "I have not heard population protection mentioned anywhere in any of these presentations. Are you talking about a system to protect populations and U.S. cities?"

"Let me answer it this way," DeLauer replied. "What we are trying to do is enhance deterrence. If you enhance deterrence and your deterrence is credible and holds, the people are protected."

"That is also true of massive retaliation," Nunn snapped.

A few minutes later Senator Barry Goldwater (Republican of Arizona) broke in to object that the American public was not going to support an expensive, open-ended defense research program. "I have," he said, "always believed that the best defense was a strong offense, and I think that will be the case for a long time."

Senator John Warner then changed the subject back to the more comfortable issue of the Soviet threat, and under questioning from him, DeLauer said that the Soviet Union was far ahead in defensive technologies and if Congress did not fund SDI it might take the U.S. a decade to catch up.[169]

Later on in the hearing Franklin Miller reported that the goal of SDI was to resolve the uncertainties involved in advanced ABM technologies and said that if the program were successful it would enhance deterrence by sowing doubt in the mind of the attacker about the effectiveness of a first strike, thus deterring the Soviets from a preemptive attack.[170]

"When do you see . . . the opportunity to reduce our offensive capability?" Senator Jeff Bingaman (Democrat of New Mexico) asked.

"I don't know," Miller replied.[171]

On the third day of the hearing, April 24, General Abrahamson gave a number of rationales for the SDI program, including deterring a preemptive strike and pressuring the Soviets to reduce their offensive forces. He also mentioned making "the President's vision a reality." But when Senator James Exon (Democrat of Nebraska) reminded him that DeLauer and Iklé had testified that eliminating the threat posed by ballistic missiles was "beyond the bounds of reasonable possibility," Abrahamson said that though Reagan's vision was the goal "we may well find it unachievable."[172]

In such company Abrahamson and the rest of his colleagues could not have claimed that a population defense was feasible for the simple reason that no weapons system—not even a rifle—could be counted upon to be 99.9-percent effective over time. "Nobody believes in a 100 percent leak-proof defense," Gerald Yonas, the chief SDIO scientist, told a journalist flatly. "Nobody believes in 100 percent anything that's ever worked on military systems."[173]

That SDI could not produce a defense of the American population was not something administration officials seemed eager to admit. Yet no official administration document and no administration expert speaking under oath ever claimed that it could. The Hoffman report, which was commissioned by Iklé to lay the strategic foundation for SDI, almost explicitly rejected the whole idea. Even its unclassified executive summary made the point that "nearly leak-proof defenses are required to provide a high level of protection for the population," and reported that "nearly leak-proof defenses may take a very long time or may prove to be unattainable in a practical sense against a Soviet effort to counter the defense."[174] This was strong language given that the White House had asked for studies on the "elimination of nuclear ballistic missiles." But Hoffman himself made an even stronger statement after the report appeared. Interviewed in *Science* magazine, he said, "If what you want defenses to do is to protect the bulk of our population against an attack by a large Soviet force that has the objective of destroying our population, then you would need everything to work. Even as a non-technician, it seems to me that the likelihood of this happening is small."[175]

The Hoffman report relegated what it called "the President's goal" off to some indefinite future and called for "intermediate" systems for the defense of missiles.

The Fletcher report, by contrast, recommended a long-term effort to develop an "effective" defense through research on exotic technologies, and for some time journalists supposed that this report contained the basis for optimism about population defenses. After all, its unclassified executive summary concluded, "The scientific community may indeed give the United States the means of rendering the ballistic missile threat impotent and obsolete." And in 1984 both Weinberger and Keyworth publicly claimed that the Fletcher team had concluded that "the dream" or "the President's objective" was a realistic goal.[176] Later a journalist discovered that the executive summary did not accurately reflect the body of the report—and that the report was pessimistic about overcoming the problems of battle management and Soviet counter-measures.[177] But whatever the report did or did not say about these issues, the Fletcher team did not promise population defenses. This was perfectly evident from the outset. In an article heralding the report, *Aviation Week and Space Technology* quoted it as saying, "It is not technologically credible to provide a ballistic missile defense that is 99.9% leakproof."[178] In summing up the panel's findings, Fletcher himself said that even the most effective ballistic-missile defense could never defend the total U.S. population. "Total is one thing, substantial is another. What you want is to minimize the casualties. There is no such thing as a nuclear umbrella." By his testimony, any hope for population defenses had to rest on a Soviet agreement to arms control.[179]

That the goal of SDI could be no more than the defense of missiles was difficult for laymen to discern beneath the technical jargon and the loose talk of "substantial" or "effective" defenses.[180] But it was clear enough to all defense experts, including the wildest technical enthusiasts, and those credited with selling the idea to the President. Daniel O. Graham, who in 1985 was feverishly, and quite unsuccessfully, trying to sell his High Frontier concept to the SDIO, spoke of the goal of "mutual assured survival," but the fine print of his prospectuses claimed merely that his system would give the U.S. a military advantage and preclude a Soviet first strike.[181] Senator Wallop and his aide Angelo Codevilla were calling for the deployment of a weapons system within five years and charging that the administration, with its talk of eliminating the threat of nuclear weapons, was pursuing a will-o'-the-wisp.[182] As for Edward Teller, he continued to make outrageous claims for the X-ray laser—but he did not promise population defenses. In an article published in October 1985, he asked the rhetorical question "Could we stop 99.9% of the incoming missiles?" and continued:

> The answer is no. A 99.9% defense cannot be attained soon. It may not ever be obtained. Even if it is attained, it will not be attained with complete certainty.
>
> But a defense does not need to be a tight umbrella. It suffices if it makes the success of an attack uncertain.

Teller did not explain that America's existing strategic triad did the same thing.[183]

Even Robert Jastrow, who, in his attacks on Richard Garwin and Ashton Carter, often seemed to be arguing the feasibility of population defenses, and who wrote a pamphlet entitled *How to Make Nuclear Weapons Obsolete,* never—technically speaking—made such a claim. In January 1985 he co-authored an article in the *New York Times Magazine* with Max Kampelman and Zbigniew Brzezinski expressing agnosticism about exotic technologies and calling for the development of a two-layer defense—one that sounded remarkably like Graham's High Frontier—for the purposes of protecting U.S. missiles and preventing the Soviets from obtaining a first-strike capability.[184]

Senator Nunn was, of course, well aware of the consensus within the defense community—and of the commonsense logic behind it.[185] In the March–April 1984 Armed Services Committee hearings on SDI, he and his colleagues had simply been trying to get the Pentagon officials to admit to it. They were fairly successful, and in hearings later that year he and other members of the committee, including the powerful Republican Senator John Warner, were more successful still. In one hearing Nunn asked how the administration would explain to the people of, say, New York City that, after a trillion dollars had been spent on strategic defenses, they still were not protected from ICBMs. "I do not believe that this is what we have ever really said," Abrahamson testified. "I think it is a defense deterrent that we are talking about . . . to prevent them from being able to hit your military capability."[186]

Nevertheless, the President went on making speeches about a security shield that would make nuclear weapons obsolete while Abrahamson and other Pentagon spokesmen continued to talk about "the President's vision" and their "hope" of making it a reality—words rarely used in an Armed Services Committee room.

WHY RONALD REAGAN KEPT TALKING about a defense that would make nuclear weapons obsolete was a question that was more or less settled for reporters by the spring of 1985. McFarlane and other White House officials often said that SDI was his favorite program, that he believed in it deeply and that he had a moral commitment to defending the nation. Reagan, they disclosed, had dreamed of a defense against missiles since his visit to NORAD in 1979, and afterwards Wallop, Teller, Graham and members of his former Kitchen Cabinet had convinced him that it could be made a reality. Don Oberdorfer, the diplomatic correspondent for the *Washington Post,* later wrote: "Reagan was fascinated with the prospect of a technological breakthrough that would create hardware that could stop incoming missiles. Reagan often called the idea 'my dream,' which suggests the magical nature of its hold on him. . . . No one was ever able to shake him in his deep belief that his dream would actually come to fruition and thus change the world for the better."[187]

What other administration officials were doing talking about population defenses was rather less clear to reporters, but, then, in late 1984 and early 1985 the administration's intentions with regard to SDI were baffling in many respects.

In mid-November 1984 Washington journalists reported that a new fight over arms control was brewing between State and Defense, and that President Reagan had not yet made up his mind on the key issues dividing his bureaucracy. The most serious bone of contention was whether the U.S. would agree to negotiate restraints on the development of space weapons. For the moment SDI was merely a research program, but it could not remain one forever, and doubtless the Soviets would never agree to reductions in their missiles while the U.S. proceeded with the development of space weaponry or anti-missile systems. The ins and outs of the debate were, however, somewhat murky, because officials from all quarters were professing loyalty to "the President's goal," and most were saying that SDI would never be traded away. Obviously the administration could not announce in advance that it was willing to abandon SDI or the program would lose its value as a bargaining chip, but if the administration refused to put limits on it, arms control was unlikely. SDI was the program the President seemed to care most about, but whether he understood that there was a conflict between it and his other goal of reducing nuclear weapons was unclear. According to officials in the State Department, the Defense Department and ACDA, no one had explained the conflict to him.[188]

In the administration's public statements the ambiguities persisted, and as far as reporters could tell, the struggle went unresolved. In late December, Margaret Thatcher visited Washington to express her concern about the Star Wars program and its implications for arms control and East-West relations. The day before meeting with her, President Reagan told reporters he would make her understand that "the only defensive weapon we have is to threaten that if they kill millions of our people, we'll kill millions of theirs," and that it was immoral not to look "for something that will make these weapons obsolete. . . ."[189] The day after the meeting, Secretary Weinberger said that the President would never give up the opportunity to develop SDI in return for Soviet arms reductions.[190] However, a White House statement, agreed to by Reagan and Thatcher, said that SDI was a research program, that the overall aim was to enhance, not to undermine, deterrence and that in view of treaty commitments SDI-related deployments would "have to be a matter of negotiation" with the Soviet Union.[191]

What had happened, it later emerged, was that over the course of the election year Secretaries Weinberger and Shultz had found their own particular uses for SDI. The goals of the two secretaries were incompatible, indeed contradictory—and yet both goals required rhetorical support for the President's "dream" of making nuclear weapons, or missiles, "impotent and obsolete."

In 1983, four days after the President's speech, Weinberger had backed up the President by calling for a "reliable and total" defense. But when the SDI program began, he offered another possibility. In a speech to the National Press Club in May 1984 he said, "The ultimate goal of the Strategic Defense Initiative is to develop thoroughly reliable defenses. This does not preclude, of course, any intermediate deployment that could provide, among other things, defense of the offensive deterrent forces, which of course we still have to maintain."[192] A number of conservatives favored deploying limited defenses, and this was the formula Fred Hoffman and his Pentagon sponsor, Fred Iklé, had found to make their goal compatible with the NSDD directing them to set up a research effort on "the elimination of the threat of ballistic missile attack." In effect, the possible would be done first and the impossible left for the indefinite future.[193] Subsequently all Pentagon officials testifying before the Armed Services Committees took this line—a tactic Harold Brown qualified as "bait and switch."[194]

But developing defenses for U.S. missiles appealed only to the right, and if that had remained the sole justification for SDI, the program might never have gotten off the ground. It was the prospect of arms talks with the Soviets that brought the entire administration around to supporting the initiative.

In his memoir George Shultz tells us that during the spring of 1984 he had noticed that the fledgling SDI program had riveted the attention of Soviet officials. Chernenko wrote Reagan to protest "the development of large-scale ABM weapons"; Gromyko and Dobrynin raised the specter of "space weapons" and "the militarization of space" at almost every meeting with U.S. officials. The Soviets were concerned not only with SDI but with the U.S. advances in the development of anti-satellite weapons (ASATs) and in the test of a new ASAT system scheduled for the fall.[195] In June the Soviets proposed talks to begin in September on preventing the militarization of space. At that point Shultz realized that the fear of potential U.S. breakthroughs in space weaponry might provide an incentive for the Soviets to make deep reductions in offensive arms. His counter-proposal that the talks should include offensive systems was rejected, but over the summer he worked at a plan to reconvene all of the arms talks under one umbrella and to create the grounds for a trade-off between space weaponry and nuclear arms. In September, Shultz, with McFarlane's cooperation, had the President discuss his plan for "umbrella talks" with Gromyko, and in November, his efforts were rewarded: Chernenko accepted the U.S. proposal for recommencing the arms talks and noted that there was an "organic" relationship between issues of offensive nuclear weapons and space weaponry.[196]

The immediate difficulty for Shultz lay not so much with the Soviets as with the Office of the Secretary of Defense.

According to Strobe Talbott, Richard Perle had taken little interest in SDI until the fall of 1984. Like the Pentagon's R&D chiefs, he took a dim view of the prospects for orbiting space weapons that would shoot down missiles in the boost phase or in their mid-course flight. Indeed, he had once called the idea of multi-layered space defenses "the product of millions of American teenagers putting quarters into video machines."[197] Along with Fred Iklé and the authors of the Hoffman report, he believed that the only candidate for near-term deployment was a system of ground-based interceptors which could be used for the defense of missile silos. Perle had always disliked the ABM Treaty—he had never concealed his desire to see it abrogated—for in his view the national interest would be served by competition with the Soviet Union in both defensive and offensive weapons. Yet in the early years of the administration he had not urged the development of a ballistic missile defense. Ground-based defenses, nuclear or non-nuclear, were not very capable against ICBMs and so expensive that they would, he feared, drive out other, more capable weapons programs. Subsequently he had opposed SDI on similar grounds: the research effort on exotic defenses would, he thought, give Congress an excuse to oppose the development of offensive systems. But now that the President was committed to SDI, and the Soviets were taking it seriously, it occurred to Perle that it might have its uses—not as a bargaining chip or, certainly, as a Star Wars defense, but, rather, as the ultimate weapon against arms control. If SDI could be turned into a development program, or simply a threat to become one, it would serve not only to block whatever plans Shultz had for an arms agreement but to wreck the ABM Treaty as well. Perle thus became a vigorous advocate of the SDI program and took to delivering reports on great progress and the promise of technical marvels to come.[198]

In November, Defense and State had begun to struggle over arms control. Yet, as much at odds as they were over the purpose of SDI, Weinberger and Shultz were united in a desire to get the SDI program through the Congress. In December, McFarlane, otherwise torn between the conflicting demands of the two Cabinet secretaries, organized an elaborate three-month-long campaign to sell SDI to the country, with the President taking the lead. In the early months of 1985 Reagan frequently referred to SDI in his speeches and gave numerous media interviews on the subject. "I have approved a research program to find, if we can, a security shield that will destroy nuclear missiles before they reach their target," he said in his second inaugural address. "It wouldn't kill people. It would destroy weapons. It wouldn't militarize space, it would help demilitarize the arsenals of the earth. It would render nuclear weapons obsolete."[199] Other officials contributed to this rhetoric. In a speech in late December, Weinberger assailed deterrence as a policy that "condemns us to a future in which our safety is based on the threat of avenging aggression" and lambasted critics of SDI for contending that "effective defense is technically unobtainable." History, he said, "is filled with flat predictions about the impossibility of technical achievements that we have long since taken for granted." He went on to quote Albert Einstein saying in 1932 that there was not the slightest indication that nuclear energy would ever become available.[200]

The campaign was highly successful. By April, Gallup and many other polls showed that the American public had taken a great interest in SDI and that a high percentage favored the development of a Star Wars defense. Over 80 percent of all Americans had heard of the program, and about half of that group—the figures ranged from 41 to 69 percent, depending on the pollster and the wording of the poll—favored the development of a defensive system.[201] The polls also showed that approval of Star Wars was directly related to the belief that it could produce a complete defense of the country. Americans did not favor partial defenses: they were not for a system that could defend only missile silos, and they were not for a system that could stop ICBMs if it left the country vulnerable to missiles fired by submarines or bombers; they were for nothing less than a perfect defense against nuclear weapons, and when asked whether scientists could come up with an effective way to protect the U.S. from a nuclear attack, two out of three Americans said they could.[202]

The poll results would not have surprised anyone who had followed the public attitudes towards defenses over the years. Since World War II, Americans had consistently told pollsters that they wanted a defense, and that they were confident that American science could create one. Between 1946 and

1949 polls showed that a majority of Americans thought that scientists could find a defense against the atomic bomb. In the 1960s, after the deployment of ICBMs, numerous polls showed that Americans favored the development of a defense against nuclear missiles and believed that it could be done. Indeed, when asked if the U.S. already had a defense against nuclear missiles, most Americans said yes, it did—except when the lack of one, or the issue of U.S. vulnerability, was in the news.[203] Apparently Americans not only had great faith in the power of science, but they could not accept the idea that the country was vulnerable to nuclear destruction. Thus, when Reagan proposed to make nuclear weapons "impotent and obsolete," he was running almost no risk of raising public incredulity. In fact, a Wirthlin poll taken two weeks after the 1983 speech showed that, as usual, only one American in three doubted that American scientists could come up with "a really effective way to destroy Soviet nuclear missiles from space."[204]

But the surveys also showed that support for anti-nuclear defenses was not unconditional. For example, Harris and other polls taken between 1970 and 1974 revealed that the American public overwhelmingly favored an agreement between the U.S. and Russia limiting, or banning, anti-missile systems. Americans still wanted population defenses, but they had come to understand that the ABM systems then in development would be hugely expensive and would protect only missile sites, not cities. Then, too, the polls consistently showed that, though Americans overwhelmingly favored keeping up with, or ahead of, the Soviets in the arms race, they also overwhelmingly favored disarmament agreements that would reduce the threat of nuclear war.[205]

The congruence between the polling data and the manner in which President Reagan and other administration officials presented SDI was remarkably precise. In 1983 the President had wanted to propose a defense against all nuclear weapons; his policy aides had insisted that he speak only of a defense against ballistic missiles, but by referring to "these nuclear weapons," he kept the original idea in the speech. In 1985 the original idea surfaced again, more or less explicitly, in his speeches and remarks.

In 1983 Reagan had presented his initiative as a means of ending the nuclear threat, but because it came in the midst of so much "evil-empire" rhetoric, it was understood as a proposal for an offensive-weapons system. In 1985 he returned to it after a year of talk about improving relations with the Soviet Union and arms reductions, and its fortunes changed. During the campaign Reagan had frequently referred to his "dream" of eliminating nuclear weapons and proposed to share SDI technology with the Soviets. Both ideas were ridiculed by sophisticates, but for the public the issue was Reagan's intentions, and both made him sound like a man of peace—and a radical disarmer. He had appropriated the rhetoric of the anti-nuclear movement, and that, plus the promise of arms control, caused the freeze movement to melt away. Polls taken in 1985 showed that, though conservatives and Republicans approved of Star Wars more than did liberals and Democrats, and though most people thought of Star Wars as a threat, or a challenge, to the Soviets, almost 50 percent of the public saw a Star Wars defense as an aid to arms control. According to poll analysts, a majority of Americans now favored Star Wars on the grounds that it would protect the U.S. from a nuclear attack, increase the chances for a disarmament agreement and reduce the risk of nuclear war.[206] With all of Reagan's talk of peace and disarmament, Star Wars had become acceptable to people far outside his core constituency.

Faced with the claims for SDI, defense experts outside the administration argued that an umbrella defense of the United States was a virtual impossibility. But their arguments made no headway with the public. Indeed, the more they explained the technological difficulties involved, the more they talked about the number of orbiting battle stations required, possible Soviet counter-measures and the like, the more they made Star Wars sound like a near-term possibility. It was, it turned out, rather difficult to argue that a defense that was 70 or 80 percent effective was worse than no defense at all. But the problem went deeper. To listen to radio call-in shows in 1985 was to hear people from all over the country assailing the experts with arguments such as: people said Alexander Graham Bell was crazy, people said we couldn't get to the moon, now you're telling us scientists can't give us defenses! Nothing in this country is impossible! When the experts insisted that science was not magic and that American technology could not do everything, they would be accused of lack of patriotism.

Curiously, Washington journalists covering national-security affairs failed to remark upon the extraordinary coincidence between Reagan's SDI rhetoric and what the polls revealed about American attitudes towards antinuclear defenses. But public opinion on these issues did not escape the notice of members of Congress.

During the Senate Armed Services Committee hearings of March–April 1984, Sam Nunn said that, if the objective of SDI was not to end the balance of terror but to add a defensive component to the arms race, it would probably lack "the general public enthusiasm" required "to justify a five-year program of the magnitude requested." In the hearing he and his fellow Democrats were so successful in forcing the Pentagon officials to drop the rhetoric about population defenses that at the end of one session Senator Pete Wilson (Republican of California), a leading advocate of SDI, burst out at Dr. Cooper, "I must tell you that I am mystified and, frankly, angry because your written testimony is at variance with, certainly the tone and, I think, even the substance of some of the responses you made." Why, he asked, had Cooper not echoed the optimism of the Fletcher report about the prospects for a "robust, multi-tiered system"—and why had he not even mentioned the goal of population defenses?

By dint of persistence, Wilson finally got Cooper to say that, although he did not see "any combination of technology we have today guaranteeing . . . the elimination of offensive strategic forces," he did hold out "the hope that it will be possible sometime in the future."

"I wish you had said it with precisely that clarity earlier," Wilson replied tartly. "I think you are going to have to say that because otherwise you are going to find there isn't support for the kind of R&D that is essential."

Clearly Wilson was not at all surprised by Cooper's testimony. He was merely warning the DARPA director that if officials did not represent the program as an attempt to create population defenses the public would not support it, and SDI would have rough sledding in Congress.[207]

Public attitudes on the subject of defenses did not escape administration officials either. Years later Edwin Meese spoke of polls showing that the public thought the U.S. had a defense against nuclear weapons already.[208] In his memoir George Shultz tells us that he realized that the initiative "provided a potent argument against . . . those who argued that the Reagan administration was heedlessly taking the nation down the path to nuclear disaster" and "spoke to national pride in American technological prowess."[209] Caspar Weinberger argued the case for SDI to NATO defense ministers by citing American public-opinion polls and, along with Abrahamson, rhapsodized about the magic of American technology, just as did callers on radio talk shows.[210] In his memoir Robert McFarlane quotes from a memorandum he gave the President, and discussed with him, in late December 1984 on the subject of the public-relations campaign for SDI. The memo reads in part:

> For a generation the world has lived under the surreal notion that we are better off being unable to defend ourselves under a balance of terror. Your concept of changing that has provoked enormous public interest and criticism. But there is no question that you have the moral high ground with the American people. In order to assure that we keep it that way, we have been preparing a "public affairs blitz" involving your speaking to the nation, and a widespread campaign involving dozens of spokesmen inside and outside of government who will carry the gospel into the fourteen major media markets in the next three months. I intend to meet with the network news directors next week to state plainly that this issue is of such historic importance as to warrant a truly vigorous national debate, and that you have directed me to make available to them our full cooperation in presenting our rationale and technical concept. As a separate but related matter, you have thrown the left into an absolute tizzy. They are left in the position of advocating the most bloodthirsty strategy—Mutual Assured Destruction—as a means to keep the peace.[211]

McFarlane knew perfectly well that technology held no alternative to deterrence—or "mutual assured destruction." (Earlier on in the memo he told the President that his "historic initiative" would "lead us toward less reliance on offensive systems and more on defensive systems.") Yet he was writing as if an alternative existed and actively encouraging the President to speak as if it did.

The McFarlane memo raises the possibility that Reagan's advisers duped the President into thinking that a security shield could be built—or at least failed to tell him otherwise. Possibly a credulous person with a deep and simple belief that scientists could save humanity with an impregnable defense might have understood the memo as a confirmation of his faith. But the memo does not sound as if it were addressed to someone of deep and simple beliefs. It is, after all, about perceptions, not substance, and at the end of it McFarlane refers to the political purpose of the 1983 speech insert and declares victory: the left—or the freeze—has been routed.

In sum, the evidence suggests that administration officials and SDI advocates in Congress were quite consciously manipulating the American public for their own ends.

Journalists thought they knew what Reagan believed, but the evidence for what he believed lies merely in what he said and wrote about the initiative, and during the 1984–85 campaign for SDI, Reagan said a great many different things. In his election-day interview with Cannon, the President spoke as if population defenses were already a reality. In a news conference in January 1985, he described SDI as a research program in its early stages, a long way from what was implied by television animations of Star Wars.[212] Sometimes, as in his 1983 speech, he spoke with conditionals—"if we can do it . . . if it can be done"—and sometimes he spoke of a security shield as his "hope" or his "dream"—rather than his expectation. On one occasion, however, he denied that he had such a dream or such a goal. In an interview with *Wall Street Journal* reporters on February 8, 1985, he was asked whether he would continue with SDI even if scientists said there could be no leakproof defense. "Oh," Reagan said, "I've never asked for 100 percent. That would be a fine goal; but you can have a most effective defensive weapon even if it isn't 100 percent. Because what you would have is that the other fellow would have the knowledge that if they launched a first strike, that it might be such that not enough of their missiles would get through, and in return we could launch a retaliatory strike."

He added, "Now that isn't really the goal of the Strategic Defense Initiative. I tie that to what I think is the goal of these arms negotiations. The Soviet Union—Chernenko and Gromyko both have publicly stated that they would like to see the elimination, ultimately, of nuclear weapons. . . . Now, if they really mean it, we can go to a table and sit down and start negotiating reductions aiming toward the elimination of these weapons."[213]

In other words, SDI would provide a defense for U.S. missiles. Or it would serve as an aid to arms reductions, with the elimination of nuclear weapons being the ultimate, though perhaps unattainable, goal.

But then, only six weeks after the *Wall Street Journal* interview, the President said in a speech to the National Space Club: "This should not and should never be misconstrued as just another method of protecting missile silos. We are not discussing a concept just to enhance deterrence but . . . research to determine the feasibility of a comprehensive non-nuclear defensive system, . . . a shield that could prevent nuclear weapons from reaching their targets."[214]

It could, of course, be argued that Reagan was saying what he truly believed in his speeches and telling sophisticated reporters what they wanted to hear. But his speeches in this period—unlike that of March 1983—were vetted by the bureaucracy. Furthermore, to look at these utterances in context is to see that all of them served the purposes of his various national-security advisers. In his speeches he was selling SDI to the public. When he called SDI a fledgling research program—nothing at all like the TV animations—he was responding directly to the complaints raised by Margaret Thatcher and the NATO defense ministers. In the *Journal* interview he was maintaining that SDI could be the bargaining chip that Shultz wanted, or the means to develop a weapons system, as Weinberger and his aides hoped. The import of his statement was that the conflict between the two secretaries had not been resolved.

What did Reagan, in his heart of hearts, believe about the potential of defense weapons? In his memoir of the presidency he writes:

> I never viewed SDI as an impenetrable shield—no defense could ever be expected to be one hundred percent effective. . . . [But] if it worked and we then entered into an era when the nations of the world agreed to eliminate nuclear weapons, it could serve as a safety valve against cheating—or attacks by lunatics who managed to get their hands on a nuclear missile. And, if we couldn't reach an agreement eliminating nuclear weapons, the system would be able to knock down enough of an enemy's missiles so that if he ever pushed a button to attack, he would be doing so in the knowledge that his attack was unable to prevent a devastating retaliatory strike.[215]

This answer is, of course, much the same as the one he gave *The Wall Street Journal,* and what it means is that the President had no more expectations for SDI than his technical experts, or Senator Sam Nunn. Still, on the basis of this evidence it would be just as unwise to assert that Reagan did not believe in a "security shield" as to maintain that he did. After all, Reagan said one thing in his speeches and another to journalists with total aplomb, and given his lack of interest in most matters of policy, it is quite conceivable that he had no beliefs on the subject at all.

Addressing a symposium on SDI in Atlanta in November 1985, Senator Nunn complained of the President's propensity to speak of a nuclear "shield." It was, he said, "essential that this debate be clearly understood. I think it would be a great tragedy if the American people were convinced that what we are building is purely a shield over the United States and if they believed . . . that shield would be impenetrable. . . . Right now that rhetoric is very popular, but in my view it is irresponsible."[216]

Nunn was reduced to pleading for the administration to stop, for under current circumstances he and his colleagues could not convince the public that SDI would not produce an impenetrable shield.

Representative Tom Foley (Democrat of Washington), later the Speaker of the House, remembered that there was far less public controversy about SDI than about the MX or the B-1 bomber. In 1985 most congressional Republicans signed onto the program, and after that all the arguments against Star Wars could be construed as purely partisan. The Democrats could no longer ridicule SDI or argue that a defense might be dangerous. "We couldn't argue the counter-intuitive," Foley said.[217]

That year the Congress gave the administration three out of the four billion dollars it had requested for the SDI program. The appropriation was something of a landmark in congressional history. The sum was not a vast one in terms of the entire military budget, or even in terms of the cost of developing strategic systems, such as the MX. Then, too, SDI was merely a research program, or, rather, a collection of research programs, that the Congress had funded quite generously before SDI began. What was more, the State Department had held out some hope that it would be a bargaining chip in negotiations.[218] All the same, SDI was surely the first military program the Congress had funded because of direct popular pressure, and the first its members had voted for knowing full well that what the public expected from it could not possibly be achieved.

CHAPTER SEVEN

Hard-Liners vs. Pragmatists

As Reagan began his second term in January 1985, many in Washington supposed that Shultz had established himself as the dominant force in administration foreign policy, and that, given Reagan's commitments to improving U.S.-Soviet relations, the administration would move towards an arms agreement that year.[1] But the hard-liners had merely been quiescent for the duration of the election year, and the battle had begun anew.

Even before the election George Shultz felt a new stirring among his opponents. The President, he discovered, had waited as long as he could before telling his staff about Gromyko's visit to the White House the previous September, lest the hard-liners try to argue him out of it. The visit had been a political boon to the President, but, Shultz writes, "the wolves were out."[2]

In early November 1984 Kenneth Adelman, the thirty-seven-year-old director of the Arms Control and Disarmament Agency, gave an interview to *The Wall Street Journal* in which he proposed that the U.S. ought to abandon the whole tedious and unreliable business of arms negotiations and explore "arms control without agreements." Adelman, who had replaced Eugene Rostow earlier in the year, was a thorn in Shultz's side. For the first three years of the administration he had been Jeane Kirkpatrick's deputy at the United Nations. That plus a year that he had spent as special assistant to Defense Secretary Donald Rumsfeld in the Ford administration constituted his experience in foreign and defense policy. Brash, irrepressible and quick on his feet, he excelled at debate of the sort carried on in young conservative circles and on the newer Washington TV talk shows. While at the Stanford Research Institute during the Carter years, he had written a number of articles deriding the SALT II treaty and arms control generally. His grasp of the subject remained incomplete. Asked at his confirmation hearings whether he believed a nuclear war could be a limited conflict, he had responded, "I have no, honestly, no thoughts in that area." The Senate had taken months to confirm him, not only because he would be the least qualified head of ACDA in the history of the agency but also because his commitment to arms control seemed questionable at best.[3]

"Little Kenny," as Adelman was known within the defense community, had been swept aside bureaucratically, but now, in the wake of Reagan's reelection, he had decided to assert himself, and "arms control without agreements" was his big idea. As he later explained it in *Foreign Affairs*, arms-control negotiations were time-consuming and led to treaties which were ambiguous, largely unverifiable and easily violated by the Soviets. Instead he proposed that the two superpowers proceed to disarm unilaterally by a series of reciprocal but uncodified steps. Why the Soviets would not violate arms control without agreements if they violated it with them he did not explain. Shultz told him the idea was dumb and bawled him out for publishing views which contradicted administration policy. Adelman went away upset, but contrition was not in his nature.[4]

It was not, of course, Adelman who posed the most danger to Shultz's fledgling policy of reengagement with the Soviet Union, but Weinberger. Curiously, Shultz tells us little about Weinberger's activities at this juncture, but in his memoir Constantine Menges, a hard-liner on the NSC staff, describes an astonishing altercation between the two secretaries in the summer of 1984.

At one NSC meeting, Menges writes, Shultz presented a plan for negotiating a settlement in Central America, for which he had clearly obtained the President's approval in advance. Weinberger denounced the plan in no uncertain terms and painted the consequences of such a negotiation in terms so dire that the President flushed with anger and exclaimed, "No!" Shultz attempted to rebut Weinberger's charges, and the arguments went back and forth ever more furiously—but Shultz had no allies in the room.

When the meeting ended, as usual without a decision, the President rose and started making his way through the narrow space between the Cabinet table and the window to go back to the Oval Office. Shultz rose at about the same time, and, blocking the passageway with his large frame, brought the President to a halt and continued his passionate defense of the plan. The President looked at him quizzically and in a genial tone said, "Very interesting, George, but I have to get to my next appointment."

According to Menges, Shultz was so angry that a few minutes later he went up to Weinberger, poked a finger at his chest and said, "If you can't support negotiations in Central America as the President ordered, you should leave the administration!"

Weinberger, in a lower key, replied, "All of us—Casey, Kirkpatrick, the president and I—favor negotiations. If you can't obey the president's clear wishes on the *objectives* of those negotiations, *you're* the one who should go."[5]

Looking ahead to battles of this sort on U.S.-Soviet relations, Shultz decided to try and force a choice on the President. In an hourlong meeting with Reagan and McFarlane on November 14, he laid out the alternatives as sharply as possible. Standing still with the Soviets, he said, was not an option. The choice was to negotiate new arms agreements or to enter a world in which there were no arms limitations at all—a world fraught with danger for the United States, a world in which the Soviets could easily double their strategic warheads in ten years, and the attempt to keep up would prove costly, both politically and financially. The U.S. needed to do better than existing agreements, he argued, for without meaningful negotiations the Congress would not fund new weapons systems and Allied support would be problematic. But, he said, most in the administration were quite comfortable with the present situation and were doing all they could to block any effort to engage with the Soviets and to achieve arms-control agreements.[6]

The President, Shultz writes, seemed to agree with him and seemed troubled by the thought that many in his administration opposed arms control. Shultz therefore pressed on. To succeed, he said, the administration needed a team, but right now there wasn't one, because Cap Weinberger, Bill Casey and Jeane Kirkpatrick and he did not see things the same way. Instead of teamwork there were leaks, end-runs and people refusing to follow through on decisions.

Going on in this vein, Shultz made it clear that if the President wanted a team he would have to fire some people. To put a fine point on the matter, he volunteered to resign himself. Reagan merely said that he wouldn't stand for the thought of Shultz leaving and did not respond to the rest of his argument.

In his diary Reagan wrote that the dispute between Shultz and those in Weinberger's camp "is so out of hand George sounds like he wants out. I can't let that happen. Actually George is carrying out my policy. I'm going to meet with Cap and Bill and lay it out to them. Won't be fun, but it has to be done."[7]

Reagan does not seem to have acted on this intention.

At around the same time, Weinberger made his own attempt to end the stalemate in the administration. As Reagan's diary shows, he lectured the President on the theme of the evil empire and the danger of negotiations. He himself named no names, but a group of the President's right-wing political supporters, whom Reagan knew to be Weinberger's allies, informed the President that Shultz had gone soft on the Russians and ought to be fired.[8]

McFarlane, too, urged the President to make a choice. For a year he had tried to mediate between the two warring secretaries, with the result that neither of them trusted him and the central issues of foreign policy remained unresolved. Traveling back from California with the President on Air Force One, he said, "I must tell you that I fear that nothing can get accomplished if you don't recognize that you face paralysis within your administration owing to the largely personal animus that exists between Cap and George."

This was, of course, something of a low blow at both secretaries, whose differences were mainly substantive. McFarlane then advised Reagan to build his team around one or the other of them. If you want to keep both, he warned, you will have discord, and you will have to play a much more active role. He concluded by offering to resign if Reagan could think of anyone more effective than he in dealing with this problem.

The President, McFarlane writes, would have none of it. He knew, he said, that there was "this thing" between Cap and George; he wished they could get along with each other better, but he didn't imagine they would, because at his age, and at theirs, "people don't change very much." Yet they were both his friends, so he couldn't fire either one of them. "I know," he said, "that means you are going to have to work a little harder. But you do it right, Bud. In all my time in public life, I don't know if I've ever found a person as indispensable as you."[9]

Flattered, McFarlane agreed to stay on, even though Reagan had not promised to do anything himself.

At the time few in Washington knew of these attempts to resolve the stalemate within the administration. Still, the state of hostilities between the two secretaries was such that many within and without the administration wondered why Reagan would not chose between the two. One theory was that, like many successful executives, he wanted people around him who disagreed so that he could choose between competing strategies. But as Stockman and other officials had observed, Reagan disliked conflicts among his advisers, and could not settle them, certainly not when the combatants were in the same room. Why, then, didn't he just get rid of one contending party and establish harmony within the administration? The answer from some within the administration was that the President was just too kind-hearted to fire anyone, even those such as Haig, whom he seemed to be happy to see go.

The latter explanation was accepted by many, but those who knew Reagan well knew that he was indifferent to the people who worked for him. He was always cordial, always courteous, but he never expressed appreciation, or acknowledged the service his closest advisers rendered him, unless they threatened to resign. "He treated us like hired help," one of the most valuable of his aides said.[10] Reagan was, of course, remote from everyone, including his own children. He didn't like it when people around him argued or made a fuss, but he could tolerate it: he just wouldn't involve himself. In the NSC meeting Menges describes, Reagan betrayed Shultz once again in the face of a hard-line majority in the room, but he would not explain his change of mind or in any way deal with his angry secretary of state.

At that moment Shultz may have felt that Weinberger, who had known Reagan since the mid-sixties, had a personal bond with the President that he, Shultz, lacked. Many people who worked with Reagan for long periods simply assumed that others were closer to him than they were, or alternately, that they had a bond with him that others did not. But Reagan treated everyone the same way.

A few weeks before the election, Colin Powell, Weinberger's military aide, was sitting opposite the secretary of defense one night on a near-empty 707 on the last leg of a grueling trip from foreign capital to foreign capital, when in the darkness he heard Weinberger say, as if to himself, "This is a lonely life. You make real enemies but few real friends. It exhausts a man in body and spirit. I try to serve the President as faithfully as my strength permits. But gratitude does not always come easily to him and his wife."[11]

Reagan's remoteness had great advantages to him as chief executive. Many of those who served him but did not know him imagined that he was deliberately standing above the fray and deliberately keeping his own counsel in order to render the lonely judgment required of the leader of the Free World. The thought that he was holding something back from them was in itself reassuring, for it suggested the self-control of a strong leader. In addition, his inscrutability allowed many of his bureaucratic servants to project upon him their fondest hopes: here was a man of wisdom and depth; here was a man who, whatever the compromises he might have to make, believed as they believed.

Reagan had, as Deaver writes, glided through life.[12] He had managed to do so in part because there had always been people like Deaver to make his way plain. The trouble was that, as Helene von Damm writes, that he really did not understand the importance of those who worked for him.[13] He never rewarded his associates in any fashion, and when his interests and theirs took different courses, he had no claim on their loyalties. It was thus that at the very same time that Reagan was calling McFarlane indispensable, all of the rest of his top aides were making plans to leave the White House.

Just after the election Chief of Staff Jim Baker and Secretary of the Treasury Donald T. Regan decided to change places. Baker wanted to get on with his career, and Regan, a successful Wall Street businessman, wanted to go where the power in the administration seemed to lie. The two of them consulted with Deaver, and just before the New Year's holiday, the three of them met with the President and asked his approval. Regan thought the decision a serious one for the President, not only because Baker had proved a successful chief of staff but because the other two members of the "troika" were leaving as well. The previous spring Reagan had nominated Ed Meese to succeed William French Smith as attorney general. The confirmation had been held up because of an investigation into Meese's financial affairs, but he would soon be moving on to the Justice Department. Michael Deaver had made known his intention to leave the administration in a few months to go into private business. Thus, with Baker's departure, Reagan would be losing all three of his closest aides, two of whom had been with him his entire political career. In place of them he would be getting a man who, in spite of his four years as secretary of the Treasury, was still a virtual stranger to him. Yet, to Regan's surprise, the President took the news with complete equanimity. Fine, he said, after Regan had told him how the idea came about. Fine, he repeated, it sounds sensible. And that was that.[14]

• • •

By the end of November it was clear to Shultz that the President was not going to fire any of the hard-liners or take charge of policy himself. With what emotions he does not tell us, he went to Weinberger and proposed that the two of them lunch once a week with Casey and McFarlane so that they could talk out the issues, particularly the Soviet issues, as they came up—and before Weinberger made up his mind on them. Weinberger agreed without much enthusiasm. The President, on the other hand, liked the idea and gave them the Old Family Dining Room in the White House residence for their meetings. Thus the group became known as "the Family Group." Weinberger, however, had made his mind up about arms control, and at the first meeting he declared himself unwilling even to have Shultz reiterate the old U.S. positions on START and INF to the Soviets. "Cap was impossible," Shultz writes. "Some family."[15]

Shultz was, however, not totally discouraged, for in the meantime McFarlane had given him an idea. In October, McFarlane had proposed that arms-control policy-making be centralized and that a "czar" be installed in the White House. Shultz had objected mightily: he was not, he told McFarlane, going to give away U.S.-Soviet relations to the White House staff—and he thought "czar" an unfortunate term. Yet, as it was, policy decisions were made in the Senior Arms Control Policy Group, an interagency committee, which, given its acronym, was known as "Sack-pig." Shultz thought the name fitting. Committees are rarely sources of inspiration, and this one not only included Kenneth Adelman but for years had been the battleground between Richard Burt and Richard Perle. Because Perle had always carried the day, the administration still had no negotiable arms proposal, and Shultz, who depended on Burt for his expertise, had lost faith in his champion. Thinking McFarlane's proposal over, he decided that having an "umbrella man" for the arms talks was an excellent idea, as long as that person was responsible to the secretary of state as well as to the President. And McFarlane had suggested just the right man for the job: Paul Nitze.[16]

Those familiar only with the role Nitze played in the late 1970s would have thought that Shultz had made a rather curious choice for an ally against the hard-liners. His Committee on the Present Danger had included most of those same hard-liners, and Nitze had not only joined them in lobbying for a major U.S. strategic buildup, but had personally led the fight against the SALT II agreement and personally constructed the doomsday scenario which bedeviled the strategic debate until the Scowcroft Commission laid it to rest in 1983. Nitze, in sum, had played a major role in devising the rhetoric and the policies which led to the breakdown of U.S.-Soviet relations in Reagan's first term.

Yet by now this period in Nitze's career had faded far into the background—journalists, certainly, no longer brought it up—for, with the election of Ronald Reagan, Nitze had become a leading advocate of arms control. Even during the campaign Nitze privately advised Reagan to take up the SALT negotiations promptly and to take no actions inconsistent with SALT I or SALT II until a new agreement could be made. He reiterated this after the election.[17] Then, on being named chief INF negotiator in late 1981, he had fought mightily for a negotiable proposal, arguing that the continued existence of NATO depended upon an INF agreement. In the summer of 1982, frustrated by the administration's refusal to move off the "zero-zero" approach, he ignored his instructions and proposed a compromise of his own design to his Soviet counterpart, Yuli Kvitsinsky, during a walk in the woods outside Geneva. His initiative was scotched by Perle and McFarlane, but the story of his "walk in the woods" was later leaked by others and widely reported.[18] Subsequently Nitze was the only ranking official in the administration to predict that the Soviets would walk out of the arms talks months before they did. And, like the moderates in Congress, he became an advocate of single-warhead missiles. As a result, arms controllers came to think of him as one of the few sensible people in the administration. By the same token, many in the administration had come to see him as soft on the Russians and dangerously independent—a man who might "stray off the reservation" at any time.

Those with some historical knowledge of Washington were not entirely surprised by this turn of events, for Nitze had gone through similar transformations before. When out of office during the late 1950s, he accused Eisenhower of allowing the U.S. to fall behind the Soviet Union in strategic weapons and raised the specter of a dangerous and growing "missile gap." Yet, in the Berlin crisis of 1961, he, as a member of the Kennedy administration, behaved as if the "missile gap" greatly favored the United States—which, of course, it did. When back in private life in 1969, he along with Dean Acheson created the Committee for a Prudent Defense Policy to defend the ABM program from its numerous critics. Then, appointed to the Nixon administration's SALT-negotiating team, he played an important part in negotiating the ABM away. Nitze could, of course, defend the consistency of his actions: the U.S. required the ABM as a bargaining chip, and so on. But over time his Washington colleagues had noticed that he far preferred to be in government than out of it. When out of it, he had a tendency to descend into Spenglerian gloom about the decline of the West in the face of Eastern barbarism, and to cry alarm about an emerging Soviet first-strike capability. When in office, he would become far more optimistic about the rationality of the Soviet leadership and the possibility of making a deal on nuclear weapons that would dispel fears of a preemptive strike. What was more, his choleric and sanguine humors tended to coincide with the cycles in which contenders for the presidency talked tough and then, upon their election, looked for a modus vivendi with the Soviet Union.

At seventy-seven, Nitze was, as Shultz writes, lean, tanned and fit from winters on the ski slopes of Aspen, summers playing tennis in Maine and weekends riding horses on his Maryland farm. In fact, he had the energy and the concentration of men half his age. Walking, he leaned forward with his shoulders back, leading with his jaw, his eyes scanning the terrain, confident but wary as a general in enemy country. There was a severity about him, relieved by flashes of humor and sheer delight. In groups of people he sometimes withdrew, his eyes hooded, the corners of his lips pulled down, as if the conversation around him was distasteful, or at least far less interesting than his own train of thought. He would remain thus immobile for a while, then suddenly look up, grinning like a boy—or like a lizard which has caught its prey. Though an elder statesman, and one quite conscious of the role, he seemed to have neither aged nor mellowed: he had the same drive and ambition he had had in his youth.

Nitze had given his previous bureaucratic superiors difficult times, but Shultz had no anxiety about appointing him. For one thing, the two were not remotely competitive: Nitze could have no hope of a Cabinet post in this administration, and Shultz did not pretend to be an arms-control expert. Indeed, Shultz made it quite clear that he would depend on Nitze not only to conceptualize the issues but to coach him in negotiating with the Soviets. Then, temperamentally and in their essential conservatism, the two were well matched. "In Paul Nitze I found a diplomatic soul mate who shared my view that strength and diplomacy had to be used together," Shultz wrote.[19] In Nitze, Shultz gained not only an arms-control expert but a black belt in bureaucratic politics, and one who, like Perle, did not always play by Marquis of Queensbury rules.

In November, Shultz had Nitze named ambassador-at-large for arms control, and moved him from the ACDA office he occupied to an office on the seventh floor of the State Department, very close to his own. To Shultz one of the benefits of this arrangement was that it downgraded Kenneth Adelman. Another was that, with any luck, it would short-circuit SAC-PG. Even in retrospect Shultz dreamed: "Interagency committees would meet and NSC members would fight for their views, but ultimately the decisions would be made through the Nitze-Shultz-Reagan line-up." Burt, predictably, was furious. "What's behind this Nitze thing?" he complained. "He's seventy-seven. He doesn't take orders. He's too iconoclastic."[20] Burt did what he could to keep Nitze on the sidelines, but Shultz wouldn't have it, and a few months later Burt accepted an appointment as ambassador to West Germany. At the same time Shultz unseated Edward Rowney as START negotiator and gave him an advisory role in the State Department.

In early December 1984 McFarlane, Shultz and Nitze set about preparing a negotiating position for the meeting with Gromyko in January 1985 on a resumption of the arms talks. All three believed that the stakes were high and that an astonishing arms-control bargain had become a distinct possibility.

After the Soviet call for talks to prevent the militarization of outer space the previous June, Shultz with McFarlane's backing had proposed that the talks also address a radical reduction of offensive nuclear weapons. Just in case the Soviets accepted, Nitze had prepared a concept paper on the relationship of offense and defense. According to Talbott, he envisioned an ambitious, open-ended agreement in which the Soviets would give up large numbers of their heavy, MIRVed ICBMs in exchange for constraints on SDI.[21] The preparations came to naught at the time, but after Reagan's reelection the Soviets responded much as the three men had hoped. In early November, Reagan sent Chernenko a forward-looking letter, and Chernenko replied in the same spirit. Shultz then drafted a longer, more substantive letter for the President to send to the general secretary proposing discussions on space weapons and offensive nuclear arms. "I think your own experts would agree that these two areas are inherently related, even though we may ultimately choose, as was the case in the past, to discuss them in separate negotiating fora," the draft read. Before Reagan's letter could be sent, a letter arrived from Chernenko proposing "new negotiations on the full range of questions concerning nuclear and outer space arms," and acknowledging that there was an "organic" relationship between the two. The text clearly pointed to a trade-off between SDI and offensive missiles, and Shultz underscored the key phrases when he spoke to Reagan about it. The joint U.S.-Soviet announcement of the Shultz-Gromyko meeting released on November 22 contained similar language: the two sides, it said, would "enter into new negotiations with the objective of reaching mutually acceptable agreements on the whole range of questions concerning nuclear and space weapons."[22]

Still, establishing even a preliminary negotiating position was not at all easy. For one thing, the hard-liners in the administration continued to oppose an arms-control treaty, and the popularity of the idea of building a Star Wars defense gave them a politically acceptable means of blocking negotiations. For another thing, Shultz and McFarlane were in a rhetorical bind. Offering to limit Star Wars weaponry in return for deep offensive reductions would cost the U.S. nothing. Yet promising Stars Wars defenses was the only way to sell SDI to the public, and without public support for the program Congress would not fund it and there would be no bargaining chip. Even within the administration, Shultz could not straightforwardly propose limiting the defense, or the hard-liners would leak the offer and denounce him as an apostate to "the President's goal." How to structure a grand compromise without offering to constrain defenses—or, rather, how to tell the Soviets what could not be said domestically—was the problem that Shultz handed Nitze.

In his memoir of 1990, Nitze tells us, somewhat elliptically, how he dealt with this conundrum. In interagency meetings, he reports, many officials urged Shultz to avoid the whole subject of defense and space when talking with Gromyko. He himself disagreed, for the following reason: when the ABM Treaty was concluded in 1972, the U.S. government stated that, if it proved impossible to negotiate restraints on offensive weapons, and if its national security were in jeopardy, the U.S. would consider itself justified in withdrawing from the treaty. The statement, he pointed out, was based on the fundamental nature of the interrelationship between the offense and the defense, and the excessive Soviet deployments of offensive systems had forced the U.S. to consider new defensive systems.

In his memoir Nitze does not tell us where these propositions should lead, and doubtless he was not more forthcoming with his colleagues at the time. But by accusing the Soviets of destroying the strategic equilibrium, he was establishing the principle of an offense-defense relationship in terms the hard-liners could not but agree to. Then, because framing an offer in the negative was a tactic often used in U.S.-Soviet negotiations, he was creating the basis for a trade-off that Gromyko would understand.[23]

Nitze then did something which mystified defense experts outside the administration, but which in context had a purpose.[24]

In interagency meetings, Nitze tells us, many officials doubted that known technologies could achieve the President's goal and argued that the SDI program should concentrate on the lesser goal of protecting U.S. nuclear weapons. Weinberger, however, maintained that the program should focus on the President's goal. "It seemed to me essential," Nitze writes, "to draft a long-term strategic concept with respect to SDI and its relationship to offensive forces, keeping in mind the President's objective of eventually eliminating nuclear weapons." Nitze did that, and the draft was just four sentences long:

> For the next five to ten years our objectives should be a radical reduction in the power of existing and planned offensive nuclear arms as well as the effective limitation of defensive nuclear arms, whether land, sea, air or space-based. We should even now be looking forward to a period of transition beginning five or ten years from now, to effective non-nuclear defensive forces, including defenses against offensive nuclear arms. This period of transition should lead to the eventual elimination of all nuclear arms, both offensive and defensive. A nuclear-free world is an ultimate objective to which we, the Soviet Union and all other nations can agree.

"I was surprised," Nitze writes, "at the reaction of SAC-PG. The representatives of the Defense Department, the JCS, the Arms Control Agency, State and the CIA, all expressed their general agreement. Somewhat revised, (e.g. five to ten years was made ten) the paragraph was approved by the President. . . ."[25]

Possibly Nitze was surprised, for in four sentences he had taken the President's fiction and transformed it into a fantastical strategy for the indefinite future—and the entire panoply of high national-security officials signed onto it. "We had gotten quite used to believing six impossible things before breakfast," one State Department official later said.[26]

Nitze does not explicate the four sentences in his book, but in retrospect the purpose of them seems fairly clear. He knew that the hard-liners could sink the current negotiations if they developed, or threatened to develop, an ABM system. But developing an effective non-nuclear defense would take a very long time, if it could be done at all. It was therefore quite safe as a goal. The "strategic concept" did not put SDI on the table, for it spoke only of reducing offensive and defensive *nuclear* arms, and SDI was advertised as a non-nuclear program. Still, it maintained SDI as a potential bargaining chip, and possibly that was the best Nitze could do.[27]

Because the President invariably took a long Christmas vacation in California, Shultz and McFarlane once again seized the occasion of the Annenbergs' New Year's Eve party to brief Reagan about the forthcoming U.S.-Soviet talks. This year Weinberger also came to Palm Springs and joined the small group in Annenberg's study. According to Oberdorfer, Shultz and McFarlane went over the negotiating strategy they had developed with Nitze. Weinberger had a long list of objections. His main point was that Shultz should not even talk about SDI with Gromyko, lest he give it away. The President seemed sympathetic to this argument, but he was also sympathetic to Shultz's argument that space defense was the primary topic of interest to Moscow and that it would be unrealistic not to discuss it. "Cap," Reagan said, "we can't know where it will all come out, but we are going to engage. So George, go over there and get it started without giving anything up."[28]

Shortly afterwards Shultz made the final preparations for the trip to Geneva. In order to show that the whole administration was united behind the negotiating position, he decided to invite a large delegation: McFarlane, Nitze and Burt, but also a number of the hard-liners, including Kenneth Adelman, Edward Rowney and Richard Perle. Shultz had some reason to believe that the hard-liners would cooperate. The ballooning deficits were causing even Republican congressmen to take a hard look at Weinberger's defense budget; the Democrats were holding funds for the MX hostage to the resumption of U.S.-Soviet negotiations, and they were haggling over the amount they would give SDI. Still, Shultz's delegation was not a happy family; on the flight to Geneva reporters dubbed the plane "the ship of feuds."[29]

On January 7 Gromyko listened glumly to Shultz's opening statement. The two sides quickly agreed to resume negotiations on INF and START, but the third area was more difficult; the Soviets wanted to call the talks "space-strike arms" but the Americans insisted on "defense and space." According to Nitze, Gromyko stated the Soviet position unambiguously. Maintaining that the U.S. was planning to achieve a first-strike capability with SDI, he called for the non-militarization of space and proposed that all research designed to develop space weapons be banned. He further stipulated that all three areas of negotiation be discussed in their interrelationship, and that no agreement on one was possible without concurrent movement on the other two. Shultz, for his part, refused to discuss banning research, and, in drafting an agreement to resume the talks, shied away from any language suggesting that the U.S. might constrain the SDI program. The meeting almost broke down over these issues, but eventually a compromise was found; the two sides agreed on a joint communiqué and announced that the talks would begin in mid-March.[30]

Shultz declared victory and sent members of his delegation to brief other governments about the breakthrough.[31] The only problem was that the central issue of the arms talks remained unresolved. The key paragraph of the U.S.-Soviet joint communiqué read: "The sides agree that the subject of the negotiations will be a complex of questions concerning space and nuclear arms, both strategic and intermediate range, with all the questions considered and resolved in their interrelationship. The objective of the negotiations will be to work out effective agreements aimed at preventing an arms race in space and terminating it on earth, at limiting and reducing nuclear arms, and at strengthening strategic stability."[32]

The vagueness of the language was the result of much bargaining. Nonetheless, the Soviets, and most outside observers, interpreted it as establishing a linkage between negotiations on offensive nuclear weapons and negotiations on "space weapons"—that is, anti-satellite weapons and the new technologies being researched under SDI—and creating the basis for a trade-off between the two. But U.S. government spokesmen rejected this interpretation. The stipulated "interrelationship," they maintained, did not mean limiting SDI: to the contrary, it meant introducing space-based defenses while reducing offensive nuclear arms and beginning a negotiated transition to a world without nuclear weapons.[33]

Neither Shultz nor Nitze tells us anything about this disagreement in their memoirs. But in effect they had done exactly what the President asked: they had engaged the Soviets in negotiations without giving anything away. The "strategic concept," which former Defense Secretary James Schlesinger described as a "strategic cover story," had become the sum of U.S. policy on arms control; and the question of what the U.S. would trade for deep reductions in the Soviet arsenal was put off for another day.[34]

But Nitze was not through yet, and in the months that followed he made an audacious attempt to maneuver the administration into a grand compromise through what might be called reverse diplomacy. First, however, he took another step to ensure that SDI remained a research program.

On the plane home from Paris after the Geneva talks, Nitze proposed to McFarlane that the administration announce that any system to come out of SDI research had to meet military standards before it was developed and deployed. He was not the first to suggest this. Since the beginning of the SDI program some Pentagon experts had worried that, given the enthusiasm for Star Wars, a development decision might be made for political reasons with results that would be militarily unsound. In July 1984 Franklin Miller, the strategic analyst in Weinberger's office who had done the third report on SDI, told a House subcommittee that any defensive system the administration supported for development and deployment would have to meet the tests of military effectiveness, survivability and cost-effectiveness. These were the criteria normally applied in the acquisition of new weapons systems, but they had not been formally adopted as standards for SDI. In January 1985 Admiral Watkins told an audience in Los Angeles that SDI should meet these same three criteria. No SDI-related system, he said, should go forward unless it was highly survivable and unless it would be "more expensive for an attacker to add warheads than for a defender to increase defensive capability."[35] Nitze, when asked about SDI, had proposed a version of these standards, using the phrase "cost-effectiveness at the margins" to cover the case of incremental additions, such as the one Watkins had described. On the plane he persuaded McFarlane to draft the criteria into an official guidance for the President to sign.

On February 20 Nitze gave a speech at the World Affairs Council in Philadelphia and with some fanfare presented the criteria of military effectiveness, survivability and "cost-effectiveness at the margins" as official policy. The speech received a good deal of attention, and in the wake of it McFarlane was able to get the standards, now known as the "Nitze criteria," accepted by the bureaucracy. He encountered no resistance, for, once the criteria had been spelled out in public, no Pentagon civilian could object: they were, after all, the Pentagon's own standards for acquisitions.[36]

Many of Nitze's former colleagues in the defense community applauded the speech, interpreting it as a coup for the arms controllers in the administration. SDI enthusiasts, including Henry Kissinger, denounced it. But in the opinion of all of them, the "Nitze criteria" precluded any SDI-related deployment. Daniel Graham complained that the criteria could be used by bureaucrats to stop the development of any system, no matter how good it was. Robert McNamara and James Schlesinger maintained that no anti-missile system could be cost-effective, and Kissinger said the criteria were not meetable—adding that strategic defenses should be deployed anyway. McNamara predicted the administration would never adhere to the cost-effectiveness criterion even if it was government policy; Schlesinger said that Nitze had killed Star Wars. Nitze, however, refused to agree. At an Aspen Institute seminar which both of them attended, Schlesinger commented that a cost-effective defense was by definition impossible, and Nitze responded vehemently, "What is your evidence, Jim? How can you be so sure? Why can't you keep an open mind on this? My own mind is totally open."[37]

Nitze's professed agnosticism annoyed his former colleagues, but it annoyed Weinberger and his deputies a good deal more. In his memoir Weinberger calls Nitze "one of the strongest opponents of SDI in the State Department." But he could not prove it, and he could not dismantle the Nitze criteria. In his memoir he argues first that the "Nitze criteria" were not Nitze's but originated in his own office and were routinely applied to all weapons systems; second, that the standard of cost-effectiveness did not apply in all cases, and certainly not in the case of SDI; and third that Nitze adopted the criteria in order to kill the SDI program. In the midst of this Lewis Carroll syllogism he writes that the phrase "cost-effective at the margins" was "strategic gibberish," which he understood but State Department officials did not. To read these pages is to see why Shultz often seemed so ill-tempered after meeting with the secretary of defense.[38]

The arms-control talks began in March with a new U.S. negotiating team headed by Max Kampelman, a lawyer, a Democrat and a former member of the Committee on the Present Danger, who had served the Carter and the Reagan administrations as ambassador to the European Security and Cooperation talks. (Weinberger had proposed that Edward Teller lead the delegation—but his suggestion was vetoed.) John Tower, who had just resigned from the Senate, was named head of the START negotiating group. Kampelman and Tower were deeply conservative, but they were not intransigent hard-liners, and Kampelman, though he had no experience in arms control, was an accomplished negotiator. Maynard Glitman, Nitze's deputy in Geneva in 1981–83, was appointed to lead the INF talks.[39] But the new team had no new instructions. In preparing the opening proposal, Shultz had not dared to bring up the matter of an offense-defense trade-off, and none of the six options that went to the President mentioned the possibility of limiting SDI. Kampelman and Tower thus went to the table empty-handed except for the 1982 INF and START proposals, and instructions to convince the Soviets of the virtues of Star Wars defenses.[40] Still, they were at the table, so the Congress authorized funds for the MX.

In his memoir Nitze tells us that in April a reporter asked how the negotiations were going. "I could only respond 'about as anticipated,' which was, at that point, no progress at all."[41]

Soon afterwards Nitze heard the message from Geneva he had been listening for.

In Geneva, Kampelman and Tower had asked their Soviet counterparts to show flexibility—to make them an offer which Washington could not refuse. In discussions they ascertained that the Soviets were primarily concerned with the space-based aspects of SDI: they did not want American battle stations hanging "like a sword of Damocles" over their heads. In this context Yuli Kvitsinsky, Nitze's counterpart in the INF negotiations who had become the head of the delegation for Defense and Space, mentioned the need for a non-withdrawal clause for the ABM Treaty. By the terms of the treaty, either side could withdraw in six months if it declared its national security in jeopardy. The Soviets, it seemed, wanted to extend the period to ten years, in order to give themselves time to react if there was a breakthrough in SDI research that would permit a deployment. In the START talks they hinted at the possibility of deep reductions in offensive weapons in return.[42]

With that information Nitze went to work drafting his own version of a grand compromise. Working with a few colleagues, and otherwise in secret, he prepared a schedule of offensive reductions which would bring both sides down to 50 percent of their current strategic arsenals over a period of ten years. Shultz thought the idea of 50-percent reductions would appeal to the President, and the ten-year period figured in Nitze's strategic concept as the first phase of the transition to a nuclear-free world. In refining the proposal Nitze broke with the administration's past efforts and with his own previous positions. Since the early 1970s Nitze had insisted on the need to reduce Soviet throw-weights, and in Reagan's first term he had backed Perle's attempt to make throw-weights the centerpiece of START. His new proposal, however, rested on the principles the congressional moderates and the Scowcroft commissioners had espoused, and the numbers he chose cut more deeply into the quantities of warheads on both sides than it did into the quantities of launchers. The purpose was clearly to encourage deMIRVing, or the development of single-warhead missiles, and to enhance "crisis stability."

The draft was finished on a Monday, and since Nitze wanted an innocuous title for his clandestine endeavor, the proposal was named "the Monday package."[43]

Nitze gave the paper to Shultz and McFarlane, and although McFarlane had reservations about some aspects of the offensive side of the plan, both approved the idea. The bargain the Soviets had suggested seemed almost too good to be true. By the estimates Shultz had, the prospects for deploying a credible strategic defense before the mid-1990s were negligible. Thus, in promising not to withdraw from the ABM Treaty for ten years, the U.S. would be giving up nothing.[44] The three decided not to breathe a word of the plan to Perle and Weinberger but to obtain the President's consent and to attempt to enlist the support of the Joint Chiefs of Staff. After that they would set up a secret back channel to Moscow, and Nitze would do the negotiating.[45]

According to Nitze, Shultz and McFarlane laid out their whole plan to Reagan and the President approved it. According to Talbott, however, the process was not quite so straightforward.

Since the start of the Geneva talks, Shultz and McFarlane had held a number of sessions with the President in which they had attempted to persuade him of the virtue of a trade-off between offense and defense. To be sure he grasped their argument, they went through the logic of the trade-off with exaggerated simplicity, starting with a *reductio ad absurdam* and working back to a "do-able deal." Their argument, McFarlane recollected, went this way: if the Soviets did not have any ballistic missiles at all, we would not need SDI; if the Soviets had fewer ballistic missiles, we would not need as much SDI; if we got the Soviets to the point where their missiles did not threaten us with a first strike, we could live with constraints on SDI.

At the end of these sessions the President would nod and say yes, that made sense. But then Weinberger would get equal time with him and insist that SDI must proceed unconstrained, arguing that it would be irresponsible to deny the American people the chance that their technology gave them to defend themselves against a Soviet attack. The President, according to McFarlane, always found this argument more appealing than the more complex one he and Shultz had presented.[46]

In McFarlane's telling of this story, and in Talbott's, the point seems to be that the President did not quite grasp the elementary logic his national-security adviser and secretary of state laid out for him. But to examine the story is to see that Shultz and McFarlane failed to make the crucial point that SDI was not going to produce anything like a "shield." Indeed, their logic was founded on the premise that it would produce weapons which could defend the United States against some significant proportion of Soviet missiles within the foreseeable future. Had they really believed this, they themselves would doubtless have had many second thoughts about trading the program away. As it was, they gave Reagan no reason to find their argument more compelling than Weinberger's.

By Talbott's account, McFarlane did not really obtain the President's consent to the Monday package. Rather, he ran the paper by the President, then summarized it for him in an offhanded fashion, as if it were entirely routine. Reagan often did not read the option papers given to him for decision but simply initialed them after an oral briefing. He approved this one with a shrug and a nod.[47]

Meanwhile, Nitze discussed the ideas in the Monday package with General Vessey and then with the Chiefs as a group, presenting the proposal as his own. The Chiefs raised no objection, but they were careful not to commit themselves to a plan that departed radically from current policy and that had as yet no official status. McFarlane had promised to give the Chiefs an official briefing and to obtain their consent, but, to Nitze's disappointment, he failed to follow through. As a result, the conspirators had no bureaucratic allies.[48]

Nevertheless, Shultz, McFarlane, Nitze and Burt met with Ambassador Dobrynin on June 17.[49] After speaking to Dobrynin of other matters, Shultz suggested that the two sides create a confidential channel to discuss arms control, broadly hinting that an offense-defense trade-off might be the subject of the discussions. During the SALT I negotiations Dobrynin himself had served as a back channel, enabling Kissinger to bypass his negotiators in Geneva—among them, Paul Nitze. The three hoped he would see the need to create another one, this one bypassing not only the Geneva negotiators but the Office of the Secretary of Defense. Then Nitze and a Soviet counterpart could work out a grand compromise in secret and present it as a breathtaking fait accompli, which Weinberger would have to accept.[50]

To their dismay, however, Dobrynin brushed aside the hint of an offense-defense trade-off and commented only on the channel. Shultz thought he did not get the point, but Nitze assured the secretary that he did. "Dobrynin *does* know what we are talking about," he told Shultz. "The Soviets just don't want to acknowledge SDI in any form."[51] In his memoir Nitze writes that in his opinion Dobrynin disliked the whole idea because of "some intrigue being played out in Kremlin politics."[52]

In fact, the intrigue on the Soviet side was plain vanilla next to the one the Americans were engaged in, and the real problem was that the Americans had committed a diplomatic blunder.

In his account of the June 17 meeting, Dobrynin tells us that he heard Shultz's message about the trade-off loud and clear, and he was most encouraged by it. However, because Shultz said that he had presidential authorization to deliver it, and because Shultz had always been extremely careful not to overstep his authority in the past, Dobrynin assumed that he must have come to some kind of agreement with Weinberger on the plan. In other words, the intrigue on the American side was so deep that even Dobrynin failed to make it out.

As to the channel, Shultz had suggested that Nitze was ready to meet with whomever the Kremlin might designate for negotiations. Dobrynin, to trust his memoir, did not even hear this suggestion. The ambassador had very keen ears, but the proposal was not one designed to appeal to him, since it was in essence a request that he set up a back channel that bypassed himself. In Dobrynin's version of events, Shultz proposed that he and Dobrynin conduct a "broad, philosophical" discussion of the key arms-control issues—a discussion that could be continued between Shultz and Gromyko when they met in July. This, in any case, was the message he passed on to Moscow. Gromyko then turned down the proposal—according to Dobrynin, because he didn't want Dobrynin to do the negotiating, and he thought that nothing good could come of "broad, philosophical" discussions involving SDI, since it might lead to a tacit Soviet acquiescence to the program.[53]

Later in the summer Nitze tried once more to establish a back channel. With encouragement from the Soviet side, he dined with his former negotiating partner, Yuli Kvitsinsky, and outlined the Monday package in some detail, presenting it not as a proposal but as his own personal view of how the negotiations should proceed. He had made the same distinction to Kvitsinsky when he proposed an INF compromise during their walk in the woods. On that occasion Kvitsinsky had passed on Nitze's proposal as an official overture, and had been badly burned when it turned out to be merely Nitze's idea. This time he took full note of the distinction and refused to relay the message. Thus Nitze's attempt at reverse diplomacy—or what Weinberger might have called the Monday Package Plot—came to a somewhat ignominious end.[54]

That Nitze and Shultz undertook such a desperate venture was a measure of their sense of the opportunity which awaited, but it was also a measure of their despair about achieving arms control by more conventional means. In the months since Reagan's reelection the hard-liners had regained their ascendancy. Taking heart from Reagan's landslide victory and interpreting it as a mandate for their own policies, they had moved the administration back into a confrontational mode. The President had reverted to crusading anti-Communist rhetoric, and his NSC staff to pressing for a resumption of aid to the contras.

In January, William Casey gave a speech calling for the support of anti-Communist insurgencies, or "freedom fighters," around the world. The President picked up the theme in his second inaugural address, and he and other administration officials returned to it often during the year as they lobbied the Congress for aid to the contras, to the Afghan rebels, to the Savimbi forces in Angola and to other insurgencies in the Third World. The "Reagan doctrine," as this theme became known, did not signify an abrupt change of policy, for Casey was already running dozens of covert operations in the Third World. Still, it implied a reversion to the proposition that the Soviets were responsible for all the trouble in the world, and it implicitly repudiated the vow Reagan had made in his speech of January 16, 1984, to engage the Soviets in a dialogue on peace in the Third World. As such it was a direct blow to Shultz's hopes of settling regional conflicts with the Soviets.[55]

Then, while Shultz, McFarlane and Nitze were planning an unprecedented new arms treaty, Weinberger and Perle were maneuvering to destroy the last two.

On February 1 the administration issued a report to the Congress on Soviet violations of the ABM Treaty and the SALT II agreement. It was the second such report prepared by Richard Perle's office at the request of Senator Jesse Helms and other right-wing Republicans in the Senate. The first had been issued in January 1984, just before the President made the conciliatory speech opening his campaign and Shultz met with Gromyko in Stockholm. Both reports charged the Soviets with a long list of violations, most of which were petty and technical, a few of which had some substance. The most serious charge was that the Soviets were building a phased-array radar near the city of Krasnoyarsk, deep inside the Soviet Union. Phased-array radars are capable of tracking incoming warheads, and under the terms of the ABM Treaty both nations were permitted to build such radars on their peripheries, where they could serve an early-warning function, but not in their interiors, where they might serve as battle-management stations for a nationwide ABM system. Under previous administrations, U.S. negotiators in Geneva had settled similar issues with their Soviet counterparts without much strife or publicity, and there was no reason to expect that they could not settle this one, except that the hard-liners refused to allow them to make an attempt.[56]

Weinberger and his aides had said little about the radar in 1984, but now they could not seem to stop talking about it. In one congressional hearing after another, Pentagon spokesmen made it the centerpiece of their testimony, citing it as evidence for a list of propositions: the Soviets were deliberately violating the ABM Treaty; the Soviets were far ahead of the United States in the development of anti-missile defenses; the Soviets were planning to break out of the ABM Treaty and establish a national ABM system, which would cripple the U.S. deterrent. In public Weinberger and his aides drew the conclusion that SDI had to be funded, and swiftly, so that the U.S. could defend itself from this new Soviet threat. But the secretary and his aides had a more immediate goal.

In early 1985 Weinberger argued within the administration that the United States should withdraw from the ABM Treaty because compliance with it was hindering SDI research. Shultz was taken aback. In his memoir he writes, "We were, in fact, nowhere *near* the point in our research where such a step was needed for the sake of the program. Furthermore, our security interests would be jeopardized more seriously than those of the Soviets. If we tried to pull out of the ABM Treaty, our allies and Congress would be enraged, and our negotiations with the Soviets would blow up in our faces."[57] Weinberger did not give voice to his opinion in public, but, along with his testimony about the Krasnoyarsk radar, his proposal was a shot across Shultz's bow.

The report on the alleged Soviet violations of SALT II had a similar purpose: that of ending the SALT regime. The hard-liners had sought to kill the policy of not "undercutting" the unratified treaty off and on ever since Reagan was first elected, but they had never been able to show there was any military advantage to be gained by it. The Joint Chiefs had supported adherence to the treaty on the grounds that it constrained Soviet forces and added "predictability" to future deployments while permitting the U.S. strategic buildup to proceed as planned. The treaty, had it been ratified, would have expired in December, but American deployments were still not running up against the limits, and the Chiefs maintained that the Soviets could deploy additional strategic warheads faster than the United States, and at less cost, if the constraints were removed. In interagency meetings Weinberger and Perle maintained that the Soviets were violating the treaty so egregiously that the U.S. had to make a response. Nitze countered that, though there were technical Soviet violations, none of them entailed going over the numerical sub-ceilings. In June the two sides agreed to a compromise: the U.S. would remain in compliance with the treaty for the time being but would also prepare "proportionate and appropriate" responses to Soviet violations.

In effect, the administration was edging closer to a decision that would remove all constraints on offensive strategic arms.[58]

WHILE THE REAGAN administration moved back to the right, important changes were taking place in Moscow that made a hard anti-Soviet stance far more difficult to sustain.

On March 10 the long-enfeebled Konstantin Chernenko died, and on the 11th Mikhail Gorbachev was named general secretary of the Soviet Communist Party. Only fifty-four years old, Gorbachev was a full generation younger than Chernenko and most of the other members of the Politburo. Simply as a matter of appearance he seemed to belong to a different country from his predecessors. Articulate, energetic and well dressed, he often appeared in public with his attractive wife, Raisa, and he had positive affinity for the media. Margaret Thatcher, who had had a five-hour conversation with him at 10 Downing Street in December 1984, had been impressed with his directness, his flare and his ability to handle complex issues. "I like Mr. Gorbachev," she announced. "We can do business together."[59]

American officials knew more about Gorbachev than they did about most Soviet officials, for he had previously made several visits to Europe and one to Canada. Still, their information about him was sketchy.

Born in the Stavropol district in the foothills of the northern Caucasus, Gorbachev had made his career in the region. He came from a peasant family that had suffered much during the purges and famines of the 1930s and during World War II. But, bright, hardworking—and the star of his school plays—he had attended the prestigious Moscow State University, where he studied law. He was thus better educated than any general secretary of the party since Lenin. On his return to Stavropol, he specialized in agriculture and rose quickly through the ranks of the party. During the seventies, when he was regional secretary, his intelligence and reputation for incorruptibility attracted the attention of high party officials, including the austere Yuri Andropov. As chief of the KGB, Andropov knew better than most what damage the slackness and corruption of the Brezhnev regime had done to the party and to the country. A true believer, he set about creating a constituency for reform, and recruited Gorbachev into his faction. Following his mentor into the inner circles of the party, Gorbachev was made a full member of the Politburo in 1980. He was then forty-nine—eight years younger than the next-youngest member and twenty-one years below the average age of his colleagues.[60]

After Brezhnev's death in 1982, Andropov moved a number of reformers into the top ranks of the party, but his health gave way before he could complete the process and make any significant changes. During his illness

Gorbachev took an increasingly important role in managing the government and the party, and when Chernenko was elected general secretary, the expectation was that Gorbachev's turn would come next. But the Brezhnev faction was far from defeated, and when Chernenko died a year and a half after taking office, there was a brief struggle for succession in which Gorbachev outmaneuvered a rival with the help of Andrei Gromyko.[61]

On a trip to Moscow for Chernenko's funeral, George Bush and George Shultz met with Gorbachev for the first time. At ten in the evening, after a long, hard day, Gorbachev launched into a wide-ranging discussion of foreign policy. He had extensive typed notes to work from, but he soon put them aside and spoke extemporaneously. The positions he took were familiar, and he challenged the American positions aggressively, but the spirit seemed different. Bush and Shultz were impressed by his intellectual energy, his expressiveness and the breadth of his interests and knowledge. He had, they thought, an engaging sense of humor, and he seemed comfortable with himself. "Gorbachev is totally different from any Soviet leader I've met," Shultz told the press. But he cautioned, "The U.S.-Soviet relationship is not just about personalities."[62]

Gorbachev, it became evident, was primarily concerned with the problem of the moribund Soviet economy. In his first few months in office he set out a number of new goals for the party—greater discipline, a brake on corruption, better management, more sobriety in the workforce. He had inherited these projects from Andropov, and the general expectation in Moscow, as elsewhere, was that he would be a younger, more forward-looking version of his mentor. Yet some in Moscow noticed that he was acting more quickly and boldly than Andropov and that he seemed to have much greater ambitions for economic renewal than could be achieved by the limited means he had proposed. In mid-May, in a speech at the Smolny Institute in Leningrad, where in 1917 Lenin had announced the construction of socialism, he spoke bluntly about the failures of the economic system and the need to change its nature, raising it to Western levels of efficiency and quality.[63] Animated, leaning forward every few minutes to explain what he meant, he reminded one American observer of a Baptist preacher.[64]

In foreign affairs Gorbachev made no precipitous moves. He endorsed the basic lines of Soviet foreign policy, though he struck a new note in calling for "civilized relations" between states. The previous year he had been instrumental in the decision to reopen the arms talks, and he had helped to reverse the course of sullen withdrawal and abusive propaganda that his government had taken in the fall of 1983. Though he criticized U.S. policies, he continued to speak positively about improving the U.S.-Soviet relationship. His main concern seemed to be arms control.[65]

In early April 1985, Gorbachev announced a six-month unilateral moratorium on the deployment of Soviet INF missiles in Europe and promised that if the United States joined him, it would become permanent.

This was not a proposal with any attractions for NATO, because the Soviet Union had apparently completed its deployments whereas NATO was still in the early stages of its own. Ten days later he proposed a bilateral moratorium on all nuclear-weapons testing.[66] In a speech on April 26 in Warsaw he said that the Soviet Union would be willing to go beyond the offensive reductions it had proposed as an opening position in the START talks in return for restrictions on SDI. The Soviet Union, he said, had "already suggested that both sides reduce strategic arms by one quarter," but it had "no objections to making deeper reductions" as long as "an arms race does not begin in space."[67]

Administration officials dismissed Gorbachev's initiatives as propaganda, but they were merely the first in a long series of proposals and unilateral arms-control measures. The previous December, Gorbachev had told Margaret Thatcher that he did not believe the Soviet Union could solve its domestic economic problems without curbing the arms race. At the plenary meeting of the Central Committee in April—"the April plenum," as it came to be known—Gorbachev took preliminary steps towards redirecting investment from the military sector into the civilian economy. The committee set out a number of new policy lines, among them a decision to make military doctrine more defensive and to limit the armed forces by criteria of "sufficiency," a decision to reactivate a series of arms-control measures and a recognition of the need to disengage Soviet forces from Afghanistan.[68] These policy lines were not made public, but in July, Dusko Doder, the *Washington Post* correspondent in Moscow, reported that there was "a clear impression that Gorbachev wants to reach some sort of accommodation with the United States that would limit the scope of the arms race." Another distinct impression, he wrote, was "that Gorbachev's interest in foreign affairs at this point is primarily linked to his domestic policies as the continued arms buildup and other foreign commitments would inevitably interfere with his plans to modernize Soviet society and improve living standards."[69]

Having decided not to go to the Chernenko funeral, President Reagan had sent a letter inviting Gorbachev to meet with him in Washington at his earliest convenience. Gorbachev replied with an expression of interest in a summit, though not necessarily one in Washington, adding that at such a meeting no major documents need be signed but that agreements on issues of mutual interest could be concluded if they could be worked out. Former Soviet leaders had never counted summits successful without a major arms agreement, and Gorbachev foresaw no immediate prospect of one.[70] In mid-May Gromyko conveyed Gorbachev's formal acceptance to Shultz, specifying a meeting in Europe in November. The decision, it later appeared, caused a good deal of dissension in the Kremlin, but Gorbachev was a man in a hurry. He knew that he would have to deal with Reagan for the next four years, and that a summit—if it was not a disaster—would give him the prestige he needed, both at home and abroad, to proceed with his plans for domestic reform.[71]

Shultz was delighted with the prospect of a summit, and he assumed the President would be, too. Reagan had, after all, pressed him hard for a summit throughout 1984, and Gorbachev, a much more promising interlocutor than Chernenko, had taken the unprecedented step of accepting without preconditions. Yet from the moment that Gorbachev expressed interest the White House began backpedaling. On April 8 an administration spokesman said that "much serious work" was needed before such a meeting, and the summit must be "carefully prepared"—a qualification which in the past had been used to fend off summit invitations. The next day Donald Regan, the White House chief of staff, explained, "We've always felt that there should be a lot of groundwork and an agenda set before any meeting between the leaders." A day later Robert McFarlane attempted to clarify the "ambiguity" by distinguishing between a "meeting," which the President would favor, and a "summit," which would take longer to prepare.[72]

Reagan told Shultz that he was being clobbered by Weinberger and the hard-liners for wanting to meet with Gorbachev. He was wavering about going to a summit; McFarlane was wavering as well. After Gorbachev made his acceptance firm and proposed a European capital as the site, McFarlane told Shultz that the President might not travel outside of the United States for a summit. "That would be insane," Shultz retorted.[73] Eventually McFarlane seemed to get the point: Gorbachev had forced the issue, and Reagan could not be in the position of refusing to meet with him.

On July 3 the two sides announced that the two leaders would meet in Geneva on November 19 and 20. The Soviets followed their announcement with another one: Gromyko was to be elevated to the ceremonial post of President of the Soviet Union, and Eduard Shevardnadze, the party chief of the Republic of Georgia, would be the next foreign minister. Shevardnadze had no experience in foreign relations, but he was reputedly an able and a trusted ally of Gorbachev's. His appointment seemed to indicate that Gorbachev wanted a break with the past, and that he was going to take foreign policy into his own hands.

A month later Shultz met with Shevardnadze at a conference in Helsinki. He and the members of his delegation, including Jack Matlock, the Soviet specialist on the NSC staff, were pleasantly surprised. Shevardnadze greeted Shultz in a friendly, informal fashion and made no bones about his own lack of experience. "I'm new at this," he said. "Please tell me if I goof." In the discussions he would state the Soviet position succinctly, and if Shultz did not agree, he would say, "All right, think about it. We think it's a good idea. Maybe you can suggest a better one." Then he would move on to the next topic. Similarly, when Shultz made arguments he could not accept, he would respond with remarks such as, "We have a different point of view on that, but we need to solve the problem. Think about what we have said, and we will study what you have said. Maybe next time we can move closer." For the American delegation it was difficult to believe that this was a *Soviet* foreign minister.[74]

In early September, after the President returned from a holiday at his California ranch, Shultz found a "sour and uncertain" mood in the White House. McFarlane was still talking about a "meeting" rather than a summit, and he seemed to be making the President feel that the whole affair would be complicated, worrisome and difficult. Shultz dressed McFarlane down. The President, Shultz told him, worked best when he was confident, comfortable and positive, but McFarlane was confusing him and making him uncomfortable and insecure. Shultz then went to work on Reagan like a coach on a demoralized ball player. "We have a strong position from which to work, and we are ready to engage with the Soviets and confident that we can represent ourselves and the free world strongly." This, he said, "is the Super Bowl."[75]

For all of Shultz's brave words, the administration had not as yet begun to gear itself up for the summit. Its arms-control proposals had hardly changed since 1982. Gorbachev, by contrast, was staking out new positions and publicizing them skillfully.

In late August, Gorbachev gave a long and candid interview to *Time* magazine, and on September 3 he met with a delegation of eight U.S. senators, including Warner and Nunn, for a three-and-a-half-hour discussion of arms control and other bilateral issues. To the senators he said that he would make "radical proposals" to reduce strategic and intermediate-range arms as soon as the U.S. agreed to prohibit the militarization of space. Both in that meeting and in the *Time* interview, he made a very precise statement about SDI.

For months the Soviet negotiators in Geneva had been calling for a complete ban on SDI research, claiming that the ABM Treaty prohibited it. This was, of course, not the U.S. understanding of the treaty, and it had never been the Soviet understanding of it either. American arms-control experts assumed that the Soviets would back off from this demand when the time came for serious negotiations. In the interview Gorbachev said that the Soviet Union opposed research outside, but not inside, the laboratory. He did not, he said, have in mind banning research in fundamental science, but, rather, research at "the designing stage . . . when they start building models or mock-ups or test samples, when they hold field tests [of systems or components] . . . that can be verified . . . by national technical means."[76]

Gorbachev had chosen his words carefully. At the Senate hearings on the ABM Treaty in 1972, the chief U.S. negotiator, Gerard Smith, had used the same words to define the difference between "research" and "development" that had been agreed upon by the SALT negotiators in Geneva. Gorbachev was saying that his government would ask only that SDI conform to the ABM Treaty as it had always been understood.[77] In other words, he seemed to be clearing the way for an offense-defense trade-off.

NOT LONG AFTER Gorbachev signaled his interest in a grand compromise, the Reagan administration vacillated and then responded by attacking the very foundation of arms control.

In mid-September 1985 administration officials held a series of high-level meetings to decide U.S. arms-control positions for the November summit. Shultz, Nitze and McFarlane tell us little about these meetings in their memoirs, but from press reports of the period it is clear that the two long-established factions in the administration waged a ferocious battle. Stories in the *New York Times* and the *Washington Post* carry with them the distant sounds of combat, the smell of cordite and almost daily predictions of imminent victory from the commanders on either side. These reports suggest that Shultz, Nitze and McFarlane were, for the first time in interagency discussions, calling directly for an offense-defense trade-off and proposing limits on SDI. Just how they were doing this was not clear, but certainly Weinberger and his aides were resisting any limits on "the President's favorite program." On September 15 the *Post* reported that, with a little more than nine weeks left before the summit, the President seemed to be far from a decision on this crucial issue, and that his own approach was still unknown.[78]

On September 17, however, the President, in a nationally televised press conference, announced that he would not accept limits on SDI research in exchange for offensive reductions. Further, he seemed to rule out any limitations on the "testing" and "development" of defensive weapons. To some analysts it sounded as though the President was talking about breaching the limits of the ABM Treaty, but there was room for doubt, since the treaty did not ban laboratory testing but only the field testing of ABM systems and components, and the President did not make the distinction. Asked whether he would rule out any deal on development and testing, he said, "I think that's a legitimate part of research, and, yes, I would rule it out.... This is too important to the world to be willing to trade off that for a different number of nuclear missiles." Asked what the President meant exactly, the State Department spokesman replied that the President was speaking merely of the testing permitted by the treaty, and that the SDI program would be conducted in full compliance with it.[79]

Whatever Reagan meant by "testing," he had apparently rejected an offense-defense trade-off—at least as a going-in position. Asked if he would change his position if the Soviets made an attractive enough offer on offensive arms, some officials said they believed the decision would stand. "I think the President never seriously entertained the idea of restrictions on SDI, beyond those which already exist in the ABM treaty," Richard Perle said. Other officials, however, said they thought it "premature" to predict what Reagan would do at the summit, and some insisted that the President's statements were not final but a part of a bargaining strategy. Because no battle in the Reagan administration ever ended, it still seemed unwise to report that there would be no agreement.[80]

A few days later, at the opening session of the UN General Assembly, the President invited the new Soviet foreign minister to visit the White House, and on September 27 Shevardnadze gave Reagan a new Soviet arms-control proposal: a 50-percent reduction in strategic weapons to a level of six thousand "charges" (defined as missile warheads and gravity bombs), accompanied by an agreement not to develop, test or deploy "space-strike weapons."[81] Administration officials labeled this a "counter-proposal," and were quick to assert that the specific reductions proposed were heavily weighted against the United States. Nonetheless, it was a radical move for the Soviets to make, and a breakthrough in principle. The administration could count this as a victory, since it had insisted on deep reductions since 1982. President Reagan said that he "welcomed" the proposal and seemed to indicate that serious negotiations could now begin.[82]

But then, on Sunday, October 6, McFarlane disclosed a new interpretation of a key provision in the ABM Treaty. In an interview on *Meet the Press,* he stated that the ABM Treaty permitted not only research but the testing and development of defensive systems based on exotic technologies, presumably such as lasers and particle beams. Though he brought the matter up quite casually, he spoke deliberately and precisely, citing the relevant articles of the treaty so that there should be no mistake: the U.S. government was reading the treaty quite differently from the way it had for the past thirteen years.

Two days later the White House confirmed that McFarlane's statement was administration policy—and a considered policy based on an examination of the negotiating record by administration lawyers, including a Defense Department attorney and the legal adviser to the State Department.[83]

The announcement, though little noticed by the public at large, scandalized the foreign-policy community in the U.S. and in Europe. Representative Dante B. Fascell (Democrat of Florida), chairman of the House Foreign Affairs Committee, called the reinterpretation "incredible" and "a fundamental decision with serious and far-reaching consequences." He promised that his committee would question Secretary Shultz about it the following week.[84] Representative Norman Dicks (Democrat of Washington), a prominent member of the House Armed Services Committee, protested the move, as did Senator Sam Nunn. The Republican-dominated Senate Armed Services Committee scheduled hearings on the issue. Gerard C. Smith, the chief negotiator of the ABM Treaty, held a news conference to object to the reinterpretation. Margaret Thatcher and Helmut Kohl wrote to the President criticizing the decision, and other NATO leaders protested in the strongest terms.[85]

As the reaction indicated, the reinterpretation was no lawyerly quibble over a technicality. The ABM Treaty was the cornerstone of all agreements on strategic weapons, and its provisions were well known. The purpose of the treaty was to ban nationwide defenses against strategic missiles, and to that end it prohibited the testing and development as well as the deployment of such defenses. The treaty explicitly prohibited space-based and other mobile ABM systems, for these were the most likely to lead to countrywide defenses, and, as a treaty of unlimited duration, it did not limit its ban to current technologies. The language of the treaty was exceptionally clear for an arms-control treaty, and U.S. negotiators had parsed it in detail to the Senate during the ratification process. Furthermore, every succeeding administration, including the Reagan administration to that point, had explicitly stated that the treaty forbade the testing and development of exotic, as well as current, technologies for all mobile systems—indeed, for all systems except the fixed, land-based systems permitted by the treaty.[86] But now the administration was claiming that it was free to go ahead with the development and testing of Star Wars weapons.

As Congressman Fascell indicated, the potential consequences of the administration's claim were vast. To "reinterpret" one of the central provisions of the ABM Treaty was surely to make the whole treaty a dead letter and to remove the foundation for any future strategic-arms agreement. But that was the least of it, for the method was more important than the result. The administration could have attempted to amend the treaty, or it could have withdrawn from it, giving the Soviets six months' notice, as the treaty required. Instead, it had chosen to argue that the treaty did not mean what it said. If the Soviets had done anything similar, administration officials would have regarded it as a demonstration that the Soviets could not be trusted and might well have responded by shutting the arms negotiations down. Whatever the Soviets chose to do in response, the implications for American foreign policy were indeed far-reaching. If the President, or the executive branch, was free to reinterpret a treaty unilaterally, keeping only the commitments which suited him, other governments could have no confidence in any agreement made by the United States. Further, the Senate could not ratify any treaty in the confidence that it meant what the executive branch stipulated at the time. The issue went not merely to practicalities but to the constitutional separation of powers, and where it would end was difficult to discern, for, in all of American history, the executive branch had never dealt with an international treaty in this way before.[87]

On October 11 there took place what was described as a "knock-down-drag-out meeting" in the Oval Office attended by Shultz, Weinberger, McFarlane, Adelman and the President, at which Shultz carried the day, reportedly by a subtle threat of resignation. On October 14 Shultz gave a speech in San Francisco in which he said that the ABM Treaty could be "variously interpreted" and that, "based on a careful analysis of the Treaty text and the negotiating record," the administration had decided that a broader interpretation was "fully justified." However, he said, the President had decided to continue to conduct the SDI program in accordance with the "restrictive interpretation" of the treaty, and therefore the whole problem was "moot." But Shultz did not say how long the administration would abide by the "restrictive" interpretation, and on October 16 Richard Perle seemed to indicate that U.S. restraint might be only temporary. "With respect to the future," he said, "it remains to be seen what will happen." Asked whether in the meantime the Soviets would be within their legal rights to test and develop exotic space weapons, Perle said, "That's correct."[88]

Shultz's speech reassured the Allies and many in Congress, but later that week the chief of the Soviet General Staff, Marshal Sergei Akhromeyev, published a detailed analysis of the ABM Treaty in *Pravda,* calling reinterpretation a "deliberate deceit" and maintaining that the treaty unambiguously banned the testing, development and deployment of all mobile systems, regardless of whether current or future technologies were used.[89]

On October 22 the House Foreign Affairs Committee began hearings on the ABM Treaty dispute. The main administration witness was Abraham B. Sofaer, the legal adviser to the State Department and a former U.S. District Court judge in New York. In his opening statement Sofaer testified that Soviet violations of the treaty, the establishment of the SDI program and the arms talks in Geneva had led him to make a detailed study of the negotiating record. That study had in turn led him to conclude that the language of the treaty was ambiguous.

The traditional "restrictive view," Sofaer explained, rested on Article V of the treaty: "Each Party undertakes not to develop, test or deploy ABM systems or components which are sea-based, air-based, space-based or mobile land-based." But this article, he argued, did not apply to systems based on future technologies, because Article II of the treaty, which defined then-current ABM systems in terms of their components, did not mention them. The only mention of future technologies, he said, lay in Agreed Statement D, one of the interpretive understandings attached to the treaty, which said that, "in the event ABM systems based on other physical principles" were created in the future, their deployment would be subject to discussion between the parties. Agreed Statement D, he argued, would be unnecessary if the other articles in the treaty applied to future technologies—thus only the deployment of exotic weapons were banned.[90]

Sofaer's reading of the treaty was outlandish. Because by 1972 the Soviet Union had already deployed point defenses, and the U.S. had plans to deploy them, the treaty explicitly permitted a hundred ABM systems in each of two sites in each country, one around the nation's capital and one around a single ICBM site. (A 1974 protocol to the treaty reduced the number of sites to one.) Agreed Statement D plainly applied to these systems. During the ratification proceedings, U.S. negotiators had made it clear to the Senate that it applied to these systems alone and was a further restriction upon them; it did not apply to space-based systems, for the treaty specifically banned the testing, development and deployment of space-based systems, and of mobile systems of all sorts, no matter what the technology involved.[91]

Sofaer acknowledged that this was the traditional interpretation of the treaty, and the one stipulated by U.S. negotiators to the Senate. But he argued that the American negotiators were mistaken: they thought they had achieved a complete ban on all mobile systems, including those based on "other physical principles," but they had not. The Soviets did not accept the ban, so neither should the U.S. Sofaer gave no evidence to support this assertion; he simply claimed that the evidence lay in the negotiating record—which, being highly classified, was not available to the committee.[92]

The argument was so bizarre the members of the Foreign Affairs Committee did not bother to quiz Sofaer about it. What they wanted to know was why the administration had taken this line as a matter of law and then taken it back as a matter of policy. This they asked of the second administration witness, Paul Nitze, who skillfully evaded the question.

As the committee members well knew, Nitze had been a negotiator of the ABM Treaty, and had worked on Agreed Statement D. Moreover, as he testified to the committee, he had been instrumental in introducing the phrase "other physical principles" into the negotiations. He had always held the traditional view of the treaty, and as recently as May 1985 he had explicitly affirmed it. Yet in his opening statement he said that Sofaer's interpretation was "fully justified." When Representative Lee Hamilton asked him why he had changed his mind, he said that he had been convinced by Sofaer's review of the negotiating record, which he qualified as "the first really solid examination of the complete record" in thirteen years. At the time of the negotiations, he said, the Soviets had taken the position that it was improper to try to limit systems whose technology was unknown, and they were only trying to limit them now because they were afraid of SDI.[93]

Gerard C. Smith, the chief SALT I negotiator; John Rhinelander, the legal counsel for the negotiating team; and Ralph Earle, an Arms Control and Disarmament Agency representative at the SALT I talks, also testified at the hearing. All three contradicted what Sofaer and Nitze had said about the Soviet understanding of the treaty in 1972. According to Rhinelander, it was the U.S. Joint Chiefs of Staff who had wanted to keep the option open for testing and developing exotic technologies on the permitted land-based systems, and the Soviets who had wanted greater restrictions. Like the committee members, the three negotiators asked why the administration would make such a strange legal interpretation and then take it back as a matter of policy. Gerard Smith recalled that the secretary of defense had called SDI "the hope of the future." Then why, he asked ironically, was the administration now exercising such self-restraint? "If the President's claim is valid that SDI leads us to arms control and the total elimination of nuclear weapons, why would we want to put off that happy day by proceeding at a more leisurely pace?" Smith suggested that the reinterpretation might be "an exercise in playing hardball" for the summit. Rhinelander, however, pointed out that it was not much of a negotiating tactic, since the administration was in effect telling the Soviets that it could reinterpret any treaty anytime it wanted—thus giving them no incentive to make an agreement reducing their offensive arms.[94]

The questions raised by the House Foreign Affairs Committee and later the Senate Armed Services Committee—plus the many others that hovered around the affair—were not answered at the time, for the reduction of the ABM Treaty reinterpretation to a legal abstraction, plus the approach of the summit, effectively silenced the congressional Democrats. But the issue surfaced again in 1987, and at that time the Senate Judiciary and Foreign Relations Committees held hearings, and the Foreign Relations Committee produced a report on the reinterpretation. The proceedings of the committees, plus journalistic investigations, went some way to explaining what had occurred: that is, among other things, who in the administration was responsible for the reinterpretation and what the purpose of it was.[95]

In late 1984, just as Richard Perle began to consider how SDI might be used to stop arms control, T. K. Jones, the deputy undersecretary of defense for research and engineering/strategic and theater nuclear forces, began to worry out loud about the constraints the ABM Treaty imposed on the program. The civil-defense enthusiast who had once maintained that with enough shovels Americans could defend themselves from a nuclear war, had, it seemed, become a strategic-defense enthusiast who wanted more leeway for the SDI program than the current interpretation of the treaty allowed. Complaining that the U.S. was holding itself to a stricter standard than the Soviets were, he pressed for "a greater flexibility of interpretation" from the Defense Department's legal staff.[96] Getting none, he sought the opinion of outsiders.

In late January 1985 Jones queried William R. Harris of the Rand Corporation. In 1977 Harris, along with Abraham S. Becker of Rand, had conceived the idea that the ABM Treaty put no limitations on the use of exotic technologies, not even a ban on their deployment. Two weeks later Harris responded to Jones with an unclassified memorandum repeating his well-known view.[97]

At around the same time, Jones asked Sidney Graybeal and Colonel Charles Fitzgerald of the Systems Planning Corporation for a study of the classified negotiating record. Graybeal and Fitzgerald had been members of the SALT I delegation. Graybeal had negotiated on Article V of the treaty, and Fitzgerald had been one of Nitze's advisers. Since 1972 their corporation had had a contract with the Defense Department to analyze issues having to do with the implementation of the treaty. Their study, submitted to Jones in March 1985, presented strong evidence for the traditional interpretation.[98]

By March, Weinberger, according to Shultz, had begun to talk about an American withdrawal from the ABM Treaty. Doubtless he was told that the Congress would never accept a withdrawal, for he did not propose it publicly. In April, however, the Pentagon gave Congress a report on the SDI program and the ABM Treaty, which alarmed arms-control advocates: it seemed to reclassify ABM components as subcomponents and thereby to stretch the limits of the "research" permitted by the treaty.[99] The report put the wind up among Democrats on the Armed Services Committees; in May, Nitze, as if to scotch the Pentagon plan, made a speech at the Johns Hopkins School of Advanced International Studies in which he gave a clear exposition of the traditional interpretation of the treaty.[100]

Stymied by the Graybeal-Fitzgerald report and the Defense Department counsels, Fred Iklé and Richard Perle went out and hired Philip Kunsberg, a former assistant district attorney from New York, as a Pentagon staff lawyer. Thirty-five years old, Kunsberg had legal experience fighting pornography and organized crime, but no experience in arms control or anything related to it. Nonetheless, he was quickly put to work analyzing the impact of the ABM Treaty on SDI, and before long he opined that the treaty and its negotiating record gave far more leeway to SDI than the administration had told the Congress. Iklé and Perle now had their own lawyer.[101]

At the end of the congressional session in late July, Senator Carl Levin (Democrat of Michigan) had asked a number of detailed questions about the compliance of the SDI program with the ABM Treaty. Perle, as chair of the interagency committee on SDI, had to formulate the administration's response, and in early September he asked Kunsberg for a report on the negotiating record.[102] In less than a week, Kunsberg produced a nineteen-page paper arguing that the Soviets had never accepted restrictions on mobile ABM systems if they employed future technologies—and thus the testing, development and deployment of Star Wars weapons were entirely consistent with the treaty.[103]

On September 17 the interagency committee on SDI met and decided to respond to Senator Levin's questions with answers which reflected the traditional interpretation. But at some point in the meeting Perle introduced Kunsberg's memorandum, and soon thereafter the matter was referred to the legal counsels of State, Defense and ACDA.[104]

Abraham Sofaer, who had joined the State Department that summer, was even newer to Washington than Kunsberg, and he, too, lacked any experience with arms control. Nonetheless, from a study of the negotiating record and several long conversations with Nitze, he arrived at the view that the ABM Treaty was ambiguous and probably allowed the testing and development, though not the deployment, of Star Wars weapons. He sent a memorandum to this effect to Shultz and Nitze on October 3.[105]

On Friday, October 4, at a meeting of the Senior Arms Control Group (the word "policy" had been stricken from its title to make the acronym the more dignified SAC-G), McFarlane, Iklé, Perle, Nitze and other officials debated what the ABM Treaty said. The Defense Department representatives argued the Kunsberg position that the treaty permitted the deployment of Star Wars weapons, but Nitze persuaded them to accept the Sofaer position that it permitted only development and testing. No one challenged this idea, but the meeting ended without any decision on how, or even if, Sofaer's "broad" interpretation should be translated into policy.[106] McFarlane's announcement of the "broad" interpretation as administration policy on *Meet the Press* two days later therefore came as a surprise to everyone.

In its investigation of the affair in 1987, the Senate Foreign Relations Committee paid particular attention to the role of the legal adviser. Sofaer had, after all, established the legal and factual grounds on which the administration based its claim for the "broad" interpretation, and in the years that followed he had elaborated his case and become the chief proponent of the "broad" interpretation before Congress. Inquiring into how he had arrived at his conclusions, the committee found that Sofaer's methodology left a good deal to be desired.

In the first place, under the canons of international law it is the text of a treaty and the subsequent practice of the parties which provide the strongest evidence for interpretation. Negotiating records are rarely consulted, even in the case of disputes between parties to an agreement, for the simple reason that negotiations are rarely, if ever, transcribed. Certainly in the case of the ABM Treaty, there was no transcription, or agreed-upon record. What the U.S. government had for a "negotiating record" was about a thousand memoranda written by the American negotiators in the years 1969 to 1972.[107]

To help with the task of collecting and analyzing these memoranda, Sofaer passed over the career State Department lawyer, who had long experience in the field, and enlisted three young lawyers, all of whom had just recently joined the department and two of whom had come with him from New York. The young lawyers worked hard, but they did not succeed in obtaining the Graybeal-Fitzgerald study from the Department of Defense, and, strangely enough, they did not find all the negotiating memoranda. They were still collecting material when Sofaer testified before the House Foreign Affairs Committee on October 22—and new memos were still turning up two years later.[108]

In the midst of the initial record search, one of the young lawyers, William J. Sims, discovered a memorandum from the SALT II negotiations which showed that a lead Soviet negotiator, Victor Karpov, interpreted Article V of the ABM Treaty as banning all mobile systems, including those based on future technologies. The memo was a critical one, because the issue of future technologies did not otherwise come up in U.S.-Soviet exchanges between the conclusion of the treaty and the advent of SDI. Sofaer, however, did not mention this document in his report. Sims also found that the counsels for the Defense Department and ACDA supported the traditional interpretation of the treaty, but Sofaer did not consult them. In fact, he failed to consult anyone with any knowledge of the treaty, except for Nitze—and yet between September 17 and October 3 he arrived at the view that the treaty did not say what the U.S. negotiators had attested it said.[109]

In its final report, the Foreign Relations Committee denounced Sofaer for having done a disservice to his office and condemned the whole reinterpretation process as "not merely unusual but so substandard as to breach the requirement of international law that a treaty be interpreted in good faith." The committee, however, did not hold Sofaer alone responsible for the reinterpretation, for it said, "Such haste and bias can only be explained by an ideological motivation on the part of certain Administration officials . . ." and it maintained that the administration "relied on Mr. Sofaer's 'studies' not to determine what is legally valid but to justify aims already decided upon."[110]

From the committee's report, as from all else that has been written on the subject, it is clear that Perle and his colleagues initiated the reinterpretation, and the closer the administration came to arms negotiations, the harder they fought for it.[111] Yet the Pentagon civilians did not call for the Sofaer report, and they did not change administration policy all by themselves. What is missing from the report is the role played by Nitze, Shultz and McFarlane.

Why Paul Nitze supported the reinterpretation was a question that puzzled and disturbed his friends and allies in Washington. In testimony to the House Foreign Affairs Committee on October 22, 1985, Nitze said that it was Sofaer's review of the negotiating record—"the first really solid examination of the complete record that has taken place in thirteen years"—that convinced him to change his long-held view of the treaty. The explanation seemed implausible to most of Nitze's former associates. As John Rhinelander put it most succinctly, "Nobody knows more about the ABM treaty than Paul Nitze. Nobody has more respect for rigorous logic. How could a couple of lawyers who don't know the first thing about arms control come along and turn him around on a dime? It's absurd to think Sofaer could teach Paul anything he didn't know."[112] The explanation is even less plausible in retrospect, for Sofaer, as it turned out, had just two weeks to collect and analyze the thousand memoranda that made up the "negotiating record." And his one expert guide to this material was Paul Nitze.

In fact, Nitze himself later denied that he had learned anything from

Sofaer. In his memoir, which appeared in 1989, he wrote that his own conversion to the "broad" interpretation began in the summer of 1985, when he read the Graybeal-Fitzgerald report. "To my surprise," he writes, "... I found I disagreed with their conclusions.... The record as summarized by them seemed to me to demonstrate that the Soviets had never agreed ... that research, development and testing of systems and components based on other physical principles were prohibited under the terms of the treaty." However, he writes, there were "certain ambiguities that needed to be addressed, so I urged the secretary to ask his legal counsel, Judge Sofaer, for an informed opinion."[113]

This is a story quite as strange as the first one. Graybeal and Fitzgerald had been colleagues of Nitze's during the SALT talks, and in the late 1970s he had had an office in their Systems Planning Corporation.[114] Nitze knew what they thought about the ABM Treaty, and he had always agreed with them. He claims to have read their report in the summer of 1985, and possibly he did. However, by William Sims's testimony, the Defense Department did not release the Graybeal-Fitzgerald report to Sofaer and Nitze until the end of October. Nevertheless, Nitze stuck to his new story and later vehemently denied that Sofaer had had anything to do with changing his mind. "How could he? I hired him!" he exclaimed.[115]

According to Talbott, many of Nitze's supporters in and out of government tried to excuse him on the grounds that at the time he was under great pressure from the right. During the summer and fall of 1985, news stories were depicting him as an arms controller under siege and in danger of losing his credibility with the President because of his impatience to make a deal with the Soviets. Perhaps, it was said, he did not want to confirm this impression, so he gave in to the Pentagon.[116]

This seemed the simplest explanation, and among those concerned with the subject, it stuck. However, there was something much more complicated going on.

In his memoir, Shultz describes himself as having been an agnostic about the meaning of the ABM Treaty even after McFarlane made the announcement on October 6. He quotes Harold Brown making a technical point to him about the testing prohibited and permitted by the treaty the following day, and jokes that he had entered "the higher realms of arms control theology."[117] His agnosticism is, however, difficult to credit. Though no arms-control expert, Shultz had been involved with the issue of the ABM Treaty and SDI since the beginning of the year, and he was smart enough to know exactly what was going on. In any case, Shultz also tells us that he was furious with McFarlane for making the announcement: "He had, in effect, *declared publicly that the U.S. was unilaterally changing its long held position on the treaty.* No such decision had been made! And now there would be hell to pay. I was appalled and angry at this arrogation of power." A few paragraphs later, he continues in this vein:

> Bud had jumped the gun. No administration position on the question of the ABM Treaty had yet been agreed upon. And what Bud stated publicly was *not* the traditional position of the United States, or the position of our allies; nor was it in accord with what the Congress had been told about the meaning of the ABM Treaty's language; nor was it the position previously taken by the administration. And it certainly was at odds with current Soviet views.[118]

This account is extremely puzzling. Shultz surely understood the grave consequences of unilaterally reinterpreting a major international treaty, yet his objections to McFarlane's announcement are tactical and procedural rather than matters of principle. And by October 9—so he tells us—he had decided that Sofaer's interpretation was correct.[119]

McFarlane, for his part, let it be known at the time that the reinterpretation was to play a role in the U.S.-Soviet negotiations. Some years later he told Strobe Talbott that the idea was to "lay down a marker" with the Soviets, warning them that they had better make offensive reductions soon, and in addition to have "something on which the U.S. could make concessions down the road in exchange for Soviet concessions."[120] McFarlane's explanation sounded far-fetched, given the scandal the reinterpretation caused. But Shultz's memoir, in combination with news reports of the period, show that not only McFarlane but Shultz and Nitze saw the "broad" interpretation as yet another bargaining chip with the Soviets, and they suggest how Shultz and Nitze thought it could be used.

In early September 1985, after Gorbachev revised the Soviet position on SDI to accord with the ABM Treaty, Shultz went to work preparing Reagan for the summit and, under Nitze's guidance, formulating a new arms-control position. On Friday, September 13, there was a meeting of top officials, and in its wake *Washington Post* correspondents reported that some of these officials—clearly those from the State Department—said that an offensive-defensive trade-off was under discussion and that Reagan had spoken with top aides about the "concept" of accepting limits on the Star Wars program. The issue of limiting SDI, the *Post* story said, was quite complex, involving the precise dividing lines between "research" and "testing," and "development"; also, the long gestation period of the program provided the President with an opportunity to accept interim restraints while allowing the research to go forward.[121]

On Tuesday, September 17, Reagan announced in his press conference that he would not trade SDI. "I'm saying that research to see if such a weapon is feasible is not in violation of any treaty. It's going to continue. That will one day involve, if it reaches that point, testing. On the other hand, I stop short of deployment because, as I said, I'm willing to talk to our allies . . . and talk to the Soviets."

Q: But development and testing, you're ruling out any deal on that?

REAGAN: I think that's a legitimate part of research, and, yes, I would rule it out. . . . This is too important to the world to be willing to trade off that for a different number of nuclear missiles.[122]

What the President meant was unclear, but in retrospect it sounds very much as if he was quoting the "broad" interpretation—two days before Nitze put Sofaer to work on it.[123]

To reporters the President's statements seemed to indicate that Reagan was ruling out a deal on SDI. However, some officials insisted that the President's statements were not final but, rather, a bargaining strategy to up the ante on SDI.[124] And at that point the secretary of state seems to have been optimistic about a grand compromise.

Shultz, according to his memoir, met with Reagan on September 19. He congratulated the President on his press conference, and handed him a memorandum with talking points for the summit concerning arms control and how to handle the sensitive issue of SDI. Going over the memo with Reagan, he argued that the choices on SDI did not come down to going full speed ahead or bargaining it away. Rather, he said, SDI should be a permanent fixture in the U.S. strategic posture, and the U.S. should seek massive reductions in offensive weapons. SDI should be positioned as the key to implementing an agreement on offensive reductions; it should continue as a research program under the terms of the ABM Treaty, and issues surrounding "the development and testing of SDI permitted by the treaty" should be clarified.[125]

That same day, "an authoritative administration official"—doubtless McFarlane—told White House reporters that the massive Soviet arms buildup had put the ABM Treaty "very much in question," and "it might be wise" to modify the ABM Treaty in the years after President Reagan left office. The official added that the administration believed that testing of the Star Wars program was permissible under the treaty.[126]

What McFarlane, Shultz and Nitze seem to have had in mind was that in return for offensive reductions the U.S. would agree not to withdraw from the ABM Treaty for a period of time, though perhaps not the ten years the Soviets wanted. In order to get the best deal possible on offensive weapons, the administration would speak of an "ambiguity" in the treaty that might permit the testing and development of space weaponry—and would argue that, the greater the Soviet reductions, the less need there would be for SDI.[127]

The question is how Shultz and Nitze thought they were to make the "broad" interpretation known to the Pentagon and the Soviets, but not to Congress and the Allies. The answer seems to lie in the ambiguity they sought to maintain about whether they were reinterpreting the ABM Treaty or simply haggling about the limits of "research" and "testing."

On October 4, SAC-G adopted the State Department's reinterpretation of the treaty, and, according to one news report, the group agreed to a five-to-seven-year period of non-withdrawal from the ABM Treaty.[128] But then, two days later, McFarlane, for reasons he has never explained, blew the whole complicated scheme out of the water by announcing the new interpretation on television.

Shultz was understandably furious at McFarlane, but in reality he and Nitze had badly miscalculated.[129] By calling for a legal review of the treaty—a review which could hardly have remained secret once its existence was known to others in the administration—they had destroyed the ambiguity they had apparently hoped to maintain. Presumably Nitze was trying to stop Perle from establishing the Kunsberg position that the ABM Treaty permitted the deployment of Star Wars weaponry. But if so, he was not thinking very clearly. According to Talbott, Perle exulted when he heard about Sofaer's memo. The administration could not, after all, have based any claim about the meaning of the ABM Treaty on the frail reed of the Kunsberg paper; the opinion of a heavyweight lawyer was just what Perle required. When the memo was circulated, Perle did not even bother to read it, for the only news in it was that he had won.[130]

Yet, even after the furor erupted, Shultz—to trust his memoir—continued to think he could use the reinterpretation of the treaty, or the threat of it, as a bargaining chip with the Soviets. Speaking of the decision to make it a matter of law but not policy, he writes: "The combination would give us the best of both worlds, I felt. We would be able to research the key questions of strategic defense. We would also have something to fall back on and to bargain with by 'clarifying' the treaty. So all this flurry of concern could be made useful to us."[131]

Possibly Shultz knew better. Possibly he and Nitze had simply been outmaneuvered by Perle and his allies. In any case, the "broad" interpretation became a part of the U.S. negotiating position, where it served as yet another block to arms control.[132]

By the end of October 1985, public attention was focused on the prospects for the Geneva summit, scheduled for November 19 and 20. Cold War summits were by definition major events, and because of the long freeze in U.S.-Soviet relations, this one was awaited with more anticipation than most. In the public imagination, the thrill of a summit lay in the idea of a personal encounter between two great world leaders who, alone together in a room, might decide the fate of the planet between them. This was, of course, a romance. Summits were not undertaken lightly, for the prestige of both men and of their powerful nations were seen to be balanced upon their discussions. At least since the disastrous Kennedy-Khrushchev confrontation in Vienna in 1961, diplomats on both sides had taken great care to see that summits were programmed and scripted so that nothing untoward would occur between the principals. In the 1970s most summits took place only when significant agreements were near completion, and all of them rested upon months, or years, of negotiations between the two sides.

In part because of this history, the great question in the press at the end of October was whether the U.S. and the Soviet Union would make a breakthrough on arms control.

Recently Gorbachev had taken a number of new initiatives. In July he had declared a unilateral moratorium on nuclear testing; in September he had proposed a 50-percent reduction in strategic warheads and suggested that Moscow might retreat from its call for a ban on SDI research. Soviet negotiators had offered to separate the INF negotiations from the strategic-weapons talks, and in early October, during a highly successful state visit to France, Gorbachev announced a unilateral reduction in the number of Soviet intermediate-range weapons targeted on Europe and proposed an interim agreement on those weapons.[133] In addition, Soviet officials offered to halt construction on the Krasnoyarsk radar if the United States would forgo plans to modernize early-warning radars in Britain and Greenland.[134] How much further he might be prepared to go was unknown, for the Reagan administration had not yet made any response.

Throughout October sounds of discord rose from the Reagan administration. State Department officials welcomed some of the Soviet initiatives and made cautiously optimistic statements suggesting that some agreement could be reached; Weinberger intimated that purported Soviet violations of SALT II cast doubt on the value of arms control generally. The President did not make his own position clear.[135]

On November 1, a few days before Shultz was scheduled to go to Moscow to make the final preparations for the summit, the administration made its own proposal for a 50-percent cut in strategic weapons. Weinberger, it appeared, had opposed making any response to the dramatic Soviet offer, but McFarlane, concerned that, in a remarkable role reversal, Ronald Reagan was losing the public-relations battle to the Soviet general secretary, had persuaded the President to overrule him.[136] The plan, presented at the arms talks in Geneva, required much larger cuts in Soviet than in American strategic forces, but as far as the Soviets were concerned, the real difficulty was that it came unaccompanied by any suggestion of an accommodation on SDI.[137]

On November 5 Shultz met with Gorbachev in Moscow. According to Dobrynin, the general secretary was agitated before the meeting. Some of his colleagues in the Politburo were asking whether there was a purpose to the summit, and with less than two weeks remaining, the agenda and possible outcome of the summit were still unclear. "We hear nothing from the Americans except generalities," he said.[138] The meeting was contentious. Shultz had brought nothing new with him. On SDI he asserted, as before, that the buildup of offensive arms had undermined the assumptions behind the ABM Treaty; but, rather than make any explicit offer of a trade-off between offense and defense, he called for a cooperative transition to defensive weapons. Gorbachev, seeing no opening, angrily objected to the new interpretation of the ABM Treaty and said that if the United States persisted in developing space weapons there would be no offensive reductions. According to Shultz, he railed about American "illusions" that the U.S. could gain strategic superiority and weaken the Soviet Union economically.[139]

After the meeting Shultz told reporters that the two sides had failed to narrow their differences on arms control or on any other substantive issues, and that the summit was unlikely to produce even a face-saving agreement on arms reductions. To reporters, a sharp clash between Reagan and Gorbachev at the summit seemed a distinct possibility.[140]

Gorbachev, however, had long ago determined to have a cordial meeting with Reagan, no matter what the prospects for arms control. Just after Shultz returned to Washington, he sent a message via Dobrynin saying in effect that he had no intention of being as argumentative with the President as he had been with Shultz.[141] He then, according to Dobrynin, went about lowering "the unduly high expectations in the Politburo." The official government instructions he took with him to Geneva declared that the principal aim of the summit was "to try, however slim the chance may be, to find a common language with the American president on the key question of his preparedness to build relations with the Soviet Union on an equal footing," and that in terms of arms control the best that could be expected was a joint statement that both sides would "proceed from the assumption that nuclear war is unacceptable and unwinnable."[142]

An optimist and a man of great confidence in his own powers of persuasion, Gorbachev hoped to convince Reagan to change his mind about SDI, yet, as the summit approached, his anxieties rose. Shultz had been working with Shevardnadze on the draft of a joint communiqué to be issued at the close of the summit stating what the two sides had been able to agree to: future summits, cultural exchanges and a few other matters. But on November 13 Shultz broke off the negotiations, leaving Dobrynin and Shevardnadze to wonder whether the summit might end without even routine diplomatic niceties.[143] Gorbachev knew he was taking a risk going into a summit without any prospect of a breakthrough, and with a president known for his virulent anti-Communism.[144]

With the approach of the meeting, anxieties ran high in the Reagan White House as well. The hard-liners were working hard to see that nothing came of the summit—Weinberger had made it impossible for Shultz to negotiate a joint communiqué in advance—and in doing so were threatening to turn it into a disaster for the President. In addition, White House aides worried about how their boss would do in an encounter with Mikhail Gorbachev. Reagan had never visited the Soviet Union, and his knowledge of it was just about the same as that of the average man in the street. Then, too, strategic weaponry was just not his strong suit. In preparation for the summit, McFarlane had given him a good deal of background material, including a series of twenty-five essays on Russian history, Soviet policy and Soviet life written by Jack Matlock, the Soviet expert on the NSC staff. Reagan complained about the amount of reading he had to do, and though some aides worried that he was learning too little, others worried that he might be learning too much. "You can put too much in the computer—he'll try to remember it all," one longtime Reagan adviser said. "Some people sift it out; it all goes into Reagan, and he's so serious and sincere that when he gets into a situation he'll try to use it all."[145]

While Reagan crammed, White House aides dealt with the public aspects of the summit. In October a special planning group had been set up, and Michael Deaver and Richard Wirthlin were called in to help. In early November the group set about lowering expectations for the summit. According to Don Regan, the President's only goals for Geneva were to establish a personal relationship with Gorbachev, to obtain his commitment to continuing the arms talks and to set the place and approximate time for another meeting.[146] The group decided that Weinberger should be kept from making television appearances and excluded from the delegation to Geneva, and that Richard Perle, who would go, should be kept under very tight wraps. It was also decided that the President would give no interviews and hold no press conferences at the summit. Rather, he would fly back to Washington via Brussels and would—dramatically—take a helicopter from Andrews Air Force Base to the Capitol, where he would address a joint session of Congress. The speech, Deaver told one reporter, would give Reagan "a chance to verbally restructure what happened if it all fell apart."[147]

In the meantime, Deaver and others organized a pre-summit public-affairs campaign for the President. Well-publicized meetings were set up. An array of noted experts on the Soviet Union were called in to give Reagan the benefit of their wisdom. This particular effort had indifferent results, for, when queried by journalists, some of the experts expressed amazement at Reagan's ignorance of the Soviet Union.[148] In addition, the President met with a group of religious leaders—a move Deaver thought would highlight the difference between the U.S. and Soviet systems—and Reagan asked the group to pray for Gorbachev.[149] More important, the President, his conservative speechwriters brought to heel, began to sound as if he actually wanted to meet with the general secretary. In speeches and in interviews with small groups of journalists, he spoke of the "misunderstandings" which existed between the U.S. and the Soviet Union, and the need for a "fresh start" in the relationship between the two countries.[150]

With regard to SDI, Reagan resurrected the proposal he had made during the debate with Mondale the year before to share technology with other nations, including the Soviet Union. "I don't mean we'll give it to them," he said with a twinkle. "They're going to have to pay for it—but at cost."[151] As before, reporters treated the proposal as one of Reagan's foibles, and, as before, the message served to reassure the American public that Reagan's intentions were good. The only problem was that the President's foreign-policy advisers did not like the thought of having to defend such a policy in the face of their Soviet counterparts. At a pre-summit meeting, Casey and Adelman brainstormed for a couple of minutes and came up with an alternative: a proposal that the U.S. would open its SDI labs to the Soviets if the Soviets reciprocated. The idea, as Adelman explains in his memoir, was no less ludicrous than the first one, but since Eisenhower had made an "open skies" proposal some thirty years before, "open labs" had a nice ring to it. The proposal was adopted and went to Geneva, where, according to Adelman, it consumed a fair amount of summit prime time.[152]

Then, too, the nearer the summit came, the more Reagan talked about the need to eliminate nuclear weapons. In an interview with four Soviet journalists, he said that the U.S. would not deploy Star Wars weapons until "we do away with our nuclear missiles, our offensive missiles."[153] This was going too far, for if SDI weapons could be deployed only after nuclear disarmament the Soviets would have a veto over the deployments. Larry Speakes, the White House press secretary, called the statement a "presidential imprecision."[154] More conventionally, Reagan declared in a televised address to the nation on the eve of his departure for Geneva: "My mission, stated simply, is a mission for peace. It is to engage the new Soviet leader in what I hope will be a dialogue for peace that endures beyond my presidency." Suggesting that U.S.-Soviet tensions had come from misunderstandings, he said, "We should seek to reduce the suspicions and mistrust that have led us to acquire mountains of strategic weapons." These weapons, he said, "pose the greatest threat in human history to the survival of the human race." And he vowed to go to Geneva "determined to search out, and discover, common ground, where we can agree to begin the reduction, looking to the eventual elimination of nuclear weapons from the face of the earth."[155]

Reagan flew to Geneva on November 16 to rest up for two days at the Aga Khan's villa and to tour Fleur d'Eau, the Swiss government's lakefront villa, where the first day's meetings were to be held. By the time Gorbachev arrived on the 18th, some thirty-six hundred journalists had assembled in Geneva and were waiting with anticipation for what many described as the most unpredictable summit in two decades.[156] According to a *New York Times* reporter, American officials did not seem to know what Reagan was thinking, or whether Gorbachev would risk a failure by insisting on an end to space weaponry.[157] Privately journalists wondered what the dynamic young general secretary, and the President, twenty years his senior, the most rhetorically anti-Communist of all Cold War presidents, would do in a room together with no agreed-upon agenda.

The sense of impending drama was only increased by a last-minute move by the administration hard-liners.

On November 13 Weinberger had personally delivered a letter to Reagan with a report charging the Soviets with a number of new arms-control violations. The report, prepared in Richard Perle's office, had for some time been slated to go into "the pre-summit mix," and according to one Pentagon official, it was designed to appear "like a turd in the punchbowl."[158] Weinberger's covering letter sharply warned Reagan against any agreement to continue to observe the SALT II treaty, any agreement restricting SDI to the "narrow" interpretation of the ABM Treaty and any communiqué which might suggest that the Soviets were committed to complying with either treaty.[159] The unclassified letter was leaked to the *New York Times* and the *Washington Post* the day Reagan left for Geneva. A furor erupted in Washington, and when asked whether the letter had been leaked in order to sabotage the summit, McFarlane said, "Sure it was."[160]

Because of a news blackout requested by Shultz, only the photographers and television cameramen captured the first meeting between Reagan and Gorbachev. It was a bitingly cold day, and the pictures they took were of Gorbachev arriving at the villa bundled up in an overcoat and wearing a fedora hat and Ronald Reagan striding out coatless and hatless to meet him, looking younger than the Soviet general secretary.[161]

If there was any tension in the air, it was soon dispelled, for the two leaders sat and stood for many more photographs, chatting in an animated and amicable fashion. Both that day and the next, there were many more photo sessions, and at each one Reagan and Gorbachev stood side by side looking more and more pleased with each other and with the turn of events. According to official spokesmen from both sides, the meetings were going well. On the morning of November 21 the two principals appeared together at a closing ceremony, wreathed in smiles, and made short, formal statements indicating that a good beginning had been made and that much hard work lay ahead.

The results of the meeting were, as expected, not very substantial. The two sides had agreed on a series of cultural and people-to-people exchanges, and they had agreed on a joint statement calling for an acceleration of the arms talks and declaring that a nuclear war could not be won and should never be fought. According to Shultz, the statement was notable for its pronouncement that "early progress" should be made towards an interim agreement on INF missiles. But there was no mention of SDI or the ABM Treaty, or of any progress on strategic-arms reductions. Nonetheless, Reagan and Gorbachev had agreed to hold two more summits—one in Washington, one in Moscow—and both spoke of the progress that had been made in improving the U.S.-Soviet relationship.[162]

According to American officials present at the meetings, the discussions between the two leaders had covered a range of issues, including bilateral relations, arms control, regional issues and human rights. There had been no changes in substantive positions except that Gorbachev had dropped a broad hint of future accommodation on Afghanistan. In the discussions of arms control, much time had been spent on SDI. On this subject, as on the others, the exchanges between the two leaders were said to have been "frank" and "tough."[163]

Still, the big news of the conference was the "bond" that developed between Reagan and Gorbachev. According to Shultz and other American officials, the two men took the meeting over in a way that none of their aides had anticipated. In a remarkable display of personal diplomacy, they had decided to spend much of their time alone together, and in the course of two days they had met five times with only their interpreters along. On the first morning a private conversation scheduled for fifteen minutes stretched out for an hour and a quarter. Then, that afternoon, Reagan asked Gorbachev if he wanted to get some air, and the two men walked to a pool house by the lakeside where a roaring fire was lit and talked for an hour about arms control. Their discussion was inconclusive, but they came back in obvious good spirits, and Reagan announced that Gorbachev had agreed to hold meetings in Washington and Moscow. In what American officials were now calling "the fireside summit," Reagan and Gorbachev spent roughly half of their meeting time in private conversation. Just as in the plenary sessions, they often disagreed heatedly, and the atmosphere became highly charged. Nonetheless, a real "personal chemistry" developed between them. The President, officials said, had learned a lot in these sessions and had come to have a healthy respect for this Soviet leader, who was a strong advocate and a good interlocutor. "[We] got very friendly," Reagan said.[164]

After the final ceremony, Reagan flew to Brussels, where he briefed NATO representatives, then continued to Washington, where he reported to Congress. His speech, a perfectly calibrated presentation, brought the congressmen and senators to their feet over and over again. "I had called for a fresh start," he said, "and we made that start. I can't claim that we had a meeting of the minds on such fundamentals as ideology or national purpose—but we understood each other better. And that's a key to peace. I gained a better perspective. I feel he did, too."[165]

For Reagan the summit was an unmitigated triumph. The press coverage was entirely favorable. Those reporters who were inclined to think of the summit as a contest declared Reagan the winner because he had worked through the American agenda and refused to give up SDI. Others gave Reagan credit for responding to a new situation with flexibility and grace. John

Newhouse, the diplomatic correspondent for *The New Yorker,* wrote, "Reagan demonstrated once again a resilience, an ability to perform in a clinch, that has marked his career in politics."[166] According to a Wirthlin poll, 83 percent of those who saw the speech to Congress approved of Reagan's performance. Other polls showed a dramatic rise in public approval for the President's conduct of U.S.-Soviet relations and nuclear-disarmament negotiations.[167]

This enthusiasm for Reagan's performance was mysterious in that nothing much happened at the summit, and certainly nothing in regard to disarmament. Possibly, Newhouse suggested, relief was the dominant emotion. After five years in office without a summit and five years of aggressive anti-Soviet rhetoric, Ronald Reagan had met with a Soviet leader, and nothing awful had happened—and that in itself was seen as a success. Still, that was clearly not all there was to it. Both hawks and doves approved of Reagan's performance, and the Congress had acclaimed him as a hero returned from the wars. For Newhouse the explanation was "the continuing power of his persona and his almost uncanny ability to connect with the American public."[168]

In fact, there was some magic involved.

Considered as a public spectacle, the meeting of Reagan and Gorbachev fulfilled the fantasy of Cold War summits: the leaders of the two superpowers meet and defend their positions, then walk off together and, finding they get along as man to man, decide they will not go to war. Then, too, Reagan had apparently behaved like a quintessentially American champion. "The pictures we saw of Reagan appearing to be getting along famously with . . . Gorbachev," Newhouse wrote, "and the details we were given of their 'frank' and 'tough' exchanges reinforced the image of Reagan as the tough guy who will stand up to an opponent but who is also quite an amiable fellow."[169]

The key scene in this spectacle was surely that of the first afternoon, when Reagan, taking the initiative, invited Gorbachev to go outside with him in the freezing weather, and the two of them walked down to the pool house together—coming back an hour later in great good spirits, having agreed to two more summits.

Interestingly, Reagan had imagined such a meeting well before it occurred. In February 1984 he had written in his diary: "I have a gut feeling that I'd like to talk to him [the Soviet general secretary] about our problems man to man."[170] Reagan was then speaking of the aged and ailing Chernenko, but apparently this was not the first time he had thought of such an encounter. In his memoir he tells us:

> Starting with Brezhnev, I dreamed of personally going one-on-one with a Soviet leader because I thought we might be able to accomplish things our countries' diplomats couldn't do because they didn't have the authority. Putting that another way, I felt that

> if you got the top people negotiating and talking at a summit and then come out arm-in-arm saying, "We've agreed to this," the bureaucrats wouldn't be able to louse up the agreement. Until Gorbachev, I never got the opportunity to try out my idea.[171]

Reagan, in other words, had written the scene of the pool-house meeting long before it happened.

At the press briefing in Geneva, journalists noted that Reagan's decision to take Gorbachev to the pool house could not have been perfectly spontaneous, because the fire was already lit. Larry Speakes conceded the point with a joke, and Mrs. Reagan was given credit for choosing the pool house the day before.[172] The preparations were, however, a good deal more elaborate than that. Over a month before, Reagan and his aides had talked about Reagan spending a considerable amount of time alone with Gorbachev at the summit.[173] The White House advance man, Bill Henkel, had looked for an appropriate setting and had found the pool house on his initial trip to Fleur d'Eau. "There are some great camera angles walking down from the big house," he told Donald Regan. "We can have a fire going in the fireplace, and the two of them can sit beside the fire and talk tête-à-tête." The day before the summit began the Reagans conducted what amounted to a set rehearsal at the villa and the pool house, with Mrs. Reagan sitting in for Gorbachev.[174]

The lack of spontaneity did not, of course, obviate the fact that Reagan had spent a great deal of time alone with the Soviet general secretary talking man to man. To those who knew the ways of diplomacy, his initiative seemed not only unorthodox but daring. As Leslie Gelb of the *New York Times* explained, "One of the worst nightmares for professional diplomats and experts is to see what they regard as their untutored bosses going off on their own; they are never quite sure what was said and whether compromises were suggested that would run counter to policy or established interests."[175]

Shultz, however, had planned for two hours of private meetings, and he was pleased when the principals stretched the time out. There was, after all, nothing to negotiate, and the private meetings distracted attention from this.[176] Shultz did not have to worry that the President would attempt to forge an agreement on his own, for Reagan, unlike other presidents, left policy entirely to others. As for the "personal chemistry" between Reagan and Gorbachev, it was, to read the subsequent accounts of the meeting, diplomatic chemistry.

According to the American officials present, Reagan was at the top of his form during the two-day summit. In his own way he had worked very hard at preparing himself. Among other things, he had watched a CIA-produced film on Gorbachev; he memorized facts about the Soviet leader, such as the name of his favorite soccer team, which he could use in private conversation; and he had rehearsed his lines, with Matlock and other experts playing Gorbachev. The Soviets were bemused by his three-by-five cards and his spurious quotations from Lenin and Stalin. Still, he had essentially mastered his brief, and in the plenary sessions he argued with verve. According to Regan, the President and the general secretary often went at it like taxi drivers after a fender-bender, and Reagan seemed to enjoy the give-and-take.[177]

In the first session, Gorbachev said in a conversational tone that the United States should have no illusions about being able to bankrupt the Soviet Union or about gaining military superiority through space weapons. The President, much sterner, talked about the origins of the Cold War and blamed the Soviet Union. On the second day, Gorbachev returned to SDI and made his points at greater length: space weapons would be hugely expensive for the United States—the government would be putting up to a trillion dollars in the hands of the military-industrial complex. And for what? Did Reagan really want a first-strike capability? If so, the U.S. was bound to fail, for the Soviet Union could match these weapons much less expensively with programs of its own. In response, Reagan brushed off the financial issue and offered to open the labs. Gorbachev dismissed the offer and went on: "You are trying to catch the firebird with technology. How can we go before the world and say we lost the chance for fifty percent reductions because we wouldn't stop research on space weapons?"

"How can you defend a chance for fifty percent reductions just because you were stubborn [about a] research [program]?" Reagan replied.[178]

Reagan gave a passionate speech about how much better the world would be if both sides could defend themselves rather than relying on the ability to "wipe each other out" to keep the peace. When he finished, there was a long silence.

Gorbachev, McFarlane later wrote, "had to conclude one of two things: either Reagan was being cynical with all his preaching about eliminating nuclear weapons, and his real intention was to bankrupt the Soviet system; or he was incredibly ignorant." But, whatever he concluded, McFarlane wrote, Gorbachev knew he had to put up with Reagan. "Mr. President," Gorbachev finally responded, "I don't agree with you, but I can see you really mean what you say."[179]

On Afghanistan, Reagan waxed eloquent about the brutalities of the war and accused the Soviets of engaging in genocide.[180] He did not pick up on Gorbachev's mention of a political settlement and a Soviet troop withdrawal from Afghanistan—only Shultz did.[181] But, then, as George Bush had warned Dobrynin before the summit, the President found it hard to think and to express his own ideas simultaneously. This meant, Bush explained, that whenever Reagan was ardently advocating an idea, he hardly grasped what his opponent was saying. He needed some time to digest the ideas and arguments coming from the other side.[182]

In private discussions with Gorbachev, Reagan showed similar verve, but he did no more negotiating than he did in the plenary sessions. In the pool house he gave the general secretary a document proposing joint instructions, or guidelines, for the negotiators at the next round of arms talks. Nitze had initially drafted these guidelines in the hopes of moving the process forward, but the final document did little more than reiterate the positions Gorbachev had already heard, and in answer to the general secretary's questions Reagan indicated that the administration was holding to the "broad" interpretation of the ABM Treaty.[183] On the way back from the pool house, Reagan invited Gorbachev to a summit in the United States. This was his only personal initiative, and Shultz was unpleasantly surprised. The U.S. and Soviet governments had already agreed to two future summits, and Shultz wanted Gorbachev to make the proposal officially so that the general secretary would look like the *demandeur*. But Reagan had jumped the gun and, by all accounts, was extremely pleased with himself. "The President," Regan writes cattily, "glowed with pride and a sense of accomplishment after this master stroke of personal diplomacy. He felt he had stolen a march on his Secretary of State and Chief of Staff and all the other advisers who hovered in the background."[184] But Reagan was, McFarlane writes, "a little shaky on the dates of what Gorbachev had agreed to."[185]

In another private session, Reagan gave Gorbachev a pre-planned lecture on human rights. Otherwise the two rehashed their established positions or chatted.

During breaks, Reagan reported some of the conversations back to his aides. According to Adelman, Reagan spent a good deal of the first private meeting reciting the history of earthquakes along the San Andreas Fault from 500 A.D. to modern times. Something Gorbachev said set him off.[186] The two of them spent another private session discussing the problems they had with their respective bureaucracies. And at one point Reagan said that if creatures from outer space invaded the planet Americans and Soviets would soon forget their national differences and get together as human beings.[187]

Reagan remained in high spirits throughout the meeting. He joked continuously when alone with his aides, and at the two small dinner parties for the Reagans, the Gorbachevs and their ranking officials, Reagan made appropriate diplomatic remarks and then told stories. Gorbachev had seen Reagan's film *King's Row* as a part of his pre-summit homework, and when he said he enjoyed it, Reagan told stories about his Hollywood days, his career in the movies, how movies were produced, how different directors worked, how various stars behaved in real life. According to Regan and Adelman, the Gorbachevs devoured the details and seemed pleased to be in the company of someone who had known Jimmy Stewart, John Wayne and Humphrey Bogart. Regan and Adelman were, however, of the opinion that all Soviet officials were fascinated by the glitter of Hollywood.[188]

Gorbachev, too, put a lot of effort into his performance. Dobrynin had told him that it was important to have the President see him in human terms even when they disagreed, and he had advised Gorbachev to use his own sense of humor and not to go into too much detail on subjects, in order not to corner Reagan or embarrass him. Gorbachev followed the advice faithfully. According to the American participants, he argued basic issues and avoided the arcana of arms control.[189] He made his points dramatically, sometimes pounding the edge of his hand on the table, raising his voice and demanding answers, sometimes turning on his considerable charm and flattering Reagan. In informal conversations he showed that he had been meticulously briefed on the manners and the interests of the Reagans. He told amusing stories at dinner even though, as Regan suspected, he had an analytical mind, and storytelling did not come naturally to him.[190]

To all appearances, Gorbachev enjoyed Reagan's company and was interested in what the President had to say. Twice it was Gorbachev who initiated the private meetings.[191] Furthermore, each session seemed to leave Gorbachev in a very good mood. But, then, as Dobrynin tells us, "Gorbachev himself was a very good actor."[192]

At the reception after the closing ceremony of the summit on November 21, a *New York Times* reporter noted that just before Reagan and Gorbachev left the conference building they retired to a private room, drank a farewell toast of champagne and shook hands warmly.[193] That's what it looked like from a distance, but Adelman, who was closer to the two men than the journalist, saw the incident differently. By his account, Gorbachev asked Reagan if he could speak with him alone, and the two went off with an interpreter into a room which Adelman thought must be a pantry or a part of the kitchen. The two reappeared fairly quickly. Gorbachev then said, pointing to the pantry, that this marked the fifth time that they had met. Reagan, not catching his meaning, said no, this was the eleventh time American and Soviet leaders had met—the eleventh summit. There followed some confusing back-and-forth with the interpreter until Reagan understood that Gorbachev meant that this was the fifth time the two of them had met alone. At this point Reagan, who seemed to have had enough of summitry, thrust out his hand and said goodbye.

Adelman thought about this scene and concluded that Gorbachev was building up the number of private meetings he had had with the President, just as an American politician might, for political purposes.[194]

Reagan, for his part, seemed quite happy to see the general secretary go: the scene had ended, and he had a schedule to follow.

On the plane back to Moscow, Gorbachev, according to Dobrynin, said that he thought Reagan a complex and contradictory person who sometimes spoke his mind but at other times mouthed propaganda dogmas, which he also believed. He was, Gorbachev said, stubborn and conservative, but not so hopeless as some imagined.

Aleksandr Yakovlev, the former Soviet ambassador to Canada and one of Gorbachev's closest advisers, had a more jaundiced view. "It seemed to me that everything looked like theater," he said of the summit, "and that in this theater there was a professional actor."[195]

Reflecting on the meeting for the *Washington Post,* Lou Cannon wrote that, though summits are normally held to be no more than formalities, and this one did not produce any notable agreement, the meeting with Gorbachev might have been "one of the best things that ever happened to Reagan." It was a good thing, he argued, because "Reagan, among the least analytical and most unread of presidents, learns deeply from personal experience. . . . He learns by doing." Cannon went on to say that in a dangerous world it was important that the leaders of the two superpowers had good personal relations, and that it was particularly important for Reagan, whose touchstone was experience.[196]

This was doubtless what many Americans believed. Yet to think of Reagan as a man who would change his views because of a personal encounter is to figure him as a naïf—the endearing, naïve American Everyman that he often seemed to be. Reagan himself, the man who treated his oldest associates like extras on a set, was immune to "personal chemistry." Years later, describing his first impression of Gorbachev, Reagan wrote: "There was a warmth in his face and style, not the coldness bordering on hatred that I'd seen in most senior Soviet officials I'd met until then."[197]

Considering that until then Reagan had met only four senior Soviet officials in his life, one of them the agreeable Dobrynin and another the amiable Shevardnadze, he was hardly drawing from personal experience but, rather, from what his particular public might imagine his experience to be.*

To enter into the myth of the summit is to miss what a remarkable construction it was and ignore what Reagan actually accomplished at Geneva. With nothing to work with except his ability to connect with the American public, Reagan had foiled the hard-liners and turned a potential political disaster into an astonishing success. Playing his part as the amiable tough guy, he had both quieted public anxieties about nuclear war and pleased the right by not giving anything away.

Later Reagan himself marked Geneva as the greatest moment of his presidency.

* In September 1984 Reagan had met the well-behaved Gromyko. In 1973, when he was governor of California, he had met Brezhnev with Nixon in San Clemente. Brezhnev, Reagan remembered, had taken his hand and assured him of his dedication to peace. "Never," Reagan wrote in 1981, "had peace and good will among men seemed closer to hand."[198]

CHAPTER EIGHT

What Happened at Reykjavik?

THE BEGINNING OF 1986 was the political apogee of the Reagan administration thus far. Reagan's own polls had not been so high since just after the assassination attempt in 1981, and on the strength of his second great electoral victory in 1984 many Republican strategists were euphorically predicting a profound and lasting political realignment in which the Republican Party would dominate the country as the Democratic Party had done in the wake of the New Deal. Yet clearly there were issues that had to be dealt with before the 1986 midterm elections.

Reagan had won his second landslide in part because he had put off all the hard fiscal choices about raising taxes and cutting the budget, permitting the deficits to rise stratospherically. The decisions could no longer be delayed. Both parties in Congress had ruled out massive tax increases, and because the Reagan administration had thus far provided no leadership on cutting the budget, they had passed the Gramm-Rudman act, which, aiming for a balanced budget in 1991, mandated huge cuts in both military and discretionary domestic spending. The cuts were far too draconian for the law to survive intact, but the act clearly indicated that cuts had to come from the military as well as the domestic side of the budget. The Republican leadership had agreed to this because domestic spending programs were popular, whereas 80 percent of Americans thought military spending high enough, if not already too high.[1]

In 1984 Reagan had indicated a solution to this problem by declaring victory: thanks to defense spending increases of the first term, the U.S. had caught up with the Russians and was ready to engage the Soviets from a position of strength. Arms control would not only provide a rationale for the necessary reductions in the military budget, but was popular in its own right. Reagan's peace-and-disarmament campaign had been brilliantly successful. It had destroyed the anti-nuclear movement, and undercut the only serious challenge Mondale could make to him. Of course, any arms agreement would upset the Republican right, but Reagan was in a better position than any other President to conclude one without a political backlash. Indeed, every time Reagan mentioned arms reductions, his polls went up. Thus far his "dream" of Star Wars had substituted for an arms accord, but the notion of putting huge amounts of super-high-tech weapons into space could hardly survive in a climate of military-budget reductions. In short, arms control was a political no-brainer. So, too, was a negotiated settlement to the hugely unpopular proxy war in Central America.[2]

But during the spring and summer of 1986 the Reagan administration moved backwards rather than forward on these issues. While endorsing Gramm-Rudman in principle, the President called for an 8-percent increase in the military budget and one hundred million dollars in aid to the Nicaraguan contras; the administration made no progress on arms control, and U.S.-Soviet tensions increased. By the fall the administration was facing a rebellion in Congress, and public opinion was turning against the Republicans. The result was Reykjavik: the most bizarre summit in the history of the Cold War.

That the administration reverted to type was not entirely surprising, for, given Reagan's refusal to fire anyone the year before, hard-liners remained a majority in the national-security bureaucracy. In 1984 and 1985 Shultz had won on a number of issues thanks to the demands of the election campaign and the influence of some members of the White House staff. But Donald Regan was not a reliable ally, and in December 1985 Robert McFarlane resigned.

Years later Reagan's first-term aides were often asked why they put the White House in the hands of a man so unsuited to the task of running it as Donald Regan. Their answer was always that the secretary of the Treasury was a man of impressive achievements, that he got along well with the President and that he had no careerist motives for taking the job. All of this was undeniably true. It was also true that Baker and Deaver wanted to move on, and, as they surely knew, there were things about Regan which suggested he would not prove an ideal chief of staff for Ronald Reagan.

Regan had come to the administration from Wall Street, where he had been the chairman of Merrill, Lynch, the largest brokerage firm in the country. Tall, lean, silver-haired and invariably dressed in well-tailored gray plaid suits, he looked like one of those old-monied establishment figures who circulated between Wall Street and Washington in the earlier days of the Cold War. But, like many of Reagan's old California friends, he was a self-made man. His family was Boston Irish and his father a railroad security guard. Given a partial scholarship to Harvard, he worked his way through college and graduated fourth in his class of 1940. During World War II he became a Marine artillery officer and fought in the Pacific campaigns. In 1946 he joined Merrill, Lynch, and then worked his way up through the firm, becoming CEO in 1968, before he was fifty, and chairman of the board two years later.[3] Brash, dictatorial and something of a prima donna, Regan was not popular with his subordinates, but he was a superb salesman and an innovator, who moved the firm into new businesses and expanded it into a wide variety of new financial services for the small investor. By the 1970s he was a major player on Wall Street, heading a firm with thirty-two thousand employees and making half a million dollars a year. Yet he remained an outsider, a loner by temperament, with something of an Irish chip on his shoulder. Not surprisingly, perhaps, it was William Casey, another Irish buccaneer, who recommended him to the Reagan transition team.[4]

Regan had been eager to go to Washington, but, as a man used to running his own show, he found much about his job as secretary of the Treasury frustrating. David Stockman had begun making economic policy well before Regan's arrival, and for the first year he had little to do but cheerlead for "the Reagan revolution." He had been told that the President favored a Cabinet government, but it soon became clear to him that all important decisions were made in the White House—and that he was being ignored. In his memoir he tells us that he had come to Washington to translate the President's economic ideas into policies and programs. He thought Reagan's ideas must differ considerably from Stockman's, but he could not say how, since he could never get near enough to the President to ask him. He saw the President at official functions and Cabinet meetings, but never alone.[5]

In early 1982 Regan was invited to lead an economic briefing session for the President every six weeks, and, as everyone who attended these sessions recognized, the President enjoyed Regan's company. Like all successful salesmen, Regan projected optimism and self-confidence. He spoke of complex issues in a simple, direct way. And because he suffered from a loss of hearing, he spoke in a booming voice which the President, who was losing his own hearing, could always understand. With Reagan he shared a liking for acerbic Irish jokes and locker-room humor—and when he saw the President's attention drifting from the subject under discussion, he would interrupt to regale him with a story or an anecdote drawn from his own successful career. Then, too, in the face of what he describes as "a rising clamor for new taxes as an antidote to fiscal disaster," he was the only one who agreed with the President that the deficits would somehow just disappear.[6]

Yet Regan's success at ingratiating himself with the President did not bring him the access he wanted. By the time of Reagan's reelection, he still had not talked with the President alone. The White House staff, he tells us, had created a wall around the President, keeping valuable people out. He fought bitterly with Jim Baker until the moment the two decided to change jobs.[7]

Regan felt confident that he could run the White House, for in his view the "troika" of Baker, Meese and Deaver, with its constant feuding, news leaks and inefficiencies, had created a case study in poor management. He intended, he told a friend, to straighten things out. On the day he moved into the White House in January 1985 he announced that he would be the "chief operating officer"—a title which presumably left the President as chief executive officer, or chairman of the board.[8] He then set about streamlining the staff and setting up the White House along strictly hierarchical lines, all of which led to his office. In place of Baker's aides he installed a collection of his own from the Treasury, a group of young men so colorless and timid they were quickly dubbed "the Mice."[9]

The difficulty—or one of them—was that Regan was by training and temperament ill-suited to a supremely political job. He had no appreciation of the amount of persuading and arm-twisting it took to get a piece of legislation passed. He was used to giving orders and having them obeyed, and he seemed to think that when the President took a position the congressional Republicans should fall into line. As a salesman, he cared a great deal about how the President was perceived, but, lacking political instincts, he relied far more heavily on polling than the troika had, and he had no idea how to handle the press.[10]

In defending their choice of a successor, former White House aides made the point that Regan wanted, as he put it, to "let Reagan be Reagan," and had no policy agenda of his own. This was true—but it was a major part of the problem. Regan knew a good deal about economics, but, having long defended the President's position on the deficits, he saw no need to mount a White House effort to deal with them. He worked at tax reform instead. Outside of the economic domain, he had limited experience of public policy; in particular, he lacked a background in defense and foreign policy. An intelligent man, he might have found a way to compensate for this, but he did not have enough interest in the issues to make the effort.[11]

After Regan had been in office a few months, the President declared on a radio broadcast from his California ranch that South Africa—still in the grip of apartheid—had "eliminated the segregation that we once had in our country, the type of thing where hotels and restaurants and places of entertainment and so forth were segregated—that has all been eliminated." Many Republicans in Congress were appalled, but Regan let the remark pass, and his executive assistant, who normally reflected his views, said of South Africa, "I couldn't care less."[12] Then, when the President was in the hospital recovering from an operation for colon cancer that summer, Regan sat in the hospital room while McFarlane briefed Reagan about undertaking a secret transfer of arms to Iran in return for Iranian help in freeing the American hostages in Lebanon. Regan had nothing to say about this perilous enterprise and later could not recall having heard anything about an arms shipment. What he did recall quite vividly was that he had had a savage altercation with Nancy Reagan over whether or not he could take a helicopter from the White House to the hospital.[13] On most issues Regan vacillated so much that congressional leaders complained they could not count on him to set an agenda for the President and stick to it. The problem, a top administration official said, "is that he hasn't thought through his own position in sufficient depth for the position to be stable."[14] What seemed to interest Regan rather more than policy were the perks of his office and the figure he cut as the President's right-hand man.

For Regan the phrase "letting Reagan be Reagan" had not at all the same meaning it did for conservatives. Regan was a moderate in the context of the administration, and he believed that the President was one as well. All the same, administration foreign policy drifted and lurched to the right during his stewardship. To appease the conservatives, he hired Patrick Buchanan, the columnist and former speechwriter for President Nixon and Vice-President Agnew, as director of communications—an important post in the Reagan White House.[15] He also gave his friend William Casey and his former Cabinet colleague Caspar Weinberger private meetings with the President without informing the NSC adviser.[16] He had nothing against Shultz, but by making no effort on his behalf, he allowed the hard-line majority to rule. Then, too, he drove McFarlane to resign and replaced him with his more conservative and far less qualified deputy.

Since Reagan's reelection in November 1984, Shultz, among others, had noticed that McFarlane was showing increasing signs of stress and distress. The diffident, colorless former Marine—a man whom Paul Weyrich, the New Right activist, said "was created by God to disappear into crowds"—seemed possessed by Walter Mitty–like fantasies.[17] He kept asking to go on secret missions to talk with foreign heads of state, such as King Hassan of Morocco, or opposition leaders, such as Jonas Savimbi of Angola; he wanted to go secretly to Cuba to work out the problems of Central America with Castro; he wanted to communicate with "moderates" in Iran to counter Soviet influence in the region and to work for a change in the regime of the Ayatollah Khomeini. Apparently his ambition was to pull off something akin to Henry Kissinger's opening to China. Then, too, this normally self-effacing man had taken to upstaging Shultz, Weinberger and the President by scooping them in background briefings and making it appear that he was in charge. But with all of this new grandiosity, McFarlane seemed increasingly tired, morose and discouraged. Between January and July 1985 he told Shultz three times that he wanted to resign.[18]

The most experienced of Reagan's NSC advisers so far, McFarlane did his best, but he lacked the deep keel of self-confidence that was necessary to do the job. Dealing with the two warring secretaries was never easy, and after Reagan's reelection it became even more difficult. His relationship with Weinberger degenerated into a personal feud. Weinberger, according to McFarlane, became increasingly hostile, challenging every decision on U.S.-Soviet relations and complaining that his own views were not being fairly represented to the President. McFarlane for his part openly criticized Weinberger, once going so far as to tell reporters that the secretary of defense had "misspent" much of the money for the military buildup and that his precious MX missile was a "turkey."[19] Shultz, whom he sided with more often, was easier to get along with, but the two of them had their flare-ups. Then, too, dealing with Ronald Reagan was not a task McFarlane was suited for.

In Michael Deaver's opinion, McFarlane was not assertive enough with the President. "He'd come to me and say, 'You know, our position on this or that is terrible,' " Deaver told a reporter. "And I'd say, 'Bud, for God's sake go tell him that.' Well, he was a soldier, you know. He'd say, 'You can't talk to the commander in chief like that,' and I'd say, 'Yeah, but you're not a soldier anymore. He hired you to give him the best advice.' "[20]

McFarlane, however, was not on the President's wavelength. Reagan listened to people who engaged him directly, who told stories and who summarized issues with pithy punch lines. But McFarlane, reserved and formal, spoke in cautious bureaucratic prose. When explaining issues, he lectured, briefing-book style, in long convoluted paragraphs, and sometimes in a deep monotone, so different from his natural voice that he seemed possessed. More than once Deaver sat McFarlane down with the President and said, "Now, Bud has just told me something that you've got to hear." The President would get interested, but then McFarlane would skirt cautiously around the issue, causing Deaver to burst out, "Goddammit, Bud, tell him the way you told me."[21]

McFarlane for his part did not understand this lack of rapport. He simply felt that the President did not value him, and he put it down to the fact that he was not wealthy and successful, like Shultz, Weinberger, Regan and others in the President's set. "It's just the way he dealt with us together," he later said. "He'd pointedly ask George, 'What do you think?' He'd be very attentive to Cap and Don. And then he'd say, 'Well, Bud, take care of that' . . . He clearly didn't see me as a person of qualification, deserving of respect."[22]

Donald Regan, however, saw things differently.

Regan had no policy dispute with McFarlane, but from the beginning he was on McFarlane's case, unable to tolerate the independent authority he had and his direct access to the President. Twice in the spring of 1985, McFarlane woke the President to alert him to some overnight development but did not call the chief of staff, assuming others would do it. On the second occasion, Regan called him abruptly to his office and told him he was not going to put up with this outrageous behavior. McFarlane apologized, but Regan, with a head of steam up, lapsed into profanity and shouted that he was not going to take such insubordination. McFarlane apologized again, but objected that he worked for the President. "The hell you do," Regan roared. "You work for me, and everything you do will come through me or you'll be out of here."[23] Later that day Regan apologized, and civility was restored, but McFarlane smoldered, and Regan could not seem to reconcile himself to the fact that he did not control the NSC staff. In the months that followed, Regan took to backstabbing McFarlane in the press.[24]

McFarlane had worked extremely hard on the Geneva summit, and after it he seemed exhausted, dispirited and on the verge of emotional collapse. Previously he had told Shultz that he would resign after the summit, but now he seemed paralyzed by indecision. Friends told him to relax, take a vacation; members of his staff pleaded with him to stay on, but on December 4, after *Newsweek* ran an item about his impending departure, he resigned. Immediately he regretted the decision. When Bill Plante of CBS asked him whether he had not made a mistake, he said, "Yes, I saw a problem, and I walked away from it, and it's a cop-out." The problem he was referring to was the Iran initiative, which had just gone seriously awry.[25]

On December 5 the President appointed McFarlane's deputy, Vice-Admiral John Poindexter, as the new NSC adviser. He was Don Regan's choice, and there seems to have been no discussion of any other candidate. The vice-admiral had served on the NSC staff since 1981, when Richard Allen appointed him as his military aide, and he had made no waves in the political currents of the administration.

The son of a small-town Midwestern banker, Poindexter had had a stellar military career. He had graduated first in his class at Annapolis in 1958 and afterwards taken a doctoral degree in nuclear physics at Cal Tech and served as the chief engineer of a guided-missile frigate. Recruited to the Pentagon to join McNamara's "whiz kids" in 1966, he served as administrative assistant to three naval secretaries before making it back out to the blue Navy as commander of his own frigate in 1974. Thereafter he spent two years as executive assistant to the chief of naval operations, Admiral James L. Holloway, and three years as commander of a destroyer squadron. Cool, steady, intelligent, punctilious, he was said to be a great boat-handler and a bureaucrat's bureaucrat.[26]

But for all his achievements, Poindexter was a man of narrow horizons. Unlike most of his predecessors in the NSC job, he had no academic training in history, economics or politics. (His doctoral dissertation was entitled "Electronic Shielding by Closed Shells in Thulium Compounds.") In all the years he spent in Washington working for policy-makers, he never made up for this deficit. His reading was scientific and technical, and even as deputy NSC adviser he did not read the *New York Times* or the *Washington Post*.[27] His knowledge of world affairs remained slight. "You see, George, the Arabs don't like the Israelis," he once lectured Shultz.[28] His understanding of Washington was slighter still. Serving under Admiral Holloway in the mid-seventies, he had conceived an abiding dislike for politicians. Curiously enough, his feeling had very little to do with the Vietnam War—he had never served in it and had never felt very strongly about it. Rather, it had to do with the way in which congressmen dealt with base closings and other military issues that affected their districts. A man who identified completely with the system he had been brought up in, he could not see the point of this form of democracy.[29]

According to Colin Powell, then serving as Weinberger's chief military aide, William Casey was upset by Poindexter's appointment because he thought the naval officer lacked the breadth and depth the job demanded. He asked Weinberger to call the President to forestall the appointment. "He's not up to it, Cap," he said. Weinberger made the call, but only on Casey's behalf, and he did not argue when the President gave him reasons for the appointment.[30] Shultz for his part seemed to accept the appointment with equanimity.[31] Since the two secretaries had a veto over each other's candidates, neither made an effort to push for someone else.

At the NSC, Poindexter was a reclusive figure. He set up a chain of command and dealt with others through his deputies—and he preferred to communicate with his deputies by e-mail rather than in person. Working a twelve-to-sixteen-hour day, he often ate all three meals alone at his desk. Poindexter did not like the press, and he did not like having to deal with the Congress. In his view the affairs of state were best carried out by professionals without interference from outsiders. Then, too, security was an obsession with him.[32] Official leaks to the press, a way of life in the ideologically divided administration, were his *bête noire.* In the first term, on request from Bill Clark, he worked up a plan whereby anyone in the executive branch giving press interviews with "national-security information" would have to have NSC approval in advance and write a memo on the conversation later. Jim Baker scotched the plan, but not before news of it leaked. As national-security adviser, Poindexter devised elaborate classification systems to foil leakers; and he tried to have controls put on commercial database companies so that unclassified government information—economic statistics and the like—could not reach the Soviet Union.[33]

On becoming national-security adviser, Poindexter accepted Donald Regan's rules and did not insist on having the kind of access to the President that McFarlane had had. In the course of 1986, he and the President spent a total of eighty-one minutes alone.[34] In Regan's view this meant that Regan controlled foreign policy in the White House. In practice, however, Poindexter had as much power as any NSC adviser, because Regan lacked interest in much of what he did and generally left him to his own devices. He understood that his job meant being an honest broker between the two secretaries, and he tried his best, but neutrality was impossible and taking Shultz's side against his nature. His instincts were conservative and unilateralist, and his definition of national security barely encompassed diplomacy and the State Department. On Third World conflicts he sided with Casey, and on U.S.-Soviet relations with Weinberger. He did not believe in a negotiated settlement in Central America—and he lacked both interest and expertise in arms control.[35]

For the first time, therefore, Shultz had no ally in the White House, and within the month of Poindexter's appointment he had to fight two major battles with the White House staff and the President. The first one was over an executive order the President signed on the advice of McFarlane, Poindexter, Casey and others instituting an extensive program of random lie-detector testing for government employees with access to sensitive information. Shultz publicly threatened to resign if the order was carried out, and once again on this issue, he prevailed.[36] The second, and more serious, battle was over the Philippines. For some time the regime of Ferdinand Marcos had been falling of its own weight, and in December a huge democratic opposition movement led by Corazon Aquino took to the streets to protest a rigged election. Shultz—belatedly, in the view of many—decided that the time had come for the U.S. to use its considerable influence to get Marcos out of the country. The President, however, thought otherwise. In the past he had bitterly criticized President Carter for abandoning President Somoza of Nicaragua and the Shah of Iran. In this case he seemed to think that Aquino was a weak woman, and that the fall of Marcos would mean victory for the small Communist insurgency in the Philippines. This was Casey's view, and also Don Regan's; it remained their view, and the President's, even after the Marcoses' defense minister and chief of staff resigned and Marcos ordered troops to assault the military base where they were holed up with supporters. Shultz eventually prevailed, and in late February 1986 he extricated Marcos from a dangerous situation. But, according to Shultz, Reagan never quite forgave him for not figuring out how to save the Marcos regime, and the event created a new distance between them.[37]

At Geneva, Reagan and Gorbachev had agreed that there would be a summit in the United States in 1986, and one in the Soviet Union the following year. After his triumph at Geneva, Reagan was eager for another meeting. Gorbachev, however, had gone to Geneva proclaiming that SDI would lead to a new and more dangerous arms race and had come away without budging Reagan on the issue of restraints. Not only was he disappointed, but reaction in Moscow suggested that he had paid a political price for coming away empty-handed. On Gorbachev's return, Vladimir Shcherbitsy, an old-guard Politburo member from the Ukraine, had expressed skepticism about the results of the meeting, and Marshal Sergei Akhromeyev, the chief of the General Staff, made public statements raising doubts about the achievements of the summit. In December, Reagan and Gorbachev exchanged letters, but merely to restate their positions. In early January 1986, Shultz proposed through Dobrynin that Gorbachev come to Washington in June. Gorbachev did not reply immediately, but Dobrynin privately told Shultz that September would be more realistic, because of the time required to work out an agreement on strategic arms.[38]

On the morning of January 15 Ambassador Anatoly Dobrynin telephoned Shultz and told him to expect an important announcement from Moscow that day. His deputy had just brought Shultz a letter from Gorbachev to Reagan containing an arms-control proposal, and Shultz sent it immediately to the White House. Three hours later the television-news anchor in Moscow spent a half-hour reading the same document aloud, while Tass distributed copies of it around the world. The proposal was nothing less than a schedule for the complete elimination of all nuclear weapons by the year 2000.

Administration officials were not a little annoyed. At the very moment the message reached the White House, officials were telling reporters that the Soviet negotiating position was unlikely to change until Gorbachev had consolidated his political position at the Communist Party congress the following month.[39] But Gorbachev had once again done the unexpected, and once again he was appealing to public opinion over their heads.

In the 1950s, at a time when the U.S. had overwhelming nuclear superiority, the Soviets had often advanced proposals for "general and complete disarmament"—proposals which had some appeal for the non-nuclear powers but none at all for the United States, which relied on the nuclear threat to counter the Soviet superiority in conventional forces in Europe. Given the Soviet resistance to on-site verification—or to allowing Americans into their facilities—these proposals had been short on details, and they had not included any provisions for reducing conventional arms. Essentially they had been demands that the United States disarm itself. But Gorbachev's proposal was a schedule for mutual disarmament with a great many details.

Poring over the text that morning, Shultz and Nitze found that Gorbachev had proposed to eliminate nuclear weapons in three stages, each one lasting five years. In the first stage the U.S. and the Soviet Union would cut their strategic weapons in half and eliminate their intermediate-range weapons in Europe. These reductions would be accompanied by an agreement to renounce "the development, testing and deployment of space-strike weapons." In the second stage the other nuclear powers—France, Britain and China—would join the disarmament process by freezing their arsenals at current levels while the U.S.S.R. and the U.S. would continue to reduce their strategic weapons, eliminate all medium-range and tactical nuclear weapons, ban all nuclear testing and ban weapons based on other physical principles, such as lasers. In the third stage all nuclear weapons would be eliminated globally. The proposal spoke of on-site verification, of the reduction of conventional forces in Europe and of a ban on chemical weapons.[40]

In the view of Shultz and Nitze, Gorbachev's nuclear-disarmament proposal was a "blockbuster" piece of propaganda—but one which could hardly be denounced as such. The President, after all, had been calling for an end to nuclear weapons since 1983, and since the previous January administration officials had been treating their Soviet counterparts to recitations of Nitze's "strategic concept" of nuclear disarmament in three stages.

Of course, both the President's "vision" and Nitze's plan were predicated upon the deployment of strategic defenses. But although Star Wars was very popular with the American public, Gorbachev's anti-nuclear proposal was rather simpler and more likely to appeal to audiences outside of the United States.

In addition, as Shultz tells us, there were one or two diplomatic niceties which stood in the way of an outright rejection of the disarmament proposal. Shultz and McFarlane had many times tried to get the President to accept a grand compromise in principle by arguing that, the more offensive weapons were reduced, the less defense the U.S. would require, starting from the logical endpoint that if there were no nuclear weapons the U.S. would need no defense. Whether or not the President understood their argument, they had put the idea into his brief for Geneva. Later the President did not remember making any such point, but, looking over the interpreter's notes of the fireside conversation at the pool house, Shultz discovered that Reagan had told Gorbachev that if there was an agreement to eliminate nuclear missiles there could be an agreement to do without defenses. So now Gorbachev had come back at them with the same argument.[41] In addition, Gorbachev's new INF proposal looked very much like the "zero option" the administration had been advocating since 1981.

With only an hour or so remaining before the Soviets announced the disarmament plan, Shultz made haste to put together an initial American response. Setting up an appointment with the President for 2:00 P.M., he asked Nitze to prepare a summary of the document, talking points for him and the draft of a presidential statement. Next he called Weinberger and Casey and asked that they send over their arms-control experts, Richard Perle and Doug George, to meet with Nitze right away. Then he left to make the speech he had been scheduled to make that noon.[42]

At two in the afternoon, Shultz met with the President in the Oval Office and went over Nitze's argument for a favorable response to the proposal. "This," he said, "is our first indication that the Soviets are interested in a staged program toward zero. We should not simply reject their proposal, since it contains certain steps which we earlier set forth."[43] Apparently Shultz did not say that he considered the proposal to eliminate nuclear weapons pure propaganda.

At first Reagan had some reservations. Weinberger had just called with objections after Perle reported to him what the State Department was proposing. But Admiral Poindexter had come to much the same conclusion as the State Department, and after registering Weinberger's views, Reagan waxed enthusiastic about a favorable response. "Why wait until the end of the century for a world without nuclear weapons?" he asked. Shultz did not answer him, and Nitze's statement welcoming the proposal and promising that it would receive "careful study" went out immediately over Reagan's signature. Conceivably the President now thought that both the Soviets and his secretary of state favored total nuclear disarmament.[44]

As Shultz and Nitze had noted, Gorbachev had front-loaded his general-disarmament plan with much more practical proposals. In addition to repeating the offers he had made on START and SDI the previous September and announcing an extension of the unilateral Soviet moratorium on nuclear testing, he had made a proposal on INF weapons that to Shultz and Nitze seemed a real advance on the bidding. Because the U.S. had by now deployed its intermediate-range missiles in Europe, the offer to eliminate the INF weapons was not as completely to the American advantage as Richard Perle's zero option had been in 1981. Still, the Soviets would have to dismantle many more missiles than the U.S. to get to zero, and whereas in the past they had asked for "compensation" for the British and French missiles aimed at the Soviet Union, they were now asking simply that the British and the French refrain from increasing their arsenals. Since the Pentagon was dead set against a nuclear-test ban, on the grounds that testing was necessary to maintaining and developing weaponry, and since the two sides were still far apart on START and SDI, Shultz decided to try to separate out an INF agreement—and to up the ante by calling for the elimination of Soviet intermediate-range weapons in Asia.[45]

The first question, though, was how to deal with the "comprehensive proposal" diplomatically. Shultz was for accepting it in principle, so that the two sides might move towards deep reductions in nuclear weapons, but there was great resistance to this, even within the State Department. Nuclear disarmament, one of his deputies, Peter Rodman, heatedly argued, would mean a neutralist Europe, the end of NATO and a disaster for the West. Shultz quieted Rodman by saying that, in spite of his own efforts, the President thought otherwise, and, besides, disarmament was "a political hot button" for the public at large.[46] That left Richard Perle, who in interagency meetings kept protesting that Gorbachev's proposal was pure propaganda, and that doing away with nuclear weapons was the worst idea in the world. Perle had, of course, endorsed nuclear disarmament when he approved the "strategic concept" the previous year. That he was objecting so strenuously now was presumably because responding positively to Gorbachev's proposal might further arms control. "You've got a problem," Shultz said to him with a laugh. "The President thinks it's a *good* idea." He had Perle there. "Don't worry," he continued, "we can say 'fine' to the three-stage approach and then front-end load our program in the first stage. Gorbachev's language makes the INF zero option operational."[47]

This, of course, was just what Perle was worried about, but he could hardly object since the "zero option" was his idea to begin with.

On February 23, after a month of bureaucratic pulling and hauling, Reagan sent Gorbachev a handwritten letter welcoming his disarmament plan and calling for an INF settlement that would be global in scope, covering the Soviet missiles deployed in Asia. The administration did not, however, advance a new START proposal; and it did not respond to Gorbachev's concerns about SDI or nuclear testing.[48]

According to Dobrynin, the Soviets considered the response disappointing. As they saw it, the administration, without rejecting the Gorbachev program directly, was selecting only those parts of it that looked attractive and trying to negotiate them separately rather than as part of a package. Through intermediaries, Gorbachev made it clear that he would not commit himself to a summit date without progress in arms control generally, but he did not immediately reply to Reagan's letter. For the moment he was occupied with the party congress and with the first major initiative in perestroika.[49]

The Twenty-seventh Congress of the Soviet Communist Party convened in Moscow on February 25 and deliberated until March 6. Officially the supreme body of the party, the congress met only once every five years, and its meetings were always important occasions, for a new Central Committee was chosen, and the leadership assessed developments and either reaffirmed or changed "the general line" of policy. Because this congress was Gorbachev's first as general secretary, American officials assumed that it was a key one for him politically, and they presumed that he would make his major policy statements at the event. They were not wrong about this. Gorbachev had prepared his disarmament proposal for the party congress, but after extensive discussions in the Politburo, he had decided to make it public ahead of time so that it would be seen as an act of the Soviet government, rather than of the Communist Party.[50] What he saved for his report to the congress was an exposition of the context for the proposal: a broad statement of principles and a framework for new approaches to foreign policy.

Much of Gorbachev's report to the congress, which took five hours to read, concerned domestic affairs, but in the first section, entitled "The Contemporary World: Its Main Trends and Contradictions," the general secretary addressed international relations—and in a radically new way. He began by giving a brief and familiar litany about the contradictions between capitalism and socialism; he then struck out into uncharted territory. There are, he said, contradictions "on a global scale, affecting the very foundations of the existence of civilization," and the first among them "the pollution of the environment, the air, the ocean and the depletion of natural resources." These global problems, he said, "cannot be resolved by one state or group of states"; rather, they required "cooperation on a worldwide scale [and] . . . close and constructive joint action by a majority of countries . . . [in compliance with] international law." Gorbachev then—rather surprisingly—commented on a remark Reagan had made to him in Geneva:

> The U.S. President said once that if our planet were threatened by a landing from another planet, the U.S.S.R. and the U.S.A. would quickly find a common language. But isn't a nuclear disaster a more tangible danger than a landing by extraterrestrials? Isn't the ecological threat big enough? Don't all countries have a common stake in finding a sensible and fair approach to the problems of the developing states and peoples?[51]

Gorbachev synthesized the two parts of his argument in a sentence: "The dialectics of present day development consists in a combination of competition and confrontation between the two systems and in a growing interdependence of the countries of the world."[52]

In the Soviet context, the proposition was shocking. The Communist Party was, after all, founded on the notion of class struggle and of the irreconcilable conflict between socialism and capitalism. But Gorbachev was saying that above and beyond the ideological division there was one world—and a world growing increasingly interdependent. Global problems, he insisted, were not going to be solved by the triumph of socialism, for capitalism was going to continue to exist for the foreseeable future. Thus, above and beyond the ideological struggle, there had to be cooperation between nations and the forging of a more integrated world. Accordingly, he did not speak of "peaceful coexistence," a phrase which in the Soviet lexicon meant a variant of the ongoing class struggle, but, rather, of "a durable peace."

Later, in another section of the report, Gorbachev described the goals of Soviet foreign policy in an equally startling way. His predecessors had spoken of the need to prevent war and to achieve disarmament, but, rhetorically at least, they had always given emphasis to the progress of the world revolutionary movement. Gorbachev, by contrast, maintained that the party's main task was to establish security for the Soviet Union. He then redefined national security as international security. "The character of present-day weapons," he said, leaves no country "any hope of safeguarding itself solely with military and technical means.... The modern world has become much too small and fragile for wars and a policy of strength.... This means the realization that it is no longer possible to win an arms race, or a nuclear war for that matter.... The task of ensuring security... can only be resolved by political means." For the U.S. and the Soviet Union, he said, security could only be mutual, since "it is necessary for all to feel equally secure." In conclusion, he called for "an all-embracing system of international security"—military, political, economic and humanitarian—to be worked out in established international fora.[53]

In his report Gorbachev was drawing from ideas that had been germinating among Soviet scholars and officials for a decade or more. At first confined to private discussions, these ideas had gradually risen to the surface in the work of academics and journalists during the early eighties.[54] But his report to Twenty-seventh Congress was a landmark event in the development of "the new political thinking," and to most party officials it came as a bolt from the blue. The delegates to the congress clapped loudly, as was their wont, but, according to Foreign Minister Shevardnadze, many of them did not take the new ideas in, much less accept them. Later there were stormy debates in the party and in the government. It was difficult, Shevardnadze wrote, for many Communists to believe that there were more important issues in the world than the conflict between classes and ideological systems. Marshal Sergei Akhromeyev, the chief of the Soviet General Staff, later confessed that he found the idea of shifting the military contest to the background of policy difficult to assimilate. "For me personally, to rethink all these things and to view the situation from a different angle was very painful," he said. "Most of my life I've thought in a different manner."[55]

Pursuant to Gorbachev's report, Shevardnadze and his colleagues in the Foreign Ministry adopted a set of guidelines for a fundamental change in Soviet foreign policy. According to Shevardnadze, these guidelines included defusing regional conflicts, bringing the Soviet troops out of Afghanistan, creating a security system in Europe, radically cutting nuclear and conventional arms, treating neighboring countries with respect for their interests and on the basis of non-interference in their internal affairs, putting Soviet-American relations on the track of "normal, civilized dialog" and rejecting "the dead, brutally rigid positions in favor of intelligent, mutually-acceptable compromises."[56]

Shevardnadze later admitted that some of the guidelines turned out to be very difficult to translate into practical policies. But he went to work immediately on the Foreign Ministry, bringing in a new group of diplomats and changing Soviet diplomatic practices to accord with those of diplomats outside the Communist world. Within the space of a year, he replaced seven out of the nine deputy foreign ministers and sixty-eight out of the 115 Soviet ambassadors posted abroad, among them Dobrynin, who was brought home as a foreign-policy adviser to Gorbachev on the staff of the Central Committee. On May 23 Gorbachev made a speech in closed session to the ranking diplomatic corps of the Soviet Union, including all of the country's ambassadors, about the need for realism, pragmatism and the spirit of compromise. It would, he said, "be inadmissible if our persistence in defending this or that position grew into senseless stubbornness, if Soviet representatives were called Mr. Nyet."[57]

In his memoir, published in 1996, Robert Gates, a career CIA Soviet analyst, head of the CIA's Intelligence Directorate in the mid-eighties and later director of central intelligence, wrote that the Twenty-seventh Party Congress was "an historic turning point," and that Gorbachev's speech and the agenda that flowed from it eventually brought such "a radical turn in Soviet foreign policy" that March 6, 1986, "should be marked as the beginning of the end of the Cold War."[58]

At the time, this was hardly the perception in Washington.

By the evidence of his memoir, George Shultz did not recognize the importance of Gorbachev's report to the Twenty-seventh Party Congress, but he did know that changes were taking place in Moscow. Personal experience had taught him that the Soviets were handling their foreign policy in a completely new way. Gorbachev, he writes, was trying "something new and bold"; Shevardnadze was a "breathtaking" contrast to Gromyko, and Soviet diplomacy had become active, forward-looking and far more flexible. In Shultz's view, Gorbachev wanted out of the morass of Afghanistan, and he had come around to adding substance to rhetoric on arms control.[59]

In late January, judging the interagency process too stultified to respond to Gorbachev's energetic diplomacy, Shultz had set up a series of weekly Saturday meetings for top officials to work out new ways to deal with the Soviets on arms control and other issues. But whatever hope he had for this new forum soon faded, for among the NSC principals he alone believed that the Soviets were changing.[60]

In 1981 Weinberger had made up his mind that the Soviets were as the Committee on the Present Danger had depicted them, and no evidence to the contrary ever caused him to question this view. In his annual report to Congress in 1985, Weinberger rejected as "inherently incredible" the "theory" that the Soviets were solely concerned with their own security. All of postwar history, he declared, "demonstrates a Soviet willingness to take advantage of any perceived weakness in the global politico-military balance." In his report of 1986, he argued that it was not enough to build forces that the U.S. would regard as a deterrent, for these would never deter the Soviets from a nuclear first strike. In his 1987 report, he described the Soviet military buildup as all the more ominous because it was coupled with "military writings which continue to reflect their belief that the USSR could prevail in a nuclear war." Gorbachev, Weinberger maintained, was a public-relations expert trying to buy time from the West while pursuing the traditional Soviet goals.[61]

William Casey, too, had made up his mind some years earlier. The Soviets, in his view, were unalterably aggressive: they understood only superior force and would take advantage of any negotiation or easing of tensions to pursue their expansionist aims.[62] Though the CIA director had a responsibility to keep intelligence separate from policy, Casey habitually gave the President policy prescriptions as well as his own personal views about the Soviet threat. In June 1985, for example, he sent the President the first major CIA analysis of Gorbachev's policies, with a cover note saying that Gorbachev and those around him "are not reformers and liberalizers either in Soviet domestic or foreign policy," and that the Soviets had to be convinced that the "original Reagan agenda" of rearmament, rollback in the Third World and ideological challenge "is here to stay."[63]

Shultz cannot have had very much hope that Weinberger and Casey would change their views. What frustrated him, he tells us, is that the official CIA line of analysis—as opposed to what he learned when he talked with lower-level CIA intelligence analysts—dovetailed with the arguments the Defense Department hard-liners were making. By his account the CIA painted a picture of "a mighty nation confronting us everywhere—confident, unchanging and determined."[64] Robert Gates was often the one to present the CIA view of the Soviet Union, and, according to Shultz, he was the most prominent in saying that the Soviets wouldn't change and couldn't change and that Gorbachev was just another in the succession of hidebound leaders. "The Soviet Union is a despotism that works," Gates once told him.[65]

In his memoir, published three years after Shultz's, Gates takes issue with the secretary's characterization of his position and defends the work of his Intelligence Directorate. His position and that of his analysts were, however, not always the same, and with respect to the former, Shultz's criticisms were, even by his account, generally on target.

In the late 1970s and early '80s, the CIA's Office of Soviet Analysis (SOVA) had reported Soviet military spending growing at the enormous rate of 4 to 5 percent a year. In early 1983, however, SOVA analysts concluded that they had been wrong and that from 1976 on the actual rate of increase had been only 1.3 percent a year.[66] In that period, they wrote, Soviet spending on weapons procurements had remained flat, and spending on offensive strategic weapons had declined by 40 percent. In other words, Soviet military spending had plateaued at exactly the same time that Washington had become the most exercised about its growth.

According to a retrospective account by two former SOVA analysts, the revised SOVA estimates proved extremely unpopular in the administration. Weinberger "went nuts," and Iklé complained. Gates did not approve the SOVA paper for months, and when he did, he warned Weinberger that the new spending estimates would not be useful in helping him sell the Defense Department budget and urged him to stop their publication. Weinberger agreed, but because of the demand for the estimates from other intelligence agencies and the Congress, the decision had to be reversed. The revised SOVA figures were made public in 1985, but a paper by SOVA analysts arguing that the Soviets had made a deliberate decision to curtail their spending on strategic forces in the mid-seventies, when they attained strategic parity with the U.S., was not circulated.[67]

Along with the inflated figures for Soviet defense spending in the late '70s and early '80s had come unrealistic projections of Soviet weapons procurements. In 1985 SOVA analysts revised their force projections downward, pointing out that the older estimates did not accord with actual Soviet output, the trends in Soviet defense spending, the slowing growth of the Soviet economy or Gorbachev's ambitious program to modernize Soviet industry.

According to the retrospective SOVA account, however, their report was ignored, and Gates refused even to put a footnote in the National Intelligence Estimate pointing to the discrepancy between the huge force projections and apparent Soviet economic realities. Instead, Gates and others began to question SOVA's economic reporting. In June 1985 Gates rejected the draft of an economic paper. "The continuing litany of 2 percent growth for the 1980s has less and less credibility with me," he wrote, and he asked about the potential for policy changes that would improve the Soviet economy. In 1987, after SOVA analysts had reported that Gorbachev's efforts to modernize industry were unlikely to succeed and might lead to lower defense spending in the late 1980s, Gates ordered SOVA to send Weinberger a memo focusing on Soviet economic strengths. Apparently all circulated reports of a decline in the Soviet threat were bad news to Weinberger and Gates.[68]

Then, too, in spite of reports to the contrary from SOVA analysts, Gates officially maintained that Gorbachev and his colleagues were pursuing as aggressive a strategy of Third World penetration as their predecessors had in the mid-seventies. Unofficially he presented a far more alarming picture. In a public speech in November 1986, entitled "War by Another Name," he went so far as to say that the ultimate targets of the Soviet drive were the oil fields of the Middle East, the Panama Canal and the mineral wealth of southern Africa.[69]

As for the new general secretary, the CIA, by Gates's retrospective account, saw him as a younger, brighter and more personable Andropov: a man who had been chosen by his peers to revitalize the economy and "recreate the detente atmosphere of the early 1970s on the same premises." This sounds like a fairly positive assessment, albeit not a very good prediction. But in the ideologically charged atmosphere of the Reagan administration, what it meant was that Gorbachev wanted to lull the West while he built up Soviet military might and planned new imperial ventures in the Third World.[70] Specifically, according to Gates, the CIA analysis completed in June 1985 stated that the changes that Gorbachev had made in the foreign-policy arena were "pretty much stylistic."[71] Eight months later Gates, at least, had not changed his mind. On February 4, 1986, he wrote in a memo to Shultz that on "fundamental policies and objectives" Gorbachev "*so far* remains generally as inflexible as his predecessors."[72]

Gates was also quite certain that Gorbachev was not disposed to concessions on arms control. He took this position in June 1985, and continued to maintain it as Gorbachev made one unilateral concession after another.[73] Briefing the President for the Geneva summit, Gates said that Gorbachev needed a respite and needed "to avoid major *unanticipated* defense expenditures"—meaning principally the need to develop defenses in space—but that the general secretary "was not prepared to pay much" for the breathing room, in part because he could foresee a decline in U.S. defense spending, and particularly in spending for SDI, after Reagan left office. "My bottom line," he tells us in his memoir, was that "Gorbachev simply intended to outwait Reagan."[74] Gorbachev's initiative of January 15 did not alter his view, for in his February 4 memo to Shultz he wrote, "The new comprehensive arms proposal, while tactically a clever stroke, did not change any basic Soviet position on START or SDI or provide a realistic approach to INF."[75] As for Gorbachev's report to the Twenty-seventh Congress, Gates does not even pretend to have paid it any attention at the time.[76]

In the face of opposition from the Defense Department, Casey and Gates, Shultz got nowhere, and in the spring and summer of 1986 the Reagan administration made a series of moves that heightened U.S.-Soviet tensions. "Our relations," Dobrynin later wrote of this period, "seemed to be sliding back to the road of mounting confrontation."[77]

On March 7, the day after the conclusion of the party congress in Moscow, the Reagan administration announced that the Soviets would have to reduce the size of their UN mission in New York from about 270 to 170 in the next two years. The reason given was security against espionage, but no charges were made against any of the diplomats. The expulsion order was unprecedented in its scale.[78]

A week later two U.S. naval warships, a cruiser armed with nuclear missiles and a destroyer carrying sophisticated intelligence-collection equipment, deliberately entered Soviet territorial waters off the coast of the Crimea, ignoring Soviet signals to withdraw. When the Soviets protested, administration spokesmen claimed the vessels were exercising the right of "innocent passage," but this was hardly "innocent passage": the two vessels were way out of the normal sea-lanes, and, according to a Pentagon official, they had entered Soviet territorial waters with the mission of collecting intelligence.[79]

To the Soviets the incident took on an even more ominous construction when, ten days later, a U.S. naval contingent—also asserting "innocent passage"—held exercises in the Gulf of Sidra, just off Libya; when attacked by Libyan missiles, U.S. planes sank several Libyan patrol boats and struck missile sites on land.[80]

A month later the U.S. launched an air strike against Libya in retaliation for a terrorist bombing attack on American servicemen in West Berlin. The Soviets were informed of the American reasons for the strike, but the bombing raid, whose targets included the barracks where Colonel Qaddafi and his family lived, seemed to them to fit a pattern of American muscle-flexing. Gorbachev called the action "piracy" and canceled a trip that had been scheduled for Shevardnadze to visit Washington and discuss prospects for a summit.[81]

That spring the administration asked for a hundred million dollars in aid to the contras, and another three hundred million for the Afghan mujahedin; it ended the decade-long congressional ban on aid to Savimbi's anti-government forces in Angola and sent shoulder-held, anti-aircraft Stinger missiles to the Afghan and Angolan rebels. A great deal of harsh anti-Soviet rhetoric accompanied the various funding requests. Among other things, the President claimed that the defeat of the contras might lead to Soviet missile bases in Central America, and that the Soviets were building a first-strike capability.[82]

Gorbachev meanwhile continued to press for an independent agreement banning nuclear testing—a measure that many Democrats in Congress favored. The administration made no official response and went ahead with its scheduled underground tests.[83]

In a letter to Reagan of April 2, Gorbachev expressed frustration with the lack of progress:

> More than four months have passed since the Geneva meeting. We ask ourselves: what is the reason for things not going the way they, it would seem, should have gone? Where is the real turn for the better?
>
> . . . we hear increasingly vehement philippics addressed to the USSR and are also witnessing quite a few actions directly aimed against our interest, and to put it frankly, against our relations becoming more stable and constructive.

All this, Gorbachev wrote, created "no favorable backdrop for the summit meeting."[84]

On April 18 Gorbachev, trying another tack, proposed negotiations for "a substantial reduction" of conventional forces in Europe, which would be verified by on-site inspections and would cover the whole area "from the Atlantic Ocean to the Urals." Washington dismissed the proposal, and for a while his efforts ceased.[85]

On April 26 one of the four nuclear reactors at the Chernobyl power station in the Ukraine blew up, sending radioactive particles high into the atmosphere. For eight days Soviet authorities, attempting to ascertain the extent of the damage, said virtually nothing about the accident while rumors of the disaster spread and soaring radiation levels were recorded in Sweden and other European countries. In the meantime Reagan attacked the Soviets for their "stubborn refusal" to provide more information; Radio Free Europe, Radio Liberty and many American newspapers estimated that there had been thousands of deaths. When the Soviets reported that there had been only two deaths, administration officials refused to accept the figure. The Soviet report was accurate; still, the disaster was unprecedented. Rescue and clean-up efforts were slow in coming. Thirty people died from radiation within a few months, and eventually two hundred thousand people were evacuated from the area, perhaps half of them exposed to high levels of radiation.

Gorbachev himself said nothing about Chernobyl until May 14, when he made a major speech explaining what had occurred and attacking the West for launching an "unrestrained anti-Soviet campaign" of "dishonest and malicious lies" about the casualties. His behavior led many in the Soviet Union and the West to believe that the old habits of secrecy and of refusing to confront unpleasant realities had prevailed over any concern for human life. But the accident came as a major shock to the leadership. The explosion and the bungled attempts at recovery revealed deeper flaws in the Soviet system than many in Moscow understood it possessed. The criticisms from the West were salt to Gorbachev's wounds, and he reacted defensively. But in June he used the shock of Chernobyl to launch a system-wide policy of glasnost, or openness, to force change upon the Communist party.[86]

In April, Reagan-administration hard-liners renewed their attack on the SALT II restrictions. The Navy was about to begin sea trials for another new Trident submarine, and the U.S. would exceed the SALT limits if it did not retire two more of the older Poseidon submarines; the U.S. would also go over the limits at the end of the year, when the Air Force deployed its 131st cruise-missile-armed B-52 bomber, if other, older launchers were not taken out of service. Left to themselves, the Joint Chiefs would have retired the older weapons more or less automatically, because maintaining them would take funds from the strategic modernization program. However, by the bureaucratic compromise of the previous spring, the administration had committed itself to "proportionate and appropriate" American responses to Soviet violations of the unratified treaty, and since then Weinberger and Perle had been assiduously advertising their list of alleged Soviet violations—while refusing to allow the State Department to take their complaints to the Soviets.[87]

In late April and May a fierce battle raged in the top ranks of the administration. In the first of two NSC meetings Weinberger, Casey and Adelman argued that Soviet non-compliance with the treaty demanded an American military response, and that the President would lose all credibility if he did not show the Soviets he meant business. State Department representatives and Admiral William Crowe, the new chairman of the Joint Chiefs of Staff, countered that there was currently no operational reason for the U.S. to exceed the SALT limits, and that the Soviets were better positioned to build up strategic warheads than the U.S. He added that if the administration decided to abandon SALT II the Congress—along with the Allies—would hit the roof and scrap parts of the strategic modernization program. The second NCS meeting began with a brutal fight between Shultz and Weinberger, which the President watched with serenity while the rest of those assembled looked on in disbelief. Later Weinberger and Nitze argued heatedly about whether the President did or did not want to scrap the ABM Treaty as well as SALT II, while Reagan listened and said nothing.[88]

As usual, the meeting ended without a presidential decision, but shortly afterwards the solution adopted by the NSC staff was to retire the two Poseidons for purely economic reasons and to break the SALT limits in December, when the 131st bomber was deployed. In effect, the decision was to break the SALT limits even though Weinberger had failed to come up with any operational reason for doing so or any "proportionate" response to the alleged Soviet violations.[89]

Once this decision was made, White House officials began to worry about the political consequences. The announcement was held up while Nitze attempted to explain the decision to the Allies, and in making it on May 27, the President gave such emphasis to the retirement of the two submarines that many reporters concluded that the administration had decided to stay within the SALT limits.[90]

When the confusion was sorted out, the reaction was far more severe than Shultz or anyone in the White House had anticipated. Allied leaders besieged the President with letters; newspaper editorials condemned the move, and the outcry on the Hill was loud and protracted. Bills and resolutions were introduced into both houses of Congress urging the President to abide by SALT limits and threatening a cutoff of funds for weapons systems that exceeded them. SDI came under siege, and there was talk of holding funds for the program hostage to progress in arms control. Donald Regan, who, typically, had not paid much attention to the SALT II debate, tried to shift the blame from the President to Poindexter. But the vice-admiral, Nitze writes, being "not particularly interested or knowledgeable in arms control," had turned the matter over to his deputy, and seemed "somewhat befuddled by the uproar."[91]

In early June the President appeared to backtrack. Both in a speech and in a news conference, he clearly indicated that the decision might be reversed, depending on Soviet behavior in the months ahead. Asked for clarification, White House Press Secretary Larry Speakes told reporters that SALT II was dead. On June 12 the President suggested for a third time that the decision was not final. But when reporters confronted him with his press secretary's statement, the President puzzlingly replied, "I think you can trust what Larry Speakes said to you."[92]

In announcing the SALT decision, Reagan promised to replace the old treaty with a new and much better agreement. But Gorbachev upstaged him once again.

In April and May, Gorbachev's deputies had been putting together a new arms-control package, and on May 29, coincidentally, just two days after Reagan's SALT II decision was announced, Soviet negotiators put the first part of it on the table in Geneva. The rest followed in June. A central feature of the package was a proposal that both sides agree not to withdraw from the ABM Treaty for fifteen to twenty years, and to confine SDI research to the laboratories. On offensive strategic arms, they retreated somewhat from the 50-percent cuts they had offered before the Geneva summit, but they abandoned their long-held position that forward-based American bombers and intermediate-range missiles capable of striking the Soviet Union should be counted as strategic arms.[93]

The President welcomed the proposal. In a speech in Glassboro, New Jersey, where in 1967 Robert McNamara had told Kosygin that ABM defenses would lead to an upward spiral in the arms race, he declared that the Soviets had made "a serious effort" in strategic-arms control that could even represent "a turning point." However, he offered no compromise on SDI, and in an ironic departure from McNamara's text, he said that the program "might one day enable us to put in space a shield that missiles could not penetrate, a shield that could protect us from nuclear missiles just as a roof protects a family from the rain."[94]

The administration had to make a substantive response to Gorbachev's proposal, and the President badly needed one that would convince the Congress he was in earnest. But, as his Glassboro speech indicated, his arms-control bureaucracy was, as usual, mired in disagreement. State Department officials proposed that the U.S. agree not to withdraw from the ABM Treaty for five to eight years, but the Pentagon civilians maintained that any constraint on SDI would kill the program in the Congress. The intramural debate was complicated by the fact that Regan and Poindexter, out of concern for leaks, had created an elaborate hierarchy of classifications with "compartments" of decreasing size and overlapping memberships. At the top of this pyramid was a compartment restricted to the President, the secretary of state, the secretary of defense, the White House chief of staff and the NSC adviser. This group contained no one with any arms-control expertise and only one member with any interest in the subject—yet its deliberations were kept secret even from Nitze and Perle.[95] In mid-June this group produced an extraordinary proposal: the U.S. and the Soviet Union should dismantle all their ballistic missiles.

The idea, later dubbed Zero Ballistic Missiles or ZBM, originated with Undersecretary of Defense Fred Iklé. In January 1973, a few months before becoming director of the Arms Control and Disarmament Agency in the Nixon administration, Iklé, in an article in *Foreign Affairs*, recommended that the nuclear powers replace their ICBMs with systems, such as airplanes, which could not reach their targets so swiftly, and which would not raise fears about a preemptive first strike. To many, perhaps, the proposal sounded humane and idealistic—and, coming from the next chief of ACDA, a radical idea. How the world could "uninvent" ballistic missiles or verify their nonexistence were questions informed readers might have asked. But, then, informed readers also knew that, because the Soviet deterrent—unlike the American strategic triad—was composed almost exclusively of ballistic missiles, it was in essence a call for Soviet disarmament.

In December 1985 Iklé met with Poindexter's deputy Donald Fortier to discuss a number of ideas he had for an arms-control proposal, and one of them was what he called a "zero missile initiative." The initiative, his meeting notes read, could be a historic proposition much like the 1946 "Baruch plan"—a Truman-administration proposal for putting the control of atomic energy under the United Nations. Of course, Iklé said, the idea would probably be attacked as impractical, but it was "not more infeasible" than 50-percent reductions in all strategic weapons. And, he said, there were likely to be important public-relations advantages.

Nothing came of this conversation, but in the spring Iklé mentioned the idea to Max Kampelman, the chief U.S. negotiator in Geneva. Kampelman, who was looking for an idea dramatic enough to match Gorbachev's January 15 disarmament proposal, urged Iklé to discuss it with the Joint Chiefs. A few weeks later Iklé told Kampelman that he had broached the "zero missile initiative" informally with the Chiefs and with Richard Perle. Perle, he said, liked the idea because he thought it would put the Soviets on the defensive. The two of them then told their respective bosses about it.[96]

Shultz knew perfectly well that a proposal to eliminate ballistic missiles was not going to get anywhere with the Soviets, but he hoped to tempt the President to limit SDI in return for a *reduction* in ballistic missiles. He had, after all, been making the argument to the President for the past year that less offense would require less defense. On May 14 Shultz talked with Reagan at length about the trade, waxing eloquent about the power of Soviet ballistic missiles and the service to the nation the President would perform if he could reduce this greatest of all threats to the country. He also spoke about the importance of SDI research and the need to keep it alive so that Reagan's successor could decide whether to deploy strategic defenses. Keeping it alive, he said, meant giving something up. If the U.S. agreed not to deploy strategic defenses for a few years, then there could be an agreement on massive reductions of ballistic missiles, and the potential for an SDI deployment would ensure continuing Soviet compliance with the reductions until they were completed. "So we should give them the sleeves from our vest on SDI and make them think they got our overcoat," he said with a flourish.[97]

The President seemed to like the idea, as did Regan and Poindexter, who were also present, and he ended the meeting on a decisive, manly grace note: he would not compromise the research program for strategic defenses, and he wanted Shultz to make sure that the sleeves given away were from our *vest.* However, two weeks later he had changed his mind. He was afraid, he told Shultz in a meeting on June 3, that *any* discussion with the Soviets about strategic defenses would be used to scuttle SDI. Hearing Weinberger's argument in his mouth, Shultz argued heatedly that the research program would not produce strategic defenses within the next five to eight years—the U.S. lacked the technical capacity—so an agreement not to deploy in that period "would be giving the Soviets the sleeves from our vest!" But the President would not agree.[98]

On June 12, the day after Reagan suggested the SALT II decision might be reversed, the President, the secretaries of state and defense, the NSC adviser and the White House chief of staff met to discuss a response to Gorbachev. Weinberger proposed that the United States and the Soviet Union, along with the other nuclear powers, eliminate all of their strategic ballistic missiles—that is, all of their ICBMs and SLBMs—leaving themselves with only bombers and cruise missiles for defense. The President looked at the secretary of state for his reaction. Smiling, Shultz complimented Weinberger for having the imagination to present such a bold idea. The President now looked interested, as did Admiral Poindexter: this was the first time the two secretaries had agreed on any strategic issue in four years. The group decided that the idea should be studied carefully and in secret, to see how it might be used as a part of the U.S. reply.[99]

On June 23 Yuri Dubinin, who was then replacing Dobrynin as Soviet ambassador to Washington, brought a letter from Gorbachev to Reagan in which the general secretary held out the promise of further flexibility in the arms talks and suggested that Shultz and Shevardnadze meet in September, during the UN General Assembly session, to review whether a summit in the late fall looked promising or not. Because Shultz was abroad, Poindexter drafted a reply which made use of the State Department's proposal for a period of non-withdrawal from the ABM Treaty and Weinberger's idea for eliminating ballistic missiles. The draft was sent to Shultz, who in turn sent it to Nitze for review.[100]

Nitze was horrified. The idea of eliminating ballistic missiles by agreement with the Soviet Union seemed to him ridiculous. The proposal was non-negotiable, but it was not therefore harmless. For one thing, it was bound to have an unwelcome impact on the strategic modernization program, because Congress, in a period of huge deficits, would be loath to fund a new generation of ballistic missiles, such as the MX, if the President had committed himself to banning them. For another, the draft spoke of *all* ballistic missiles—and that presumably meant that the U.S. would be offering to eliminate not only its own missiles but those of Britain, France and China as well. Given the sensitivities of the European allies at having the U.S. negotiate over their heads, the proposal might, Nitze said, destroy the alliance.[101]

Nitze attempted to see Poindexter, but the admiral refused even to return his phone call. Irritated, Nitze called Colonel Robert Linhard, Poindexter's deputy for arms control, who in Nitze's estimation was "the only person in the White House with a depth of knowledge in the field," and showed him the draft letter. Linhard, who had not seen the draft before, was as appalled as Nitze, but there was little they could do about it, since Poindexter did not want to submit it to an interagency review. Dispatched to London and Paris to consult with the Allies, Nitze reported back that British and French officials in outrage insisted that their missiles not be mentioned in any such communication with Gorbachev. They wanted no part of the plan.[102]

The proposal, mentioning only U.S. and Soviet missiles, was sent to Gorbachev on July 25. But in mid-July leaks to the press, apparently from the White House, suggested that it would include an offer to "delay the deployment" of SDI in return for deep reductions in strategic weapons.[103] This was encouraging news to many in Congress. But what the proposal actually said was that the two sides would agree not to withdraw from the ABM Treaty for five years, during which time they would make 50-percent cuts in their strategic forces and would proceed with SDI research, development and testing, "which is permitted" by the treaty. After that period, the sides would have two years to negotiate a treaty to share the benefits of their strategic-defense research and to dismantle all their ballistic missiles. If no agreement was reached, either side would then be free to deploy strategic defenses on six months' notice.[104]

When the proposal was made public a month later, journalists focused on the "radical" idea of eliminating ballistic missiles and on the period of non-withdrawal from the ABM Treaty. According to official sources, the President himself had made the proposal to do away with the most dangerous weapons on the planet, and many officials thought the President had gone much too far.[105] Yet in essence the administration had put forth a plan for deploying strategic defenses, with or without an agreement on eliminating ballistic missiles, and seven and a half years (the five years of non-withdrawal, the two years of negotiations and the six months' notice required by the ABM Treaty) hardly constituted any "delay," since neither side could possibly deploy any effective strategic defense system in that period. In addition, the administration was insisting upon the "broad" interpretation of the ABM Treaty. Once again Shultz's attempt to create a negotiating position out of a Pentagon proposal had done the opposite of what he had intended, and once again he found himself endorsing yet another block to a strategic-arms-control agreement.[106]

When Gorbachev finally replied to Reagan's letter on September 15, he called the proposal a step backwards, ignored the whole idea of banning ballistic missiles and focused on the attempt to "nullify" the ABM Treaty.[107]

On August 5 George Shultz handed the President a letter of resignation. It was his third offer to resign, but for the first time he made no particular demand that the President might respond to. "You might well be better off without me," he said.[108]

In his memoir Shultz tells us that White House officials were uneasy with him, and he was "uneasy, too, with them." But, according to a contemporary source, he was close to despair that summer. "I have no influence at the White House," he told a visitor after the SALT II decision.[109] In mid-July he fought a bruising battle with William Casey and Patrick Buchanan over policy towards South Africa. The Congress had voted for sanctions against the apartheid regime, and though Shultz thought the President could not agree to congressionally mandated sanctions, he wanted the President to give a strongly anti-apartheid speech and to take some of the same steps by executive order. But Casey and Buchanan got their way, and in his speech on July 22 the President actually praised the regime while calling upon it to end apartheid. The speech so inflamed the Congress that the Republican-controlled Senate overrode Reagan's veto of the sanctions by a vote of seventy-eight to twenty-one.[110]

The President refused to accept Shultz's resignation. Shultz did not insist but, rather, went off for a few days' vacation. He did not really want to resign: as always, he was trying to put pressure on the President and his staff. Don Regan, with whom he had a perfectly cordial relationship, promised him, not very convincingly, that things would change. Shultz was still mulling over the problem during another short vacation at the end of August when a Soviet-American crisis erupted. It was the first in a series of crises that would occupy him completely for the rest of the year.[111]

By the end of August, White House officials began to voice optimism about a summit. They badly wanted one before the end of the year. The midterm elections were coming up, and the President was in deep trouble with the Congress on foreign policy and arms control. Not only had the Senate rebuffed Reagan on South Africa, but the administration's decision to scrap SALT II at the end of the year, combined with the lack of progress towards a new arms treaty, had created a near-mutiny in the House of Representatives. In August the House passed five amendments to the Defense Authorization Act repudiating the President's strategic policies. One of them denied funds for the deployment of strategic weapons that would break the SALT II sublimits; another mandated a continued moratorium on anti-satellite weapons testing; a third imposed a one-year moratorium on all but the smallest nuclear-weapons tests, provided the Soviets continued to observe their moratorium; yet another put a hold on the production of chemical weapons; and the fifth held SDI funding to the level of the previous year, with only an increase for inflation. Given Reagan's identification with SDI, this last amendment was a serious matter for the President.[112]

Still, with the hard-liners in control of policy, wanting a summit and getting one were two different things. Since the beginning of the year Gorbachev had insisted that there could be no summit without substantial progress on arms control or other issues. After Shevardnadze's May visit to

Washington was canceled because of the U.S. bombing of Libya, the President had proposed that Shultz and the Soviet foreign minister meet in midsummer to begin summit preparations. Gorbachev rejected the idea, but in late July he proposed a "work program" of consultations between high-level experts on arms control and other bilateral issues, so that when Shultz and Shevardnadze met in mid-September they could decide whether or not there was any basis for a summit. Shultz accepted the invitation. In mid-August a delegation of U.S. arms-control experts, including Nitze and Perle, went to Moscow—it was Perle's first trip to the Soviet Union—and met with their Soviet counterparts. No notable progress was made, and although a second meeting was scheduled for early September, the two sides seemed an unbridgeable distance apart. In late August teams of experts on regional conflicts met in Washington, but could reach no agreement. After the meeting the senior Soviet official present said that his government had not yet decided on a summit and repeated what Gorbachev had been saying all year: "We are not interested in an empty summit. . . . It has to have results—concrete results."[113]

Then a crisis erupted.

On August 23 the FBI arrested Gennadi Zakharov, a Soviet scientific attaché assigned to the UN Secretariat, on a Queens subway platform, where he was meeting with a Guyanese student and exchanging money for documents from a U.S. defense contractor. The student was an FBI informant, and Zakharov, who did not have diplomatic immunity, was charged with espionage, put in jail and scheduled for trial. The event was not much remarked upon in the United States until August 30, when the KGB arrested Nicholas Daniloff, a correspondent for *U.S. News & World Report* in Moscow, just after a Soviet acquaintance handed him a packet with classified materials on Soviet activities in Afghanistan. Daniloff, a bona-fide journalist, was jailed and charged with espionage. The Soviets then turned around and offered to exchange Daniloff for Zakharov.[114]

Daniloff's arrest created a political firestorm in the United States. Concerned about the seizure of one of their own, the news media put the story at the top of the news and kept it there. Editorialists and columnists expressed indignation at the entrapment of an innocent American journalist and the cynical offer to exchange him for a Soviet spy. The first word from the administration was a statement from a spokesman in Santa Barbara, where Reagan was staying at his ranch, saying that a swap might be arranged. The statement was soon contradicted by other officials. On September 5 Secretary Shultz voiced "outrage" at Daniloff's arrest; he likened it to hostage-taking and said, "Let there be no talk of a trade."[115]

Amidst the furor, the administration took a series of diplomatic initiatives on Daniloff's behalf. Officials offered to have Zakharov released to the custody of the Soviet ambassador while awaiting trial if Daniloff were tried quickly and expelled from the Soviet Union. The President wrote Gorbachev a personal letter assuring him that Daniloff was not a spy. Gorbachev, however, replied that the journalist had long been engaged in impermissible activities, and Soviet officials continued to insist that he would be prosecuted to the full extent of the law if Zakharov was not released.[116]

On September 8 the administration raised the stakes. Speaking out for the first time in public about the case, the President sternly warned that if Daniloff was not let out soon his imprisonment would become a "major obstacle" in U.S.-Soviet relations. "Whatever the Soviet motive," he said, ". . . their action violates the standards of civilized international behavior. There will be no trade." An administration official added, "I think our time is exceedingly short to limit the damage from this, and I see the summit receding very rapidly into the distance."[117] From both inside and outside the administration, pressure was mounting for retaliatory measures, from the cancellation of the Shevardnadze visit to the expulsion of all Soviet diplomats at the UN mission. Shultz refused to call the Shevardnadze visit off, but officials were saying that the Daniloff case could dominate the meeting and prove as disruptive to U.S.-Soviet relations as the Soviet downing of the Korean airliner in 1983.[118]

But then, on September 12, the administration agreed to a Soviet proposal it had previously turned down, and Daniloff and Zakharov were released into the custody of their respective ambassadors. Both men still awaited trial, but the equivalent treatment accorded to them suggested quite strongly that a trade was in the works. Many in Washington heaved sighs of relief: the Reagan administration was, it appeared, not going to create a serious confrontation with the Soviets over the case, and Daniloff might be freed. Conservatives, however, objected angrily. The columnist George Will charged that the administration had paid the first installment of a "ransom" to the "hostage-takers" and quoted a former CIA analyst as saying that the U.S. placed "a mantle of protection over Soviet spies."[119] Representative Jack Kemp, who was planning to seek the Republican presidential nomination in 1988, charged that the administration was giving up its principles for the sake of a summit and proposed that Shultz should refuse to speak with Shevardnadze until Daniloff was unconditionally freed. William Safire of the *New York Times* compared the deal the administration had made to Yalta and, referring to Gorbachev's refusal to accept Reagan's assurance that Daniloff was not a spy, he wrote, "Never in such a personal way has a Russian leader put a thumb in the eye of an American president."[120]

In fact, the Zakharov and Daniloff cases were more complicated than they seemed, and the U.S. government bore some responsibility for Daniloff's arrest.

The years 1984–86 had been ones of frenetic activity for the intelligence services of the two superpowers—and for the first time there had been a host of spy scandals involving Americans. Until then the U.S. intelligence services could boast of the loyalty of their people, certainly by contrast to the Soviet services, which had seen many of their members defect or become double agents. But in October 1984 an FBI agent was arrested and indicted for espionage, and a month later a CIA contract employee was arrested for working with the Czech intelligence service. In 1985 spies were exposed right and left. In May, John Walker, Jr., a retired Navy warrant officer, was arrested, and it was found that he and several members of his family had been giving the Soviets important cryptographic information for seventeen years.[121] In June one of the CIA's most valuable Soviet agents, an engineer involved with Soviet aerospace and weapons programs, was arrested, and his handler, a U.S. Embassy officer, was expelled from the Soviet Union.[122] In July the tide seemed to turn with the successful exfiltration from Moscow of Oleg Gordievsky, the KGB chief of station in London, who had been working for the British since 1974. The British expelled thirty-one Soviet spies, including the entire twenty-five-man KGB station. Then, on August 1, Vitaly Yurchenko, the KGB general responsible for Soviet espionage in the U.S., defected to the United States. He tipped off the CIA to two American intelligence officers who had sold vital information to the Soviet Union and then, on November 2, unaccountably redefected to the Soviet Union.[123]

In the midst of these embarrassments, the CIA's Intelligence Directorate released a study showing that many Soviet officials assigned to the UN Secretariat were working for the achievement of Soviet foreign policy and intelligence goals. The study was hardly a revelation. American officials had always assumed that to be the case; in fact, if there had been evidence to the contrary, the CIA analysts would have been shocked. But once the paper was circulated, it created pressures upon the administration and the Congress to do something about it. Since the UN Secretariat had a fixed quota of Soviet employees, the solution adopted was to reduce the size of the Soviet mission to the UN. Neither the State Department nor the CIA's clandestine services liked the idea because the Soviets always responded to expulsions by throwing American diplomats or spies out of the Soviet Union. But the decision was made to go ahead. After the order went out in March 1986, the Soviets quickly arrested an official of the U.S. Embassy in Moscow, caught in a clandestine meeting with a Soviet source, and expelled him from the country. In May they expelled another embassy officer. Then, in June, the U.S. arrested and expelled the Soviet air attaché in Washington after publicly accusing him of espionage.[124]

The arrest of Gennadi Zakharov was a part of this tit-for-tat series of arrests and expulsions. Yet, from the perspective of the KGB, the U.S. had in this instance broken the well-established rules. Zakharov was a spy in the sense that his job was to recruit science students and others who might in the long run provide Moscow with information on American technology. But the scientist was not, strictly speaking, an espionage agent, for it was not his job to handle the transfer of information. On both sides only professional agents with diplomatic immunity engaged in espionage—a criminal offense in both countries. The FBI, which had been following Zakharov for three years, knew that he was not an espionage agent, and knew that the student had no access to classified material. Yet the bureau, with the approval of an NSC staffer and an undersecretary of state, entrapped Zakharov with classified documents, arrested him on criminal charges and, in another departure from standard practice, denied him bail.[125]

The administration did not, however, trade Zakharov for Daniloff because officials had second thoughts about Zakharov. Rather, after a week of scouring its files, the Operations Directorate of the CIA came up with the disturbing news about its connection to Daniloff. The story was a murky one. In December 1984 a man claiming to be a Russian Orthodox priest had contacted Daniloff and a month later left an envelope in Daniloff's mailbox containing a sealed letter addressed to the U.S. ambassador, Arthur Hartman. With some misgivings Daniloff delivered the letter to the U.S. Embassy. Inside there was another sealed envelope, this one addressed to Casey, with information on Soviet rocketry. The handwriting on all the materials was identical to that on a document the CIA had received in 1981—a document which in the analysts' opinion contained the most significant piece of information the agency had ever received on Soviet strategic missiles.[126] Desperate to establish contact with the informant, a CIA officer asked Daniloff for the priest's phone number. That this supposed priest called himself "Father Roman Potemkin" ought perhaps to have inspired some caution, but the bait was apparently too strong. In attempting to contact the man, CIA agents used Daniloff's first name in a phone call and a letter, both of which were intercepted by the KGB. In April a Soviet informant told CIA agents that they had approached the wrong person and that the KGB was convinced Daniloff was working for the CIA.[127]

Informed of much of this by Casey on September 8 and 9, Shultz consulted his legal counsel and was told that Daniloff could be convicted of espionage under Soviet law—and that similar evidence against a Soviet journalist would be sufficient to convict him in an American court. Shultz realized that the administration would have to make the trade, and since nothing could be said about the reason for it, the administration would be castigated for abandoning its principles. Complaining bitterly about the clumsiness and irresponsibility of the CIA in compromising the journalist, he made the arrangements for the release of Daniloff and Zakharov to their embassies. The President seemed relieved that Daniloff would be getting out of jail, but Poindexter, who did not appear to understand the danger Daniloff was in, kept arguing for the expulsion of more Soviet diplomats, and on September 17 twenty-five more Soviet officials from the UN mission were ordered to leave.[128]

Shultz worried that Shevardnadze would not come to Washington given the ceaseless criticism of the Soviet Union in the American press. But on September 18 the foreign minister arrived on schedule, ready to work on the trade and bringing a letter from Gorbachev proposing a meeting with Reagan the following month in Europe.

Shultz and Shevardnadze had not met since the Geneva summit, but over the next two weeks, first in Washington and then in New York during the UN General Assembly, the two of them spent many hours together and developed a close working relationship founded on mutual trust. By September 28 they had worked the terms of a Daniloff-Zakharov exchange.[129]

On September 29 Nicholas Daniloff boarded a plane for the United States. A Reagan aide said that there had been no trade and that the reporter's release was an "independent event" with "no conditions" attached to it. "They blinked," the President said. However, the following day Gennadi Zakharov pleaded no contest to the charges against him and left for Moscow. That same day Shultz announced that Yuri Orlov, a prominent Soviet dissident, would be allowed to leave the Soviet Union with his wife, and that the President would meet with General Secretary Gorbachev in Iceland's capital, Reykjavik, in ten days' time.[130]

The last announcement came as more of a surprise to those within the administration than to those outside of it. Since August the administration had been advertising the Shultz-Shevardnadze meeting as one which might set a date for a summit. Yet, until Shevardnadze delivered Gorbachev's letter on September 19, neither Shultz nor anyone else in the administration had any real reason to believe that Gorbachev would meet with Reagan that fall. The second meeting of arms-control experts in early September had produced no results. In an interview with a Czech newspaper just after that meeting, Gorbachev said, "We have not moved an inch closer to an arms reduction agreement, despite all the efforts made by the USSR," and again insisted that a summit depended on a change in U.S. policies. Still, administration officials continued to voice optimism about a summit, and since Daniloff was arrested on August 30, they had spoken as if only his detention stood in the way.[131] Their purpose, it seemed, was to persuade the Congress and the public that the President wanted a summit—and if no summit took place, they could always blame the Soviets.

The letter Shevardnadze brought was quite different from any letter Gorbachev had sent Reagan before. In all of his past communications, including that of April, Gorbachev had extended cordial greetings, couched policy differences in diplomatic language and expressed optimism that the differences could be resolved. But in this letter he denounced the President for launching a "massive, hostile campaign" against the Soviet Union and upbraided him for refusing to match the Soviet moratorium on nuclear testing. In addition, he rejected Reagan's proposal of July 25 to eliminate ballistic missiles and repeated his own proposal that all work on anti-missile systems be confined to the laboratories. Poindexter found the letter insulting in tone. However, Gorbachev wrote that, since there had been no movement on arms control since the Geneva summit, the negotiations needed a "major impulse," and he proposed a two-day meeting with Reagan—perhaps in London or Reykjavik—to see if progress on the unresolved issues could be made in preparation for a Washington summit.

To Poindexter's surprise, the President wanted the invitation accepted immediately; he made it clear to Shevardnadze that he would accept, and it was only after some argument that he agreed to hold off on an official acceptance until the Daniloff affair could be settled.[132]

Gorbachev's proposal was kept under wraps, but White House officials continued to talk of a "summit," and when the exchange was negotiated and the announcement made, they spoke as if the impromptu Reykjavik meeting were the "summit" they had expected all along. To all those outside the administration who had followed the affair it seemed quite obvious that the President had traded a Soviet spy not just for Daniloff's freedom but to clear the way for superpower diplomacy.[133] Conservatives, predictably, denounced the whole maneuver. In rhetoric better saved for the Iran affair, the columnist Charles Krauthammer charged: "The Soviet capacity to manufacture hostages . . . is unlimited. Against an endless supply of hostages, the West will need an endless supply of principles in exchange." Kissinger and Brzezinski called the trade unconscionable and warned of the dangers of an ill-prepared summit. But most commentators expressed relief that the confrontation had come to an end.[134]

In attempting to explain why the President wanted a summit, administration officials maintained that arms-control negotiations were in a "sensitive stage." On September 30 Reagan endorsed this view. "I've said for a long time that chances are better than they've been for many years for reaching some agreement on arms reductions," he said.[135] On background, White House officials added that the President's attitude towards the Soviets had softened since the Geneva meeting, when he had come to realize the depth of Soviet distrust of the United States. They also said that the President liked summits, because he felt he was a good communicator and could persuade Gorbachev in a one-on-one meeting.[136] Republican political strategists, however, pointed to more practical considerations. A summit, they said, would give the President a club to beat back the Congress, and it would help the GOP retain control of the Senate. "A political masterpiece, a real coup," one declared. "For what? For winning the November congressional elections on a peace plank."[137]

On the campaign trail before the summit, Reagan argued that the House amendments restricting his strategic-weapons programs would weaken his bargaining position at Geneva. The House obliged and withdrew all of its amendments except for the long-standing ban on anti-satellite weapons testing.[138]

THE REYKJAVIK SUMMIT was "one of the strangest episodes in the annals of nuclear diplomacy," Strobe Talbott wrote sometime after the event. For defense experts it was a "lost weekend," as Talbott put it, in which Reagan and Gorbachev, caught up in a frenzy of enthusiastic and muddle-headed bargaining, nearly brought down the temple of nuclear deterrence. For others it seemed an unseasonal midsummer night's dream in which the two leaders shared an amazing vision of peace and disarmament—only to wake up with all of their previous concerns and animosities intact. Yet what actually happened at Reykjavik was not at all clear, certainly not in the immediate aftermath, when officials, unsure of what to reveal and what to conceal, kept raising and lowering the scrims. Then, too, disconcertingly, there was no prologue and no preparation for what took place.

Shortly after the summit was announced on September 30, the White House made a concerted effort to diminish expectations for the meeting. According to officials, Reykjavik was to be merely "a planning session for the full-dress summit in Washington." Officials expressed vague hopes that the two sides might find avenues of compromise for the arms negotiators in Geneva to pursue, and said that the INF negotiations and nuclear testing showed the most promise. The President assured his conservative critics that he would press the issues of Soviet human-rights violations and Soviet military intervention in regional conflicts. Iceland, he promised, would be merely "a base camp" for the summit.[139]

Journalists who traveled to Reykjavik with the American delegation on October 9 found no reason to question this assessment. The administration had had little more than a week to prepare for the meeting, and for some of that time the President had been on the campaign trail. There had been no official exchanges about the agenda. The American delegation, numbering 267, was a quarter the size of those sent to previous summits. No ceremonies or social events were planned, and the meeting schedule was short: the two leaders were to confer twice on Saturday, October 11, and once the following morning, then fly home Sunday afternoon.[140]

Reykjavik, a town the size of Sioux City, Iowa, was cold and rainy when the delegations arrived. For security reasons the meetings were held at Hofdi House, a two-story villa some miles out of town on a bleak plain overlooking the North Atlantic. Just as at Geneva, there was a press blackout for the duration of the talks, so on the first day of the meeting, the assembled journalists had little to report. But at the lunch break the following day, Larry Speakes reported that working groups from the two sides had spent the night in negotiations and that the President and the general secretary would hold an extra session that afternoon. The Soviet press spokesman, breaking the embargo, said that the two sides were close to agreement on deep cuts in strategic weapons and on a zero-zero INF treaty. Thus alerted, reporters waited with anticipation for the announcement of a major breakthrough in the talks.[141]

Just before 7:00 P.M., Reagan and Gorbachev emerged from Hofdi House, both of them tight-lipped and grim. According to American officials, the two sides had developed tentative agreements on all the outstanding arms-control issues, among them on drastic reductions in strategic and medium-range weapons, but at the last minute the talks had foundered on the Soviet insistence that the U.S. scrap its plans for space-based defenses. As a result, no date had been set for a full-fledged summit, and the future of the negotiations was in doubt. At the American press briefing, at which Reagan did not appear, Shultz, his lips quivering, declared himself "deeply disappointed" by the outcome. He and other senior American negotiators looked drawn and exhausted; Kampelman was fighting back tears. "It's been a failure," Gorbachev said at the Soviet press conference. "We missed an historic chance. Never have our positions been so close."[142] Both Shultz and Gorbachev assured the press that efforts to get an agreement would continue, but their demeanor was anything but reassuring.

According to American officials, the talks had been exhilarating, exhausting and ultimately frustrating. On Saturday, Gorbachev had laid out new proposals on START and INF; the experts had worked through the night and by morning had come very close to a tentative agreement on START, making significant progress on the issues of how weapons would be counted, and on the overall numerical limits for ICBMs. They had been unable to resolve their differences on medium-range missiles, but in the morning the Soviets changed their position and agreed not only to eliminate INF missiles in Europe, but to cut their Asian forces back to one hundred missiles. With that, an INF accord was in sight. But then Gorbachev had tied this package of important potential agreements to a demand that both sides adhere to the ABM Treaty for ten years, during which time all SDI research and testing would remain confined to "the laboratory." After consultation with aides, Reagan proposed that the two sides remain within the treaty for ten years; in the first five years they would cut their strategic forces in half, and in the second five they would eliminate all ballistic missiles. But Gorbachev insisted that SDI research be confined to the laboratory and Reagan would not agree to that. It would, he said, "have killed our defensive shield."[143]

In Washington that evening a number of Democrats, including Senators Sam Nunn, Gary Hart and Claiborne Pell, expressed disappointment that no accord had been reached and criticized Reagan for refusing to limit SDI in exchange for deep offensive reductions. Apparently an extraordinary opportunity had been lost, and a rift had opened up between the two sides. "There can be no disguising the aura of collapse and the bleak prospect that hangs over the Soviet-American scene now,"[144] a *Washington Post* editorial reported.

Yet, the following day, in a televised address to the nation, the President gave a much sunnier view of the summit. The United States, he said, had made "perhaps the most sweeping and generous arms control proposal in history"—the complete elimination of all ballistic missiles by 1996—and the proposal was still on the table. We are, he declared, "closer than ever before to agreements that could lead to a safer world without nuclear weapons." He had, he said, proposed to share the benefits of SDI technology with the Soviets, but the general secretary had wanted wording that would have kept the United States from developing SDI for ten years, in effect "killing" SDI. "I told him," Reagan said, "that I had pledged to the American people that I would not trade away SDI—there was no way I could tell our people their government would not protect them against nuclear destruction. I went to Reykjavik determined that everything was negotiable except for two things, our freedom and our future." Nonetheless, he remained optimistic that a way would be found to "begin eliminating the nuclear threat." The door, he said, was open, and U.S. negotiators would be ready to go forward when the Soviets were. We would, he asserted, "continue to make progress if we pursue a prudent, deliberate, and above all, realistic approach with the Soviets." The President uttered the word "progress" eight times in the speech.[145]

That same day, all the senior officials present at the Reykjavik meeting began to speak with enthusiasm of the progress that had been made and the promise of future negotiations. "Momentous," "historic" and "breakthrough event" were some of the words used.[146] Poindexter, in one of his rare interviews on the record, told reporters that U.S. negotiators would attempt to hold the Soviets to the deep cuts in strategic and intermediate-range missiles. Donald Regan said that it was possible that the President would appoint a special envoy on arms control to revive the negotiations; a State Department spokesman said that Shultz and Shevardnadze would discuss arms control when they met in Vienna in early November.[147] Shultz, who had appeared dejected the previous evening, was smiling and optimistic when he met with reporters after briefing the NATO allies. He later termed the Iceland meeting unexpectedly successful and a "serious and positive step" in the direction of arms agreements. Richard Perle suggested that the Soviets might be more flexible on SDI in future negotiations. "Things look much brighter than they did before," Kenneth Adelman said.[148]

In the days that followed, the administration's arms-control experts fanned out across the United States and Europe to deliver the good news of the summit, or, as Helen Thomas of UPI put it, "to reverse the perception that President Reagan had struck out in extraordinary nuclear arms negotiations with Soviet leader Mikhail Gorbachev."[149] In what Larry Speakes later called "an unprecedented news blitz . . . the super-blitz of all [news] blitzes," officials made some ninety press appearances within the week. Shultz went to New York to meet with the editorial boards of the *Times* and *The Wall Street Journal,* and with key people at the three television networks; Buchanan, Adelman, Nitze, Kampelman and Poindexter gave television interviews and prepared Op Ed pieces for the major newspapers. The President and the secretary of state conducted lengthy briefings for members of Congress, and the White House dispatched what Speakes called a "truth squad" of Nitze and others to London, Paris, Rome and Bonn.[150] Donald Regan, who himself gave fifty-three broadcast and print interviews, said of the effort, "Some of us are like a shovel brigade that follows a parade down Main Street, cleaning up."[151]

Meanwhile, the President went on the campaign trail and gave speeches for Republican senatorial candidates across the country, making Star Wars the centerpiece of his campaign. "SDI is America's insurance policy that the Soviets will begin living up to the arms control agreements that they have agreed to," he said in Baltimore on October 15. "SDI is one of the chief reasons the Soviets went to the summit and is one of the primary reasons that they will come back again." SDI scientists, he had maintained in his report on the summit, were certain that an anti-missile system was practical and that "several years down the road we can have such a system ready to deploy." In Baltimore he attacked congressional liberals for wanting to "take a meat axe" to the program, thus handing over to the Soviets "free of charge what we refused to hand over across the negotiating table at Reykjavik." Nonetheless, he insisted that the negotiations had been successful: "Far from being a defeat, Reykjavik was a milepost, a turning point in the disarmament negotiations. It will lead to eventual agreements. It is not the end but a furthering of the process."[152]

The "news blitz" had the intended effect on public opinion.[153] According to Wirthlin's polls, the percentage of Americans who thought Reykjavik a success rose every day between October 13 and October 17. By the end of that period the President's approval rating had jumped six points, and about 70 percent of the American public believed that the U.S. and the Soviet Union had made major progress towards arms reductions.[154] Reykjavik did not become the triumph for the President that Geneva had been, but a week later Donald Regan had reason for some self-satisfaction. "We took Reykjavik and turned what was really a sour situation into something that turned out pretty well," he said.[155]

Reagan's campaign for SDI was equally successful. In mid-October public approval of the program reached an all-time high of 73 percent. More than two-thirds of all Americans accepted the proposition that research on defenses increased the chances of an arms-control agreement, helped deterrence and reduced the risk of war. According to polling experts, the public reasoned that if the Soviets feared SDI, then a space defense must be possible, and if SDI was causing the Soviets to make concessions, it was a good thing. Americans generally thought the President's refusal to compromise on SDI admirable: their President was a tough guy who stood up to the Russians and would get a disarmament agreement because of it.[156]

During the White House public-relations blitz, officials added many more details to their account of the dramatic two days at Reykjavik. They described the diminutive meeting room where Reagan and Gorbachev, Shultz and Shevardnadze sat face to face for hours across a small dining table, and the adjoining suites upstairs crowded with officials of the two delegations. For lack of a copy machine, the American team at one point had to borrow carbon paper from the Soviets, and in the final hectic hours Perle and Linhard had put a board over a bathtub on which to draft a proposal for drastic nuclear reductions. Officials also described the nightlong working session in which the seventy-nine-year-old Paul Nitze, and Marshal Sergei Akhromeyev, the last veteran of World War II on the Soviet General Staff, had conducted the most intensive and far-reaching negotiations on record. The American side had had hardly any preparation. "We were really given very little instruction," Nitze said. "We were told to go out and do battle." Yet by 7:00 A.M. the two sides had resolved a number of issues which had been roadblocks to progress for years.[157]

In the Sunday-morning session, according to officials, Gorbachev had stunned the Americans by accepting the U.S. proposal on INF weapons. But the two leaders could not agree on SDI, so an afternoon session was added to the schedule. The President then raised the bidding: the U.S. would abide by the ABM Treaty for ten years if strategic weapons were reduced by half in the first five years and ballistic missiles eliminated in the second five years. "The Soviets," Perle said, "were taken aback by the proposal. They did not reject it on the spot." But, he added, they responded by toughening their stance on SDI. There ensued what Shultz called "the highest stakes poker game ever played." Reagan, David Hoffman of the *Washington Post* reported, "had allowed his hopes to soar—it had seemed that he might achieve the greatest arms control agreement in history." But then, according to the President, the Soviets had given up the agreement over "only one word, only one word"—and the word was "laboratory."[158]

The more administration officials spoke about Reykjavik, the more questions they raised about what really had gone on at the summit. Though some, including Shultz, claimed that the preparations had been impeccable, it appeared that American officials had been taken completely off guard: they had expected some movement on INF and possibly on nuclear testing but nothing like the sweeping concessions the Soviets had made. What had been seen as merely a "base camp" to a summit had suddenly exploded into a full-fledged bargaining session in which the American side had proposed, or agreed to, a great many things which had not been vetted in the interagency process or approved by the Joint Chiefs. Then, too, American officials seemed to disagree about what had happened at key moments, and Gorbachev's report on the summit, which he gave in a speech on October 14, differed significantly from all of the American accounts—particularly in regard to what had happened in the final negotiation session.[159]

On October 17 Senator Sam Nunn announced that a genuine question existed as to whether the President of the United States and the general secretary of the Communist Party of the U.S.S.R. had, or had not, reached a verbal agreement to eliminate all strategic nuclear arms by the year 1996. In a speech on the floor of the Senate, he described the sequence of events that had led him to this idea.[160]

The first indication that such an agreement might have been reached came to Nunn while he was listening to Shultz's press conference just after the summit. In a sentence which required some parsing, Shultz had said, "as the agreement that might have been said, during this ten-year period in effect all offensive strategic arms and ballistic missiles would be eliminated."[161] That same evening, Donald Regan was quoted as saying: "We said to the Soviets, we will do away with all nuclear weapons—nuclear bombs, nuclear shells for artillery. Everything was on the table." Since these statements were at odds with what arms-control experts told the press that evening, Nunn supposed them to be imprecisions which owed to great fatigue. Still, having noted them, Nunn listened carefully to what administration officials said about Reykjavik thereafter.

On October 14 the President and the secretary of state briefed the congressional leadership on the summit. In his introductory remarks the President said that he and his team had put on the table a proposal to eliminate within ten years all nuclear ballistic missiles and all other nuclear weapons, including bombs. Later in the briefing, Secretary Shultz revealed that, after the American proposal to do away with ballistic missiles was presented, Gorbachev had made a counter-offer: he had proposed that in the second half of the ten-year period all remaining strategic nuclear arms be eliminated. The U.S. had compromised, Shultz said, and agreed that the language of the agreement would refer to "strategic nuclear arms and ballistic missiles."[162]

In the question period, Nunn, wanting to be certain of what he had heard, inquired whether the President and the general secretary had agreed to eliminate all strategic offensive nuclear arms by 1996. The President nodded affirmatively. Nunn then asked what should be done to correct the balance in conventional arms, which so dramatically favored the Soviet Union. The President did not answer the question directly, but Shultz, intervening, defended the concept of eliminating all strategic arms by 1996, contending that NATO could find a way to provide a conventional balance vis-à-vis the Warsaw Pact.

Subsequently Nunn spoke with a number of other senior administration officials and military leaders, all of whom had insisted that the U.S. offer was to eliminate ballistic missiles. Yet he had found no one who could authoritatively rebut the considerable evidence that the leaders had agreed to eliminate all strategic arms by 1996.

Nunn's speech prompted a flurry of denials and counter-claims from the administration. Larry Speakes, aboard Air Force One with the President, told reporters that the President might have "misspoken" in the meeting with the congressional leaders. Speakes later corrected himself: the President might have been "misunderstood." Shultz released the text of two proposals given to Gorbachev, both of which called for the elimination of ballistic missiles in ten years, and, apparently reversing himself, said that the U.S. had proposed only that.[163]

On October 22 Gorbachev, in a televised speech, accused U.S. officials of deliberately misrepresenting the Reykjavik negotiations and said that the President had consented, albeit reluctantly, to the elimination of all—and he emphasized all—strategic arms.[164] The next day, in another attempt at "clarification," Larry Speakes said that Reagan had discussed the total elimination of nuclear weapons as an "ultimate goal" but without a timetable, and that the formal American proposal called only for the elimination of ballistic missiles.[165] Two days later, however, a Soviet deputy foreign minister, Aleksandr Bessmertnykh, reading from what seemed to be the Soviet minutes of the meeting, quoted Reagan as agreeing to the Soviet plan for the elimination of all strategic weapons and saying: "If we agree that by the end of the ten-year period, all nuclear arms are to be eliminated, we can refer this to our delegations in Geneva to prepare an agreement that you can sign during your visit to the United States."[166] American officials indignantly denounced the Soviets for breaching diplomatic protocol, and refused to release the U.S. minutes of the session. One senior White House official said that he "would not quarrel" with the Soviet contention, but added that the talks ended without time to "get down to the nuts and bolts" of a ban on strategic arms.[167]

Washington journalists and others following the story were flabbergasted. Had Reagan almost bargained away the entire U.S. nuclear deterrent or only a part of it? The very question sent shock waves through the American defense community. In the weeks that followed, Richard Nixon, Henry Kissinger, James Schlesinger, Brent Scowcroft, Zbigniew Brzezinski, Jim Woolsey, Les Aspin, Dick Cheney, Dante Fascell and others took to the airwaves and wrote articles in the major newspapers and foreign-policy journals on the folly of Reykjavik. Members of the House and Senate Armed Services Committees called for hearings and voiced astonishment over what had occurred. If agreement had not fallen apart over Star Wars, Senator Nunn said, "it would have been the most painfully embarrassing example of American ineptitude in this century, certainly since World War II." Reykjavik, Schlesinger wrote, was "a near disaster from which we were fortunate to escape."[168] The "mélange of agreements, near-agreements and contradictory proposals," Kissinger wrote, "run the risk of undermining deterrence and the cohesion of the Western alliance."[169] But the consternation of the American defense experts was nothing beside that of the NATO allies. "It was like an earthquake," Margaret Thatcher said. "There was no place you could put your political feet, where you were certain that you could stand."[170]

What scandalized the defense establishments on two continents was not just what the President might have said in the last session but the proposal the U.S. had certainly made to cut strategic weapons by 50 percent in five years and eliminate all ballistic missiles—long-, medium- and short-range—in ten. That proposal, which was apparently still on the table, defied the logic of strategic planning since the early 1960s. "Without warning, without consultation with Congress or its allies, indeed without any prior analysis, the Administration proposed the abandonment of two of the three traditional legs of the triad," Schlesinger wrote.[171] In articles and speeches, he and other defense experts spelled out what they saw as the dire consequences for U.S. and European security:

If land- and sea-based ballistic missiles were eliminated, the only strategic and theater nuclear weapons the U.S. would have left were bombers and cruise missiles. The American weapons were significantly more capable than the Soviet bombers and cruise missiles, but the Soviet Union had an elaborate system of air defenses with thousands upon thousands of anti-aircraft missiles and interceptor aircraft. Given the 50-percent cut in strategic weapons that would take place in the first five years after the agreement, the Soviets might be able to beef up their defenses so that none of the remaining U.S. bombers or cruise missiles could get through. U.S. air defenses were, by contrast, skeletal, and without a prolonged and expensive effort to upgrade them, the U.S. bomber fleet itself might become vulnerable to a preemptive attack. On top of that, the danger to Western Europe would be extreme. At Reykjavik nothing had been said about the missile forces belonging to other nuclear powers, but unless the U.S. and the Soviet Union were going to allow Britain, France and China to become nuclear superpowers in their stead, the European missiles would have to go, Europe would be effectively denuclearized and the Soviets, with their great superiority in conventional forces, would have the capacity to dictate the terms in Europe. The Reykjavik edifice, Kissinger wrote, "puts the entire postwar structure of deterrence into question because it makes even more doubtful that the United States would use nuclear weapons in defense of its allies." Schlesinger concurred. "For a generation," he wrote, "the security of the Western world has rested on nuclear deterrence. Its goal has been to deter not only nuclear attack but also massive conventional assault from the East. . . . The American position at Reykjavik seems to have reflected no understanding of these simple fundamentals."[172]

Kissinger and Brzezinski, who had become staunch advocates of SDI, praised Reagan for his principled stance in refusing to trade the program away. But to Scowcroft, Schlesinger and the congressional Democrats the insanity of Reykjavik was compounded by the President's position on missile defenses.[173] SDI was "no more than a collection of technical experiments and distant hopes," Schlesinger wrote, and yet, though apparently prepared to sacrifice the strategic arsenal of the United States, Reagan had refused to make any compromise on outside-the-laboratory testing. Of course, Schlesinger continued, his inflexibility in this matter had rescued the negotiators from the folly upon which they were embarked. In that sense, he wrote, SDI "has probably now done more to protect the United States and its allies than it will ever do in the future."[174]

Notably, however, the alarm over what had happened at Reykjavik, and the anguish of such as Kissinger and Schlesinger over the possible loss of ballistic missiles, were not shared by many outside the defense establishment. Even among *New York Times* readers, a great many people were thrilled by the idea that Reagan and Gorbachev had cut through the pettifogging accountancy of arms control and had almost negotiated radical cuts in the vast nuclear arsenals. Many regretted that the two leaders had not made a historic decision to renounce nuclear weapons, and many, including those who thought such a step probably couldn't be taken, considered the establishment's rush to the defense of nuclear weapons the ultimate irony.

In November the House Armed Services Committee, under the chairmanship of Representative Les Aspin, began hearings on the Reykjavik summit and its implications for arms control. The testimony from Nitze, Perle, Adelman and other officials only reinforced the impression that the summit had been marked by confusion and enthusiastic disarray. Aspin, who knew most of the witnesses well, could not get over what had happened. "This one will go down in the annals of history," he said. "In graduate schools all over the country, people will be teaching the Reykjavik summit as the prime example of why you don't wander into something without knowing what you are talking about and put out proposals without thinking it through."[175]

The administration, it appeared, had made few preparations for the summit, and Gorbachev's proposals took the negotiators completely by surprise. With no planned responses, they had improvised ad-hoc positions without consulting the Allies or the Joint Chiefs. The proposal which Reagan had called "the most sweeping and important arms reduction proposal in the history of the world" had apparently been scratched out on a legal pad by two American officials during an unscheduled session on Sunday afternoon.[176] What happened at the climactic last session was still in dispute. At a press conference on November 19 the President, speaking of Reykjavik, said, "For the first time there was an agreement reached on the desirability of eliminating all strategic nuclear missiles in a five-year period and then dealing with the intermediate-range missiles in Germany."[177] There had been no official denial of this statement, but no one had referred to it again.

"Ronald Reagan gets up at a national press conference on Wednesday night, gives some totally different view of what our position is, and nobody bothers; doesn't matter!" Aspin exclaimed.[178] Later he asked Adelman who spoke for the administration. "Everyone," Adelman replied, adding that the President was of course the authoritative spokesman. "We all know that the one person we cannot listen to is the President," Aspin said. "We all know that this is an unreliable source as to what our position is. . . . The details . . . are not his strong suit."[179]

Yet, as far as the committee could discover, Ronald Reagan had taken a very active role in the Reykjavik negotiations. Among other things, he had, the committee wrote, "contributed to the momentum of the summit by his initiative in setting up the all-night working session," an initiative which "contributed more than anything else to the sense of exaggerated progress and inflated expectations that finally undermined the meeting itself." In the judgment of the committee, it was in part because of the President's interventions that "the excessive rigidity that characterized the U.S. position throughout most of the Reagan administration was suddenly transformed at Reykjavik into incautious and impatient enthusiasm."[180]

By the time Aspin's committee released its report in January 1987, the revelations of the Iran-contra affair had eclipsed the whole subject of Reykjavik. The picture of the negotiations was still far from complete, but little further effort went into establishing exactly what had occurred. The result was that Reykjavik remained in the public imagination as a "lost weekend," in which Reagan and Gorbachev either casually gambled with the security of their own countries and of Europe or nearly brought the senseless nuclear-arms race to an end.

Years later, however, new accounts of the summit appeared in the memoirs of officials and in journalistic histories, all of which differed considerably from those put forth in the post-summit public-relations blitz. Some of them seem to reinforce the initial impression of disarray. Yet, read together, along with Gorbachev's much-neglected account of the meeting, they suggest another interpretation entirely. What they suggest most strongly is that there was no "impatient enthusiasm" on the part of most in the American delegation, and that the final bargaining session was not the make-or-break gamble with nuclear weapons that it seemed to be.

By these later accounts the Soviets, as many at the time believed, made extensive preparations for the Reykjavik meeting. On August 19, Gorbachev, frustrated by the lack of movement on arms control, had called Shevardnadze from his vacation villa on the Black Sea and suggested a preliminary meeting with Reagan in a third country "to try and get some breakthrough." Shevardnadze then drafted a letter from Gorbachev to Reagan, to be presented when the foreign minister went to Washington in September, and launched a major planning exercise.[181]

The result of the exercise was a package of dramatic proposals on INF and START—all of them dependent on Reagan's acceptance of curbs on

SDI. Gorbachev and his advisers wanted the offensive reductions for their own sake: it was not SDI which brought them to the table. Still, the consensus in the Soviet military establishment and the Politburo was that there could not be deep reductions in Soviet offensive forces if the U.S. abandoned the ABM treaty and built space weapons that could be used either defensively or offensively.[182] Judging that the American side could not be easily persuaded to agree to a long period of nonwithdrawal from the treaty, they offered significant concessions in other areas.

With these concessions Gorbachev hoped to persuade Reagan to curb SDI, but, failing that, he planned to embarrass the administration. As he later put it, "In advancing the package, we wanted to show to the world that SDI was the main obstacle to an agreement on nuclear disarmament." The package was kept secret, and after Reagan agreed to the Iceland meeting, Soviet diplomats put out the word that the discussions would focus on Euromissiles and nuclear testing.[183]

The Reagan administration, by contrast, did merely perfunctory planning for Reykjavik. Time was limited. All the same, there were no interagency reviews of START or defense and space, and only cursory discussions of other issues. In September the administration had made a largely cosmetic counter-proposal on nuclear testing, and in deference to the NATO allies, it had proposed an "interim" INF agreement whereby both the U.S. and the Soviet Union would retain a token force of medium-range missiles in Europe; it had also made minor adjustments in its START proposal. None of these positions were changed. The administration, Aspin's committee determined, went to Reykjavik with only the proposals already tabled at Geneva and without any fallback positions or negotiating strategies.[184]

Gorbachev's sweeping proposals certainly took administration negotiators by surprise: they could hardly have failed to do so. Yet Gorbachev had given the administration plenty of warning about his desire for agreements on strategic weapons and SDI, as well as on Euromissiles and nuclear testing. In his letter to Reagan proposing the meeting and a "major impulse" on arms control, he had described his positions on these issues in some detail and called for an agreement in all three areas. Then, too, the CIA had put the negotiators on notice. In a briefing to the NSC on October 7 Casey said, "We think Gorbachev will press hardest on limiting SDI. . . . He will have to use the appeal of nuclear reductions to get you to agree to constraints that would effectively block SDI and eventually kill the program."[185] In addition, the fact that the chief of the Soviet General Staff was on the list of Soviet participants should have signaled that the Soviets were prepared to make arms-control decisions on the spot.[186]

Still, Shultz, Perle and Adelman later insisted that the administration was well prepared for the meeting, and the chairman of the Joint Chiefs, Admiral Crowe, told the House Armed Services Committee that he had not supposed that any great progress would be made at Reykjavik.[187] What this suggests is that the administration went to Reykjavik well prepared to do nothing at all.

Contrary to what some U.S. officials said in the immediate aftermath of the summit, Gorbachev explained his position on SDI in the very first session. Reading from a thick stack of papers, he outlined a series of new proposals, making it clear that they depended on an agreement to remain within the ABM Treaty for ten years and to confine space-weapons research to "the laboratories."[188] According to Shultz, the President commented briefly on the shortcomings of Gorbachev's offers, reacting with particular sharpness to the ABM Treaty proposal, maintaining, "Success with SDI would make the elimination of nuclear weapons possible." He went on to say that, if testing showed a defensive system to be practicable, there would be an obligation to share technology with the other side and to eliminate ballistic missiles. Gorbachev seemed somewhat taken aback. He said that he had put a good many new ideas on the table and that he hoped the President would study them carefully.[189]

At the luncheon recess Shultz and Reagan went to the U.S. Embassy with a text of Gorbachev's statement and joined their aides in the embassy's "security bubble," a small vaultlike enclosure mounted on blocks. Shultz and Nitze were elated. "It's the best Soviet proposal we have received in twenty-five years," Nitze said. Perle and Adelman, less enthusiastic, raised a number of objections. The group discussed the fact that Gorbachev was maintaining the position he had held since the previous spring on confining SDI to the laboratories. "He's brought a whole lot of proposals, but I'm afraid he's going after SDI," the President reportedly said.[190]

In the afternoon session Reagan read from a seven-page single-spaced paper that had been prepared for him. He spent some time on the "interim" INF proposal, but, according to Shultz, most of his exposition concerned the July 25 proposal to eliminate ballistic missiles and deploy space defenses in seven and a half years. He was, he said, willing to sign a treaty that would "supersede" the ABM Treaty.[191]

Gorbachev fumed. The President, he later said, was "offering us the same old moth-eaten trash ... from which the Geneva talks are already choking."[192] In the course of his response he insisted on the elimination of INF missiles from Europe. He also attacked Reagan's offer to share SDI technology. "I do not take this idea seriously," he said. "You do not even want to share with us oil equipment or equipment for the dairy industry, and you still expect us to believe your promise to share the research developments in the SDI project. That would be something like a Second American Revolution, and revolutions do not occur that often." But he reserved his harshest words for Reagan's proffer of a new agreement to "supersede" the ABM Treaty. He was not going to support scrapping the ABM Treaty, he said.[193]

Nonetheless, the President proposed, and Gorbachev agreed, that the two sides should establish working parties to continue the talks that evening, one to deal with arms control and the other to discuss regional issues and human rights.

The nightlong arms-control discussion proceeded much as Nitze and other U.S. officials described it to the press immediately after the summit. But the point they might have made somewhat more clearly was that virtually all the concessions were made by the Soviet side.

In the START discussion, Akhromeyev initially proposed that the two sides simply slice each category of weapons in half. Because that would leave the Soviets with superiority in heavy, MIRVed missiles, Nitze argued that this was the wrong way to proceed: what was wanted was not equal cuts but equal results in each category. The argument over this issue went on for almost six hours. "Ours were not the most erudite of arguments," Adelman writes; "we merely echoed the Chinese expression, 'No problem, we can't do that.' "[194]

At one-thirty in the morning, Akhromeyev requested an adjournment and said that he would be back at three.

Nitze, Linhard, Edward Rowney, the State Department special adviser on arms control, and several others woke up Shultz at his downtown hotel and crammed themselves into his small sitting room. To get the Soviets to accept equal ceilings on strategic launchers and warheads, Nitze wanted to adjust the sub-ceiling on ICBM warheads upwards from three thousand to thirty-six hundred. During the negotiating session Rowney had strenuously objected: "But ICBMs are the Soviet speciality."

"I *know* that, Ed," Nitze replied, exasperated.

Rowney went on about the dangers of an American retreat until Nitze could take it no longer. "You're forcing me to be as rigid as the Russians are at their worst. I'm absolutely furious," he said.

Shultz overruled Rowney and told Nitze that he had the authority to adjust the sub-ceilings.[195]

When the session resumed, Akhromeyev came with permission from his boss to agree to equal ceilings, and the two sides settled on overall ceilings of sixteen hundred launchers and six thousand nuclear charges.[196]

The session continued until around six-thirty in the morning, and by the end of it the Soviets had made a major concession on bomber-counting rules and resolved a host of other issues on strategic and intermediate-range weapons. But there was a complete impasse on SDI. At one point Nitze put forward a version of the administration's July 25th proposal, and Akhromeyev, his voice heavy with sarcasm, asked Nitze how it differed from the one already tabled in Geneva. After an awkward pause Nitze replied that it did not differ from it because "it was a good proposal."[197]

The House Foreign Affairs Committee later noted that there had been no attempt to discuss what might constitute a mutually agreeable interpretation of the ABM Treaty at the summit.[198] However, the U.S. negotiating position, based on the broad interpretation of the treaty and the July 25th proposal, was cast in stone. In his memoir Adelman writes, "No American official at Reykjavik dared to suggest a compromise on SDI, no matter what he may have thought personally."[199] As for the Soviet proposal to confine SDI research "to the laboratories," this was a way of making it plain that the Soviets would not agree to the "broad" interpretation.

Nitze reported to Shultz at seven-ten that morning. He was full of praise for Akhromeyev and exhilarated by the progress achieved on START. "Damn good!" Shultz exclaimed, pumping Nitze's hand. "It's what we came for."[200]

The Soviets, however, were disappointed. "It was becoming clear," Gorbachev later said, "that the U.S. representatives had come to Reykjavik with nothing at all to offer. The impression was that they had come there empty-handed to gather fruit in their basket."[201] The impression was correct. Of the overnight session Adelman writes, "We came with nothing to offer and had offered nothing; we merely sat there while the Soviets unwrapped their gifts."[202]

The following morning, Gorbachev changed his position on INF weapons, proposing a limit of one hundred Soviet warheads in Asia and one hundred American warheads in the U.S. (presumably in Alaska) aimed at targets in Soviet Asia. At this point Shultz dropped the "interim proposal" and accepted the elimination of INF missiles in Europe.[203] There was discussion of other issues including nuclear testing and the work accomplished on START. Gorbachev then insisted that there could be no agreement on deep cuts in offensive weapons without an agreement on defense and space. Reagan and Shultz proposed that the two teams work out language to describe their progress on START and INF and turn their disagreement on SDI over to their negotiators in Geneva. Gorbachev refused, saying it would be "kasha forever"—meaning that they would be eating the same porridge forever. At one point Gorbachev said, "We've accomplished nothing. Let's go home." But he stayed, and the session ran ninety minutes overtime. At the last minute Reagan accepted Gorbachev's suggestion that an unscheduled afternoon session be held to try again for agreement on space weapons. It was now 1:30 P.M.[204]

As the President left Hofdi House for the U.S. Embassy, Shultz called in five of his advisers: Poindexter, Nitze, Perle, Kampelman and Bob Linhard of the NSC staff. "We're at a very serious impasse," the secretary said, explaining that the tough issue was SDI. The Americans had little time to talk before Shevardnadze and his aides came in and joined them at the conference table. Shultz began speaking about nuclear testing, but Shevardnadze stopped him cold and insisted that there was only one issue before them: whether or not the President would agree that for a period of ten years there would be "no withdrawal from the ABM treaty and strict adherence to its terms." Turning to Kampelman, Shevardnadze said imploringly, "You are a creative person—can't you think of something?" Then, turning to Nitze, he said, "You are so experienced—can't you come up with something?"[205]

Perle and Linhard were whispering to each other at one end of the table. Linhard wrote something on a piece of paper and handed it to Poindexter, who gave it to Shultz. The secretary read it carefully, then gave it to Nitze and Kampelman for their opinions. When no objections were raised, he told the Soviets, "You have seen some writing at that end of the table. This is an effort by some of us here to break the impasse." He then read out what Reagan later called "the most sweeping and important arms control proposal in the history of the world."

> Both sides would agree to confine itself *[sic]* to research, development and testing which is permitted by the ABM Treaty, for a period of 5 years, through 1991, during which time a 50% reduction of strategic nuclear arsenals would be achieved. This being done, both sides will continue the pace of reductions with respect to the remaining ballistic missiles with the goal of the total elimination of all offensive ballistic missiles by the end of the second five-year period. As long as these reductions continue at the appropriate pace, the same restrictions will continue to apply. At the end of the 10-year period, with all offensive ballistic missiles eliminated, either side would be free to deploy defenses.[206]

The proposal was sweeping, but far from original—being no more than a reworking of the ZBM proposal of July 25. The new offer differed from the old one in that the period of non-withdrawal from the ABM Treaty was ten years instead of seven and a half; it incorporated the administration's proposal for a 50-percent reduction in strategic weapons, and it proposed a precise timetable for the elimination of ballistic missiles. But it was still a proposal for getting rid of all the Soviets' best weapons and "superseding" the ABM Treaty.

The proposal was also not quite as impromptu as it appeared. At dinner the previous evening with Reagan, Regan and Shultz, Poindexter had said that, unless the American side proposed something dramatic, the U.S. would be in the difficult position of having been offered large-scale Soviet concessions and having no response other than to reject them because of the restrictions the Soviets wanted to place on SDI. He suggested presenting a new ZBM proposal, and since the President did not object, he told Linhard about his plan.[207]

The next day, when Shevardnadze asked for new ideas, Poindexter leaned over to Shultz and whispered, "We ought to consider what we talked about last night." Linhard had simply anticipated his boss.[208]

When the proposal was translated, Shevardnadze, taken aback, asked why the U.S. would want the right to deploy defenses in ten years. The discussion ended there because it was almost 3:00 P.M., and the two leaders had returned to Hofdi House. The two sides caucused.[209]

In an upstairs room Shultz and Poindexter presented Reagan with the new proposal and explained it to him in some detail, stressing its consistency with his July 25 letter.[210] According to one source, Reagan asked Perle if eliminating ballistic missiles in ten years was practical: could it be done fast enough? Perle said he thought so and explained that the stealth bombers and the advanced cruise missiles that would be coming on line within ten years would provide for the security of the United States. Reagan then asked the JCS representative, General John Moellering, if the Chiefs would support the proposal. Moellering, who had no instructions on the matter, was non-committal.[211] "This wasn't supposed to be a summit. We aren't supposed to be in these negotiations," Reagan complained at one point.[212]

At 3:30 P.M. Reagan, Gorbachev, Shultz and Shevardnadze went back to the negotiating table. In the half-hour Gorbachev and his aides had had to consider the American proposal, they had drawn up an extremely simple counter-proposal: the two sides would remain within the ABM Treaty for ten years and confine the testing of space weapons to the laboratories; meanwhile, they would eliminate all strategic offensive arms, 50 percent in the first five years, the rest in the second.[213]

Outside in the hallway Kampelman asked Adelman what the chances were that Gorbachev would buy the American proposal. None, said Adelman—"he wouldn't even buy his own proposal!" Bewildered, Kampelman asked, "Then why do we do this? Why propose something he'd never accept, something even we might not want?" Adelman shrugged.[214]

In the meeting Gorbachev led off by reading the Soviet counter-proposal, making no mention of the American proposal. When he finished, the President responded, "This seems only slightly different from the U.S. position." "There are important differences," Shultz interjected.[215]

Apparently Reagan had not digested the American proposal as thoroughly as all that.

Reagan then presented the U.S. proposal, and he and Gorbachev went back and forth about space weapons and the ABM Treaty. At one point Gorbachev told Reagan that he would be regarded as "the village idiot" in Moscow if he agreed, even in principle, to deep cuts in offensive weapons without a clear and restrictive understanding about what the defensive half of the agreement would entail.[216] At another point Reagan said, "We obviously have a different interpretation of the ABM Treaty, and we have for a long time. Let's just say that we will take this up again in Washington when you come to Washington for the summit." "No, then there will be no package," Gorbachev replied bluntly.[217]

According to Shultz, Reagan periodically drove the tension up with pronouncements about the aggressive intentions expressed by Marx and Lenin. Having heard this litany before, Gorbachev let it pass—though at one point he said with a laugh, "Well, at least we've gotten past Marx and are on to Lenin."[218]

At 4:30 P.M. another recess was called. The Americans decided to stick with their own proposal but to put it into the Soviet format. Perle and Linhard then went to an upstairs bathroom and redrafted the text, using a board placed over the bathtub as a desk.[219]

While this was going on, Reagan called Regan aside and murmured that it was taking too long. He wanted to get back to Washington. He had planned to have Sunday-night dinner at home and was annoyed at the delay. When Regan suggested it might be necessary to stay on another night—the Soviets having made it known that they were willing to continue the next day—Reagan said with some exasperation, "No, we just can't do that." He added, "Hell. He doesn't want to set up a summit. He wants to have a summit. Right here."[220]

When the meeting resumed, Reagan read out the new text of the old proposal calling for the elimination of ballistic missiles. There followed a series of extremely confusing exchanges.

According to the Soviets, Reagan suggested that the cosmetically revised American proposal was the Soviet position as well.[221] Gorbachev replied that this was at best a misunderstanding and explained that he had proposed eliminating all strategic weapons, including bombers and cruise missiles. Reagan then said a bit grudgingly, "Apparently we misunderstood you. But if that is what you want, all right."[222]

By one American account, Gorbachev asked why the American proposal spoke of "strategic" weapons with regard to the first five years and "ballistic missiles" with regard to the second. "I thought you were interested in missiles," Reagan said.

By the same account, Reagan made a series of other bewildering remarks which suggested that he had lost his grip on which proposal was which and on what "strategic weapons" meant. According to both sides, Reagan went on to talk about the elimination of all nuclear weapons.

"We can do that," Gorbachev shot back. "Let's eliminate them. We can eliminate them."

Reagan repeated that he really thought Gorbachev was mainly interested in missiles, but added that, if all nuclear weapons were to be eliminated, "we can turn it all over to the Geneva people and they can draft the agreement and you could come to the United States to sign it."[223]

The rest of the discussion concerned SDI, and since neither Reagan nor Gorbachev changed his position by one iota, the two went round and round on this subject until, at six-thirty, Reagan unceremoniously closed his briefing book and stood up. "The meeting is over," he said. "Let's go, George, we're leaving." With that he walked out of the room.

As the two leaders put on their coats in the hallway, Gorbachev said, "Can't we do something about this?"

"It's too late," Reagan said.[224]

Reagan was angry. In his diary that night he wrote, "He tried to act jovial, but I was mad, and I showed it. Well, now the ball is in his court and I'm convinced he'll come around when he sees how the world is reacting."[225]

What all of these newer, and surely more reliable, accounts of the summit suggest is that on the American side the high stakes had mainly to do with perceptions, not arms, and that in the last sessions the stakes were the same for the Soviets.

In his memoir Larry Speakes tells us, "Reykjavik was to have been just another opportunity for Reagan and Gorbachev to meet in person; we embarked on the trip to Iceland without any great expectation of actually concluding an arms control agreement. Given the hostility over the Daniloff-Zakharov affair, the mere fact that the two leaders were meeting so soon afterwards was enough of an accomplishment."[226] In other words, Reagan's White House advisers hoped to have another summit just like that in Geneva to boost Reagan and his party in the polls. As for the U.S. negotiators, they went to Reykjavik with proposals designed to block an agreement. When the Soviets "unwrapped their gifts," Shultz and Nitze were delighted and allowed themselves to hope that an unprecedented deal could be made. But they had little flexibility on any issue, and none on the main sticking point for the Soviets: the "broad" interpretation of the ABM Treaty. What followed the overnight session was a piece of theater played to the galleries.

On the evening of the first day, Poindexter, for one, realized that the Soviets were going to score a propaganda coup if the U.S. did not respond to their dramatic initiatives. Linhard and Perle then concocted a new version of the July 25 proposal to put Gorbachev in the position of having to reject an even more sweeping agreement than the ones he proposed. Gorbachev and his aides clearly understood the ploy, for, without giving a half-hour's thought to it—and certainly without consulting the Politburo—they raised the bidding with a proposal that departed so radically from the serious negotiations that had gone on all the previous night that Adelman, and presumably most on the American side, regarded it as pure propaganda: in other words, a fitting response to the ZBM proposal.

Reagan did not grasp the details but he understood the essence: that in the court of world opinion he might be seen to be the recalcitrant one if he turned down a more radical Soviet proposal. So he accepted it, or brushed it off, and went on to up the ante with the proposal he had publicly espoused for years: the elimination of nuclear weapons. When Gorbachev agreed to that, there was nowhere else for Reagan to go but back to the old issue of SDI and the ABM Treaty—and an argument he had down pat after dozens of repetitions.

Reagan was furious when he walked out, and small wonder. Gorbachev had forced him to say *nyet.* Gorbachev had been quite prepared to continue the discussions—he was not going to be the one who walked out—but there were only so many sacrifices Reagan was willing to make on the altar of public opinion, and staying in Reykjavik another night was not one of them. Besides, the scene had played itself out. So he got up and left.

Shultz, Nitze and Kampelman looked crushed when they emerged from the meeting, but, then, Gorbachev had offered them the Grand Compromise Shultz and Nitze had been working for two years to achieve, and they were incapable of making the deal.

Adelman, on the other hand, was not a bit depressed. By his own account, his thought at the time was that Reykjavik would help Reagan with the American public. "Sure," he writes, "the American people like their president to sit down with the Russians, but they like it even more when he stands up to the Russians."[227]

Gorbachev for his part was angry that he had been unable to shake the President from his absurd position on strategic defenses. He was angry all over again a few days later, when the American propaganda machine turned out to be far more effective than his own, and the American public, unused to giving any credence to a Soviet leader, refused to believe his version of events and embraced SDI.[228]

THE WHITE HOUSE won the public-relations battle over Reykjavik, but the victory was evanescent and it left much debris.

Reagan's efforts on behalf of a Republican victory on November 4 was successful only in regard to Reykjavik and SDI: the polls led several Democratic senatorial candidates to pledge reluctant fealty to the program. Otherwise, his speeches were extremely short on substance, and for reasons which had more to do with domestic issues than with foreign policy, nine of the thirteen Republicans Reagan campaigned for lost their bids, and the Democrats regained control of the Senate.[229]

In the meantime, as Poindexter admitted to Senator Nunn, the administration had "some tidying up to do."[230]

In their haste to reverse the perception that the President's obsession with Star Wars had wrecked the summit, administration officials had not paid enough attention to the way the broadcasting of their own proposals would affect the defense community. Richard Perle's previous inventions, such as the "zero option," had been seen for what they were, but in the hurly-burly just after Reykjavik, many defense experts had to wonder whether Reagan might not actually be serious about total disarmament. Somewhat untidily, Poindexter and others had managed to sweep Reagan's verbal agreements under the rug. But it was not so easy to dispose of the written no-ballistic-missiles offer, particularly since the President had called it "the most sweeping and important arms reduction proposal in the history of the world."

In his memoir, Admiral William Crowe, the chief of the JCS, writes eloquently of the attempt to solve this problem, for nothing remotely like it had ever happened to him before:

> When the American delegation returned to Washington, the events of Reykjavik were handled in an oddly secretive fashion. Although accounts of what had happened made their way through the rumor mill and into the newspapers, the administration never did inform the Joint Chiefs of what had transpired. No one called to discuss the proposals that had been made, or to ask for an opinion. By inference, I concluded that various people in the President's inner circle had become agitated that he had gone too far, and that the political tacticians had decided the best way to manage the situation was to act as if it had never happened. The President's zero–ballistic missiles–in–ten–years (ZBM) formula was being treated as a non-event—the idea apparently being that if it were ignored long and hard enough it would eventually go away (which is essentially what did happen).[231]

However, the proposal did not go away immediately. Instead it became the object of impassioned protests from the Allies, the defense pundits and the Congress, and within a few days Crowe realized that he would have to do something about it. He would, he knew, be called before the House Armed Services Committee and asked if he had been consulted about the proposal before Reykjavik. When he answered no, Chairman Les Aspin would undoubtedly ask what he thought of the idea and whether he had subsequently given the President the benefit of his advice. "It was," Crowe writes, "important to avoid having to say no to that question." So he gathered the Chiefs and told them he would have to tell the President what they thought of the proposal even though their opinion had not been solicited. After some grumbling, they agreed. Weinberger, however, was dead against the idea of Crowe's telling Reagan that ZBM was a mistake. "Why tell the President that?" he asked. "We all think it's a mistake. But it's going to go away, don't worry about it." Crowe explained that it was not going to go away for him, given Aspin's well-known curiosity. Weinberger reluctantly gave his assent.[232]

Crowe was, he confesses, quite nervous about telling the President that his proposal was a terrible idea: he laid awake for several nights worrying about it and wondering if it would cost him his job. But it was, after all, of some importance that the United States not agree to give up its ballistic missiles, so he decided to take his chances.

On October 27 the NSC principals gathered in the White House for a National Security Planning Group meeting. The discussions ranged over a number of issues, and at the end, when the President asked if anyone had anything more to say, Crowe asked for the floor and said he would like to speak about Reykjavik. In the silence that descended upon the room, Crowe read out a statement he had carefully prepared with a four-page summary of the objections made by all of the Chiefs. He laid out a number of the arguments against the ZBM proposal, two of them striking enough to be recorded by Adelman: first, that the elimination of ballistic missiles would pose high risks to the security of the nation; second, that, given the need for new bombers, air defenses and cruise missiles to protect the country, a 12-percent real increase in military spending would be required each year for the next ten—putting the defense budget well over a trillion dollars a year by 1996.[233]

"As your chief military adviser," Crowe concluded, "I do not recommend that you submit this proposal, Mr. President. It is not my intention to make your burdens any greater than they normally are, but this subject is of sufficient significance that I feel I would not be carrying out my responsibilities without informing you."

"I agree with him!" Adelman burst out.

Everyone turned to stare at Adelman. Then all eyes turned to the President, and Crowe, by his account, thought, "Well, I've done my duty. Now here it comes."

"Admiral," the President said, "I really love the U.S. military. I have always loved it. Those young men and women do a wonderful job for our country, and everywhere I go I tell people how proud I am of our armed forces. You oversee a superb organization, one that is not adequately appreciated. But I am constantly trying to get the country to recognize and understand the true value of our military."

Did the President not know what Crowe was talking about? Or was he simply filling the air because there was nothing to be said in the defense of the ZBM? No one knew, but Crowe and Weinberger felt hugely relieved.[234]

The administration could not, however, publicly reverse itself so soon after the summit, and the flap continued.[235]

On November 5 Shultz went to Vienna with a huge delegation of military and civilian arms-control experts to meet with Shevardnadze and his aides. In the preceding weeks American officials had voiced optimism about the possibility of a breakthrough at this meeting. But that was merely part of the public-relations blitz. Both during the Reykjavik negotiations and in his speeches thereafter, Gorbachev had insisted that everything he had offered on INF and START was part of a package that included confining SDI to the labs. "No package, no concessions," he said.[236] The Reagan administration's misrepresentations did not incline him to be any more conciliatory, and then, just after the summit, the espionage conflict had flared up again. In a delayed response to Reagan's September 17 decision to expel twenty-five members of the Soviet UN mission, the Soviets expelled five American diplomats from Moscow; the administration responded by ousting fifty-five more Soviets, and in a final move the Soviets expelled five more Americans. In his speech on October 22, Gorbachev had charged that the United States "does not even have a desire to maintain the atmosphere which is essential for the normal continuation of the dialogue."[237]

In Vienna, Shultz and his colleagues attempted to pocket everything the Soviets had offered at Reykjavik and to press for further concessions on START. The Soviets would have none of it. Their negotiators—a small group that did not include Marshal Akhromeyev—were adamant about the package, and actually took back some of the concessions they had proposed in Iceland. The meeting ended in bitter disagreement.

Nitze realized that it would be some time before there was any further progress in the arms talks.[238]

On Friday, November 14, Margaret Thatcher descended like a thundercloud upon Washington. Uninformed about the intentions of the administration, she had to take the Reykjavik proposals seriously. She did not like the zero-zero INF proposal, but it had been NATO policy for years, and she herself had paid lip service to it, so she could hardly object now that the Soviets had finally agreed to it. But the proposal to eliminate ballistic missiles was another matter entirely. It appalled her that the United States would be willing to propose a deal that would dismantle extended deterrence—the basis of European security for the past forty years. Though there had been no mention of British or French missiles at Reykjavik, it was quite clear that British missiles would go as well, for it was inconceivable that the U.S. would continue to sell Britain the very missiles it was phasing out. When the news broke, she wasted no time in consulting with other NATO leaders, going so far as to call French President François Mitterrand to a meeting with her at 10 Downing Street. All agreed that Reykjavik had been a folly and that Europe should not be denuclearized.[239]

The year before, Thatcher had spent a weekend in Washington attempting to quash the "broad" interpretation of the ABM Treaty, and this trip was an almost exact repetition of the first. On Friday afternoon she assailed Shultz and Weinberger with the objections of all the European allies; the next morning she went up to Camp David like a nanny in pursuit of her errant charge. In no time, she maneuvered the President into going off alone with her in a golf cart. For an hour or so her aides wrung their hands, wondering what was going on. Just before lunchtime she and the President reappeared, and Thatcher was smiling. Taking a piece of paper out of her handbag, she read off a list of the positions she had come with. The President had agreed to all of them.

After luncheon she returned to Washington and held a press conference in which she read out a statement of "agreed views." The statement reaffirmed the President's support for "the arrangements made to modernize Britain's independent nuclear deterrent" and confirmed that NATO strategy would continue to require "effective nuclear deterrents based upon a mix of systems"; it also said that the "priorities" for arms-control negotiations with the Soviets were agreements on INF weapons, a chemical-weapons ban and a 50-percent reduction in strategic arms. There was no mention of eliminating ballistic missiles.[240]

On Monday, November 17, George Shultz delivered a speech in Chicago that was billed as an attempt to reassure the NATO allies. Thatcher's visit had caused a good deal of embarrassment at the State Department, and Shultz wanted to make the ZBM proposal disappear without seeming to do so. In his speech he defended a ban on ballistic missiles as a "significant plus for NATO," but he said that, even after the elimination of these weapons, the alliance would need "insurance policies to hedge against cheating or other contingencies," including possibly "an agreed-upon retention of a small nuclear ballistic missile force." According to Adelman, Shultz had put together the European horror at the thought of scrapping ballistic missiles with the opinion of pollsters that the notion of "insurance" was appealing to the public, and he had come up with a proposal for ballistic missiles to provide insurance for the elimination of ballistic missiles.[241]

The speech did not go unnoticed by the defense establishment.

A couple of weeks later James Schlesinger, testifying before the House Armed Services Committee, remarked, "Breathtaking as the [Reykjavik] proposals were, it is equally breathtaking how quickly they have been withdrawn. We have been engaged in shedding the substance of these proposals while attempting to maintain an upbeat mood."[242]

The satirical note suggested that Schlesinger had divined the purpose of the ZBM proposal—if not of Reagan's whole performance in the last sessions of the Reykjavik summit.

During his committee hearings Les Aspin, too, allowed himself a satirical sally. After his old friend Richard Perle had tried his patience for too long with the official line about sharing SDI technology with the Soviets, Aspin called the administration's negotiating positions a "combination of Richard Perlism and Mike Deaverism: Richard Perle in putting forth proposals to screw things up, and Mike Deaver in putting forward ideas that look good PR-wise."

"I don't know whether zero ballistic missiles is like that or not," he continued, "but I think you have got to be careful." The Soviets, he said, had accepted the zero-zero INF proposal, and "I wouldn't be surprised to see them come back and say, 'Gentlemen, we want our share of the technology of SDI,' and so forth. I mean be very careful. I just think that you are dealing with a different crowd. Throwing things out there because they can't be negotiated, you know."[243]

But this was inside baseball—and not something Aspin could explain to the public, even if he wanted to.

CHAPTER NINE

Falling Stars

> "In the summer of 1985 Senator Bennett Johnston went to the floor of the Senate without any preparation—just cold—and asked if anyone believed in an astrodome defense. A dead silence followed."
>
> —JIM BRUCE[1]

ACCORDING TO MICHAEL DEAVER, Ronald Reagan was superstitious. He consulted his horoscopes in the newspapers and habitually carried around a pocketful of lucky charms that people had sent him. A dog that he had for a period in the White House was named Lucky. In addition, he entertained all kinds of ideas, from UFOs to ghosts in the Lincoln bedroom of the White House. Deaver did not understand how anyone as secure and comfortable with himself as Reagan seemed to be could believe in luck and fate and events beyond human control.[2] But, then, Deaver did not know much about actors. He did not know that the world of the theater has always been filled with superstitions, because for actors virtually everything, from sets to the audience to the pace of a performance on a given evening, is beyond their control.

In the fall of 1986, around the time of Reykjavik, Reagan's luck seemed to be running out. Just as the President was walking away from the most sweeping nuclear-disarmament agreement in history for the sake of an unconstrained SDI program, the bubble of Star Wars was collapsing, the dream of a perfect defense against Soviet missiles giving way to an untidy residue of claims for some form of space defenses. At about the same time came the revelations of the Iran-contra affair. Because of them, Reagan's public-approval ratings plunged twenty points in the month of November and remained at a low ebb for most of the following year.

The idea of a perfect defense was Reagan's invention, but he could not sustain it alone. During the midterm-election campaign he boosted the popularity of SDI to record heights in the polls, but by that time the program was already under attack in Washington from two sides: on the one hand, from Democrats and moderate Republicans concerned with the mounting budget deficits; on the other, from the conservatives who worried that SDI would not survive the Reagan presidency if it remained a research program.

The attacks were effective, for by that time many in Congress and the Washington press had taken the measure of the SDI program.

In 1984 and 1985 most congressmen and senators, including those on the committees charged with overseeing the military budget, had found it extremely difficult to come to grips with the SDI program. The technologies were outside the ken of all but a few experts on the Armed Services Committees. Beyond that, it was a huge, diffuse endeavor whose very objectives were elusive.

The Strategic Defense Initiative Organization had been chartered to conduct research to determine the feasibility of "an effective ballistic missile defense," and SDIO officials had promised that they would complete this task by the early 1990s, at which point a decision on whether to develop strategic defenses could be made. But what was an "effective" ballistic-missile defense? There had been no definition of "effective" apart from the one the President often advertised, and that was impossible to achieve. The SDIO seemed to have high ambitions. Officials and scientists spoke of a multi-layered defense designed to stop missiles in their boost phase and warheads in their mid-course trajectories, and occasionally officials talked about 80- or 90-percent-effective defenses: that is, defenses that would stop 80 percent of the Soviet missile fleet, as opposed to saving 80 percent of the U.S. population from an attack. Yet, when pressed, General Abrahamson, the SDIO director, and his aides would say only that the goal of the program was to "enhance deterrence"—or, in other words, to do something of some military value.[3]

Then, too, the constituents of a ballistic-missile defense had yet to be decided upon. Would it be made up of directed-energy weapons, such as lasers and particle beams, or kinetic-energy weapons, which destroyed targets by the force of impact? What kind of sensors would be used to detect an enemy attack, track the warheads, discriminate between warheads and decoys and acquire the warheads so they could be destroyed? And what of battle management? What kind of computational power would be needed to coordinate and control the individual weapons and sensors in combat? Could a human be in the loop? The Fletcher panel, which provided the intellectual basis for the program in 1983, had provided no answers: it had simply recommended a crash program of research into BMD-related technologies and concepts to see if something would pan out. Accordingly, the SDIO had amalgamated the existing programs from the armed services and Defense Advanced Research Projects Agency (DARPA) and added to them. Then, not knowing what it was looking for, it hired ten contractors to make competitive blueprints, or systems architectures, for an integrated anti-missile defense.[4]

The costs of this enterprise, too, were unknown. The Fletcher panel had recommended a "technology-driven" research program—that is, a program limited only by technological progress—and had estimated the cost as somewhere between eighteen and twenty-seven billion dollars over five years. When the program began in 1984, the figure given was twenty-six billion, but this was merely an improvisation. Under pressure from Senator Nunn to come up with a number, Richard DeLauer, the undersecretary of defense for research and engineering, had estimated that 20-to-25-percent growth per year was the most the program could absorb, and had done the arithmetic.[5] Given the open-ended nature of the program, the research costs could well go higher. As for developing and deploying a space-based defense, James Schlesinger and Harold Brown had put the cost at a trillion dollars. SDIO officials insisted that this figure was far too high, but they refused to make any cost projections of their own. Instead, they were working on estimates of what elements of the system *should* cost if the whole was to be affordable and cost-effective.[6]

In sum, SDI was a program in search of technologies for an undesigned system at a price the nation might be willing to pay.

In 1984 the SDIO requested almost two billion dollars for fiscal year 1985; the following year it asked for a total of almost four billion. The Congress did not give the SDIO what it wanted, but it appropriated $1.6 billion in the first year and almost three billion in the second—thereby tripling the annual funding for BMD work in three years. Abrahamson and Weinberger deplored the "cuts" in the budget, and on occasion lamented that the Congress had all but crippled SDI, but they nonetheless maintained the Fletcher deadline for a decision on the development of strategic defenses in the early 1990s.[7]

In the fall of 1985, Weinberger, Abrahamson and other officials began to give glowing reports of progress. In November, Abrahamson spoke of "genuine breakthroughs" in SDI research and said that recent experiments had exceeded the most optimistic expectations. He also claimed that there was no longer any doubt about the feasibility of strategic defenses. "The question is no longer can we do such a thing, but when, how fast and at what cost," he said in a speech to the National Space Foundation. The same month, Weinberger publicly asserted, "We are making much greater progress than we anticipated. The barriers we saw to progress are crumbling."[8] Administration and SDIO officials were somewhat more circumspect in their testimony before Congress, but they spoke of technical marvels and showed videotapes of spectacular experiments: a low-powered laser beam bouncing off the space shuttle, a chemical laser hitting the mock-up of a Titan booster and a hypervelocity weapon—said to be a railgun—destroying a missile airframe under simulated conditions. The code name for these telegenic demonstrations was Beacon, or Bold Experiments to Advance Confidence.[9]

The experts on the Armed Services Committees greeted these reports and demonstrations with a good deal of skepticism. In December 1985 Les

Aspin somewhat acidly remarked that the "commitment to SDI has grown substantially, even though its feasibility and good sense have been no better demonstrated today than when the President first spoke of the idea."[10] Yet for most in Congress and in the press the SDI program was a black box out of which anything might come. For the Democrats in the Senate, where the Republicans controlled the Armed Services Committee, the question of what the Congress was paying for was a pressing and practical one. During the debates over the defense-authorization bill in mid-1985 five Democrats had made attempts to stem the growth of the SDI budget, choosing figures ranging from $1.4 billion to $2.7 billion; none of their amendments gathered much support, since the figures were more or less arbitrary. Senator John Glenn, who had more of a grasp on SDI technologies than most, was hard put to explain his own figure of $2.7 billion. "I feel better at $2.7 billion," he told colleagues.[11]

In the summer of 1985 Senator William Proxmire (Democrat of Wisconsin), a member of the Defense Appropriations Subcommittee, had decided that it was necessary to look to the long term and to educate himself and his colleagues about the program. Enlisting the support of two other members of the subcommittee, Senators J. Bennett Johnston and Lawton Chiles, two moderate Southern Democrats, he organized informal briefings by SDIO officials and outside experts. That fall his staff assistant, Douglas Waller, along with James Bruce from Johnston's staff and Douglas Cook from Chiles's staff, visited a number of the major SDI installations across the country, from the Army's Ballistic Missile Defense Command to the Sandia and Lawrence Livermore National Laboratories, and talked with over fifty scientists as well as with SDIO officials.[12]

One of the questions Waller and his colleagues asked the SDI scientists in the course of interviews was whether they had seen the great progress that Abrahamson and others talked about. To their surprise the answer was a resounding "no." Instead of lobbying for their projects, the scientists scoffed at the exaggerations coming out of Washington and expressed concern that the hype would undermine their credibility and create a backlash against the program as a whole. To the Senate staffers they freely admitted that they still had no firm idea of what an "effective" strategic-defense system would look like.[13]

On their return to Washington the three staffers spent several months writing up a detailed technical assessment of the program. Their report, which they presented in March 1986, was difficult to assail, since it was based entirely on briefings from scientists at work on the program. SDIO officials did not like it, but with another Senate vote on appropriations coming up, they agreed to declassify it and offered no official rebuttal. The report led to further congressional inquiries, and it helped journalists with their own investigations of the program. The result was a flood of unclassified information about SDI.[14]

According to SDI scientists, some progress had been made in the past two years, but there had been no major breakthroughs, and in some technologies—most notably in those advertised to Reagan by the original Star Wars enthusiasts—there had been serious setbacks. The X-ray laser, which Teller and his Livermore protégé Lowell Wood had claimed would be able to shoot down the entire Soviet ICBM fleet, had recently proved weaker by a factor of ten than was previously believed.[15] Furthermore, it was scandal-ridden. In 1985 Teller and Wood had claimed that in a test performed in March the laser had achieved weapons-level brightness, and on the strength of these claims had won an extra hundred million dollars for the program; but scientists from Los Alamos and Livermore had later discovered that the test was so seriously flawed that there was some question whether it had demonstrated the existence of the laser. The expensive underground nuclear tests continued, but the X-ray laser was no longer thought of as a potential SDI weapon.[16] As for the chemical laser which Senator Malcolm Wallop and his aide Angelo Codevilla had promoted as a silver bullet, further testing had confirmed the inefficiencies experts had already pointed to, and it was no longer judged to have any military utility.[17] Other directed-energy programs proceeded on track, but there was much basic science to be done on them. The work was of interest, but in the opinion of SDIO program managers laser and particle-beam weapons were "too Buck Rogers" and "too much in the 'if' stage" to be counted upon for the foreseeable future.[18]

Kinetic-energy, or hit-to-kill, weapons were not so speculative, but they were hardly "off the shelf," as General Daniel O. Graham and his High Frontier colleagues maintained. Formidable engineering problems remained to be solved. By 1986 the SDIO was working on three hit-to-kill interceptor systems: a space-based system of chemically powered rockets, or "smart rocks," launched from orbiting platforms to attack Soviet ICBMs in their boost phase; a ground-based interceptor, known as ERIS (the acronym for Exoatmospheric Reentry Vehicle Interceptor Subsystem), to attack Soviet warheads in space during the late mid-course phase of their flight; and another ground-based interceptor, known as HEDI (High Endoatmospheric Defense Interceptor), to attack warheads as they descended through the atmosphere.

Of the three interceptors, the ERIS was the most technically mature. In June 1984 the Air Force had launched a rocket from Kwajalein Island in the Pacific and intercepted in mid-flight a mock warhead launched from California. The demonstration, known as the Homing Overlay Experiment, was still the most spectacular success SDI advocates could point to. According to the Air Force it had proved that "a bullet can hit a bullet in space." But the test had succeeded only after three failures, and the old Titan booster used as an interceptor was only a crude prototype of the ERIS: it was far too heavy and expensive for operational purposes, and its instruments were too delicate for use in combat.[19] A suitable homing rocket might be engineered, but the real problem was that of target acquisition and discrimination in space. It was one thing for a "bullet to hit a bullet," but that achievement paled before the task of finding the bullet when it was surrounded by chaff, decoys and debris—and thus far the solution was still merely theoretical.[20]

The HEDI interceptor was less far along. The challenge in this case involved propulsion and timing. When a warhead entered the atmosphere, descending at the speed of sixteen thousand miles an hour, the HEDI sensor would have four seconds to find it and guide an interceptor to the target before it hit earth; and it would have to find it amidst the remaining decoys and the atmospheric turbulence that would attend a nuclear war. The first experiment to determine the feasibility of such an interceptor was not planned until 1989.[21]

As for the space-based interceptors, they were even further into the future. According to the program manager for kinetic-energy weapons, the SDIO would only be capable of completing "near-term validation experiments"—or a host of subtests with computer simulations and modelings—by the early 1990s, and only years after that could there be a demonstration of the system as a whole.[22]

Whether space-based interceptors could be developed remained an open question, but if they could, there would remain the tremendous problem of transport and logistics. For an "effective" boost-phase defense against the current Soviet ICBM fleet, the U.S. would have to put thousands of battle stations in orbit plus hundreds of other satellites for surveillance, tracking and so forth. The space shuttle could carry twenty to fifty thousand pounds into orbit, depending on the height of the orbit, but to lift and maintain a strategic-defense system of any degree of effectiveness, the U.S. would have to put millions of pounds of equipment into space every year. The task would be something like that of pulling the *Titanic* from the ocean floor and putting it into orbit. It might conceivably be done if a new heavy-lift launch vehicle were built, but even so it might take as much as eight years to deploy the system—and it would require NASA and the aerospace industries to mass-produce satellites and launchers.[23]

The U.S. might succeed in creating this armada and lifting it into space, but then the question was why anyone would want to do it. As fast as kinetic-energy weapons were, they were still only barely fast enough to hit an SS-18 in the five minutes it took the missile to climb out of the atmosphere, and in the opinion of SDI scientists they would "fail catastrophically" against solid-fuel, or fast-burn, boosters, such as the U.S. possessed. According to the Defense Intelligence Agency, the Soviets were already developing fast-burn boosters and were likely to replace their liquid-fuel ICBMs within seven years. If that were the case, the space-based interceptors would be obsolete before they could be deployed.[24]

In the view of the numerous SDI scientists with whom Waller and his colleagues talked, much of the progress that had been made in the program over two years lay in a greater understanding of the difficulties involved in mounting an effective strategic defense. SDI scientists now judged that discriminating hundreds of warheads from decoys and debris in space was beyond the scope of current technology, and that the computing requirements for battle management of a centralized three-tiered system could not yet be met. But the real problem—the show-stopper, in the opinion of many—was that of survivability. As Teller and others had pointed out three years before, any space-based system was essentially a sitting duck, and the cost of shooting it down was minimal compared with that of building and deploying it. Though some SDIO officials voiced optimism that this problem could eventually be overcome, there was as yet no conceptual solution, and the scientists at the Sandia Laboratory, who had studied the problem intensively, had come to the conclusion that space-based defenses could never be made survivable unless an agreement was reached with the Soviets to make them so.[25]

By the time the report by Waller and his colleagues was released in March 1986, it appeared that, in order to reach the Gramm-Rudman deficit-reduction targets, the Senate would cut the administration's defense-budget request by twenty billion dollars, leaving the Pentagon with only enough increase to cover inflation. Yet the administration had requested $5.4 billion for SDI for fiscal year 1987—an increase of 77 percent over the previous year—and almost six billion dollars for fiscal 1988. Funded at that level, SDI would be the largest military-research program the Department of Defense had ever undertaken. The total research costs would be in excess of the full deployment costs of many major weapons systems.[26] In the past the service chiefs had regarded the SDI budgets with complacency, but now the mutterings in the Pentagon could be heard all the way up to Capitol Hill.

In late May, Senators Proxmire and Johnston circulated a letter calling upon the Senate Armed Services Committee to check the spiraling costs of SDI. Arguing that the budget increases had "out-paced the progress of technology" and "begun to impinge on other military research and development," Proxmire and Johnston urged the committee to hold SDI to a 3-percent real increase. Speaking of his concern about the disproportionate funding for the program, Johnston said that almost all of his colleagues believed that Reagan's goal of making nuclear weapons impotent and obsolete was "unrealistic," yet they continued to pour money into SDI for fear of being tagged "anti-defense, anti-technology and anti-Reagan." This fear had apparently diminished, for forty-six senators, including nine Republicans, signed the letter, and later two others endorsed the arguments it made.[27]

In response to the letter, Senator Nunn, working closely with Republican Senator William Cohen of Maine, proposed to reduce the administration's request of $5.4 billion to $3.9 billion and offered an amendment known as the Balanced Technology Initiative to channel funds requested for SDI into research on conventional arms. The committee debate over the amendment was partisan and acrimonious. While it proceeded, sixteen hundred scientists, many of them involved in military research and some in the SDI program, delivered an open letter to Congress calling SDI wasteful and a spur to the arms race. At the same time, Lowell Wood and a group of pro-SDI scientists gave press interviews outside the hearing room. The amendment squeaked through the committee—with Cohen casting the deciding vote—and passed the Senate with the rest of the defense bill. The House later voted a budget of $3.1 billion, and in conference the two chambers split the difference at $3.5 billion.[28]

The votes were important ones, for they showed unequivocally that the Congress preferred to fund SDI in the three-billion as opposed to the five-billion-dollar range. Just as important was a recommendation made by the Senate Armed Services Committee. In its report on the defense bill the committee called for a redirection of the SDI program from research on comprehensive population defenses to research on survivable cost-effective defenses for U.S. strategic forces. The purpose of the program, the report made clear, should be the traditional one of developing options to serve as a hedge against the possibility of a Soviet breakout from the ABM Treaty, as well as providing leverage in the START negotiations.[29]

These legislative moves, and the fact that the Reagan administration had only two years more in office, galvanized Star Wars advocates in and out of Congress. General Graham and his colleagues, who had spent the past two years trying to pressure the SDIO to move from research into development, now became frantic that nothing would be built. "If you scratch someone in the SDI office, he bleeds RESEARCH," wrote one High Frontier advocate. "The administration must make an unequivocal decision in favor of deploying defenses."[30] Senator Wallop and his aide Angelo Codevilla, who had long agitated for development and deployment, also began to despair of the administration. Wallop and his congressional allies had always worked within the context of support for the President. But with the defeat of the administration's SDI budget, and with Reagan soon to become a lame duck, they decided to make an open break with the President and to lead a public campaign for building strategic defenses.

In July, Wallop and seven other Republican members of Congress, including Senators Dan Quayle and Pete Wilson and Representatives Jack Kemp and Jim Courter, wrote Reagan urging that he repudiate the ABM Treaty and begin the production and deployment of "near term" strategic-defense systems. "Mr. President," they wrote, "if the administration keeps on defining SDI as a faraway dream for the next millennium, no one will support it, including us. But if we begin now, as we must, to build the antimissile devices we can build, the American people would soon enjoy real and growing protection."[31] By the end of the month they had yet another grievance to air: in his letter to Gorbachev of July 25 Reagan had proposed to "delay" the deployment of strategic defenses for seven and a half years.

On August 6 the legislators met with the President. The meeting was not a success from their point of view. White House officials had invited nine congressional Republicans who opposed early deployment to the meeting, and the group was given only a half-hour with Reagan. Taking the floor, Wallop and his allies told the President that any agreement with the Soviets on SDI would kill the program; Courter then asked rather rudely whether U.S. astronauts would ever have gotten to the moon if Kennedy had treated the Apollo program as Reagan had treated SDI.[32]

Backed up by Weinberger, the President took the outburst in stride. He promised that SDI would not be a bargaining chip, but turned down their bid for early deployment. "I know there are those who are getting a bit antsy," he said, "but to deploy systems of limited effectiveness now would divert limited funds and delay our main research. It could well erode support for the program before it's permitted to reach its potential."[33]

Shortly afterwards Wallop and Kemp wrote an Op Ed piece for the *New York Times* complaining that SDI might never be built because the President had offered to delay the deployment, and Congress would not vote funds for a program that might be negotiated away. They added that the U.S. had the capacity to deploy a system that would defend U.S. missiles and disrupt a Soviet first strike by introducing uncertainty into the attack planning.[34]

As the Op Ed piece demonstrated, the right-wing push for a weapons deployment entailed an important rhetorical shift. In the past, right-wingers had always advertised strategic defenses as population defenses and had used language suggesting that they would be a substitute for offensive deterrence, or "Mutual Assured Destruction." This was, after all, what the majority of Americans, including many in the conservative rank-and-file, wanted from the SDI program, and the conservative leaders could read the polls as well as anyone else.[35] But in calling for an early deployment, the conservatives unmasked themselves. Interestingly enough, Martin Anderson, one of the principal authors of "the President's vision," was among the first to do so. In an Op Ed piece in *The Wall Street Journal* on May 19, he had called upon the administration to deploy a limited defense of one hundred ground-based ERIS missiles to protect the U.S. against an accidental launch or a small-scale nuclear attack. He did not promise that a perfect defense would follow.[36] Then, in July, Senators Quayle and Wilson called for an early deployment of antimissile systems to protect military assets in Europe from attack by Soviet intermediate-range missiles—a far cry from an astrodome defense of the United States.[37] In their Op Ed piece, Kemp and Wallop made a clean break with rhetorical orthodoxy by calling for weapons that would protect U.S. strategic forces.

In speaking thus plainly, the conservatives were, of course, endangering the popularity of SDI, for, along with the Senate Armed Services Committee, they were calling it down from its moral heights and the mythic sphere of technological "magic" into the secular realm where weapons were just weapons and the logic of cost-effectiveness ruled. But they were in a hurry, and they had allies within the administration.

At a Ditchley conference in England in the summer of 1985, Kenneth Adelman, the director of ACDA, had told assorted U.S. and European dignitaries that the real aim of SDI was to create a point defense for American ICBMs, and that the rationale of population defenses was merely public relations for the program. The remark caused a flap, but because of the venue, and because it was Adelman speaking, the perturbation passed over quickly. But in June 1986 Richard Perle told an American audience much the same thing. Presidents, he said, "give expression to long-term hopes and dreams," and that was as it should be, but "the rendering of nuclear weapons impotent and obsolete is not a short-term proposition, and it may not be possible in the long term." There were, he said, "more immediate goals, more tractable problems to be solved," among them "the defense of America's capacity to retaliate," or the defense of U.S. missiles and command-and-control facilities. Later in the summer he was asked point-blank whether SDI could replace retaliatory weapons. "Who said anything about getting rid of deterrence?" he replied coolly.[38]

By that time a number of conservatives within the administration had decided that the moment of truth had come for SDI. In the Office of the Secretary of Defense, some were urging that the SDIO perform tests that would violate the limits of the ABM Treaty; others urged that Weinberger announce plans to develop defenses immediately.[39]

All through the summer of 1986 Weinberger continued to vow support for "the President's dream." In June he told the Senate Defense Appropriations Subcommittee that the goal of SDI was to protect the entire United States, and its purpose "to have a system that will destroy [Soviet] missiles before they get near any target," adding, "I am confident that we can do it." Two months later, in response to calls for early deployment, Weinberger again protested that there was only one SDI, and it was Ronald Reagan's.[40] Weinberger, however, had begun to consider plans for a deployment. In his memoir he tells us that in August the Defense Department, under the direction of Iklé, Perle and Abrahamson, conducted an analysis of the "likely availability of SDI technology," and that, in the course of some four or five briefings throughout the fall, the analysis "became a search for the best route to effective defenses."[41]

The search was not, however, immediately successful. Most deployment advocates in and out of the administration regarded the ERIS program, designed by Lockheed, as the most likely candidate for early deployment. But Weinberger, who sometimes defended "Reagan's dream" to European officials by citing U.S. polling data, did not want a ground-based interceptor that could do no more than defend U.S. military assets. In meeting after meeting, he writes, options for near-term ground-based defenses were presented, and always he rejected them because they "offered little improvement on the ground-based point defenses available by the late 1960s." In his view, the early deployment of such systems "would do little more than recapitulate the ABM debate of 1969–72—with the same result." In other words, an administration proposal to build ground-based defenses would be politically disastrous. "Time and again," Weinberger writes, "I directed General Abrahamson and the staff assistants in OSD Policy to continue to look for the first point from which we could build effective defenses." What the secretary wanted was a system with some space-based elements. He insisted upon this, and he insisted that the proposal not be called "early deployment"—a term he associated with ground-based systems—but, rather, "Phase One" of a phased deployment that could be said to be the first step towards "the President's goal."[42]

In the fall the movement for early deployment gathered force. The Coalition for SDI, an umbrella group led by Graham, which claimed a membership of 196 organizations, campaigned for a deployment, as did the Center for Peace and Freedom, an offshoot of the Heritage Foundation.[43] Henry Kissinger opined that the strategic balance had worsened so much that the only solution was to deploy defenses. Deputy CIA Director Robert Gates suggested that the Soviets were about to deploy an ABM system with laser weapons. On October 1 Jack Kemp, Jim Courter, Republican Senator Rudy Boschwitz, former ACDA Director Eugene Rostow, Edward Teller and Lowell Wood wrote a letter to the President urging speedy deployment and making the reason plain. "We are," they wrote, "deeply concerned that a SDI program which has no definite consequences for a defense of America within the next ten years will not be politically sustainable. . . . We believe that imperfect but significant defensive options have already been laid before the American leadership by the SDI, and that they must not only be continued to perfection but also prudently exercised, while the political will to do so undeniably exists."[44]

That same month, the Heritage Foundation released a report calling for the speedy deployment of one hundred ERIS missiles at Grand Forks, North Dakota, at a cost of $3.5 billion, and the High Frontier organization made yet another proposal for the deployment of a system of ground- and space-based interceptors.[45]

The administration, however, made no response: the President was going to the Reykjavik summit, and the Republicans had the midterm-election campaign to fight. Then, in November, the administration was rocked by the Iran-contra affair.

On October 5, 1986, a C-123 cargo plane bearing arms for the contras was shot down over Nicaragua, and one crew member, Eugene Hasenfus of

Marinette, Wisconsin, survived. Documents on board the plane connected it with Southern Air Transport, a former CIA proprietary charter based in Miami, Florida. For over a year there had been rumors that Oliver North, a Marine colonel on the NSC staff, had been running a covert operation designed to circumvent the congressional ban on aid to the contras, so there was speculation in Washington that the Hasenfus plane had some connection to the White House, the CIA or both. Briefed by his NSC adviser, John Poindexter, on the shoot-down, the President said that there was "no government connection with the plane at all . . . absolutely none."[46] However, the FBI, the U.S. Customs Service and the press began to look into the matter, and eventually, under pressure from the Congress, Attorney General Edwin Meese appointed an independent counsel to investigate the involvement of the NSC staff and CIA Director William Casey with the contras.[47]

On November 3 the Hezbollah, an Iranian-backed terrorist group, released one of the Americans it had been holding hostage in Lebanon; the same day, a Beirut weekly, *Al Shiraa,* claimed that the White House had been selling arms to Iran in exchange for the hostages and described a trip that former National Security Adviser Robert McFarlane had made to Teheran in May with a cargo of weapons. The Iranian prime minister, Holjistan Rafsanjani, confirmed the account the following day and added that McFarlane had brought a Bible inscribed by Ronald Reagan and a cake decorated with a key.

The revelation caused an outcry across the country, and among Republicans as well as Democrats: selling arms to Iran for hostages contradicted not only long-established administration policies but much of what Ronald Reagan stood for.

In any other administration the attempt to ransom American hostages might not have been seen as a scandalous act. Where hostages are concerned, governments normally deal with enemy governments and terrorists. The Carter administration had, after all, negotiated the release of the embassy personnel in Iran, and even the Israeli government often exchanged prisoners with groups it deemed terrorist. But Ronald Reagan, who had come to office in part because of the perceived weakness of Carter, had ruled out any such deals. A week after his inauguration, at a welcoming ceremony for the embassy hostages just returned from Teheran, he said, "Let terrorists beware: when the rules of international behavior are violated, our policy will be one of swift and effective retribution."[48] His administration had maintained a strict embargo on Iran. But the U.S. intervention in Lebanon in 1983 had prompted a series of attacks on Americans, including the bombing of the U.S. Embassy, the bombing of a Marine barracks near Beirut and the capture of hostages. The administration had proved incapable of retaliating effectively against these outrages, but the tough talk continued. In July 1985 the President said, "Let me make it plain to the assassins in Beirut and their accomplices that America will never make concessions to terrorists." And he pointed to Iran as the source of most of the trouble, declaring it to be a part of a "confederation of terrorist states . . . a new international version of Murder Incorporated."[49]

It now appeared that Reagan and his staff had been secretly selling arms to "Murder Incorporated" for more than a year. Three American hostages had been ransomed in this fashion, but three more Americans had been captured to serve as further bait for the arms sales.

Poindexter's reaction to the breaking news was to deny there had been arms shipments to Iran and to continue the arms-for-hostages negotiations. On November 4 he put out an official statement saying, "As long as Iran advocates the use of terrorism, the U.S. arms embargo will continue."[50] A flood of news stories soon contradicted him. According to well-informed sources, McFarlane had initiated the venture for large but muddled geo-strategic purposes; the President, however, had been interested only in getting the hostages out, and as time went on he had become more and more determined on the operation, even though both his secretary of defense and his secretary of state strongly opposed it.

The revelations triggered a political crisis, and several congressional committees called for investigations into the affair. Poindexter, however, decided to stonewall, and White House Chief of Staff Don Regan, who had paid small attention to the arms deals, did not object.

On November 13 Ronald Reagan made the biggest mistake of his political career. In a televised address to the nation he said that the charge that the U.S. had shipped arms to Iran as ransom payment for hostages was "utterly false." Instead, he explained, the White House had authorized the shipment of small amounts of "defensive weapons" in the course of an initiative designed to "restore a relationship with Iran, to bring an honorable end to the Gulf war [the Iran-Iraq war under way since 1980]. . . ." And he insisted, "We did not—repeat—did not trade weapons or anything else for hostages, nor will we."[51]

But there was already plenty of evidence on the record to show that that was just what had occurred. An ABC news poll taken immediately after the speech showed that 56 percent of the public thought that arms had been swapped for hostages and 72 percent opposed selling arms to Iran for any reason whatever.[52]

In the days following the speech, the White House put on a "media blitz" similar to that which Regan had orchestrated after Reykjavik, but, when interviewed by the reporters, Regan and Poindexter managed to contradict the President on key details and in general to make matters worse. Shultz, who since November 4 had feared that a Watergate-style cover-up was in the works, then began what he later described as a "battle royal" to stop the operation and get the facts out.

Meeting with the President on November 14, Shultz found the President adamant that what was done had been right and it had not been a trade with terrorists for hostages. Shultz then realized that reason would not prevail: Reagan truly did not believe that what had happened had in fact happened. "I had seen him like this before on other issues," Shultz tells us in his memoir. "He would go over the 'script' of an event, past or present, in his mind, and once that script was mastered, that was the truth—no fact, no argument, no plea for reconsideration, could change his mind. So what Reagan said to the American people was true to him, although it was not the reality."[53]

On November 16 the secretary went on the CBS Sunday-morning talk show, *Face the Nation,* and told its moderator, Lesley Stahl, that he opposed further shipments of arms to Iran but, no, he could not speak for the administration.

To reporters the answer meant that the arms-for-hostages operation was still going on, that Shultz was not in control of it and that he was willing to stake his job on bringing it to a halt.

As Shultz had hoped, the White House responded with a statement that the President had no plans to send further arms to Iran. However, the planning continued, and so, too, did attempts by Poindexter, North and others to cover up the illegalities, this time with a series of fake chronologies of the transactions.

On November 19 Reagan gave a televised press conference in which he again assured the country that there had been no arms-for-hostages transactions and made a number of new erroneous statements, including one of his own invention, that Israel had not been involved with the arms shipments. By that time Poindexter had told him so many different stories that, according to Don Regan, "This sort of confused the Presidential mind as to what he could say and couldn't say. . . ."[54]

Shultz went to see Reagan the following evening and had what he later described as "a long, tough discussion. Not the kind of discussion I ever thought I would have with the President of the United States."[55] Yet, for all of his efforts, Shultz could not get the President to see that there was a problem. "I didn't make a dent on him," he later told his executive assistant.[56]

In light of the investigations that followed, it is difficult to imagine how North, Poindexter and others thought they could conceal anything about the Iran operation, for vast numbers of people knew at least something about it. Outside the U.S. government, those in the know included high Iranian officials, high Israeli officials, Israeli intelligence, British intelligence (which had bugged one negotiation) and an entire world of international arms dealers. Inside the U.S. government, the list of those who knew a good deal about the operation included Vice-President Bush, Director Casey and a number of CIA officials; Secretary Weinberger and other Pentagon officials; Secretary Shultz and several of his close aides. In addition, the operation had been monitored electronically by the National Security Agency. The astonishing thing was that among the principals only Shultz understood that it could not be covered up.[57]

On November 21 Poindexter and Casey, testifying before a joint session of the House and Senate intelligence committees, gave mutually contradictory accounts of the most legally fraught of the arms transactions—that of November 1985—each one claiming not to have been informed by the other's agency. That afternoon, Attorney General Edwin Meese went to the President and told him that the administration did not have a coherent picture of the Iran initiative; he asked for, and obtained, authorization to gather the facts in one place.

The purpose of Meese's inquiry, as it later appeared, was to cover up the President's role in the November transaction. While Meese interviewed officials, Colonel North and his staff purged computer files and shredded many cubic feet of documents. However, the investigation turned up a document indicating that North, with Poindexter's knowledge, had illegally diverted some of the profits from the Iran arms sales to the contras. On November 25, Meese announced his discovery to the press. The President, he said, had not been informed of the diversion of funds, and North and Poindexter were leaving the NSC staff.[58]

The Meese press conference sent shock waves through Washington and across the country. The following day, the administration appointed a three-member commission, headed by former Senator John Tower, to "conduct a comprehensive study of the future role and procedures of the National Security Council staff" and announced that the criminal division of the Justice Department would conduct an inquiry into the diversion of funds from the arms sales.[59] But these efforts were quickly seen to be inadequate. House and Senate leaders decided to form select investigating committees to look jointly into the affair, and under pressure Meese reluctantly agreed to appoint an independent counsel to take the investigation over from the Justice Department. Meanwhile, the House Foreign Affairs committee and the intelligence committees of both houses held hearings, and more information about North's secret operation to support the contras came to light.

On December 1 a *New York Times*-CBS poll showed the effect the scandal had had on the American public. In a single month, Reagan's overall approval rating had dropped from 67 percent to 46 percent—the largest one-month collapse in a president's rating ever recorded. What was more, a vast majority of the country did not believe that Reagan was telling the truth about what he knew of the Iran-contra affair.[60]

After November 25 the goal of the President and all his advisers was to put the scandal behind them, but the goal was not so easy to achieve, for, with the exception of Shultz, none of them seemed to understand what the problem was.

Sometime after Shultz's interview with Lesley Stahl on November 16, Nancy Reagan had decided that the secretary of state was disloyal to her husband and had to go. She also wanted Regan and Poindexter out, because they had failed to protect her husband. As was her practice in such matters, she called her husband's old California friends for help. William Clark, Reagan's former NSC adviser; William French Smith, his former attorney general; Jaquelin Hume, the promoter of strategic defenses; and Senator Pete Wilson responded with calls to Reagan or the press.[61]

Meese, too, felt that Shultz should be fired, and while his investigation continued he and three other ranking administration officials did their best to unseat the secretary of state. On November 23 William Casey wrote the President: "The public pouting of George Shultz, and the failure of the State Department to support what we did inflated the uproar on this matter. If we all stand together and speak out I believe we can put this behind us quickly. . . . You need a new pitcher! A leader instead of a bureaucrat. I urge you to bring in someone like Jeane Kirkpatrick or Paul Laxalt. . . ."[62]

Weinberger did not lobby the President directly, but he was a part of the California network, and he saw the anti-Shultz campaign as an opportunity for himself. After a call from his old friend Bill Clark on Friday the 21st, Weinberger noted in his diary, "Bill Clark . . . also wants me to be the Secretary of State + if so he'd come back as N.S.C. adviser to the President."

On the 25th Weinberger wrote: "Bill Casey—on secure [phone]—thinks Shultz should go to [o]—suggests Kampleman [sic], Scowcroft, Tower or Eagleburger should be NSC head. I suggested Bill Clark—Bill Clark also mentioned Bob Gates and [CIA Deputy Director] John McMahon."

Later that day he added: "[Called] Bill Clark in San Luis Obisbo [sic] —Bill Fr. [French Smith] + Pete Wilson both will call President + urge that he dump Shultz."[63]

That same day, Vice-President Bush added his voice to the chorus. In his tape-recorded diary he noted, "I . . . went in and told the President that I really felt Regan ought to go, Shultz should go, and he ought to get this all behind him in the next couple of months."

Advising the President to fire the only top official who was not implicated in the cover-up was hardly sage counsel, but apparently it accorded with Reagan's feelings about the secretary of state. "The President," Bush reported, "is very unhappy. He keeps worrying about the people at the State Department. And he thinks that Shultz is not backing him."[64]

Donald Regan's initial strategy to deal with the political disaster was to "distance" the President from the affair and lay the blame on the NSC staff. The President, however, refused to cooperate. On November 26 he told Hugh Sidey, the *Time* columnist, that he did not feel in the least "betrayed" by North. "He has a fine record. He is a national hero," he said. "My only criticism was that I wasn't told everything." By Thanksgiving most of Reagan's advisers were urging the President to offer a public explanation and some words of apology. But Reagan continued to maintain that he had never traded arms for hostages and that what he had done was right. Puzzled and aggrieved by the drop in his polls, he blamed the press for the outcry against the initiative.[65]

Then, too, the Iran initiative went on as before. After Poindexter's resignation, the President formally handed control of the negotiations with the Iranians over to Shultz, who insisted there would be no more discussion of arms for hostages. But then, under pressure from Casey, the President reneged on the agreement. In mid-December, Casey was hospitalized with a brain tumor; it was still several weeks before Shultz could gain control over the negotiations.[66]

In the meantime, Weinberger and his allies continued their intrigues against Shultz.

On Thursday, November 27, Thanksgiving, Weinberger noted: "Bill Clark fm San Luis Obisbo [sic]—Bill Casey, Bill Smith, Hume, etc. all calling President + Nancy to urge changes at State—Told Bill my name should not be used— + that I wanted him [Bill] to come east as NSC, etc."[67]

On Sunday the 30th, Weinberger had a conference call with William Clark, William French Smith and Pete Wilson about their hopes for a "change at State," during which Smith said that he had spoken for forty minutes with Nancy Reagan and Wilson promised to call the President. "Bill Casey," Weinberger noted, "says fate of Western world depends on what we do in 72 hours."

On December 18 Weinberger wrote, "Bill Clark in office—says Shultz is losing all credibility."[68]

In fact the reverse was the case, and the campaign to oust Shultz died away. George Bush recorded its passage on December 21: "Given Shultz's public differing with the President, coming down 'on the right side.' You can't make a change there."[69]

By mid-December, Wirthlin's polls were showing that even the Republican Party faithful thought the President should answer questions, take charge and make a clean sweep. In particular they thought he should fire his chief of staff. But Regan, who seemed surprised that anyone would consider him responsible for the actions of the NSC staff, dug his heels in. Now concerned that her husband might be impeached, Mrs. Reagan enlisted the help of Michael Deaver and Stu Spencer, who in turn orchestrated a public and private campaign to persuade the President that Regan must go. However, the President seemed incapable of grasping what had happened and the dangers he faced. The political problem, he insisted, was exaggerated and would be over in a week. "He couldn't confront anything. He was living in a dream world," one senior aide later said.[70] Regan, whose job now depended on Ronald Reagan alone, joined him in this state of denial.

On December 22 Bush noted: "Morning meeting with the President. A certain unreality now—Don and the President, it seems to me. I mention to the President my concern that we did look like arms for hostages, and he reiterated his view that he was convinced he didn't."[71]

Ronald Reagan never really admitted that he ordered the sale of arms for hostages—although, as the independent counsel years later discovered, his own diary for 1985 and 1986 contained numerous entries describing the transactions as they went on.[72] Why he was so determined on the operation therefore remained something of a mystery. Most assumed that he was concerned with the fate of the hostages but did not want to bargain for them publicly, given what had happened to Carter in 1980 and his tough antiterrorist stand. But the explanation that he gave his principal advisers at a meeting on December 7, 1985, was somewhat different.

At that meeting both Weinberger and Shultz argued vehemently against the arms-for-hostages transfers. They came out with different views about how effective their arguments had been, but both noted that, when Weinberger pointed out that the initiative violated the embargo on Iran and the Arms Export Control Act, the President made light of the legal problems involved and jokingly indicated that he was willing to take the heat for the decision. According to Weinberger's notes, Reagan said that he could answer the charges of illegality but couldn't answer the charge that "big, strong President Reagan passed up a chance to free the hostages."[73]

What was at stake for Reagan, in other words, was not the hostages, but his own public image as a tough guy. His bravado about breaking the law was merely a part of the tough-guy act—but McFarlane and Poindexter might well have assumed that he was giving them permission to break laws if necessary and would take responsibility for the consequences.

By March 1987, the Reagan White House had taken on a new complexion. Frank Carlucci, Weinberger's first deputy secretary of defense, had taken over Poindexter's job in December. Bringing in General Colin Powell, Weinberger's former executive assistant, as his deputy, he had completed a housecleaning of the NSC staff. Donald Regan had resigned. The new chief of staff, former senator Howard Baker, was a moderate Republican and an experienced politician who had retired a year earlier as Senate majority leader. In addition, William Casey, fatally ill with brain cancer, had resigned, and William Webster, another moderate Republican who had headed the FBI, had taken over as DCI. By then, too, it was clear that Reagan was not going to be able to put the Iran-contra affair behind him for a very long time.

In the months of December, January and February, there was an interregum, a period of uncertainty, in which some in the administration harbored the illusion that Reagan would magically shed the scandal and others slowly absorbed the full implications of what had occurred. In this period the White House drifted as it were in a Sargasso Sea, with no wind behind it and no one at the helm. The President, though still unrepentant, was depressed by his polls. In early January he had a minor prostate operation, and Mrs. Reagan, citing the authority of an astrologer, refused to allow him to travel or to make speeches other than the State of the Union address. Donald Regan, preoccupied with his own struggle for survival, no longer gave media interviews or insisted that he was in charge. Frank Carlucci, the first thoroughly competent NSC adviser of Reagan's presidency, was in the process of reorganizing the battered NSC staff, attempting to find a way to cope with the rival baronies at Defense and State and trying to understand Ronald Reagan.[74] In this period Weinberger made his move to deploy SDI weapons and to end the ABM Treaty regime.

On December 17, at a time when the NSC staff was more than usually disorganized, Weinberger, accompanied by General Abrahamson and Richard Perle, met with the President and gave him a glowing report on the progress of SDI. Unveiling charts and vu-graphs, the group informed Reagan that the Pentagon was now ready to take the first step towards making his dream of a nuclear-free world a reality: they were ready to begin building the first phase of a defensive system for deployment in the early 1990s.[75]

Nothing was said publicly about the meeting at the time, or for the next few weeks, and Shultz was not informed of it. But in early January, Weinberger began to air the idea of an early deployment both to congressional committees and to the public at large. "I think a firm commitment can be made in the next couple of years to deploy," he told television correspondents on January 7.[76] Testifying before the Senate Armed Services Committee on the 12th, he said that, rather than wait for the perfection of population defenses, the administration might deploy "Phase One" of a defensive system as soon as it could be built.[77] In a speech in Colorado Springs on the 22nd he said, "Today we may be nearing the day when decisions about the deployment of the first phase can be made. We are now seeing opportunities for earlier deployment of the first phase of strategic defenses than we previously thought.... Our bags are packed." He added that the first phase was not designed to protect military assets but rather to be "one piece of an entire system that provides a thoroughly reliable defense for the free world."[78]

Star Wars advocates in the Congress cheered the promise of early deployment, but others on the Hill wondered what Weinberger was up to. The SDIO had been aiming for a development decision in the early 1990s, but now Weinberger was saying that a decision to deploy a "Phase One" system would be made while Reagan was in office and that deployment would begin shortly afterwards. Further, he was claiming that the technical problems had been solved. "Some elements of our research have proved successful beyond the expectations of the most optimistic scientists and engineers," he told his audience in Colorado Springs. "In fact our research has progressed so well that we now have an unprecedented degree of confidence in the feasibility of defense against Soviet missiles—for ourselves and our allies." According to officials, the President was impressed with the results.[79]

In his public remarks Weinberger did not specify what kind of a system he was talking about, but two proposals had recently been made by conservatives close to the SDIO. In December the newly formed George C. Marshall Institute had issued a report, written in part by Robert Jastrow, the Star Wars enthusiast, calling for two thousand satellites, each carrying five interceptor rockets; ten thousand ERIS missiles and three thousand HEDI missiles; and at the end of the month, Lieutenant Colonel Simon P. Worden, who had served as Abrahamson's assistant and was now stationed in the White House science office, published an article in *The National Review* maintaining that by 1995 the U.S. could have a system of several thousand space-based rockets plus a few thousand ground-based missiles with the capacity to disrupt a Soviet first strike at a cost of less than a hundred billion dollars. According to officials, Weinberger had a system of this type in mind.[80]

To Proxmire, Johnston and those others in the Congress who had been following SDI closely, the idea sounded familiar. It sounded in fact like the ballistic-missile boost intercept (BAMBI) concept developed by the Pentagon in the 1950s, and very much like General Daniel O. Graham's High Frontier proposal, which Weinberger had rejected in 1982, and which General Abrahamson had repeatedly dismissed when queries about it came up in the Armed Services Committees. That Weinberger and Abrahamson were now proposing to start building such a system for deployment in the early nineties seemed to suggest a venture more political than technological in nature. And indeed, a week after Weinberger made the announcement, Edwin Meese urged that the administration deploy the first stage of SDI quickly, "so it will be in place and not tampered with by future administrations."[81] A few days later Allen Mense, the chief scientist for the SDIO, gave a similar explanation for early deployment. "Like it or not," he said, "we see a political reality staring us in the face. If we don't come up with something specific, people are not going to let us play in the sandbox for ten years."[82] Asked his opinion of Weinberger's call for deployment, former Defense Secretary Harold Brown said, "It's aimed either at locking in the program or retaining the support of the right wing in Congress."[83]

Congressional Democrats lit into the deployment scheme, as did outside experts, such as Ashton Carter and Richard Garwin.[84] More surprisingly, the plan was only weakly defended by SDIO officials. In December, Abrahamson had admitted that a first partial capability "probably wouldn't even act as a deterrent all by itself." In January, after Weinberger's announcements, Dr. Louis Marquet, now Abrahamson's chief deputy for technology, said it would cost a hundred billion dollars merely to reach the starting point for the production of the necessary equipment for Phase One. As for the Joint Chiefs of Staff, they rejected the whole idea of a near-term deployment. Testifying before the Senate Armed Services Committee in early January, Admiral William Crowe said, "SDI is a research project.... We still have to determine whether it is technically feasible and then whether it is financially possible." He added, "A lot of what I read makes it sound as if SDI is just out sitting in the parking lot. That's not true. . . . It will be some time before the decision is made to begin deployment."[85]

What, then, was Weinberger talking about?

On February 3, the *Washington Post*'s defense correspondent, R. Jeffrey Smith, reported that in an NSPG meeting that day Weinberger would ask the President to authorize detailed planning for the development of a "near-term" ballistic-missile defense and to authorize planning for SDI tests in space that would exceed the limits of the "narrow" interpretation of the ABM Treaty. Secretary Shultz was expected to express strong opposition to both proposals on the grounds that they would be fiscally irresponsible, a disaster on Capitol Hill and destructive of the Geneva negotiations.[86]

Shortly after the meeting, Shultz appeared before the Senate Armed Services Committee. Apparently announcing the results of the meeting, he said that the time was not ripe for a decision on deployment and that he doubted it would be made before the end of the year. However, he said, action might be considered on "certain items" that might have to be launched now in order for a future president to make a deployment decision five, six, or even more years into the future. The President, he said, might wish to shift to the "broad" interpretation of the ABM Treaty sometime soon, but "until then I'll just tell him what I think on the subject." According to a White House spokesman, the President had made no decision at the meeting.[87]

On February 5 Smith reported that Shultz had not directly opposed the "broad" interpretation at the NSPG meeting, but instead had initiated a new study of the ABM Treaty by Abraham Sofaer that was expected to call into question the legality of that interpretation—a study which might take six months to complete.[88]

Shultz, it appeared, had scotched the talk of a deployment, and though he had seemed to give way on the decision to authorize testing beyond the limits of the ABM Treaty—or the treaty as the Soviets and almost everyone outside the administration understood it—he had at least managed to delay the decision. A day later, however, it appeared he had failed to delay it.

On February 6 Gregory Fossedal, an activist for SDI and other conservative causes, published a portion of the minutes of the February 3 meeting in the *Washington Times* under the headline "NSC Minutes Show President Leaning to SDI Deployment." The minutes had clearly been leaked by a Weinberger supporter. Consisting mainly of indirect quotes, they read as follows.[89]

> WEINBERGER: Do we want to deploy? The answer, obviously, is yes. Nothing comprehensive is available now, but we should deploy something integral to the whole system.

Carlucci: Incremental deployment is correct, militarily and strategically. Is it politically?

Admiral Crowe: "The chiefs support SDI and support phased deployment. But we don't have enough in hand to decide now."

Weinberger: "But we need to make some decisions now."

Shultz: A decision is not yet appropriate.

Weinberger: "We've made great progress for kinetic kill vehicles for boost phase. Do we deploy incrementally or all at once?" Let's deploy 60 vehicles that can destroy 2,000 warheads. Delta 181 will test if the missiles can be hit. If so, we could deploy by 1993.

Shultz: 1993 "is Abe's view" [a reference to General Abrahamson.] Others are more skeptical. Add a couple of years to that date.

Weinberger: Question is: "Do we deploy incrementally? Go to the LCI? [That is, the "broad," or what Weinberger had taken to calling the "legally correct," interpretation of the ABM Treaty] Later we could go with lasers, particle beams and so forth. But we need a specific program.... We need the phased deployment because you can't do it all at once." (Reminds president of the December briefing on phased deployment.) "It's an area defense, not a point defense, and it's stabilizing."

Shultz: "I didn't know we made decisions in December, but I talked to Abe twice, and all the chiefs individually and am impressed by what I heard." Notes that "the chiefs have been skeptical about going back on the ABM treaty." Don't start on phase 1 unless "you have some idea on where you're going beyond. I agree with Crowe that we're not in a position to confront the decision."

Reagan inquires about Soviet reaction.

Shultz: "It's hard to say what the Soviets would do." There have been no indications from Geneva, and we should feel them out. The problem with deployment even for 1993 is that some tests (Delta 181) require broad interpretation of the ABM treaty, or LCI.

Weinberger: The Soviets have an agenda.... They want to prohibit something. "We shouldn't debate with the Soviets what can and can't be prohibited."

Shultz: "We can see what we can find out, if we can find it, then negotiate with the Soviet Union."

Reagan: "Why don't we just go ahead on the assumption that this is what we're doing and it's right.... We're not going nearly as far as them." (Notes a magazine article on the Soviet "star wars" program.) "Don't ask the Soviets. Tell them." The United States can move ahead. "I'll say I've reevaluated. I see the price tag, and I'm willing to pay."

Apparently Reagan wanted to go ahead with deployment, or testing, or both, and he didn't care what the Soviets thought.

An uproar ensued. That day, a Friday, the British foreign secretary, Geoffrey Howe, sent a message that his government would not support either "near-term" SDI development or the "broad" interpretation of the treaty. More ominously, Senator Sam Nunn wrote the President that if the administration decided to reinterpret the ABM Treaty without the consent of NATO and the Congress the consequences would be "extremely adverse." The decision, he wrote, would be taken on Capitol Hill "as the end of arms control under your administration"; it would cause "much deeper SDI [budget] cuts than would otherwise occur," and it would provoke "a Constitutional confrontation of profound dimensions."[90]

On Sunday, February 8, Shultz appeared on ABC's *This Week With David Brinkley* and indicated that he now accepted the need to adopt a more permissive interpretation of the ABM Treaty in order to test key elements of the SDI program. It was clear, he said, that, "given the progress that has been made, you'd be able to pursue the program much more effectively—and perhaps only—if a different pattern of testing is permitted." But the administration, he promised, would not adopt the "broad" interpretation until it had consulted with Congress and the NATO allies.[91]

On Tuesday, February 10, the President met with Shultz, Weinberger and his senior arms-control advisers. The upshot of the meeting, officials later said, was a series of decisions: the President would direct the Defense Department to produce a detailed list of missile-defense experiments it would conduct under the "broad" interpretation of the ABM Treaty; he would formally authorize the State Department to go ahead with an additional analysis of the legal justification of that interpretation; the administration would put off a final decision on the "broad" interpretation until after consultations with the Congress and the Allies, but the Soviet Union would not be consulted. "We don't think any further negotiations are necessary," Shultz said. "Rather, we will proceed on the basis of what we think [the treaty] says."[92]

These statements only increased the uproar. Several influential senators and congressmen joined Nunn in warning the administration against the adoption of the "broad" interpretation, and before the week was out formal protests were lodged by Britain, West Germany, Canada, Japan and the Soviet Union.[93]

What the administration was planning was not clear to reporters, but certainly it had little to do with what officials were talking about.

According to official statements and the minutes of the February 3 meeting, Weinberger had attempted to persuade the President to make a decision to deploy his "Phase One" system. He had talked about deploying sixty kinetic-kill vehicles in space "that can destroy 2,000 warheads" and a second phase of deployment involving "lasers, particle beams and so forth." But this was nonsense. In the first place, sixty orbiting hit-to-kill vehicles could hardly destroy two thousand warheads, and in the second there was nothing to deploy, and everyone in the room, with the possible exception of the President, knew that. As Crowe had told the Armed Services Committee, SDI was a research program, and even a decision to *develop* "first-phase" defenses lay some years into the future.[94]

Then, too, according to officials, Weinberger and Shultz thought it necessary to adopt the "broad" interpretation of the ABM Treaty in order to permit advanced testing of SDI technologies. In the February 3 meeting, Shultz said that the problem with deployment even for 1993 was that some tests (such as Delta 181) required the broad interpretation of the ABM Treaty. Yet in 1985 the Congress had required the SDIO to certify that all SDI tests complied with the traditional interpretation of the treaty, and since then all the scheduled tests, including Delta 181—which involved launching sensors to observe ballistic-missile launches from space—had been designed to be compliant with the treaty. Shultz certainly knew this.[95] Yet four days after the meeting he said that the program required "a different pattern of testing" in order to be effective—and thus the need for the "broad" interpretation. Both he and Weinberger strongly implied that the SDIO was ready to go forward with non-compliant tests in order to turn "Phase One" into a reality. But this was not the case either. Interviewed by R. Jeffrey Smith a few days later, Colonel Raymond Ross, the director of the SDIO kinetic-energy weapons program, said that research in KEWs could profitably continue for three years without bumping up against the ABM Treaty limits.[96] Other SDIO scientists and technical experts told Smith that the President's request for a list of tests to be conducted under the "broad" interpretation could not be fulfilled quickly, because there had as yet been no assessment of the need. They expressed concern that a push for accelerated testing would distort their research programs and create a damaging political backlash.[97]

There was yet another piece that did not fit the picture. The "broad" interpretation, as Abraham Sofaer had defined it in the fall of 1985, permitted the development and the space-testing of weapons based on "other physical principles." But Weinberger's "Phase One" involved kinetic-energy weapons, whereas weapons based on "other physical principles" were understood to be exotics—laser weapons and so forth—none of which had been invented yet. The "broad" interpretation was thus irrelevant to any conceivable SDI test.[98]

When reporters inquired about this matter, senior Pentagon officials asserted that the SDI's kinetic-energy weapons were based on "other physical principles." State Department experts, lawyers for the Arms Control and Disarmament Agency and negotiators of the ABM Treaty scoffed at the idea. After all, kinetic-energy weapons had existed from the time the first stone was thrown, and the BAMBI program was more than a decade old by the time the ABM Treaty was signed. Furthermore, just the previous spring, General Abrahamson had maintained that kinetic-energy weapons were not exotic technologies. "It's a nutty argument," one State Department official said of the Pentagon's contention; "the whole thing is specious in the extreme."[99]

But redefining kinetic-energy weapons as exotics was no more specious than the "broad" interpretation itself, and no more of a fiction than the promise of a defense that would render ballistic missiles obsolete. Since 1983 little that high administration officials said about SDI had anything to do with reality. In this latest go-round, Weinberger seemed to be urging Reagan to make a decision about deployment and non-compliant testing, but what he was really doing was urging the President to speak about these things.

Since January, Weinberger and his aides had shown an imaginative streak far richer than most would have thought they possessed. In 1985 they had tried to destroy the ABM Treaty with the "broad" interpretation, but McFarlane's announcement was so sudden and so bald that the maneuver failed. This time the preparations were far more elaborate: Weinberger and Abrahamson's reports of "amazing progress" in SDI, Weinberger's dramatic announcement that an SDI system would soon be ready for deployment and his call for a new pattern of testing to make sure the system worked. The presentation was fabulous, in the original sense of that word, and it might have been more fabulous had the President designed the rhetoric himself.

Weinberger failed to induce the President to talk about deployment because Carlucci refused to let him go behind Shultz's back, and the Chiefs put a public damper on the whole idea.[100] But with the help of the leaked minutes of the February 3 meeting, he did move Shultz one step further into the world beyond the looking-glass. In 1985 Shultz had agreed that the "broad" interpretation was "legally correct"; now he was calling for the "broad" interpretation to accommodate the testing necessary to progress in the SDI program. That was enough for Weinberger's purposes.

Of course, the SDIO was in no position to conduct tests that fit the "broad," rather than the "narrow," interpretation, but, then, reality made little difference to the outcome. All the administration had to do was to *call* any given test, such as Delta 181, non-compliant. Who, after all, could say for sure that a reconfigured Delta 181 test was compliant if Weinberger and Abrahamson said it was not? At that point the Soviets would have to react; the ABM Treaty as a whole would be called into question; arms control would be doomed, and SDI would have to be put on the track towards some form of deployment.

• • •

On February 4 Shultz had one of his regularly scheduled meetings with Reagan. The President, he writes, was "far more subdued and realistic than Cap" and "seemed to realize that Weinberger's zeal . . . had needlessly stirred up a potentially devastating resistance to the entire SDI program." Apparently Reagan had given his usual he-man response to Weinberger's challenge at the February 3 meeting, but under Shultz's coaching he thought better of it.[101]

Shultz did not advise the President to reject the "broad" interpretation—that die had already been cast—but he had a strategy for returning the administration to the traditional, and generally accepted, interpretation of the treaty. The strategy was Nitze's.

Since Reykjavik, Nitze had been at work on a means of reconciling the U.S. and Soviet positions on SDI. In the wake of the summit the Soviets had signaled that they would drop Gorbachev's stark demand that all testing be confined to the laboratory; they proposed setting an "experts group" to conduct talks about what forms of development and testing should be permitted or prohibited under the ABM Treaty. The idea was to forge an agreement on the technical issues not dealt with by the treaty negotiators—and to make sure that the U.S. interpreted the treaty as they did. Nitze favored such talks. The two sides, he said, must "figure out a way to fill in the holes in the treaty . . . to fix it where it needs fixing . . . to make it whole . . . to perfect it." Clearly this meant filling the hole he himself had helped to dig in the fall of 1985, since a formal agreement with the Soviets on the meaning of the treaty would make the "broad" interpretation a dead letter. On January 22, while Weinberger was speaking of early deployment in Colorado Springs, Nitze was talking informally with Gorbachev's science adviser, Evgeny Velikhov, in the State Department about such arcane issues as establishing parameters for the brightness of lasers.[102]

Coming to terms with the Soviets was, however, only one part of the battle. The other part was dealing with Weinberger and his allies, who kept insisting that the "broad" interpretation was legally correct. Nitze had a plan for that as well.

Before McFarlane announced the reinterpretation on October 11, 1985, Judge Sofaer had based his claims for the reinterpretation on his analysis of the treaty language and a study, assisted by Nitze, of the sheaves of classified U.S.-government memoranda he called "the negotiating record." However, by the canons of international law, the meaning of a treaty depends first on its language and, if that is disputed, on subsequent practice of the parties—that is, their statements as well as their actions in regard to the treaty. Only if the practice is unclear is the negotiating record invoked, and in the United States, where the Senate must give its consent to all treaties, the probative part of the negotiating record is what the executive branch tells the Senate it has agreed to. Sofaer had initially ignored the ratification record and the subsequent statements of the parties, but when testifying before the Congress in late October and November 1985, he claimed that both records were generally consistent with the "broad" interpretation. Nitze did not support him in these claims—he was not called upon to do so—but at the request of the Foreign Affairs Committee, Sofaer prepared a detailed memorandum arguing his case and later published it in the *Harvard Law Review.* This was a mistake, for, unlike the negotiating memoranda, the record of subsequent practice and the ratification proceedings before the Senate were in the public domain, and Nitze, among others, knew that his analysis of these records could not stand up to scrutiny.[103]

In his account of the controversy over the ABM Treaty in early 1987, Nitze, in his memoir, tells us that the "broad" interpretation "might indeed" be fully justified based on the negotiating record, but that the ratification record supported the "narrow" interpretation. He then makes the following argument. Because Congress had approved the treaty based on that record, the "narrow" interpretation had become the law of the land—even if the Soviets did not recognize it as binding upon themselves. The President, he continues, has the "right to interpret treaties" but the "practical consideration" was that the Congress holds the purse strings and could cause an "unmanageable stalemate." This consideration, Nitze tells us, led him to recommend that the President authorize additional studies of the ratification record and on subsequent practice of the parties and consult with Congress before making any decision to implement the "broad" interpretation.[104] In other words, Sofaer would have to admit that he was wrong about everything except the negotiating record.

Apparently Shultz and Sofaer adopted Nitze's strategy, for on February 3 Shultz went into the NSPG meeting with a memorandum on the ratification record and on subsequent practice composed by Nitze and Sofaer. According to a senior State Department official, the memo "strongly suggested" that both the U.S. and the Soviet Union had endorsed and followed the narrow interpretation, since the treaty was signed. There was, Shultz later said, "a large and difficult record" on the ABM Treaty that would be shared with Congress, and it was "important to reach a broadly supported interpretation of what we're dealing with."[105]

From Nitze's memoir it would seem that he and Shultz hoped that the Congress would accept the notion that the "narrow," or traditional, interpretation of the treaty was legally binding on the United States, though not on the Soviet Union, while they worked out an agreement that would bind the Soviets. The idea, and the reasoning behind it, however, involved so many novelties in international and constitutional law—among them the proposition that the President had the right to interpret treaties just as he saw fit—that it is possible they merely hoped that the Congress would save the administration from itself. In any case, the plan was scotched when the minutes of the February 3 meeting were leaked and it appeared that Reagan had come out for deployment, or non-compliant testing, or both, and no negotiations with the Soviets over the meaning of the ABM Treaty. With the President's position thus firmly fixed, Sofaer could not go to the Congress and say that the "broad" interpretation was illegal under U.S. law.

After February 6 all Shultz could do was to attempt to put the final decision on the "broad" interpretation off into the indefinite future. The hawks, however, refused to cooperate. Shultz had proposed that Sofaer be given six months to complete his study, but Meese, after a cursory examination of the treaty, declared that the "broad" interpretation was correct and insisted that the study couldn't possibly take that long. Sofaer was given three months.[106] The form the consultations with the Congress would take was not decided upon, but consultation with the Allies was quickly defined as informing the Europeans of the American decision. Adelman, who had grown used to dismissing the uproar from abroad, publicly said that, though the Allies had made clear their disapproval of the reinterpretation, their views would not count for much, because they did not have access to the negotiating record and were not qualified to interpret the treaty. When Shultz asked that Nitze be sent to talk with the Allies, Weinberger insisted that Perle accompany him. Meanwhile, Max Kampelman, the chief U.S. negotiator in Geneva, was instructed not to talk with the Soviets about any constraints on SDI that would impinge upon the "broad" interpretation.[107]

Some congressional Democrats favored a compromise with the administration. On February 28 Senators Al Gore and Claiborne Pell, on a visit to the Geneva talks, went so far as to work out a tentative agreement with Nitze, Kampelman and Perle. The administration would refrain from carrying out non-compliant SDI tests for a year and would make a commitment to arms control, in exchange for which the Senate would support a "respectable" level of funding for SDI research and forgo legislation locking in the "narrow" interpretation. Nitze thought they had a deal, but back in Washington, Weinberger dismissed it and Gore failed to sell it to his Democratic colleagues.[108]

Sam Nunn, Carl Levin and a number of other Senate Democrats were in no more of a mood for compromise than the hawks. The administration had reneged too many times before on informal pacts with the Congress over arms control; the Iran-contra affair had destroyed the modicum of trust that was left, and there was a matter of constitutional principle involved. By the end of February the Senate Judiciary Committee and the Committee on Foreign Relations had drafted a bill on interpretation of the ABM Treaty and scheduled joint hearings to begin on March 11. Nunn had scheduled a series of floor speeches to begin the same day.

On February 6, when the minutes of the February 3 meeting appeared, Nunn was as angry as his aides had ever seen him. Sam Nunn was not an ABM Treaty fundamentalist. Given a Soviet challenge to the treaty or the promise of an ABM weapon that would make the country more secure, he would have considered abrogating the treaty. But he was a true believer in the constitutional separation of powers, and for the administration to reinterpret the treaty unilaterally seemed to him a fundamental challenge to the power of the Senate. By that time he had been involved with the issue for over a year.[109]

In the fall of 1985, after Sofaer testified on the reinterpretation to the Senate Armed Services Committee, Nunn had asked the State Department to provide the Senate with classified documents that Sofaer had assembled and was calling "the negotiating record."[110] His request was rebuffed, but he persisted, making one request after another. Finally, on August 6, 1986, shortly after the administration incorporated the "broad" interpretation into its START negotiating position, Secretary Shultz released the documents to the Senate along with a new and expanded Sofaer study arguing for the reinterpretation.[111] The documents, all highly classified, were stored in room S407, a windowless room under the dome of the Capitol to which only senators and six designated staff members had access. Nunn delegated Robert Bell, an arms-control specialist and one of his chief aides on the Armed Services Committee, to review them. This was no small task, for there were thousands of pages of memoranda and cables between the negotiators in Geneva and officials in Washington. It took Bell almost six months to read and analyze the documents. What he found was that Sofaer's claims about the negotiating record were virtually groundless.[112]

In the meantime, Nunn and his colleague Carl Levin did their own research on the ratification proceedings and discovered that the claims Sofaer had made in his 1985 memorandum and repeated in his *Harvard Law Review* article were based on flagrant misrepresentations of the record.[113] In December 1986 Senator Levin sent Shultz a detailed critique of Sofaer's analysis.[114] Shultz responded the same day with a letter defending the work of the legal adviser. His subsequent promise that Sofaer would do a new study of the ratification record, however, suggested that Levin's critique had made an impression.[115] But then the minutes of the February 3 meeting were leaked. Nunn fired off a letter that made no mention of deploying or testing SDI weapons; it spoke only of the ABM Treaty reinterpretation and the constitutional crisis it would provoke. To Nunn it was obvious what the administration was after.

On March 9, two days before Nunn was to give his first speech before the Senate on the reinterpretation, Sofaer sent him a letter saying that the memorandum on the ratification record he had written in October 1985 "did not provide a complete portrayal of the ratification proceedings" and that he "did not review this material personally." He admitted that some statements in the ratification record might "have a bearing on the President's obligations to the Senate," but maintained that "the U.S. internal ratification process cannot by itself create international obligations under the Treaty." He promised a fuller study by the end of April.[116]

Sofaer's letter struck Nunn as nothing short of scandalous. In 1985 the legal adviser had made statements about the ratification record that he could fairly easily have determined were false. He had published these statements in the *Harvard Law Review,* and now, more than a year later, he was backing off. But he had not thought better of the "broad" interpretation. Instead he claimed that the interpretation given to the Senate had no bearing on the meaning of the treaty with the Soviet Union—thus making explicit the constitutional issue that had been implicit in his initial argument about the negotiating record.

Shultz, according to State Department sources, had been "very concerned" about Nunn's letter and had commented, "We should respond to Nunn with the attention his position merits and not be shooting off from the hip."[117] But because of the leaked minutes of the February 3 meeting, he and Sofaer had no way to pull back from the "broad" interpretation, and no way to appease Nunn.

On March 11, 12 and 13 Nunn made successive speeches on the Senate floor and submitted two lengthy reports, one on the ratification record, the other a classified study of the negotiating record.[118] The speeches were masterworks of textual analysis and legal argument: elegant, precise and comprehensive. In the first two, Nunn demonstrated that Sofaer's claims about the ratification proceedings and the subsequent practice of the United States rested on a total misrepresentation of the record. Sofaer, he showed, had simply omitted all the evidence that supported the traditional interpretation of the treaty, sometimes by dint of quoting only one side of a dialogue or only half of a sentence. Having failed to identify a single statement that explicitly supported the "broad" interpretation, Sofaer had built his case on statements by Nixon-administration officials that did not spell out the entirety of the traditional interpretation and on distortions of the text. In the third speech, Nunn summarized the classified analysis he had made of the negotiating record. Judge Sofaer, he said, had identified some ambiguities in the vast assemblage of memoranda, but these ambiguities were not "of sufficient magnitude to demonstrate that the Nixon administration reached one agreement with the Soviets and then presented a different one to the Senate." Further, he said, Sofaer had ignored the "substantial and credible" evidence that the Soviets agreed to the traditional interpretation of the treaty.[119]

Having dismantled Sofaer's factual claims, Nunn examined the issues Sofaer had raised with his claim that the ratification record could be disregarded because it had "absolutely no standing with the Soviets." This novel doctrine, he said, implied that the executive branch was free to reach secret understandings with other governments, or to mislead the Senate about the meaning of a treaty. In either case it was a direct challenge to the treaty-making power of the Senate under the Constitution and the doctrine of checks and balances. Further, if a president could maintain that a treaty meant one thing before ratification and afterwards insist it meant something else, the United States could not make treaties, for the Senate could hardly ask the public to support a treaty if the executive branch deemed formal representations by senior officials irrelevant as to its meaning. If the administration persisted in this line of argument, Nunn warned, it would create a constitutional confrontation that would go far beyond the ABM Treaty; it would also create a backlash in which the Congress might use its power of the purse and its power to raise and support armies to restore the original meaning of the treaty.[120]

Nunn's speeches caused a major stir in Congress and in Washington generally. Knowing Nunn, his colleagues had expected a trenchant critique, but the exhaustiveness of Nunn's analysis, and the devastation he had wrought on the administration's case, far exceeded all expectations. The performance was a tour de force: nothing like it had been heard in the Senate for many years. Nunn "savaged" Sofaer's arguments, a *Washington Post* editorial reported, adding, "The administration has lost for good the legal basis" for the "broad" interpretation.[121]

The administration had lost much more than a legal argument. According to congressional leaders, Republicans as well as Democrats, Nunn's speeches had reshaped not only the debate on the ABM Treaty but the politics of SDI. Nunn's case for the traditional interpretation "sets SDI back considerably and delays the decision-making well into the next administration," Representative Jack Kemp acknowledged. "The bottom line is that [the President] will have to adhere to the traditional interpretation or see SDI funding cut dramatically from current levels," Carl Levin said. Senator John Warner, the ranking Republican on the Armed Services Committee, observed that Nunn's "most scholarly" study had helped to crystallize congressional skepticism about SDI. Senator Warren Rudman, another Republican member of the committee, queried the purpose of the SDI program: "The question is whether it's possible to deploy a feasible system in the near future . . . and I think the answer is no. So why borrow trouble by pushing for the unattainable?" Senator John Chafee, a moderate Republican from Rhode Island, said that he was "shocked" and "horrified" by Sofaer's admission that his study of the ratification record was flawed, adding, "It's going to make anyone take a look at anything they say" on arms control.[122]

In mid-April, Bob Dole, the Senate minority leader, organized a Republican counter-offensive, and over the course of ten days eighteen GOP senators paraded onto the Senate floor to challenge Nunn's arguments. The effort, however, backfired. In the first place, none of the eighteen attempted to refute Nunn's analysis of the reinterpretation: they merely denounced it as legal sophistry whose real aim was to "kill" SDI. Their inability to find flaws in the analysis made other Republicans take Nunn's argument about the administration's challenge to the treaty-making powers of the Senate more seriously. In the second place, the eighteen Republicans did not agree among themselves. At one end of the spectrum, Senator Lugar urged the Congress and the White House to adopt an informal agreement to retain the "narrow" interpretation and to support a "well-funded SDI program"; at the other end, Senator Jesse Helms called for the abrogation of the ABM Treaty and the deployment of an anti-missile system.[123] The Republican Party was split over SDI.

Nunn had hoped to convince the administration to make an official declaration of support for the traditional interpretation of the treaty and for the constitutional principle that the Senate had a role in interpreting treaties. In this he was unsuccessful. According to Nitze, Howard Baker, the new chief of staff, tried to get the President to work out a compromise with Nunn and his colleagues, but the President refused. "I suspected that Baker had found the President a much more determined and forceful man than he had anticipated," Nitze writes.[124] Shultz, who knew the President better than Baker did, apparently made no attempt to change the President's mind on this point. Reagan was obdurate about positions he had taken in public: he would never admit that he had sold arms for hostages; he would never admit he had increased taxes; and he would not take back what was perceived as his endorsement of the "broad" interpretation at the February 3 meeting.

For Nunn the only appropriate response lay in the passage of the legislation proposed by the Judiciary and Foreign Relations Committees: a binding resolution affirming the traditional interpretation of the ABM Treaty and the treaty-making power of the Senate. But since Sofaer did not present his study on subsequent practice until September, there was a delay. In the meantime, Nunn joined Levin in sponsoring an amendment to the defense-appropriations bill prohibiting funds for SDI tests that violated the traditional interpretation of the ABM Treaty for the two remaining years of the Reagan administration.* The issue, as they knew, was as much a matter of perception as of reality. The amendment not only precluded an actual violation of the treaty but prevented Weinberger from asserting that a given test had exceeded the limits of the "narrow" but not the "broad" interpretation. The amendment passed with the defense bill in the fall, and it preserved the ABM Treaty.†

* Nunn was celebrated by the arms-control community until, at the Arms Control Association dinner in early 1988, he proposed what he called an accidental launch-protection system (ALPS), a land-based ABM defense against a Soviet missile fired by mistake. ALPS was to be ABM Treaty–compliant, but arms controllers saw it as the thin end of the wedge that would lead to a national missile defense. Why he made the proposal puzzled many, for the Pentagon judged the Soviet system of safeguards excellent and the possibility of an accidental launch extremely low. Possibly he was simply trying to climb down off the pedestal the Arms Control Association had put him on. In any case, he soon let the idea drop.

† The SDIO could violate the ABM Treaty in ways which had nothing to do with the "broad" interpretation. It could, for example, test a component of an ABM system. It was this consideration that led to the initial congressional stricture that SDI be treaty-compliant.

On March 19, 1987, the week after Sam Nunn made his speeches, Douglas Waller and Jim Bruce produced a second detailed review of the SDI program for Senators Proxmire and Johnston. The study, which appeared just a year after the first, caused consternation in the Congress.

Interviewing SDIO officials in January and February, Waller and Bruce had been assured that the SDIO was still researching the feasibility of "effective" strategic defenses for a development decision in the mid-1990s. According to officials, the program was proceeding as it had in the past, with funding spread out over near- and far-term weapons technologies. In looking through the various program budgets, however, Waller and Bruce discovered that in December the program as a whole had been abruptly redirected towards the near-term technologies. The previous year, the funding emphasis had been on lasers and other exotics, as opposed to kinetic-energy weapons; in the fall of 1986, SDIO officials, faced with budgetary constraints, had actually proposed to cut the KEW budget in the next fiscal year. But after the budgets were revised, the new figures showed a hefty increase for kinetic-energy weapons in fiscal 1987 and an increase in fiscal 1988 that would triple the funding for these weapons.[125] On the other hand, funding for exotic weaponry showed a comparative decline, as did funding for experimental sensor technologies for mid-course interception. What was more, the funding within certain programs had shifted to the achievement of short- over long-term goals. In the ground-based interceptor program, for example, money had been moved from advanced technological research into near-term validation experiments.[126]

Program managers insisted that these changes were occasioned by congressional budget cuts and had nothing to do with any plans for development or deployment. Yet there was one fact that could not be explained in this fashion: the new budgets showed major sums allocated for a heavy-lift launch vehicle, or "space truck"—$110 million in fiscal 1987, and $434 million in fiscal 1988. In the past, SDIO officials had maintained that a concerted effort to solve the problem of lifting millions of pounds of weaponry into orbit every year should wait until the larger challenge of developing the weaponry was met. But now they were asking contractors to design a heavy-lift launch vehicle that would be ready to go by the mid-1990s, even though they could not make the planned cost reductions by that time.[127]

More interesting still, there was now a "black" program in the SDIO, a program so secret that only a few members of Congress would be allowed to review it, if they knew of its existence. The program, Waller and Bruce discovered, was a study laying out a preliminary, or reference, architecture for a strategic-defense system to be deployed in the mid-1990s. The architecture, as it was described to them, looked nothing like the design concepts the SDIO had been working on when the goal was 80- or 90-percent effectiveness. Rather than a plan for tens of thousands of weapons, most of them based in space, it was a blueprint for four hundred to a thousand ground-based interceptors and a token deployment of space-based missiles.[128]

Weinberger and Abrahamson, it appeared, were working on a plan for an early deployment of strategic defenses, even though they had failed to persuade the President to come out for a deployment.

Waller and Bruce very much doubted that the SDIO could deliver on the plan for a deployment by the mid-1990s: the technical hurdles remained formidable even for the weapons envisaged, and according to one source, the reason the reference architecture had been put "in the black" was that it was so immature it could not stand close scrutiny.[129] In their view, what Weinberger and Abrahamson could do was to begin a development program that would inexorably lead to some form of deployment at some point in the future. Congress could require the administration to keep SDI testing within the limits of the ABM Treaty, but it was ill-equipped to prevent the SDIO from moving any particular piece of technology into development. And it was a well-known rule that once any weapons system went into development—once its managers began to "bend metal" and to spend serious money—political and bureaucratic pressures would mount to keep the program going. It was this prospect which alarmed Proxmire, Johnston and many others in the Congress.

The senators were, however, not alone in their anxiety. The reorientation of the SDI program was even more worrisome to the Joint Chiefs of Staff.

As an institution, the JCS bore a great deal of responsibility for the SDI program. In 1983 Admiral Watkins and his colleagues had promoted a well-advertised strategic-defense initiative as an answer to the freeze movement and to their embarrassment over their inability to base the MX missile in an acceptable fashion. They did not object when the President promised that the initiative would make nuclear missiles obsolete, and the rhetoric served their purposes: the freeze movement died away, the MX missiles were built and all the controversial strategic programs they had pressed for, including the B-1 and B-2 bombers, continued unhampered by public protest. In 1984 they did not fight to put SDI under their own control, and later they left it to Nitze to establish responsible military criteria for deployment. As a research program SDI had given the services everything they wanted, including support for their own anti-missile research and a potential bargaining chip in the START negotiations. But then, like some genie released from a bottle, it began to get out of hand.

Appointed chairman of the Joint Chiefs in June 1985, after all the major decisions about the SDI program had been taken, Admiral William Crowe had for a year or so looked askance at the program and at its director.

General Abrahamson, Crowe tells us in his memoir, had come to the SDIO with a superb record as a program manager; he was a fine technician and a powerful advocate, but he had come to believe that his job was not just to run the SDI program but to sell it as well. Abrahamson reported directly to Weinberger, but Crowe would often sit in on his briefings, as would General Robert Herres, the vice-chair of the Joint Chiefs and a former head of the U.S. Space Command, who had considerable expertise in SDI technologies. On these occasions, Crowe writes, there was always an "upbeat atmosphere" in the secretary's office, and Abrahamson, playing to a friendly audience, would exude optimism and speak of the tests that worked but not of those that failed. Herres would always ask a few hard questions to try to keep the enthusiasm at least partly in check, but Weinberger and his policy advisers would make it clear that they did not want to hear them and that they thought Herres the conduit for the "negative" views of the Chiefs.[130]

This is a nice scene, and doubtless it was played out in just this fashion, even though Weinberger's top policy advisers, Fred Iklé and Richard Perle, had no more faith in a space-based SDI system than did the JCS.

In what can be read as an attempt to take Abrahamson to the woodshed for these slanted briefings, Crowe invited him to brief the Chiefs and their specialists in "a more neutral setting": the secure inner sanctum of the Pentagon, known as the Tank. These sessions, he writes, bore little resemblance to what went on in Weinberger's office in that the chiefs and the specialists would take "vigorous exception" to much of what the SDI director said. At some point the Chiefs stopped relying upon Abrahamson's reports and invited scientists working on the program to tell them what was actually going on.

Crowe of course understood that Abrahamson was not the real source of the problem. "To put the best face on it," he writes, "we knew that Abrahamson himself was under great pressure from the advocates to put developments in the most optimistic light. I complained to Weinberger about this, but he just sort of brushed me off."[131]

According to Crowe, Weinberger saw to it that the President received only the most encouraging news about SDI. Instead of presenting information about the program at NSPG meetings, Weinberger would set up special meetings with the President in which he and his key advisers would hype test results and exaggerate the progress being made. Apparently they believed that the President could not be given a fair and balanced picture of the program, lest his enthusiasm for it flag.

Crowe sometimes attended these briefings, and on one occasion, he heard the secretary of defense, after announcing some recent test results, say, "Mr. President, your dream is here."

"I thought," Crowe writes, "I was going to choke."[132]

In 1986 conservatives in and out of government began calling for an SDI deployment. The advocates, Crowe writes, were determined to get the nation committed before the public lost interest and SDI disappeared like "a shooting star" into the night. They did not seem to care much about the cost, and they did not seem to care that the preliminary research had not been done. Indeed, Crowe writes, they seemed afraid that "in doing the research we might even discover that a space-based missile defense was not technically feasible. And they did not want that to happen: the political and military stakes were far too high."[133]

When Weinberger himself began to call for early deployment in January 1987, Crowe did something JCS chairmen rarely do to their secretaries of defense: he flatly contradicted him in public, telling the Congress in so many words that there was nothing to deploy. When the issue of the ABM Treaty came up, he ignored the rhetoric about the "broad" interpretation and told the President that abandoning the ABM Treaty would prove more advantageous to the Soviet Union than to the United States. In response to the reorientation of the SDI program and the possibility that Weinberger and Abrahamson would force some SDI technology into premature development, Crowe did two things. In public he warned that the huge expense of developing SDI weapons would completely unbalance U.S. military forces. Privately he pressed Weinberger and Abrahamson to bring the "Phase One" concept into conformity with the procedures of the Defense Acquisitions Board.[134]

The Defense Acquisitions Board is, as its name suggests, the panel which reviews new weapons systems for the Pentagon. Composed of senior military officers from all the armed services and the JCS, the DAB subjects all programs to a detailed review in a series of steps, known as "milestones," from their initial design stages to full-scale development. As a first step, the Chiefs define an "operational requirement"—that is, they make a statement attesting to the need for a weapon that can perform certain specified tasks. As a part of the DAB process, the Chiefs can call upon the Defense Science Board, the senior scientific advisory group to the Pentagon, to review the program.

Having managed other weapons programs in the past, Abrahamson saw the entry into the DAB process as a way to advance his deployment scheme and the SDI program generally. He believed it would give SDI more legitimacy in the Pentagon and help him raise funds from Congress.[135] Thus, after some fencing with Weinberger, Crowe succeeded in gaining his end.

The news that Abrahamson's deployment concept would be going into the DAB process set off alarm signals in the Congress. In June, Senator Gore wrote the DAB chairman seeking his assurance that "Congress will not . . . be suddenly confronted with a sea change in SDI, moving it from a research program to a weapons system on the way to development."[136] Gore's concern was understandable, but by persuading Weinberger and Abrahamson to accept the DAB process, the Chiefs, who formerly had no control over the SDI program, gained jurisdiction over the development of any SDI weapon.

Taking their first step in the DAB process, the JCS created a "requirement" for a system that could stop 30 percent of a limited "first-wave" Soviet attack. In their view this was the minimum capability a defense would have to have in order to make any contribution to deterrence. The SDIO then came up with a "Phase One" architecture to meet that requirement. In June, Abrahamson testified that "Phase One" would be made up of hundreds of space-based battle stations and hundreds, or thousands, of ground-based interceptors; deployment could begin in 1994, and the total cost would be forty to sixty billion dollars. "Phase One," he said, would protect only a limited number of military installations, not cities, but it could later be supplemented by more effective defenses.

After the many months of talk about an SDI deployment, there was for the first time a specific plan on paper for outsiders to look at. And it did not look like much. The panel of the Defense Science Board which first examined it found it less an architecture than a list of components, and so "sketchy" that neither level of effectiveness nor cost could be determined from it. The panel recommended that the DAB withhold its approval for the next year or two, or until the SDIO filled in the substantial "gaps in system design and key technologies."[137]

The recommendation was not followed, because the chairman of the Defense Science Board panel, apparently under political pressure to keep "the President's program" alive, decided to remove the most devastating criticisms from the report and to pass the "Phase One" architecture on to the DAB.[138] The architecture passed its first milestone in September, and SDI advocates cheered. "With adequate funding for the SDI program, we could confidently anticipate that phased deployment could begin as early as 1994 or 1995," Weinberger wrote in an Op Ed piece for the *New York Times.* "In my view, no technical road blocks stand in the way."[139]

Yet "Milestone One" was just the beginning of the process, and as the design was elaborated, it looked no better to DAB reviewers than it did to the Defense Science Board. Abrahamson had publicly estimated the cost of the "Phase One" deployment at \$40–60 billion, but his real estimate, later revealed, was \$75–\$150 billion. The Chiefs thought even that estimate far too low.[140] In the fall of 1987, after three months of briefings by SDI contractors, the DAB Milestone Panel concluded that the plan was too formless to provide any guide to the cost of a "Phase One" system. "As a consequence of the current gaps in systems design and technology, none of the current cost estimates can be relied upon," the panel reported.[141]

By the end of the year it had become obvious that "Phase One" was still not much more than a concept, and that there could be no deployment of a system that would meet the Chiefs' operational requirement by the mid-1990s. A year later the plan for a BAMBI- or High Frontier–style deployment simply faded away, and the SDIO went back to the drawing boards.[142]

"In retrospect," Crowe writes, the activation of the DAB process "may have been the chiefs' most significant accomplishment on SDI."[143]

The Chiefs had succeeded in turning SDI back into a research program. But in the world of public discourse, there was no way to restore SDI to its former position—that is, to reinvest it with Reagan's magic. In the past, SDI had held the promise of putting an end to the fear of nuclear weapons and making America invulnerable. In calling for deployment, Weinberger had excited the hopes of many Americans, leading some to imagine that "the President's dream" was coming true. By luring Abrahamson into making a definite proposal, Admiral Crowe had performed the reverse alchemy of turning gold into dross—or magic into a weapons system that would cost billions upon billions of dollars and still let 70 percent of Soviet missiles through. The DAB process did not, of course, kill SDI. It did not even bring the worlds of science and of public discourse much closer together, for, with all the talk about cost estimates and capabilities, the "Phase One" plan took on a concreteness it did not possess, creating hopes, or simply unexamined assumptions, that there was something, after all, to space weaponry. Nonetheless, "the President's dream" was clearly seen to be fading, and the popularity of SDI went into a gradual decline.[144]

AT THE SAME TIME that SDI was losing its magic in the United States, the spell of it was lifting in the Soviet Union as well.

From the time of Reagan's reelection, or from the time the administration began promoting Star Wars defenses and pouring money into the program, SDI had mesmerized the Soviet leadership. In 1985 SDI was the main subject, and the sticking point, of every arms control negotiation. At the Geneva summit Gorbachev had spent half his time trying to argue Reagan out of SDI. At the Reykjavik summit it was the focus of his efforts. Exactly why the Soviets were so concerned about SDI is not easy to explain. They did not believe that the U.S. would suddenly deploy an umbrella defense of the United States. Having worked on lasers and other exotic technologies for years, their scientists were as skeptical as American scientists about the feasibility of population defenses. The notion that the U.S. might develop ground-based ABM systems capable of defending missile silos did not worry them either. Having deployed nuclear-tipped ground-based ABMs around Moscow in the late 1960s, they had far more experience than the U.S. with point defenses. What worried them was that the U.S. might deploy weapons of some sort in space. This concern was not entirely unreasonable: the U.S. was already far ahead of the Soviet Union in the development of anti-satellite weapons, and it was just plausible that the SDI program might sooner or later produce space weaponry that could be used to destroy their ICBMs on the ground. Still, there was some element of magical thinking involved, for their assessments were contradictory. On the one hand, like the American critics of SDI, Soviet scientists and military men pointed to the vulnerability of space-based weapons and asserted that even exotic defenses in space could be easily, and relatively cheaply, overcome by countermeasures, such as the addition of more offensive weapons. On the other hand, they accused the United States of attempting to gain a first-strike capability, and behaved as if they really were frightened of the SDI program. Possibly McFarlane was right that the Soviets had such respect for American science and technology that they could only imagine that the expenditure of billions of dollars in research funds would lead to some kind of technical breakthrough. Certainly it would have been difficult for them to imagine the U.S. was spending billions of dollars for nothing at all.

Gorbachev, who had a logical mind, apparently wondered about the contradictory assessments himself. In February 1986, according to Dobrynin, he confided in his assistants: "Maybe it is time to stop being afraid of SDI? The United States is counting on our readiness to build the same kind of costly system, hoping meanwhile that they will win this race using their technological superiority. But our scientists tell me that if we want to destroy or neutralize the American SDI system, we only would have to spend 10 percent of what the Americans plan to spend."[145]

According to Dobrynin, the Soviet military-industrial complex had persuaded Gorbachev to drop this idea and return to the attempt to get rid of SDI. Given the nature of military establishments, this sounds plausible, and since Gorbachev did not want to start a Soviet SDI program or an offensive buildup to counter the threat, he may have felt that he had to try to negotiate the American program away.[146]

In 1985 and 1986 the Soviet negotiating position went through a series of changes and tergiversations. Some of them were tactical responses to American moves, but, generally speaking, the emphasis in 1985 was on getting the U.S. to give up SDI, whereas in 1986 Soviet negotiators focused on "strengthening" the ABM Treaty with a non-withdrawal clause and stricter limits on R&D. Gorbachev and his colleagues wanted a START agreement, and they did not think they could make deep offensive reductions without strengthening the ABM Treaty so as to prevent an American breakout for some period of years. That offenses and defenses were interrelated, and that offensive reductions depended on stability in the defensive arena, was classical strategic doctrine: it was the logic that McNamara had tried to teach Kosygin in 1967, the logic that led to the ABM Treaty of 1972 and the logic that U.S. officials still espoused with as much conviction as their Soviet counterparts. That there were no anti-missile devices on the horizon that could compete with even a small percentage of the thousands of deployed ICBM warheads somehow made no dent in this logic for either side.

At the Reykjavik summit Gorbachev offered a series of breathtaking concessions on INF and START in order to get Reagan to confine SDI "to the laboratory." Soviet negotiators subsequently made it clear that the phrase was an oversimplification of their actual position. Nonetheless, for months after the summit they continued to link progress on INF and

START to limits on SDI. But Reykjavik was the last opportunity the Reagan administration had to use SDI to exact serious concessions on offensive arms. By the end of February 1987 the spell of SDI on the Soviet leadership had been broken, and, with the kind of poetic justice that rarely obtains in life, it was broken by Andrei Sakharov.[147]

On December 23, 1986, Andrei Sakharov returned to Moscow from internal exile in the city of Gorky. The return of the renowned dissident and winner of the 1975 Nobel Prize for Peace was a major event in the capital. The physicist who had helped create the Soviet hydrogen bomb had been exiled without trial in 1980 for speaking out against the invasion of Afghanistan and for condemning Soviet human-rights violations. He and his wife, Yelena Bonner, had spent nearly seven years in exile, deprived of work and companionship and subjected to constant harassment by the police. Both were now in frail health.

Gorbachev had personally ordered Sakharov's release—he himself called the physicist to tell him that he was free to return. The gesture, it soon became clear, heralded a major turning point in Soviet policy. By the end of 1986 Gorbachev had come to the conclusion that he and his allies could not change the entrenched Soviet bureaucracy from the top down, that he required popular pressures for change and the only way to get it was by political reform, greater freedom of expression and glasnost, or "openness," on the part of the government and the Communist Party. In 1987 he opened up much of Soviet history to critical review, granted a greater measure of religious freedom, loosened the controls on the press and on speech and released political prisoners—140 of them in the first few weeks of the year—creating the political space for the growth of a reformist movement to the left of him. The amnesty for Sakharov was his first step in carrying out this policy.

On his return to Moscow, Sakharov immediately had a political stage on which to operate. Admirers crowded into his apartment, and Western journalists besieged him for interviews. On December 28, just five days after his return, he spoke with several reporters, and to the surprise of most, he took the opportunity not just to press for the release of other prisoners of conscience but to criticize Gorbachev's policy of tying offensive-arms reduction agreements to restrictions on SDI research.

During his exile Sakharov had always spoken his mind on arms-control issues, as though he were a citizen of the planet rather than of any particular nation. In 1983 he had argued in an open letter to an American colleague, Sidney Drell, that the U.S. should field the MX missile in order to force the Soviet government to put its heavy land-based missiles on the negotiating table. He had also criticized the Reagan administration for using SDI to stop arms control. This time he criticized Soviet policy, speaking, as he always did, from a high plane of reason but with such simplicity it seemed like common sense.

Strategic defenses, Sakharov explained, would never be able to stop a powerful opponent. "I think," he said, "that in the distant future this [an SDI system] will be a practical possibility, but it will always be impossible from the point of view of military strategy." It was a pity, he said, to see "so much money being wasted on such things." He then made a distinction between the attempt to develop strategic defenses and SDI research on new and exotic technologies. It was, he said, impossible to expect a complete renunciation of this research, for it was intimately connected with the prospect of military technology for the next century. Eventually this new technology would have to be taken into account in the negotiations, but for the moment, he said, there should be a compromise in which other issues were not too closely linked to SDI. With time, he said, the problem would "simply die on its own, quietly and peacefully."[148]

Sakharov returned to work at the Lebedev Institute of Physics. In mid-February, at the invitation of Evgeny Velikhov, he attended an international forum on disarmament that Gorbachev had assembled in Moscow. After listening to Gorbachev attack SDI and the "broad" interpretation of the ABM Treaty, Sakharov, speaking to fellow scientists in a closed session, again called for breaking the linkage between limits on SDI and progress on START and INF. An SDI system, he said, would never be militarily effective against a well-armed opponent; rather, it would be a kind of "Maginot line in space"—expensive and vulnerable to counter-measures. It would not serve as a population defense, or as a shield behind which a first strike could be launched, because it could be easily defeated. Possibly, he said, SDI proponents in the United States were counting on an accelerated arms race to ruin the Soviet economy, but if so they were mistaken, for the development of counter-measures would not be expensive. SDI proponents also argued that the existence of the SDI program spurred the U.S.S.R. to disarmament negotiations, but this was not so: on the contrary, SDI was impeding negotiations, though there was no reason that it should. "I believe," Sakharov concluded, that "a significant cut in ICBMs and medium-range missiles and battlefield missiles and other agreements on disarmament should be negotiated as soon as possible, independently of SDI, in accordance with the understanding laid out at Reykjavik. I believe that a compromise on SDI can be reached later. In this way the dangerous deadlock in the negotiations can be overcome."[149]

Sakharov thought he had made no impression on his colleagues. Before the conference Velikhov had said that he opposed untying the Reykjavik package, and afterwards he seemed angry that Sakharov had argued against that position, for he told him that scientists shouldn't engage in politics. But then, on February 28, Gorbachev proposed an agreement to eliminate INF missiles in Europe independent of any agreement on SDI. "This represented considerable progress," Sakharov later wrote, "but I continued to press for abandonment of the package with respect to ICBMs as well."[150] By December he had succeeded.

Journalists and historians of the period have speculated that Gorbachev's decision to break the linkage came from a sense of the weakness of his own position—or the weakness of Reagan's, in the midst of the Iran-contra affair. But the fact was that the spell of SDI had been lifted, and that was not a matter of calculation but revelation. It was like finding something hidden in plain sight. According to Aleksandr Yakovlev, Gorbachev's reformist ally, it happened because "some scientists came to Gorbachev and said 'We could be making a fuss about nothing. We suspect that this SDI is nothing but a bluff.' "[151]

Gorbachev's science advisers never gave Sakharov credit for persuading them that SDI was not a serious threat. How could they, when what Sakharov said was not new to them, and when in his exile he had far less information about the program than they did? Yet, hardly a month after Sakharov's return to Moscow, Velikhov and Roald Sagdeyev, the head of the Institute for Space Research, began to dismiss SDI as a military threat. They then changed their minds about linking SDI with INF, and as the year went on they came around to his view that explicit restrictions on SDI, though eventually necessary to strategic stability, need not stand in the way of a START treaty. "We came to realize," Sagdeyev said, "that we had not helped ourselves by screaming so much about SDI. We had encouraged some Americans to think that anything the Russians hate so much can't be all bad. And we had overestimated how much damage SDI could do to strategic stability in the short and even the medium term."[152]

How Sakharov managed to dispel the fear of SDI was mysterious—but, then, Sakharov played the same role in everything he did in that period of thaw in the Soviet system. He always told the truth as he saw it with clarity and simplicity, and, given the ellipticism and obfuscation in even ordinary discourse in the Soviet Union, his truth-telling appeared as a searchlight, or a radar beacon in the fog. There was something uncanny about it, David Remnick wrote; "through him [people] saw the hollowness of the old propaganda and the system itself." In the three years he had left to live, Sakharov became the intellectual leader and the conscience of all the reform groups in Moscow. A one-man loyal opposition, he continually harried Gorbachev and constantly annoyed him by pressing him to do all that the logic of his position entailed and everything that he was most reluctant to do. "He was the only one among us who made no compromises," one leading dissident said. "For us he was a figure of the inner spirit." According to Remnick, ordinary people came to love and trust Sakharov; he was the most popular political figure in the Soviet Union by the time of his death, and many thought of him as a saint or a prophet—though he resembled few saints in his balance, his liberalism and his rationality.[153]

In mythology it is the pure of heart who slay the dragons, and so it was that in the Soviet Union Sakharov dispelled the fear of SDI.

CHAPTER TEN

Reagan and Gorbachev

"The Iran thing has taken a personal toll on the President, I know that. You have to understand—it goes right to the heart and soul of this President to read that most of the American people 'don't believe he's telling the truth.' It hits him where he hurts the most—his popularity. He cares deeply about that."

—a former senior White House official, June 1987

On February 27, 1987, Donald Regan resigned in high dudgeon. In November he had told the President that he would leave whenever Reagan wanted him to go, but since he was sure the Tower report would exonerate him, he had made it clear that he did not want to leave before it came out. For three months Nancy Reagan did her utmost to get him to go, but Regan refused to resign, and the President refused to fire him. Throughout January, Regan attempted to persuade the President to make speeches, talk to the press and put the affair behind him, but the President had decided he would not say anything about Iran until the report came out, and every time Regan tried to schedule him for a speech on some other subject, Mrs. Reagan would tell him that her astrologer had found the day inauspicious. In fact, all days seemed to be inauspicious. After a month of arguing over astrology, the First Lady and the chief of staff ceased to speak. Finally, the President seemed to notice the warfare going on around him and acceded to the wishes of his wife.

On February 23, just days before the Tower report was due to appear, the President broached the subject of resignation to Regan. "I think it's time we do that thing you said when we talked in November," he said, apparently unable to utter the word.

"You can't do that to me, Mr. President," Regan exploded. "If I go before that report is out, you throw me to the wolves. I deserve better treatment than that."

The President backed off.[1]

Senator Tower presented his report to the President on the morning of the 26th, just before releasing it publicly. To Regan's enormous surprise, the commissioners had assigned him a share of responsibility for the debacle: "More than almost any chief of staff in recent memory," they wrote, "he asserted personal control over the White House staff and sought to extend this control to the National Security Adviser. He, as much as anyone, should have insisted that an orderly process be observed.... He must bear primary responsibility for the chaos that descended upon the White House" when the affair came to light.[2]

That afternoon Vice-President Bush told Regan the President had asked about his plans for leaving. "Does he want me out today?" Regan said in a temper. "If I go now, I'm part of the scandal." Bush spoke with the President again and reported that it would be fine if Regan left the following week, as planned.

But the next day Regan discovered that his successor would be coming to the White House shortly, and CNN was about to broadcast the news. Regan resigned with a one-sentence note. When the President called him to apologize for the abruptness of the decision, Regan exploded at him again.[3]

"My prayers have really been answered," the President wrote in his diary. Regan never heard from him again.[4]

Regan's successor, Howard Baker, had been brought in by Paul Laxalt. Able, mild-mannered, politically experienced and above all a grown-up, the former Senate majority leader took the job merely because he thought the beleaguered President needed help. His very arrival restored sanity to the White House. Losing no time, he dismissed Regan's assistants and replaced them with savvy professionals. Ken Duberstein became his deputy chief of staff, and when Pat Buchanan resigned on March 1—having failed in an unlikely bid to become ambassador to NATO—Thomas Griscom, a former Baker aide, succeeded him as communications director. For the President the staff changes came just in the nick of time.

The Tower Commission report did not blame the President for the operational disasters of the Iran initiative. In the judgment of the commissioners, only the NSC staff and William Casey had been directly involved in the arms deals, the diversion of funds to the contras and the subsequent attempt at a cover-up. The report was nonetheless damning, for it showed that the operation had gone on for fourteen months in a virtual vacuum of authority. Not only had Donald Regan failed to supervise the NSC staff but, according to the report, the secretaries of state and defense had "simply distanced themselves from the march of events" and "were not energetic in attempting to protect the President from the consequences of his commitment to free the hostages." That Ronald Reagan needed protection went without saying. As R. W. Apple of the *New York Times* wrote, the Tower Board had painted a picture "of a man confused, distracted, so remote that he failed utterly to control the implementation of his vision ... the inhabitant of a never-never land...." The President, the commissioners wrote more tactfully, "did not seem to be aware of the way in which the operation was implemented and the full consequences of U.S. participation."[5]

Reagan, the commissioners reported, had initially told them that he authorized the first shipment of arms to Iran, but in a second interview, after a conversation with Donald Regan, he told them he had not. Later he wrote them that his recollection had been influenced by that of others, and that, try as he might, he could not recall "anything whatsoever" about the event. The President, former Senator Tower said, "clearly didn't understand the nature of this operation, who was involved and what was happening."[6]

Before the Iran-contra revelations, it was well known that Ronald Reagan had a less-than-hands-on management style; it was known that he was often inattentive to policy details, that he sometimes made factual errors and that he occasionally fell asleep during long meetings at international economic gatherings. Few thought ill of him for these lapses: it was easy to imagine doing the same in his place. But that he could have ignored what his own NSC staffers were doing for well over a year seemed incredible. Polls showed a widespread belief that the President had not told the Tower Board everything he knew. "What did the President forget, and when did he forget it?" comedians asked, and "What did the President not know, and when did he decide not to know it?"[7] Reagan's job-approval rating, already low, fell further, and his "negatives," in the pollsters' jargon, rose to 53 percent.[8]

On March 4 the President, at the recommendation of all of his advisers, made a public act of contrition in a televised address: "A few months ago, I told the American people I did not trade arms for hostages. My heart and my best intentions still tell me this is true, but the facts and the evidence tell me it is not. As the Tower Board reported, what began as a strategic opening to Iran deteriorated, in its implementation, into trading arms for hostages. This runs counter to my own beliefs, to administration policy, and to the original strategy we had in mind. There are reasons why it happened, but no excuses. It was a mistake."[9]

Reagan, however, believed none of this. In briefing the President on the report on February 26, former Senator Tower had taken great pains to convince him that he had sold arms for hostages. Reagan had signified that he understood, but the next morning he told Regan and Bush that he would explain to the nation in his address that he had never sold arms for hostages or dealt with terrorists. "Reagan was dug in on this position," Regan wrote, "face flushed, lips pursed, voice strained." It was only later that day, when Senator Tower, worried about impeachment proceedings, urged him to hire his own counsel, that the President changed his mind about what he was going to say.[10] But he never changed his mind about what he had done. "For the rest of his term," Colin Powell writes, "we learned to avoid the subject. . . . Once anybody accidentally hit the trip-wire, Reagan would launch into a twenty-minute monologue on why the deal had not been arms-for-hostages, and how did we know there were no Iranian moderates?"[11] Still, the March 4 speech, with its apparently heartfelt admission of error, was well received, and Reagan's job-approval rating jumped nine points.[12]

The speech encouraged Reagan's supporters, but the President's troubles were far from over. In a search of the White House computers, the

Tower commissioners had found evidence of other covert operations by the NSC staff; the congressional hearings were due to begin in May, and the investigation by the independent counsel had hardly begun. Nancy Reagan was worried that her husband might be impeached. That word hardly ever appeared in the press, and Reagan's personal popularity remained high. However, two-thirds of the American public said that the controversy over the Iran-contra affair would make it difficult for Reagan to be an effective president for the next two years, and almost a third thought he should consider resigning before his term was out.[13]

What Reagan could do to put the affair behind him and demonstrate that he ought to remain in office was, of course, the issue. It had been the issue since the end of November, and as yet no solution had been found. Since Reagan's reelection in 1984, the administration had had virtually no domestic policy, and at this juncture it was pointless to assemble one. Congress had taken over fiscal policy in 1985, and now that the Democrats were in control of both houses of Congress, they were actively pursuing their own legislative agenda. In late January 1987, they had passed an eighty-billion-dollar extension of the Clean Water Act over Reagan's veto and crushed a Republican attempt to curb Medicare.

The administration had, of course, a number of firmly held foreign and defense policies, but the Congress had turned against all of them. In March the Congress voted to suspend further aid to the contras until the White House came up with an accounting of the private funds it had raised for them. That same month Weinberger's dogged efforts to boost military spending were dismissed out of hand, and the administration's attempt to break the ABM Treaty was checked by Sam Nunn. It was useless to appeal to the country on these issues, for, as the biannual Gallup survey for the Chicago Council on Foreign Relations showed, administration officials held views strikingly at odds with public-opinion leaders outside the government and with the public as a whole. For example, 100 percent of the administration officials polled favored giving military and economic aid to rebels against Communist-supported governments—or the Reagan doctrine—but only 48 percent of the leaders outside government and 24 percent of the public favored such a policy. On the issue of military spending, 91 percent of administration officials thought the goal of matching Soviet power "very important," compared with 56 percent of the other leaders, and 43 percent of officials wanted to spend more for the national defense, compared with 21 percent of the public. What was more, administration officials had a different view of reality. Asked which of the superpowers was militarily stronger, only 9 percent of administration officials said the U.S., as opposed to 30 percent of the non-governmental leaders and 30 percent of the public. (The majority of the public thought the two powers were about equal in military strength.) Then, too, Weinberger and the rest of the Pentagon civilians were making their bid to stop arms control forever at a time when over 80 percent of the public and of other leaders favored arms agreements with the Soviets.[14] Donald Regan had urged the President to get out on the hustings, but Mrs. Reagan and her astrologer had wisely confined him to the family quarters, for he had nothing to say.

In February it crossed the minds of some in the administration that a disarmament initiative might be the way to put the presidency back on track. According to Shultz, the President "was focused on moving forward with the Soviets."[15] Weinberger, however, was trying to get the President to speak about testing and deploying strategic defenses. When—thanks to the leaked minutes of the February 3 meeting—he succeeded in getting the President to endorse SDI testing under the "broad" interpretation of the ABM Treaty, the prospects for an arms-control agreement seemed at best dim.

At the National Security Planning Group meeting of February 10, the second one called to consider Weinberger's proposals, the agenda included Nitze's idea for talks with the Soviets on the unresolved technicalities of the ABM Treaty. According to Adelman, Shultz was in a very poor humor at the meeting. He refused to discuss Nitze's idea, or anything else, maintaining that he could not give the President confidential advice if it was going to be leaked to the press. Weinberger took the opportunity to denounce Nitze's idea, and others followed suit.

That idea dispensed with, the President hushed the group and said that he had been doing some hard thinking about all of this. With what Adelman describes as a "pensive but strained look," suggesting that this thinking had cost him some effort, Reagan proposed that the group develop the idea of sharing SDI technology with the Soviet Union and combine it with the total elimination of nuclear weapons. These things, he said, could be done through an international body, and it made sense to do them together, because no one would need nuclear weapons if they had SDI.

He was about to continue when Adelman broke in and argued that neither of these things could be done: you couldn't share SDI technology with the Soviets, you couldn't get rid of nuclear weapons. The President argued back; Adelman argued some more. Then, Adelman writes, the President revealed what was bothering him. We're just fiddling around in Geneva, he said. Nothing ever happens there, with all these numbers going back and forth and all that. Our fellows over there should change what they're doing and present this scheme.

Carlucci, nudging the argument off center, asked what the Soviets would think of the idea. When Shultz maintained his self-imposed silence, Weinberger jumped in to say that the proposal would "electrify the Europeans" and enable the President to seize the moral high ground.

"Electrify the Europeans?" Adelman blurted out. "It would electrify them all right. Just like Reykjavik!"[16]

In his memoir Adelman waxes indignant that Shultz and Weinberger did not argue with the President—as he so courageously did—but of course he did not understand what was happening. Another Reykjavik or another Geneva was precisely what the President wanted, and that was all he was saying. Reagan had gone to both summits talking about sharing SDI technology and eliminating nuclear weapons—so why shouldn't he do it again?

On February 28 Gorbachev offered to untie the Reykjavik package, in which all agreements on offensive weapons were linked to an agreement on SDI, and to conclude a separate INF treaty "without delay." The offer was a godsend to the President, particularly since, according to the State Department, it meant that Gorbachev wanted a summit before the end of the year. On March 3 Reagan welcomed the offer, making his first appearance in the White House press room since November 25. Three days later the White House announced that Shultz would travel to Moscow in mid-April to "maintain momentum" towards an INF accord.[17]

In mid-March, Richard Perle announced that he would resign later that spring. In an interview he predicted that Reagan and Gorbachev would hold a full summit meeting that year and would conclude a treaty eliminating INF missiles in Europe.[18] The prediction suggested that Weinberger had decided not to block the treaty that Reagan needed so much.

The major impediments to an INF agreement had been removed, but Shultz still had a number of obstacles to overcome, one of them quite unexpected.

On March 24 Shultz learned there had been a catastrophic security breach at the U.S. Embassy in Moscow. Back in December, Sergeant Clayton Lonetree, a U.S. Marine guard at the embassy, had confessed to passing classified information to a Russian woman with whom he had been having an affair. Subsequently a second Marine guard was said to have confessed to conspiring with Lonetree to allow KGB agents to roam freely through the embassy at night. Since the Marines had the combinations to all the safes in the embassy, the KGB would have had access to every secret the embassy possessed.

The news threw the State Department and U.S. intelligence agencies into turmoil. The entire Marine security detachment guarding the embassy was replaced, and, on the assumption that the KGB had installed bugs everywhere inside the embassy, officials communicated in whispers and wrote their dispatches in longhand to be sent to Washington in the diplomatic pouch. Counter-intelligence experts told Shultz that this was the worst intelligence defeat since World War II. Lieutenant General William Odom, head of the National Security Agency, wanted the embassy closed altogether, and he, along with Weinberger, wanted Shultz to meet with Shevardnadze in Western Europe. Henry Kissinger told people that Shultz should not go to Moscow under these circumstances, and Congress was up in arms. In early April seventy senators, including all but ten of the Republicans, voted for a resolution opposing Shultz's trip.[19]

Shultz, however, insisted on going to Moscow. He could not meet with Gorbachev anywhere else, and if security concerns were linked to his agenda, the INF agreement would be delayed, if not derailed. Howard Baker, his only ally on the White House staff, argued that the U.S. should not be "run out of town" by the embassy scandal. The President seized gratefully upon this phrase and, over Weinberger's objections, decided that Shultz should make the trip.[20]

Some months later it transpired that, though Sergeant Lonetree had given away some classified information, he and his fellow Marine had never let Soviets into the embassy. Rather, the Naval Intelligence Service had pressured the Marines into making false confessions, which they later repudiated, and the rest of the counter-intelligence services, rattled by all of the spy scandals of the previous years, had failed to examine the body of evidence, electronic and otherwise, which showed that there had been no Soviet penetration of the embassy. The intelligence agencies had simply panicked and assumed the worst.[21]

The President had sided with Shultz on the Moscow visit, but in the matter of Shultz's instructions he sided with his secretary of defense. When Shultz left for Helsinki and Moscow on April 11, he took with him an NSDD cast in strong language instructing him, among other things, to stick with the "broad" interpretation of the ABM Treaty, and to offer only a seven-year period of non-withdrawal from the treaty—as opposed to the ten years offered at Reykjavik. The President had rejected all of Shultz's proposals for moving forward on START and other issues and had given him so little flexibility in the INF negotiations that he feared he could not make any progress towards an agreement. However, the President had authorized him to talk in positive terms about a summit.[22]

In Moscow, Gorbachev asked Shultz whether the U.S. still accepted the INF formula that had been agreed to at Reykjavik: zero missiles in Europe, one hundred apiece globally. The question was an important one. The administration wanted all INF missiles eliminated, and Shultz believed that Gorbachev would eventually accept the idea; Gorbachev, however, needed some evidence that the administration was not just going to pocket Soviet concessions and ask for more, as it had so often done, but would agree to less than exactly what it wanted. Shultz replied that the U.S. preferred to have no intermediate-range missiles in Asia, but the answer was yes. There followed a discussion of the short-range INF missiles. The U.S. had no weapons in this category, but the Soviets had ninety-two of them and the West Germans had seventy-two very old Pershing Ia missiles armed with U.S. nuclear warheads that fit the category. Within a few minutes Gorbachev proposed eliminating all these weapons on a global basis. Shultz replied that he would consult with NATO and deliver a prompt response.[23]

Returning to Washington via NATO headquarters outside Brussels, Shultz found the NATO governments—principally Kohl's and Thatcher's—

concerned about the prospect of losing the American weaponry. The "zero option" had been NATO policy since 1983, but since no one believed the Soviets would accept it, the implications of an agreement had not been thought through. With all the medium-range missiles gone, the only ground-based nuclear weapons left would be the tactical weapons deployed in and around Germany, and the Germans did not want their country to become Europe's nuclear battlefield. The British as well as the Germans worried that the proposed treaty would "decouple" Europe from the U.S. strategic nuclear deterrent, and that an INF treaty would lead inexorably to a denuclearization of the continent, leaving Western Europe vulnerable to the superior conventional forces of the Soviet Union. The NATO governments wanted an arms-control agreement, but the Reykjavik summit and all Reagan's talk of eliminating nuclear weapons had shaken them badly.[24]

Back in the United States, Shultz found that the Republican right in Congress did not like the proposed treaty, nor did a number of influential former officials. Alexander Haig, Brent Scowcroft and James Woolsey, who had opposed the "zero option" in 1983, argued that the administration should go back to the original NATO position created by the Carter administration and leave a hundred INF weapons in Europe.[25] Henry Kissinger, who had taken to criticizing the administration from the right, delivered a series of thundering broadsides against the INF agreement. In March, Kissinger had infuriated many in Europe by calling for the testing and deployment of SDI, and for the "broad" interpretation of the ABM Treaty, but on the INF issues he seemed hypersensitive to European concerns. "The so-called 'zero option,' " he wrote, "reduces in no significant way the Soviet nuclear threat to Europe. It eliminates completely the American means of retaliating from Europe. . . . It does represent an important step in decoupling Europe from the United States politically."[26] In April, Kissinger and Richard Nixon, speaking out jointly for the first time since they left office, warned Reagan in Kissinger's syndicated column in the *Los Angeles Times* that it would be "a profound mistake" to sign an INF agreement unless Moscow accepted major changes in the formula under negotiation, including the elimination of INF missiles in Asia and of the "huge" Soviet superiority in conventional arms. The wrong agreement, they wrote, could leave Western Europe vulnerable to Soviet attack with conventional forces or to nuclear blackmail with Soviet-based weapons. If the administration struck the wrong deal, it would "create the most profound crisis of the NATO alliance in its 40-year history."[27]

Weinberger, for his part, insisted that the Soviets agree to a zero outcome in Asia as well as in Europe, and in a public statement virtually endorsed Nixon and Kissinger's suggestion of linking an INF treaty to conventional-force reductions.[28]

Shultz, however, had Admiral Crowe on his side, and he believed the Allies would eventually come around. The Soviet Union would, after all, be taking out many more nuclear weapons than the U.S. because it had several times more intermediate-range weapons deployed.[29] The British and French nuclear forces would remain intact, and when the U.S. removed its medium-range weapons, there would still be many other types of U.S. nuclear weapons in the European theater—not only battlefield weapons but sea-launched ballistic and cruise missiles, and nuclear-capable bombers. In addition, the presence of three hundred thousand American troops in Europe would remain a guarantee that the U.S. would intervene if the NATO allies were threatened. In his talks with the West German officials, Shultz made it clear that the only alternative to an elimination of short-range INF missiles was a U.S. buildup of SRINFs to the Soviet level: a compelling argument, since Kohl did not want to deal with the political trauma that would result from the deployment of more U.S. nuclear weapons in Germany.[30]

Over the late spring and summer, the Europeans and the Soviets removed a number of the obstacles to a treaty. In early June, Kohl privately agreed to the U.S.-Soviet proposal, and on June 12, NATO formally accepted the elimination of long- and short-range INF weapons. In July, Gorbachev agreed to eliminate the INF weapons in Asia as well, and the agreement became the "double global zero" Shultz had predicted it would. Gorbachev also called for discussions on "radical reductions" in the levels of conventional military forces in Europe, though in a speech that was largely ignored. In August, Kohl announced that he would dismantle the Pershing Ia missiles after the INF agreement was signed and implemented. Henry Kissinger continued to complain, but in Europe all the talk of decoupling and denuclearization drifted slowly off into the ether.[31]

Then a new objection cropped up from within the U.S. military. The Pershing II's had been deployed at great expense, and some military men had initially contended that the U.S. should not give up so significant a system—one that was able to reach the Soviet homeland—without extracting more concessions from the Soviets. In midsummer General Bernard Rogers, the Supreme Allied Commander in Europe, resurrected this contention and argued with passion that, since the Pershings had already been integrated into the U.S. war plans, to take them out would be to take out an important rung on the ladder of escalation and to interfere with the planning for "flexible response." Logically, he argued, the bottom rung of the ladder should go first, so it would be better to keep the Pershings until the Soviets were willing to throw in their tactical nuclear weapons as well. Two of the Chiefs had some sympathy with this view, so a new debate started up in the Pentagon. Crowe and others pointed out that the 108 deployed Pershings did not constitute that much of a bargaining chip, and that, though it might be more logical to eliminate the bottom rung of the ladder first, no one had thought to propose this until just now. Besides, since the Soviets would be eliminating far more weapons than the U.S., the U.S. would have far fewer targets to hit on its escalation ladder. This view eventually prevailed.[32]

There remained the problem of verification. For years the hawks in the administration had called for strict verification measures for any agreement, including on-site inspections. The Soviets had always rejected the idea of Americans' inspecting their military facilities, so it could be assumed that such requirements would serve as a block to any treaty. In April, Shultz had gone to Moscow with a plan for very strict and intrusive verification measures, including on-site inspection of the destruction of the missiles, perimeter monitoring of missile-production facilities and the right to make spur-of-the-moment challenge inspections of these facilities—anytime, anyplace—for up to thirteen years. To the amazement of American officials, the Soviets accepted the plan without demur. This put the administration in a terrible quandary, for the last thing U.S. military and civilian intelligence agencies wanted was to have the Soviets making "anytime, anyplace" inspections of U.S. defense plants.

In August the administration came up with a new and much-modified inspection plan and presented it at the Geneva talks. The Soviets agreed to it, and U.S. officials took credit for having convinced Moscow to accept strict verification procedures.[33]

In mid-September, Shevardnadze came to Washington for three days of intensive talks with Shultz. The talks focused on the unresolved issues of the INF treaty, but in a private meeting with Shultz, Shevardnadze made a dramatic announcement: the Soviet troops would be leaving Afghanistan within the next twelve months.[34]

For the Soviet Union the seven-year-long war in Afghanistan had proved a debacle: it had cost the lives of thousands of soldiers, sapped the morale of the Soviet army, antagonized Pakistan and many other Muslim countries, served as a major obstacle to the normalization of relations with China and badly impaired Soviet-U.S. relations. Ever since he came to power in 1985, Gorbachev had been actively searching for a way to extricate the Soviet troops—but without having to accept a humiliating defeat that would destroy the credibility of Soviet armed forces and precipitate a bloodbath of Soviet allies in Kabul. His dilemma was much the same as that Nixon had faced in his attempt to extricate American troops from Vietnam—with the additional complication that a hostile Muslim regime in Kabul might cause a great deal of trouble in the neighboring Muslim republics of the Soviet Union. Since 1985 Gorbachev and his allies had tried a variety of approaches, including the use of massive firepower to gain a military advantage, attempts to shore up the Kabul regime politically, efforts to get the Pakistani government to help and the encouragement of UN mediation efforts to bring about a negotiated end to the war. In May 1986 they ousted Babrak Kamal, the Afghan leader their predecessors had installed, because he would not cooperate by broadening his political base, and replaced him with the more flexible Mohammad Najibullah. In December they officially told Najibullah to prepare for a Soviet withdrawal within two years, and in July 1987 Gorbachev publicly said that the withdrawal had been decided upon "in principle."[35]

The Soviets did not, of course, suppose that the Najibullah regime could survive indefinitely without them. What they wanted, therefore, was a negotiated settlement, and as their previous efforts had shown, they could not get one without the United States. Shevardnadze's hope lay in the personal relationship he had developed with Shultz. The Soviet Union, he told Shultz on September 16, would accept a neutral, non-aligned government, but it did not want an Islamic fundamentalist regime. He asked for American help in preventing such an outcome. Shultz said that a neutral, non-aligned government would be acceptable to the United States but offered no assistance.[36]

By the end of their three days of meetings, Shultz and Shevardnadze had agreed in principle on an INF treaty and on a summit meeting later that year in Washington, with the date to be determined when Shultz visited Moscow in October. But they made no progress on START.

In deference to the weakness of the President's political position, the hard-liners had allowed the INF agreement to get through the gauntlet of objections, but they had seen to it that nothing else would. In April, Weinberger had successfully blocked the half-dozen new arms initiatives Shultz had proposed and held the line on the "broad" interpretation of the ABM Treaty. At the time, Major General William Burns, an arms-control expert in the State Department's Bureau of Politico-Military Affairs, had told a colleague, "Cap and Richard see the INF as something we can afford to give away because it'll give the arms controllers something to chew on while the tough guys circle the wagons on SDI and START."[37] In September, just before Shevardnadze was to come to Washington, Weinberger advised the President to make no compromises on strategic-arms issues. Reagan agreed, apparently swayed by the thought that if he made any concession on SDI it would look as if he were weakened by the pressures of the Iran-contra affair.[38] The same logic seemed to apply to other issues as well.

In numerous speeches over the spring and summer, Reagan had expressed readiness to meet with Gorbachev and to improve relations, but he had continued to belabor the Soviet regime on human rights, its role in regional conflicts and other matters. On occasion he pointed to changes in Soviet policy, but, rather than crediting Gorbachev, he attributed them to U.S. military strength and the firmness of American leadership. Then he called for further reforms and concessions, suggesting that he would take credit for them as well. On June 12, at the Brandenburg Gate in Berlin, he challenged Gorbachev to make one "unmistakable sign" that his policies were not just "token gestures intended to raise false hopes in the West or to strengthen the Soviet system without changing it." Mr. Gorbachev, he cried, "tear down this wall!"[39] In September, just a few days after Shevardnadze told Shultz the Soviet troops would soon be leaving Afghanistan, Reagan, in an address to the UN General Assembly, criticized the Soviet Union at some length for its occupation of that country. He recalled that he had urged the Soviets to set a date for their withdrawal, and he said, "There is no excuse for prolonging a brutal war or propping up a regime whose days are clearly numbered."[40]

The speeches played well with American conservatives, but they made the task of reformers in Moscow more difficult than they already were.

In 1987 Gorbachev and his allies pushed ahead as quickly as they could with perestroika. They enacted economic-reform laws decentralizing the command economy and opening it up to foreign trade and investment; they attempted to break the stranglehold of the party on economic management and called for democratization of the party through secret ballots and multiple candidates. But without a majority in the Central Committee and with virtually no control over the vast, sluggish Soviet bureaucracy, their economic-reform efforts were largely frustrated. In the meantime, glasnost was taking effect in Moscow: dissident views appeared regularly in the press, hundreds of independent civic and social clubs sprang up and political groupings to the left of Gorbachev took shape. Glasnost was far more successful than perestroika, but it was a mixed blessing as far as the reformers were concerned. As Gorbachev had hoped, it exposed some of the corruption and inefficiency of the Soviet system, but it also showed how difficult it would be to transform the system, and how painful. In addition, it encouraged nationalist ferment in the Asian and European republics of the Soviet Union. These developments emboldened party conservatives and permitted them to create a constituency of dissent from the entire reform program under the banner of Russian nationalism. By their account, Gorbachev was attempting to "Americanize" Soviet society and was knuckling under to pressures from the West.[41]

On October 21 Shultz and Carlucci arrived in Moscow with a large delegation of experts expecting to wrap up the INF negotiations and set a date for the summit. The discussions with Shevardnadze went smoothly. Meeting with Gorbachev on the 23rd, Shultz found him smiling and positive in his manner. The two discussed U.S.-Soviet cooperation on bringing an end to the seven-year-old Iran-Iraq war, and then moved on to arms control. Gorbachev asserted that the INF treaty could be completed soon; the main issues should be resolved while Shultz was in Moscow, with only the technical details left for the Geneva negotiators to clear up. Turning to strategic arms, he proposed that the two sides adopt "the essence" of the Reykjavik formula: 50-percent reductions in offensive strategic arms to achieve equal levels, and a ten-year period of non-withdrawal from the ABM Treaty. Shultz summarized what had already been agreed to on offensive weapons, and Gorbachev proposed a further set of sublimits. Under questioning from

Shultz, the general secretary called for adherence to the traditional interpretation of the ABM Treaty and discussions of what could and could not be tested in space. Agreements on key provisions of a strategic-arms agreement could, he said, be ready in time for a Washington summit, and a statement of principles could be signed at the summit by Reagan and himself.

Shultz demurred. His instructions did not permit him to make an agreement of any kind on strategic arms.

Gorbachev turned sour and complained angrily about a piece of anti-Soviet literature put out by the State Department. When the discussion of arms control resumed, Carlucci said he was troubled by Gorbachev's emphasis on linking the "narrow" interpretation of the ABM Treaty to START, since Reagan would not be willing to accept "artificial restraints" on SDI. What was needed, he said, was a way to assure the Soviet Union of greater predictability about SDI without trying to restrain it through the ABM Treaty. Gorbachev then expressed concern about the forthcoming summit, observing that, apart from the INF treaty, an arms-control agenda had not yet emerged. "People," he said, "will not understand if the two leaders keep meeting and have nothing to show for it, especially since both agreed and said publicly that strategic arms were the key."

Gorbachev was clearly attempting to make progress on strategic arms a precondition for the summit, but Shultz could not promise anything. When the meeting ended, Gorbachev had still not set a date for his visit to Washington, and the summit was in doubt.[42]

During the meeting Shultz felt that there was something distinctly different about Gorbachev, and he surmised that for the first time the general secretary had run into domestic political trouble. "This boxer," he said, "has been hit." Shultz was right. A week later it became known that a major confrontation had taken place at a Central Committee plenum on the eve of his visit. Boris Yeltsin, the Moscow party chief, a candidate-member of the Politburo and the most ardent reformer in the topmost ranks of the party, had delivered a blistering attack on Yegor Ligachev, the leading conservative in the Politburo. Yeltsin had broken all the rules, and whether he wanted to or not, Gorbachev had to fire him from his party posts, thereby weakening his own position vis-à-vis the conservatives. Seizing their opportunity, the conservatives had turned on Gorbachev, accusing him of making repeated concessions to the Americans, who in turn ignored Soviet interests.[43]

Gorbachev's refusal to set a summit date was a blow to the Reagan White House. For months the President had been looking forward to a summit, though in some detachment from the preparations required to produce one. In May the Reagans had talked with Carlucci about having Gorbachev come to the United States and visit their California ranch over Thanksgiving. In September, just before Shevardnadze's arrival in Washington, when diplomatic diffidence about a summit remained advisable, Shultz found that the President and the First Lady had made extensive plans for Gorbachev's visit. "She's already bought the groceries for Thanksgiving," Colin Powell said wryly. "Gorbachev's going to the ranch whether he wants to or not."[44] Ever since the Geneva summit, Reagan had talked about taking Gorbachev up in a plane or a helicopter over the United States to show him how well the average American lived.[45] As part of the preparations, Shultz discovered, White House advance men were planning a flight path to the ranch for the general secretary and his wife that "would take them over all sorts of Southern California real estate, endless private houses, many with swimming pools."[46]

By the third week in October, Reagan needed a summit more than ever. The congressional hearings on the Iran-contra affair had hurt him politically by reinforcing the judgment of the Tower commissioners. North and Poindexter, it appeared, had been running a variety of covert operations through a private corporation, known as "The Enterprise," with its own ship, its own planes, pilots and Swiss bank accounts. The President, it appeared, had known nothing of this, and nothing of the diversion of funds to the contras. In their final report the joint congressional committees had charged Reagan with failing to fulfill his constitutional duty to uphold the law, but they had not come close to recommending impeachment. For one thing, it was difficult to imagine impeaching a president for sheer lack of attention to what was going on; for another, Reagan's personal popularity and the politics of the moment dictated a general agreement to let him serve out his term.

The President was safe in his job, but congressional Republicans and Democrats alike had come to regard his presidency as moribund, and that was fine with the Democrats. In September the Senate Foreign Relations Committee had released its report calling the ABM Treaty reinterpretation "the most flagrant abuse of the Constitution's treaty power in 200 years of American history."[47] The Armed Services Committees agreed on a defense bill that reduced military spending and cut the administration's SDI budget by a third. In early October the Senate handed Reagan what in the opinion of many was the worst defeat of his presidency by rejecting his nominee for the Supreme Court, Robert H. Bork, on the grounds that his jurisprudential views were radically right-wing. As the Congress defied him on measure after measure, Reagan vowed to fight on, but in metaphors, as Sidney Blumenthal noted, that suggested that his presidency was already posthumous: "over my dead body," "as long as there is breath in this body." [48] After the defeat of the Bork nomination some conservatives jested bitterly, "This never would have happened if Reagan were still alive."[49]

On October 19, later known as Black Monday, the stock market crashed, losing over 20 percent of its value, the largest collapse of prices in a single day since 1929. The following day, the market went into a free fall, creating a panic on Wall Street. The Fed stepped in and the crisis passed, but the crash jolted lots of ordinary investors and ended the economic euphoria of the past few years. To many, it now appeared that the Reagan administration had created a false prosperity based on tax cuts and military Keynesianism. In the sobering aftermath the prospect of an INF treaty and a summit seemed to be the administration's only good news.

However, Gorbachev, too, wanted a summit, and, finding the Reagan administration immovable, he altered course and signaled Shultz that he was ready to proceed. On October 30 Shevardnadze arrived in Washington with a letter from the General Secretary proposing that the summit begin on December 7, that the two leaders sign the INF treaty and set in motion a START treaty to be completed at a Moscow summit the following spring. Shultz and Shevardnadze went to work on the INF treaty, and after another meeting in Geneva in mid-November they resolved virtually all of the remaining technical issues.[50]

Shultz, to trust his memoir, felt relieved, even triumphant, about the INF agreement, and he had reason to be satisfied with it. The treaty did what the Reagan administration had proposed in 1981: it eliminated an entire class of nuclear weapons. Of course, the proposal had been somewhat different in 1981, when the U.S. had no INF weapons deployed, but still the reductions would be disproportionate: the Soviets would eliminate about 1,280 warheads, and the U.S. about 429. The sum of them amounted to only 4 percent of the fifty thousand warheads the two sides possessed, but the benefits were as much political and psychological as military. Then, too, the verification procedures were far more extensive and intrusive than any that had been achieved in the past. The treaty could be said to demonstrate the efficacy of Reagan's initial policy of toughness with the Soviet Union; it also could be said to show that the President was not an opponent of arms control.[51]

Shultz had reason to be pleased with a few other recent developments as well.

On November 5 Caspar Weinberger announced his resignation, citing the persistent ill-health of his wife. The decision was by all accounts a difficult one for him to make. He was a fighter, and he did not want to concede the field to Shultz, yet, as was clear to all in Washington, there was little point in his staying on. In the past year or so he had lost most of his influence in the Pentagon and on the Hill. He could no longer bring the Chiefs along with him on important issues, and in a period of fiscal deficits his no-compromise approach to defense spending alienated even the Republicans on the Armed Services Committees. He had become a marginal figure in the debate. In addition, he had lost at least some of his influence in the White House. According to Colin Powell, Nancy Reagan viewed his unremitting hostility to the Soviet Union as "swimming against the tide." The First Lady increasingly took Shultz's side in the ongoing struggle between the two secretaries, and, Powell writes, Weinberger was "enough of a performer to recognize an exit line."[52]

With Weinberger's departure, Shultz regained the place of influence he had held in 1984, and the ideological balance of forces within the administration changed again, this time decisively. On the advice of Baker and Shultz, Carlucci was appointed secretary of defense, and Powell moved up to become national security adviser. Richard Perle had left the administration in June. Kenneth Adelman had made known his plans to resign in December, and a Nitze ally, General William Burns, was nominated to take his place. In the national-security arena the administration, for so long dominated by the right, was now at its top levels manned by "pragmatists," and by a group which Shultz considered "by far the best team, and in fact, the first genuine team, assembled in the entire Reagan presidency."[53]

Thus far Shultz's main role as secretary of state had been to provide a moderate front for the administration while the hard-liners set the agenda. His opportunity to make policy had finally come.

THE SUMMIT MEETING of December 1987 was the first U.S.-Soviet summit to be held in Washington in fourteen years, and for the American public it seemed to mark a turning point in U.S.-Soviet relations. Not long before it, Robert Gates, the deputy director of the CIA, told Shultz that the Soviets were merely resting up for another round of Cold War hostilities. The American public thought otherwise. Back in September a Gallup poll had shown that 54 percent of all Americans and 70 percent of all college graduates had a favorable opinion of Gorbachev. Not only was this the highest approval rating for any Soviet leader in the post-war period, but it was higher than Reagan's—then at 49 percent.[54] The fact that Gorbachev was coming to Washington at the invitation of the most right-wing of presidents only confirmed the public belief that the Soviet Union was changing and that the Cold War was coming to an end.

When Gorbachev arrived on December 7, Washington, a city normally quite blasé about visiting dignitaries, was in the grip of what Tom Shales, the television critic of the *Washington Post,* called "Gorby fever." Congressmen, former high officials, publishers, intellectuals and media celebrities were falling over themselves to get into the official receptions and dinners, and all three TV-network anchors were on hand. The night of his arrival Gorbachev, accompanied by his wife, Raisa, dined at the Soviet Embassy with an eclectic group of celebrities that included Henry Kissinger, Reverand Billy Graham, John Denver and Yoko Ono; on the succeeding days he attended two state dinners, one at the White House, one at the Soviet Embassy, a huge luncheon-reception at the State Department, and a meeting with a group of American publishers. Acting, reporters wrote, "like an American politician," Gorbachev asked about the Iowa caucuses, discussed recent books on the Soviet Union with their authors and joked about the dubious virtues of moonshine whiskey with Howard Baker and Sam Nunn. Never defensive, and only once nettled by aggressive questioning, he charmed audiences with his vigor, his candor and his good will. The cameras followed him everywhere, and the networks preempted soap operas to show footage of him shaking hands, schmoozing and responding to letters from American children. As he traveled around town in his black Zil limousine, huge crowds lined his route. There were demonstrators for the rights of national minorities in the Soviet Union and demonstrators for peace, but these were far outnumbered by people who just wanted to catch a glimpse of this interesting new Soviet leader who was changing so much at home and abroad. Ripples of applause swept through the crowds as he went by. "In my two decades in Washington, I had never seen anything like it," Robert Gates later wrote.[55]

On the third day of the summit Vice-President Bush, who was traveling with Gorbachev from the Soviet Embassy to the White House, looked out at the crowd at Connecticut and L Streets and said, "It's too bad you can't stop and go into some of these stores because I think you'd find warm greetings from the American people." At this invitation Gorbachev halted the motorcade, bounded out of the Zil and plunged into the crowd, shaking hands. Bush got out of the car belatedly and stood next to it, looking slightly dazed. Few people noticed him. They were in front of Duke Zeibart's restaurant, one of the power lunch spots in Washington, and Zeibart was on the balcony yelling an invitation to Gorbachev to come in for borscht. Gorbachev was mobbed. "Do you do this a lot?" Bush asked him when they got back into the Zil. "Oh," Gorbachev said, "I do it a lot in Moscow, and I do it every time I go to the provinces."[56]

In public Reagan gave a skilled performance, and one that perfectly complemented Gorbachev's. If he minded the adulation of the Soviet leader, he did not show it. A few days before the general secretary's arrival, he said charmingly, "I don't resent his popularity. Good Lord, I co-starred with Errol Flynn once."[57] Apparently happy to watch the star at work, he gave the television audiences to know that he was the host and he had a personal relationship with Gorbachev that went way back. Welcoming the general secretary to the White House on the morning of December 8, he suggested that the two address each other by first names. "I'm Ron," he said, to which his guest responded, "I'm Mikhail."[58] At the ceremonial signing of the INF treaty—which both Reagan and Gorbachev described as a historic event—the two leaders displayed an easy familiarity with each other, their friendliness setting off the grand drama of an accord between the nuclear superpowers.

In his opening remarks Reagan said, "We have listened to the wisdom of an old Russian maxim. The maxim is *doverai, no proverai*—trust but verify."

"You repeat that at every meeting," Gorbachev interjected, chuckling.

"I like it," Reagan answered, and the room erupted in laughter.[59]

At the closing ceremonies Ron and Nancy, smiling and shaking hands with the Gorbachevs, looked, Shales reported, like the neighbors or a benign pair of in-laws. "It could have been any parting of hosts and houseguests," Shales wrote, "except that the two men had spent a part of the week tossing around the future of the world. . . ."[60]

Shales, like most people, imagined the President in closed sessions with Gorbachev speaking solemnly about SS-18s and submarine-launched cruise missiles, and laying out considered new approaches to the problems of global security. But according to the memoirs of George Shultz, Colin Powell and the White House press secretary, Marlin Fitzwater, this is not what occurred. By these accounts, Reagan, after his polished public performances, seemed to slip out of gear, or out of touch, and in the closed sessions behaved in a fashion that was, well, surreal.

The first official meeting between the President and the general secretary took place the morning of December 8. The meeting was brief, because Mrs. Reagan had insisted that the INF treaty be signed at precisely 1:45 P.M. Her astrologer had told her that that was the most propitious time, and she insisted it be done then even though it made lunch early and disrupted the morning's schedule.[61]

Reagan began by presenting Gorbachev with a pair of gold cuff links, the match of his own, on which figures were beating swords into plowshares. He had thought a lot about this gift. A California friend had given him two pairs of these links, and at a pre-summit briefing a few days before, he had interrupted Powell's disquisitions on economics and arms control to talk about them. Powell tried to tell him gently that the Russians did not wear French cuffs, but the President was not deterred: he talked about the cuff links every time Powell came to brief him.

Gorbachev, however, seemed to be thinking about something else, for, with hardly a look at the links, he said "thank you" and put them in his pocket.[62]

Reagan then launched into a stern lecture about human-rights abuses in the Soviet Union. In the past year the Soviets had talked quite freely about human-rights issues with Shultz, but Reagan's aggressive manner caused Gorbachev to reply that he did not like to be lectured to, that he was not the accused standing at the dock and Reagan was not the prosecutor, and, besides, the domestic affairs of the Soviet Union were no business of the United States. Reagan gave a sharp reply, and the two argued from a script of summits past until the end of the meeting.[63]

The afternoon meeting was scheduled for the Oval Office, but because Shultz wanted to invite a number of people from both delegations, it was changed to the Cabinet Room. By 2:30 P.M. there were people sitting all along the walls as well as at the Cabinet table. The two principals, just come from the INF-treaty signing, swept into the room and, after shaking hands all around, took their seats at opposite ends of the long table. President Reagan, who, Shultz could see, regarded the meeting as an anticlimax to the signing ceremony and was not concentrating, asked his guest to lead off. Pulling a small spiral notebook out of his pocket and putting it beside his briefing books, Gorbachev flipped through the pages and spoke from handwritten notes. He spoke briefly about the importance of the INF treaty and then gave a short introduction to the issues he was going to talk about and which he hoped the summit would address: the START treaty, the need to reduce conventional forces in Europe and the need to control chemical weapons.[64] Powell, who had not seen the Soviet leader in action before, jotted down his impressions: "Bright. Fast. Quick turning radius. Vigorous. Solid. Feisty. Colorful speech."[65] Gorbachev then launched into a discussion of the problems of the Soviet Union and spoke with pride of his efforts to reform the system through perestroika. Shultz was pleased he had opened up this subject, for it offered an opportunity to probe his ideas on domestic reform.[66]

The President, who had been listening with a fixed, pleasant expression, suddenly interrupted, saying that he had a story to tell. Powell knew that Reagan had a stack of Soviet jokes on file cards, most of them gags fed to him by the U.S. Embassy in Moscow. Gorbachev yielded the floor.

"An American professor was in a cab on his way to the airport for a flight to the Soviet Union. It turns out the cab driver was a student. 'When you finish your studies, what do you want to do?' the professor asked. 'Don't know,' the cabbie said. 'I haven't decided yet.'

"At the other end of the flight the professor was taking a cab into Moscow and struck up a conversation with the Russian cab driver. He was a student, too. So the professor asks what he's going to do when he finishes school. 'Don't know,' the cabbie says, 'they haven't told me yet.' " That, the President concluded pleasantly, "is the basic difference between our systems."

During the telling of the story, Gorbachev stared ahead, expressionless. He had heard a number of the President's anti-Soviet stories before, and he had often responded with jokes of his own about the stodginess of the Soviet bureaucracy. But at the end of this one he colored and said nothing. The Americans in the room wanted to drop through the floor. "It was offensive," Powell later told Cannon.[67]

On resuming, Gorbachev dropped the subject of perestroika. He suggested that the two sides move on to discuss conventional-arms reductions, noting that some opponents of the INF treaty in the United States were interested in the issue. The President agreed, and Gorbachev led off the discussion. Afterwards he spoke about chemical weapons, citing facts about U.S. production facilities and the dimension of artillery shells that even Powell did not know.

The President had nothing to say about any of this. On arms-control issues he would turn to Shultz and ask for his comments; on military matters he would turn to Carlucci and say, "Frank, I'm sure you would like to address that point." Shultz was upset. The President should have been the main interlocutor, but Reagan was not well informed about these subjects, and Shultz had no written material to give him for guidance. When the need to say something became intense, Reagan made remarks about the goodness of America. At one point he said, out of the blue, "There have been four wars in my lifetime, and we've never taken an inch in any of them."[68]

When the meeting ended, the Americans retreated to the Oval Office and Shultz said bluntly, "Mr. President, that was a disaster. That man is tough. He's prepared. And you can't just sit there telling jokes."

The President knew the session had not gone well, but he was not devastated. "What do we do now?" he asked. "No more big meetings in the Cabinet Room," Shultz replied. "You do much better in smaller groups and in the intimacy of the Oval Office." Powell promised to get him a better set of talking points for the next day, so that he could lay down the main arguments before inviting others to fill in the details.

"I better go home and do my homework," the President said; "Mikhail has all those details."

Powell and Baker urged him to take a rest before dinner instead.[69]

Reagan performed well at the dinner, and the next morning Powell found him brisk and businesslike. Powell came with three pages of talking points that he and other members of the NSC staff had worked up overnight and laid out double-spaced, like a script. He briefed the President on them, then slipped the pages into a drawer and told Reagan to take them out when Gorbachev opened his briefcase and took out his steno pad with his handwritten notes. "Just make sure, sir, that you speak first," he said.[70]

When Gorbachev arrived, the President greeted him at the entrance to the White House, and the two men and their staffs went to the Oval Office. Following Powell's directions, the President pulled the pages out of the drawer and, speaking naturally, followed the talking points: Yesterday had been a proud day, but, as the general secretary said, there was still much to do. He was encouraged by the Soviet willingness to limit ballistic missiles to between forty-eight and fifty-one hundred warheads. Offensive missiles had kept the peace for over forty years, but our people deserved better. This was the purpose of SDI: it would improve world stability by removing any incentive to strike first in a crisis.

"The scene," Powell writes, "was playing perfectly." But Powell could see that Gorbachev understood exactly what had been done to change the President's performance.

When Reagan finished, Gorbachev, by Powell's account, put his steno pad aside and, speaking without a trace of condescension, gave a fact-filled presentation out of his head. He stated his objections to SDI but said that, if the U.S. wanted to proceed down that path, that was its business; the Soviets would have a response. He then spoke positively about the need to continue the search for agreements to reduce nuclear arsenals.

The discussion went on for an hour and a half, with Powell, Shultz and Carlucci backstopping the President on details. Then Shultz took Gorbachev off to the State Department for lunch.[71]

The following morning Gorbachev was late for his meeting with the President because he had taken some time to make a report to the Politburo and had stopped his motorcade to shake hands with people on the street. The meeting was therefore brief, and after it, the two went for a "photo-opportunity" walk together in the Rose Garden. A few days later the President said that the discussion had been about Nicaragua, and that at his urging Gorbachev had agreed to halt Soviet shipments of arms to the Sandinistas. Gorbachev, however, had done no such thing, and the misunderstanding took some days to clear up.[72]

There was to have been a large working luncheon for the principals and their staffs, but the arms-control experts, who had met for about twelve hours the previous day, had not yet agreed on a ballistic-missile-warhead sub-ceiling and were having trouble coming up with a way to handle ABM-related issues in the final joint statement.[73] Shultz, Carlucci, Powell and their Soviet counterparts had to skip the luncheon to join the expert groups.

Gorbachev was scheduled to leave at 2:30 P.M., and when the luncheon ended, the two leaders went to the Red Room, a ceremonial sitting room on the main floor, to wait for their wives and for the moment when the Reagans and the Gorbachevs would go outside and publicly say their farewells. Gorbachev, nervous and fidgety, asked several times where George and Eduard were. "Working on communiqué," former Ambassador Dobrynin said. Howard Baker was nervous as well. The President always liked to keep to his schedule, and he was ready for the summit to be over. Baker called Shultz in the Cabinet Room and told him that, communiqué or no, the President was leaving at 2:30 P.M.

Baker returned to the group to find Reagan telling Gorbachev about a twelve-hundred-pound man who never left his bedroom. Reagan had read about the man in *People* magazine. "This is a real man," he said. "He went to the bathroom one day, and he fell in the doorway and got stuck. It frightened him so much to get stuck that he went on a diet."

Vice-President Bush and Treasury Secretary James Baker, sitting on a couch across from the President, were doing their utmost not to show incredulity.

"Is this real fact?" Gorbachev said, looking strangely at his interpreter.

"Yes," the President said. "Since his diet, his knee measurement shrank to one and one-third meters around. When the diet is complete, he wants to visit the grave of his mother."

Gorbachev asked Dobrynin about a men's room, excused himself and walked off, gesticulating wildly at Dobrynin.

Minutes before the President's deadline, Shultz and Shevardnadze returned with the communiqué. Gorbachev read and approved it, and Reagan, who said he could see no difference between it and the previous drafts, approved it on the advice of Shultz and Powell. Finally, the Reagans were able to show the Gorbachevs to their waiting Zil.[74]

The entry in Reagan's diary for December 10, 1987, reads, "Well, at last it's over. They've departed and I think the whole thing was the best summit we've ever had with the Soviet Union."[75]

In their accounts of the Washington summit, Shultz, Powell and Fitzwater tell us much about Reagan's behavior, but almost nothing about the substance of the negotiations. For Shultz this is a curious omission, but, then, the performance of "the first genuine team" of the Reagan administration left something to be desired. In preparation for the summit, the "pragmatists" had managed to take several steps backwards from previous administration positions and commitments. Then, when Gorbachev, as usual, presented an array of new proposals for resolving some of the outstanding Cold War conflicts, they were unprepared. Apart from a few advances on START—and a decision to hold a summit in Moscow by June—the negotiations were not much more consequential than those at the Geneva summit of 1985.

In his memoir Shultz tells us that in the fall of 1987 he thought that a "profound and historic shift was under way" in the Soviet Union: the Soviets were practically begging for help to get them out of Afghanistan, they were admitting that the Brezhnev Doctrine was dead, their policy towards Eastern Europe was changing and Boris Yeltsin was charging that perestroika was not going fast enough. The Soviets, he writes, were not just resting up for round two of the Cold War, they were "turning a corner." The administration, he thought, should "work with Gorbachev in order to pull him in the right direction—and as fast as possible."[76]

This view was hardly a radical one, but if Shultz fought for it going into the summit, he lost: the administration had no new agenda for dealing with Gorbachev. The President's secret policy guidance for the summit—since declassified—stated: "While seeking concrete agreements in arms reductions which serve our national interests, we must not foster false illusions about the state of U.S.-Soviet relations." And "Our conduct at the Summit and the framing of its results must in no way complicate our efforts to maintain a strong defense budget and key programs like SDI; they must help us maintain support for the Contras, Mujahedin, UNITA [the Angolan guerrilla movement] and the democratic resistance in Cambodia; and they must reinforce Alliance unity."[77] In other words, the first priority of the administration at the summit was to preserve the defense buildup and the Reagan doctrine. Both of these policies were history in the Hollywood sense of that word, yet administration officials followed the guidance quite faithfully.

When Shevardnadze asked for American help in getting out of Afghanistan in September, Shultz had promised none, but in December 1985 the Reagan administration had made a commitment to halt military assistance to the mujahedin when the Soviets withdrew their forces. Possibly the administration had made the undertaking in the same spirit in which the Europeans had approved the proposal for eliminating INF missiles in 1981. Certainly few in the administration thought that the Soviets would voluntarily move out.[78] In any case, when a journalist mentioned the pledge on the eve of the summit, Reagan, who appeared to be hearing of it for the first time, rejected the idea, saying that he'd never betray the mujahedin. This was thought to be another presidential error, since a State Department spokesman publicly reaffirmed the commitment. But Shultz had decided to renege on the undertaking before the summit, and shortly afterwards the administration publicly repudiated its pledge.[79]

On Nicaragua the administration officials simply missed the boat.

Since the Iran-contra scandal, the administration had lost control over policy in Central America. The Democrats in Congress wanted a negotiated settlement to the conflict, but even after the Congress turned down the administration's request for contra aid in March, Shultz's Assistant Secretary of State Elliott Abrams and other hard-liners continued to press for aid and to resist attempts by Shultz and Baker to reestablish a negotiating track. The result was that the administration could make neither war nor peace. Stepping into this vacuum, President Oscar Arias of Costa Rica took up where previous mediation efforts of the Latin American Contadora Group had left off, put together a peace plan and united all five Central American presidents behind it. Arias and his colleagues asked that the U.S. continue to suspend contra aid to give the plan a chance to succeed. Because Shultz could not hold a policy together, the Speaker of the House, Jim Wright, became their U.S. interlocutor.[80]

In one of the working sessions of the summit, Reagan suggested that the joint communiqué should report that the Soviet Union had agreed to stop sending arms to Nicaragua. Gorbachev made a counter-proposal: the two sides should say they supported the Contadora accords and the Arias plan and that they agreed to look at practical measures that would contribute to implementing them. He added that, in the process of working together, the two sides could agree to stop supplying arms to Nicaragua.[81]

Gorbachev's proposal should have been very good news to the administration. The Soviets had long supported the Contadora process, and now the general secretary was declaring his support for the Arias plan as well. Since few, if any, in the administration believed that the Congress would restore contra aid if the Arias plan succeeded, his proposal that both sides halt their arms shipments in accord with it was almost as good as the promise of a unilateral suspension of Soviet aid—or the concession Reagan mistakenly claimed he had exacted. Administration officials, however, did not take up the offer. Abrams and his colleagues were determined on a showdown with the Democrats in Congress, and the last thing they wanted was a deal with the Soviet Union.

While the administration retreated into the past, Gorbachev took the opportunity of the summit to propose a move forward on a new front. In the meeting in the Cabinet Room on December 8, he spoke of his desire for drastic reductions in conventional forces and for the elimination of chemical weapons. This was not the first time he had brought these matters up. In April 1986 he had proposed "a substantial reduction" of conventional forces in Europe to be verified by on-site inspections in the whole area "from the Atlantic to the Urals." During a visit to Prague in April 1987 he called for a meeting of the foreign ministers of the member countries of the European Conference on Security and Cooperation to open discussions aimed at "radical reductions" in conventional forces. At the same time he announced that the Soviet Union had halted chemical-weapons production and was ready to eliminate its stockpiles as a part of an international agreement. The administration had paid little attention to these proposals; NATO had no position on them, and clearly Shultz was surprised when Gorbachev brought them up at the summit, for, as he tells us, he had no written material on hand. In their memoirs both Shultz and Powell complained that the President was ill-prepared for a discussion of these issues, as though it were somehow his fault that they had not prepared him. To Gorbachev, who by now knew Reagan's limitations pretty well, the significance of the meeting was surely not that the President had made a fool of himself but that the administration had not thought seriously about these issues.[82]

On the second morning of the summit, Reagan, his three pages of talking points firmly in hand, presented an outline of the U.S. positions on the strategic-arms treaty and SDI. Here the administration had come up with a few novelties.

In the meetings leading up to the summit, the two sides had made little progress on START or SDI, in great part because Weinberger had refused to countenance any. But since Weinberger's departure, the administration had moved towards a compromise on limiting ballistic-missile warheads and had developed positions on a few other START issues. It had also come up with a new demand on the Soviets with regard to SDI, one so egregious that even Weinberger had not thought of it. The position had been adopted at an NSPG meeting on the eve of the summit, just days after the President had signed the defense bill with the Levin amendment confining SDI testing to the traditional interpretation of the ABM Treaty.[83]

In Adelman's account of this meeting, Shultz and Carlucci both argued that the administration should ask the Soviets for their explicit agreement to a "broad" SDI testing program, as well as to an eventual SDI deployment.

The proposition surprised even Adelman. For one thing, Adelman writes, there was no "broad" SDI testing program because the SDIO program managers had "never managed to define precisely what tests they needed or to justify all possible needed tests as within the [broad] interpretation of the ABM treaty." For another thing, the administration had always refused to negotiate what the ABM Treaty permitted or prohibited with the Soviets—so why should the Soviets suddenly concur with its interpretation of the ABM Treaty? Then, too, the Congress had just banned testing under the "broad" interpretation.

After listening to Carlucci and Shultz argue for their position, Adelman was moved to ask why the Soviets would be more generous with SDI than the U.S. Congress, some of whose members had American interests at heart. There was general laughter at this sally—but no answer to his question.[84]

According to Talbott, the explanation for this step backwards lay with the new secretary of defense. Carlucci was of a mind with the Joint Chiefs when it came to the development and deployment of SDI weaponry. "I never believed in SDI," he told former Soviet officials years later.[85] Yet, according to Talbott, Carlucci was "genuinely skeptical" about how far the U.S. should go in accommodating Soviet concerns about SDI, and he did not want SDI enthusiasts to accuse him of giving away the store at the first opportunity. In other words, Carlucci thought he himself needed some political protection from the hard right. Why Shultz went along with these proposals is unclear—according to Talbott, he said he would have preferred "a somewhat more realistic approach"—but he did. Colin Powell certainly concurred, for the day that Gorbachev arrived in Washington the President instructed his negotiators to ask for the maximum and to see what they could extract.[86]

But Gorbachev also had a surprise for Reagan and his advisers. In his own presentation in the Cabinet Room he did not mention SDI, and the issue did not come up until Reagan made his own—or, rather, Powell's—presentation the following morning. According to Talbott's account of the exchange, the President said, "We are going forward with the research and development necessary to see if this is a workable concept and if it is, we are going to deploy it."

Gorbachev listened intently, looking Reagan hard in the eye, and when the President had finished, he said without sarcasm or rancor, "Mr. President, you do what you think you have to do. . . . And if in the end you think you have a system you want to deploy, go ahead and deploy it. Who am I to tell you what to do? I think you're wasting money. I don't think it will work. But if that's what you want to do, go ahead." He added, however, "We're moving in another direction, and we preserve our option to do what we think is necessary and in our own national interest at the time. And we think we can do it less expensively and with greater effectiveness."

Having reproduced Sakharov's argument exactly, Gorbachev said, "Let's talk about something else."[87]

How many pages of his script the President then had to skip is not recorded, but apparently the argument served to finesse the rest of the SDI litany, for, according to Powell, the discussion then turned to START.

In the meantime, the working groups on arms control had begun their discussions on START and SDI. Nitze, who headed the American team, disapproved of the administration's step backwards on SDI, but he had his instructions, and in the discussions with Akhromeyev he at one point offered to agree to a sub-ceiling on ballistic-missile warheads that was closer to the Soviet figure of fifty-one hundred than to the American one of forty-eight hundred if Akhromeyev would agree to the American language on SDI.[88] This was the ultimate irony. For the past three and a half years Nitze had been working on a grand compromise in which the U.S. would use the SDI bluff as a bargaining chip to extract major concessions on offensive weapons from the Soviet Union. But now he was offering the Soviets a concession on offensive weapons for the sake of a non-existent defense.

Akhromeyev, however, refused to agree to the American language, since it meant agreeing to the "broad" interpretation of the ABM Treaty. When the American negotiators threatened that, without an agreement, the United States would test and deploy SDI at will, he responded that the Soviet Union would feel free to withdraw from any offensive agreement if it judged that the U.S. testing violated the ABM Treaty.[89]

The struggle over the communiqué continued until after midnight that night and resumed in the morning. At some point in this exercise Nitze decided to try to find language that would paper over the disagreement. Members of his delegation, notably Dr. Henry F. Cooper, Max Kampelman's hard-line deputy at the defense and space talks in Geneva, and the President's current science adviser, William Graham, objected and dug their heels in. But Shultz did not want the summit to end in public discord, so on the last day of the summit the two sides agreed on a sub-ceiling of forty-nine hundred warheads and a formula that finessed their differences on SDI.[90] The statement in the final text of the joint communiqué read:

> Taking into account the preparation of the Treaty on strategic offensive arms, the leaders of the two countries also instructed their delegations in Geneva to work out an agreement that would commit the sides to observe the ABM treaty, as signed in 1972, while conducting their research, development, and testing as required, which are permitted by the ABM treaty, and not to withdraw from the ABM treaty for a specified period of time. Intensive discussions of strategic stability shall begin not later than three years before the end of the specified period, after which, in the event the sides have not agreed otherwise, each side will be free to decide its course of action.[91]

The formula was, strictly speaking, meaningless. The period of non-withdrawal from the ABM Treaty was not settled, and the language relating to what the treaty permitted was so perfectly ambiguous that each side could interpret it as it liked. The U.S. side later claimed that it referred to the "broad" interpretation of the treaty; the Soviets later claimed that it invoked the traditional interpretation. Yet at the time spokesmen from both sides admitted that meaninglessness had been achieved, or, as Max Kampelman put it, the two sides had agreed to "kick the can down the road."[92]

In a televised address later on, Reagan called the summit "a clear success" and said that it had made more progress to halt the arms buildup than any meeting since World War II.[93] This was hardly the case, but it was the impression American officials wanted to convey, and certainly it was a public-relations triumph for both leaders.

In his few days in the United States, Gorbachev had turned "Gorby fever" into "Gorbymania." Polls taken just after the summit showed that 65 percent of the American public had a favorable impression of him; *Time* magazine named him its "Man of the Year," and for the first time in the history of Gallup polling the general secretary of the Soviet Communist Party appeared on the list of the ten most admired men in the country. (He came in at eighth place, in a tie with Lee Iacocca, the flamboyant head of Chrysler.) But it was Reagan's poll numbers that showed the greatest gains from the summit. Though the President still trailed Gorbachev at 61 percent, the figure represented a twelve-point jump since September. What was more, 77 percent of the public approved his handling of U.S.-Soviet relations—the highest percentage of his presidency—and his overall job-approval rating rose to a respectable 58 percent.[94]

Gorbachev for his part said that a good deal had been accomplished at the summit. This was not just diplomacy, for, as he himself suggested, what happened outside the negotiating sessions greatly compensated for what happened within them.[95] The price of Reagan's restoration was precisely what the conservatives had so strenuously attempted to avert for a decade: a general sense in the United States that there was no serious Soviet threat and the Cold War was coming to an end. The crowds on the streets were far ahead of the administration in this perception, but by calling the INF treaty "historic," Reagan made it so, and by playing his part in the buddy movie of Mikhail and Ron, he destroyed the caricature of the Soviets he himself had done so much to create over the past thirty years.

SOME TIME AFTER Reagan left office, Republican right-wingers began to look back on the Reagan years as the golden age of conservatism and to enshrine the fortieth President as their patron saint. Conveniently forgotten at that stage was their own apostasy after the Washington summit and during the last year of his presidency.

Conservative dissatisfaction with Reagan began with the revelations of the Iran arms deals; it grew in 1987 with his choice of new advisers and with the realization that even in his second term he was making no effort to legislate anti-abortion measures, prayer in the schools and the other elements of the conservative social agenda. But it was the INF treaty and the Washington summit that drove them to public protest. Paul Weyrich, head of the Free Congress Committee, said, "Reagan is a weakened president, weakened in spirit as well as clout, and not in a position to make judgments about Gorbachev at this time." Less temperately, others called the President "Regachev" and "nothing more than a useful idiot for Soviet propaganda." Still others spoke of "creeping Nancyism" and of the influence of the "appeasing pragmatists." Beneath the hyperbole there was a genuine concern that out of weakness, or a desire for popular approval, the President and his administration would make wholesale retreat from conservative policies, and in particular from the pursuit of the Cold War.[96]

In the domestic arena the fears of the conservatives were more or less justified, for there the administration had ceased to exist as a political force. After the Republicans lost the Senate in 1986, Reagan's record for getting his programs through Congress sank below that of any president in the post-war era. Efficiently and without much fanfare, the Democrats of the hundredth Congress passed a series of controversial bills including the Omnibus Trade Bill, a civil-rights restoration bill and legislation strengthening the bargaining power of labor; they also expanded the food-stamp program, voted aid to the homeless, provided protection against catastrophic illness and bolstered elementary and secondary education.[97]

In terms of foreign policy, however, conservatives need not have been quite so worried, for in the months following the Washington summit the "pragmatists" shored up all the old policies that could be maintained. Not all of them could.

In early 1988 the administration presented another request for military aid to the Nicaraguan contras, and on the eve of the House vote, scheduled for February 3, the President made his twentieth speech for contra funding in five years. By that time the Sandinistas had taken steps to comply with the Arias peace plan and had acceded to the administration's request that they enter into direct talks with the contras. The President said that the Soviets were continuing to give military assistance to Nicaragua and that the "freedom fighters" were "preventing the permanent consolidation of a Soviet military presence on the American mainland." Maintaining that the Sandinista concessions were the result of military pressure, he called for the aid package as an insurance policy for the peace plan.[98] The Democrats, however, contended that the package would be a "death warrant" for the Arias initiative, and on February 3 the House rejected the request by an eight-vote margin. The vote was understood to be decisive. In February the Soviets renewed their offer of an agreement on mutual military disengagement from Central America, but Elliott Abrams, who had claimed that the House vote would lead to the "dissolution of Central America," refused to meet with the Soviet embassy official charged with making the offer. That left the Soviets and the Cubans as the sole suppliers of military aid to Nicaragua. However, the peace process continued, a cease-fire was declared, and at the end of 1988 Gorbachev unilaterally halted Soviet military aid to the Sandinistas.[99]

Shultz in his memoir maintains that he and the President had long labored for democracy and peace in Nicaragua, but for seven years the only policy the administration pursued with any consistency was support for the contras and the hopeless attempt to unseat the Sandinistas by force. The Central American presidents, the Congress and Mikhail Gorbachev had finally taken the fate of Nicaragua out of the administration's hands.

In southern Africa, too, the Reagan doctrine was all but a dead letter. In 1986 the Congress legislated sanctions against South Africa and sustained them over a presidential veto, handing Reagan a major foreign-policy defeat and dealing a serious blow to the apartheid regime. In Angola the Reagan doctrine entailed support for UNITA, the rebel group led by Jonas Savimbi, against the government in Luanda, which was in turn supported by Cuban troops and Soviet military aid. Since South African forces were supporting Savimbi, this policy was in danger as well. The administration hard-liners had no solution to this problem, so the State Department was free to act, and in 1988 Chester Crocker, the assistant secretary of state for Africa, managed, with the help of his Soviet counterpart and by dint of long and patient negotiations, to achieve an agreement whereby Cuba withdrew its troops from Angola, and South Africa withdrew its forces from Angola and Namibia, giving Namibia its independence. It was a masterful piece of diplomacy—the only one of the Reagan administration—and an important contribution to peace in the region. Still, the U.S. continued to supply arms to Savimbi while the Soviets supported the Luanda government, and the civil war in Angola raged on.

With regard to Afghanistan, the conservatives preferred that the war continue, so that it would keep on bleeding the Soviet Union and end with a triumph for the mujahedin. But on February 8 Gorbachev announced in a national television broadcast that the Soviet troops would begin to move out of Afghanistan on May 15 and would complete their withdrawal in ten months' time. By then the Soviets had given up hope that the U.S. would help with a political settlement to establish a neutral, non-aligned government in Kabul. Gorbachev merely asked that the U.S. work for the signing and implementation of a UN-sponsored agreement between Pakistan and Afghanistan and honor its previous commitment to halt military aid to the mujahedin. The administration, however, decided it would sign the agreement as a guarantor, but would reduce or terminate its arms shipments only in a symmetrical fashion, as Moscow drew down or halted its aid to the government in Kabul. Gorbachev could not renege on his commitment to Najibullah, certainly not at this late date, so, as the Soviet troops moved out, the U.S. continued to aid the mujahedin, the Soviets continued to arm the regime in Kabul and the bloody civil war continued.[100]

At the time few in Washington complained of this arrangement. There had always been strong bipartisan support for the mujahedin; Shultz's insistence on reciprocity seemed fair enough; and it was generally supposed that the Najibullah government would fall soon after the Soviets left and the war would end. However, Najibullah held out for three years after the Soviet troop withdrawal; he held out even after the U.S. and the Soviets agreed to halt military aid to Afghanistan in 1991; he remained in office longer than Gorbachev, and his regime survived the demise of the Soviet Union. After his fall the civil war continued among the mujahedin factions; only in 1997, when a radical fundamentalist regime took power in Kabul, did it begin to peter out.

In December 1987 Shultz did have one ambition that departed radically from the program of the hard-liners: he wanted to conclude a START treaty before Reagan left office and, if possible, before the Moscow summit, scheduled for the following June. In mid-February the President said that the administration should "go for the gold" and complete the treaty by the time of his visit to Moscow.[101] But February passed, then March, then April, and the prospective date for the completion of the treaty moved further and further into the future.

In his memoir Shultz—again uncharacteristically—does not discuss the START negotiations or tell us what the obstacles were. He merely reports that the battle over the ratification of the INF treaty took a "real pint of blood" out of the administration's efforts to conclude a START treaty.[102] This certainly was the case.

In January, Shultz had felt fairly confident that the INF treaty would be ratified without much ado. After all, the Soviets had accepted the proposal that Reagan had made in 1981, and the administration was in the enviable position of having complete support from the opposing party, with its majority in the Senate, plus considerable support from its own. True, Henry Kissinger and other establishment figures had raised all kinds of objections to the treaty, but by February they managed to surmount them, Kissinger with the argument that, although the treaty was flawed, it should be ratified lest the Soviets see weakness and division in Washington.[103] That left only the diehard right-wingers in the opposition.

Still, the administration had a great deal of trouble getting the treaty ratified. As expected, right-wing organizations campaigned against it, and Senate conservatives, led by Jesse Helms and Steven Symms, proposed a series of amendments, any one of which would have killed the treaty. But most of the difficulties were of the administration's own making.

In early February Senator Nunn refused to take testimony on the INF treaty for the Senate Armed Services Committee until Shultz assured him that administration testimony would be authoritative and that the President would not later reinterpret the treaty without the consent of the Senate. The position was not an unreasonable one, for the administration was still holding to the "broad" interpretation of the ABM Treaty and to Sofaer's argument that the executive branch's representations to Congress during the ratification process did not establish the meaning of a treaty. Under pressure from Republican senators who complained that such an assurance might undermine the "broad" interpretation of the ABM Treaty, and therefore the prospects for SDI, Shultz declined Nunn's request. This put him in the absurd position of refusing to attest that what he and the rest of the treaty negotiators would be telling the Senate was true. He changed his mind in short order and gave the assurance, but by the time he did, Senator Biden, the chair of the Judiciary Committee, and Senator Pell, chair of the Foreign Relations Committee, had decided to resolve the issue in principle and as a matter of law. Referring back to the final report of the Foreign Relations Committee on the ABM Treaty dispute, they proposed a treaty reservation, later known as the Biden Condition, whereby the INF treaty would take effect only if the administration agreed to the constitutional principle that treaties must be carried out in accordance with the understanding of the text shared by the executive branch and the Senate at the time of ratification.[104]

On March 30 the Senate Foreign Relations Committee voted to report the INF treaty favorably to the full Senate with the Biden Condition attached. But the Armed Services Committee had further questions. Because the "broad" interpretation of the ABM Treaty permitted the testing and development of weapons based on "other physical principles," Nunn asked whether the INF treaty banned weapons based on "other physical principles." Shultz was preparing to reply in the affirmative when Senator Quayle, who favored an "option" to develop cruise missiles armed with lasers, obtained letters from several former officials, including Weinberger and Adelman, averring that the question of exotic weaponry had not been addressed during the negotiations. Administration officials had to acknowledge that this was perfectly true. In the context of the INF treaty, administration officials had given no thought to laser weapons—or any weapons based on "other physical principles"—for the simple reason that these weapons did not exist. That they were at the same time claiming they needed the "broad" interpretation of the ABM Treaty in order to test SDI weaponry somehow slipped their minds.

In the interests of forestalling yet another "broad" interpretation, Senator Nunn insisted that the administration and the Soviet government give the Senate a written statement that the INF treaty banned exotic weapons.

This was done, causing Quayle to complain bitterly and repeatedly about his non-existent lost option. Finally, Shultz said to him, "Dan, you have to shut down! We can't have the president's achievement wrecked by Republicans!"[105]

Quayle piped down, but by then it was May, and there remained several technical problems of the sort that normally surround arms treaties plus the "killer amendments," one of them proposed by the President's erstwhile ally Pete Wilson, that had to be cleared away before the ratification vote.

The struggle to get the INF treaty ratified cost Shultz a good deal of time and effort, but that was hardly the main obstacle to the conclusion of START. What confounded him was resistance from the Pentagon, a resistance that, as Admiral Crowe tells us quite frankly, was led by the Joint Chiefs of Staff and the secretary of defense.

In his memoir Crowe recalls that, just after the signing of the INF treaty at the Washington summit, Shultz had suggested in a closed meeting with the Chiefs that the START treaty could be completed before the 1988 elections. This sent a tremor through the room. The Chiefs believed that it was not possible, and Frank Carlucci shared their view. A strategic-arms treaty was, Crowe writes, orders of magnitude more complex than an INF treaty, and there were "a large number of significant issues we had not begun to explore in depth." The Chiefs, he writes, were prepared to support deep reductions in strategic weapons, but strategic-arms-control treaties with the Soviet Union were of a different character from other international agreements, in that they struck to the heart of the country's security. Time and patience were therefore required, and many careful studies had to be done, or mistakes with intolerable consequences might be made. Shultz, Crowe writes, had an electoral timetable in mind, but he came to see that START was just not going to move as rapidly as he wished. "In a sense," he writes, "Carlucci and I had thrown our bodies across the tracks."[106]

Crowe's brief account suggests how determined the opposition was, but it does not adequately capture the alarm in the Pentagon at Shultz's proposal, nor does it explain the cause of the consternation.

The strategic-arms agreement was, as Crowe writes, many times more complex than the INF treaty with its simple ban on medium-range weapons. Still, the START negotiations had been going on since 1982, and on those occasions when he was allowed to negotiate, Nitze had worked out a number of difficult issues with the Soviets, among them overall ceilings on strategic launchers and warheads, and sub-ceilings that tightly constrained ballistic missiles. As a result of Soviet concessions, the proposed treaty gave the U.S. what its negotiators had always seen as their goal: deep reductions in Soviet heavy-missile forces and incentives for the Soviets to move to slower, less threatening delivery systems, such as bombers. In Nitze's view, the major issues had been resolved. "The main thing," he said after the Washington summit, "is that we've broken the back of what we mean by 50% reductions. And that means we've solved 90 percent of the problem in START."[107]

The Chiefs did not object to what had been done. In February, Crowe told Nitze, Shultz and Kampelman that the Chiefs were "basically in favor of this treaty as it is shaping up." They complained, however, of the pace. In meeting after meeting, Crowe warned that "the arms control dialogue is acquiring a momentum of its own" and argued for "applying the brakes" until the Pentagon's own defense planning for the future could catch up. "Diplomacy," Crowe said at the time, "has gotten out in front of planning."[108]

In his memoir Crowe tells us that the main impediment to a START treaty was establishing a verification regime for Soviet weapons, including its mobile ICBMs, and its far-flung—and up until now secret—network of manufacturing and support facilities. This was a challenge, but the greater challenges lay elsewhere.

By April 1988 U.S. and Soviet negotiators were agreed on the main issues that stood in the way of an accord. Apart from SDI there were, as Shevardnadze put it, four "knots." All of them involved verification, but Soviet resistance to U.S. demands for strict verification measures did not figure in any of them.[109]

One of the "knots" involved the inspection of strategic-arms production plants, and just as in the INF negotiations, the knot lay in Washington. On the one hand, the hard-liners—this time in the Congress—insisted on intrusive inspections; on the other hand, the Chiefs and the U.S. intelligence agencies did not want the Soviets snooping around U.S. defense plants. "Verification," Carlucci said, "has proved to be more complex than we thought it would be. The flip side of the coin is its application to us. The more we think about it, the more difficult it becomes. . . ."[110]

Another "knot" involved sea-launched cruise missiles. The U.S. held the lead in SLCM technologies, and, partly for that reason, the Soviets had long sought to constrain them severely, if not to ban them outright. Many American military experts, including Nitze, thought the U.S. would be well advised to ban them: when the Soviets caught up technologically, these missiles would pose a far greater danger to the United States than to the Soviet Union. Nuclear-armed SLCMs could, after all, be used to neutralize American naval superiority and could threaten U.S. coastal cities—whereas most major Soviet cities lay inland and were surrounded by air defenses. Carlucci and the Chiefs, however, thought SLCMs were necessary to bolster the forces of NATO after the ground-based INF weapons were removed. The problem, then, was that these small, low-flying drones were easy to hide, and there was no obvious way to distinguish between nuclear- and conventionally armed cruise missiles except by having inspectors go aboard the ships that were carrying them. The Soviets favored such inspections, but since the U.S. Navy did not want Soviet inspectors on advanced U.S. nuclear submarines, the U.S. proposed that each side simply declare how many SLCMs it was going to deploy. As Strobe Talbott pointed out, President Reagan repeated the Russian proverb "Trust but verify" at every meeting with Soviet officials, yet on SLCMs the American position was "Trust," period. The Soviets, however, insisted on verification.[111]

Another point of contention was the counting rule for air-launched cruise missiles, or ALCMs. The Pentagon position was that, because there could be no sure way of verifying how many nuclear-armed cruise missiles were aboard any given plane, each ALCM-carrying bomber should be supposed to be carrying six cruise missiles, even though the American bombers were capable of carrying two or three times that number. Nitze pressed for a number that corresponded more closely to the U.S. load capability, but by April the Pentagon still had not budged.[112]

The fourth issue involved mobile land-based ICBMs. Since 1985 U.S. negotiators had proposed to ban these missiles. The Soviets had rejected the ban, and for reasons that were entirely understandable to American planners: most of the Soviet strategic forces were land-based, and the mobile missiles they had deployed served much the same function as the U.S. submarine-based ballistic missiles in that they were, in the jargon, survivable. In the context of deep reductions in strategic forces, survivability was important because, the fewer the targets, the greater the danger was that in a crisis one side or the other might be tempted, or feel forced, to launch a first strike. Nonetheless, U.S. negotiators argued that mobile land-based missiles should be banned, because the smaller ones could be easily hidden and verification would be impossible. The real problem, however, lay with Weinberger's failure to find a survivable basing mode for the MX in 1982.

In late April, U.S. negotiators abruptly dropped their demand for a ban on mobile ICBMs. The shift came a day after Carlucci announced that the Air Force had come up with a new plan for the MX: in times of crisis fifty MXs would be loaded onto railroad cars and, leaving the military bases in which they were stored, would travel the nation's railroad network amidst the civilian freight traffic. However, Les Aspin and other Democrats on the Armed Services Committees did not think much of the idea, and U.S. negotiators, though admitting that the problem of verifying Soviet mobiles was not insoluble, did not come up with a solution.[113]

Frustrated by the endless internal debates over technicalities, Robert Linhard, Powell's deputy for arms control on the NSC staff, made what Talbott considered a stunning acknowledgment of the core problem of America's arms-control policy. "Even if the Soviets did not exist," he remarked, "we might not get a START treaty because of disagreements on our side." Interviewed by John Newhouse, another senior official said, "If they [the Soviets] came to us and said, 'You write it, we'll sign it,' we still couldn't do it."[114]

For those who understood the ways of the Pentagon there was nothing either surprising or troubling about what was going on. The Chiefs *were* dragging their feet. But, then, although the START negotiations had gone on for six years, the Pentagon under Weinberger's leadership had never taken the completion of a START treaty seriously and had not begun to contemplate force reductions or the force structure the U.S. should have in the decade after the treaty was signed. Looming before the Chiefs was the question of what forces to retain and deploy under the START ceilings. The dilemma was that, if the U.S. retained its most modern and accurate weapons, such as the MX, it would retain those most heavily MIRVed, and because numerous warheads would be loaded onto a relatively small number of missiles, its strategic forces would become less survivable. The Democrats in Congress had long been agitating for the development of a mobile, single-warhead ICBM, the Midgetman, but with the declining military budgets, it was not clear where the funds would come from. On top of this uncertainty, there were many finer points of strategic doctrine to be resolved, and a host of questions about the missions and the budgets of the individual services in the years ahead. Crowe was too much of a diplomat to explain this in his memoir, but that was what he meant when he said at the time, "Diplomacy has gotten out in front of planning." In a sense, then, the START negotiations had just begun in January, and in large measure they had nothing to do with the Soviet Union.[115]

Still, Shultz's initial sense of confidence that the remaining issues of START could be resolved before the end of Reagan's term, if not before the Moscow summit, was not entirely unreasonable. What was required was leadership from the President and his senior advisers. It was not, after all, the job of the Chiefs to force the START treaty to conclusion, and it was not within their power to forge an agreement with Congress on the budgets for years to come. Only the administration could do that. But in spite of the harmony that reigned among Shultz, Carlucci and Powell, the leadership was not there. Carlucci joined the Chiefs in urging delay and did little to settle the issues that concerned them; Shultz became more cautious as the months went on; Colin Powell, a temperamentally cautious man, sided with his colleagues in the Pentagon.[116] As a result, the President made no public or private effort to move the process along. The one decision attributed to him with regard to START put a spoke in its wheels that even the Chiefs did not want.

At the Washington summit Shultz and Shevardnadze had finessed the dispute over SDI and the ABM Treaty with the ambiguously worded joint declaration. Both apparently hoped to complete the START treaty and to put off what one Soviet official later described as the "conceptual dispute" over the ABM Treaty into the indefinite future. But the ambiguity could not be sustained.[117]

Appearing at a background briefing the day the summit ended, Powell said that the joint communiqué permitted the U.S. to go ahead with SDI testing under the "broad" interpretation of the ABM Treaty, and that the general secretary had understood that. Asked if the general secretary had committed himself not to raise any objections, Powell said, "I would not find [the joint communiqué] to be an adequate basis for him to disagree with us."[118]

Soviet spokesmen, including Gorbachev himself, objected strongly to Powell's reading of the communiqué, and when Reagan and Powell reaffirmed it, members of Congress became interested to know what had actually been said at the summit. In a letter to Congress a few weeks later Powell acknowledged that the Soviets had not accepted unrestricted testing of SDI but had explicitly reserved the right to "suspend implementation" of an offensive-arms treaty if the U.S. conducted tests that violated the traditional interpretation of the ABM Treaty.[119]

The admission raised alarm signals for the Joint Chiefs of Staff. At the Washington summit Admiral Crowe accepted the joint communiqué as a diplomatic face-saving device, but now it appeared that the ambiguous formula might be used in lieu of an agreement on defense and space. In a formal letter he told Powell that the communiqué was unacceptable as a basis for future policy. The U.S., he wrote, could not conclude an offensive-arms treaty if the Soviets reserved the right to withdraw from it anytime they decided that an SDI test violated the ABM Treaty. Further, the U.S. could not allow the Soviets to test defensive weapons in ways that the Congress would not permit the U.S. to match. Since the administration could not simply turn around and reject the "broad" interpretation of the ABM Treaty, Crowe suggested that the administration might negotiate a detailed list of tests permitted under the treaty, or that it agree not to withdraw from the treaty for five years—instead of the seven previously proposed—given that little or no SDI technology was likely to be ready for weapons testing within that period.[120]

As Crowe's letter indicated, the Chiefs, though not at all eager to conclude a START treaty any time soon, did favor an agreement on defense and space. Crowe did not embarrass the administration by advocating this position in public, but two of the key military officers in charge of SDI issues did. At a forum on space and national security at the Brookings Institution in March, Vice-Admiral William E. Ramsey, the vice-commander of NORAD and the deputy commander of the Space Command at Colorado Springs, bluntly declared that he favored a negotiated ban on all space weapons. "If we could outlaw weapons in space," he said, "it would be a damn worthy goal." At the same forum Air Force General Robert Herres, the vice-chair of the JCS and the former head of the Space Command, whom Crowe had charged with overseeing SDI, declined to offer an opinion on a ban, but said that the "chances are we would like to see" a negotiated limit on space weapons. Asked about the proposal to negotiate a list of tests permitted by the ABM Treaty—an approach that Nitze had been advocating since early 1987—he said it was "not without merit" and "certainly should not be summarily cast aside."[121]

Just nine years after Ronald Reagan had his revelation about anti-missile defenses at NORAD, the deputy commander and the former chief of the Space Command at Colorado Springs were openly calling for "the President's dream" to be put back in its box.

The White House, however, turned down Crowe's proposals to negotiate limits on SDI and reaffirmed the policy the administration had adopted before the summit. In mid-January, Powell sent the State Department a draft of new instructions for the American team in Geneva requiring negotiators to seek Soviet acceptance of the "broad" interpretation of the ABM Treaty before agreeing to any period of non-withdrawal from the treaty. The title of the U.S. draft treaty on defense and space spoke of "Measures to Facilitate the Cooperative Transition to the Deployment of Future Strategic Ballistic Missile Defenses."

"This is a real strategic arms treaty buster," one U.S. official said. It was just that. The Soviets refused to agree to the "broad" interpretation, and the Chiefs would not accept offensive-arms reductions without a defense-and-space agreement, so the impasse was complete.[122]

On the principle that no issue was ever finally settled in the administration, Nitze continued to fight for the "list approach" to testing under the ABM Treaty, but the White House remained adamantly opposed. In early May, Colin Powell, speaking to a group of defense officials and contractors in the Old Executive Office Building, specifically rejected it, promising that the administration would reject any "deal" or "arrangement" that would "cripple" SDI. The President, he said, was committed to building strategic defenses.[123] What this meant was that administration officials were unwilling to take the political risks involved in moving the President off the "broad" interpretation.

In the months leading up to the Moscow summit, an extraordinary round of high-level U.S.-Soviet meetings took place. In February, Shultz, accompanied by Colin Powell, met with Gorbachev as well as Shevardnadze in Moscow; in March, Shevardnadze came to Washington, and Carlucci held an unprecedented meeting with Soviet Defense Minister Dmitri Yazov in Bern, Switzerland; in April, Shultz and Powell returned to Moscow and again saw Gorbachev; in May, Shultz and Shevardnadze met in Geneva. In addition, there were several meetings between U.S. assistant secretaries of state and their Soviet counterparts. Although in late February the President, on the advice of Howard Baker, had attempted to lower expectations for the completion of a START treaty by the time of the summit, all of this activity quite naturally created the impression that progress was being made on all kinds of issues, particularly since U.S. officials never publicly expressed disappointment with the lack of it.[124]

In reality, however, the high-level meetings were occasions for disagreements on Afghanistan, on NATO plans for new military programs to "compensate" for the INF missiles being destroyed, on a wide range of START issues, and on the "broad" interpretation of the ABM Treaty. There was also a disagreement on the Krasnoyarsk radar, which the administration had long insisted violated the ABM Treaty. In 1987 Shevardnadze had admitted that it was a violation; construction on it was stopped, and three American congressmen and a team of experts were permitted to visit it. They found that, though the radar was designed to track missiles, it was not designed to serve as a part of an ABM system. Nonetheless, the Administration now insisted that the enormous radar facility be dismantled as a condition for START.[125] Shevardnadze tried to engage Shultz on the subject of conventional-force reductions in Europe, but since American officials did not believe the Soviets were ready to make any real concessions, Shultz put him off.[126] There was progress on southern Africa and on a few peripheral issues; and the Moscow summit was set for May 29 to June 2.

Gorbachev was impatient, and said so. "Doesn't it seem to you that we are just marking time?" he asked Shultz on one occasion. On another occasion he criticized the virtue Americans seemed to pride themselves in. "The United States," he said, "needs a more philosophical approach. The inertia that is inherent in pragmatism makes the United States look only to its own advantage. It needs to look at things more broadly. Unless it does, the two sides would fail on the specifics: there will be a dead end on specific issues."[127]

Gorbachev was in a hurry—and not just in regard to the negotiations. In the spring of 1988 he was formulating plans for a restructuring of Soviet relations with Eastern Europe and a normalization of relations with China. He was also preparing to take a giant step in his domestic-reform program. A year and a half before, he had proposed that a party conference, a major gathering of party representatives from across the Soviet Union, be convened to take decisions that otherwise could not be made until the next five-yearly party congress in 1991. The proposal was controversial—the last party conference had been held in 1941—but the Central Committee eventually agreed, and the conference was scheduled for June 1988. Gorbachev's initial aim had been to obtain an authoritative resolution in favor of perestroika and to change the membership of the Central Committee so as to gain a majority in favor of his economic reforms. In the meantime, he had decided that there could be no economic reform without a transformation of the Soviet political system.[128]

For most of the spring the auspices for the party conference appeared unfavorable. The economy was not responding to the first series of reforms taken under perestroika; there were ethnic and nationalist disturbances in the Baltic States, Transcaucasia and Central Asia, and in Azerbaijan violent protests had broken out over the Armenian-populated enclave of Nagorno-Karabakh. In addition, the conservatives in the party leadership were mounting a serious effort to roll back Gorbachev's reforms.

In mid-February, Ligachev, who had become the leader of a powerful conservative constituency in the leadership, launched a scathing attack on glasnost, holding it responsible for the expressions of nationalism, the blackening of Soviet history and the pernicious effects of rock and roll. On March 13, when Gorbachev and his ally Aleksandr Yakovlev, the Politburo chief for press and propaganda, were out of the country, a conservative newspaper, *Sovetskaya Rossiya,* published a long letter attributed to a Leningrad chemistry teacher, Nina Andreyeva, attacking the Gorbachev reform policies, defending Communist orthodoxy and Stalin and suggesting that Gorbachev and his allies were not Communists but "left-wing liberal socialists." The following day, Ligachev praised the Andreyeva letter at a meeting of Soviet editors, drawing the attention of editors all over the country and in effect instructing them to reprint it. For three weeks the letter was reproduced and distributed widely while conservative party propagandists suggested that the letter represented the new party line and a victory for Ligachev and his supporters. Afraid that the balance of forces in the upper ranks of the party had changed, the reformers made no response.[129]

On his return to Moscow, Gorbachev consulted with Defense Minister Dmitri Yazov and with Marshal Akhromeyev, the chief of staff, to be sure he had the support of the armed forces. Yakovlev drafted a reply to the Andreyeva letter, and in early April, Gorbachev took the matter to the Politburo. Discovering that an alarming number of his colleagues had some sympathy with the sentiments expressed in the Andreyeva letter, he nonetheless insisted that a formal rebuttal be made, arguing that he could not continue without an unequivocal endorsement of his policy—in effect putting his leadership on the line. The conservatives backed down; Yakovlev's rebuttal appeared in *Pravda* on April 5, and afterwards the reform movement reemerged in a more powerful and more radical form.[130]

Strengthened by the outcome of the Andreyeva affair, Gorbachev in April conducted a series of intensive discussions with his reformist allies in and out of the Politburo and emerged with a blueprint for a revolutionary change in the Soviet political system. Laid out in a series of detailed proposals, or "theses," for the party conference, the plan called for the replacement of Leninist "democratic centralism" with a government based on individual rights and the rule of law. At the federal level there was to be a president and a bicameral legislature, chosen by an elected Council of People's Deputies, with a prime minister and a Cabinet responsible to it. Elections for the council, the local soviets and the local leadership posts were to be held by secret ballot; there were to be multiple candidates for each post and term limits for all elected officials. Gorbachev had pressed for a multi-party system, but this proved too radical for the Politburo. However, the plan called for an independent judiciary, and it contained a lengthy proposal for the codification of individual rights, including the right to remain innocent until proven guilty, and provisions for freedom of speech, freedom of assembly and freedom of conscience.[131]

What would happen to this plan in the Central Committee and in the party conference was Gorbachev's main concern in April and May. Glasnost had provided a foundation for institutional change, in that there were now heated debates in the press, ordinary people felt free to criticize government policies and public opinion had become a factor in politics. However, it also made party politics a good deal less predictable and less amenable to fiat from the Politburo. As a result, Washington had a role to play in the outcome of the party conference. Gorbachev wanted arms reductions for economic and diplomatic reasons, but he also wanted them because his reform program had a far greater chance of success if the Soviet public believed that the nuclear threat was receding and the normalization of Soviet relations with the West was under way.[132]

But in Washington almost no one was in a hurry—and certainly not with regard to START. The Pentagon was still ruminating upon its force "requirements"; the administration was putting no pressure upon it, nor was the defense community. Sam Nunn agreed with the Chiefs that it was probably unwise to proceed to a START treaty when there was so much division and uncertainty about the future of American strategic programs. Henry Kissinger, who ever since the Washington summit had deplored the "euphoria sweeping Washington," warned that it was not realistic to think that Gorbachev was moving in a radically new direction. He called for a replacement of ideological politics by *Realpolitik* and opposed concluding START unless an agreement to reduce Soviet conventional forces in Eastern Europe was reached at the same time.[133] What Kissinger apparently did not know was that the administration was stalling Gorbachev's efforts to negotiate a reduction of conventional forces and arms.

In public, administration officials spoke of Gorbachev and the Soviet Union much as they had two and three years before. Robert Gates, as always, saw nothing but danger ahead from "a more competitive and stronger adversary . . . whose aggressive objectives abroad and essential totalitarianism at home remain largely unchanged." Shultz objected to Gates's assessment, but in public even he took a negative line. In a major speech on February 8 he said that a Soviet Union that was ready to deal with other countries and its own people through dialogue rather than intimidation was a prospect for the "distant" rather than the "foreseeable" future. Hence, he said, "I find it difficult to believe that our relations with the Soviet Union will ever be 'normal' in the sense that we have normal relations with most other countries."[134] As for the President, he, when speaking informally, praised glasnost and perestroika and expressed sympathy with the problems Gorbachev faced in reforming the Soviet "bureaucracy." But in his speeches he often took a very hard line. Addressing an audience in Springfield, Massachusetts, on April 21, he extolled the virtue of speaking bluntly about the superior morality of the West, ridiculing the idea that this kind of candor could be dangerous or worsen U.S.-Soviet relations and claiming that it had had practical results. "We learned long ago," he said, "that the Soviets get down to serious negotiations only after they are convinced their counterparts are determined to stand firm. We knew the least indication of weakened resolve on our part would lead the Soviets to stop the serious bargaining, stall diplomatic progress, and attempt to exploit this perceived weakness." He noted that the Soviets had pledged to get out of Afghanistan, but suggested that they would not. "We believe that they still hope to prop up their doomed, discredited puppet regime, and they will still seek to pose a threat to neighboring Pakistan," he said.[135]

Shultz and Powell were, as it happened, in Moscow on April 21, and in a meeting with them the following day, Gorbachev began by delivering a tirade about the speech. The U.S. administration was taking a backward step and attempting to preach. Did Reagan really intend to bring this ideological baggage to Moscow? If so, the Soviet side would have to answer back, and there would be an argument such as would negate everything that had been achieved.

Shultz and Powell were stunned. The President's speech had been routinely cleared by the State Department, and Powell, who had cleared it for the NSC staff, had paid it small attention, for it seemed to him a perfectly normal effort by White House speechwriters to anchor the Republican right wing before the summit.[136]

Having delivered his warning, Gorbachev changed his approach. He promised that Reagan would receive a warm reception when he came to Moscow and went on to other matters. Later, according to Powell, he spoke about his plans for changing the Communist Party and ending the ideological struggle at home and abroad. When he had finished, he looked at General Powell and, with eyes twinkling, said, "What are you going to do now that you've lost your best enemy?"[137]

Gorbachev's message for the White House was noted, and on May 4 Reagan gave what the *Washington Post* described as an "unusually conciliatory speech" in which he praised recent Soviet achievements in human rights and—quite exceptionally—criticized American failings in such areas as homelessness and racial injustice.[138]

White House officials had no intention of endangering the summit. They had begun preparations in early February, when Colin Powell and Thomas Griscom, the White House communications director, put together a planning group, and since then the advance work had taken up much of their time. In February the President's pollster Richard Wirthlin had assembled a focus group of suburban-Philadelphia voters as a testing ground for the themes the President might use in his speeches, and in March a summit advance team had gone twice to Moscow to work out the President's schedule.[139]

As these preparations suggested, White House aides had more than a passing interest in the domestic impact of the summit. In the wake of the Washington summit, Reagan's polls had slumped once again. Americans complained of the budget deficits, of administration policy in Central America—and in fact about almost everything except his new policy towards the Soviet Union. The spring brought further bad news to the White House. The administration botched an attempt to oust the Panamanian dictator, Manuel Noriega, who had been indicted for drug trafficking by an American court. Donald Regan published a memoir with unflattering portraits of Ronald and Nancy Reagan. More important, Attorney General Edwin Meese was threatened with indictment on charges of conflict of interest, and senior congressional Republicans were calling upon him to resign. The Meese affair was only the latest in a string of scandals involving Reagan's appointees and close associates, and a rank smell was rising from the administration. According to aides, the President looked forward to the summit as a way to divert attention from these embarrassments and to "restore the luster of his presidency."[140]

At the end of his April visit to Moscow, Shultz acknowledged that the START treaty could not be completed in time for the summit. The two sides were moving towards each other on the verification of mobile missiles and air-launched cruise missiles, but they had come no closer on sea-launched cruise missiles. And there remained the impasse on SDI. In late May, State Department and ACDA officials expressed doubt that the summit would produce a breakthrough on START. White House officials, however, seemed far more optimistic. Reagan raised the possibility that he might meet again with Gorbachev if the treaty were ready for signing before the end of his term. Just before the summit began, Colin Powell told the traveling White House press: "If we make some progress on sea-launched cruise missiles—if not a breakthrough, we might make sufficient progress that we can return to work in Geneva, finish it over the summer, and in the fall at a ministerial meeting or higher, should that come about, we could go to closure on it." This optimism heightened the sense of anticipation about the meeting of the two world leaders and Reagan's first visit to Moscow.[141]

On May 26, three days before the summit was to begin, the Senate passed the Biden Condition to the INF treaty by a vote of seventy-two to twenty-seven. The following day the majority leader, Senator Robert Byrd, cleared the "killer amendments" off the schedule, and the Senate voted ninety-three to five to ratify the INF treaty.[142]

President Reagan left Washington on May 26 for Helsinki, where he spent two days resting up before going on to Moscow. This time the President's advisers had left little to chance: the degree of detailed planning was said to be unprecedented in the Reagan administration. The President's schedule had been set almost two months in advance, and White House speechwriters, armed with the conclusions drawn from the focus group, had already prepared the fourteen sets of remarks the President was to make over the ten-day period that included the Helsinki stopover and a visit to London on the way back.[143] According to *New York Times* sources, the presidential aides had set out to construct a summit scenario that would resemble an American political campaign, with strong emphasis on visual impressions and on the emotional impact the President would make as he went out among the Soviet people. They wanted, sources said, to emphasize the President's "incomparable skill" at carrying out the ceremonial functions of the presidency while playing down his weakness in grasping and explaining the details of public policy.[144]

On May 27 Gorbachev's "theses," forwarded by the Central Committee, appeared in *Pravda.* Jack Matlock, the U.S. ambassador to Moscow and a career State Department Soviet specialist, read them in Helsinki, where he was helping to brief Reagan for the summit. He was not surprised by their appearance, for there had been discussions of reform in the Central Committee and in Gorbachev's speeches. But the contents astonished him—most particularly the sections on the separation of powers, judicial independence and the rights of citizens. To Matlock some of the language seemed to have been lifted from the U.S. Constitution. The "theses" stopped short of a multi-party democracy, but still they described something closer to a European-style social democracy than to a Communist state, and Matlock had no doubt that, if enacted, they would bring the Communist Party monopoly on power to an end. Briefing Reagan on them that afternoon, he said that, if the "theses" turned out to be real, the Soviet Union could never again be what it had been in the past.[145]

On the 29th Reagan flew to Moscow and had his first meeting with Gorbachev that afternoon. What happened in this meeting, and at the three other formal meetings between the two leaders, is largely unrecorded in the memoirs of Reagan's advisers, for, as was not the case with the Washington summit, all the preparations paid off, there were few surprises and almost everything proceeded according to plan. Over the past six months American officials had become extremely familiar with the Soviet agenda: progress on START, a ban on chemical weapons, conventional-force reductions, an expansion of U.S.-Soviet trade and so on. In Moscow, Gorbachev made only one major new offer: a proposal for conventional-force reductions in Europe that would remove the Soviet advantage and then cut a half-million men from the NATO and Warsaw Pact forces. U.S. officials rebuffed the offer; they later told reporters that they considered it designed more for political appeal than serious negotiations, and the American press paid small attention to it. As was also not the case at the Washington summit, the President was well briefed and well rehearsed. Just as at Geneva in 1985, all he had to do was to follow the script through the U.S. agenda, and this he did pretty well.[146]

In the first session Gorbachev expressed a desire for an increase in U.S.-Soviet trade. "I was ready for him," Reagan writes. "I'd thought about what I was going to say when he brought up the issue: One reason we have trouble increasing trade with your country is that many members of Congress as well as many other Americans oppose it because of what they consider Soviet human rights abuses." Rather than specify what these abuses might be, Reagan delivered a disquisition about America as a nation of immigrants united against discrimination on the basis of ethnic origin or religious belief. That finished, he said that Americans were encouraged by the changes in the Soviet Union, but wouldn't it be a good idea to tear the Berlin Wall down? Gorbachev, Reagan reports, said nothing harsh in rebuttal. Later the two leaders pledged to do their best to complete the START treaty and to conclude agreements on chemical weapons and conventional forces.[147]

In the rest of the formal sessions Reagan apparently took a less aggressive approach, and on one occasion he permitted Gorbachev to talk at length about perestroika. But in what passed for negotiations the pattern remained the same: Gorbachev would make a familiar proposal, Reagan would register familiar objections or change the subject and Gorbachev would then go on to talk about something else. In conclusion, the two of them would agree that they had come a long way, or that their one-on-one discussions had done so much to dispel misconceptions and build trust and understanding. This ritual was disturbed only once.

In a plenary session on the last day of the summit Gorbachev asked Reagan to approve the brief statement he had given him in the first session affirming the belief of the two leaders in the peaceful resolution of disputes and in the principles of peaceful coexistence and non-interference in the internal affairs of others. Reagan had said that he liked it, but, when consulted, his advisers most emphatically did not like it. Shultz and other U.S. officials understood "peaceful coexistence" to be a Soviet slogan which implied a truce between governments while the class struggle continued; to them it sounded like the Basic Principles of Mutual Relations, signed in 1972 and associated with the now much-despised Nixon-Brezhnev détente. In addition, Colin Powell thought that Gorbachev would use the word "non-interference" to denounce American support for the "freedom fighters" under the Reagan doctrine. In subsequent meetings with their Soviet counterparts, U.S. officials had redrafted the declaration and had thought the matter disposed of, but now Gorbachev had put it back on the table and was challenging Reagan to take the initiative. "You had no objection to this last Sunday," he said. Reagan, who still could see nothing wrong with the statement, was about to agree to sign it when Shultz and Carlucci objected and called for a recess. The American team huddled, and Shultz once again explained his objections to the President. Obediently Reagan went back to Gorbachev and turned the last of the Soviet proposals down.[148]

This was not high drama, but, then, the drama of the summit took place in public in a series of speeches, performances and tableaux vivants, all of them perfectly scripted and choreographed in advance.

For lack of any negotiating objectives, Reagan's advisers had some months before decided to make human rights, as Shultz put it, the "overriding and powerful theme of the Moscow summit." The President announced this theme in Helsinki in a speech criticizing the Soviets for suppressing religious freedom and restricting the right of emigration for Soviet Jews. In Moscow he visited the Danilov Monastery, a thirteenth-century sanctuary of the Russian Orthodox church, where he spoke of his commitment to religious freedom and the "deep faith that lives in the hearts of the people of this land." He also attended a much-publicized reception for ninety-eight "refuseniks" and human-rights activists at the U.S. ambassador's residence, at which he praised the positive steps Gorbachev had taken and insisted that more remained to be done.[149]

Human rights was not Reagan's only theme. In a luncheon with Soviet intellectuals from many fields, he spoke about democracy and freedom of artistic expression. Then, in an address to students at the prestigious Moscow State University, he spoke about the blessings of democracy, individual freedom and free enterprise. Standing on a podium in front of a monumental bust of Lenin—so monumental it could not be removed by his advance men—he waxed eloquent about the great economic engine of the United States, the "continuing revolution of the market place," the creativity of capitalism and the information age in which "one individual with a desktop computer and a telephone commands resources unavailable to the largest government just a few years ago." He concluded with a quotation from Gogol and the remark, "Your generation is living through one of the most exciting and hopeful times in Soviet history."

With a few amendments the speech could have been given at any American college commencement that year, but certainly nothing like it had ever been heard in Moscow. The students gave him a standing ovation.[150]

Except in his speeches on human rights, Reagan avoided any direct criticism of the Soviet Union, and as the days passed, a new theme developed: that of approval for Gorbachev and his works. Under its influence Reagan muted the criticisms he had made. In answer to a question from a student at Moscow State University, he blamed the bureaucracy—as opposed to Soviet policy—for the fact that the dissidents he met had not been allowed to leave the country.

At Shultz's instigation Reagan walked through Red Square one morning, with Gorbachev acting as his guide. Followed closely by photographers and television cameras, the two leaders chatted easily with each other and with the small groups of people the KGB allowed in the square. Gorbachev was heard to propose civil space cooperation and a joint U.S.-Soviet mission to Mars. A few feet from Lenin's tomb, Reagan put his arm over the general secretary's shoulder. Gorbachev then lifted a small boy up in his arms and invited him to "shake hands with Grandfather Reagan." The two leaders cuddled the child as if campaigning for election together. Back inside the Kremlin grounds, a reporter asked the President what had become of the "evil empire" he had warned about in 1983. "I was talking about another time, another era," the President replied.[151]

As usual, Reagan appeared more intimate with Gorbachev in public than he actually was in private. Gorbachev, for his part, treated Reagan in a respectful but somewhat patronizing fashion, as the elder statesman who was about to retire. In the negotiating sessions he and his colleagues seemed impatient with all the old disagreements and impatient for new leadership on the American side.[152] Still Gorbachev played the genial host, honoring the President with a state dinner and entertaining the Reagans in a more personal fashion. On the last evening of the summit the Reagans attended a special performance of the Bolshoi Ballet, where "The Star-Spangled Banner" was played, dined privately with the Gorbachevs at their dacha on the outskirts of Moscow and afterwards drove through Red Square again so that Nancy could see the floodlit cathedrals and the towers of the Kremlin.

Reagan grew tired during the last days of the summit: he dozed off in public at the ballet and while Soviet intellectuals droned on; his final press conference was perfunctory, and at one point he seemed so bewildered by the questions of reporters that Gorbachev stepped forward and protectively cut off the questioning. But for the most part Reagan played his part very well. In his speech at House of Writers he seemed to be reflecting upon his performance, for he spoke about being an actor and how in the movie business it was easy to get typecast. "Well, politics," he said, "is a bit like that, too. So I've had a lot of time and reason to think about my role." Then he quoted Sergei Eisenstein, a filmmaker not much cited in Hollywood, on the importance of having a vision and holding it. "You must see and feel what you are thinking. You must see and grasp it." In practice, Reagan seemed to be having some difficulty grasping the reality of what he was doing. "There is no way I can really explain how I came to be here," he told Hugh Sidey on his fourth day in Moscow.[153]

The sense of unreality was, however, shared by many of the reporters who accompanied him. Here was Ronald Reagan talking to Moscow State University students as if they were an American graduating class. Here was Ronald Reagan walking through Red Square arm-in-arm with the general secretary of the Soviet Communist Party. What was more, the Soviet public was clearly taking to him. Crowds gathered wherever he went. Merely curious at first, they warmed towards him, until, on the last day, they lined the streets and applauded him steadily, much as the crowds in Washington had applauded Gorbachev. There was, one reporter wrote, a dreamlike quality to the whole experience.[154]

At the ceremonial exchange of the instruments of ratification for the INF treaty, Gorbachev said that each of the four summit meetings had "dealt a blow to the foundations of the Cold War." Later, at Reagan's press conference in the U.S. ambassador's residence, a reporter asked the President a question on the lips of many: could he "now declare the Cold War over?" Reagan hesitated. "I think right now, of course," he began slowly, as though debating whether or not to take the leap. Then he decided against it. "As I've said, *doverai no proverai,* trust but verify." But his hesitation said much to reporters, as did the fact that he blamed "the bureaucracy" rather than the Soviet leadership for the restrictions on emigration.[155]

In taking his leave the following day, Reagan gave a sentimental speech in which he called Gorbachev a friend and spoke of "hope for a new era in human history, an era of peace." In thanking his Soviet hosts, he said that he and Mrs. Reagan had been "truly moved" by the warmth and hospitality the Gorbachevs had shown them and were most grateful for the reception given them by the Soviet people. He had, he said, mentioned to the students at Moscow State University "that they appeared to my eyes exactly as would any group of students in my country, or anywhere in the world. So, too, did Nancy and I find the faces, young and old, here on the streets of Moscow." As for the summit itself, he said, "I would like to think that our efforts during these past few days have slayed a few dragons and advanced the struggle against the evils that threaten mankind, threats to peace and to liberty."[156]

Gorbachev responded by thanking the President and his colleagues for their cooperative and businesslike approach, and recalling that they had "come a long way" since the Geneva meeting two and a half years ago. But he did not call Reagan a "friend" or extol the results of the negotiations. In his press conference the evening before, he had called the summit a meeting of "missed chances" and complained that the U.S. was not prepared to break deadlocks on START and the reduction of conventional forces. "Our dialogue has not been easy," he now said, "but we have mustered enough realism and political will to overcome obstacles and switch the train of Soviet-U.S. relations from a dangerous track to a safer one. It has, however, so far been moving much more slowly than is called for by the real situation in both our countries." And he added, "For our part I can assure you we will do everything in our power to continue moving forward."[157]

At the end of four days American and Soviet officials had few substantive achievements to report. In the START negotiations there was considerable progress on the verification of mobile ICBMs and on ALCMs, but none on SLCMs or SDI. Just as at summits past, there were a few minor agreements on matters such as fishing rights and student exchanges. As Jim Hoagland of the *Washington Post* put it most succinctly, the diplomatic business done at the summit "could have been accomplished by a couple of assistant secretaries of state in Geneva before lunch."[158]

Reagan-administration officials, however, wanted a different verdict on the summit. Briefing NATO foreign ministers on his way home, Shultz said that "in a curious way" the fact that there was no START agreement "has caused people to reflect on what may be the more important, the deeper and more significant meaning of what the President and the General Secretary have managed to put together. Because underneath it all, what we are looking for is an East-West relationship, or a U.S.-Soviet relationship, that is broad, that is solid, manageable. . . ." In an interview with reporters on the trip back to the United States, Colin Powell bridled at suggestions that the summit was primarily spectacle with little substance. "Is there substance in the president speaking at the Danilov Monastery? To students at Moscow State University? At the House of Writers?" he asked. "I submit to you that there's real substance . . . that goes well beyond style." It was not, he added, something that could be accomplished by an assistant secretary of state.[159]

Reagan, for his part, waxed euphoric about the summit. In a major speech in the Guildhall in London on his way home, he celebrated it as marking a turning point in East-West relations and said that "a world-wide movement toward democracy" was ushering in "the hope of a new era in human history, and, hopefully, an era of peace and freedom for all." He praised perestroika and for the first time mentioned that Gorbachev had initiated a "democratic reform" which included "such things as official accountability, limitations on length of service in office, an independent judiciary, revisions of the criminal law and lowering taxes on cooperatives." To "all those familiar with the postwar era," he said, "this is a cause for shaking the head in wonder. Imagine the president of the United States and the general secretary of the Soviet Union walking together in Red Square, talking about a growing personal friendship and meeting, together, average citizens, realizing how much our people have in common." Quite possibly, he said, "we are entering an era in history, a time of lasting change in the Soviet Union. We will have to see." On his arrival back in Washington he called the summit "momentous" and said that it produced "real progress on human rights, on regional conflicts, on greater contacts between the people of the Soviet Union and the United States."[160]

Later Reagan compared the summit to a Cecil B. DeMille extravaganza and said he felt he had "dropped into a grand historical moment."[161]

CHAPTER ELEVEN

The End of the Cold War

For Reagan the Moscow summit was a personal triumph. All the concern for the domestic impact of his performance had clearly paid off, for his popularity rating climbed to almost 70 percent, or to that of the early days of his presidency, and 77 percent of the American public approved his conduct of U.S.-Soviet relations. In the White House the news was particularly welcome because, according to Gallup, a majority of Americans gave the President bad marks on the economy, the deficit and other issues, and only the perception of his success at the summit allowed his job-approval rating to remain relatively stable at 51 percent. At the same time—and for reasons clearly related to his performance—"Gorbymania" reached new heights: on the eve of the summit 72 percent of Americans had a favorable impression of the general secretary, and after it 83 percent registered their approval of Gorbachev.[1]

Reagan had done exactly what the country wanted, but he had also changed the perception of the Soviet Union in the United States.

On the day the Moscow summit opened, a *Washington Post* editorial predicted that after Reagan's visit to Moscow there would be "few Americans left who refuse to lend Moscow at least some legitimacy, some psychological parity in their minds," for the reason that "probably no one else—no, not Richard Nixon, who was himself in Moscow 14 years ago—could carry this sort of heavy symbolic baggage. No one else so well represents the American temper, with its provincial tinge and its ingrained skepticism but also with its hope and openness." That was Reagan's text exactly. From the focus group the President's aides had learned that Americans favored the President's efforts to improve U.S.-Soviet relations and liked Gorbachev but remained suspicious of Soviet intentions.[2] In Moscow, Reagan acted out a voyage of discovery, beginning with his skepticism about human rights, proceeding with the apparent intimacy of his relationship with Gorbachev and ending with his apparent discoveries that ordinary Soviet citizens were much like Americans, that the general secretary had made substantial reforms and that "a new era" was dawning. Reagan did not announce that the Cold War was ending in so many words, but his performance convinced many Americans that this was exactly what was happening.

The American public applauded Reagan's performance, and the press reviews were generally laudatory. But in Washington the enthusiasm was muted. The day the summit ended a *Washington Post* editorialist wrote: "It was exciting to have President Reagan in Moscow, but, truth be told, it will be good to have him out. . . . He was becoming less an attentive observer than something of an uncritical booster of Soviet reform." The editorial praised Reagan for not permitting Gorbachev to "force the pace of decision" on a strategic-arms accord "for which there was not yet sufficient preparation or agreement." We are, the editorial concluded, "glad Mr. Reagan went to Moscow and glad he is coming home without any unfortunate additional baggage."[3] Conservatives had harsher words for the President. Not fringe right-wingers but such as Henry Kissinger, William Safire and George Will accused Reagan of being unduly influenced by his personal encounters with the seductive Gorbachev and guilty of creating a false "euphoria" that would give a breathing space to the unchanging enemy.[4]

Watching the summit on television at home in Kennebunkport, Maine, George Bush did not applaud. "The Cold War isn't over," he was heard to remark.[5] In a press interview he said, "I don't agree that we know enough to say that there is that kind of fundamental change . . . on the part of the Soviet Union." Asked if a redefinition of the Soviet threat could lead to a reduction in defense spending, he replied that he disagreed with the premise. Gorbachev, he said, is "stylistically different," but as for his intentions, "my view is that the jury is still out."[6]

This was a jarring note. For a vice-president to criticize the President while he was representing the United States in Moscow was unheard of, and Bush had been a most loyal VP. Still, Bush was running for President, and journalists covering his campaign were not surprised by his remarks. Earlier in the year he had taken public issue with the administration's handling of the Noriega affair, and he had taken quite a hard line on the Soviet Union. In a speech at the National Press Club in January he had mentioned Gorbachev's name in the same breath with Hitler's and said that the general secretary was not a "freedom-loving friend of democracy" but, rather, an "orthodox, committed Marxist." Later he had expressed great skepticism about the Soviet experiment, warning against a "euphoric, naively optimistic view of what comes next." To the political press his jaundiced remarks about the Moscow summit seemed to be just another awkward attempt to move out from under Reagan's shadow and at the same time to curry favor with the Republican right, where he had no base of support.[7]

The START talks continued after the summit. Over the summer some progress was made on technical issues, but the two major obstacles to an agreement, the differences on SLCMs and the ABM Treaty, remained intact, as did the American position on ALCMs. Still, the summit had engendered such anxiety on the right that twenty Republican senators urged the administration to declare the Krasnoyarsk radar a "material violation" of the ABM Treaty. In effect, they were asking the administration to transform its long-standing objection to the radar into a formal assertion that would give the U.S. the right to withdraw from the treaty at any time, thereby introducing yet another obstacle to START. Several top administration officials, including Carlucci, Meese and Treasury Secretary James Baker, argued for the proposal—Baker on the grounds that it would prevent the administration from appearing weak. Shultz and Nitze objected and eventually killed the idea with the help of the Chiefs, but the administration continued to insist that the Soviets dismantle the huge radar complex.[8]

On September 21 Shevardnadze came to Washington, where he met with Reagan and Bush and held his last scheduled negotiating session with Shultz. At the end of their meeting both he and Shultz expressed disappointment that the treaty could not be concluded during the Reagan administration. Shultz promised that the two sides would continue to work in Geneva during the remaining months and "turn over to our successors a very good package from which they can continue on and work, and they don't have to start all over again."[9]

Shultz hoped that the next administration would take up where he had left off and build on the progress that had been made. But the prospects for an early conclusion of the START treaty dimmed when Bush won the presidential election in November, defeating the Democratic contender, Michael Dukakis. Bush and his advisers had no stake in Reagan's "dream" of effective defenses—in fact, they deeply disapproved of what the "dream" had done to U.S. defense planning—still Bush came out for the "broad" interpretation of the ABM Treaty and the "option" of deploying SDI. Bush also said that he wanted to take a more restrained approach to START and accelerate talks on conventional weapons. The meaning of this utterance remained obscure to many, but, as those within the administration knew, Bush could hardly be more restrained than Reagan on START; then, too, senior Reagan-administration officials, having dismissed Gorbachev's conventional-arms initiative as propaganda, were estimating that an agreement on conventional forces would take five or perhaps ten years to complete.[10] In effect, Bush was promising to do nothing for a very long time.

Meanwhile, between June and November, Gorbachev had moved swiftly to enact his political-reform program. He had failed to get a START agreement, but Reagan's performance at the summit had, with the help of some editing by Soviet television censors, convinced much of the Soviet public that an improvement in Soviet-U.S. relations was under way. After a series of heated debates, the party conference approved his "theses," and over the summer Gorbachev cut back and reorganized the Central Committee apparatus. He scheduled elections at local and regional levels for the end of the year and elections for the national legislature for the following spring. In the fall the Supreme Soviet approved a new legal code based on the rights of the individual and, giving earnest that power was passing from party to government, made Gorbachev president of the U.S.S.R.[11]

During these same months Gorbachev laid the groundwork for transforming the relationship of the Soviet Union to its neighbors. At the party conference he spoke about "freedom of choice" (or self-determination) as a universal principle of international relations and about "managing civilized relations among *all* peoples and states on the basis of democratic principles of equal rights, non-interference in the affairs of one another, and the recognition of the sovereign right of peoples to determine their own destiny." At a Foreign Ministry conference in July, Shevardnadze and his deputies spelled out a concept of security that did not rely principally on military might, and a concept of international relations in which the Soviet Union, renouncing its claim to be the vanguard in a worldwide class struggle, would act as a state among other sovereign states. In the fall Gorbachev removed the last obstacles standing in the way of a normalization of relations with China and proposed a summit to end the conflicts which had marked Soviet-Chinese relations since the 1950s.[12]

On November 13 Gorbachev sent word through Ambassador Dubinin that he had decided to come to the United Nations in early December to make an important address and asked if he could meet with the President and the President-elect. The request for a meeting in the interregnum between administrations irritated Shultz and Powell. But since they could not stop Gorbachev from coming to the UN, they arranged for a luncheon with Reagan on Governor's Island, an easily secured Coast Guard base in New York Harbor, making it clear to the Soviets that this was to be a purely social meeting and they wanted no surprises. Bush agreed to attend the luncheon, though he did not seem to welcome the invitation.[13]

Gorbachev's appearance at the UN on December 7 was a major event, because no Soviet general secretary had come to the United Nations since 1963, when Khrushchev had spoken and, famously, banged his shoe on the table. Gorbachev entered the assembly hall to thunderous applause. But it was his speech that sent reporters and editorial writers in the U.S. running to their word processors.

For those who had not listened to Gorbachev before, the rhetoric itself was electrifying. With hardly a concession to the old Soviet language, Gorbachev spoke about freedom, the rights of the individual, national self-determination, the globalization of the world economy, the threat of environmental destruction, the reach of international communications and the debt crisis in the Third World. He spoke of the need for a more effective United Nations and for a settlement in Afghanistan. In addition, he described his own domestic-reform program: perestroika and a "socialist state built on the rule of law," with freedom of expression, freedom of conscience and democratic elections.

For the American press, and for American officials, the big news of the speech came towards the end, with Gorbachev's announcement that the Soviet Union would be unilaterally reducing its armed forces by a half-million men and undertaking a major withdrawal from Eastern Europe and the European part of the U.S.S.R. Fifty thousand troops, Gorbachev said, including six tank divisions, would be withdrawn from East Germany, Hungary and Poland, and the remaining troops reorganized into defensive formations; in all, ten thousand tanks, eighty-five hundred artillery systems and eight hundred combat aircraft would be withdrawn from the European theater, and there would be significant reductions in the forces stationed in Mongolia and the Asian part of the Soviet Union.

Less noticed in the U.S. was Gorbachev's statement that "the use or threat of force cannot be and should not be an instrument of foreign policy. . . . Freedom of choice is a universal principle that should allow for no exceptions. . . . This applies to both the capitalist and the socialist systems." The language was abstract, but for Gorbachev to say that self-determination was a universal principle meant that he was repudiating all the doctrines under which his predecessors had intervened in conflicts abroad. More concretely, it was an announcement that Moscow would not intervene to save any of the Communist regimes in Eastern Europe from domestic challenges.[14]

According to Colin Powell, the luncheon on Governors Island was warm and intimate. Reagan chatted amicably with his guest. He told Gorbachev that he was leaving office with only one mission unaccomplished: he had not been able to reinstate the horse cavalry in the Army. Nothing, he said, was better for the inside of a man than the outside of a horse. Gorbachev politely replied that he wished he could have helped: the Soviet Union was full of horses.[15]

That evening Reagan wrote complacently in his diary: "The meeting was a tremendous success. A better attitude than at any of our previous meetings, Gorbachev sounded as if he saw us as partners making a better world."[16]

But to Powell, as to everyone else in the party, it was clear that Gorbachev had no interest in Reagan—Fitzwater thought he treated him like a piece of furniture—and that he had asked for the luncheon in order to have a preliminary talk with the President-elect. Bush, however, kept dodging Gorbachev's questions and turning attention back to the President. He addressed Gorbachev for the first time as the luncheon was drawing to a close. "We're a nation of investors," he said, "and an investor wants to know what conditions are like today. But an investor is even more interested in the prospective situation. So, Mr. General Secretary, what is it going to be like in the Soviet Union three or four or five years from now?"

"Mr. Vice President," Gorbachev replied without missing a beat, "even Jesus Christ couldn't answer that question."[17]

Later Gorbachev said to Bush: "I know what people are telling you now that you've won the election: you've got to go slow, you've got to be careful, you've got to review." But, he said, "you'll see soon enough that I'm not doing this for show and I'm not doing this to undermine you or to surprise you or to take advantage of you. I'm playing real politics. I'm doing this because I need to. I'm doing this because there's a revolution taking place in my country. I started it. And they all applauded me when I started it in 1986 and now they don't like it so much, but it's going to be a revolution, nonetheless."[18]

In the year that followed, Gorbachev kept the promises he had made, and the revolution occurred. In March 1989 elections were held for the new Soviet legislature, opening new frontiers in freedom of political speech; numerous reformers, including Andrei Sakharov, were elected, and deep fissures appeared within the Communist Party. At the same time, the unintended consequences of glasnost and perestroika shook the very foundations of the Soviet Union. The economy went into a steep decline. There was significant labor unrest, including a strike by several hundred thousand miners. In many regions ethnic tensions erupted into demonstrations and in some cases violence; in the three Baltic States, Georgia and Moldavia there was overt nationalist agitation. Meanwhile, Communist rule in the Warsaw Pact countries of Eastern Europe came to an end. Within the space of six months, free elections brought Solidarity to power in Poland, the reformist Hungarian government cut down the barbed wire on its Austrian border, the Honecker regime in East Germany collapsed, the Berlin Wall opened, the "velvet revolution" took power in Czechoslovakia, the Bulgarian party boss was replaced and the Romanians overthrew the Ceaușescu regime. Gorbachev, who had precipitated these events with his encouragement of reform in Eastern Europe and his promise not to intervene, did not expect the complete repudiation of the Communist parties and the disintegration of the Warsaw Pact. Yet all through these upheavals he continued to reaffirm his acceptance of freedom of choice for the peoples of Eastern Europe and to speak of a "common European home" and a "common civilization" uniting Eastern and Western Europe.[19]

In his 1996 memoir Robert Gates writes that Gorbachev's revolution, which ended with the collapse of the Soviet Union in 1991, had been essentially accomplished by December 1988.

> By the end of the Reagan administration, Gorbachev and the forces he had set loose had shattered the myths and the fear that sustained the rule of the Communist Party. He had broken the political monopoly of the party and its apparatus, had removed the party from day-to-day administration of the Soviet Union, and

> had created an alternative structure of power and political legitimacy in the country. Step by tactical step, he had carried out one of the most far-reaching, and bloodless, political revolutions in history. Finally, his political revolution undermined, and then largely destroyed, the administrative structure that had managed the Soviet economy.

It was Mikhail Gorbachev, Gates adds, who broke the fear in Eastern Europe.[20]

This was hardly Gates's view at the time. The deputy director of the CIA remained adamant that Gorbachev was using détente to revamp the Soviet military machine, and that, if perestroika created further domestic turbulence, he would be overthrown by the right. "The dictatorship of the Communist party remains untouched and untouchable," he said in an October 1988 speech. He continued in this opinion well into 1989.[21]

The American public, however, believed that the Cold War was over. After Gorbachev's speech at the UN, opinion polls showed that 54 percent of Americans believed the Soviet Union was either "no threat" or "only a minor threat." Two-thirds of those polled said that the Soviet Union was primarily concerned with protecting its own national security, and only 28 percent that it was bent on world domination. Polls conducted in Europe showed the same, or less, concern about a Soviet threat.[22]

In December and January, Reagan gave a series of farewell addresses and press interviews in which he extolled the advance of freedom and the record of his administration for the past eight years. The speeches were well crafted but far from memorable, and some historians expressed disappointment that Reagan did not take the opportunity to reflect upon his presidency. "They weren't farewell speeches, they were his last campaign speeches," one scholar complained. Reflection was not, however, an activity that Reagan was given to. In one of his final press interviews he defended himself from Safire's charge that he had "embraced" Gorbachev too quickly by repeating all his old lines: previous Soviet leaders called for a one-world Communist state and asserted the right to lie, cheat, steal; he knew that because he had fought the Communists in Hollywood when they tried to take over the motion-picture business after World War II; détente was wrong, peace through strength was right, *doverai no proverai.*[23]

Reagan left office with a 68-percent job-approval rating—the highest of any post-war President at the end of his term. Seventy-one percent of the public approved his handling of foreign relations with the emphasis on U.S.-Soviet relations.[24] Yet, in assessing the record of his two administrations, the pundits gave him uniformly poor reviews. Both liberals and conservatives focused on the $1.6 trillion he had added to the national debt, and while the former decried the "Reagan revolution" for redistributing income from the poor to the rich, the latter pointed out that, in terms of reducing the size of government, there had been no "revolution" at all. In regard to U.S.-Soviet relations, the liberals gave him no credit for doing what in their view he should have been doing all along, and pointed to the Iran-contra affair as the source of his change of heart. The conservatives agreed that popularity counted the most with Reagan and that it was his political debilitation that had led him into the arms of Mikhail Gorbachev. "He professed to see in Mr. Gorbachev's eyes an end to the Soviet goal of world dominance," Safire of the *New York Times* wrote scornfully. In a lengthy assessment of the Reagan years in *Newsweek,* George Will exclaimed, "How wildly wrong he is about what is happening in Moscow," adding, "Reagan has accelerated the moral disarmament of the West—actual disarmament will follow—by elevating wishful thinking to the status of political philosophy."[25]

But Reagan was not through yet. In the months that followed his inauguration, George Bush, quite inadvertently, gave his predecessor the tribute Reagan had failed to devise for himself and enhanced the glow around his last year in office. Nothing, in fact, showed Reagan off better than the behavior of a president who was far better equipped to deal with the Soviets than he. Then, after the Soviet Union collapsed, the conservatives changed their minds about Reagan once again.

Leaving Washington on Air Force One after the Bush inauguration, Reagan, as if at last released from his White House captors, said bluntly, "The Cold War is over." Two days later Bush's closest defense adviser, Brent Scowcroft, appeared on ABC's *This Week with David Brinkley* and just as bluntly contradicted Reagan. Scowcroft, who had headed Ford's NSC staff and chaired the commission on strategic forces for Reagan in 1983, had come from Kissinger's consulting firm to become Bush's campaign adviser and to head the NSC staff. Asked about Gorbachev's UN speech, he said that the general secretary might be "interested in making trouble within the Western alliance," and "until we have better evidence to the contrary, we ought to operate on that expectation." He added, "I think the Cold War is not over."[26]

On February 13 Bush signed a directive calling for a full-scale "strategic review" of U.S.-Soviet relations and announced that all policy decisions would be postponed until he rethought how to deal with Gorbachev.[27] In the meantime, the administration virtually shut down communications with Moscow. The START talks were suspended, the frequent meetings between officials at various levels of the two governments came to an end; Bush said nothing, and no proposals or responses came from the American side. It was as if the circuits had all gone dead.

"The pause," as this policy came to be known, went on for months and surprised almost everyone in Washington. Bush was, after all, no hard-liner by the standards of the Reagan administration, nor were his chief advisers, Brent Scowcroft and James A. Baker III, who had left his Treasury post the previous summer to become Bush's campaign manager and then his secretary of state.* Furthermore, to many moderates in Washington it seemed that Reagan had left Bush with a clear course of action. Before the inauguration a bipartisan group of policy professionals, known as the Annapolis Group, presented the President-elect with a memorandum of recommendations based on interviews with 125 key national-security players, including members of Congress, former high officials, generals and experts. According to the group, the consensus view was: "You possess a unique inheritance from Ronald Reagan: a strategic arms reduction negotiation which is very far advanced. If you accept and embrace this inheritance, you may enhance American security and your own political fortunes at the same time."[28]

But Bush and his advisers clearly wanted nothing to do with any inheritance from Reagan.

At the time of the transition it was generally known that there was a good deal of ill-feeling between "the Bush people" and "the Reagan people." These feelings were never explained, but they were certainly vented, for as Jack Matlock, the ambassador to the Soviet Union, later wrote, the Bush-Reagan transition "resembled a hostile take-over rather than a cooperative transition." In the space of a few weeks hundreds of Reagan appointees found themselves without jobs. Bush made a clean sweep of the Reagan foreign-policy team, and for a normally gracious man, he did it quite brutally. The very day after the election, Bush called Shultz and then publicly announced that he was nominating Baker for secretary of state, thus undercutting Shultz's effectiveness for the remainder of his term. He did not even call Carlucci but had an aide call him to say that the choice of his successor was about to be announced. In his memoir Shultz writes mildly about the abruptness of his dismissal and reports, "George Bush and Jim Baker seemed concerned and wary that Ronald Reagan and I had become too impressed with Soviet personalities—Gorbachev and Shevardnadze—too ready to believe that genuine change was occurring in the Soviet Union." That was the least of it. Baker let it be known that he thought Shultz had been a flabby negotiator during his last year in office, paying for Soviet concessions that Gorbachev might have made for free.[29]

Scowcroft and Baker urged caution, yet, unlike Reagan's hard-liners, they did not seem to have an alternative policy in mind—or any fixed view of what was happening in the Soviet Union. Baker, who was taking on his first foreign-policy job, was an agnostic on what he describes in his memoir as the "theological" issue of whether perestroika was a "breathing space" or a fundamental shift in Soviet policy.[30] Scowcroft made Gates his deputy, but, unlike Gates, he did not actually predict that the Soviets would revert to

*Bush's first choice for secretary of defense was former Senator John Tower. When the Senate failed to confirm Tower's nomination, Bush picked Representative Richard Cheney, but because of the delay, Cheney did not join the administration until March.

type. In mid-February he told colleagues that, ideologically and economically, the Marxist-Leninist threat was over, that even the military threat was changing and that "there's a new world out there." His directive ordering the strategic review proposed that the U.S. "might stand at the door of a new era" of "reduced military forces and peaceful resolution of conflicts," but cautioned that the USSR remained "an adversary with awesome military power" and that it would be "thoughtless to abandon policies that have brought us this far." After reading Scowcroft's draft, Bush added a sentence: "My own sense is that the Soviet challenge may be even greater than before, because it is more varied."[31]

Completed on March 14, the strategic review gave guarded approval to perestroika but warned that the Soviets still aspired to become "a more competitive superpower"; it found Gorbachev's effort to create a "less confrontational" relationship "double-edged" because it might divide the Western alliance. Clearly the authors could not decide whether Gorbachev was Gorbachev or Brezhnev. The policy recommendations of the review were so bland and unspecific that Baker called them "mush." Baker complained to Bush that the bureaucracy was simply dredging up ancient positions. Couldn't anyone come up with something "creative and new"? Scowcroft told members of his staff that he wanted them to "stretch," to break out of old habits and patterns. He chided them for their "lack of imagination" and said, "You are being too conservative. You've become a bunch of old curmudgeons."[32] But no new ideas materialized, and another strategic review was soon ordered up.

The paralysis was mysterious, except that, as became increasingly clear, Bush and his advisers were not very well focused on current events.

Relations between American presidents and their vice-presidents have rarely been easy. For seven years Bush had conducted himself as a model vice-president, never criticizing administration policy, rarely proffering his own views at meetings and never complaining. But he and Reagan could hardly have been more different, and he would hardly have been human had the years of enforced silence not left a mark. Bush's long suit was foreign policy, and in that domain Reagan had offended his deepest sensibilities.[33]

In Reagan's first term, Bush and Scowcroft had been concerned about the President's harsh rhetoric on the Soviet Union, the administration's intransigence over arms control and the incoherence of its strategic-weapons programs. Scowcroft had counseled moderation and worked out a bipartisan accord on the MX and arms control. But instead of modifying his hard-line policies, Reagan had simply escaped from the political consequences of them in Houdini fashion with his anti-nuclear rhetoric and his claims for SDI. Scowcroft, like many of his colleagues, thought the rhetoric deeply irresponsible. He was appalled by what he saw as Reagan's "spirit of enthusiastic confusion and mixed purposes" at Reykjavik, and had many reservations about the INF treaty.[34] Bush supported that treaty, but when Reagan went to Moscow and declared the Cold War over, Bush and Scowcroft were once again scandalized.

In a book published many years later, Robert Hutchings, the Eastern Europe expert on Scowcroft's NSC staff, reported that the main goal of the Bush administration in 1989 was "to restore public support for the principle of nuclear deterrence, including extended nuclear deterrence."[35] In this period Bush and Scowcroft seemed to be following Kissinger's lead, and this was Kissinger's oft-stated concern. In his attack on START the previous spring, Kissinger had warned that the START process might "mark yet another major step away from the deterrent strategy pursued for the entire post-war period" and "another step towards stripping away the legitimacy of nuclear weapons."[36] According to Hutchings, *the* issue for Bush-administration officials was "how to make the case for nuclear deterrence to an American public whose views had been conditioned by the nuclear freeze movement, the television docudrama *The Day After* and the specter of 'nuclear winter,' the INF agreement, and President Reagan's proposal at Reykjavik for the elimination of all strategic nuclear weapons . . . together with the false promise of SDI. . . ."[37]

This anguish about the legitimacy of nuclear deterrence was on the face of it puzzling. In the first place, Bush—though not Scowcroft—had, like Kissinger, supported Reagan on SDI; in the second, the Reagan administration had just conducted the greatest peacetime military buildup in history, including a major nuclear-weapons buildup, which had gone on irrespective of SDI. The defense budgets were now on the decline, because of the huge budget deficits and, to a lesser extent, because the public felt that enough was probably enough. However, the foreign-policy establishment had worried about public support for deterrence since the Cold War began. From Acheson to Kissinger, its major figures had bemoaned the inconstancy of the American public with, as Kissinger put it, its cycles of "exuberant overextension and sulking isolationism . . . each conceived in moralistic terms."[38] Its members saw it as their Sisyphian task to maintain public support for deterrence, and every few years for the past forty they had taken it upon themselves to roll this particular stone back up the hill. Participation in this endeavor was a sure sign of membership in the establishment, and for those who had engaged in it more than once, it was a ritual, one perhaps almost as comforting as the words so often used to describe the goal of the effort: "a stable, predictable" relationship with the Soviet Union and "prudent" defense policies.

In May 1988, just as Reagan left for Moscow, George Bush gave a speech at West Point in which he placed himself squarely in the establishment tradition. He began by hailing the "great bipartisan consensus" of the early Cold War; he then lamented that it had shattered in the 1970s because of "the death of Kennedy, Vietnam, the lure of the old desire to once again leave the world and turn inward." "The reasons," he concluded lamely, "would take another speech." There were "changes," he continued, but the "great bipartisan consensus endured." "The logic," he explained, "still applies."

As with so many Bush utterances, the speech lacked something in coherence—particularly since he proceeded to read "the liberal elite" out of the old consensus. But the gaps in its logic pointed to what could not be said: Bush was looking back with nostalgia to the period before the mid-1970s—to the time before Reagan came on the scene—and promising that he would put the consensus together again.[39]

Like soldiers after a war, the Bush people longed for a return to normalcy: to the restoration of the pre-Reagan, pre-lapsarian foreign-policy establishment—presumably that of the Nixon administration—and to the task of maintaining support for deterrence with the promise of a stable, predictable relationship with the Soviet Union. The trouble was that they could only do this if Gorbachev was Brezhnev.

While the Bush administration waffled, Gorbachev began to disarm: Soviet divisions prepared to move out of Europe; tanks, planes and artillery were retired; production of weapons-grade uranium was halted and two plutonium plants were shut down. Gorbachev announced a 10-percent cut in Soviet defense spending; the East German government followed suit; in May he said he would take five hundred nuclear missiles out of Eastern Europe in order to improve the prospects for the elimination of all short-range nuclear weapons in Europe.

These moves seemed only to irritate the Bush administration. Officials responded by accusing Gorbachev of playing politics and attempting to split the Western alliance. Marlin Fitzwater, now Bush's press secretary, called Gorbachev "a drugstore cowboy" playing "a PR game" and not matching "words with deeds."[40]

Meanwhile, the administration proceeded with plans inherited from the Reagan administration to modernize the short-range Lance missiles in West Germany. The year before, NATO had requested the upgrade as a sign that Reagan was not going to denuclearize Europe, but since Gorbachev now seemed intent on denuclearizing Europe, the West German public protested and Helmut Kohl pleaded with the Bush administration to call it off. A barrage of criticism went up from members of Congress, the press and the rest of the NATO allies. The Bush administration, however, stood firm, posing the issue as a test of political will: if the Germans rejected the missiles, Gorbachev would have achieved his goal of undermining Western resolve and splitting the Alliance.

Ronald Reagan, now at home in California, told friends that he had an "uneasy" feeling about Bush's "foreign policy indecisiveness." He was, his friends told Lou Cannon, concerned about Bush's excessively cautious approach to nuclear-arms-reduction talks with the Soviets. He believed, they said, that Bush's "hesitancy" had allowed Gorbachev to regain the initiative in world opinion and had created a "needless crisis" in the NATO alliance over the short-range missiles in Germany.[41]

Reagan's comments, reported in the *Washington Post* on May 6, naturally infuriated Bush-administration officials. In a column that clearly reflected their views, Jim Hoagland of the *Post* railed at the injustice of Reagan's reported charge that they had created a "needless crisis" in NATO: The charge was not just ungracious but flat wrong. It was not the Bush team that had caused the crisis in NATO; rather, Bush, Scowcroft and Baker were simply trying to moderate a dispute that became inevitable when Reagan signed the INF treaty—a dispute that Scowcroft had foreseen at the time, etc., etc.[42]

Bush-administration officials were spluttering. Here was Reagan accusing them of creating a crisis in NATO when for eight years he had done nothing but create crises in NATO! However, by repudiating Reagan's course of action, they were implicitly criticizing him. In addition, they were casting aside what was at least the most expedient way of dealing with the Soviet Union. Reagan's "embrace" of Gorbachev horrified the conservatives, but all the Reagan administration had ever done was to talk to the Soviets, pocket the concessions they made and take credit for having forced Gorbachev to do what he was doing anyway for his own purposes.

In reporting Reagan's comments, Cannon maintained that Bush, by contrast to Reagan, merely reacted to events. But the reverse was the case. Bush refused to react. He wanted to figure out exactly where the Soviet Union was going before he made his first move—though Gorbachev had told him on Governors Island that even Jesus Christ did not know.

At the end of May, Bush and his advisers pulled themselves out of their state of paralysis—not because they had made their minds up about Gorbachev (that came later) but because, under considerable pressure from Congress and the Allies, they finally realized that they had to react.

Galvanized by Baker, a relative newcomer to the foreign-policy community, Bush made a substantive response to the Soviet proposals for conventional-force reductions in Europe. Thereafter the two sides reengaged. That summer and fall, as the Communist governments in Eastern Europe fell in rapid succession, Bush did much to ease the transition by reassuring Gorbachev that the U.S. would not take advantage of the Soviet retreat and by refusing, as he put it, to "dance on the Berlin Wall." Baker and Shevardnadze were soon working closely together, and, beginning with the Malta summit in December, Bush and Gorbachev developed a real personal bond and a degree of trust that permitted Gorbachev to accept the reunification of Germany, the entrance of Germany into NATO and the breakaway of the Baltic States without fear that the U.S. would exploit these losses.[43] The START treaty was belatedly concluded in July 1991—a month before a coup attempt against Gorbachev precipitated the breakup of the Soviet

Union. It was the first strategic-arms agreement signed since 1979, and the first to be ratified by the Congress since 1972.

George Bush dealt in substance and achieved far more with Gorbachev than Reagan ever did, but the "pause" of 1989 did lasting harm to his reputation and much to enhance Reagan's. By contrast to Bush, Reagan seemed a model of decisiveness and farsightedness about Gorbachev's reforms. The legend he and his advisers had created around the four summits was only enhanced by the complaints of Bush-administration officials about Shultz's soft-headedness and Reagan's eagerness for START. It was further enhanced by Gorbachev, who for the purposes of getting Bush off the dime complained that the strategic review was endangering the "momentum" of the arms negotiations—not a word he had used while Reagan was in office.[44]

Memory being what it is, many chroniclers of the period later reproduced this legend. By one account: "It would take George Bush and his associates most of the year to restore the momentum in U.S.-Soviet relations that had been such a notable feature of the Reagan administration's last year."[45] By another: Scowcroft was "more cautious about the pace of arms control and less starry-eyed than Reagan about the prospect of drastic cuts in the strategic nuclear arms."[46] Hutchings writes of Bush's START agreement as "codifying further deep reductions in strategic nuclear weapons," as though deep reductions had already been made.[47] Kissinger, of course, was not fooled. With what might be imagined as a degree of resentment, he told Gorbachev's close adviser Yakovlev in early 1989 that improvements in U.S.-Soviet relations under Reagan had been largely cosmetic.[48] But he did not say this publicly.

As a result, many Americans continued to associate Reagan, not Bush, with nuclear disarmament, even when, paradoxically, they came to associate Reagan's military buildup with the demise of the Soviet Union.

No one in Washington foresaw the collapse of the Soviet system, but the conservatives were the very last to see that the system was vulnerable and that it was changing. In his memoir, published in 1990, Caspar Weinberger wrote, "In a world in which there are two superpowers, one of which has the governmental structure and military might of the Soviet Union, it is essential for our very survival that we retain the military strength we acquired in the 1980s. . . ." And "My feeling has always been that no general secretary of the Communist Party of the Soviet Union will be allowed to alter in any fundamental way the basically aggressive nature of Soviet behavior."[49]

Yet, as soon as the Soviet Union collapsed, conservative pundits began to advance the argument that the Reagan administration had played a major role in its downfall. Among others, George Will and Irving Kristol argued that SDI, Reagan's military buildup and the ideological crusade against Communism had delivered the knockout punch to a system that had been on the ropes since the early 1980s. A parade of former Reagan-administration officials, including Weinberger and Richard Perle, came forward to assert that Reagan had known all the time that the Soviet Union was on its last legs and had aggressively foreclosed Soviet military options while pushing the Soviet economy to the breaking point. According to conservatives, the combination of military and ideological pressures gave the Soviets little choice but to abandon expansionism abroad and repression at home, and SDI was the key to this winning strategy. The Star Wars initiative had put the Soviets on notice that the next arms race would be waged in areas where the West had a decisive technological advantage.[50]

This argument contrasted sharply with previous conservative complaints about Reagan's embrace of Gorbachev, and it did not persuade scholars of the Soviet Union. Yet, since it is the inveterate propensity of Americans—or at least of American pundits—to relate the fall of sparrows in distant lands to some fault or virtue of American policy, it went against the grain to deny the argument entirely and to propose that the enormous military buildup of the Reagan years had no role at all in the demise of the Soviet Union. Thus a vague and unexamined version of the conservative thesis entered the public discourse: SDI and the U.S. military buildup forced the Soviets to spend more than they could afford on their defenses and/or convinced them of the inherent weaknesses of their system. But the evidence for this proposition is wanting.

From 1983 to 1987 the Strategic Defense Initiative alarmed Soviet leaders because it threatened to reverse what they saw as the trend towards strategic stability and stable costs. Nonetheless, they did not respond to it by creating their own SDI program. That is, they continued their existing research programs on lasers and other advanced technologies, plus their existing design-work on space weaponry, but they did not mount an effort to test or develop SDI-type weapons. In addition they studied counter-measures to space-based weaponry, but since the SDIO never designed a plausible system, they had nothing specific to study, and their military spending was unaffected.[51] Between 1985 and 1987 Gorbachev spent a great deal of effort trying to convince the Reagan administration to restrain the program, presumably because he thought his own military-industrial complex would eventually force him to adopt a program of some sort to counter SDI, but by the end of 1987 the Soviet leadership no longer regarded SDI as a threat.

Then, too, the Soviets did not respond to the Reagan administration's military buildup.

As CIA analysts discovered in 1983, Soviet military spending had leveled off in 1975 to a growth rate of 1.3 percent, with spending for weapons procurements virtually flat. It remained that way for a decade. According to later CIA estimates, Soviet military spending rose in 1985 as a result of decisions taken earlier, and grew at a rate of 4.3 percent a year through 1987. Spending for procurements of offensive strategic weapons, however, increased by only 1.4 percent a year in that period. In 1988 Gorbachev began a round of budget cuts, bringing the defense budget back down to its 1980 level.[52] In other words, while the U.S. military budget was growing at an average of 8 percent a year, the Soviets did not attempt to keep up, and their military spending did not rise even as might have been expected given the war they were fighting in Afghanistan.

During Reagan's first term, some in the Kremlin were concerned about the possibility that the U.S. was gaining a first-strike capability and might actually launch a nuclear war. This was, of course, the mirror image of the fears expressed in Washington in the mid-seventies. Nonetheless, though the strategic arsenals on both sides grew like Topsy in the 1980s, the strategic balance remained extremely stable. Without any spending increases, the Soviets continued to turn out and deploy strategic warheads at about the same rate the U.S. did. When the START I treaty was signed in 1991, the U.S. had 12,646 deployed strategic warheads, the Soviet Union 11,212—the numbers so large as to be almost meaningless in terms of deterrence.[53]

At the beginning of Reagan's first term, some conservative enthusiasts in the administration might have believed that the U.S. could spend the Soviets under the table in an all-out strategic-arms race. But the Joint Chiefs of Staff never thought this, nor did the CIA, for the simple reason that Soviet spending on strategic weapons was a very small fraction of the overall Soviet military budget. According to one MIT expert, Soviet spending for the procurement, operations and maintenance of its strategic offensive forces amounted to only 8 percent of its entire defense budget. In other words, had Gorbachev achieved the 50-percent reductions he was seeking at Reykjavik, he would not have made savings of any significance in terms of the Soviet economy.[54]

What did happen in the 1980s was that the Soviet economy continued to deteriorate as it had during the 1970s. The economic decline, of course, resulted from the failures of the system created by Lenin and Stalin—not from any effort on the part of the Reagan administration. Without Gorbachev, however, the Soviet Union might have survived for many more years, for the system, though on the decline, was nowhere near collapse. It was Gorbachev's efforts to reverse the decline and to modernize his country that knocked the props out from under the system. The revolution was in essence a series of decisions made by one man, and it came as a surprise precisely because it did not follow from a systemic breakdown.[55]

At the time the American public understood this better than most in Washington—and thanks in large part to Ronald Reagan. Reagan had no idea what Gorbachev was up to, but he always described the world in terms of individuals rather than institutions and portrayed U.S.-Soviet relations as the personal relationship between two heads of state. His own officials considered this naive. But it was Gorbachev who changed the Soviet Union, and Reagan's "embrace" of him as an individual was surely the most important contribution the United States made to the Soviet revolution until after the disintegration of the Warsaw Pact.

Reagan did not see exactly what he had done, but in 1989 he described his first meeting with Gorbachev over and over again, the story growing more dramatic with each telling.

In an interview with Mike Wallace on CBS's *60 Minutes*, on January 15, 1989, just before he left office, Reagan spoke about the first day of the 1985 Geneva summit. He had, he said, been told by "our more experienced people in diplomacy" that the meeting would be a success if it resulted in only one thing: the setting of another summit. He told his people in advance that he was going to do something about that summit, and in the midst of the negotiations on arms control, he said to Gorbachev across the table, "Why don't you and I just step out and get some fresh air, and let them, for a while, go on with this subject?" Gorbachev accepted immediately, and the two of them walked down to a pool house by the lake shore. "I made it sound as if it were impromptu," he said, "[but] the fire was going in the fireplace." In the pool house he told Gorbachev: "We don't mistrust each other because we're armed; we're armed because we mistrust each other." Here we are, he continued, two men in a room, with the power to start World War III but also the power to bring peace to the world. On the walk back to the villa he invited Gorbachev to come to the United States, and the general secretary not only accepted but invited him to come to the Soviet Union the following year. "I want to tell you," Reagan said, "when . . . I told our people that there were going to be two more summits, in the United States, and in Moscow, they fell down. They couldn't believe it."[56]

In reality, of course, the two future summits had been negotiated in advance, and Shultz and McFarlane were annoyed that Reagan had popped the question because they wanted to force Gorbachev to make the official request.

Two months after the *60 Minutes* broadcast, Morton Janklow, the literary and theatrical agent, visited the former President in his new home in Bel Air. Janklow, who had signed a multi-million-dollar deal with Simon & Schuster for Reagan's memoirs, had brought Robert Lindsey, a prospective ghostwriter for the book. The two of them found Reagan dressed in jeans and cowboy boots, relaxed and ebullient. It was St. Patrick's Day, and, possibly to put the writer at ease, Reagan put on a comical green hat and did a few steps of a soft-shoe routine. That afternoon he told a story: On the first day of the Geneva summit in 1985, he and Gorbachev, surrounded by their advisers, had been in formal negotiations for hours and were getting nowhere. On an impulse he asked Gorbachev to take a walk with him down to a pool house by the lake, where they could talk man to man. Max Kampelman, his senior arms negotiator, expressed concern at this breach of diplomatic procedures. But Reagan and Gorbachev went off together, and during their tête-à-tête in the pool house, Reagan convinced Gorbachev to adopt strict verification procedures for the arms treaty they were negotiating.[57]

No arms agreement was signed at Geneva, but Janklow, who, understandably did not remember this, found the story fascinating. Possibly *doverai no proverai* had suggested verification to Reagan, and Janklow, who is tall, distinguished-looking and Jewish, may have brought Kampelman to his mind.

Some months later Michael Korda, the editor-in-chief of Simon & Schuster, and the editor of Reagan's memoir, met with the former President to discuss the book. Reagan, who, to the despair of his ghostwriter, had proved no more introspective than he had in his farewell addresses, had only one suggestion to offer: his memoir should begin with the most important moment of his presidency—his first meeting with Gorbachev, on November 19, 1985. Reagan then proceeded to tell much the same story he had told Janklow, but this time subtracting Kampelman and adding a few other touches: The negotiations had been going nowhere, so Reagan tapped Gorbachev on the shoulder and invited him to go for a walk. On the way down to the pool house he turned to Gorbachev and said, You and I are old men, grandfathers, and the peace of the world is on our shoulders. So why can't we just sit down and talk things out, man to man? So they went into the pool house, just the two of them, and lit a fire. At the end of a long and heartfelt discussion, Gorbachev agreed to mutual inspection and verification, which Reagan had established as the sine qua non of any arms treaty. Gorbachev then promised to take steps towards nuclear disarmament, and agreed to two more summit meetings. It just went to show, the President said, his eyes moist, how important a person-to-person approach was.

Reagan, Korda later wrote, told the story as if it were a scene from a movie, with vivid detail and real feeling; his sincerity was so obvious that all of those listening to him were touched.

Korda, who did not remember the Geneva summit any better than Janklow, saw only two problems. First, he couldn't remember whether Reagan and Gorbachev were grandfathers at the time. (They were.) And second, since Reagan spoke no Russian and Gorbachev spoke no English, the two could not have been alone in the pool house for this man-to-man discussion. "They *weren't* alone," one of Reagan's aides whispered. "There were interpreters, security men—a whole bunch of people. That's just the way the President likes to remember it."

Korda put the story down to the President's selective memory and his well-known tendency to place himself in the foreground of events and to confuse fiction and reality. "He had the ability," Korda wrote, "rare even among actors, to convince the listener that something had happened the way he told it when it hadn't, and this was because he believed it with complete sincerity himself."[58]

Korda had apparently missed the *60 Minutes* interview in which Reagan had told the pool house story fairly accurately.

• • •

In 1989 Reagan wanted his memoir to begin with the story of how he had first met Gorbachev, and at that time he was surely right. The Geneva summit was his summit—the others were dominated by the general secretary—and in Geneva he put his great gift to work. His man-to-man talk with Gorbachev in the pool house was itself a story, which he made up long before he acted it out, and the story convinced the American public that something substantive had happened, when nothing had. In embellishing this story for Janklow and Korda, he was not only pointing up his own personal contribution to ending the Cold War but performing this feat all over again.

Ten years later, however, Reagan might have wanted to begin with his speech of 1983 calling for a defense against ballistic missiles. By then the Soviet Union had receded into history, while the program to provide the United States with an anti-missile defense remained alive and on the track to deployment, even though, after an expenditure of sixty billion dollars, it had yet to produce a capable weapons system. But that is another story.

Afterword: National Missile Defenses, 1989–99

"Most Americans are shocked to discover that our country is unshielded from the accidental or ruthless launch of even a single missile over our skies."

—Representative Steve Largent (Republican of Oklahoma), January 19, 1999[1]

In 1988 many in Washington and Moscow predicted that the Strategic Defense Initiative would not survive the Reagan administration: that the effort to deploy anti-missile defenses would soon end and that the research programs in defensive technologies would return to the relatively obscure place in the military budget from which they had come. But the initiative defied these expectations. Throughout the decade after Reagan left office, spending on anti-missile defenses remained at the level it had attained in the second Reagan administration, that is, at three to four billion dollars a year. Then, except in the first three years of the Clinton administration, the U.S. government was never without a plan to deploy a missile defense for the United States. Over the years program managers beat a gradual retreat from the technical goals of the Reagan administration, and by the late 1990s the anti-missile system envisioned for deployment was a pale shadow of its former self: a network of ground-based interceptors with the capability to stop a few ICBMs. Whether even this goal could be achieved by the target date of 2005 remained uncertain. Nonetheless, in the spring of 1999 the Clinton administration and both houses of Congress committed themselves to deploying a national missile-defense system as soon as technically feasible, and the administration began negotiations with the Russians to revise the ABM Treaty. For the first time many expert observers felt that at least some elements of the system would be deployed in the next few years.

Much, of course, happened within the decade to alter the purpose and military requirements of an anti-missile system. Still, the persistence of the push for deployment was in many ways phenomenal. It survived declining defense budgets. It survived a fall-off of public interest so complete that many consistent newspaper readers thought the program had died. It survived the collapse of the Soviet Union. It survived despite the fact that there was no technological breakthrough, and that by 1999 the prospects for deploying an effective interceptor remained not very much brighter than they had been in 1983. In a sense the history of the initiative in the 1990s is even more remarkable than that of its origins. Every time the program seemed ready to expire, or collapse of its own weight, something would happen to bring it to life again.

At the beginning of 1989 there was some reason to suppose that the Bush administration would quietly let the Strategic Defense Initiative fade away. During the 1988 campaign Bush had blown hot and cold on the issue of deployment, but he was not thought to have much enthusiasm for his predecessor's project, and his closest defense adviser, Brent Scowcroft, was a major critic of SDI. In 1988 Scowcroft and three colleagues from the Aspen Strategy Group had criticized the structure of the program, rejected the idea of near-term deployment and endorsed the traditional interpretation of the ABM Treaty.[2] Then, a few days after the inauguration, former Senator John Tower, Bush's first choice for secretary of defense, said in a Senate hearing that the Bush administration was going to take a more modest view of SDI than its predecessor. "To begin with," he said, "I don't believe that we can devise an umbrella that can protect the entire American population from nuclear incineration."[3]

The remark made headlines across the country. Tower was merely acknowledging the obvious, but as a spokesman for the Bush administration he was violating the taboo on official speech that had held for the past four years. Tower did not become secretary of defense, but Richard Cheney, the Wyoming congressman who did, took the same line, and so did all senior Bush-administration officials.[4] Apparently the President and his aides had deliberately decided to burst the bubble their predecessors had spent so much breath inflating.

Then, too, the auspices in Washington were favorable to a restructuring of the SDI program. The Democrats retained control of both houses of Congress, and by this time the heads of the Armed Services Committees and the Joint Chiefs were thoroughly fed up with Star Wars. The Pentagon's acquisition process had shown that Abrahamson's "Phase One" architecture was nothing but a concept, and yet, because of the Reagan administration's deadline for a deployment decision in 1993, the SDI budgets continued to climb off the charts. Carlucci had cut Weinberger's proposed budgets way back, and the Congress appropriated less than he asked; still, the last Reagan-administration budget showed the Pentagon spending over forty billion dollars on SDI from fiscal 1990 through fiscal 1994.[5] In a time of declining military budgets the sum appeared chimerical.

During the strategic review that began shortly after Bush's inauguration, the Joint Chiefs took a hard look at SDI and made three recommendations: first, the administration should continue the research and testing of SDI technologies but make no commitment to deployment; second, it should refrain from violating the ABM Treaty; third, it should take a meat ax to the proposed SDI budgets. In May, Admiral Crowe added a fourth recommendation: that the administration change the U.S. position at the Geneva talks and no longer insist upon the U.S. right to deploy anti-missile defenses.[6] The Chiefs were, in other words, proposing that SDI be returned to the status quo ante and to its mission as a research program on the weapons of the future, so that they could go about their business of strategic-force planning and the START talks could proceed.

The Chiefs' recommendations added up to a coherent change of policy. They also added up to a repudiation of Reagan-administration policies on strategic defenses—and a potential confrontation with the Republican right.

Presented with this clear alternative, the Bush administration rejected it. In the course of the strategic review, the President decided to maintain the Reagan administration's negotiating position on strategic defenses: the "broad" interpretation of the ABM Treaty, and the call for an agreement on deploying defenses after a period of years. Bush also decided to proceed with work on "Phase One" for a deployment decision in 1993. At the same time, recognizing that the Reagan budgets could not be sustained, Secretary Cheney cut seven billion dollars out of the forty Carlucci had proposed for the next five years.[7]

Bush had made some decisions, but they did not add up to a plausible policy for the SDI program. Thirty-three billion dollars was an enormous sum—doubtless too big for the Congress—yet it would not begin to pay for Abrahamson's "Phase One," with its hundreds of ground-based interceptors and hundreds of space-based "garages" full of kinetic kill vehicles, supposing these weapons could be built. But just at the moment, there appeared a new concept in space weaponry, one that promised an affordable defense: a swarm of tiny kinetic-energy weapons stuffed with miniaturized computers and high-technology sensors known as Brilliant Pebbles.

In February 1989 General Abrahamson, who had decided to retire as director of the SDIO, wrote an end-of-tour report for the incoming secretary of defense recommending a radical change in the "Phase One" system. The system, he noted, had passed the Defense Acquisitions Board, but now there was a new opportunity for "improved performance and dramatic cost reductions" in Brilliant Pebbles. In an effusive five-page memorandum, which soon became public, he described an architecture made up of several thousand tiny interceptors floating around the earth in low orbits waiting for the signal to attack enemy rockets rising out of the atmosphere. Each interceptor would have its own optics and sufficient computer capability to make its own targeting decisions; once cleared for release, it would select the nearest target, fly towards it on an intercepting orbit, then ram into it at high speed. These tiny interceptors, Abrahamson wrote, could be proven in two years and deployed three years later; with them, he wrote, an entire SDI "Phase One" system that met the JCS requirements would cost not more than about twenty-five billion dollars.[8]

This concept, it transpired, was the brainchild of Edward Teller and his protégé Lowell Wood.

In the fall of 1986 Teller and Wood breakfasted with Gregory Canavan, the Los Alamos physicist, who had defended the concept of Star Wars in the "science wars" of 1984. In the course of a discussion, Canavan offered an idea: why not make a miniature smart rock that would be so intelligent that it could operate on its own, and so small it would be easy to launch into space and difficult for the Soviets to go after? The idea, as Canavan later acknowledged, was not a fundamentally new one. It had been conceived in the late 1950s, and in the early 1980s, with the revolution in microchip technology, Richard Garwin—one of Canavan's opponents in the "science wars"—had brought the idea up again, only to dismiss it as unworkable. Teller and Wood had long argued that space-based defenses could not be made survivable, but since the demise of the X-ray laser they had been looking for new ideas, and this one, they decided, was worth exploring.

Wood put the Livermore Lab to work on Canavan's concept, and by the fall of 1987 he had a model of the interceptor, blueprints, computer simulations and a name: Brilliant Pebbles. He and Teller then began to sell the project in much the same way they had sold the X-ray laser.[9]

In 1987 the SDIO had decided to put a little money into the concept, but by the fall of 1988 Brilliant Pebbles was still a low-level project and something of a curiosity in the organization. Still, after taking office in March 1989, Defense Secretary Cheney decided to accept Abrahamson's glowing end-of-tour recommendation and to give emphasis to the Livermore program. In April the SDIO unveiled the project with some fanfare.[10] Just as with concepts past, schematic drawings of Brilliant Pebbles appeared in the press, and journalists quoted officials on the devastation the system might wreak on Soviet ICBMs. The unveiling was heralded by Vice-President Quayle, who, in a speech on the sixth anniversary of Reagan's Star Wars address, praised the affordability of the system, its survivability and "its use of available, largely demonstrated technologies." Brilliant Pebbles, Quayle said, "could revolutionize much of our thinking about strategic defense."[11]

The interceptor, as it was now described, was not quite the weapon Wood had touted the year before. From a five-pound "pebble" it had become a hundred-pound, three-foot-long boulder with a "protective cocoon." Wood now had to use a cart to take its mock-up around Washington. Also, it was not quite so autonomous as it had been. Apparently the Pentagon was uneasy about the idea of unleashing thousands of robots into space without any human controls. Then, too, the estimate for each copy had gone up from one hundred thousand dollars to somewhere between a half and one and a half million, exclusive of launching costs.[12] Still, even by the new estimates, the interceptor promised to be cheap compared with its predecessor, and in an effort to match the stated goal of a deployment decision in 1993 with some politically plausible expenditure of funds, the administration made what one Senate staffer described as "the technological equivalent of a Hail Mary pass." In 1989 the SDIO asked for a sevenfold increase in funding for the Livermore program; in 1990 it abandoned the old concept for a space-based interceptor and substituted Brilliant Pebbles. The new "Phase One" architecture showed a system made up of forty-six hundred pebbles plus one to two thousand ground-based interceptors. The funding request for the pebbles rose to $392 million for fiscal 1991.[13]

Brilliant Pebbles did not, however, fare well with the Pentagon review boards, and by the summer of 1990, when the Congress came to consider the defense budget for the following year, the purpose of the deployment scheme had become even more mysterious than the virtue of the technology under consideration.[14] The Cold War in Europe was over. Bush and Gorbachev were working together on regional issues, including Iraq's invasion of Kuwait. They were still wrangling over the side issues of the START treaty, but they were looking forward to making deeper reductions in START II. The Soviets had already agreed to dismantle many more of their ICBMs than the "Phase One" scheme was designed to stop, and on the defensive side their only condition was that the U.S. abide by the ABM Treaty: the administration could have arms reductions or "Phase One" but not both.[15]

Bush-administration officials acknowledged that warmer U.S.-Soviet relations and the imminent prospect of a START treaty diminished concerns about a Soviet nuclear attack. But, they did not therefore question their goal of an SDI deployment. Rather, they and other Republicans came up with new rationales. In February 1990, during a trip to California in which he visited the Livermore Lab and was briefed on Brilliant Pebbles, President Bush had suggested that the U.S. faced threats beyond the traditional one from the Soviet Union. SDI, he said, might protect the U.S. from ballistic missiles in the hands of renegade nations, terrorists or "narco-gangsters," who he maintained were taking on "the pretensions of a geopolitical force."[16] Around the same time, Richard Perle testified to the Senate that the U.S. could "safely reduce the investment we make in protecting against a massive surprise Soviet nuclear attack" and "reorient the program towards missiles launched by accident or by rogue states in the Third World."[17] With the outbreak of ethnic violence in the Soviet Union that spring, some Republicans raised the prospect that terrorists or madmen might gain control of a few Soviet long-range missiles. When Saddam Hussein invaded Kuwait that summer, a number of Republicans called for an SDI deployment to defend the United States against attack by a "rogue state."

Pentagon and CIA analysts did not think much of these new rationales. General Colin Powell, who had succeeded Admiral Crowe as chairman of the JCS the previous year, came down hard on the idea of accidental launches or terrorists' gaining control of Soviet ICBMs. "Based on my knowledge of how the Soviets manage their nuclear systems and the safeguards they have," he said, "I'm fairly comfortable that those weapons will not get into improper hands"; if they did, "the systems they have to protect those weapons would make them pretty much unusable."[18] As for the "rogue state" threat, it was not yet on the horizon of U.S. military planning. True, Iraq and a number of other Third World countries, including India and Pakistan, were developing ballistic missiles as well as nuclear weapons, but all of them seemed to be developing relatively short-range missiles to threaten their regional rivals, not intercontinental missiles for suicidal attacks on superpowers. Besides, if any rogue state or terrorist group wanted to attack the U.S., it could accomplish the task far more easily—and with far less risk of retaliation—by delivering a bomb in a suitcase or from an offshore vessel. As Harold Brown suggested, the U.S. would gain more protection from Third World threats by beefing up the U.S. customs service than by deploying SDI.[19]

In early August the Senate, by a vote of fifty-four to forty-four, passed an amendment to the defense bill that for the first time imposed some congressional control over how SDI funds were expended. The amendment, proposed by two Democrats and backed by Nunn, cut the administration's request for Brilliant Pebbles by almost two-thirds and refocused the program on ground-based interceptors and long-range research on exotic technologies. In October the Democrats cut back SDI funding by almost a billion dollars from the previous year, a reduction that clearly doomed "Phase One"[20]

On January 3, 1991, Bush and his advisers approved a new deployment plan presented by Dr. Henry F. Cooper, the new head of the SDIO. Cooper, who had been chief negotiator at the moribund defense and space talks, was the choice of the conservatives to succeed the Bush administration's first director, Lieutenant General George L. Monahan. The plan Cooper presented was as great a step down from "Phase One" as that limited system had been from Reagan's promise of a perfect defense. Known by its acronym, GPALS, for Global Protection Against Limited Strikes, the proposed deployment was designed to protect the United States from an attack by Third World countries or accidental Soviet launches of under a hundred ballistic missiles. Approximately a thousand Brilliant Pebbles and between five hundred and a thousand ground-based interceptors were to be involved in this enterprise, and the cost was estimated at forty billion dollars.[21]

On January 3 the chances that the Congress would fund GPALS seemed extremely low. However, on January 16 the UN deadline for an Iraqi withdrawal from Kuwait ran out, and the Gulf War began. For five weeks U.S. aircraft and naval vessels pounded Iraq, before the ground troops moved into Iraq and Kuwait. During this period the American public watched U.S. military videos of cruise missiles and smart bombs acquiring their targets and homing in on them unerringly. The public also watched televised pictures of U.S. Patriot-missile batteries firing at Iraqi Scud missiles aimed at cities in Israel and Saudi Arabia and creating spectacular fireworks in the sky. The Patriots, it appeared, had achieved the first destruction of enemy ballistic missiles in a combat situation, and, according to exultant Army briefers, they had intercepted almost all the Scuds they had attempted to hit.[22] Along with General Norman Schwarzkopf and the American troops, the Patriot missile became a hero of the Gulf War, and with it the fortunes of SDI soared.

Just hours after the first Scud fell out of the Arabian sky on January 18, *The Wall Street Journal* called the event "a great advertisement for SDI." A few days later Patrick Buchanan wrote, "Using SDI technology, the United States has shown it can attack and kill ballistic missiles." President Bush, he said, "ought to insist on the restoration of full funding for SDI." Other conservative commentators followed suit.[23] On January 29, with the air war still less than two weeks old, President Bush in his State of the Union address cited the "remarkable" success of the Patriot in defending Israeli and Saudi citizens and announced his decision to refocus the SDI program "on providing protection from limited ballistic missile strikes, whatever their source." The administration asked for a 77-percent increase in the SDI budget, and conservatives in Congress roared approval. "While the images [of the Patriot streaking skyward] are fresh in our mind," wrote Representative John Kyle, an Arizona Republican on the House Armed Services Committee, "we should focus on what these events teach us: Americans and our allies should never again be defenseless against a ballistic missile attack; and we need not be."[24]

In the midst of this excitement Senator John Warner, the ranking Republican on the Armed Services Committee, proposed a resolution directing the secretary of defense to begin the development of space-based defenses immediately, regardless of the ABM Treaty. After some discussion with administration officials, he modified the resolution so that it called for a prompt renegotiation of the ABM Treaty and directed the secretary of defense to prepare to develop and test space-based systems while the negotiations continued. In floor speeches and a letter to colleagues, Warner invoked the Patriot missile and said his amendment would free American genius to devise new, more advanced systems to defend U.S. territory and fighting forces from a "world-wide proliferation of ballistic missiles."[25]

Senators Nunn and Cohen and others on the Armed Services Committee persuaded Warner to withdraw the proposal and began discussions to work out a compromise. In July, Nunn and Warner offered a bill, known as the Missile Defense Act of 1991, which called for the deployment of one hundred ground-based ABM interceptors at a single site in five years' time. The deployment was to be a first step towards an anti-missile system with multiple sites to defend the entire United States against a limited nuclear attack. The bill called upon the administration to begin negotiations to modify the ABM Treaty so as to permit the deployment, and it authorized $4.6 billion for the SDI program—or just seven hundred million less than the administration had asked. The bill mandated only ground-based deployments, but it included $625 million for the accelerated development of Brilliant Pebbles.[26]

In retrospect, these events would seem to suggest that a major misunderstanding had taken place. The Patriot and SDI interceptors were both intended to shoot down missiles, but the similarity ended there. The Patriot was an Army program begun during the Ford administration with technology conceived in the 1960s; originally designed as an air-defense system, it was upgraded in the 1980s to defend troop concentrations or military bases against primitive, short-range missiles, such as the Iraqi Scuds, by exploding in their path. The SDIO had displayed no interest in the Patriot since it was technically irrelevant to the mission of defending the United States. The task of blowing aside a Scud in its short trajectory through the atmosphere and that of hitting a warhead traveling through space and descending into the atmosphere were two different things. To say that, because the Patriot worked, an ABM defense of the U.S. should be deployed, was the equivalent of saying that anyone who could build a barn could build a skyscraper.[27]

In fact, there was very little misunderstanding about this issue in Washington. Not long after the first announcement of a Scud shoot-down, Army spokesmen crowed that the Patriot was an Army program and "not even a spinoff of SDI," and Dr. Henry Cooper acknowledged forthrightly that the Patriots were "not some product of 'Star Wars' technology or 'Star Wars' funding." Subsequently numerous journalists and experts explained the differences between the two programs.[28] With a few exceptions, conservative commentators did not assert that there was any real technological connection between the two programs but merely argued by analogy.[29]

What had happened was that the conservatives had seized upon the apparent success of the Patriots to push for space-based defenses at a time when the Democrats were in disarray. In January the Congress had debated the wisdom of an immediate attack on Iraq, and on January 12, just a few days before the expiration of the UN deadline, both houses voted on whether or not to give Bush the authorization he needed for the use of force. The Pentagon had estimated that the war might produce thousands of American casualties, and Nunn, who had previously insisted that the President needed the consent of Congress to go to war, argued that the Bush administration should allow some time for the sanctions to take effect before committing U.S. troops to battle. Nunn voted against the authorization, and so did a majority of the Senate Democrats.[30] When the worst-case Pentagon estimates proved spectacularly wrong, and NATO forces quickly routed the Iraqi troops, taking very few casualties, Nunn and the rest of the Democratic nay-sayers were roundly denounced. In Nunn's home state of Georgia, the reaction was harsh. A billboard went up proclaiming Nunn "Saddam Hussein's Best Friend." In February many commentators pronounced him politically dead.[31]

The Nunn-Warner bill passed the Armed Services Committee on July 17 with only Senators Glenn, Gore, Kennedy and Levin opposed. The same day, Bush and Gorbachev wrapped up the START treaty, and attached to it was a unilateral Soviet declaration that the U.S.S.R. might withdraw from START if the U.S. abrogated or substantially violated the ABM Treaty.[32] The Senate nonetheless passed the Missile Defense Act without debate, and when Les Aspin came out for the deployment plan, the House passed a similar bill. SDI funding for fiscal 1992 went to $4.15 billion—a 43-percent increase over the previous year and a record high for the program.[33]

Senate Democrats assumed that this deployment plan superseded not only Warner's first proposal but GPALS, the administration's plan that included a space-based deployment. Henry Cooper, however, did not interpret the Nunn-Warner bill in quite the same way. He agreed that the bill gave priority to a ground-based system, but, he pointed out, it did not order him to abandon GPALS, and the Congress had always asked for a balanced defense, so he saw no reason to shelve his earlier approach. Nunn argued with him, but to little effect: the Republicans wanted a space-based defense. Thus, in December 1991, when the Soviet Union broke up, the SDIO was working not on one deployment plan but on two.[34]

A year later both deployment plans had been abandoned and an air of scandal surrounded the SDI program.

The SDIO had planned for a GPALS deployment in the mid-1990s, and for over a year SDI enthusiasts spoke as if the project were well under way. But in March 1992 GAO investigators reported that GPALS still had no stable architecture, and that Brilliant Pebbles was still unproven and "tremendous technical challenges" lay ahead. Interpreting this language for a reporter, Representative John Conyers (Democrat of Michigan), the chairman of the House Government Operations Committee, said, "The Star Wars program is floundering. They haven't a clue where they are going or how to get there."[35]

By contrast to GPALS, the congressional plan to deploy ground-based interceptors had seemed eminently feasible. Certainly it was described in that way. When the Nunn-Warner bill was proposed, Defense Department officials told Congress that they were ready to forge ahead with an ABM Treaty–compliant defense located at a single site. They assured Nunn's committee they could field one hundred interceptors by the target date of 1996 without much technical risk. The evidence they presented to that effect included the spectacular success of a January 1991 test, in which a prototype ERIS missile had hit a mock warhead in space. According to SDIO estimates, the first site could be built for ten billion dollars, and the network of sites needed to cover the United States could be completed for twenty-five billion.[36]

However, when the Senate Armed Services Committee took up the matter in the spring of 1992, the cost estimate for the first site had mysteriously doubled; a second ERIS test, conducted in March, failed because of technical errors; and in the testimony of Henry Cooper, small warning signals began to appear.[37]

On June 2 the *New York Times* revealed that the Pentagon's top program analyst had conducted an internal Pentagon review of the deployment plan and found it a disaster in the making. In the leaked report, dated May 15, Dr. David S. C. Chu, the assistant secretary of defense for program analysis and evaluation, wrote that, in order to meet the target date, the interceptor system would have be exempted from more than a dozen laws and regulations governing weapons procurements; it would have to skip important performance tests, with the result that it could end up with crippling defects. Dr. Chu, an economist who had directed program analysis in the Pentagon since 1981, recommended that the system not be built until it could be thoroughly tested and that the deployment target be moved to 2002 or 2003.[38]

On June 4, two days after the *Times* article came out, Donald J. Atwood, the deputy secretary of defense, appeared before a subcommittee of the Senate Armed Services Committee. Senator Nunn was angry. "We've been substantially misled," he told Atwood. "There was considerable evidence, in fact overwhelming evidence, that the '96 goal was achievable, based on all the testimony we had." The SDI program, he said, "is already in enough trouble without these kind of background exaggerated claims that are now proven to be totally erroneous and false."

Atwood did not deny Nunn's accusation. He replied that those responsible for the program had assumed that critical parts of the testing program could be skipped. This, he added, was "a terrible mistake," and on reflection the original schedule "didn't appear to be realistic at all."

Duly warned, the Armed Services Committees set the deployment date back to 2002.[39]

How Sam Nunn could have been so misled about the feasibility of missile defenses became rather clearer in September, when the GAO released another report on SDI. After studying the seven major flight tests of SDI interceptors conducted between January 1990 and March 1992, GAO investigators found that SDIO officials had at least exaggerated the success of four of them. The other three tests were correctly depicted by the SDIO as either complete failures or only partly successful. According to the GAO, no Brilliant Pebbles test had succeeded, in spite of SDIO claims that one had "accomplished all of the main objectives." Also, according to the GAO, the Army had misrepresented the ERIS test of January 1991, claiming that the missile had met its key goal of discriminating between a warhead and decoys, when it had not.[40]

The four SDI tests studied by the GAO were, it later appeared, not the only ones that had been misrepresented. In August 1993 four former Reagan-administration officials, including two military officers and a scientist, told the *New York Times* that the HOE test of 1984 had been rigged. This was big news, since that test, fourth in a series known as the Homing Overlay Experiment, was the first—and for many years the only—example of a missile hitting a missile in space. Coming just a year after Reagan's Star Wars speech, it was cited as proof that "the President's dream" could come true.

The Pentagon, and later the GAO, investigated the charge, only to discover that, though the four former officials did not have all of the facts right, there had been not one but many attempts to rig the test results. In the first three of the HOE tests, Pentagon officials had installed a small bomb on the target missile, which they planned to explode if the interceptor flew past it, simulating the effect of a direct hit. The idea, it appeared, was to deceive the Soviets about U.S. capabilities. But the plan was not carried out, because the interceptors flew so wide of their mark that the Soviets would not have been fooled by an explosion. The fourth test was not rigged in this way. Instead, officials, afraid that another failure would doom the entire program, had "enhanced" the target by heating it and turning it sideways in flight, so that it appeared twice its normal size to the interceptor sensors, thereby doubling the likelihood of a hit. SDIO officials thought these "enhancements" reasonable, but they had failed to inform the Armed Services Committees.[41]

In addition to these discoveries, it was found that the Patriot missiles had not done nearly as well as was claimed. In the midst of the war, President Bush said that the Patriots had intercepted forty-one out of the forty-two Scuds they engaged, and at the end of it the Army claimed a 96-percent success rate. But when independent American experts and Israeli Defense Force officials took a look at the evidence for this claim, they concluded that there was no clear evidence of even a single successful Scud interception. Looking again at the data, the Army twice revised its estimates downwards. By April 1992 Army officials said that the Patriots had intercepted 70 percent of the Scuds fired at Saudi Arabia and 40 percent of those fired at Israel.[42] But even these figures were, it turned out, not based on hard evidence. Prodded by a congressional investigation, the Army found that it had "high confidence" in warhead kills in only 25 percent of the Patriot engagements. The GAO, however, reported that, except in 9 percent of the cases, the Army could prove only that the Patriots had come close to the Scuds, not that they had destroyed them.[43]

The news that anti-missile weapons were not as successful as previously thought had a depressing effect on some SDI promoters but a positively liberating effect on others. From the beginning it had been clear to many experts that Star Wars technologies were much better suited to the offense than to the defense, and among SDI enthusiasts there were a number who had always thought that the goal of the program should be to establish U.S. control over space. The subject was taboo while the nuclear-arms race with the Soviet Union continued, and while the idea of Star Wars defenses had popular support in the U.S. But the end of the Cold War and the demise of the Soviet Union permitted space-weaponry advocates to come out of the closet—even as it encouraged those who had been working on missile-defense technologies to design new uses for their products.

In 1991–92 one center of this new thinking was the Heritage Foundation. Another was the Lawrence Livermore Laboratory, where Edward Teller and Lowell Wood were gearing up for another campaign. In their view the SDI surveillance satellites known as "Brilliant Eyes" could be equipped with radars, lasers and telescopes, antennae and sensors to allow military commanders to peer through clouds and darkness to see troop movements and bombing targets. As for Brilliant Pebbles, the system could be reconfigured to attack targets on the ground or in space. One proposal Wood was shopping to the Pentagon involved ordering the pebbles, which for these purposes he called "Endo-Pebbles," to leave their orbits and hit targets on the surface of the planet: enemy tanks, artillery emplacements, airplanes, command bunkers and so forth. Another proposal involved using Brilliant Pebbles as anti-satellite weapons and as "battleships" to enforce a space blockade, standing ready to destroy any rocket launched to put a satellite into orbit.[44]

Yet another center of this thinking was the National Space Council, a White House panel created by Bush to oversee the space program and directed by Vice-President Dan Quayle. In 1992 Quayle proposed to break down the traditional barriers between the military and civilian space programs. In January 1993 he issued a final report calling upon the nation to develop space weapons to exploit the high ground of space for future wars. His report said nothing at all about missile defenses. Rather, he raised the specter of America's foes using spacecraft "to overfly and threaten U.S. forces with impunity" and called for a comprehensive "space control" capability, including space-based surveillance systems and anti-satellite weapons that could destroy enemy communications, navigation and weather satellites.[45]

These ideas were shelved.

By the time of Bill Clinton's inauguration in January 1993, the fortunes of SDI were at an all-time low. The Cold War was over; the Gulf War had receded into the past; the economy had been in recession for over a year; some in Congress were pressing for major cutbacks in defense spending; the public had turned its attention to domestic issues, and SDI did not figure in the election campaign. In January, just before he left office, Bush signed an agreement with Russian president Boris Yeltsin to eliminate two-thirds of the strategic nuclear warheads on both sides by 2003. The START II treaty required the elimination of MIRVed land-based missiles and tacitly affirmed the traditional interpretation of the ABM Treaty.[46]

On taking office, the Clinton administration conducted a bottom-up review of the defense budget. In May 1993 Les Aspin, the new secretary of defense, declared that the era of Star Wars was over and that the Strategic Defense Initiative was dead. The SDIO would, he said, become the Ballistic Missile Defense Organization (BMDO) and would report to the assistant secretary of defense for acquisitions and technology instead of to the Office of the Secretary of Defense. These changes, Aspin said, represented a shift away from a crash program to deploy space-based weapons. His plan, he said, was to develop and acquire systems for defending U.S. forces against shorter-range battlefield missiles while continuing research on national missile defenses. He asked $3.8 billion for the program—or the sum the Congress had appropriated for it the previous year—but suggested that, with diminishing defense budgets, there might be leaner years ahead.

Aspin's announcement went down rather better with SDI supporters than with SDI critics, both of whom had been expecting more radical surgery and now judged that the program would go on much as before. Frank Gaffney, who had been Perle's assistant in the Weinberger Defense Department and had become a one-man SDI lobby, said with unconscious irony that Aspin was "rearranging the deck chairs." Senator Jim Sasser, a Democrat, charged that SDI was being put through the equivalent of a "witness protection program."[47]

Aspin, however, made substantial changes. He halted plans for the deployment of a national missile defense and drastically reordered the priorities for the program as a whole. After the Gulf War the Bush administration had put 20 percent of the SDIO's budget into theater missile defenses; Aspin reversed the proportions, putting only 20 percent into R&D on national missile defense and 80 percent into an aggressive program to develop theater missile defenses to protect American allies and U.S. troops in the field.[48]

At the time, the changes seemed to please almost everyone in Washington. The Democratic-led Congress gave the Ballistic Missile Defense Organization a billion dollars less than Aspin requested; nonetheless, there was substantial bipartisan support for the development of theater missile defenses. The Republican right was quiescent, and for two years the only audible complaint about the program came from the arms-control community.

Long before the Gulf War, the Army, the Navy and the Air Force had begun to develop their own theater missile defenses. The Army and the Navy were both working on two types of systems: a point, or "lower-tier," defense to intercept short-range missiles in the lower regions of the atmosphere, and an "upper-tier" defense to intercept missiles of greater ranges high in the atmosphere. The Air Force was working on an array of programs, including a boost-phase laser intercept to be carried on a piloted aircraft. From the plethora of competing programs the BMDO chose to push three towards deployment: two "lower-tier" systems, the Army's upgraded Patriot (known as PAC-3), the Navy's Aegis program and one "upper-tier" system, the Army's Theater High Altitude Area Defense, known as THAAD.

Unlike most of the shorter-range systems, THAAD was a new program; it drew on concepts developed in the 1980s for the SDI's High Endoatmospheric Defense Interceptor (HEDI) and was designed to intercept missiles at altitudes in excess of forty kilometers and to protect an area a few hundred kilometers in diameter.[49] Since its planned capabilities would cross the agreed demarcation line between "theater" and "strategic" defenses, the Clinton administration, which had repudiated the "broad" interpretation of the ABM Treaty, decided to ask the Russians for a "clarification" of the treaty that would establish the demarcation line high enough so that THAAD and all the other upper-tier systems could be tested and deployed.[50] The Arms Control Association criticized both the building of an interceptor that could be used as a part of a national missile-defense system and the administration's attempt to pressure the Russians into accepting a substantial modification of the ABM Treaty, particularly when, in a period of nationalist reaction, the Russian parliament was refusing to ratify SALT II.[51]

In the 1994 congressional elections the Republicans, led by the right, made a surprise sweep through both houses of Congress, winning the House of Representatives for the first time in forty years. The comfortable majorities the Democrats had held in both houses since 1986 now belonged to the Republicans. Senator Jesse Helms of North Carolina became the chair of the Foreign Relations Committee, Senator Strom Thurmond of South Carolina the chair of the Armed Services Committee. In the House, Speaker Newt Gingrich presided over a large freshman class whose members were far to the right of most Republicans elected in previous years. Flushed with success, Gingrich made his pre-election manifesto, the Contract with America, a platform for Republicans. Among the provisions of the contract was a directive to the administration to deploy "a highly effective defense" of the United States "at the earliest practical date." Frank Gaffney had persuaded Gingrich to include the directive on the grounds that there was latent political support for it.[52] The result was another fierce partisan battle over the deployment of national missile defenses.

By the end of 1995 the Republicans had succeeded in passing legislation mandating the development of a multi-site ground-based national missile-defense system to be deployed by 2003. President Clinton vetoed the legislation, but he signed an appropriations bill that gave him $745 million for national missile defenses—or more than double what the Pentagon had asked for.[53]

The next year was a presidential election year, and the Gingrich Republicans were in a triumphal mode. Senator Dole, the leading Republican candidate, entered into the spirit of the moment to the extent of co-sponsoring a Gingrich bill entitled the Defend America Act. The bill called for the deployment of a "highly effective" national defense against limited attacks by the end of the year 2003; further, it specified a mix of ground- and space-based systems and directed that this system be "augmented over time to provide a layered defense against larger and more sophisticated ballistic missile threats as they emerge." The layers were to be composed of ground-based missile interceptors, sea-based interceptors, space-based kinetic-energy weapons and space-based directed-energy systems: the whole Star Wars extravaganza. The House Republicans had somehow lost track of the expense of such undertakings, and when the Congressional Budget Office estimated the deployment would cost either thirty-one or sixty billion dollars, the Defend America Act was withdrawn.[54]

In the meantime Senator Dole ran on the issue of deploying national missile defenses. He had never displayed much enthusiasm for deployment in the past, but, according to pundits, the issue would clearly differentiate him from Clinton without being one of those Gingrich issues, such as outlawing abortion or repealing the gun-control laws, that would alienate two-thirds of the voters. More important, perhaps, the Gingrichites had made it a loyalty test for Republicans in Congress. As Jeane Kirkpatrick, the former UN ambassador, put it, "It's not so much a matter of [Dole's] choosing the issue. He's really reflecting a widespread, deeply felt concern in the Republican community. It's the defense issue on which there is the greatest conviction among those Republicans who think about national security matters."[55]

In practice, the deeply felt concern seemed to be confined to Washington, for with the Cold War over and no international crisis at hand the public did not fear a ballistic missile attack enough to pay attention to the issue. In numerous polls and focus groups, including a half-dozen conducted by Frank Gaffney and his Coalition to Defend America, voters expressed puzzlement that anyone would bring up such a matter. When informed that the U.S. had no defense against ballistic missiles, they manifested disbelief. In one Gaffney-sponsored focus group, two women protested they had seen Patriot missiles shooting down Iraqi Scuds on TV, and one man, an auto engineer, said, "You couldn't pay me enough to believe you. After all, you see it in the movies."[56] Other participants responded much as they, or their parents, had in the days before SDI: they assumed "defense," as in "the Defense Department," meant defense. When persuaded that there was no national ABM system and told that a Chinese rocket could land on an American city, they tended to react positively to the idea of a defense—at least until told how much it would cost.[57]

Dole soldiered on with the issue. "The United States has no defense—and I repeat—no defense against ballistic missiles," he kept repeating. But in vain. "National security issues are not on people's screens at all," one foreign-policy polling expert said. "When you do finally scratch around for a threat, people see terrorism, not ballistic missiles as the problem."[58]

Clinton and the congressional Democrats, however, took the Republican challenge on missile defenses seriously enough to adopt a compromise plan for deployment known as "three-plus-three." The administration agreed to spend three years designing and testing a system that could be fielded in another three years if the go-ahead was given. The system, which in theory could be deployed by 2003, would initially consist of twenty ground-based interceptors capable of blocking the few missiles that might be launched intentionally by "rogue states," or accidentally by Russia or China. Officials pointed out that no Third World country yet had a missile capable of hitting the United States, and, according to U.S. intelligence analysts, none was likely to get one for a decade or more. In any case, they argued, the U.S. would have at least three years' warning of any deployment, so the U.S. could afford to hold off on building a system while it improved the design. According to Senator Levin, who helped forge the compromise, the deployment decision would depend not only on the threat but on the effectiveness of the system, its cost and its compliance with the ABM Treaty.[59]

In the meantime the Clinton administration continued to press for a "clarification" of the ABM Treaty to accommodate THAAD and other planned "upper-tier" theater missile-defense systems. The Russians resisted, but in 1997, with their economy in need of a bail-out, they agreed to something much less than the U.S. had asked. In effect the agreement, signed in September, exempted THAAD but not the other, faster, upper-tier systems from the treaty. The agreement infuriated the Helms-Gingrich Republicans, who complained that it prohibited the Navy and Air Force systems and did not permit an effective ground-based national missile-defense system or defenses in space. Calling for an abrogation of the ABM Treaty, they mustered enough votes to block the administration from submitting the agreement to the Senate for approval.[60]

All this diplomatic and political pulling and hauling had, however, remarkably little to do with the anti-missile defense program. For one thing, the Clinton administration had for years been operating as if its THAAD testing was compliant with the ABM Treaty. For another, the THAAD interceptor had failed to hit its target in all four of its tests. "This is really rocket science," Lieutenant General Lester Lyles, the director of the Ballistic Missile Defense Organization, said apologetically in a congressional hearing that spring.[61]

In July 1998 a bipartisan commission established by the Congress to assess the ballistic-missile threat to the United States reported that "rogue states," such as Iran and North Korea, had the capacity to develop and deploy long-range ballistic missiles "with little or no warning" in about five years' time. The report contradicted the official CIA assessment that no small, hostile country, with the possible exception of North Korea, could field an ICBM before 2010. The commission, headed by Donald H. Rumsfeld, secretary of defense in the Ford administration, had reviewed U.S. intelligence and concluded that nations such as Iran and Iraq had obtained sensitive missile technologies with the help of loosened export controls among industrialized nations and the assistance of other rogue states. In addition, the panel reported, the suspect countries had become so adept at concealing their missile programs that it was difficult for Western analysts to gauge the extent of their progress.[62]

The CIA reaffirmed its previous assessment, but its position was undermined when, in August, North Korea surprised U.S. analysts by test-firing a three-stage ballistic missile out over the Pacific. The rocket, whose purpose was ostensibly to launch satellites, fizzled in space, but it indicated that North Korea might develop a weapon capable of reaching Alaska and parts of Hawaii in the next few years.[63] In September all fifty-five Senate Republicans voted for a bill introduced by Senator Thad Cochran (Republican of Mississippi) calling for the deployment of a national missile-defense system as soon as technologically possible. "There could very well be a missile heading in our direction as we speak," Senator James M. Inhofe (Republican of Oklahoma) said during the debate. Only the threat of a filibuster by the Democrats stopped the passage of the bill.[64]

By that time THAAD—the only long-range anti-missile system being tested—had failed to hit its target for the fifth time and was four years behind schedule. In February an outside panel of experts headed by Larry D. Welch, a former Air Force chief of staff, had issued a blistering report on the program, finding failures rooted in poor design and fabrication, lax management and lack of rigorous government oversight. The main point the report made was that the test schedules had been so compressed that the program became "a rush to failure."[65]

However, the Democrats were once again on the defensive. In December, House Republicans voted to impeach President Clinton on various charges associated with his attempt to cover up an affair with a White House intern, Monica Lewinsky. In January 1999 Republicans from the House Judiciary Committee took their impeachment case to the Senate for a trial of the President.

On January 20 the Clinton administration pledged an additional $6.6 billion over five years for the deployment of a national missile-defense system. William Cohen, the former senator, who had become secretary of defense in 1996, cited the threat of a ballistic-missile attack from rogue nations and pointed in particular to the North Korean missile test. "We affirm that there is a threat and the threat is growing," he said. According to Pentagon officials, the system of ground-based interceptors probably could not be fielded until 2005, two years later than originally predicted, but a deployment review would be made in June 2000. The system, which would initially consist of twenty interceptors, might be sited in Alaska or North Dakota. According to Cohen, it had not yet been determined whether the whole U.S. could be defended from a single site, but if not, two or more sites would be built and more interceptors added. Cohen said that the administration would talk to the Russians about amending the ABM Treaty, but that if Russia refused the U.S. would abandon the treaty and build the anti-missile system anyway.[66]

Senator Thad Cochran expressed satisfaction with Secretary Cohen's statements but reintroduced his bill requiring the Pentagon to deploy a national anti-missile system "as soon as it is technologically possible."[67] Republicans in the House introduced a bill that did not fuss around with technical feasibility but simply stated, "It is the policy of the United States to deploy a national missile defense."[68]

In mid-March, after the Senate Democrats had blocked the Republican efforts to remove President Clinton from office, the Senate took up the Cochran bill with amendments added by the Democrats stating that money for the system had to go through the regular appropriations process and that the system had to be consistent with policies to reduce Russia's arsenal. The Democratic leaders told Clinton's aides that this was the best they could do, and that they probably could not muster the votes necessary to sustain a veto. The administration then dropped its objections, and the bill was passed by a vote of ninety-seven to three. According to White House officials, the administration's support for the bill would help to defuse a potent political issue for the Republicans in the campaign of 2000.[69]

The prospect of an American ABM deployment immediately raised a number of diplomatic and arms-control issues.

Shortly after the funding decision was taken in January, the President and Secretary of State Madeleine Albright attempted to reassure Yeltsin and other Russian officials that the system slated for deployment was to deal merely with threats from rogue states; Albright proposed that the two sides begin talks on altering the ABM Treaty. The initial Russian reaction was not reassuring. A top Russian general accused the U.S. of exaggerating the threat from rogue states and of violating its treaty commitments; the Russian Foreign Ministry issued a statement calling the deployment plan "a serious threat to the whole process of nuclear arms control as well as strategic stability."[70] In June, Clinton offered to resume the dialogue on a START III treaty to supersede the still-unratified START II in combination with talks on the ABM Treaty. Yeltsin, who wanted a new START treaty because his government could not afford to maintain the launchers for the three thousand single strategic warheads each side was allowed to keep under START II, agreed to listen to American proposals for amending the ABM Treaty, but by November Russia had not budged on the issue. "We aren't negotiating any kind of amendments to the ABM [Treaty]," a foreign ministry spokesman said. "There can be no compromise on this issue," the deputy chief of the Russian General Staff told reporters.[71]

Possibly the Russian leadership would eventually consent to amending the treaty, but the problem for Russia was how to retain its deterrent when its fleets of submarines, missiles and bombers were aging, and when it could not afford to modernize them. According to administration sources, Russia had developed only one new ICBM system and could afford to field forty or fifty copies of it per year. But if it relied merely on this new system, it would—in theory—fall behind the deployments of U.S. ABM systems and lose its deterrent. On the other hand, if it extended the life cycle of its older weapons, these weapons would become less and less safe. One possible solution under discussion within the Russian General Staff was for Russia to MIRV its launchers. The solution would contradict the logic of arms control since the late 1980s, doom Start II and, unless the U.S. went along, it would preclude a Start III accord.[72]

Not only Russia but China regarded the proposed deployments as a threat. After the March votes in the Congress, Chinese leaders expressed "grave concern" about upsetting the "global strategic balance." China also warned the U.S. against deploying a theater missile defense in Taiwan, saying that this would be a military provocation that would threaten security throughout the Asia-Pacific region.[73] China had never built more than a couple of dozen ICBMs in the past, but, to retain its small strategic deterrent, it might begin an arms race with the American ABM systems. A Chinese test-launch of a new, mobile, ICBM that year showed that China was entirely capable of building more strategic missiles, and statements from Chinese spokesmen suggested that was what its government would do.[74]

America's NATO allies also opposed the American anti-missile deployment and any amendment of the ABM Treaty. What worried the Europeans, along with the Chinese, the Russians and others, was that in mounting missile defenses the United States would undermine the entire system of treaties designed to restrict and control nuclear weapons, among them the Comprehensive Test Ban Treaty, which the U.S. Senate had voted not to ratify in October, the Nuclear Non-Proliferation Treaty and the START accords. If Russia did not proceed with disarmament, European security would again be threatened. And if China deployed more ballistic missiles, how could India or Pakistan be persuaded to restrict their nuclear programs? The ABM Treaty, which many in Washington considered irrelevant after the end of the Cold War, appeared to many Europeans as a bulwark against a new nuclear arms race.[75]

Proponents of missile defenses in Congress clearly believed arms control to be less important than building defenses and countering the potential threat from small "rogue states." Why a country such as North Korea or Iran would attack the U.S. with an ICBM when the U.S. could retaliate by destroying the country, and whether there weren't ways to persuade such countries not to develop ICBMs and nuclear weapons, were questions the proponents never seemed to consider. Nor did they seem to consider the technical obstacles to building a national missile defense.

Between 1983 and the fall of 1999 the U.S. had spent sixty billion dollars on anti-missile research, and though technical progress had been made in a number of areas, there was still no capable interceptor on the horizon. In that period the U.S. had conducted nineteen intercept tests outside, or at the upper edges, of the atmosphere, and in fourteen of them the interceptor had missed its target. Of the five successful intercepts, three of them were in 1999: after five failures, the THAAD had hit its target in its sixth and seventh tests, and the kill vehicle for the national missile-defense system had made a hit on its first test.[76] As these successes suggested, the BMDO and its contractors were learning how to hit a bullet with a bullet in space. Whether they could do it every time was another issue, for everything in the complex system of radars and battle-management software, as well as the rocket and the kill vehicle, had to work perfectly. But even if they could, hitting a target on a test range was only the first step on the way to the development of a capable ABM system. In the view of many expert observers, that next step was much longer than the first one.[77] As Theodore Postol and others pointed out, the Patriot missile had a perfect test record before the Persian Gulf War, yet it failed in most, or all, of its attempts to destroy Iraqi Scud missiles.[78] Then, unlike the Patriot, a national missile-defense system would have to cope with counter-measures that any country capable of building an ICBM could take to defeat it, and it would have to work the first time it was used.[79]

Common sense would, of course, suggest that if the national interceptor system could not reliably and consistently hit incoming warheads, it would not be deployed. Yet, as history has shown, big military programs are rarely canceled once Congress and the contractors are on board, and, in combination with the Clinton administration's pledge to fund the development of the system, the two congressional votes in the spring of 1999 for the first time convinced several long-term observers of the program that some form of national ABM system would be built in the coming years. "The political momentum is probably irresistible," John Pike said. Joseph Cirincione, a senior fellow of the Carnegie Endowment for International Peace, also felt that a deployment had become virtually inevitable. "This system is going to be built," he told one reporter. "Politics and the politics of defense procurement will see to that."[80]

Indeed, by November Clinton-administration officials were talking about an initial deployment of two hundred interceptors in Alaska in 2005, a hundred more in a second site by the end of the decade.[81] They were hoping to make a formal decision on the plan in June 2000—just a few weeks before the Democratic convention—and begin work that summer, with the official ground-breaking, which would breach the ABM Treaty, in the spring of 2001. However, by June only three of the nineteen scheduled tests on the interceptor could be completed, and because some of the technology for the system had not been developed yet, the tests would have to be made with jury-rigged rockets. Back in January Secretary Cohen had offered no certainty of a full deployment by 2005, and in the fall the panel of defense experts which had called the THADD "a rush to failure" said the same of the national missile-defense system.[82] These were the usual warning signals. Yet all major candidates for the Democratic and Republican presidential nominations were promising to build a national anti-missile system, and none were asking whether it was worthwhile to renegotiate or to break out of the ABM Treaty without the assurance that a capable interceptor could be built.

One of the curious things about the decisions on the national ABM system taken in 1999 was that there was no public pressure on the administration or Congress to make them. Indeed, there had been so little public discussion of the ABM program for the past several years that many consistent readers of the major newspapers did not know that the anti-missile program was still extant, much less that the U.S. was nearing a deployment decision. Both Republicans and Democrats in Washington seemed to assume that the public would favor such a system. Or, rather, they seemed to assume that, if asked whether America should be defended, the public would say yes. Possibly they were right. But in 1996 Bob Dole had failed to make missile defenses a campaign issue, and in 1999 Americans were no more fearful of a ballistic missile attack than they had been three years earlier. In September, Senator Mitch McConnell, the chairman of the Republican senatorial fund-raising committee, sent out a letter to thousands of potential donors asking for "a generous emergency gift of $25 or more" to help Senate Republicans "do what President Clinton will not" and defend the United States from the threat of a nuclear attack by North Korea. The response to this unprecedented appeal was apparently disappointing.[83]

What this suggested was that the pressures to deploy were far more ideological than political—or, as ABM proponents might put it, deployment was a matter of principle. Why principle should dictate the deployment of a system that might not work would seem to be the question, but many proponents did not care if the initial deployment worked well or not. A Heritage Foundation "backgrounder" of March 23, 1998, for example, declared, "If the United States is to be defended against the growing missile threat," Congress must "mandate the deployment of a national missile defense by a certain date"—making no mention of feasibility.[84] But then for many Republicans in Washington the initial deployment was not an end in itself. In their view the "thin" defense would have to be thickened as time went on. "It's better than having nothing," Republican Representative Curt Weldon of Pennsylvania said of the Clinton program, but "we're probably going to have to use space-based assets."[85] As always for the Republican right, the goal was weapons in space—that is, weapons which, if they materialized, could contribute to an offense, as well as provide a defense for the United States.

Glossary

ABM: Anti-ballistic missile.
ABM Treaty: Anti-Ballistic Missile Treaty. A treaty of unlimited duration signed in 1972 by Nixon and Brezhnev, designed to ban nationwide ABM defenses. Specifically the treaty banned the development, testing and deployment of sea-based, air-based, space-based or mobile land-based ABM systems, and their components, that could be used to counter strategic ballistic missiles in flight. Article III of the treaty permitted the U.S. and the Soviet Union to have two ABM sites with no more than one hundred fixed, land-based interceptors. A 1974 protocol to the treaty reduced the number of sites to one.

"broad" interpretation—Developed by Reagan-administration officials in September–October 1985, this interpretation of the ABM Treaty permitted the development and testing, but not the deployment, of ABM systems based on "other physical principles"—that is, based on technologies such as lasers and particle beams.

"narrow" interpretation—The term used by Reagan-administration officials to refer to the traditional interpretation of the ABM Treaty, or the understanding of the treaty that U.S. and Soviet negotiators agreed upon when the treaty was signed and that the Nixon administration and the Senate agreed upon when it was ratified. According to this "narrow," or traditional, interpretation, the treaty permitted the development and testing of ABM weapons based on "other physical principles," but only for the fixed, land-based systems permitted by Article III of the treaty. (Agreed Statement D of the treaty called for discussions of further limitations on such weapons if they were created.)

ACDA: Arms Control and Disarmament Agency.
ACLM: Air-launched cruise missile.
ALPS: Accidental launch protection system.
ASAT: Anti-satellite weapon.
BAMBI: Ballistic missile boost intercept. A category of defensive concepts developed in the early 1960s for attacking ICBMs shortly after they were launched. These concepts relied upon space-based as well as ground-based interceptors plus tracking and scanning satellites.
BMD: Ballistic missile defense.
BMDO: Ballistic Missile Defense Organization, successor to SDIO.
boost phase: The first phase of a ballistic missile's trajectory as the missile rises through the atmosphere.
booster: A rocket or missile that boosts a payload into space.
Brilliant Pebbles: The concept for a space-based anti-missile system composed of thousands of tiny, independently targeted interceptors under study in the late 1980s and early 1990s.
C^3: Command, control and communications.
CNO: Chief of Naval Operations.
cruise missile: A jet-powered, low-flying drone designed to penetrate enemy air defenses, capable of being launched from the ground, a ship or an airplane.
DAB: Defense Acquisitions Board.
DARPA: Defense Advanced Research Projects Agency.
Dense Pack: A concept for basing the MX missile.
DEW: Directed energy weapon, such as a laser or particle beam.
DSB: Defense Science Board.

ERIS: Exoatmospheric reentry interceptor sub-system.
fast-burn booster: A rocket powered by a solid-fuel propellant that rises quickly out of the atmosphere.
GPALS: Global protection against limited strikes, a less extensive form of BMD.
HEDI: High endoatmospheric defense interceptor.
HOE: Homing overlay experiment.
ICBM: Intercontinental ballistic missile.
INF: Intermediate-range nuclear forces.
INF Treaty: A treaty signed in December 1987, banning U.S. and Soviet intermediate-range nuclear missiles in Europe. Negotiations began in the last year of the Carter administration.
JCS: Joint Chiefs of Staff.
KKV: Kinetic kill vehicle.
launchers: Missiles and bombers.
LoAds: Low altitude defense system.
MAD: Mutual assured destruction.
Minuteman: A U.S. ICBM.
MIRV: Multiple independently targeted reentry vehicles. Multiple warheads carried on a ballistic missile, each one of which is guided to a separate target.
MX: Missile Experimental. A heavy U.S. ICBM capable of carrying ten independently targeted warheads.
MX-MPS: A concept for basing the MX involving multiple protective shelters.
NORAD: North American Aero-space Defense Command.
NSA: National Security Agency.
NSC: National Security Council.
NSDD: National Security Decision Directive.
NSPG: National Security Planning Group.
Nuclear freeze: A proposal by peace activists that the U.S. and the Soviet Union agree to freeze the testing, development and deployment of nuclear weapons as a first step towards disarmament.
OSD: Office of the Secretary of Defense.
Patriot: A U.S. short-range non-nuclear interceptor.
Pershing II: A U.S. intermediate-range ballistic missile with a single warhead.
RV: Reentry vehicle, which contains a warhead.
SAC-PG or SAC-G: Senior Arms Control Planning Group.
SALT I: The first strategic arms limitation agreements, including the ABM Treaty and an interim accord freezing the number of U.S. and Soviet ICBM launchers. Both agreements were signed by Nixon and Brezhnev in 1972.
SALT II: The second Strategic Arms Limitation Treaty, signed by Carter and Brezhnev in June 1979. The first formal treaty limiting U.S. and Soviet offensive strategic weapons, it set an initial overall ceiling of 2,400 ICBM launchers, submarine-based missiles, heavy bombers and air-to-surface missiles, with the ceiling to be lowered in later stages. It included subceilings for the various forms of launchers and their warheads. SALT II was not ratified by the U.S. Senate, but both countries abided by its provisions until 1987, when the U.S. exceeded its limits. The treaty had been due to expire in December 1985.
SDIO: Strategic Defense Initiative Organization.
SLBM: Submarine-launched ballistic missile.
SLCM: Submarine-launched cruise missile.
START I: Strategic Arms Reduction Treaty I, in negotiation through most of the Reagan administration and signed in July 1990 by Bush and Gorbachev. Reduced the number of Soviet long-range nuclear warheads from 11,012 to 6,163 and U.S. warheads from 12,646 to 8,556.
START II: Strategic Arms Reduction Treaty II, signed by Bush and Yeltsin in January 1993 and ratified by the U.S. Senate but not by the Russian Duma (as of 1999). Would reduce U.S. and Russian strategic arsenals to 3,000–3,500 warheads and bombs.
SS-18: The U.S. designation for a type of Soviet heavy ICBM capable of carrying ten independently targeted warheads.
SS-20: The U.S. designation for the Soviet intermediate-range ballistic missile deployed in the late 1970s as the successor to the antiquated SS-**4s and -5s.** A solid-fuel rocket, it could carry three independently targeted warheads.
THAAD: Theater High Altitude Area Defense. A U.S. intermediate-range interceptor tested during the 1990s.
Throw-weight: The total weight of the payload a ballistic missile can carry over a given range.
Trident: A U.S. nuclear-armed submarine that replaced the smaller Poseidon submarine.
Trident II: SLBM carried on the Trident sub; also known as the D-5.
UNITA: National Union for the Total Independence of Angola.
ZBM: Zero Ballistic Missiles, shorthand for the proposal advanced by the Reagan administration in July 1986 that both the U.S. and the Soviet Union eliminate all of their ballistic missiles, leaving only cruise missiles and gravity bombs in their strategic arsenals.

Notes

Abbreviations Used in Notes

AP: Associated Press
LAT: Los Angeles Times
NYT: New York Times
PPP: Public Papers of the Presidents
WP: Washington Post
WSJ: Wall Street Journal

ONE: The American Everyman

1. Martin Anderson, *Revolution* (New York: Harcourt Brace Jovanovich, 1988), pp. 80–86.
2. Janne E. Nolan, *Guardians of the Arsenal: The Politics of Nuclear Strategy* (New York: Basic Books, 1989), p. 156.
3. Lou Cannon, *President Reagan: The Role of a Lifetime* (New York: Simon & Schuster, 1991), pp. 58–59.
4. Ibid., pp. 487–88.
5. Philip M. Boffey, William J. Broad, Leslie H. Gelb, Charles Mohr and Holcomb B. Noble, *Claiming the Heavens: The New York Times Complete Guide to the Star Wars Debate* (New York: Times Books, 1988), pp. 3–5.
6. Strobe Talbott, *Master of the Game: Paul Nitze and the Nuclear Peace* (New York: Alfred A. Knopf, 1988), p. 188.
7. G. Simon Harak, "One Nation Under God: The Soteriology of SDI," *Journal of the American Academy of Religion,* 56, no. 3 (Fall 1988).
8. Richard V. Pierard and Robert D. Linder, *Civil Religion and the Presidency* (Grand Rapids, Mich.: Academie Books, 1988), pp. 273–79, contains all the Reagan quotes above.
9. Robert Scheer, *With Enough Shovels: Reagan, Bush & Nuclear War* (New York: Random House, 1982), p. 99.
10. Michael Lieb, *The Children of Ezekiel* (Durham, N.C.: Duke University Press, 1998), pp. 109–12.

    Senator James Mills, formerly the president pro tem of the California State Senate, told the following story: In 1971 he was sitting next to Reagan at a banquet; Reagan was telling stories, but when the lights dimmed and the waiters brought on flaming dishes of cherries jubilee, Reagan asked him if he had read Ezekiel 38 and 39. When Mills said yes, Reagan recited the end-times prophecy and concluded, "Do you understand the significance of that? Libya has now gone Communist, and that's a sign that the day of Armageddon isn't far off."

    Reagan often spoke of Armageddon; he knew the eschatology rather better than he knew Libyan politics. Many people, including Mills, wondered whether his belief affected his actions as President. But it is not clear that Reagan believed in Armageddon any more than he believed in astrology or ghosts in the Lincoln bedroom; besides, Armageddon is something that mortals can't do anything about.
11. Cannon, *President Reagan,* p. 41.
12. Paul D. Erickson, *Reagan Speaks* (New York: New York University Press, 1985), p. 67.
13. Anderson, *Revolution,* p. 71.
14. Ronnie Dugger, *On Reagan: The Man and His Presidency* (New York: McGraw-Hill, 1983), p. 423.
15. Laurence Olivier, *On Acting* (New York: Simon & Schuster, 1986), p. 29.
16. Bill Boyarsky, *The Rise of Ronald Reagan* (New York: Random House, 1968), p. 101.
17. Ronald Reagan with Richard G. Hubler, *Where's the Rest of Me?* (New York: Duell, Sloan and Pearce, 1965) [hereafter Hubler], p. 266.

18. Ibid., pp. 308–9.
19. Erickson, *Reagan Speaks,* p. 23.
20. Hubler, pp. 302–12.
21. Boyarsky, *Rise of Reagan,* p. 137.
22. Richard Hofstadter, *The Paranoid Style in American Politics and Other Essays* (New York: Vintage Books, 1967), p. 30.
23. Quoted in Frances FitzGerald, "The American Millennium," in *Estrangement,* ed. Sanford J. Ungar (New York: Oxford University Press, 1985), p. 271.
24. Ibid., p. 272.
25. *Public Papers of the Presidents: Ronald Reagan* [hereafter *PPP*], Vol. 1, U.S. Government Printing Office, 1983, pp. 442–43.
26. Cannon, *President Reagan,* p. 51.
27. Talbott, *Master of the Game,* p. 188.
28. Erickson, *Reagan Speaks,* pp. 39–49.

TWO: The Making of an Orator

1. Anne Edwards, *Early Reagan* (New York: William Morrow, 1987), p. 163.
2. Ibid., p. 69; Norman E. Wymbs, *Ronald Reagan's Crusade* (Boca Raton, Fla.: Skyline Publications, 1997), p. 135.
3. Ronald Reagan, *An American Life* (New York: Simon & Schuster, 1990), p. 21; Edwards, *Early Reagan,* pp. 23–25; Hubler, p. 7.

   Reagan calls his father a "first generation black Irishman." But according to Edwards, Jack was a third-generation immigrant. His grandfather came to the United States around the time of the Civil War.
4. Reagan, *American Life,* p. 35.
5. Hubler, p. 7; Garry Wills, *Reagan's America: Innocents at Home* (Garden City, N.Y.: Doubleday, 1987), pp. 12–13.
6. Reagan, *American Life,* p. 29.
7. Ibid.
8. Hubler, pp. 7–9; Reagan, *American Life,* p. 33.

   In his 1965 memoir (Hubler) Reagan describes coming home once when he was eleven years old to find his father out cold—dead drunk on the front porch, with his arms spread out as if he had been crucified and his hair soaked with melting snow. The boy had always known about his father's drinking—he had heard angry voices coming from his parents' room—but he had never had to deal with it before. "I wanted to let myself in the house and go to bed and pretend he wasn't there," Reagan writes, but there was no one else in the house. "I felt myself fill with grief for my father at the same time I was feeling sorry for myself." Leaning over Jack and smelling the sharp odor of whiskey on his breath, Reagan got a fistful of his overcoat and managed to drag him inside and get him into bed. He never mentioned the incident to his mother. (Hubler, pp. 7–8.)
9. Hubler, pp. 7–9.
10. Wymbs, *Reagan's Crusade,* pp. 17–22, 39–50; Wills, *Reagan's America,* pp. 17–25; Edwards, *Early Reagan,* pp. 56–57, 104.
11. Edwards, *Early Reagan,* p. 36.
12. Ibid., pp. 44, 68; Lou Cannon, *President Reagan: The Role of a Lifetime* (New York: Simon & Schuster, 1991), p. 29.
13. Edwards, pp. 62–63.
14. Ibid., pp. 52–53.
15. Reagan, *American Life,* p. 31.
16. Lou Cannon, *Reagan* (New York: Perigee Books, 1982), p. 29.
17. Wymbs, *Reagan's Crusade,* pp. 57–58.
18. Hubler, p. 28.
19. Edwards, *Early Reagan,* p. 92.
20. Ibid., p. 110; Hubler, p. 41.
21. Hubler, pp. 42–45.
22. Ibid., pp. 66–67.
23. Edwards, *Early Reagan,* p. 99.
24. Ibid., pp. 130–57.
25. Ibid., pp. 165–68, 184–85, 232, 253.
26. Wills, *Reagan's America,* p. 159; Edwards, *Early Reagan,* pp. 193–202; Hubler, pp. 132–33.

   According to Edwards, Reagan joined SAG because of Helen Broderick in 1938 and the SAG board in 1941, with Wyman promoting his candidacy.
27. Wills, *Reagan's America,* pp. 173–74.
28. Ibid., pp. 174–75.
29. Edwards, *Early Reagan,* pp. 258–72.
30. Hubler, pp. 125, 138; Wills, *Reagan's America,* p. 167.
31. Wills, *Reagan's America,* pp. 172–79; Reagan, *American Life,* p. 104.
32. Edwards, *Early Reagan,* pp. 193, 197; Cannon, *Reagan,* p. 65.
33. Ibid., pp. 226, 230.

34. Hubler, p. 201.
35. Edwards, *Early Reagan,* pp. 171, 228–31, 335.
36. Hubler, p. 139.
37. Ibid., pp. 169–70; Wills, *Reagan's America,* pp. 245–47; Edwards, *Early Reagan,* pp. 302–3.
38. Wills, *Reagan's America,* pp. 224–50; Edwards, *Early Reagan,* pp. 314–17.
39. Hubler, p. 162.
40. Robert Scheer, *With Enough Shovels: Reagan, Bush & Nuclear War* (New York: Random House, 1982), p. 41.
41. Edwards, *Early Reagan,* pp. 342–49.
42. Wills, *Reagan's America,* p. 254.
43. Ibid., pp. 253–57.
44. Cannon, *Reagan,* p. 85; Edwards, *Early Reagan,* pp. 334–35, 350–51.
45. Edwards, *Early Reagan,* pp. 425–27.
46. Ibid., pp. 196–97, 488.

    Dart's first wife was a Walgreen from Dixon, and his second wife was the actress Jane Bryan, who appeared with Reagan in one film. Dart later described himself as a "big-issues guy . . . interested in the national economy and our defense ability, not all these crappy little issues like equal rights or abortion or the Moral Majority or whatever." (Ibid.)
47. Ibid., p. 231, for quote; Bill Boyarsky, *The Rise of Ronald Reagan* (New York: Random House, 1968), p. 75.
48. Wills, *Reagan's America,* p. 258.
49. Edwards, *Early Reagan,* pp. 417–18.
50. Ibid., pp. 408, 435–37; Wills, *Reagan's America,* pp. 265–66.

    In 1960 Reagan made another agreement with MCA on TV residuals. MCA had just bought seven hundred Paramount films for TV release; SAG agreed that MCA would not have to pay TV residuals on any films made before 1960 and got MCA to make a $2.65-million contribution to the pension-and-welfare fund for actors. Many within SAG thought the contract sold out the older actors. (Edwards, *Early Reagan,* p. 472; Wills, *Reagan's America,* p. 277.)
51. Wills, *Reagan's America,* pp. 271–75; William E. Pemberton, *Exit with Honor* (Armonk, N.Y.: M. E. Sharpe, 1997), p. 37.

    On the one hand, he said that the waivers were so ordinary he could not remember granting them; on the other, he said that because the circumstances were so special—meaning that he was an MCA client—he had done his best to duck the meetings and therefore could not remember them.

    According to Wills, MCA executives had arranged a series of real-estate deals and tax shelters for Reagan, which made him for the first time a rich man.
52. Cannon, *Reagan,* p. 89; Nancy Reagan, with William Novak, *My Turn* (New York: Random House, 1989) [hereafter, Nancy Reagan], pp. 88–92; Edwards, *Early Reagan,* p. 376.
53. Hubler, pp. 233–35.
54. Edwards, *Early Reagan,* p. 394.
55. Hubler, p. 236.
56. Nancy Reagan, pp. 99–101.
57. Kenneth W. Thompson, ed., *Leadership in the Reagan Presidency* (New York: Madison Books, 1992), p. 76.
58. Helene von Damm, *At Reagan's Side* (New York: Doubleday, 1989), p. 60.
59. Nancy Reagan, p. 106.

    Paul Laxalt, when running for the Senate in Nevada in 1974, said that Reagan spoke to his friends in private as if giving a speech to the multitudes: "Same stories, same one-liners," Laxalt said. (Cannon, *Reagan,* p. 200.)
60. Michael K. Deaver, *Behind the Scenes* (New York: William Morrow, 1987), p. 40.
61. Nancy Reagan, pp. 108–9.
62. *Reagan* in *The American Experience* series, WNET, February 23 and 24, 1998, produced by Adriana Bosch, narrated by David McCullough.
63. Hubler, p. 251.
64. Pemberton, *Exit with Honor,* p. 49, for quote; Cannon, *Reagan,* p. 93.
65. Hubler, p. 261.
66. Wills, *Reagan's America,* p. 283.
67. Ibid.
68. Boyarsky, *Rise of Reagan,* p. 101; Edwards, *Early Reagan,* p. 475. Speech to the Phoenix Chamber of Commerce quoted in Edwards.
69. Pemberton, *Exit with Honor,* p. 49; Edwards, *Early Reagan,* p. 457.

    Reagan attacked TVA, a client of the company, and the GE executives were not at all happy—though they did not censor him. Hearing of their concern, Reagan quickly volunteered to drop the TVA reference, saying that he could make his speech just as effectively without it. (Hubler, p. 269.)
70. Wills, *Reagan's America,* pp. 283–84; Jules Witcover, *Marathon* (New York: Viking, 1977), p. 100; Reagan, *American Life,* p. 132.
71. Edwards, *Early Reagan,* p. 17.

    Just before the war Reagan took to rattling defense figures off at a dizzying pace. "No one was quite sure he was accurate, but he sure as hell sounded accurate," another colleague said (ibid., p. 228).
72. Ibid., p. 171.
73. Wymbs, *Reagan's Crusade,* p. 165.

74. "America the Beautiful," commencement address, William Woods College, Fulton, Mo., June 1952, in Edwards, *Early Reagan,* pp. 539–54.
75. Norman Wymbs, a supporter who wrote two books about Reagan's childhood, makes this point (Wymbs, *Reagan's Crusade,* pp. 165–69).
76. Wills, *Reagan's America,* p. 284; Hubler, p. 273.

    The reason GE gave was that the show had fallen behind in the ratings; Reagan in his 1965 memoir suggests that a key but nameless GE executive thought him too controversial. Garry Wills, however, points out that GE dropped Reagan's contract just a few weeks before Reagan was summoned to the grand jury on the MCA case and the possibility of conflict-of-interest litigation raised its head.
77. Wills, *Reagan's America,* p. 287; J. Allen Broyles, *The John Birch Society: Anatomy of a Protest* (Boston: Beacon Press, 1964), p. 33.
78. Lyn Nofziger, *Nofziger* (Washington, D.C.: Regnery Gateway, 1992), p. 28; Pemberton, *Exit with Honor,* pp. 64–65.
79. Boyarsky, *Rise of Reagan,* p. 104.
80. Edwards, *Early Reagan,* pp. 561–70, for text; Wills, *Reagan's America,* p. 29.
81. Wills, *Reagan's America,* p. 291.
82. Boyarsky, *Rise of Reagan,* p. 158.

    Years later Salvatori said, "We knew then, as we know now, that Reagan didn't have any depth, but he was sure good on his feet." (Pemberton, *Exit with Honor,* p. 65.)
83. Edwards, *Early Reagan,* p. 489.
84. Boyarsky, *Rise of Reagan,* p. 104.
85. Cannon, *Reagan,* pp. 101, 107.
86. Joseph Lewis, *What Makes Reagan Run? A Political Profile* (New York: McGraw-Hill, 1968), p. 109.
87. Boyarsky, *Rise of Reagan,* pp. 142–45; Wills, *Reagan's America,* pp. 296–98.
88. Pemberton, *Exit with Honor,* p. 65, Boyarsky, *Rise of Reagan,* pp. 161–62.
89. Pemberton, *Exit with Honor,* p. 67.
90. Cannon, *Reagan,* p. 115.
91. Boyarsky, *Rise of Reagan,* p. 139.
92. Cannon, *Reagan,* p. 115.
93. Nofziger, *Nofziger,* p. 42.
94. Cannon, *President Reagan,* p. 47.
95. Cannon, *Reagan,* p. 113; Thomas C. Reed interview, June 23, 1998.
96. Cannon, *President Reagan,* p. 48.
97. Cannon, *Reagan,* p. 122.
98. Ibid., pp. 123–36; Wills, *Reagan's America,* pp. 310–11.
99. Cannon, *Reagan,* p. 167.
100. Ibid., pp. 132–38, p. 134 for quote; Nofziger, *Nofziger,* pp. 78–83.
101. Cannon, *Reagan,* p. 134.
102. Ronald Brownstein and Nina Easton, *Reagan's Ruling Class* (New York: Pantheon Books, 1983), pp. 643–46.
103. Deaver, *Behind the Scenes,* pp. 47–51.
104. Cannon, *Reagan,* p. 120.
105. Ibid., p. 125.
106. Wills, *Reagan's America,* p. 313.
107. Thompson, ed., *Leadership,* p. 83; Nofziger, *Nofziger,* p. 47, for quote, p. 57 on hiring; interview with Reed, June 23, 1990.

    "He is an endorser," Sears wrote later. "Reagan sat with his California cabinet more as an equal than as its leader. Once consensus was derived or conflict resolved, he emerged as the spokesman, the performer." Deaver quotes this and tells us that Reagan would probably not quarrel with this statement. Deaver himself does not. (Deaver, *Behind the Scenes,* p. 73.)
108. Cannon, *Reagan,* pp. 124–25.
109. Ibid., pp. 128–32.
110. Lewis, *What Makes Reagan Run?,* p. 176.
111. Thompson, ed., *Leadership,* p. 72.
112. Pemberton, *Exit with Honor,* p. 76; Wills, *Reagan's America,* pp. 308–9; Cannon, *Reagan,* pp. 159–60.
113. Pemberton, *Exit with Honor,* p. 76.
114. Ibid., p. 76; Cannon, *Reagan,* p. 161.
115. Pemberton, *Exit with Honor,* pp. 76–77; Cannon, *Reagan,* pp. 161–62.
116. Pemberton, *Exit with Honor,* p. 77.

    At the time, William F. Buckley explained that Republican conservatives had asked Reagan to stand by to guard against the possibility that Nixon would collapse in the primaries, but that Reagan's entourage, understandably seized with "royalist passions," pressed the candidate forward and at the last moment pushed him over the brink. It was many years before Reagan's conversations with other Republican leaders came into the public domain. (Cannon, *Reagan,* pp. 163–64.)
117. Haldeman, H. R. *The Haldeman Diaries: Inside the Nixon White House* (New York: G. P. Putnam and Sons, 1994), pp. 447–78.
118. Interview with embassy official; Kitty Kelly, *Nancy Reagan: The Unauthorized Biography* (New York: Simon & Schuster, 1991), pp. 182, 201–3, 208.

119. Pemberton, *Exit with Honor,* pp. 77–78.
120. Deaver, *Behind the Scenes,* p. 44; Pemberton, *Exit with Honor,* p. 78.
121. Pemberton, *Exit with Honor,* pp. 79–80; Cannon, *Reagan,* p. 184; Wills, *Reagan's America,* pp. 312–13.
122. Cannon, *Reagan,* p. 185, for figures; yearly income taxes rose from $6.64 to $7.62 on every hundred dollars of personal income. For withholding, see Nicholas Lemann, "The Peacetime War," *Atlantic Monthly,* October 1984, p. 82. See also Pemberton, *Exit with Honor,* pp. 78–79; Wills, *Reagan's America,* pp. 314–15.

    In the eight years of the Reagan administration, two analysts concluded, "government entrenched itself in many ways as a strong, effective force in California society." Reagan did try, unsuccessfully, to pass a bill putting a legal limit on state taxes. But, like that perennial in Washington, the balanced-budget amendment, the bill was a political substitute for cutting expenditures and taxes. (Wills, *Reagan's America,* pp. 314–15.)
123. Wills, *Reagan's America,* p. 314; Cannon, *Reagan,* p. 201.

    Years later Jesse Unruh said to Nofziger, "You know the difference between Reagan and most politicians is that Reagan believes what he says. He can say 'two and two are four' and he can say 'two and two are six' ten minutes from now, and he absolutely believes two and two are six.... I'm not going to sound sincere when I tell you that two and two are six because I know it isn't true. Ronald Reagan is convinced that it is." (Thompson, ed., *Leadership,* p. 81.)
124. Cannon, *Reagan,* p. 191.
125. Ibid., pp. 187–88.
126. Deaver, *Behind the Scenes,* pp. 52–53.
127. Wills, *Reagan's America,* p. 328. This is what Meese and Salvatori argued.
128. Cannon, *Reagan,* p. 188.
129. Ibid., p. 192; Witcover, *Marathon,* p. 66.
130. Cannon, *Reagan,* p. 194.
131. Ibid., p. 195.
132. Ibid., p. 196. Cannon estimated Reagan made eight hundred thousand dollars in 1975.
133. Ibid., pp. 196–97. Hannaford served as Reagan's director of public affairs in 1974; before that he ran a small public relations firm.
134. Ibid., p. 200.
135. Witcover, *Marathon,* p. 67.
136. Cannon, *Reagan,* p. 212.
137. Cannon, *Reagan,* pp. 202–3; Witcover, *Marathon,* pp. 373–76; Nofziger, *Nofziger,* pp. 173–74; Wills, *Reagan's America,* p. 328..
138. Nofziger, *Nofziger,* p. 174; Witcover, *Marathon,* pp. 373–77.

    All, or most, of Reagan's top staffers had read the speech in advance, and all later denied having any responsibility for it.
139. Cannon, *Reagan,* pp. 212–19 for first quote; William G. Hyland, *Mortal Rivals: Superpower Relations from Nixon to Reagan* (New York: Random House, 1987), p. 164, for second quote.
140. Cannon, *Reagan,* p. 219.
141. Witcover, *Marathon,* p. 422 on Wallace; Hyland, *Mortal Rivals,* p. 164; John Newhouse, *War and Peace in the Nuclear Age* (New York: Alfred A. Knopf, 1989), p. 262.
142. Martin Anderson, *Revolution* (Harcourt Brace Jovanovich, 1988), p. 71.
143. *Public Papers of the Presidents: Carter,* Vol. 1, U.S. Government Printing Office, 1980, pp. 1, 235–41. Carter's speech was on July 15, 1979.

THREE: Doubling the Volume

1. Hedrick Smith, "Reagan's World," in Hedrick Smith, Adam Clymer, Leonard Silk, Robert Lindsey and Richard Burt, *Reagan, the Man, the President* (New York: Macmillan, 1980), pp. 95–126. For Reagan's Taiwan issue and its consequences, see also Cannon, *Reagan,* p. 272.
2. Smith et al., *Reagan,* p. 109.
3. Ibid., p. 102.
4. Charles D. Hobbs, *Reagan's Call to Action* (Nashville, Tenn.: T. Nelson, 1976), p. 37.

    In this interview Reagan praises General Douglas MacArthur and claims that the U.S. could have easily won the Vietnam War if at the beginning the Air Force had been permitted to carry out its plan to hit sixty-five military targets in ninety days, destroying the North Vietnamese war-making capability.
5. Michael M. Miles, *The Odyssey of the American Right* (New York: Oxford University Press, 1980).
6. James T. Patterson, *Mr. Republican* (Boston: Houghton Mifflin, 1972), p. 197.
7. Selig Adler, *The Isolationist Impulse* (New York: Free Press, 1966), pp. 98–99, 102–3.
8. Ibid., p. 49.
9. Miles, *Odyssey,* p. 159.
10. Patterson, *Mr. Republican,* pp. 198–211.

    The America First Committee, founded by Midwestern Republicans, held that "The United States must build an impregnable defense for America" (Miles, *Odyssey,* p. 67). It stressed naval power supplemented by air power.

    The Taft Republicans had no more sympathy with fascism than did the Progressives: National Socialism was in their view just another form of socialism, but to them Communism was just as great a menace, and as they saw it the two great tyrannies should be allowed to battle each other to the death without American interference.

11. Patterson, *Mr. Republican,* pp. 495–96.

    The strategy was codified by John Foster Dulles.

12. In *The Conscience of a Conservative,* his political testament of 1960, Barry Goldwater wrote that the U.S. had to be prepared to undertake military operations against "vulnerable" Communist regimes. If there were a major uprising in Eastern Europe (presumably such as that in Hungary in 1956), the U.S., he wrote, should issue an ultimatum against Soviet intervention, and if the demand were rejected, the nation should prepare to move "a highly mobile task force equipped with nuclear weapons" to the scene of the revolt to compel a Soviet withdrawal. "An actual clash," he wrote, "would be unlikely—the mere threat would probably be enough"—because "we would invite the Communist leaders to choose between the total destruction of the Soviet Union and accepting a local defeat." (Barry M. Goldwater, *The Conscience of a Conservative* [Shepardsville, Ky.: Victor Publishing, 1960], p. 121.)

    The interest of the proposal is its atavism. Clearly it was a translation of the nineteenth-century Republican vision of an expeditionary force with overwhelming naval firepower sailing smartly into Shanghai or Manila Bay and cowing the natives into submission without firing a shot. It was the "thin red line" with superior technology––and the promise of a victory on the cheap.

13. Carol Felsenthal, *The Sweetheart of the Silent Majority* (New York: Doubleday, 1981), pp. 171–77, 218–25.

    Every delegate to the 1964 convention was sent one or more copies of *A Choice Not an Echo* (Alton, Ill.: Pere Marquette Press, 1964), many by their constituents, and a million copies were distributed in California. The thesis was that Taft's victory in 1952 was stolen from him by Wall Street and the businesses associated with it. This was Taft's view at the time.

    Schlafly's books on nuclear weapons are: Phyllis Schlafly and Chester Ward, *The Gravediggers* (Alton, Ill.: Pere Marquette Press, 1964); *Strike from Space* (Alton, Ill.: Pere Marquette Press, 1965); *The Betrayers* (Alton, Ill.: Pere Marquette Press, 1968); *Kissinger on the Couch* (New Rochelle, N.Y.: Arlington House, 1975); *Ambush at Vladivostock* (Alton, Ill.: Pere Marquette Press, 1976).

14. Leslie H. Gelb, "Domestic Change and National Security Policy," in *The Next Phase in Foreign Policy,* ed. Henry Owen (The Brookings Institution, Washington, D.C., 1973), p. 268.

15. Strobe Talbott, *Master of the Game* (New York: Alfred A. Knopf, 1988), p. 152; Paul Warnke, "Apes on a Treadmill," *Foreign Policy,* no. 18, spring 1975.

16. Jerry W. Sanders, *Peddlers of Crisis* (Boston: South End Press, 1983), p. 196.

    "For the past few years the United States has been going through a difficult period with respect to domestic morale, and this lower morale has had a direct impact upon the nation's attitudes toward national security issues," Paul Nitze wrote in 1976. In his view, the low point had come in 1974.

17. Talbott, *Master of the Game,* pp. 146–47, 59.

    The first Committee on the Present Danger was formed in December 1950 by a group of private citizens—the principal founder a friend and former colleague of Nitze's. The group echoed NSC-68 (to be discussed later in text) and called a new resolve to "prevent a 'Korea' " in Western Europe; it pressed for a strengthening of America's ability to fight a conventional war and lessening of reliance on nuclear deterrence.

18. David Callahan, *Dangerous Capabilities* (New York: HarperCollins, 1990), p. 374, for CPD formation (also pp. 407–9); Talbott, *Master of the Game,* pp. 146–47; Committee on the Present Danger, *Alerting America: The Papers of the Committee on the Present Danger,* ed. Charles Tyroler II (Washington, D.C.: Pergamon-Brassy's, 1984), pp. i–xx; Sanders, *Peddlers,* pp. 154–60, for list of board members.

19. Talbott, *Master of the Game,* pp. 139–40.

20. Ibid., p. 149.

21. Richard Pipes, "Team B: The Reality Behind the Myth," *Commentary,* October 1986, and "Why the Soviets Think They Can Fight and Win a Nuclear War," *Commentary,* July 1977; Talbott, *Master of the Game,* pp. 144–47; Robert Scheer, *With Enough Shovels: Reagan, Bush & Nuclear War* (New York: Random House, 1982), pp. 53–65, p. 60 for Graham quote; Paul Nitze, *From Hiroshima to Glasnost: At the Center of Decision—a Memoir* (New York: Grove Weidenfeld, 1989), p. 352.

22. Committee on the Present Danger, *Alerting America,* p. 3.

23. Sanders, *Peddlers,* p. 266.

24. William Hyland, *Mortal Rivals: Superpower Relations from Nixon to Reagan* (New York: Random House, 1987), p. 210.

25. McGeorge Bundy, *Danger and Survival: Choices About the Bomb in the First Fifty Years* (New York: Random House, 1988), p. 565.

26. John Newhouse, *War and Peace in the Nuclear Age* (New York: Alfred A. Knopf, 1989), p. 301.

27. Interview with Zbigniew Brzezinski, 8/24/93.

28. Newhouse, *War and Peace,* pp. 318–20; Talbott, *Master of the Game,* pp. 119–24.

29. Talbott, *Master of the Game,* p. 158.

30. Newhouse, *War and Peace,* pp. 318–23.

31. Committee on the Present Danger, *Alerting America,* p. 20.

32. Janne E. Nolan, *Guardians of the Arsenal: The Politics of Nuclear Strategy* (New York: Basic Books, 1989), p. 136; Sanders, *Peddlers,* pp. 260–64; Callahan, *Dangerous Capabilities,* pp. 407–9.

    CPD members testified seventeen times before the Senate. Lloyd Cutler, who managed the ratification process for the Carter administration said that Nitze was "the leading opponent of the treaty." Charles

Walker of the CPD said that Nitze "was the Committee when it came to SALT II." (Callahan, *Dangerous Capabilities,* pp. 407–9.)

33. Talbott, *Master of the Game,* pp. 156–61; Nitze, *From Hiroshima to Glasnost,* pp. 364–65; Bundy, *Danger and Survival,* p. 558.
34. Sanders, *Peddlers,* p. 260, for quote; Talbott, *Master of the Game,* p. 157; Callahan, *Dangerous Capabilities,* p. 409.

    Nitze on other occasions suggested as much. In one CPD forum he said, "In summary I believe the issue is not so much whether a SALT II treaty can be negotiated and ratified, but rather what the United States should be doing to correct the currently adverse trends in our strategic posture" (Committee on the Present Danger, *Alerting America,* p. 28).

    In an essay of October 1, 1979, "Considerations Bearing on the Merits of the SALT II Agreements as Signed in Vienna," he wrote, "The SALT process, regrettably, has contributed to this tendency [to underestimate Soviet military growth] by creating the illusion that a fundamentally new era in the strategic competition has arrived" (Committee on the Present Danger, *Alerting America,* p. 142).
35. Committee on the Present Danger, *Alerting America,* contains this collection, p. 4 for quote.
36. Ibid., p. 42.
37. Ibid., pp. 58–61.
38. Ibid.
39. Ibid., p. 41.
40. Ibid., p. 5.
41. Ibid., p. 65.
42. Ibid., p. 183; Sanders, *Peddlers,* p. 280, for cost.
43. Steven L. Rearden, *The Evolution of American Strategic Doctrine: Paul H. Nitze and the Soviet Challenge* (Boulder, Colo.: Westview Press, 1984), pp. 89–92. Text of NSC-68 in Appendix, pp. 89–92.
44. Ibid., pp. 111–12.
45. Ibid., pp. 95, 98, 111.
46. Ibid., p. 124.
47. Ibid., p. 111.
48. Talbott, *Master of the Game,* p. 56.

    In 1950 the Soviets had no atomic stockpile, and their strategic bombers could have reached the United States only on a one-way suicide mission. By 1954 they still did not have a bomber of true intercontinental range. The Air Force and the CIA had made a series of projections that were little more than educated guesses—and naturally they did not want to guess too low.

    In 1980 Nitze, in reply to critics, wrote that his committee had no choice but to accept these estimates. However, had the committee members been interested in reducing the defense budget rather than increasing it, they would doubtless have pointed to the uncertainties and unknowns.

    George Kennan and Charles Bohlen, the two leading Soviet-experts in the State Department objected to the document. For discussion, see Paul Y. Hammond, "NSC-68: Prologue to Rearmament," in Warner R. Schilling, Paul Y. Hammond and Glenn H. Snyder, *Strategy, Politics and Defense Budgets* (New York: Columbia University Press, 1962), pp. 309–10; John Lewis Gaddis and Paul H. Nitze, "NSC-68 and the Soviet Threat Reconsidered," *International Security,* vol. 4, no. 4 (Spring 1980), p. 173.
49. Dean Acheson, *Present at the Creation* (New York: W. W. Norton, 1969), pp. 374–75.

    Acheson refers to the Hammond study in his memoir; clearly it is the reason he felt it necessary to explain the heightened language of NSC-68.

    Nitze was always more circumspect than Acheson about NSC-68. In interviews with historians he said only that the document was "a product of its time," and, "We wrote it that way for clarity." However, Professor Paul Y. Hammond, who interviewed participants in the debate over NSC-68 a decade after it was written, describes the contretemps between Bohlen and Nitze as follows:

    > Bohlen wanted to make the draft at least more precise and accurate in the hope or expectation that greater accuracy in formulating the problem would result in more accurate conclusions, upon which policy could be based. Nitze adopted quite the opposite view. Anticipating that the military threat would be discounted, he wanted to sacrifice a degree of rationality in the analysis of NSC-68 in order to exaggerate the threat, with the hope that the reaction of opinion leaders would be commensurate with the threat—that is to say, would be rational as measured against the actual threat, though not against the portion of NSC-68 which purported to describe the threat." (Hammond, "NSC-68," p. 371.)

    Nitze, who participated in subsequent studies of NSC-68, never objected to Hammond's characterization of his tactics. (See Gaddis and Nitze, "NSC-68 and the Soviet Threat Reconsidered.")
50. Acheson, *Present at the Creation,* p. 219, for first quote; Joseph M. Jones, *The Fifteen Weeks* (New York: Viking 1955), pp. 139–40, for second quote. Jones, who was Acheson's aide, gives a fuller account of the speech.

    That Acheson thought the scenario he outlined was at least an exaggeration is suggested by the fact that the word "Armageddon" in his memoir refers not to the U.S.-Soviet conflict but, rather, to his own confrontation with the gentlemen of the Congress.
51. Jones, *Fifteen Weeks,* pp. 141–42.

    Six days later Vandenburg wrote a colleague: "I am frank in saying that I do not know the answer to the latest Greek challenge because I do not know all the facts. . . . But I sense enough of the facts to realize that the problem in Greece cannot be isolated by itself. On the contrary, it is probably symbolic of the world-wide ideological clash between Eastern communism and Western democracy. . . ." (Ibid.)

52. Ibid., pp. 139–42.

    Jones later wrote of Vandenburg's "conversion" from isolationism (ibid., p. 193).
53. Talbott, *Master of the Game,* pp. 68–69; Callahan, *Dangerous Capabilities,* pp. 169–71; Robert H. Johnson, "Periods of Peril," *Foreign Affairs,* vol. 61 (Spring 1983), p. 954.

    The estimates were so alarming that a member of the Gaither Committee said that he had spent ten hours a day staring straight into hell.

    The study also predicted a final period of peril, beginning in 1970–75, characterized by an "extremely unstable equilibrium" in which temporary technical advantages, such as an effective ABM system, "could give either nation the ability to come near annihilating the other" (Johnson, "Periods of Peril," p. 958).

    Johnson asks what was so attractive about these doomsday scenarios. His answer is that they offered a readily available solution: a strategic buildup.
54. Bundy, *Danger and Survival,* pp. 543–48; Nolan, *Guardians,* p. 82.
55. Bundy, *Danger and Survival,* p. 548. General Le May's successor as commander of SAC, General Thomas Power, said this candidly, as did his successor, General Richard Ellis.
56. Ibid.; Nolan, *Guardians,* pp. 85–86.
57. Paul Nitze, "Assuring Strategic Stability in an Era of Détente," *Foreign Affairs,* vol. 54, no. 2, January 1976, pp. 224–26.
58. Committee on the Present Danger, *Alerting America,* p. 41.
59. Scheer, *With Enough Shovels,* pp. 115–18.

    According to Scheer and to Talbott, the calculations were done by T. K. Jones, one of Nitze's technical advisers during his tenure on the SALT I delegation (Talbott, *Master of the Game,* pp. 145, 149).
60. Lawrence Freedman, *The Price of Peace: Living With the Nuclear Dilemma* (New York: Henry Holt and Company, 1986), p. 44.
61. See Pipes, "Team B," for the same usage.
62. Committee on the Present Danger, *Alerting America,* pp. 42–43.
63. Talbott, *Master of the Game,* p. 96.
64. Bundy, *Danger and Survival,* p. 549; Newhouse, *War and Peace,* p. 205, for quote.
65. Bundy, *Danger and Survival,* pp. 552–53.
66. Conversation with Leslie H. Gelb, 7/2/90.
67. Sanders, *Peddlers,* p. 202.
68. Bundy, *Danger and Survival,* p. 558.
69. Interview with Richard V. Allen, 6/4/98; Michael K. Deaver, *Behind the Scenes* (New York: William Morrow, 1987), p. 129, on China.
70. Interview with Richard V. Allen, 6/4/98.
71. Ibid.
72. Talbott, *Master of the Game,* p. 151; Sanders, *Peddlers,* p. 282.
73. Kenneth W. Thompson, ed., *Foreign Policy in the Reagan Presidency: Nine Intimate Perspectives* (Charlottesville, Va.: University Press of America, 1993), p. 22; Peter Hannaford, *The Reagans: A Political Portrait* (New York: Coward-McCann, 1983), p. 200; Sanders, *Peddlers,* p. 217.

    Hannaford puts the date of this dinner as January 22, 1979. Sanders tells us that Reagan visited Washington in January 1979 and was made a board member of the CPD at that time.
74. Sanders, *Peddlers,* p. 282.
75. An avid mountain climber, Morrow took part in the physiological training program of NASA. He was a member of NASA's advisory council. *(NYT,* 9/29/94.)
76. B. Bruce-Biggs, *The Shield of Faith* (New York: Simon & Schuster, 1988), pp. 95–96, 156–57, 265–69, 337–38, 409–10.
77. Martin Anderson, *Revolution* (New York: Harcourt Brace Jovanovich, 1988), p. 84.
78. Interview with John Sears, 10/25/90.
79. Policy Memorandum No. 3, "Reagan for President," Los Angeles, Calif., August 1979, courtesy of Martin Anderson.
80. Anderson, *Revolution,* p. 86.
81. Interview with John Sears, 10/25/90.
82. Lou Cannon, *Reagan* (New York: Perigree Books, 1982), pp. 241–55.
83. Scheer, *With Enough Shovels,* pp. 232–34, for all below. Scheer gives us a transcript of the interviews.
84. Ibid., p. 105.
85. Ibid., p. 250.
86. Ibid., pp. 250–51.
87. Ibid., p. 105.
88. Ibid., p. 68.

    John F. Lehman, Jr., a CPD board member and later Reagan's secretary of the Navy, must have made a strong impression on the candidate, for Reagan kept confusing his arguments for a stronger navy with strategic nuclear issues and "the window of vulnerability."
89. Ibid., pp. 235, 234, 245.
90. Smith et al., *Reagan,* pp. 99–100, 116, 119; Rowland Evans and Robert Novak, *The Reagan Revolution* (New York: E. P. Dutton, 1981), p. 159, for vacillation quote.
91. Sanders, *Peddlers,* p. 283.

92. Ibid.; Smith et al., *Reagan,* pp. 119–21; Ronnie Dugger, *On Reagan: The Man and His Presidency* (New York: McGraw-Hill, 1983), pp. 365–66, 396; Evans and Novak, *The Reagan Revolution,* p. 160.
93. Smith et al., *Reagan,* p. 87.
94. Ibid., p. 57.
95. Ibid., pp. 87–91.
96. Jack W. Germond and Jules Witcover, *Blue Smoke and Mirrors* (New York: Viking, 1981), pp. 205–6.
97. Cannon, *Reagan,* pp. 271–75, p. 282 for "secret weapon."
98. Ibid., pp. 274–78.
99. Germond and Witcover, *Smoke and Mirrors,* p. 280.

    David Stockman reports that in 1981 the very word "Medicare" would trigger a discourse from Reagan about how the whole program had been a mistake (David Stockman, *The Triumph of Politics: How the Reagan Revolution Failed* [New York: Harper and Row, 1986], p. 310).
100. Richard Reeves, "America's Choice: What It Means," *NYT Magazine,* 11/4/84; Germond and Witcover, *Smoke and Mirrors,* pp. 26–27, 284.

    In 1979 Carter's own pollster had found that almost half of all Americans were pessimistic about the future.

    A CBS poll taken before and after the debate showed that the percentage of voters concerned that Reagan "would get us into a war" had declined from 43 to 35 (Germond and Witcover, *Smoke and Mirrors,* p. 286).

    Another poll showed that the percentage had dropped from 39 to 31 (Smith et al., *Reagan,* p. 143).
101. Smith et al., *Reagan,* pp. 95–99.
102. Robert Scheer, *LAT,* 6/25/80. This was what Meese was telling reporters.
103. Cannon, *Reagan,* pp. 374–75.
104. Bob Schieffer and Gary Paul Gates, *The Acting President* (New York: E. P. Dutton, 1989), pp. 78–79; Deaver, *Behind the Scenes,* pp. 124–32.
105. Schieffer and Gates, *Acting President,* pp. 79–80; Deaver, *Behind the Scenes,* pp. 123–26; Cannon, *President Reagan,* pp. 70–71.
106. Schieffer and Gates, *Acting President,* pp. 82–85.
107. Jonathan Kwitney, *WSJ,* 10/28/80.
108. Ibid.
109. Schieffer and Gates, *Acting President,* pp. 100–101.

FOUR: Space Defense Enthusiasts

1. Donald R. Baucom, *The Origins of SDI 1944–1983* (Lawrence, Kans.: University Press of Kansas, 1992), pp. 3–7, 16.
2. Erik K. Pratt, *Selling Strategic Defenses: Interests, Ideologies and the Arms Race* (Boulder, Colo.: Lynne Rienner, 1990), pp. 18–19.
3. Baucom, *Origins of SDI,* pp. 17, 20–21.
4. Ibid., p. 22.
5. Ibid., p. 26; Janne E. Nolan, *Guardians of the Arsenal: The Politics of Nuclear Strategy* (New York: Basic Books, 1989), p. 92.
6. Baucom, *Origins of SDI,* pp. 25–71; Nolan, *Guardians,* pp. 96–97; McGeorge Bundy, *Danger and Survival: Choices About the Bomb in the First Fifty Years* (New York: Random House, 1988), p. 550.
7. Frank Hoeber, "Active Defenses: U.S. Strategic Options in the 1980s," in William R. Van Cleave and W. Scott Thompson, eds., *Strategic Options for the Early Eighties: What Can Be Done?* (New York: National Strategic Information Center, 1978), p. 79; Herbert Scoville, Jr., *MX: Prescription for Disaster* (Cambridge, Mass.: MIT Press, 1981), p. 164, for cost.
8. Pratt, *Selling Strategic Defenses,* pp. 36–37, 53, 59.
9. See Van Cleave and Thompson, eds., *Strategic Options* (Van Cleave and other Reagan advisers considered an ABM to protect land-based missiles); interview with Sears, 10/25/90 (according to Sears, Laird and Bryce Harlow mentioned ABM defenses during the campaign).
10. Pratt, *Selling Strategic Defenses,* pp. 54–56. It was conceivable that an MX defense could be made ABM Treaty–compliant.
11. Scoville, *MX,* pp. 1–23, 161, 169; John Newhouse, *War and Peace in the Nuclear Age* (New York: Alfred A. Knopf, 1989), pp. 322–23.
12. Scoville, *MX,* p. 183.
13. *Congressional Quarterly Weekly Report,* vol. 38, no. 29 (July 19, 1980), p. 2049.
14. Angelo Codevilla, *While Others Build* (New York: Free Press, 1988), pp. 240–41; interview with Richard V. Allen, 6/4/98. These people all wanted a stronger statement, but Senator John Tower would not have it.
15. Richard Burt, "Arms and the Man," in Hedrick Smith, Adam Clymer, Leonard Silk, Robert Lindsey and Richard Burt, *Reagan, the Man, the President* (New York: Macmillan, 1980), p. 88. The paper also said that, rather than basing mutual deterrence on the capacity of nuclear weapons to kill millions of Americans and Russians, the United States should aim at military targets in the Soviet Union in time of war, not civilians. In other words, more counter-force weapons were required.

16. Baucom, *Origins of SDI,* p. 134; *NYT,* 1/16/81.
17. Baucom, *Origins of SDI,* p. 135.
18. Caspar Weinberger, *Fighting for Peace* (New York: Warner Books, 1990), p. 300.
19. Interview with Thomas C. Reed, 6/23/98.
20. *NYT,* 10/3/81; Pratt, *Selling Strategic Defenses,* pp. 54–57. But the Pentagon did increase the funding for the Army's low-altitude nuclear-tipped interceptor, LoADs.
21. Donald M. Snow, "Ballistic Missile Defense: The Strategic Defense Initiative," in *The Reagan Defense Program: An Interim Assessment,* ed. Stephen J. Cimbala (Wilmington, Del.: Scholarly Resources, 1984), p. 148.

    In Weinberger's report to Congress in early 1983, the entire discussion of BMD was confined to two sentences. The report said, "Active defense could protect some high-value strategic assets from ballistic missile attack.The program is structured, therefore, to sustain our understanding of the technology so that we could field an advanced and highly effective BMD system should the need arise."
22. *NYT,* 3/30/83; David Hoffman, *WP,* 3/3/85; William J. Broad, *NYT,* 3/4/85; George W. Ball, "The War for Star Wars," *New York Review of Books,* April 11, 1985; Gregg Herken, "The Earthly Origins of Star Wars," *Bulletin of the Atomic Scientists,* October 1987.
23. Malcolm Wallop, "Opportunities and Imperatives of Ballistic Missile Defense," *Strategic Review,* Fall 1979, pp. 13–21.
24. B. Bruce-Biggs, *The Shield of Faith* (New York: Simon & Schuster, 1988), pp. 350–51; Codevilla, *While Others Build,* pp. 22–36.
25. Baucom, *Origins of SDI,* pp. 119–21; see also Bruce-Biggs, *Shield of Faith,* p. 408; Codevilla, *While Others Build,* pp. 63, 69–70.
26. Bruce-Biggs, *Shield of Faith,* p. 351, for "philosopher's stone"; Baucom, *Origins of SDI,* p. 124; Codevilla, *While Others Build,* pp. 61–62, 66.
27. Wallop, "Opportunities," pp. 19–20; Baucom, *Origins of SDI,* p. 128.
28. Baucom, *Origins of SDI,* p. 125.
29. Codevilla, *While Others Build,* pp. 69–70. According to Baucom, Hunter said that eighteen laser battle stations could defend U.S. Minutemen against the threat of Soviet SS-18s *(Origins of SDI,* p. 126). Wallop's *Strategic Review* article, which Hunter apparently read and corrected, said that ten battle stations would suffice to fend off a small-scale attack, such as one by three hundred SS-18s ("Opportunities," p. 19). The numbers are not consonant. In any case, Hunter seems not to have been promising population defenses. According to Codevilla, he claimed that the first copy of the battle station would cost only two to three billion dollars.
30. Codevilla, *While Others Build,* pp. 70–72; Pratt, *Selling Strategic Defenses,* pp. 69–70.
31. Codevilla, *While Others Build,* pp. 73–75.
32. Ibid., pp. 67–68, on the Reagan-Wallop meeting; William J. Broad, *Teller's War* (New York: Simon & Schuster, 1992), pp. 102–3; see also Broad in *NYT,* 3/4/85.
33. Interview with Richard V. Allen, 6/4/98.
34. Baucom, *Origins of SDI,* p. 132; interview with Graham, 6/29/90; interview with Allen, 6/4/98. According to Allen, Graham was called in to brief Reagan on Team B. Allen favored ABM defenses, but he did not want the candidate to talk about them.
35. Interview with an intelligence official; interview with Graham, 6/29/90; Nolan, *Guardians,* p. 10.
36. Nolan, *Guardians,* p. 151, for quote; interview with Paul Nitze, 6/21/90.
37. Baucom, *Origins of SDI,* p. 131.
38. Interview with Graham, 6/29/90.
39. Lieutenant General Daniel O. Graham, "Toward a New U.S. Strategy: Bold Strokes Rather Than Increments," *Strategic Review,* Spring 1981, pp. 9–16.
40. Ibid.; Daniel O. Graham, letter to Alexander M. Haig, Jr., July 21, 1981. Courtesy of the office of Senator J. Bennett Johnston.
41. Broad, *Teller's War,* p. 50.

    Teller argued that, if the Soviets were certain that the U.S. would not launch a nuclear attack, they would continue to support Communist rebels in such places as the Congo and would "step by step, nation by nation . . . conquer the world eventually."
42. Nolan, *Guardians,* pp. 76–77.
43. Broad, *Teller's War,* pp. 97–98.
44. Edward Teller, "Technology: The Imbalance of Power," in *The United States in the 1980s,* ed. Peter Duignan (Hoover Institution, Stanford University, Palo Alto, Calif., 1980).
45. Broad, *Teller's War,* pp. 94–95.
46. Ibid., pp. 78–89.
47. Ibid., pp. 23–26, 73.
48. Quote is in ibid., p. 92; William J. Broad, *Star Warriors* (New York: Simon & Schuster, 1985), p. 121.
49. Codevilla, *While Others Build,* pp. 77–78; quote in Nolan, *Guardians,* p. 163.
50. Codevilla, *While Others Build,* pp. 80–81.
51. Ibid., p. 79. Warner brought Foster to Wallop's office, and Wallop and Codevilla argued technology with Foster. Codevilla maintains they won.
52. Baucom, *Origins of SDI,* p. 146; Broad, *Teller's War,* pp. 38, 97–98, 105–6; interview with Caspar Weinberger, 9/11/90.

    Teller was a fellow and Bendetsen an overseer of the Hoover Institution. Weinberger said that he introduced Teller to Reagan after having the scientist on a radio show to debate civil defenses.

53. Interview with Allen, 6/4/98; see also Richard V. Allen, "The Man Who Changed the Game Plan," *National Interest,* no. 44, Summer 1996; Burt, "Arms and the Man," p. 87; Codevilla, *While Others Build,* p. 241; Martin Anderson, *Revolution* (New York: Harcourt Brace Jovanovich, 1988), p. 87.

The same confidential paper prepared for him during the campaign which called for investments in civil and ABM defenses and counter-force targeting also said that Soviet military gains in Afghanistan, or for that matter Eastern Europe, should not be accepted as a "permanent historical fact."

54. Interview with Allen, 6/4/98; Baucom, *Origins of SDI,* p. 141.
55. Baucom, *Origins of SDI,* pp. 149–50.
56. Anderson, *Revolution,* pp. 88–95.
57. Lieutenant General Daniel O. Graham (ret.), *High Frontier: A New National Strategy* (Washington, D.C.: High Frontier, 1982) pp. 122–28; Pratt, *Selling Strategic Defenses,* p. 24, on Stanford Research Institute.
58. Baucom, *Origins of SDI,* p. 150.
59. Anderson, *Revolution,* pp. 94–95. Anderson has the phrases reversed, making it sound as if it is easier to protect the country than to protect missile sites. Notes provided by Anderson.
60. Ibid.
61. Herbert Reynolds, Office of the Under Secretary of Defense, "Point Paper on Global Ballistic Missile Defense," September 28, 1981, released in 1987 at the request of Senator J. Bennett Johnston.
62. Baucom, *Origins of SDI,* pp. 233–38; Broad, *Teller's War,* pp. 304–6.
63. Baucom, *Origins of SDI,* p. 151.
64. Ibid.; Broad, *Teller's War,* p. 108; Gregg Herken, "The Earthly Origins of Star Wars," *Bulletin of the Atomic Scientists,* October 1987, p. 22.
65. Broad, *Teller's War,* pp. 109–10. Wallop's phrase was "assured protection."
66. Interview with Graham, 6/29/90.
67. Broad, *Teller's War,* pp. 112–13.
68. Baucom, *Origins of SDI,* pp. 157–59.
69. Broad, *Teller's War,* pp. 114–15; Baucom, *Origins of SDI,* p. 153.
70. Broad, *Teller's War,* p. 114.
71. Anderson, *Revolution,* pp. 95–96.
72. Broad, *Teller's War,* pp. 114–15, n. 64 on p. 305; Baucom, *Origins of SDI,* pp. 153, 234; Anderson, *Revolution,* p. 97.

Anderson tells us that Bendetsen, Hume, Coors, Wilson and Teller came to the meeting. But according to Bendetsen's "Report to Members of the High Frontier Project Panel" of January 9, 1982, only Bendetsen, Hume and Coors went. Evidence as to whether Teller participated in the meeting is mixed, according to Broad. Bendetsen's report does not put him there, but in an interview with Broad in 1985, Bendetsen said he was there. Edwin Thomas, who set up the meeting, at first said he was there but later changed his mind. Keyworth said that in his recollection Teller was not there. Teller's later statements indicate that he was not there. According to Broad, it is possible that Teller was there but his presence was downplayed to minimize friction with Graham. But Baucom does not put him there, and in my view it is implausible that he was. The White House staff—as reconstituted—seemed to want to please Reagan's old friends with the meeting, not introduce the President to strategic defenses. Also, had Teller been there, he would have dominated the meeting—and no one remembers that. In fact, no one quotes him at all.

73. Baucom, *Origins of SDI,* pp.166–67.
74. Lou Cannon, *President Reagan: The Role of a Lifetime* (New York: Simon & Schuster, 1991), pp. 188–91.
75. Ibid., pp. 190–93; *WP,* 3/19/93; Frances FitzGerald, "Death of a Salesman," *Rolling Stone,* February 25, 1988, pp. 47–48.
76. Interview with Thomas C. Reed, 10/14/98.
77. Anderson, *Revolution,* pp. 90–91.
78. Gregg Herken, *Cardinal Choices* (New York: Oxford University Press, 1992), pp. 199–200.
79. Anderson, *Revolution,* p. 90.
80. Herken, *Cardinal Choices,* p. 201.
81. Broad, *Teller's War,* p. 116.
82. Baucom, *Origins of SDI,* p. 154.
83. Ibid., p. 155.
84. Broad, *Teller's War,* p. 111.
85. Baucom, *Origins of SDI,* p. 154.
86. Philip Boffey, William J. Broad, Leslie H. Gelb, Charles Mohr and Holcomb B. Noble, *Claiming the Heavens: The New York Times Complete Guide to the Star Wars Debate* (New York: Times Books, 1988), p. 19; Herken, *Cardinal Choices,* p. 116.
87. Pratt, *Selling Strategic Defenses,* pp. 64, 99–100 on Science Applications, Inc.; Baucom, *Origins of SDI,* p. 107, on Charles Townes; Broad, *Teller's War,* p. 116.
88. Anderson, *Revolution,* p. 96.
89. Department of the Air Force, "Global Ballistic Missile Defense Examination," January 1982.
90. Reynolds, "Point Paper."
91. Daniel O. Graham, letters to Caspar Weinberger of February 11, March 17, 31, April 13, 14, November 5, 1982.
92. Caspar W. Weinberger, letter to Daniel O. Graham, November 24, 1982. Courtesy of office of Senator J. Bennett Johnston.

93. Interview with Angelo Codevilla, 5/4/92.
94. Codevilla, *While Others Build,* pp. 83–87.
95. Interview with Codevilla, 5/4/92.
96. Codevilla, *While Others Build,* p. 87.
97. Ibid., pp. 84–92.
98. Broad, *Teller's War,* pp. 127–28.
99. Ibid., pp. 129–30.
100. Ibid., p. 117.
101. Ibid., pp. 118–19.
102. Herken, *Cardinal Choices,* n. 61 on p. 295.
103. Baucom, *Origins of SDI,* p. 169; Broad, *Teller's War,* p. 120.
104. Quoted in Gregg Herken, "The Early Origins of Star Wars," p. 22.

FIVE: To the Star Wars Speech

1. Raymond L. Garthoff, *The GreatTransition* (Washington, D.C.: Brookings Institution, 1994), p. 56; Strobe Talbott, *The Russians and Reagan* (New York: Vintage Books, 1984), pp. 24–26.
2. Cannon, *President Reagan,* p. 282; Alexander Haig, *Caveat: Realism, Reagan and Foreign Policy* (New York: Macmillan, 1984), p. 103, for Dobrynin quote.
3. Anatoly Dobrynin, *In Confidence: Moscow's Ambassador to America's Six Cold War Presidents (1962–1986)* (New York: Times Books, 1995), pp. 484–85.
4. Murrey Marder, *WP,* 8/8/86; John Newhouse, *War and Peace in the Nuclear Age* (New York: Alfred A. Knopf, 1989), p. 336; Garthoff, *Great Transition,* pp. 60–62.

   According to Garthoff, the Soviet leadership did not expect that the U.S. would actually launch a nuclear war, and most officials continued to hope for an improvement in the relationship. Still, they were nervous. Off the record Dobrynin said that the period was the most dangerous time in his twenty years in Washington.
5. David Stockman, *The Triumph of Politics: How the Reagan Revolution Failed* (New York: Harper and Row, 1986), pp. 118–19; Nicholas Lemann, "The Peacetime War," *Atlantic Monthly,* October 1984, p. 72.
6. Lemann, "Peacetime War," p. 72; Ronald Brownstein and Nina Easton, *Reagan's Ruling Class* (New York: Pantheon Books, 1983), pp. 450–55; Hedrick Smith, "How Many Billions for Defense?," *NYT Magazine,* 11/1/81, p. 90.
7. Smith, "How Many Billions"; Lemann, "Peacetime War," p. 90.
8. Brownstein and Easton, *Reagan's Ruling Class,* pp. 456–57, Smith, "How Many Billions," p. 79, for quote.
9. Brownstein and Easton, *Reagan's Ruling Class,* p. 549.
10. Cannon, *President Reagan,* p. 298; Newhouse, *War and Peace,* pp. 339–40.
11. Garthoff, *Great Transition,* pp. 24–28.
12. Robert Scheer, *With Enough Shovels: Reagan, Bush & Nuclear War* (New York: Random House, 1982), pp. 29–30.
13. Newhouse, *War and Peace,* p. 337; Brownstein and Easton, *Reagan's Ruling Class,* pp. 47, 560.

    In addition, Eugene Rostow in his confirmation hearings spoke about the prospects for the American population's surviving a nuclear war.
14. Scheer, *With Enough Shovels,* p. 29.
15. *NYT,* 8/14/81, quoted in ibid., n. 7 on p. 130.
16. Newhouse, *War and Peace,* p. 337, for Weinberger quote; Mark Green and Gail MacColl, *Reagan's Reign of Error* (New York: Pantheon Books, 1987), p. 46, quotes Reagan's statement of April 13, 1982.
17. Scheer, *With Enough Shovels,* p. 12.
18. Ibid., p. 6.
19. Ibid., p. 18.
20. *NYT,* 5/30/82.
21. Theodore Draper, *Present History* (New York: Random House, 1985), p. 40.
22. Haig, *Caveat,* pp. 105–11; Garthoff, *Great Transition,* pp. 46–49; Talbott, *Russians and Reagan,* p. 74, for quote.

    The Reagan administration had no ambassador in Moscow until October 1981.
23. Strobe Talbott, *Deadly Gambits: The Reagan Administration and the Stalemate in Nuclear Arms Control* (New York: Alfred A. Knopf, 1984), pp. 221–27, p. 225 for quote; Newhouse, *War and Peace,* p. 340.

    Reagan had denounced the treaty during the campaign; he had also pledged to negotiate a replacement for it. In the interim the Joint Chiefs wanted the administration to continue the Carter administration's policy of adhering to the terms of the treaty as long as the Soviets did the same.
24. Talbott, *Deadly Gambits,* pp. 44–48.
25. Newhouse, *War and Peace,* pp. 243–44.
26. Talbott, *Deadly Gambits,* p. 46.
27. Newhouse, *War and Peace,* p. 343.
28. Ibid., pp. 354–55; Haig, *Caveat,* p. 229.
29. Douglas C. Waller, *Congress and the Nuclear Freeze* (Amherst, Mass.: University of Massachusetts Press, 1987), p. 91.
30. Ibid., pp. 95–99, for quotes; Talbott, *Deadly Gambits,* pp. 263–73.

    The next day the *New York Times* called the plan "sweeping and dramatic," and the *Washington Post* said that Reagan had called for the "dismantling of the nuclear menace." Even supporters of the freeze movement had to agree that, by calling for deep reductions in the strategic arsenals, the President had regained the initiative.

31. Text in Talbott, *Russians and Reagan,* pp. 89–104.
32. Ibid., pp. 72–73. In a series of off-the-record lectures, W. Scott Thompson, a USIA official, maintained that the world had moved into the "post-containment era" and it was time to "take the struggle directly to the enemy."
33. Garthoff, *Great Transition,* p. 38.
34. Lemann, "Peacetime War," pp. 86–88, 93; Smith, "How Many Billions," pp. 90–91; Theodore H. White, "Weinberger on the Ramparts," *NYT Magazine,* 2/6/83, p. 19 for quote.
35. Smith, "How Many Billions," p. 89; Lehman quoted in U.S. House of Representatives, *National Security Policy, Hearings before the Defense Policy Panel of the Committee on the Armed Services,* 100th Cong., March 11, 1987; Lemann, "Peacetime War," p. 93; White, "Weinberger on the Ramparts," pp. 19–20.

    "As a nation we can afford anything," a former defense secretary observed. "Security is first priority. But then you have to start with foreign policy and then you make defense strategy and then you get down to force budgets. . . . Cappy's like a little kid going to F.A.O. Schwarz and buying all the toys on the shelf. The services aren't being managed."
36. Garthoff, *Great Transition,* p. 38.
37. William Schneider, "Rambo and Reality," in *Eagle Resurgent,* eds. Kenneth A. Oye, Robert J. Lieber and Donald Rothschild (Boston: Little, Brown, 1987), p. 43.
38. Lemann, "Peacetime War," p. 75; John Lehman, *Command of the Seas* (New York: Scribner, 1988), pp. 102–8.
39. Brownstein and Easton, *Reagan's Ruling Class,* pp. 501–2; Newhouse, *War and Peace,* p. 340.
40. Newhouse, *War and Peace,* p. 613; Robert M. Gates, *From the Shadows* (New York: Simon & Schuster, 1996), pp. 199–204.
41. Brownstein and Easton, *Reagan's Ruling Class,* pp. 505–6, 511–12.
42. Scheer, *With Enough Shovels,* p. 8.
43. David Stockman, *The Triumph of Politics: How the Reagan Revolution Failed* (New York: Harper and Row, 1986).
44. Ibid., p. 9.
45. Ibid., p. 116.
46. Ibid., pp. 117–18.
47. Ibid.
48. Ibid., p. 296.
49. Ibid., p. 345.
50. Ibid., pp. 297–98.
51. Ibid., pp. 385, 406.
52. Ibid., pp. 82–83, 96–97, 139.
53. Ibid., p. 97.
54. Ibid., p. 116.
55. Ibid., pp. 302–17.
56. Ibid., p. 119.
57. Ibid., pp. 312–13.
58. Ibid., p. 317.
59. Ibid., p. 318.
60. Ibid., pp. 318–19.
61. Ibid., pp. 319–21.
62. Brownstein and Easton, *Reagan's Ruling Class,* p. 433; *Newsweek,* 12/22/80.
63. Lemann, "Peacetime War," p. 82.
64. Ibid., pp. 82, 85.
65. Brownstein and Easton, *Reagan's Ruling Class,* pp. 436–37.
66. Lemann, "Peacetime War," p. 74.
67. *U.S. News & World Report,* 11/24/80; *Newsweek,* 12/22/80, for direct quote.
68. Lemann, "Peacetime War," p. 86.
69. Ibid., p. 85.

    Weinberger's zeal was such that he sometimes seemed unbalanced. Challenged on the law of impoundment in a congressional hearing by the distinguished constitutional scholar, Alexander Bickel, he questioned whether residual power lay with the Congress rather than with the President. He then said, "There can even be an argument made that the courts themselves have no power to interfere with the President or with the Executive power." This was to question the central constitutional principle of checks and balances.
70. Ibid., p. 90.
71. Vincent Davis, "Reagan's Defense Program," in *The Reagan Defense Program: An Interim Assessment,* ed. Stephen J. Cimbala (Wilmington, Del.: Scholarly Resources, 1984), p. 40.
72. Lemann, "Peacetime War," p. 71, for quote; *WP,* 7/10/86.
73. Colin Powell, *My American Journey* (New York: Random House, 1995), pp. 258–59; Lemann, "Peacetime War," p. 72.
74. Lemann, "Peacetime War," p. 76.
75. Ibid.

76. Caspar Weinberger, *Fighting for Peace* (New York: Warner Books, 1990), pp. 19–21.
77. Cannon, *President Reagan,* p. 310.
    To Admiral Crowe, Weinberger added a corollary: "Never, never, never, never, never admit you made a mistake" (Admiral William J. Crowe, Jr., *The Line of Fire* [New York: Simon & Schuster, 1993], p. 221).
78. Weinberger, *Fighting for Peace,* p. 61; Lemann, "Peacetime War," p. 91.
    Three former secretaries of defense criticized this as unprofessional behavior.
79. Weinberger, *Fighting for Peace,* pp. 60–64, 69.
80. Haig, *Caveat,* pp. 6–7.
81. Cannon, *President Reagan,* p. 78.
82. Brownstein and Easton, *Reagan's Ruling Class,* p. 543; William Bundy, *A Tangled Web: The Making of Foreign Policy in the Nixon Administration* (New York: Hill and Wang, 1998), pp. 512–13.
    Weinberger had also served with MacArthur, but in a relatively low-level position during World War II.
83. Bundy, *Tangled Web,* p. 512; Brownstein and Easton, *Reagan's Ruling Class,* pp. 540–42.
    Haig was far too loyal to Nixon, in the view of many, since he had carried out his boss's orders to wiretap journalists and other staff members in order to stop "national-security" leaks. He also drove Elliot Richardson to resign as attorney general during the Watergate investigations by cobbling together an attempt to foreclose further requests for the presidential tapes.
84. Haig, *Caveat,* pp. 53–58, 74–76, 85; Cannon, *President Reagan,* p. 194.
85. Haig, *Caveat,* p. 71.
86. Quote in ibid., pp. 143–49; see also Cannon, *President Reagan,* p. 197.
87. Talbott, *Deadly Gambits,* p. 12.
88. Haig, *Caveat,* pp. 26–31, for all quotes but last, pp. 122–37 on Cuba; Robert C. McFarlane with Zofia Smardz, *Special Trust* (New York: Cadell and Davies, 1994), pp. 177–81; Ronnie Dugger, *On Reagan: The Man & His Presidency* (New York: McGraw-Hill, 1983), p. 344, for parking-lot quote; Weinberger, *Fighting for Peace,* pp. 30–31.
    According to Weinberger, Haig, at a meeting with the President and the Cabinet before the inauguration, said it was quite clear the U.S. would have to invade Cuba and, one way or another, put an end to the Castro regime.
89. Cannon, *President Reagan,* p. 197.
90. Frances FitzGerald, "Memoirs of the Reagan Era," *New Yorker,* January 16, 1989.
91. Haig, *Caveat,* pp. 155–59 for quotes; Cannon, *President Reagan,* p. 198; FitzGerald, "Memoirs."
    Others in the Situation Room, including Donald Regan, have confirmed Haig's account of his discussion with Weinberger. In *Fighting for Peace,* pp. 86–88, Weinberger does not describe this discussion. He does, however, tell us that he made a phone call to the chairman of the Joint Chiefs outside the Situation Room and was told that alert status was normal. The chairman, General David C. Jones, also told him that the position of the Soviet forces was more or less normal except that two of the Soviet submarines patrolling the Atlantic coast were "outside the box" of normal operations. This was not out of the ordinary, but Weinberger, thinking that something might be up, queried Jones about the difference between Defcons 3, 4 and 5 and decided to raise the alert status of the Strategic Air Command but not the Defcon.
    On television Haig also made the mistake of saying that the secretary of state came after the vice-president "constitutionally," when he meant "by tradition" (Haig, *Caveat,* p. 164). Weinberger not only objected to this, but he thought *he* was in control militarily, so another argument resulted.
92. Haig, *Caveat,* p. 85; see pp. 67, 84–86, 93, 115 for obstacles.
93. Cannon, *President Reagan,* p. 195.
94. Haig, *Caveat,* p. 116, for quote; FitzGerald, "Memoirs."
95. Cannon, *President Reagan,* p. 195.
96. Garthoff, *Great Transition,* pp. 28–30; Haig, *Caveat,* pp. 96–98, 105; see Brownstein and Easton, *Reagan's Ruling Class,* p. 526, for Rostow's much tougher formulation of the same idea and pp. 562–63.
97. Haig, *Caveat,* pp. 105–10; Garthoff, *Great Transition,* pp. 46–49; Dobrynin, *In Confidence,* p. 483.
98. Garthoff, *Great Transition,* p. 30.
99. Brownstein and Easton, *Reagan's Ruling Class,* p. 459; Gates, *From the Shadows,* pp. 193–97.
100. Haig, *Caveat,* pp. 26, 240.
101. Ibid., pp. 238–41; Gates, *From the Shadows,* p. 228.
    According to Gates, measures harsher than trade sanctions and warnings were not even discussed. The approach of the Reagan administration was almost identical to that of the Carter administration.
102. Haig, *Caveat,* pp. 81, 115–16, 240, 256; Garthoff, *Great Transition,* pp. 44–45.
    The grain exports had always been the lion's share of U.S. trade; the value of annual U.S. exports of industrial goods was only three hundred million dollars.
103. Garthoff, *Great Transition,* pp. 49, 548–50; Haig, *Caveat,* pp. 246–56, 304–5; George Shultz, *Turmoil and Triumph* (New York: Scribner, 1993), pp. 135–45, for an explanation of what later transpired.
104. Garthoff, *Great Transition,* p. 31; Gates, *From the Shadows,* pp. 237–38.
    Carl Bernstein has written of the "Holy Alliance" between the Reagan administration and the Vatican to aid Solidarity *(Time,* February 24, 1992). According to Gates, there was no "covert alliance" between CIA, the Vatican and the AFL-CIO (the latter had been helping Solidarity before the crackdown). At most there was a modicum of coordination at the highest levels, so that the three institutions would not trip over one another. According to Gates, Casey paid little attention to it once it was under way. See also Jonathan Kwitney, *The Man of the Century* (New York: Henry Holt, 1997), for the view of some in Solidarity that the aid was of minimal help.

105. Richard V. Allen, "The Man Who Changed the Game Plan," *National Interest,* no. 44, Summer 1996, pp. 60–65; interview with Richard V. Allen, 6/4/98.
106. Interview with Henry Kissinger, 2/12/97; see also Talbott, *Deadly Gambits,* pp. 75–76.

In his memoir Robert Gates, a career CIA Soviet analyst who became William Casey's executive assistant and later director of central intelligence, tells us that in the early years of his administration President Reagan was extremely receptive to briefings on the Soviet economy, because he thought that the U.S., and the West more generally, could bring serious economic pressure to bear on the Soviet Union through the defense buildup and trade restrictions that would adversely affect its ability to keep the system going while maintaining ambitious military programs. Most experts, Gates writes, including those in CIA, "would have argued—and did—that such a campaign would not work, that despite Soviet economic problems they were not vulnerable to outside pressure. Indeed, the handful of people who wrote that the United States could spend the Soviets into the ground on defense and thereby speed bringing the system to its knees were dismissed by most in Washington as right-wing kooks.... But at the end of the day, the President believed that a tottering regime could be pushed further off balance by such pressures." Reagan, he writes, "nearly alone, truly believed in 1981 that the Soviet system was vulnerable, not in some vague, long-range historical sense, but right then." (Gates, *From the Shadows,* pp. 194–97.)

Writing in retrospect, Gates, like so many others before and since, figured Reagan as an inspired fool or a prophet—as opposed to one of the right-wing kooks he mentions. But, then, all successful politicians are optimists, and Gates, like Stockman, did not take Reagan's political problems into account. The administration had decided on a huge military buildup and against negotiations; the hard-liners had determined not to reestablish détente with the Soviet Union but, rather, to work for its overthrow. Thus the only good news Reagan could offer the American public was evidence pointing to a Soviet collapse—and, if possible, within the years of his administration. When the CIA offered him only the kind of evidence that had caused the Trilateral Commission to maintain that as an economic power the Soviet Union was becoming increasingly irrelevant to the world, he made do with that.

Left to himself, Reagan occasionally engaged in wishful thinking. In October 1981, for example, Reagan said in an interview, "They [the Soviets] cannot vastly increase their military productivity because they've already got their people on a starvation diet.... They've been building the greatest military machine the world has ever seen. But now they're going to be faced with [the fact] that we could go forward with an arms race and they can't keep up." (Garthoff, *Great Transition,* p. 11.)

Haig stuck close to the evidence. In August 1981 Haig noted that the "economies of Moscow's East European allies are in various stages of decline. The Soviet economy itself may have lost its capacity for the high growth of the past," and concluded, "Ambitious foreign and defense policies are therefore becoming more of a burden." (Brownstein and Easton, *Reagan's Ruling Class,* p. 563.) In June 1982 he spoke of the 1980s as a decade in which the Soviets would experience "greater economic difficulties and growing international isolation" (Garthoff, *Great Transition,* p. 29).

107. Brownstein and Easton, *Reagan's Ruling Class,* p. 502.
108. Ibid., p. 500.
109. Ibid., p. 497.
110. Talbott, *Deadly Gambits,* p. 44.
111. Ibid., pp. 44–48.
112. Ibid., pp. 47–49.
113. Ibid., pp. 56–58.
114. Ibid., pp. 59–60.
115. Ibid., pp. 61–62.
116. Waller, *Congress and the Nuclear Freeze,* p. 14.

When speaking of arms control, Reagan often cited *The Treaty Trap* by Lawrence Beilenson, a conservative who had been the lawyer for SAG.

117. Journalists who wrote of Reagan as a nuclear abolitionist include John Newhouse (in *War and Peace*), Lou Cannon (in *President Reagan*) and Strobe Talbott himself in a later book, *Master of the Game: Paul Nitze and the Nuclear Peace* (New York: Alfred A. Knopf, 1988).
118. Talbott, *Deadly Gambits,* pp. 72–74, 77.
119. Bob Schieffer and Gary Paul Gates, *The Acting President* (New York: E. P. Dutton, 1989), p. 327.
120. Talbott, *Deadly Gambits,* pp. 79–80.
121. Brownstein and Easton, *Reagan's Ruling Class,* p. 527.
122. Ibid., p. 528.

In March, Eugene Rostow told Congress: "The Soviet Union is not yet convinced of the need to negotiate seriously. Until it comes to accept that necessity ... it will continue to conduct INF negotiations not as a part of a quest for stability and peace ... but as a tactical effort to divide the United States from Europe, Japan and from its other allies and vital interests."

123. Garthoff, *Great Transition,* p. 504.
124. Waller, *Congress and the Nuclear Freeze,* pp. 38–41.
125. Edward Tabor Linenthal, *Symbolic Defense: The Cultural Significance of the Strategic Defense Initiative* (Urbana, Ill.: University of Illinois Press, 1989), p. xv; Jonathan Schell, *The Fate of the Earth* (New York: Alfred A. Knopf, 1982), p. 5.
126. Linenthal, *Symbolic Defense,* p. xv.

127. Waller, *Congress and the Nuclear Freeze*, pp. 76–78, for all quotes above.
128. Ibid., p. 70.
129. Talbott, *Deadly Gambits*, p. 247.
130. McFarlane, *Special Trust*, p. 198.
131. Talbott, *Deadly Gambits*, pp. 235–39.
132. Ibid., pp. 238–40, 246–48.

    In writing up the formal terms of reference for the proposal, the nearest Burt got to the word "negotiability" was "sustainability"—a term which, as Haig later used it, seemed to mean that the goal was to keep the Soviets at the negotiating table long enough to impress the Congress and the American public of the administration's desire to negotiate.
133. Ibid., pp. 248–51.
134. Ibid.
135. Ibid., pp. 253–56, 263–67.
136. Waller, *Congress and the Nuclear Freeze*, p. 99.
137. Ibid., p. 99; Talbott, *Deadly Gambits*, pp. 273–74.
138. Draper, *Present History*, p. 38.
139. In "Dear Mr. Weinberger," the *New York Review of Books* essay of November 4, 1982, reprinted in ibid., Theodore Draper wrote, "The search for nuclear superiority, and the goal of prevailing in such a war, all fit together on behalf of a master plan that goes far beyond deterrence; it is the vision of an apocalyptic nuclear war to decide once and for all the issue of world power." (Ibid., p. 47.)
140. Janne E. Nolan, *Guardians of the Arsenal: The Politics of Nuclear Strategy* (New York: Basic Books, 1989), pp. 85–87.
141. For a more extended discussion of these issues, see Lawrence Freedman, *The Evolution of Nuclear Strategy* (New York: St. Martin's Press, 1989); McGeorge Bundy, *Danger and Survival: Choices About the Bomb in the First Fifty Years* (New York: Random House, 1988); Nolan, *Guardians*.

    Harold Brown explained PD-59 as a deterrent to any illusion the Soviets might have that war-fighting might be an option. But even on that issue he was skeptical. In 1979 he wrote: "Counterforce and damage-limiting campaigns have been put forward as the nuclear equivalents of traditional warfare. But their proponents find it difficult to tell us what objectives an enemy would seek in launching such campaigns, how these campaigns would end, or how any resulting [a]symmetries could be made meaningful" (Freedman, *Evolution*, p. 393).

    In fact the 1982 Defense Guidance, raised the same question itself, for it stated that, if the Soviet Union attacked U.S. naval forces with nuclear weapons, U.S. policy was that the attack would "not necessarily remain limited to the sea" *(NYT*, 5/30/82).
142. Scheer, *With Enough Shovels*, p. 13.

    Perle's whole statement was as follows: "I'm always worried less about what would happen in an actual nuclear exchange than the effect that the nuclear balance has on our willingness to take risks in local situations. It is not that I am worried about the Soviets attacking the United States with nuclear weapons confident that they will win that nuclear war. It is that I worry about an American President feeling that he cannot afford to take action in a crisis because Soviet nuclear forces are such that, if escalation took place, they are better poised than we are to move up the escalation ladder."
143. Freedman, *Evolution*, pp. 403–7; interviews with Allen, 6/4/98, and Thomas C. Reed, 6/23/98.
144. *NYT*, 5/30/82; Freedman, *Evolution*, pp. 393, 406.

    "Decapitation" would, if successful, ensure that there was no one to negotiate with for an end to hostilities. The theory was that the Soviet command structure was so centralized that eliminating the leadership would end the Soviet capacity to continue the war. But it was only a theory, and later evidence suggested that it was not correct.
145. Garthoff, *Great Transition*, p. 37, quotes *WP* account.
146. Nolan, *Guardians*, p. 241.

    According to Nolan, the target base consisted of an estimated fourteen hundred Soviet ICBM silos, seven hundred leadership "bunkers" and assorted other hard-point targets.

    The administration initially planned for a vastly expanded civil-defense program, which involved building blast shelters in urban areas and planning for the evacuation of urban populations. The OMB estimated it would cost ten billion dollars; a number of municipalities refused to take proposed measures, and the Congress eventually turned the plan down. (Scheer, *With Enough Shovels*, pp. 107–10.)

    As a part of the plan, the administration launched an eight-billion-dollar program in command, control, communications and intelligence—C^3I—to remove U.S. leaders from Washington and to enable them to communicate with the U.S. strategic forces for the duration of a long nuclear war. Initially run by Colonel Oliver North of the NSC staff, the program, known as the Doomsday Project, involved a great deal of expensive communications equipment, a network of bunkers, convoys of lead-lined trucks and two hundred special-operations commandos to secure the surviving leaders. The difficulty with it was that the various elements of the project were so secret that even in peacetime they could not be coordinated between the White House and the various government agencies. *(NYT*, 11/18/91 and 4/18/94.)
147. Scheer, *With Enough Shovels*, p. 9.
148. Cannon, *President Reagan*, pp. 165–66.
149. Newhouse, *War and Peace*, pp. 321–22; Donald R. Baucom, *The Origins of SDI 1944–1983* (Lawrence, Kans.: University Press of Kansas, 1992), p. 117; interview with Harold Brown, 11/5/90.

150. Cannon, *President Reagan*, p. 167; Weinberger, *Fighting for Peace*, p. 301. Weinberger kept calling MPS "the multiple protective system."
151. Cannon, *Reagan*, p. 390.
152. Ibid.; Talbott, *Deadly Gambits*, p. 300; B. Bruce-Biggs, *The Shield of Faith* (New York: Simon & Schuster, 1988), p. 399.
153. Cannon, *Reagan*, pp. 391–92.
154. Cannon, *President Reagan*, p. 169. Reagan said that "a window of vulnerability is opening" that would jeopardize "our hopes for peace and freedom."
155. Ibid.
156. Scheer, *With Enough Shovels*, pp. 78–79; Baucom, *Origins*, p. 177.
157. Baucom, *Origins*, p. 180; Nolan, *Guardians*, p. 152.
158. Newhouse, *War and Peace*, p. 358; Cannon, *President Reagan*, pp. 323–24.
159. *NYT*, 5/30/82.
160. McFarlane, *Special Trust*, p. 198; Mark Hertsgaard, *On Bended Knee: The Press and the Reagan Presidency* (New York: Farrar, Straus and Giroux, 1988), p. 280. McFarlane gave Hertsgaard these figures; he has slightly different ones.
161. Waller, *Congress and the Nuclear Freeze*, p. 79; Mark Green and Gail McColl, *Reagan's Reign of Error* (New York: Pantheon Books, 1987), p. 47, for Reagan quote.
162. William A. Au, *The Cross, the Flag and the Bomb*, Contributions to the Study of Religion, no. 12 (Westport, Conn.: Greenwood Press, 1985), pp. 202–8.
163. Waller, *Congress and the Nuclear Freeze*, pp. 163–65.
164. Rebecca S. Bjork, *The Strategic Defense Initiative: Symbolic Containment of the Nuclear Threat* (Albany, N.Y.: State University Press of New York, 1992), pp. 47–48 for polls; Gregg Herken, *Cardinal Choices*, n. 71 on p. 296; Dobrynin, *In Confidence*, p. 515.
165. McFarlane, *Special Trust*, p. 228.
166. Cannon, *President Reagan*, p. 324; McFarlane, *Special Trust*, p. 224.
167. Talbott, *Deadly Gambits*, p. 303; Newhouse, *War and Peace*, p. 359; James Woolsey, "The Politics of Vulnerability: 1980–3," in *The Nuclear Controversy*, a Council on Foreign Relations Publication, ed. William Bundy (New York: New American Library, 1985), pp. 211–25.

    Thomas C. Reed resigned from the White House staff, but not from the commission, after questions arose about his having engaged in insider stock trading.
168. Woolsey, "Politics of Vulnerability," pp. 218–23; Talbott, *Deadly Gambits*, pp. 304–5.
169. Interviewed in 1990, Weinberger seemed even to have forgotten what the "window of vulnerability" was. Asked to define it, he said it "had to do with the fact that they [the Soviets] had a modern, accurate missile while we had a missile that was twenty years old and did not have that accuracy or that yield." In other words, Weinberger had redefined the problem so that the MXs based in fixed silos was the solution to it. (Interview with Caspar Weinberger, 9/11/90.)

    This was not exactly new. Weinberger had redefined the "window of vulnerability" in 1982, when it became clear that the basing-mode problem might never be solved. At that time he defined it as "the period of substantial imbalance in the strategic forces between the Soviets and ourselves," and maintained that cruise missiles would "help close it more rapidly than anything else." (Brownstein and Easton, *Reagan's Ruling Class*, p. 456.)
170. *NYT*, 3/24/83; *NYT*, 3/25/83; *NYT*, 3/30/83.

    The President, Teller wrote, "did not lightly accept the idea that these can be made to work. He wanted to know a vast number of details. He asked questions of his science adviser, George Keyworth, and many other scientists, myself included. He then decided that something must and can be done." (Teller spoke of Reagan's visit to the Livermore Lab in 1967 in much the same way.)

    See *NYT*, 4/3/85, for William Broad's story on the Bendetsen group. Broad reported that Reagan had met with Teller and the Bendetsen group in early 1983. He later discovered from the Bendetsen papers that this was not the case. (See previous chapter.)
171. William J. Broad, *Teller's War* (New York: Simon & Schuster, 1992), pp. 123, 126; Baucom, *Origins*, p. 183.
172. Accounts in Broad, *Teller's War*; Baucom, *Origins*; Cannon, *President Reagan*; Nolan, *Guardians*; Talbott, *Master of the Game*; Weinberger, *Fighting for Peace*; Gregg Herken, "The Earthly Origins of Star Wars," *Bulletin of the Atomic Scientists*, October 1987, p. 22; Herken, *Cardinal Choices*; Frederick H. Hartmann, *Naval Renaissance: The U.S. Navy in the 1980s* (Annapolis, Md.: Naval Institute Press, 1990); Hedrick Smith, *The Power Game* (New York: Random House, 1988); also in *The Reagan Legacy*, pt. II, "Star Wars," Discovery Channel, documentary, produced by Nick Gold, world premiere November 4, 1996, with Garrick Utley; interviews with Robert McFarlane, 6/20/90; Admiral James R. Watkins, 4/6/95; Captain Linton Brooks, 6/30/98; Theodore Postol, 6/30/98.

    Martin Anderson, of course, tells us that Ronald Reagan was the main protagonist in the drama, and that he launched SDI as a result of the report he received from the High Frontier group. He sustains this thesis by telling us that Reagan met privately with the Joint Chiefs in December 1982 and himself brought up the issue of strategic defenses. "What if . . . what if we began to move away from our total reliance on offense to deter a nuclear attack and moved toward a relatively greater reliance on defense?" he reportedly asked them. On the way back to the Pentagon one of the Chiefs—according to Anderson—called Clark and asked if he had just gotten instructions to take a hard look at missile defenses. Clark said yes, he had;

he then asked McFarlane to study the issue (Martin Anderson, *Revolution* [New York: Harcourt Brace Jovanovich, 1988], p. 97).

But the overwhelming evidence is that no such meeting occurred. The President was in the habit of meeting with the JCS on a quarterly basis. Thus, if he had met with them in December, there would not have been a February meeting. None of the Chiefs remember a December meeting; it was not on their schedules, and Watkins's account, not to mention McFarlane's, would not make sense if it had occurred. Baucom, who made an investigation of this putative event, found that a December meeting with the Chiefs had been put on the White House schedule but the meeting was canceled. Anderson was not in Washington at the time, so his source was surely Clark. The chairman of the Joint Chiefs did call Clark after the February 11 meeting to ask whether the President wanted them to take a look at missile defenses. So Clark, who did not attend the February 11 meeting because he was out of town, may have confused the dates (Baucom, *Origins,* n. 61 on p. 243).

173. Baucom, *Origins,* p. 181; McFarlane, *Special Trust,* p. 226. The latter writes of the Soviet capability "to destroy all of our ICBM forces in one fell swoop leaving us without a plausible means of striking back." See also Smith, *Power Game,* p. 606.
174. Interview with McFarlane, 6/20/90.
175. Baucom, *Origins,* p. 183; Hartmann, *Naval Renaissance,* p. 257; McFarlane, *Special Trust,* pp. 226–27.
176. McFarlane, *Special Trust,* pp. 226–27; Smith, *Power Game,* p. 606.
177. Smith, *Power Game,* p. 606; Broad, *Teller's War,* p. 124; Baucom, *Origins,* p. 183; Nolan, *Guardians,* p. 14; Cannon, *President Reagan,* p. 326;Talbott, *Master of the Game,* p. 204, for quote; interview with McFarlane, 6/20/90.
178. Baucom, *Origins,* p. 184.
179. Cannon, *President Reagan,* p. 327; Hartmann, *Naval Renaissance,* pp. 252–53.
180. Baucom, *Origins,* pp. 188–89, for quote; Hartmann, *Naval Renaissance,* p. 253; Cannon, *President Reagan,* p. 328.
181. Baucom, *Origins,* p. 190; Smith, *Power Game,* p. 606; Hartmann, *Naval Renaissance,* p. 254.
182. Nolan, *Guardians,* pp. 164–65; Baucom, *Origins,* p. 190; Cannon, *President Reagan,* p. 328, for Vessey quote; Herken, "Earthly Origins," p. 24, for the other options.
183. Baucom, *Origins,* p. 191; Cannon, *President Reagan,* p. 329, for quote; Smith, *Power Game,* p. 607.
184. Cannon, *President Reagan,* p. 329; Weinberger, *Fighting for Peace,* p. 304; Nolan, *Guardians,* p. 164; Hartmann, *Naval Renaissance,* p. 255, for quotes.
185. Cannon, *President Reagan,* p. 329.
186. Ibid., p. 330; Baucom, *Origins,* p. 192; McFarlane, *Special Trust,* pp. 229–30; Smith, *Power Game,* p. 608; Hartmann, *Naval Renaissance,* pp. 255–56; Weinberger, *Fighting for Peace,* p. 304. Each source has a slightly different version of this interchange. I have used McFarlane's. Some report that Watkins made the presentation and summed up his proposal by asking, "Wouldn't it be better to protect the American people rather than to avenge them?" Reagan said, "Don't lose those words."
187. McFarlane, *Special Trust,* p. 230.
188. Ibid., pp. 230–31; Nolan, *Guardians,* p. 13; Herken, *Cardinal Choices,* p. 211; interview with McFarlane, 6/20/90.

    McFarlane does not give a date in his book; he told me he spoke with the President on March 16; Nolan and Herken have him meeting with Clark and Reagan at Camp David on March 18.
189. Smith, *Power Game,* p. 610; McFarlane, *Special Trust,* p. 230; Cannon, *President Reagan,* p. 331.
190. Interview with McFarlane, 6/20/90.
191. Herken, "Earthly Origins," pp. 25–26.
192. Cannon, *President Reagan,* pp. 330–31.
193. McFarlane, *Special Trust,* p. 232; Smith, *Power Game,* pp. 613–14; Herken, *Cardinal Choices,* p. 213.
194. Interview with McFarlane, 6/20/90. McFarlane said he knew of the Pentagon's 1981 study.
195. Baucom, *Origins,* pp. 181–82.
196. Ibid., pp. 182–83, 179.
197. Baucom, *Origins,* p. 177.

    Reagan's announcement of the Defense Department plan for strategic force modernization of October 2, 1981, included a discussion of missile defenses as a possible solution to the vulnerability of U.S. ICBMs.

    On November 22, 1982, the President said, "We plan to continue research on ballistic missile defense technology—the kind of smart, highly accurate, hopefully non-nuclear, weapons that utilize the microelectronic and other advanced technologies in which we excel" (Baucom, *Origins,* p. 179).
198. *NYT,* 5/30/82.

    The NSC staffers also knew that Reagan had evinced interest in missile defenses in the past. Even an Air Force colonel on the staff had heard about the NORAD visit (Hartmann, *Naval Renaissance,* p. 257).
199. Baucom, *Origins,* p. 183; interview with Watkins, 4/6/95.

    Watkins said McFarlane was not talking about a bargaining chip at the time. McFarlane in his memoir does not mention a bargaining chip in connection with the beginning of the initiative. Baucom and Hartmann do not mention it.

    McFarlane told Congress in 1988 that he and Pentagon officials had been talking "frankly about just stressing the Soviet system," and their concept was subsequently transformed by the President into a much more ambitious nationwide anti-missile defense. (Herken, *Cardinal Choices,* n. 72 on p. 296.)
200. Baucom, *Origins,* p. 183.

201. Interview with Thomas C. Reed, 6/23/98.

202. McFarlane, *Special Trust,* p. 227; Baucom, *Origins,* n. 72 on p. 245.

Baucom says Watkins denied that he coordinated his efforts with McFarlane over the issue, but concludes on the basis of other interviews that there was probably some coordination between Watkins and McFarlane before the February 11 meeting.

Hartmann does not describe any advance coordination.

Smith quotes Watkins as saying that he was encouraged by McFarlane and Poindexter to put forward his view to the Chiefs (Smith, *Power Game,* p. 606).

In 1995 Watkins told me that he knew McFarlane well and did lunch with him on the occasion McFarlane describes (interview, 4/6/95).

In 1996 Watkins said on television, "He [McFarlane] said to me that the President really wants an alternative. Can't you give him another option?" (*The Reagan Legacy,* pt. II, "Star Wars.")

According to Baucom, Watkins did not begin work on the project until January 10, when Clark invited the Chiefs to the White House (Baucom, *Origins,* p. 188).

203. Telephone interview with Theodore Postol, 6/30/98.

204. Brock Brower, "Semper Fi," *NYT Magazine,* 1/22/89; Cannon, *President Reagan,* p. 327; McFarlane, *Special Trust,* p. 227.

205. Baucom, *Origins,* pp. 186–87; interview with Watkins, April 6, 1995.

206. Cannon, *President Reagan,* p. 327.

207. Hartmann, *Naval Renaissance,* p. 254; Baucom, *Origins,* p. 190.

208. Interview with Watkins, 4/6/95.

By another account, Watkins did not neglect the role of the Navy, for one of the five options the Chiefs recommended to the President was shifting the emphasis from land-based ICBMs to submarine-launched ballistic missiles (Herken, "Earthly Origins," p. 24).

209. Cannon, *President Reagan,* p. 329.

In 1985 Watkins toned down the presidential directive on SDI to read that it would enhance deterrence by frustrating a Soviet first strike (interview, 4/6/95).

In *The Reagan Legacy* he said: "We believed that we had reached that point in technical maturity when we could move into a defensive system and prevent any missiles from hitting the United States."

A few minutes later in the film he reported that when he got the draft of the speech (on March 20) he discussed it with General Vessey and "Jack was worried about it, and I was worried for the same reason. We were concerned that the President would be reaching beyond the real technology available within the near timeframe and would be implying that we could field this soon. We knew this was not the case."

The filmmakers apparently did not notice the contradiction.

210. Interview with Watkins, 4/6/95.

211. Baucom,*Origins,* p. 189, for quote; Hartmann, *Naval Renaissance,* p. 254.

According to Hartmann, Watkins's aim was to put the MX basing-mode problem "into perspective" and to give arms-control advocates what they so avidly sought: "a way to draw the fangs off the weapons that threatened mankind's survival by making the success of a first strike questionable." This suggests a defense for ICBMs.

212. Baucom,*Origins,* pp. 189–90; Hartman, *Naval Renaissance,* p. 255; interview with Brooks, 11/15/95.

213. Smith, *Power Game,* pp. 609–10, for quotes; Nolan, *Guardians,* pp. 164–65.

214. Hartmann, *Naval Renaissance,* pp. 255, 259.

215. Ibid., pp. 255–56.

McFarlane told Hartmann, "The Chiefs hadn't intended to stress it alot. They were going to make a mild statement of interest without any implication of major resource investment at the time." Hartmann also quotes McFarlane as saying that, though Watkins endorsed his expression of presidential support for the project, the other Chiefs were less enthusiastic.

216. Interview with Postol, 6/30/98.

217. By one of McFarlane's accounts, the NSC staff went to work on the project; by another, the Pentagon did (Baucom, *Origins,* p. 192; McFarlane, *Special Trust,* p. 230). In fact, nothing much seems to have happened until mid-March, when the President began to press McFarlane to have the strategic-defense proposal completed quickly.

218. Baucom, *Origins,* p. 193; Nolan, *Guardians,* p. 14.

219. *PPP*, Reagan, 1983, pp. 437–38, for quotes; Waller, *Congress and the Nuclear Freeze,* p. 192.

220. Baucom, *Origins,* p. 193.

221. Smith, *Power Game,* p. 609.

222. Baucom, *Origins,* p. 193.

Clark, Meese and Deaver were backing the proposal—only Baker was opposed (Weinberger, *Fighting for Peace,* p. 305; interview with Michael Deaver, 12/5/95).

223. Interview with McFarlane, 6/20/90.

224. Herken, "Earthly Origins," p. 25; Herken, *Cardinal Choices,* pp. 211–12, for quotes.

225. Herken, *Cardinal Choices,* pp. 212, 207.

226. Ibid., p. 212; Baucom, *Origins,* pp. 194–95; Broad, *Teller's War,* pp. 131–33.

227. Herken,*Cardinal Choices,* p. 212; Broad, *Teller's War,* p. 132.

228. Herken, *Cardinal Choices,* pp. 212–13.

229. Smith, *Power Game,* p. 614, for the "lunatic" quote; Shultz, *Turmoil and Triumph,* pp. 246–55, for the rest.
230. McFarlane, *Special Trust,* p. 233.
    McFarlane later wrote that he could hardly keep from laughing: "Neither before nor since had Richard Perle ever cared a whit about the allies and coordination."
231. Keyworth, in *The Reagan Legacy;* Herken,*Cardinal Choices,* p. 213, for quote; Herken, "Earthly Origins," p. 26.
232. George W. Ball, "The War for Star Wars," *New York Review of Books,* April 11, 1985.
233. Cannon, *President Reagan,* p. 333.
234. Ronald Reagan, *An American Life* (New York: Simon & Schuster, 1990), p. 571.
235. Draft of insert to speech given by Ronald Reagan March 23, 1983, dated 9:30 A.M., March 22. (Dr. Keyworth's draft with President Reagan's handwritten changes.) Courtesy of Martin Anderson.
    This contains rewrites in Reagan's distinctive handwriting, and one sentence—the Watkins question, slightly reworded—in a hand that is neither Reagan's nor McFarlane's. Possibly Keyworth had simply forgotten to type this sentence in from a previous draft. But there is no evidence that Reagan put it in.
236. Reagan, *American Life,* p. 571.
237. Herken,*Cardinal Choices,* p. 297; Broad, *Teller's War,* p. 133.
238. Reagan, *American Life,* p. 572. This is all that is quoted from the March 24 entry.
239. Ibid., p. 572.
240. Dobrynin, *In Confidence,* p. 529; interview with Deaver, 12/5/95.
241. *PPP,* Reagan, 1983, vol. 1, p. 448.
242. Ibid., p. 465.
243. Ibid., p. 448.

SIX: Selling the Strategic Defense Initiative

1. On the reaction of the Chiefs, Hedrick Smith, *The Power Game* (New York: Random House, 1988), p. 603; Strobe Talbott, *Master of the Game: Paul Nitze and the Nuclear Peace* (New York: Alfred A. Knopf, 1988), p. 193; Lou Cannon, *President Reagan: The Role of a Lifetime* (New York: Simon & Schuster, 1991), p. 331. On DeLauer, Janne E. Nolan, *Guardians of the Arsenal: The Politics of Nuclear Strategy* (New York: Basic Books, 1988), p. 5.
    "The speech caught us all by surprise," Vessey later said. He had expected that the White House would initiate an "orderly reexamination of resources to put more emphasis on defense." He wondered where the money would come from, and had reservations about the timing, but it was clear that the President was determined to make the speech, and that was enough for him (Cannon, p. 331).
2. Larry Pressler, *Star Wars: The Strategic Defense Initiative Debates in Congress* (New York: Praeger, 1986), p. 63; Nolan, *Guardians,* p. 8; Brent Scowcroft, John Deutch and R. James Woolsey, "A Way Out of Reykjavik," *NYT Magazine,* 1/25/87, pp. 40 ff. The Scowcroft Commission quote is in Joseph J. Romm, "The Problems with the Strategic Defense Initiative," in *The Arms Race in the Era of Star Wars,* eds. David Carlton and Carlo Schaerf (New York: St. Martin's Press, 1988).
3. Douglas C. Waller, *Congress and the Nuclear Freeze* (Amherst, Mass.: University of Massachusetts Press, 1987), p. 191.
4. *Newsweek,* April 4, 1983. Representative Jim Leach said this.
5. Ibid. The House cut the proposed increase from 10 to 4 percent.
6. Ibid.; *Time,* April 4, 1983.
7. George Shultz, *Turmoil and Triumph* (New York: Scribner, 1993), p. 259; *Time,* April 4, 1983.
8. *NYT,* 3/27/83. Hedrick Smith, in the News of the Week in Review, does a wrap-up of editorials; see also Leslie Gelb, *NYT,* 3/25/83, p. 1.
9. Leslie Gelb, *NYT,* 3/25/83.
10. *PPP,* vol. 1 (1983), pp. 466–67.
11. *New Republic,* April 18, 1983.
12. Gerald M. Steinberg, ed., *Lost in Space* (Lexington, Mass.: Lexington Books, 1988), p. 2.
    The Manhattan Project and the Apollo Project cost thirteen billion and fifty-seven billion dollars respectively in 1984 dollars. And the costs in both cases included development.
13. Gelb, *NYT,* 3/3/85, p. A1.
14. Cannon, *President Reagan,* p. 205.
15. Don Oberdorfer, *The Turn: From the Cold War to the New Era: The United States and the Soviet Union 1983–1990* (New York: Poseidon Press, 1991), pp. 42–43; Shultz, *Turmoil and Triumph,* pp. 24–29.
16. Michael Deaver, *Behind the Scenes* (New York: William Morrow, 1987), p. 173; Shultz, *Turmoil and Triumph,* p. 8, tells of meeting Reagan in 1974 and 1978; Martin Anderson, *Revolution* (Harcourt Brace Jovanovich, 1988), p. 169, for the 1978 meeting.
17. Cannon, *President Reagan,* p. 79.
18. Don Oberdorfer, *The Turn,* p. 44; Bob Schieffer and Gary Paul Gates, *The Acting President* (New York: E. P. Dutton, 1989), p. 212.
19. Shultz, *Turmoil and Triumph,* p. 5.
20. Ibid., pp. 31, 155.
21. Schieffer and Gates, *Acting President,* pp. 212–15; Vincent Davis, "The Reagan Defense Program: Decision Making, Decision Makers and Some of the Results," in *The Reagan Defense Program: An Interim Assessment,*

Stephen J. Cimbala, ed. (Wilmington, Del.: Scholarly Resources, 1984), p. 35; see also Anatoly Dobrynin, *In Confidence: Moscow's Ambassador to America's Six Cold War Presidents (1962–1986)* (New York: Times Books, 1995), p. 509.

22. Shultz, *Turmoil and Triumph*, pp. 305–7; interview with a senior White House official.
23. Raymond L. Garthoff, *The Great Transition* (Washington, D.C.: Brookings Institution, 1994), pp. 32–33; Robert C. McFarlane with Zofia Smardz, *Special Trust* (New York: Cadell and Davies, 1994), pp. 272–80, for text of NSDD-75.
24. Dobrynin, *In Confidence*, p. 509.
25. Donald Regan, *For the Record* (New York: Harcourt Brace Jovanovich, 1988), pp. 49, 71, 270–76; Larry Speakes with Robert Pack, *Speaking Out: The Reagan Presidency from Inside the White House* (New York: Scribner, 1988), pp. 111–14; Nancy Reagan, pp. 244–63; Cannon, *President Reagan*, p. 528.
26. Regan, *For the Record*, p. 247.
27. Leslie Gelb, "The Mind of the President," *NYT Magazine*, 10/6/85, pp. 21 ff.
28. Regan, *For the Record*, pp. 247–48.
29. Colin Powell, with Joseph E. Persico, *My American Journey* (New York: Random House, 1995), p. 333; Peggy Noonan, *What I Saw at the Revolution* (New York: Random House, 1990), p. 150.
30. Noonan, *What I Saw*, pp. 154–58, 174–75; interview with White House official.
31. Regan, *For the Record*, p. 271; Speakes, *Speaking Out*, p. 114.
32. Regan, *For the Record*, pp. 271–72; Helene von Damm, *At Reagan's Side* (New York: Doubleday, 1989), p. 60.
33. Speakes, *Speaking Out*, p. 306; Regan, *For the Record*, p. 226, 271.
34. Von Damm, *At Reagan's Side*, p. 188.
35. *Newsweek*, January 9, 1989.
36. Cannon, *President Reagan*, p. 182.
37. Anderson, *Revolution*, pp. 289–92.
38. Schieffer and Gates, *Acting President*, pp. 89–91, for quote; see Regan, *For the Record*, pp. 266–67; Powell, *My American Journey*, p. 336; and McFarlane, *Special Trust*, p. 288, for similar experiences.
39. Schieffer and Gates, *Acting President*, p. 89; see William E. Pemberton, *Exit with Honor* (Armonk, N.Y.: M. E. Sharpe, 1997), p. 114, for the self-evaluation that Reagan sent a high-school teacher on his leadership style.
40. Regan, *For the Record*, p. 268.
41. Powell, *My American Journey*, p. 334.
42. Cannon, *President Reagan*, p. 362.
43. Ibid., p. 361.
44. Powell, *My American Journey*, p. 334; Smith, *Power Game*, p. 584, for quote; Schieffer and Gates, *Acting President*, p. 85.
45. Shultz, *Turmoil and Triumph*, p. 126.
46. Ibid., p. 159.
47. Ibid., pp. 159–60.
48. Ibid., pp. 162–63.
49. Ibid., p. 164. It was at this impromptu dinner that Reagan told Shultz about his desire for a defense initiative.
50. Ibid., pp. 164–65; Cannon, *President Reagan*, p. 312.
51. Shultz., *Turmoil and Triumph*, pp. 164–65, for quote; Dobrynin, *In Confidence*, pp. 518–20.
52. Cannon, *President Reagan*, p. 312.
53. Shultz, *Turmoil and Triumph*, pp. 165–66.
54. Ibid., pp. 166–67.
55. Ibid., pp. 167–68.
56. Ibid., pp. 265–66.
57. Ibid., p. 267.
58. See stories by Howard Kurtz in *WP*, 2/9/84, 3/22/84, 5/10/84 and 5/16/84.
59. Shultz, *Turmoil and Triumph*, pp. 267–68.
60. Ibid., p. 268.
61. Ibid., pp. 268–69.
62. Ibid., pp. 269–70.
63. Ibid., pp. 270–71; Gallup polls. In January, 36 percent of the public approved Reagan's handling of foreign policy; in May, the number had gone down to 32 percent.

    In mid-March, Richard Wirthlin asked a sample group of Americans two questions. The first was which statement was closest to the respondent's opinion: (A) "We must build as many nuclear weapons as quickly as we can so that we won't be pushed around by the Russians anymore," or (B) "Once the Soviets and the United States have about the same strength in nuclear weapons then nuclear weapons must be reduced dramatically to assure lasting peace and security." The second question was which of these two statements best reflected Ronald Reagan's position. Of those polled 72 percent said that statement (B) best represented their position and 56 percent said that statement (A) represented Reagan's position. (Wirthlin archives.)
64. Shultz, *Turmoil and Triumph*, pp. 274–75.
65. Ibid., p. 275; Dobrynin, *In Confidence*, p. 530.
66. Geoffrey Smith, *Reagan and Thatcher* (New York: W. W. Norton, 1991), p. 114, for Shultz quote; Shultz, *Turmoil and Triumph*, pp. 270, 276–80, for the rest. Don Oberdorfer of the *Washington Post* thought it confrontational, and Philip Taubman of the *New York Times* thought it conciliatory. Shultz told his State Department press briefers to go with the *Times'* interpretation.

Shultz tells us it was also supposed to signal that the administration was ready to discard the principle of "linkage" and to attempt to resolve regional conflicts and arms-control issues independently and on their merits, but this message does not come through in his own quotations from the statement.

67. Shultz, *Turmoil and Triumph,* p. 281.
68. Ibid., pp. 358–60.
69. Ibid., pp. 281–82.
70. Strobe Talbott, *Deadly Gambits: The Reagan Administration and the Stalemate in Nuclear Arms Control* (New York: Alfred A. Knopf, 1984), p. 305.
71. Ibid., p. 308.
72. Ibid., pp. 307–13.
73. Ibid., p. 263.
74. Ibid., pp. 179–82.
75. Ibid., pp. 191–92.
76. Shultz, *Turmoil and Triumph,* pp. 362–64; Garthoff, *Great Transition,* pp. 118–19, 124; Oberdorfer, *The Turn,* pp. 55, 59.
77. Dobrynin, *In Confidence,* pp. 536–38.
78. Shultz, *Turmoil and Triumph,* pp. 361–71; Cannon, *President Reagan,* p. 318; Oberdorfer, *The Turn,* pp. 61–65; Dobrynin, *In Confidence,* pp. 538–40; Talbott, *Deadly Gambits,* p. 193.
79. Talbott, *Deadly Gambits,* pp. 194–95.
80. Oberdorfer, *The Turn,* pp. 65–67; Garthoff, *Great Transition,* pp. 138–39.

The information became public after Oleg Gordievsky, deputy KGB chief in London and an agent for the British, defected to the West in 1985.

According to Oberdorfer, the original plan was to include the JCS, the President, the vice-president and the supreme commander of NATO, but because of McFarlane's concern about the state of Soviet nerves, the war game was scaled back. Oberdorfer also reports that McFarlane initially discounted the reports of a war scare in the Kremlin.

81. Shultz, *Turmoil and Triumph,* pp. 374–75.
82. Ibid., p. 376.
83. Ibid., p. 317.
84. Ibid., pp. 306–10.

Shultz also found that Clark had drafted an NSDD, which he got the President to sign, one sentence of which suggested that the Congress was not providing adequate security assistance to Central America, and that the executive branch would have to make up for this deficit. Shultz pointed out that this raised a serious constitutional issue and stopped Clark. The following year, McFarlane secretly raised money for the contras from Saudi Arabia.

85. Ibid., pp. 310–13.
86. Ibid., pp. 311, 317; Oberdorfer, *The Turn,* p. 42; Roy Gutman, *Banana Diplomacy: The Making of American Policy in Nicaragua 1981–1987* (New York: Simon & Schuster, 1988), pp. 146–47.

A Gallup poll in August showed that 55 percent of the public opposed giving military assistance to Central America.

87. *LAT,* 12/19/83.
88. Ibid., Cannon, *President Reagan,* pp. 424–26.

The leak was of the President's authorization to the U.S. Marines in Lebanon to call in air strikes against forces shelling their positions. Clark told the President that the identification of McFarlane as the official who argued for a change in the rules of engagement had put McFarlane's life in danger. The FBI carried out the investigation—without the specific authorization for polygraph testing—and found that so many people knew of the order given the Marines that it was impossible to know who had been the source of the story.

89. Cannon, *President Reagan,* pp. 427–28; Shultz, *Turmoil and Triumph,* p. 319.
90. Cannon, *President Reagan,* pp. 428–29.
91. Ibid., pp. 429–33.
92. Ronald Reagan, *An American Life* (New York: Simon & Schuster, 1990), p. 448.
93. Cannon, *President Reagan,* pp. 433–35; *LAT,* 12/19/83.
94. Reagan, *American Life,* p. 448.
95. Shultz, *Triumph and Turmoil,* pp. 275, 466.
96. Sidney Blumenthal, *The Rise of the Counter-Establishment* (New York: Times Books, 1986), p. 279.
97. Cannon, *President Reagan,* pp. 513–15.
98. Oberdorfer, *The Turn,* pp. 70–71. According to Wirthlin's polls, 43 percent versus 42 percent thought Reagan was increasing the chances of war.
99. Gallup polls; see also Cannon, *President Reagan,* pp. 344, 510; Jane Mayer and Doyle McManus, *Landslide* (New York: Houghton Mifflin, 1988), p. 15, for Wirthlin quote.

Gallup polls showed that 49 percent disapproved of the administration's policies in Central America—as opposed to 29 percent in favor; and they showed that 59 percent disapproved of the policy in Lebanon, versus 28 percent in favor. They also showed that, by a margin of 30 to 45 percent, the public thought the Democrats more likely to keep the country out of war.

100. Cannon, *President Reagan,* pp. 480–81.
101. Ibid., p. 514.

According to Cannon, Reagan loved the commercials made about him. His favorite showed him in front of the service flags for all the wars of the twentieth century saying that he hoped American boys would never have to go to war again. Thus did he succeed in associating himself with the U.S. armed forces and with a hope for peace.

102. *WP,* 1/17/84, for partial text.
103. *WP,* 8/24/84; *WP,* 12/16/84.
104. *WP,* 12/16/84; James K. Oliver and James A. Nathan, "The Reagan Defense Program: Concepts, Continuity and Change," in *The Reagan Defense Program: An Interim Assessment,* ed. Stephen J. Cimbala (Wilmington, Del.: Scholarly Resources, 1984), p. 16, Defense expert Coral Bell wrote: "The almost universal impression is that President Reagan has achieved—not merely proposed—an unprecedented increase in U.S. military muscle. But I would argue that since the image of U.S. military weakness was created chiefly by words . . . it is logical that more words from the same sources should have been effective readjusting that somewhat distorted image to reflect the reality of effective (though asymmetrical) superpower parity."
105. Oberdorfer, *The Turn,* pp. 70–71.
106. Transcript in *Congressional Quarterly Texts,* October 27, 1984, pp. 2828–38.

Reagan also spoke of "our rendez-vous with destiny," a phrase of Franklin Roosevelt's that he had used in his 1964 speech for Goldwater.

107. Ibid.; see also Shultz, *Turmoil and Triumph,* pp. 466–67; see *WP,* 1/17/84 for partial text; and *WSJ,* 1/16/84; see also Reagan, *American Life,* p. 592.
108. Shultz, *Turmoil and Triumph,* p. 466.

Shultz and Gromyko did not get this far in the discussion.

109. Reagan, *American Life,* pp. 591–92.
110. Dobrynin, *In Confidence,* p. 551.
111. Shultz, *Turmoil and Triumph,* p. 472.
112. Ibid., pp. 472–73.
113. Ibid., pp. 473–74.
114. Ibid., pp. 475–77.
115. Ibid., pp. 473–76; Dobrynin, *In Confidence,* p. 554.

The Soviets succeeded to some degree. In May the Italian prime minister, Bettino Craxi, suggested that NATO halt its deployments if the Soviets resumed negotiations, and the Dutch government put off a vote on the deployments in the Netherlands because it could not count on gaining a majority in the Parliament.

116. Reagan, *American Life,* pp. 588–90.

Reagan had also learned that the collapse of the Geneva arms talks had worried many people around the world, so it was necessary to go on a propaganda offensive.

117. Ibid., pp. 591–92.
118. Ibid., pp. 592–94.
119. Ibid., pp. 594–95.
120. Ibid., p. 595.
121. Ibid., pp. 599–602; McFarlane, *Special Trust,* pp. 297–98.

On March 6 Reagan wrote Chernenko indicating that he believed "an improvement in United States–Soviet relations is feasible," and stressing "the importance of communicating with you directly and confidentially."

Shultz tells us that he himself favored "a serious summit after the elections" (Shultz, *Turmoil and Triumph,* p. 479).

Dobrynin speaks of a three-hour meeting with Shultz and other American officials on June 20, 1984, in which Shultz spoke of a summit between Reagan and Chernenko, but does not say that any date was mentioned (Dobrynin, *In Confidence,* p. 533).

122. Cannon, *President Reagan,* p. 741.
123. Transcript in *Congressional Quarterly Texts,* October 27, 1984, pp. 2828–38. Reagan also spoke of "our rendezvous with destiny," a phrase of FDR's that he had used in his 1964 speech for Goldwater.
124. Cannon, *President Reagan,* p. 536.
125. Shultz, *Turmoil and Triumph,* p. 480.
126. Ibid., pp. 480–82; Garthoff, *Great Transition,* p. 161, for quote.
127. Shultz, *Turmoil and Triumph,* pp. 481–83.
128. Ibid., p. 484; Dobrynin, *In Confidence,* pp. 556–57.
129. Shultz, *Turmoil and Triumph,* p. 483.
130. *WP,* 11/7/84.
131. Shultz, *Turmoil and Triumph,* pp. 499–500.
132. *WP,* 6/19/84.
133. Interview with Richard Wirthlin, 4/4/95.
134. Angelo Codevilla, *While Others Build* (New York: Free Press, 1988), p. 131.
135. *NYT,* 4/8/84.
136. *Congressional Quarterly Texts,* October 27, 1984, p. 2834.
137. *WP,* 6/19/84.
138. *WP,* 11/7/84.

Reagan also said that he believed the Soviets were ready to negotiate because they could no longer afford the arms race. Previously this had been the hard-line argument for building more weapons and not negotiating.

139. George W. Ball, "The War for Star Wars," *New York Review of Books,* April 11, 1985.
140. Ibid.
141. Steinberg, ed., *Lost in Space,* pp. 63–64; Codevilla, *While Others Build,* p. 115, for the Defense Department posture statement; Philip M. Boffey, William J. Broad, Leslie H. Gelb, Charles Mohr and Holcomb B. Noble, *Claiming the Heavens: The New York Times Complete Guide to the Star Wars Debate* (New York: Times Books, 1988), p. 66, for Iklé quote.
142. Quote of March 12, 1985, in Arms Control Association, ed., *Star Wars Quotes* (Washington, D.C.: Arms Control Association, 1986), p. 2.
143. Steinberg, ed., *Lost in Space,* pp. 2–3, p. 55 on NSSD 6–83; see also Nolan, *Guardians,* p. 175.
144. Arms Control Association, ed., *Star Wars Quotes,* p. 3.
145. The declassified portions of the Fletcher Report, Defensive Technologies Study, "The Strategic Defense Initiative," Department of Defense, March 1984, can be found in Senate Foreign Relations Committee, *Strategic Defense and Anti-Satellite Weapons: Hearing,* 98th Cong., 2nd sess., April 25, 1984, pp. 94–175.

    The Hoffman report, "Ballistic Missile Defenses and U.S. National Security," prepared for the Future Security Strategy Study, October 1983, Institute for Defense Analysis, Alexandria, Va., can be found in the same hearing.
146. Nolan, *Guardians,* pp. 197–98; *Congressional Quarterly,* March 1985, p. 75; Douglas C. Waller, James T. Bruce and Douglas Cook, *The Strategic Defense Initiative* (Claremont, Calif.: Regina Books, 1987), p. 25.

    The figures mentioned include not only the Department of Defense but the Department of Energy budgetary component, much of it for the X-ray laser tests. The Energy requests went from three hundred million dollars in fiscal 1985 up to $508 billion the next year, and then gradually declined.
147. Sydney D. Drell, Philip J. Farley and David Holloway, *The Reagan Strategic Defense Initiative: A Technical, Political and Arms Control Assessment* (Cambridge, Mass.: Ballinger Publishing Co., 1985), p. 63 for quote.
148. Arms Control Association, ed., *Star Wars Quotes,* p. 43.
149. Ibid.
150. Broad, *Teller's War,* p. 156; Wayne Biddle, "Star Wars Technology Is More Than a Fantasy," *NYT,* 3/5/83, p. 1; Boyce Rensberger, *WP,* 3/3/85.
151. Boffey et al., *Claiming the Heavens,* p. 74; *Aviation Week and Space Technology,* vol. 123 (October 14, 1985), pp. 22–23, for Abrahamson quote; John Tirman, ed., *Empty Promises* (Boston: Beacon Press, 1986), p. 17.
152. Defense Technologies Study, "Strategic Defense Initiative," p. 6; Tina Rosenberg, "The Authorized Version," *Atlantic,* February 1986.
153. Pressler, *Star Wars,* p. 133; Nolan, *Guardians,* p. 204 for quote; Steinberg, ed., *Lost in Space,* pp. 93–94. Ashton Carter was a consultant on the Hoffman report.
154. Nolan, *Guardians,* pp. 204–5; Steinberg, ed., *Lost in Space,* pp. 95–96.

    William H. Taft IV, who succeeded Carlucci as Weinberger's number two, took the unprecedented step of asking OTA to withdraw the report. In response, the OTA appointed a senior bipartisan panel to review the report. The panel stood behind the study (Nolan, pp. 204–5).
155. Rensberger, *WP,* 3/3/85.
156. Rensberger, *WP,* 3/3/85; Steinberg, ed., *Lost in Space,* p. 95.
157. Haley and Merrit, eds., *Strategic Defense Initiative,* n. 12 on p. 106; Sidney D. Drell, Philip J. Farley and David Holloway, *The Reagan Strategic Defense Initiative,* pp. 57–68; Boffey et al., *Claiming the Heavens,* p. 72; Talbott, *Deadly Gambits,* p. 239.

    The Soviets had a total of twenty-three hundred ICBM silos and SLBM tubes in 1982 under the SALT II agreement.
158. Boffey et al., *Claiming the Heavens,* pp. 169, 64.
159. Ibid., pp. 64–65.
160. Arms Control Association, ed., *Star Wars Quotes,* p. 41.
161. Ibid., pp. 41, 56.
162. Ibid., p. 41.
163. *NYT,* 8/23/85; *WP,* 10/4/85.
164. Philip M. Boffey, "Star Wars Is Coming, but Where Is It Going?," *NYT,* 3/8/85.
165. U.S. Senate Committee on Foreign Relations, *Strategic Defense and Anti-Satellite Weapons: Hearing,* 98th Cong., 2nd sess., April 25, 1984, pp. 69–74.
166. Nolan, *Guardians,* p. 208.
167. Nixon quote from July 1, 1984, in *Star Wars Quotes,* ed. Arms Control Association, p. 80.
168. U.S. Senate Committee on Armed Services, *Department of Defense Authorization for Appropriations for Fiscal Year 1985: Hearing on S. Hrg. 98–724,* pt. 6, 98th Cong., 2nd sess. (Strategic Defense Initiative), March 8, 22, April 24, 1984, p. 2904.
169. Ibid., pp. 2926–30.
170. Ibid., pp. 2948–53.
171. Ibid., pp. 2978–80.
172. Ibid., pp. 3028–39; Steinberg, ed., *Lost in Space,* p. 60.
173. *LAT,* 9/22/85, in *Star Wars Quotes,* ed. Arms Control Association, p. 28.
174. Hoffman report, "Ballistic Missile Defenses," pp. 2, 3, 7.
175. Rosenberg, "Authorized Version," pp. 26–30.

176. Ibid.

In May 1984 Secretary Weinberger said, "We have some of America's finest scientists who were members of the Fletcher Commission.... They found the dream to be indeed possible, after a study of about a year." (The study took five months.)

Keyworth, at a speech at the Brookings Institution that year, said that the Fletcher team had determined that "the President's objective is not an unrealistic goal and they concluded it probably could be obtained."

177. Ibid.

178. *Aviation Week and Space Technology,* October 24, 1983, p. 51.

179. Ball, "War for Star Wars"; McGeorge Bundy, George Kennan, Robert S. McNamara and Gerard Smith, "The President's Choice: Star Wars or Arms Control," *Foreign Affairs,* Winter 1984–85, p. 272. The authors of the latter quote Fletcher as testifying before Congress that "the ultimate utility ... of this system will depend not only on the technology itself but on the extent to which the Soviet Union agrees to mutual defense arrangements and offense limitations."

The presidential policy statement issued by the White House in December called SDI "a research program ... [to] provide a future President and a future Congress with the technical knowledge required to support a decision on whether to develop and later deploy advanced defensive systems" (from a statement by President Reagan on December 28, 1984, published in a White House document, "The President's Strategic Defense Initiative," January 1985, reprinted in *Congressional Digest,* March 1985, pp. 70–71; statement prepared by the Pentagon). See also Frederick H. Hartmann, *Naval Renaissance: The U.S. Navy in the 1980s* (Annapolis, Md.: Naval Institute Press, 1990), p. 263.

180. Abrahamson once said, "A perfect astrodome defense is not a realistic thing. The point is to get a thoroughly reliable and effective system. What does this mean? We haven't quantified it yet." *Science,* vol. 225 (August 10, 1984), pp. 600 ff.

181. Lieutenant General Daniel O. Graham (ret.), *High Frontier: A New National Strategy* (Washington, D.C.: High Frontier, 1982), pp. 88–89.

182. Steinberg, ed., *Lost in Space,* p. 66; Codevilla, *While Others Build,* p. 115.

183. Edward Teller, "SDI: The Last, Best Hope," *Insight* (magazine of the *Washington Times),* October 28, 1985, in *Strategic Defense Initiative,* eds. Haley and Merrit, p. 127.

In 1987 Teller wrote, "The most popular argument is that defense against nuclear missiles is useless unless it is 100 percent effective—the damage would be enormous if only a few rockets penetrated the defense. The argument is correct, but it is an argument not against defense but against war.... The main purpose of defense is to deter aggression by making its outcome dubious." (Edward Teller, *Better a Shield Than a Sword: Perspectives on Defense and Technology* [New York: Free Press, 1987], p. 8.)

184. Zbigniew Brzezinski, Robert Jastrow and Max Kampelman, "Defense in Space Is Not Star Wars," *NYT Magazine,* 1/27/85.

185. Arms Control Association, ed., *Star Wars Quotes,* p. 106.

"I don't know a single scientist in this country who agrees with the President's definition of the program," Senator Nunn said on June 9, 1985.

186. U.S. Senate Committee on the Armed Services, *Department of Defense Authorization for Appropriations for Fiscal Year 1986,* February 21, 1985, "Strategic and Theater Nuclear Forces."

In one hearing in late 1985, Senator Warner said to Fred Iklé: "One of the purposes of this series of hearings is to really try and remove some of the points from the overall record of the SDI that we in the Congress frankly feel to be somewhat incredible. The program has suffered, if I may say respectfully, from a credibility gap. The thing that has bothered me from the very earliest has been the representation that through this program we could, and I quote your testimony today, eliminate the awful threat posed by ballistic missiles." (Nolan, *Guardians,* p. 212.)

187. Oberdorfer, *The Turn,* p. 25.

In their books, Lou Cannon, Strobe Talbott and John Newhouse also wrote that Reagan deeply believed in his dream of a perfect defense.

188. *WP,* 11/18/84; *WSJ,* 11/16/84. Talbott, *Master of the Game,* p. 213.

189. *WP,* 12/22/84.

190. *WP,* 12/24/84.

191. Shultz, *Turmoil and Triumph,* p. 509.

192. Speech of May 1, 1984, in *Star Wars Quotes,* ed. Arms Control Association, p. 12.

193. Interview with Fred Iklé, June 28, 1990. Iklé called Star Wars "half a Potemkin village."

194. Nolan, *Guardians,* p. 186.

One official said that Star Wars—meaning perfect defenses—had become something like a "loyalty oath" within the administration, and there was not enough discussion of its deterrent value *(WP,* 2/14/85).

195. Shultz, *Turmoil and Triumph,* p. 477.

Others make it clear that at this stage the Soviets were complaining about ASATs (see Garthoff, *Great Transition,* p. 158; John Newhouse, *War and Peace in the Nuclear Age* [New York: Alfred A. Knopf, 1989], p. 372). But they soon dropped the issue—possibly because they felt it less important, but possibly because ASAT weapons could be used against space weaponry (see Walter Pincus, *WP,* 2/7/85).

196. Shultz, *Turmoil and Triumph,* p. 500.

197. Talbott, *Master of the Game,* p. 231.

198. Ibid., pp. 231–34. According to Talbott, Perle turned interagency meetings into pep rallies for SDI. "Spring is breaking out all over," he once said. "It's the young people who are working on this program. You almost

get the sense that they're relieved to be working on defense rather than lethal weapons. These are weapons of life."

199. Arms Control Association, ed., *Star Wars Quotes,* p. 1.

   Aides told Lou Cannon that Reagan himself had insisted on making SDI the centerpiece of the address. (*WP,* 1/22/85).

   McFarlane told me he couldn't say that he wanted SDI as a bargaining chip because the program needed to have content and substance, and that meant getting funded by Congress (McFarlane interview 6/26/90).

200. *WP,* 12/20/84.

201. An ABC–*Washington Post* poll showed that 41 percent approved (*WP,* 8/14/85); Wirthlin's polls of early March showed that 81 percent had heard of Star Wars and of those 69 percent thought it a good idea and 29 percent thought it a bad idea. Wirthlin group survey no. 3100/699/-02-103). In February, before the issue was well reported, a Gallup poll showed 52 percent in favor of developing defenses; the November Gallup poll showed 61 percent in favor. See Ronald H. Hinckley, *People, Polls and Policy-Makers: American Public Opinion and National Security* (New York: Lexington Books, 1992), pp. 72–78, for the partisan split and other poll figures.

202. On perfect defenses, see M & K poll taken September 1985, in Thomas Wallace Graham, "The Politics of Failure: Strategic Nuclear Arms Control, Public Opinion and Domestic Politics in the United States—1945–1980," unpublished Ph.D. thesis, Department of Political Science, MIT, June 1989, p. 464; Hinckley, *People, Polls,* pp. 72–78, for last statement.

203. Graham, "Politics of Failure," pp. 443–65, for numerous polls taken over the years on anti-nuclear defenses.

204. Wirthlin poll taken April 1983, survey no. 2930/699-02-60.

205. Graham, "Politics of Failure," pp. 443–65.

   Pollsters always speak of "disarmament"—arms control being apparently too confusing an issue. Reagan, too, spoke of "disarmament," and START was to be different from SALT—reductions as opposed to limitations.

   Public opinion on all of these issues was very stable over the years.

206. Gallup polls taken in February and November 1985 showed that 47–48 percent of those who said they knew something about Star Wars thought it would help arms control. Possibly this was not just the influence of the President but that of the arms-control advocates, who were saying that SDI could be a bargaining chip. The difference between the research program and the development of defenses was surely too subtle for a public-opinion poll on Star Wars.

207. U.S. Senate Committee on the Armed Services, *Defense Authorization for Appropriations for 1985,* pp. 2937–38.

208. Interview with Edwin Meese III, 10/25/90.

   Public attitudes did not, of course, escape Martin Anderson either. "If you talk to the American people about defense, they naturally believe in it," he told a reporter in January 1985 (*WP,* 1/20/85).

209. Shultz, *Turmoil and Triumph,* pp. 259–60.

210. Caspar Weinberger, *Fighting for Peace* (New York: Warner Books, 1990), p. 315.

211. McFarlane, *Special Trust,* pp. 302–3.

212. *WP,* 1/10/85.

213. *WSJ,* 2/8/85.

   A few days later Reagan was asked by the national-security reporters of the *New York Times* why he thought that the defense might be able to prevail over the offense. His answer was that an anti-missile defense could be used as an insurance policy after the superpowers had eliminated their nuclear weapons—or, to prevent a first strike. But when the *Times* reporters asked him directly whether he was advocating a defense for U.S. missiles, he said that he wanted a defense that would stop "all, or the bulk," of "those weapons" from getting through (*NYT,* 2/12/85).

214. Dorinda G. Dallmayer, ed., in association with Daniel S. Papp, *The Strategic Defense Initiative: New Perspectives on Deterrence* (Boulder, Colo.: Westview Press, 1986), p. 8, quoted by Nunn, last phrase in Boffey et al., *Claiming the Heavens,* p. 235.

215. Reagan, *American Life,* p. 608.

   In August 1985 Reagan told a gathering of Republicans, "Looking to the future, we're moving forward with research on a project that offers us a way out of our nuclear dilemma—the one that has confounded mankind for four decades now.... The Strategic Defense Initiative research program offers us the hope of protecting ourselves and our allies from a nuclear ballistic missile attack." (Arms Control Association, ed., *Star Wars Quotes,* p. 2.)

216. Dallmayer, ed., *Strategic Defense Initiative,* p. 12.

217. Interview with Tom Foley, 4/3/95.

218. *WP,* 1/11/85.

   Representative Les Aspin (Democrat of Wisconsin), chairman of the House Armed Services Committee, signaled his decision to vote for the program in January by saying that SDI would make a far better bargaining chip than the MX missile.

SEVEN: Hard-Liners vs. Pragmatists

1. Don Oberdorfer in *WP,* 2/8/85.
2. George Shultz, *Turmoil and Triumph* (New York: Scribner, 1993), p. 490.

3. *WP,* 1/28/83.
4. Shultz, *Turmoil and Triumph,* p. 496.
5. Constantine C. Menges, *Inside the National Security Council* (New York: Simon & Schuster, 1988), pp. 93–94, 129.
6. Ibid., pp. 496–97.
7. Ibid., pp. 496–98; Ronald Reagan, *An American Life* (New York: Simon & Schuster, 1990), p. 606.
8. Reagan, *American Life,* pp. 605–6.
9. Robert C. McFarlane with Zofia Smardz, *Special Trust* (New York: Cadell and Davies, 1994), pp. 285–87.

   McFarlane says in his memoir that the meeting with Reagan on the plane was on the Sunday after the election—that is, November 11. But apparently he told reporters that it was shortly before the inauguration. (Jane Mayer and Doyle McManus, *Landslide* [Boston: Houghton Mifflin, 1988], p. 56.)

   Interviewed by reporters from *George* magazine many years later, McFarlane revised the story somewhat, quoting Reagan as saying, "I know that if I build the team around Cap, I would not get policy that would achieve anything, and if I build it around George, I would lose a good friend in Cap." *(George,* February 1999.)
10. Interview with top aide.
11. Colin Powell with Joseph Persico, *My American Journey* (New York: Random House, 1995), pp. 314–15.

    Powell was nonetheless surprised when Reagan did not bother to thank him and other White House aides for the considerable effort they put into the Moscow summit (Powell, pp. 380–81).
12. Michael Deaver, *Behind the Scenes* (New York: William Morrow, 1987), p. 39.
13. Helene von Damm, *At Reagan's Side* (New York: Doubleday, 1989), p. 224; and see Cannon, *President Reagan* (New York: Simon & Schuster, 1991), p. 435.
14. Donald Regan, *For the Record* (New York: Harcourt Brace Jovanovich, 1988), pp. 219–27.
15. Shultz, *Turmoil and Triumph,* p. 503.
16. Ibid., pp. 491, 495, 498–99, 503.

    Shultz quotes a friend to the effect that Burt's leaks to Talbott had helped create "a miasma of distrust" over Washington and that Burt was the real author of *Deadly Gambits* (Ibid., pp. 498–99).
17. Paul H. Nitze with Ann M. Smith and Steven L. Rearden, *From Hiroshima to Glasnost: At the Center of Decision—a Memoir* (New York: Grove Weidenfeld, 1989), p. 365.
18. Strobe Talbott, *Deadly Gambits: The Reagan Administration and the Stalemate in Nuclear Arms Control* (New York: Alfred A. Knopf, 1984), p. 168.

    Eugene Rostow leaked it to the press, implying—quite falsely—that he had something to do with it.
19. Shultz, *Turmoil and Triumph,* p. 502.
20. Ibid., pp. 498, 504.
21. Nitze, *From Hiroshima to Glasnost,* p. 402; Shultz, *Turmoil and Triumph,* p. 479; Strobe Talbott, *Master of the Game: Paul Nitze and the Nuclear Peace* (New York: Alfred A. Knopf, 1988), p. 211.
22. Shultz, *Turmoil and Triumph,* pp. 495, 499–500.
23. Nitze, *From Hiroshima to Glasnost,* p. 403. Nitze writes merely that, when he included the argument in a draft of Shultz's talking points for Geneva, the secretary of state "was pleased with the idea of taking what had appeared to be a weak and vulnerable point in our position and turning it into a springboard for attack."
24. Talbott, *Master of the Game,* p. 214.
25. Nitze, *From Hiroshima to Glasnost,* pp. 404–5.
26. Interview with State Department official, June 21, 1990.

    The official was explaining bureaucratic reactions to all such statements about SDI.
27. Paul Nitze, "On the Road to a More Stable Peace," Department of State bulletin, in P. Edward Haley and Jack Merrit, eds., *The Strategic Defense Initiative: Folly or Future?* (Boulder, Colo.: Westview Press, 1986), p. 37.

    In explicating these sentences on the public record, Nitze wrote that an effective non-nuclear defense might prove an illusory goal.

    Shultz in his memoir tells us that nuclear weapons in space were Gromyko's bête noire. But he then drops the subject, and there is no other evidence to suggest that the Soviets would make a deal that involved only nuclear weapons. After all, they had a nuclear-tipped ABM system protecting Moscow, and they seemed to be afraid of more high-tech American weapons (Shultz, *Turmoil and Triumph,* p. 507).
28. Don Oberdorfer, *The Turn: From the Cold War to the New Era: The United States and the Soviet Union 1983–1990* (New York: Poseidon Press, 1991), p. 102.
29. Shultz, *Turmoil and Triumph,* pp. 511–12.
30. Ibid., pp. 514–18; Nitze, *From Hiroshima to Glasnost,* pp. 405–6.
31. Nitze, *From Hiroshima to Glasnost,* p. 406; Kenneth Adelman, *The Great Universal Embrace: Arms Summitry, a Skeptic's Account* (New York: Simon & Schuster, 1989), pp. 118–19.
32. Shultz, *Turmoil and Triumph,* p. 519.
33. Talbott, *Master of the Game,* p. 216.
34. U.S. Senate, *Department of Defense Authorization for Appropriation for FY 1986: Hearings Before the Committee on the Armed Services,* February–March 1985, "Strategic and Theater Nuclear Forces," March 15, 1985.
35. Talbott, *Master of the Game,* p. 217.
36. Ibid., pp. 217–18; Nitze, *From Hiroshima to Glasnost,* pp. 406–7.
37. Talbott, *Master of the Game,* p. 218.

    Nitze maintained this position ever afterwards. In his memoir he writes coolly, "Just because most research and development programs in the past had run into difficulties did not mean this one would." (Nitze, *From Hiroshima to Glasnost*, pp. 407–8.)

38. Caspar Weinberger, *Fighting for Peace* (New York: Warner Books, 1990), pp. 320–22.
39. Shultz, *Turmoil and Triumph*, pp. 521–22; Talbott, *Master of the Game*, p. 273.
40. Talbott, *Master of the Game*, pp. 254–55.
41. Nitze, *From Hiroshima to Glasnost*, p. 409.
42. Ibid., pp. 410–11; Talbott, *Master of the Game*, p. 257.
43. Nitze, *From Hiroshima to Glasnost*, p. 411; Talbott, *Master of the Game*, p. 262.
44. Shultz, *Turmoil and Triumph*, p. 583.
45. Nitze, *From Hiroshima to Glasnost*, pp. 411–12.
46. Talbott, *Master of the Game*, pp. 263–64; interview with Robert McFarlane, 6/26/90.
47. Talbott, *Master of the Game*, p. 265; Shultz, *Turmoil and Triumph*, p. 570; interview with Robert McFarlane, 6/26/90.

    Shultz says that he kept the President fully informed.
48. Talbott, *Master of the Game*, p. 266; Nitze, *From Hiroshima to Glasnost*, p. 412.
49. Nitze, *From Hiroshima to Glasnost*, p. 412.

    Richard Burt, who was about to leave for West Germany, had not been in on the preparation of the Monday package, and, according to Nitze, his presence in the room hampered the discussion a good deal.
50. Ibid., Talbott, *Master of the Game*, pp. 264–66.
51. Shultz, *Turmoil and Triumph*, p. 570.
52. Nitze, *From Hiroshima to Glasnost*, p. 412.
53. Anatoly Dobrynin, *In Confidence: Moscow's Ambassador to America's Six Cold War Presidents (1962–1986)* (New York: Times Books, 1995), p. 573.

    However, since Gorbachev was by now in command and wanted to be in full charge of policy himself, Gromyko may have been following his orders.
54. Talbott, *Master of the Game*, pp. 268–70.

    Later in the summer McFarlane consulted with a group of Rand experts, who on their own initiative were developing a plan for trading SDI for deep offensive cuts. But McFarlane was so afraid of the hardliners that he did not enter their visit on his schedule and told the experts they should not speak to anyone else on his staff.
55. Shultz, *Turmoil and Triumph*, p. 525.

    On February 22 Shultz gave a speech announcing moral support for "democratic revolutionaries" struggling not only against Communist regimes but against non-Communist governments such as those in South Africa and Korea. But little attention was paid to this interpretation of the "Reagan doctrine." And Reagan himself repudiated it in deed—most remarkably in the case of anti-Marcos revolt in the Philippines. (See Shultz's account, ibid., pp. 608–42.)
56. Talbott, *Master of the Game*, pp. 224–25.

    During 1985 the Soviets made it clear that they were looking for a face-saving way to "remove the obstacle" of the radar. Nitze proposed a possible solution within the administration, but he was forbidden to work on the problem.
57. Shultz, *Turmoil and Triumph*, p. 523.
58. Talbott, *Master of the Game*, pp. 220–26; Shultz, *Turmoil and Triumph*, pp. 567–69.
59. Dobrynin, *In Confidence*, p. 566; Geoffrey Smith, *Reagan and Thatcher* (New York: W. W. Norton, 1991), p. 146.
60. Jack Matlock, *Autopsy on an Empire* (New York: Random House, 1995), p. 50; John Newhouse, *War and Peace in the Nuclear Age* (New York: Alfred A. Knopf, 1989), p. 378, Oberdorfer, *The Turn*, pp. 108–9; Mikhail Gorbachev, *Memoirs* (New York: Doubleday, 1995), pp. 22–40.
61. Oberdorfer, *The Turn*, p. 109; Raymond L. Garthoff, *The Great Transition* (Washington, D.C.: Brookings Institution, 1987), p. 203; Matlock, *Autopsy*, pp. 45–49; David Remnick, *Lenin's Tomb* (New York: Vintage Books, 1994), pp. 191–93; Dusko Doder and Louise Branscom, *Gorbachev* (New York: Viking, 1990), p. 52.
62. Shultz, *Turmoil and Triumph*, pp. 528–33.

    "Confident," Shultz wrote of Gorbachev at the time, "but not over-bearing—and probably a strong person" (Adelman, *Great Universal Embrace*, pp. 121–22).
63. Dusko Doder, "New Leader Shows Youth, Energy," *WP*, 7/30/85.

    Doder reported: "In a relatively short time span, Gorbachev seems to have become more than a mere heir and executor of the Andropov political estate. He has acted more quickly and boldly in pushing his program and consolidating his power than any of his predecessors."
64. Shultz, *Turmoil and Triumph*, p. 568. The observer was the U.S. ambassador to Moscow, Arthur Hartman.
65. Doder, "New Leader"; Garthoff, *Great Transition*, pp. 213–15.
66. Garthoff, *Great Transition*, pp. 213–14.
67. Talbott, *Master of the Game*, pp. 258–59.

    In Geneva the Soviet START negotiator suggested that his government might accept ceilings on the number of warheads atop its heavy missiles, a concession the Soviets had been resisting since the START talks began.

    The Soviet Union also made a proposal at the eleven-year-old talks on conventional weapons that the Soviets would withdraw twenty thousand troops from Western Europe if the U.S. withdrew thirteen thousand, and for the first time proposed verification methods. The proposal answered former U.S. concerns, and it was welcomed by U.S. negotiators, but nothing came of it *(WP*, 2/15/85).

68. Robert M. Gates, *From the Shadows,* p. 340; McFarlane, *Special Trust,* p. 301, for Thatcher conversation; Garthoff, *Great Transition,* p. 214, for April plenum; John Newhouse, "The Abolitionist II," *New Yorker,* January 9, 1989, p. 54; Dobrynin, *In Confidence,* p. 570, for Gorbachev's thinking.
69. Doder, "New Leader."
   Gates, *From the Shadows,* pp. 331–32, quotes the CIA's "first comprehensive look at the new leader's policies" in mid-June 1985 as saying that a variety of sources had told them that Gorbachev was not disposed to concessions in arms control. But Matlock, in *Autopsy,* p. 88, writes: "The Soviet leaders considered arms control to be the central issue and insisted repeatedly that a major arms control agreement be reached before other issues of importance could be addressed. It was clear why they wanted it that way: they hoped to moderate the arms race and thus relieve the pressure on their economy without being forced to undertake fundamental reforms."
70. Reagan, *American Life,* pp. 613–14.
   Dobrynin also says Shultz told him in March that there was hardly any hope of solving arms-control questions at a first summit (Dobrynin, *In Confidence,* pp. 568–69).
   Publicly, Gorbachev said that the Geneva talks had "given ground for concluding that Washington was not following a course directed at an agreement" (Garthoff, *Great Transition,* pp. 215, 221–22).
71. Dobrynin, *In Confidence,* p. 569; Garthoff, *Great Transition,* pp. 221–22.
72. Garthoff, *Great Transition,* pp. 215–16.
73. Shultz, *Turmoil and Triumph,* pp. 535, 565.
   Max Kampelman later told a reporter, apropos of Shultz's summit planning, "Reagan had lots of trouble with that approach. He had problems with his own White House staff, he had problems with his friends, and he had problems with the right wing of the Republican party." (Smith, *Reagan and Thatcher,* p. 173.)
74. Shultz, *Turmoil and Triumph,* pp. 573–74 for quotes; Matlock, *Autopsy,* pp. 73–74.
75. Shultz, *Turmoil and Triumph,* p. 575.
76. *Time,* September 9, 1985, for quote; *WP,* 9/4/85.
77. Talbott, *Master of the Game,* pp. 277–78.
   The Soviet delegation in Geneva did not, however, change its position until after the summit.
78. Oberdorfer, *WP,* 9/15/85.
79. *PPP,* vol. II, pp. 1106–07, for text of press conference; Don Oberdorfer in *WP,* 9/18/85, quotes Reagan thus.
   Congress, in its 1984 and 1985 appropriation bills, specifically required that SDI remain in conformity with the ABM Treaty.
80. Oberdorfer and Hoffman in *WP,* 9/19/85, for quotes, Walter Pincus in *WP,* 9/22/85; Leslie Gelb in *NYT,* 10/18/85.
81. Shultz, *Turmoil and Triumph,* p. 576; Garthoff, *Great Transition,* p. 228.
   The Soviets defined a "charge" as an explosive weapon that could hit the other country. The definition therefore included U.S. INF weapons in Europe but not the Soviet medium-range weapons trained on Europe.
82. Shultz, *Turmoil and Triumph,* p. 577; Don Oberdorfer in *WP,* 9/29/85.
83. Shultz, *Turmoil and Triumph,* p. 578; *WP,* 10/9/95, 10/13/85.
84. *WP,* 10/10/85.
85. *WP,* 10/13/85; Shultz, *Turmoil and Triumph,* p. 581; Garthoff, *Great Transition,* p. 230; U.S. Senate Committee on Foreign Relations, *The ABM Treaty Interpretation Resolution* (Washington, D.C.: Government Printing Office, 1987) [hereafter *ABMTIR],* p. 26.
86. *ABMTIR,* pp. 2–19.
87. Ibid., pp. 46–48, 66.
88. *WP,* 10/17/85; Shultz, *Turmoil and Triumph,* p. 582.
   Shultz later denied that he had threatened to resign (Talbott, *Master of the Game,* p. 247).
89. *NYT,* 10/18/85; *ABMTIR,* p. 27.
90. U.S. House of Representatives Committee on Foreign Affairs, *ABM Treaty Interpretation Dispute: Hearings Before the Subcommittee on Arms Control, International Security and Science,* 99th Cong., 1st sess., October 22, 1985, CIS no. 86:381:33 [hereafter *ABMTID],* pp. 5–6.
91. *ABMTIR,* pp. 4–13.
   Article II defines an ABM system as "a system to counter strategic ballistic missiles or their elements in flight trajectory, currently consisting of" interceptor missiles, launchers and radars—the implication being that they could one day consist of something else.
   Agreed Statement D refers to Article III of the treaty, which defines and limits the permissible fixed, land-based systems.
92. *ABMTID,* pp. 5–6.
93. Ibid., p. 52.
94. Ibid., pp. 23, 52.
95. U.S. Senate, *The ABM Treaty and the Constitution: Joint Hearings Before the Committee on Foreign Relations and the Committee on the Judiciary,* 100th Cong., 1st sess., March 11, 26, April 29, 1987 [hereafter ABMTC].
   Don Oberdorfer's article in *WP,* 10/22/85, was the first piece of investigative reporting. Talbott added a good deal of information in *Master of the Game,* and Garthoff added to the sum of it, as did Senator Nunn in his speeches to Congress in March 1987. (See Raymond Garthoff, *Policy Versus the Law: The Reinterpretation of the ABM Treaty* [Washington, D.C.: Brookings Institution, 1987]. And Nunn testimony in *The Congressional Record,* March 11, 12, 13, 1987, U.S. Senate, p. 3092.

The Senate Armed Services Committee held hearings in November 1985. Senator Nunn requested the negotiating record, but the administration put him off.

96. Talbott, *Master of the Game,* p. 242.
97. Garthoff, *Policy Versus the Law,* p. 6; *WP,* 2/6/87.

As it happened, Donald Brennan of the Hudson Institute, the coiner of the acronym MAD, conceived the same idea quite independently at the same time. Becker surfaced the idea in the letters column of the *International Security Journal,* and there followed a round-robin correspondence between Becker and Brennan and several members of the SALT I negotiating team, including Smith, Rhinelander, Nitze and Raymond Garthoff, the executive secretary of the team. Brennan ended the exchange by capitulating. In a letter to Rhinelander, Brennan wrote: "In the face of this level of analysis . . . any further insistence that the Treaty does not necessarily ban the development of (among others) space-based exotic ABM systems would have to be reckoned willful, indeed obstinate, stupidity." Harris, however, had persevered. See also Nunn testimony in *Congressional Record,* 1987, U.S. Senate, p. 3092.

98. *ABMTC,* pp. 202–3; *ABMTIR,* p. 25.
99. Oberdorfer in *WP,* 10/22/85.
100. *ABMTIR,* p. 25; Garthoff,*Policy Versus the Law,* p. 101.

Others in the conservative network got into the act. In April the Heritage Foundation released a background paper arguing for a new interpretation of the ABM Treaty that would permit the development, testing and deployment of mobile ABM systems using future technologies. The author was said to be someone in the administration "who requests anonymity." The author, it later transpired, was Bretton Sciaroni, a young counsel to the President's Intelligence Oversight Board, who two years later told the Iran-contra committees that in his legal opinion the NSC staff was exempt from the restrictions of the Boland Amendment governing aid to the contras.

101. Oberdorfer in *WP,* 10/22/85; *ABMTIR,* p. 25.
102. Perle testimony, *ABMTC,* p. 325.
103. Oberdorfer in *WP,* 10/22/85.
104. *ABMTIR,* p. 25; Garthoff, *Great Transition,* pp. 7, 26. ACDA circulated a paper previously prepared by Nitze reflecting the traditional view, and the Defense Department formally responded with the traditional interpretation.
105. *ABMTIR,* p. 26.
106. Ibid. McFarlane asked the various agencies represented for further comments in writing. See also Talbott, *Master of the Game,* p. 246; Nitze, *From Hiroshima to Glasnost,* p. 413.
107. Garthoff, *Policy Versus the Law,* p. 18; Nunn testimony, March 13, 1987, p. 3171.

The Legal Adviser to the State Department is not just a counsel to the State Department but effectively the Legal Adviser to the whole U.S. government on matters relating to treaties and other international obligations *(ABMTIR,* p. 65).

108. *ABMTIR,* pp. 49–50; *ABMTID,* p. 7.

Sofaer testified that no single agency had collected the negotiating record in a readily usable form, but this was not the case. The MEMCONS from the negotiating team were all numbered and could have been located fairly easily. (Interview with Raymond Garthoff, 9/27/99.)

See *ABMTC,* p. 219, on the three young lawyers and the Graybeal/Fitzgerald study.

109. *ABMTC,* p. 215, for Sims discovery; pp. 219–20 for counsels; p. 204 for young lawyers. *ABMTIR,* p. 26, for Karpov statement; p. 64 for committee's conclusion.

Of the three young lawyers, Sims was the only one Sofaer had not brought with him from New York.

110. *ABMTIR,* pp. 27, 62, 64. The committee added that Richard Perle had testified that he had not read the Sofaer memo, and that his "driving curiosity concerning the legality of the 'reinterpretation' set the standard for the Administration."
111. Ibid., p. 25. Perle testified that he asked Kunsberg for a review of the treaty in early September because of the need to respond to Senator Levin's questions. But it was in early September that Gorbachev outlined his arms-control proposals, and since the Defense Department responded to Levin with the traditional interpretation of the treaty, it seems altogether likely that Perle had the forthcoming summit meeting in mind.
112. Talbott, *Master of the Game,* p. 248. Talbott, when writing his book, was inclined to accept the explanation. Sofaer, he writes, was a skilled jurist and an expert in contract law, and Nitze was always "susceptible to the persuasive powers of real experts." Sofaer, he concludes, persuaded Nitze that the ABM Treaty "had been the object of a thirteen-year-old misunderstanding on Nitze's own part as well as everyone else's" (ibid., p. 244).
113. Nitze, *From Hiroshima to Glasnost,* p. 415.
114. During this period, Nitze had a round-robin correspondence with Abraham Becker, Donald Brennan, and others, during which he called Agreed Statement D "a work of supererogation, and not strictly required"—or the opposite of what Sofaer later contended. (Nunn testimony, March 12, 1987, p. 3093. See also Garthoff, *Policy Versus the Law,* p. 6.)
115. Interview with Paul Nitze, August 14, 1990. Nitze said that this was the only point on which Talbott's book was wrong. But Talbott quotes Nitze on the point. Recalling his sessions with Sofaer, Nitze said, "I came away one hundred percent convinced that the permissive, or broad, interpretation was correct." (Talbott, *Master of the Game,* p. 249.)

See *ABMTIR,* p. 27, for Sims's testimony on the Graybeal-Fitzgerald report.

116. Talbott, *Master of the Game,* pp. 248–49; Walter Pincus, quoting *U.S. News & World Report,* in *WP,* 9/22/85.
117. Shultz, *Turmoil and Triumph,* p. 579.
118. Ibid., pp. 578–80.
119. Ibid., p. 581. Shultz also here summarizes quite effortlessly the difference between the traditional and the "broad" interpretations of the treaty.
120. Talbott, *Master of the Game,* p. 245.

Interviewed by Talbott after he left office, McFarlane said that he supported the "broad" interpretation for three reasons: one, he hoped to co-opt, and at the same time maneuver around, the Pentagon civilians, making it look as if he were on their side, so that he would be in a better position to argue them out of conducting SDI tests that would violate the ABM Treaty; two, it would "lay down a marker" to the Soviets, etc.; and, three, he hoped it would convince Reagan to make concessions on SDI.

Whether or not this was exactly what went through his head on October 4 (the congress had banned tests that would violate the ABM Treaty), McFarlane was saying with remarkable candor that Sofaer's legal argument had nothing to do with his decision.

121. *WP,* 9/15/85.
122. *PPP,* vol. II, pp. 1106–7.
123. *WP,* 9/19/85.

The State Department spokesman, Bernard Kalb, said that the President was speaking merely of the testing permitted by the treaty, and that the SDI program would be conducted in full compliance with it. Kalb may well not have known about the "broad" interpretation at the time; probably he was repeating what he had been asked to say. But he, too, could have been speaking of the "broad" interpretation.

124. Pincus in *WP,* 9/22/85.
125. Shultz, *Turmoil and Triumph,* p. 575.
126. David Hoffman in *WP,* 9/20/85.
127. On September 26, the *Washington Post* reported that, in his meeting with Shevardnadze, George Shultz had sought to reassure the Soviet foreign minister that the goal of the United States was to "reinforce" the ABM Treaty, not to change it. Shultz, it appeared, had called for continued adherence to the treaty for now, and a gradual move away from it later. The issue of whether the treaty permitted space-based defenses came up at the meeting, and according to one official would "certainly" come up again at the Geneva summit.

In his memoir, Shultz writes: "We didn't need to gut the treaty in order to do what we needed and wanted to do on SDI. We would be in the research stage for ten years. And, during that time, we could use the strength of SDI to press the Soviets into deep offensive weapons cuts. It made no sense for McFarlane to fuel the controversy now." (Shultz, *Turmoil and Triumph,* p. 580.)

According to a State Department source, Sofaer told an aide who protested the reinterpretation, "Your commander in chief needs this to bargain away Soviet missiles" (David Ignatius, in *WP,* 2/6/87).

128. Walter Pincus reported in *WP,* 10/23/85, that, according to Defense Department sources, one of the decisions taken during the October 4 SAC-G meeting was that the administration was prepared to give the Soviets five to seven years' notice before withdrawing from the ABM Treaty.
129. Nitze, *From Hiroshima to Glasnost,* pp. 413–14.

Nitze seems to have realized that at the time. In his memoir he tells us that he lay awake the night of October 4 worrying about his part in the SAC-G discussion. Though pleased that he had won on the deployment issue, he worried that the new interpretation would put the administration in an awkward position vis-à-vis the Congress and the NATO allies.

On Saturday morning Nitze drafted a memorandum to McFarlane expressing his concerns. He intended to give it to McFarlane on Monday. But by Monday it was too late. After McFarlane made his announcement on *Meet the Press,* all he could do was to warn Shultz of the reaction and advise him to say that as a matter of policy SDI would not be expanded beyond the traditional interpretation of the treaty.

Talbott, *Master of the Game,* p. 246, has much the same account.

130. Talbott, *Master of the Game,* p. 243.

Perle said that word had been spread around that Sofaer was his "plant" inside the State Department. But of course this was not the case.

That Perle never bothered to read the Sofaer memo comes from *ABMTIR,* p. 64.

131. Shultz, *Turmoil and Triumph,* p. 581. In using quotation marks around "clarify," Shultz suggests that he had something other than clarification in mind.
132. Talbott, *Master of the Game,* p. 333; Nitze, *From Hiroshima to Glasnost,* pp. 467–74.

The reinterpretation was not formally rescinded until after the Clinton administration took office in 1993. Bush and Gorbachev sidestepped the issue on signing the START I treaty in 1991.

133. Garthoff, *Great Transition,* p. 229; *NYT,* 10/24/85; Cannon, *President Reagan,* p. 749; Dobrynin, *In Confidence,* p. 579.

Gorbachev promised to retire some of the older SS-4s and -5s and to cap the number of SS-20s at the number reached in July 1984.

134. *NYT,* 10/29/85.
135. *NYT,* 10/24/85, 10/25/85.

Weinberger contended that the SS-25 was the Soviet's second new type of ICBM. SALT II permitted the deployment of only one new type. The Soviets contended that the SS-25 was merely a modification of an older missile, the SS-13. (Garthoff, *Great Transition,* p. 224.) In another provocative move, Pentagon officials in August announced a test of an anti-satellite weapon in space.

136. Dobrynin, *In Confidence,* pp. 579–80; R. W. Apple in *NYT,* 10/25/85; Leslie Gelb in *NYT,* 11/1/85; *WP,* 11/3/85.
137. *NYT,* 11/2/85; *Financial Times,* November 4, 1985; *WP,* 11/3/85.
    The plan was much criticized in Congress, because it called for a ban on mobile missiles: the very weapons that the Scowcroft Commission and the moderates in Congress favored for strategic stability.
138. Dobrynin, *In Confidence,* p. 582.
139. Oberdorfer, *The Turn,* pp. 134–36; Shultz, *Turmoil and Triumph,* pp. 589–94; Garthoff, *Great Transition,* p. 233.
    Gorbachev nonetheless proposed that the two sides cut two to three hundred ICBMs as an earnest of radical reductions to come, but Shultz did not pick up on the idea. The proposal was tabled in Geneva.
140. *NYT,* 11/6/85; *WP,* 11/8/85; Oberdorfer, *The Turn,* p. 139.
141. Shultz, *Turmoil and Triumph,* p. 595; Dobrynin, *In Confidence,* p. 584.
142. Dobrynin, *In Confidence,* p. 586.
143. Ibid., p. 584; Shultz, *Turmoil and Triumph,* pp. 596–97; Garthoff, *Great Transition,* p. 232.
144. Dobrynin, *In Confidence,* pp. 584–86.
145. John Newhouse, "A Reporter in Washington," *New Yorker,* December 9, 1985, p. 137.
    Mrs. Reagan had a horoscope of Gorbachev prepared by her astrologer, Joan Quigley (Regan, *For the Record,* p. 300), so perhaps Reagan read that, too.
146. Regan, *For the Record,* p. 304.
    According to the Harris survey of November 18, 1985, they succeeded in lowering expectations; five out of six Americans felt an accord highly unlikely. That, Harris reports, was good for Reagan. The downside for him at the summit was that fears of nuclear war might rise, and eight out of ten Americans wanted an arms accord.
147. Newhouse, "Reporter in Washington," pp. 138–39.
148. Ibid., p. 138.
149. Ibid., p. 138; McFarlane, *Special Trust,* pp. 312–13.
150. Garthoff, *Great Transition,* p. 235 for "misunderstandings"; Shultz, *Turmoil and Triumph,* p. 582 for "fresh start."
151. Newhouse, *War and Peace,* p. 387.
152. Adelman, *Great Universal Embrace,* p. 136.
153. *NYT,* 11/4/85.
    Reagan went on to explain that defenses would be an insurance policy, like poison-gas masks, after the abolition of nuclear arms. He also said that the strict definition of the ABM Treaty permitted research and testing.
154. *NYT,* 11/5/85; Garthoff, *Great Transition,* p. 232.
    Reagan made a number of other mistakes in the interview. He claimed that the Soviet Union was "occupying" Angola, Ethiopia and South Yemen; that the government of Grenada had asked for U.S. military assistance; and that two Vietnamese states had been created by the Geneva Conference of 1954.
155. Transcript of speech, in *NYT,* 11/15/85.
156. Oberdorfer, *The Turn,* p. 140; Oberdorfer in *WP,* 11/24/85.
157. *NYT,* 11/17/85.
158. *WP,* 9/22/85. The *Post* blanked out the word, but the expression was a familiar one in Reagan's Washington.
    The report had been requested in June, after the decision to continue compliance with SALT II as a sop to the Pentagon civilians.
159. *NYT,* 11/16/85.
160. Shultz, *Turmoil and Triumph,* p. 598.
    According to Shultz, Casey also made an attempt to block any progress at the summit. Casey objected to any effort to improve relations with the Soviets on the grounds that a new Nixon-Kissinger style détente would enable the Soviets to strengthen themselves at home while giving up none of their international objectives. Shultz does not say in what form he made this objection. Also, thirty-nine senators sent Reagan a letter urging him not to give up SDI. (*WP,* 11/15/85.)
    In addition, a collection of Star Wars advocates including Edward Teller, Daniel O. Graham, Lewis Lehrman and Gregory Fossedal visited the President ten days before he went to Geneva. An editorialist for *The Wall Street Journal,* Fossedal, twenty-seven years old, was one of the leading publicists for Graham's High Frontier concept. Fossedal, by his account, gave Reagan a Darth Vader doll that he said was a likeness of Gorbachev; Reagan thanked him and said, "You know, they really are an evil empire." (Sidney Blumenthal in *WP,* 11/22/85.)
161. Shultz, *Turmoil and Triumph,* p. 600; Regan, *For the Record,* p. 305; Adelman, *Great Universal Embrace,* p. 139.
162. Shultz, *Turmoil and Triumph,* pp. 604–5; Oberdorfer, *The Turn,* p. 153; *NYT,* 11/22/85; Newhouse, "Reporter in Washington," p. 130.
    The anti–nuclear-war language was from Reagan's speech to the Japanese Diet in 1983.
163. Shultz, *Turmoil and Triumph,* pp. 601–3; *NYT,* 11/22/85; Newhouse, "Reporter in Washington," p. 130.
164. *NYT,* 11/22/85; Shultz, *Turmoil and Triumph,* pp. 602–3.
    Reagan also said, "Neither side got everything they wanted." This was a strange remark, in that neither side got much of anything, but Reagan, who often spoke of his long experience as a negotiator during his SAG days, often said that successful negotiations ended with neither side getting everything it wanted. (See Reagan, *American Life,* p. 637.)
165. Text of speech, in *NYT,* 11/22/85.

166. Newhouse, "Reporter in Washington," p. 130.
167. Mayer and McManus, *Landslide,* p. 160.

According to the Gallup polls, the approval rating for Reagan's handling of relations with the Soviet Union remained steady at around 52 percent from January to October 1985. After Geneva, it jumped to 65 percent—by far its highest level in his presidency so far—and almost double what it was in 1983. Fifty-seven percent of those polled approved his handling of nuclear-disarmament negotiations. (Poll taken in January 1986.)

Going into the summit, the Harris poll showed that, though more than half of the American public thought Gorbachev more likely than his predecessors to make an agreement on arms control, over 80 percent of the public was wary of the general secretary and felt that the President had better be careful not to be taken in by him (Harris survey, October 3, 1985).

168. Newhouse, "Reporter in Washington," p. 130.
169. Ibid.

Reagan, by the evidence of his memoir, was narrating the myth of the summit even as it was being played out. In the pool house, as they sat before a roaring fire, he told Gorbachev that the two of them were in a unique situation: they were probably the only two men in the world who could bring about World War III, and they were possibly the only two men who might be able to bring peace to the world. They thus owed it to the world to build the kind of trust and confidence in each other that could lead to genuine peace. (Reagan, *American Life,* p. 636.)

170. Reagan, *American Life,* p. 592.
171. Ibid., p. 634.

After the attempt on his life in 1981, Reagan wrote a handwritten note to Brezhnev calling for a constructive dialogue. Apparently he saw a summit meeting as a part of the narrative of his presidency. (See Cannon, *President Reagan,* pp. 298–301.)

172. Larry Speakes with Robert Pack, *Speaking Out: The Reagan Presidency from Inside the White House* (New York: Scribner, 1988), p. 133; see also Shultz, *Turmoil and Triumph,* p. 599.
173. Newhouse, "Reporter in Washington," p. 140.
174. Ibid., p. 130; Regan, *For the Record,* pp. 308–9 for quote; Speakes, *Speaking Out,* p. 130.
175. *NYT,* 11/22/85.
176. Shultz, *Turmoil and Triumph,* pp. 600–607. Shultz writes that the "big day" for Ronald Reagan was November 21—the day after the summit, when Reagan had to talk about it.
177. Newhouse, "Reporter in Washington," p. 137; Garthoff, *Great Transition,* pp. 234–35; Oberdorfer, *The Turn,* p. 154; Regan, *For the Record,* p. 316.

McFarlane praised Reagan in somewhat fainter terms. At the Geneva summit, he said, Reagan had proved "almost unique in his ability to sustain a conversation for more than five minutes" (Cannon, *President Reagan,* p. 751).

According to McFarlane, Reagan at some point in the proceedings leaned over to Shultz and said, "Now tell me again, George, what's the difference between a ballistic missile and a cruise missile?" (Robert Timberg, *The Nightingale's Song* [New York, Simon & Schuster, 1995], p. 286.)

178. McFarlane, *Special Trust,* p. 318.
179. Ibid.; Shultz, *Turmoil and Triumph,* p. 603.

McFarlane writes, "Reagan did not realize that our military and intelligence officials would never go along with open labs."

180. Adelman, *Great Universal Embrace,* p. 141.
181. Shultz, *Turmoil and Triumph,* p. 601.

But, then, apparently no one else on the American side did either. Certainly Adelman did not, and he says that everyone else dismissed the idea. (Adelman, *Great Universal Embrace,* p. 141.) Only Shultz was listening for such a statement.

182. Dobrynin, *In Confidence,* pp. 580–81.
183. Oberdorfer, *The Turn,* pp. 145–46; McFarlane, *Special Trust,* p. 319.

The U.S. interpreter's notes served as a transcript of the private discussions.

Oberdorfer quotes the document as saying, "The sides should provide assurances that their strategic defense programs shall be conducted as permitted by, and in full compliance with, the ABM Treaty. The sides should agree to begin exploring immediately means by which cooperative transition to greater reliance on defensive systems, should such systems prove feasible, could be accomplished." As Oberdorfer points out, the first sentence evaded the issue of what interpretation of the ABM Treaty the administration had in mind.

By Oberdorfer's account, and by McFarlane's, Gorbachev asked Reagan detailed questions about how he interpreted the ABM Treaty, and Reagan indicated that he was talking about the broad interpretation. According to Oberdorfer, Gorbachev reminded Reagan that it had been agreed the previous January, in the Shultz-Gromyko meeting, that there must be an "interrelationship" between offense and defense, but it was not in this document. Reagan said that he didn't see that the two subjects were linked.

Nitze evades the issues of the treaty interpretation (Nitze, *From Hiroshima to Glasnost,* p. 320).

184. Regan, *For the Record,* p. 311.
185. Cannon, *President Reagan,* pp. 752–53; see Dobrynin, *In Confidence,* p. 589, for agreement on summits, and Adelman, *Great Universal Embrace,* p. 157, for reasoning.
186. Adelman, *Great Universal Embrace,* p. 124.

187. Ibid., p. 137; Regan,*For the Record,* p. 312; see Reagan, *American Life,* p. 640, on talk of problems with bureaucracy, and Oberdorfer,*The Turn,* p. 144, on creatures from outer space.
188. Regan, *For the Record,* p. 313; Adelman, *Great Universal Embrace,* p. 137.
189. Dobrynin, *In Confidence,* p. 588; Adelman, *Great Universal Embrace,* p. 137.
190. Regan, *For the Record,* pp. 316–17.
191. Shultz, *Turmoil and Triumph,* p. 602; Adelman, *Great Universal Embrace,* pp. 155–56.
192. Dobrynin, *In Confidence,* p. 588.
193. *NYT,* 11/22/85.
194. Adelman,*Great Universal Embrace,* p. 156.
195. Dobrynin, *In Confidence,* p. 592; Oberdorfer, *The Turn,* p. 154.
196. *WP,* 11/25/85.
197. Reagan, *American Life,* p. 635. Reagan also writes that Gorbachev did not speak of a "one world Communist state" the way every other Soviet leader he had heard of did, and he tells us that Gorbachev reminded him of Tip O'Neill (ibid., pp. 641, 639). Otherwise, Reagan reported only what others said about the general secretary.
198. Ibid., p. 272. This comes from a handwritten letter Reagan sent Brezhnev just after the assassination attempt in April 1981.

EIGHT: What Happened at Reykjavik?

1. John E. Rielly, ed., *American Public Opinion and U.S. Foreign Policy* (Chicago: Chicago Council on Foreign Relations, 1987), p. 29.
2. Post-midterm-election analysis by Hoffman in *WP,* 11/30/86.
3. Donald Regan, *For the Record* (New York: Harcourt Brace Jovanovich, 1988), pp. 101–34.
4. Ibid., p. 140; Jane Mayer and Doyle McManus, *Landslide* (Boston: Houghton Mifflin, 1988), pp. 38–39; Cannon, *President Reagan,* p. 563.
5. Regan, *For the Record,* pp. 153–62.
6. Ibid., pp. 175, 190–91; David Stockman, *The Triumph of Politics: How the Reagan Revolution Failed* (New York: Harper and Row, 1986), pp. 269–70, 377, 393–94; Cannon, *President Reagan,* pp. 562–63.
7. Regan, *For the Record,* pp. 218–20; Cannon, *President Reagan,* pp. 555–56.

   Later, when Ed Rollins asked Regan why he would leave one of the most prestigious jobs in the administration to become a staffer, Regan reportedly said, "Well, I've sat over here for four years being ordered around by assholes like you at the White House. I've learned where the power is." (Ed Rollins, *Bare Knuckles and Back Rooms* [New York: Broadway Books, 1996], p. 158.)
8. Mayer and McManus, *Landslide,* p. 39.
9. Cannon, *President Reagan,* pp. 567–69.
10. Rollins, *Bare Knuckles,* p. 157; Mayer and McManus, *Landslide,* pp. 43–44, 131.

    Knowing that he lacked experience in the political domain, he kept on Ed Rollins, Reagan's campaign manager, and Max Friedersdorf, his congressional-liaison director, to tend to political affairs and congressional relations, but when both told him he could not pass a budget without cutting middle-class entitlements and without raising taxes, he let them go. The White House was irrelevant to the budgetary process from then on.
11. Mayer and McManus, *Landslide,* p. 161.

    In his memoir Regan tells us a lot about the dinner parties and almost nothing of the substantive discussions at the Geneva summit. With respect to the proposals at Reykjavik, he is ludicrously wrong, as will be discussed later.
12. Ibid., p. 131; Hedrick Smith, *The Power Game* (New York: Random House, 1988), p. 381. Reagan made the comment after Pretoria imposed martial law, causing weeks of racial violence.
13. Regan, *For the Record,* pp. 13–14; Mayer and McManus, *Landslide,* p. 114; U.S. Congress, *Iran-Contra Investigation: Joint Hearings Before the House Select Committee to Investigate Covert Arms Transfers with Iran and the Senate Select Committee on Secret Military Assistance to Iran and the Nicaraguan Opposition,* 100th Cong., 2nd sess., testimony of Donald T. Regan, July 30, 1987, p. 10.

    Mrs. Reagan contended that only the President and foreign heads of state used the helicopter pad on the White House lawn.
14. Smith, *Power Game,* p. 371.
15. Regan, *For the Record,* pp. 243–44; Cannon, pp. 570–71.

    Buchanan was responsible for most of Reagan's utterances on South Africa.
16. Mayer and McManus, *Landslide,* p. 162.
17. Cannon, *President Reagan,* p. 596.
18. George Shultz, *Turmoil and Triumph* (New York: Scribner, 1993), pp. 524, 536, 561, 572, 585; McFarlane, *Special Trust,* p. 33; Mayer and McManus, *Landslide,* p. 64.
19. Mayer and McManus, *Landslide,* p. 64; Robert Timberg, *The Nightingale's Song* (New York: Simon & Schuster, 1995), p. 360.
20. Mayer and McManus, *Landslide,* p. 60 for quote; Timberg, *Nightingale's Song,* pp. 361–62.
21. Timberg, *Nightingale's Song,* p. 362.
22. Cannon, *President Reagan,* p. 597; quote in Mayer and McManus, *Landslide,* p. 165.

23. McFarlane, *Special Trust,* pp. 327–28 for quote; Timberg, *Nightingale's Song,* pp. 362–63.
24. McFarlane, *Special Trust,* pp. 328–29; Mayer and McManus, *Landslide,* pp. 133, 162–64.
25. McFarlane, *Special Trust,* p. 332, for quote; Mayer and McManus, *Landslide,* pp. 161, 169–70.

    Later he explained his decision in a variety of ways. He told Meyer and McManus, for example, that he had deceived the press by portraying Reagan as a Soviet expert and on top of matters in Geneva, and when it was over he just didn't want to be any part of that struggle anymore.
26. Timberg, *Nightingale's Song,* pp. 166–71, and 240–48; Mayer and McManus, *Landslide,* p. 174.
27. Mayer and McManus, *Landslide,* p. 174; Timberg, *Nightingale's Song,* p. 107; Cannon, *President Reagan,* p. 625; Colin Powell, *My American Journey* (New York: Random House, 1995), p. 309.
28. Shultz, *Turmoil and Triumph,* p. 822.

    At a time when he was making recommendations to the President opposing sanctions on South Africa, he made the astonishing statement to Lou Cannon that the African National Congress had a very small following in South Africa (Cannon, *President Reagan,* p. 625).
29. Timberg, *Nightingale's Song,* pp. 242–48.
30. Powell, *American Journey,* pp. 308–9.
31. Cannon, *President Reagan,* p. 625.

    According to Deaver, Shultz said, "I think he'll be good." According to Bob Woodward, Casey was glad to see the change, because Poindexter was another hard-liner (Bob Woodward, *Veil* [New York: Simon & Schuster, 1987], p. 427).
32. Timberg, *Nightingale's Song,* p. 373; Cannon, *President Reagan,* p. 625; Mayer and McManus, *Landslide,* pp. 174–75; Smith, *Power Game,* p. 436.

    On occasion he deliberately misinformed the press. On the eve of the Grenada invasion, when Larry Speakes, attempting to answer a reporter, asked him for guidance, he, rather than saying "No comment," said, "No invasion of Grenada. Preposterous. Knock it down." Speakes, who knew nothing of the invasion, repeated his words verbatim to the press.

    Then, in the summer of 1986, he involved the American press in a "disinformation" campaign to persuade Qaddafi that the U.S. was planning another attack.
33. Mayer and McManus, *Landslide,* pp. 174–75; Frances FitzGerald, "Death of a Salesman," *Rolling Stone,* February 25, 1988.
34. Mayer and McManus, *Landslide,* p. 30.
35. Roy Gutman, *Banana Diplomacy: The Making of American Policy in Nicaragua 1981–1987* (New York: Simon & Schuster, 1988), p. 317; Timberg, *Nightingale's Song,* p. 377.

    As an active-duty Navy admiral, Poindexter was technically Weinberger's subordinate. If he expected further promotion—and particularly if he expected to become CNO—he had to be mindful of Weinberger's views. One of the first things he did on becoming NSC adviser was to institute weekly meetings with the President for the secretary of defense.
36. Shultz, *Turmoil and Triumph,* pp. 798–802.
37. Ibid., pp. 614–40.

    In the 1984 campaign debate, Reagan had said that the Marcoses faced "a large Communist movement" and therefore it was better "to retain our friendship and help them right the wrongs we see rather than throwing them to the wolves and then facing a Communist power in the Pacific." (Ibid., p. 611.)

    Though the CIA analysts reported otherwise, Casey continued to press the view that the Communists were extremely strong—along with his view that Cory Aquino was a weak woman who could not conceivably stand up to them. According to Woodward, his influence on the President was decisive. (Woodward, *Veil,* pp. 437–38.)

    Shultz says nothing about Casey in this context. But he tells us that, in January, A. M. Rosenthal, the executive editor of the *New York Times,* came to Washington after a trip to the Philippines and told him that Aquino was "an empty-headed housewife" and "a dazed and vacant woman." Rosenthal repeated this assessment at a White House dinner, and according to Shultz his words made a deep and lasting impact on the President, Mrs. Reagan and Don Regan. (Shultz, *Turmoil and Triumph,* p. 617.)
38. Strobe Talbott, *Master of the Game: Paul Nitze and the Nuclear Peace* (New York: Knopf, 1988), p. 289; Don Oberdorfer, *The Turn: From the Cold War to the New Era* (New York: Poseidon Press, 1991), pp. 156–57; Ronald Reagan, *An American Life* (New York: Simon & Schuster, 1990), p. 649.

    In early February, Gorbachev told Senator Edward Kennedy in Moscow that he would not commit himself to a date for the summit until there was some indication of progress. Elsewhere, Gorbachev maintained that he was not establishing any precondition for a summit, but that real progress on arms control was necessary, and there would be no sense holding "empty talks." (Raymond L. Garthoff, *The Great Transition* [Washington, D.C.: Brookings Institution, 1987], pp. 265–66.)
39. Talbott, *Master of the Game,* p. 289; Shultz, p. 699.
40. Mikhail Gorbachev, *Socialism, Peace and Democracy* (Atlantic Highlands, N. J.: Zwan Publications, 1987), pp. 36–46.
41. Shultz, *Turmoil and Triumph,* p. 700; Talbott, *Russians and Reagan,* p. 284.

    This was the line Reagan was taking before Geneva.
42. Shultz, *Turmoil and Triumph,* pp. 699–700; Paul Nitze with Ann M. Smith and Steven L. Rearden, *From Hiroshima to Glasnost: At the Center of Decision—a Memoir* (New York: Grove Weidenfeld, 1989), p. 422.
43. Shultz, *Turmoil and Triumph,* p. 700.
44. Ibid.; Nitze, *From Hiroshima to Glasnost,* p. 422.

45. Nitze, *From Hiroshima to Glasnost,* pp. 421–22; Shultz, *Turmoil and Triumph,* pp. 701–2.
46. Shultz, *Turmoil and Triumph,* pp. 701, 704.
47. Ibid., pp. 701–2; Nitze, *From Hiroshima to Glasnost,* p. 422.
48. Reagan, *American Life,* p. 657, for text of letter.

Reagan repeated in writing what he had said to Gorbachev in Geneva: "If there were no nuclear missiles, then there might also be no need for defenses against them." But then he added, "What I am convinced is that some non-nuclear defenses could make a vital contribution to security and stability."

Shultz almost did not prevail. The text proposed by the NSC staff for Reagan's letter did not even mention INF—and Shultz discovered that a "high-level official," apparently from the Defense Department, had urged French and Japanese officials to put pressure on their governments to oppose the INF agreement he was seeking. (Shultz, *Turmoil and Triumph,* pp. 708–9.)

49. Anatoly Dobrynin, *In Confidence: Moscow's Ambassador to America's Six Cold War Presidents (1962–1986)* (New York: Times Books, 1995), p. 599, for objections; Garthoff, *Great Transition,* p. 22; Shultz, *Turmoil and Triumph,* pp. 708–9; Mikhail Gorbachev, *The Challenges of Our Time* (New York: International Publishers, 1986), pp. 77–79.
50. Oberdorfer, *The Turn,* p. 159.
51. Gorbachev, *Challenges of Our Time,* pp. 1–86, for text of report to the congress.
52. Ibid., pp. 19–22.
53. Ibid., pp. 72–86 for quotes; see also Garthoff, *Great Transition,* pp. 258–59.

Gorbachev justified the Soviet intervention in Afghanistan—which he characterized as a "bleeding wound"—on the grounds of the Soviet need for secure borders and peaceful neighbors. He mentioned no other Third World country in his report. (Gorbachev, *Challenges,* p. 80.)

54. Garthoff, *Great Transition,* pp. 261–63; Oberdorfer, *The Turn,* p. 158.
55. Eduard Shevardnadze, *The Future Belongs to Freedom* (New York: Free Press, 1991), pp. 48–49; for Akhromeyev quote, Oberdorfer, *The Turn,* p. 161.

Shevardnadze writes that even at the Nineteenth All-Union Party Congress, in July 1988, "peaceful coexistence" was still understood by many as a specific form of class struggle rather than as simply peace.

56. Shevardnadze, *Future,* p. 51; Garthoff, *Great Transition,* p. 263 for quote.
57. Oberdorfer, *The Turn,* pp. 162–64; Dobrynin, *In Confidence,* p. 619.
58. Robert M. Gates, *From the Shadows* (New York: Simon & Schuster, 1996), p. 380.
59. Shultz, *Turmoil and Triumph,* pp. 702–7; phone interview with Morton Abromowitz (chief of the State Department Policy Planning Staff under Shultz), 7/11/96.
60. Shultz, *Turmoil and Triumph,* pp. 702–3, 706–7.
61. Garthoff, *Great Transition,* pp. 531–32; Caspar Weinberger, *Fighting for Peace* (New York: Warner Books, 1990), pp. 332, 347–48.
62. Gutman, *Banana Diplomacy,* p. 269.

In his "Reagan-doctrine" speech of January 9, 1985, Casey put the behavior of Marxists in the Third World on a par with the Nazis. He spoke of Afghanistan, Angola, Cambodia, Ethiopia and Nicaragua as "occupied countries," and said of them, "In the aggregate there has occurred a holocaust comparable to that which Nazi Germany inflicted in Europe some forty years ago." He did not differentiate Nicaragua from Afghanistan, or stop to say that the Vietnamese occupiers of Cambodia had stopped the holocaust perpetrated by the Khmer Rouge—whose seat in the UN the U.S. continued to support.

63. Gates, *From the Shadows,* p. 332.

According to Bob Woodward, Casey for years used intelligence data on Soviet military planning to help Weinberger sabotage arms control (Woodward, *Veil,* pp. 489–90).

U.S. Senate, *Nomination of Robert M. Gates to Be Director of Central Intelligence: Report of the Select Committee on Intelligence,* 102nd Cong., 1st sess., October 24, 1991, p. 175.

Casey also attempted to change intelligence estimates to support his own policy goals. According to John McMahon, the Deputy Director of CIA before Gates, Casey wanted the CIA to show that Mexico was falling apart because of internal and external pressures. This would have made the case that leftist groups in Central America were destabilizing the entire region and menacing the United States. But this the Intelligence Directorate refused to do.

64. Shultz, *Turmoil and Triumph,* p. 711.
65. Ibid., pp. 703, 710.
66. *WP,* 2/22/85, 2/23/85, 2/26/85; Garthoff, *Great Transition,* nn. 6 and 7 on p. 506.
67. Noel E. Firth and James H. Noren, *Soviet Defense Spending: A History of CIA Estimates, 1950–1990* (Texas: Texas A&M University Press, 1998), pp. 75–79, 88–89, 102 (page 78 for quote). See also *WP,* 2/22/85, 2/23/85, 2/26/85, 3/31/86.

Firth and Norman were SOVA analysts for many years, and their book was sponsored by the CIA's Center for the Study of Intelligence.

More precisely, Soviet outlays for intercontinental strategic forces declined 40 percent between 1974 and 1981.

Firth and Norman do not say this, but Team B was largely responsible for the overly high estimates of the late 1970s.

68. Firth and Norman, *Soviet Defense Spending,* pp. 82–87, 94–96 (page 94 for quote). See also Douglas J. MacEachin, "CIA Assessments of the Soviet Union: the Record versus the Charges," *Studies in Intelligence,* vol. 01, no. 1, (1997), pp. 4–5.

The 1985 National Intelligence Estimate declared that economic considerations alone would not "lead the Soviets to abandon major strategic-weapon programs, to forsake force modernization goals, or to make substantial concessions in arms control." Even the 1987 NIE took almost no account of the possibility that economic constraints might affect Soviet strategic programs in the late 1980s (Firth and Norman, *Soviet Defense Spending,* pp. 86–87).

There are numerous discrepancies between Gates's memoir and the subsequent book by Firth and Norman. For example, Gates implies that he criticized SOVA's economic reporting because he suspected that Soviet economic growth was lower than 2 percent per year. He also implies that the difference over the force projections was within SOVA rather than between SOVA and the national intelligence officers, of which he was one (Gates, *From the Shadows,* pp. 332, 386–87; Firth and Norman, *Soviet Defense Spending,* p. 240 n.82).

69. Gates, *From the Shadows,* pp. 336–37, 381; U.S. Senate, *Nomination of Robert M. Gates,* pp. 129–33, 178.

At the hearings on Gates's confirmation as director of intelligence in 1991, analysts at the CIA's Office of Soviet Analysis testified that all the indices of Soviet intervention in the Third World—military and economic aid, advisers, ship visits and so on—were level or declining by 1985.

Gates's speech could have been better timed. He made it on November 26, the day after Meese's revelation of the diversion in the Iran-contra affair. In 1991 Gates said that this was his own analysis, not the CIA's—though the distinction must have been somewhat obscure to his audience—and that he was using "poetic license" (U.S. Senate, *Nomination of Robert Gates,* p. 178).

70. Gates, *From the Shadows,* pp. 330–36, 343, 375–76; interview with Gates, 7/16/96.
71. Gates, *From the Shadows,* p. 331.
72. Ibid., p. 377.
73. Ibid., pp. 331–33.
74. Ibid., p. 343.
75. Ibid., p. 377.
76. Ibid., pp. 342–43.

In my interview, I asked Gates about the memo to Casey he quotes on p. 343, which seems to conflict with his advice to Reagan; he assured me it did not.

In *From the Shadows* (p. 404) Gates writes, "Everyone knew by the end of 1985 that Gorbachev . . . needed to constrain the arms race, and new strategic programs in particular, to avoid new Soviet military expenditures and perhaps even allow some reductions in spending." But apparently this was not what he said at the time.

Gates in his memoir writes that for Casey "there was no line between policy advocacy and intelligence." But he says that the documentary record shows that the Intelligence Directorate in this period preserved its objectivity and integrity. "We were honest," he says, "even if we were not always right." (Ibid., pp. 332–33, 386–87.)

Yet, in Gates's confirmation hearings as director of central intelligence in 1991, CIA analysts from the Office of Soviet Analysis (SOVA) presented a good deal of evidence to show that Gates repeatedly turned back reports which Casey did not like and created an agency view of the Soviet Union which ignored Soviet weaknesses and exaggerated its aggressiveness abroad.

In 1991 Mel Goodman, formerly a manager and senior CIA analyst in the Office of Soviet Analysis, testified that on more than twenty issues Gates attempted to impose his views—or, more precisely, Casey's—on the DI. Goodman, who had been in charge of the estimates on Soviet involvement in the Third World, may have had it in for Gates, but in most cases his allegations were backed up by the testimony of others or by documentary evidence. In the hearings Gates had the opportunity to refute these charges, but—at least in the unclassified report of the Senate Intelligence Committee—many of his explanations seem weak. For example, he often attempted to shift the blame to others rather than acknowledging responsibility for what indisputably occurred. Goodman was removed from his job as manager and Soviet–Third World analyst in SOVA; he charged Gates with having him removed, and Gates said that Douglas MacEachin, the chief of SOVA, was responsible. But MacEachin, still a CIA employee, testified that Gates told him to remove Goodman from the Office of Soviet Analysis entirely.

The public record also shows that at least on one occasion Gates gave the kind of policy advice that Casey wanted to hear.

In a memo to Casey dated December 14, 1984, Gates, then Casey's chief of staff, writes that Nicaragua is a "Marxist-Leninist regime" closely aligned with the Cubans and Moscow. "Hopes for causing the regime to reform itself for a more pluralistic government are essentially silly and hopeless," so what we face is "a second Cuba in Central America." What is happening in Central America, he writes, "calls to mind our attempt to reach an accommodation with Castro [in 1959–60]" and "our Vietnam strategy of half-measures" ending in negotiations which became "a cover for consolidation of Communist control."

Judging, as most in the CIA and the military did at the time, that the contras were incapable of defeating the Sandinistas, Gates called for American air strikes on the "Nicaraguan military build-up." (Peter Kornbluh and Malcolm Byrne, eds., *The Iran-Contra Scandal: The Declassified History* [New York: New Press, 1993], pp. 45–49.)

76. Shultz, *Turmoil and Triumph,* pp. 703–7.
77. Dobrynin, *In Confidence,* p. 600.
78. Gates, *From the Shadows,* pp. 359–60; Garthoff, *Great Transition,* p. 269; Oberdorfer, *The Turn,* pp. 165–66.
79. Oberdorfer, *The Turn,* p. 166; Garthoff, *Great Transition,* pp. 269–70, 273–74; Woodward, *Veil,* p. 456; Shultz, *Turmoil and Triumph,* p. 713.

According to Oberdorfer, the administration had sent ships provocatively close to the Soviet coasts since early in the first term, always asserting "the right of innocent passage." This case was different because of the type of vessel and because their mission was clearly to collect intelligence. The Soviets lodged a strong protest and warned that any repetition of such an act could have "serious consequences." The mission had, as usual, been cleared with the State Department in advance. Though Pentagon officials probably did not know it, Gorbachev was in the leadership dacha in the town of Livadia, not far away.

According to Woodward, the U.S. had plans to send a U.S. nuclear submarine not only into Soviet territorial waters but up one of their rivers.

80. Garthoff, *Great Transition,* p. 270.
81. Shultz, *Turmoil and Triumph,* p. 713; Geoffrey Smith, *Reagan and Thatcher* (New York: W. W. Norton, 1991), pp. 190–97; Garthoff, *Great Transition,* pp. 270, 274–75.
82. Garthoff, *Great Transition,* pp. 271–72; Gutman, *Banana Diplomacy,* p. 322; *PPP* RR, vol. I (1986), p. 835, for Soviet base.

On March 14 Reagan sent a message to Congress asking for support for arming "freedom fighters" around the world to resist "Soviet expansionism." Continuing Soviet "adventurism" in the developing world was, he said, "an obstacle to fundamental improvement of Soviet-American relations."

In a message to Congress on the strategic modernization program on June 3, Reagan said that the Soviets "in building a first-strike capability never accepted the premise that the West should be allowed to possess secure retaliatory forces" (*PPP* RR, vol. I [1986], p. 709).

83. Reagan, *American Life,* pp. 660–61; Oberdorfer, *The Turn,* p. 184.
84. Reagan, *American Life,* pp. 662–64, for partial text.

In this letter Gorbachev wrote that the cessation of nuclear tests could be accompanied by a "specific, single-purpose meeting"—one that "would not be a substitute for the new major meeting that we agreed upon in Geneva."

85. Garthoff, *Great Transition,* p. 275.

In June the Warsaw Pact nations followed the offer up with a formal proposal, suggesting that a new forum be created under the Conference on Security and Cooperation in Europe to deal with conventional disarmament. Washington, however, dismissed the proposal as another Soviet propaganda stunt, and it was not until two years later, when the Soviets reintroduced it—this time offering to make asymmetrical reductions to bring the larger Soviet and Warsaw Pact forces to parity with the NATO forces—that the negotiations got under way.

86. Ibid., pp. 276–78; Oberdorfer, *The Turn,* pp. 129–41, 167–68; Dusko Doder and Louise Branscom, *Gorbachev* (New York: Viking, 1990), pp. 129–41.

The Soviet report on Chernobyl to the International Atomic Energy Agency four months later was candid.

87. Talbott, *Master of the Game,* pp. 227, 230, Kenneth Adelman, *The Great Universal Embrace: Arms Summitry, a Skeptic's Account* (New York: Simon & Schuster, 1989), pp. 267–71.
88. Adelman, *Great Universal Embrace,* pp. 271–78.

By the time of the first NSC meeting the only options the hard-liners had managed to come up with were to drydock the Poseidons, to put three-warhead ICBMs into silos containing one-warhead missiles and to boost research on chemical weapons. As Adelman later admitted, none of these measures had much military support or much military rationale.

After the first meeting fifty-two members of the Republican-controlled Senate wrote the President advocating that he stay within the SALT terms, and thirty-four wrote asking him to end "interim restraint." Poindexter's comment was that the first group consisted mainly of those who often opposed the administration on controversial defense issues, and the latter consisted of stalwart administration supporters. This was true, but the first group controlled the defense budget.

89. Ibid.; Smith, *Power Game,* pp. 591–92.

At some point the following exchange took place:

Weinberger: "I've never liked SALT II, and neither have you, Mr. President."

Meese: "Mr. President, you gave a hundred speeches against SALT II and never liked it."

Reagan: "Never liked it at all."

90. Adelman, *Great Universal Embrace,* p. 285; Talbott, *Russians and Reagan,* p. 228.
91. Nitze, *From Hiroshima to Glasnost,* p. 424; Talbott, *Russians and Reagan,* p. 305.

Perle made the uproar worse by telling a House Armed Services subcommittee, "Either the Congress will stand with the Administration . . . or the Congress will stand with the Soviets" on the SALT II decision—and by blandly predicting that the Soviets would not increase their strategic forces because "there is no military rationale for deployment by the Soviets of more weapons than they are permitted to have under the SALT II treaty." This, of course, was the case the Joint Chiefs had been making about the American forces. (Pincus in *WP,* 6/6/86; second quote from *WP,* 6/13/86.)

92. *PPP* RR, vol. I (1986), pp. 711, 749, 759–60.

In his June 3 speech to Congress, Reagan said that the U.S. would, technically speaking, remain in compliance with SALT II for some months, "thus giving the Soviet Union more time to correct their erosion of SALT. If they do, I will take this into account." In other words, he appeared to condition a final SALT II decision on Soviet behavior in regard to SALT II. In a June 11 press conference he seemed to condition it on Soviet behavior in the START talks. On June 12 reporters tried several times to pin him down, but Reagan kept changing the subject and talking about replacing SALT with a better treaty. Finally, one of them said,

"Larry Speakes told us very definitely that [SALT II] is dead, and yet you won't say it." It was to this that Reagan replied, "I think you can trust what Larry Speakes said to you."

93. Talbott, *Russians and Reagan*, pp. 300–302; Nitze, *From Hiroshima to Glasnost*, pp. 426–27; Shultz, *Turmoil and Triumph*, p. 718.

The Soviets wanted to discuss the term "development" as it applied to ABM components and prototypes. They also called for a ban on ASAT weapons and space-to-earth weapons. In regard to offensive strategic weapons, they now called for ceilings of twelve hundred launchers and eight thousand charges, which would allow them to keep more of the heavy MIRVed ICBMs. But they loosened their proposed constraints on cruise missiles, agreeing to permit them on heavy bombers and submarines.

94. *PPP* RR, vol. I (1986), pp. 809–10; Garthoff, *Great Transition*, pp. 278–79.

95. Nitze, *From Hiroshima to Glasnost*, pp. 423–25; Talbott, *Russians and Reagan*, pp. 306–7.

96. Oberdorfer, *The Turn*, pp. 170–72. Oberdorfer, who saw the notes, tells us that the "zero missile initiative" was listed under the heading "public relations"—as opposed to other categories of initiatives discussed.

97. Shultz, *Turmoil and Triumph*, p. 716.

98. Ibid., pp. 717–18.

Two days later Weinberger gave the first American response to the Soviet proposal that the two sides remain within the ABM Treaty for fifteen to twenty years. He called the offer a "side door" to killing SDI. "The Soviets," he said, "know you can't get funding for a program if you've said you're not going to use it for 10 years." Such an agreement, he added, would cause SDI research "to lose a great deal of momentum" and cause a "loss of all public support for the possibility of ever deploying a strategic defense." (*WP*, 6/5/86.)

Reagan's diary for June 17 reads: ". . . Cap and George Shultz differ on some elements [of the letter to Gorbachev], such as what to say about the ABM treaty. On this I'm closer to Cap. I want to propose a new treaty for what we do if and when SDI research looks like we have a practical system." (Reagan, *American Life*, p. 666.)

99. Shultz, *Turmoil and Triumph*, pp. 719–20. See also Talbott, *Russians and Reagan*, p. 311.

Apparently Kampelman persuaded Shultz that Perle might eventually be co-opted into supporting a strategic-arms agreement. They were mistaken.

100. Shultz, *Turmoil and Triumph*, pp. 723–24; Talbott, *Russians and Reagan*, pp. 306–7; Nitze, *From Hiroshima to Glasnost*, p. 424.

Nitze says he became aware of the draft around the end of May, but he must mean June (Nitze, *From Hiroshima to Glasnost*, p. 424).

No source gives the exact text of the first draft, but according to Nitze and Talbott, the first draft was not very different from the last one. Only Shultz intimates that it was different.

101. Nitze, *From Hiroshima to Glasnost*, pp. 425–26; Talbott, *Russians and Reagan*, p. 308.

102. Nitze, *From Hiroshima to Glasnost*, p. 426; Oberdorfer, *The Turn*, p. 174.

Admiral Crowe was given the final draft and informed that, since Shultz and Weinberger had approved it, he should not rock the boat. He did not, because he thought the Soviets were likely to reject it anyway, and he thought it nothing more than an "abstract principle." (Oberdorfer, p. 174.)

103. Shultz, *Turmoil and Triumph*, p. 723.

104. Ibid., p. 724; Nitze, *From Hiroshima to Glasnost*, pp. 427–28; Talbott, *Master of the Game*, pp. 307–10.

Shultz, bewilderingly, tells us that it was "a different version of the approach Nitze and I had advocated: a restriction on SDI that did not really restrict us and the reductions we sought in strategic weapons." Nitze, who certainly did not see it as such, says nothing of Shultz's calculations or role in the discussions. But he does say that Weinberger wanted to "novate" the ABM Treaty—that is, change it by agreement with the Soviets. That was the essence of the proposal.

105. *WSJ*, 8/21/86; Associated Press, 8/21/86; *WSJ*, 8/25/86.

106. Nitze, *From Hiroshima to Glasnost*, p. 427; Talbott, *Master of the Game*, pp. 307–10; Shultz, *Turmoil and Triumph*, p. 723.

Shultz does not admit that the "broad" interpretation was involved; Nitze spells it out.

107. Oberdorfer, *The Turn*, p. 174; Reagan, *American Life*, pp. 669–72, for text of Gorbachev's letter; Shultz, *Turmoil and Triumph*, p. 724.

108. Shultz, *Turmoil and Triumph*, p. 725.

109. Talbott, *Master of the Game*, p. 230.

110. *PPP* RR, vol. I (1986), pp. 984–88, for text of speech; Shultz, *Turmoil and Triumph*, p. 725.

To add insult to injury, Jonathan Miller, one of Regan's "Mice," had started refusing Shultz's routine requests for military aircraft to take him on his trips abroad. This was the reason Shultz gave the Iran-contra committees for his offer to resign—presumably in order to avoid discussing his policy differences with the President. The result was that a number of journalists and historians, including Theodore Draper, thought he was threatening to resign for trivial reasons. (Theodore Draper, *A Very Thin Line* [New York: Hill and Wang, 1991], p. 260.)

111. Shultz, *Turmoil and Triumph*, pp. 726–27.

112. Nitze, *From Hiroshima to Glasnost*, p. 428; Dante B. Fascell, "Congress and Arms Control," *Foreign Affairs*, vol. 65, no. 4 (Spring 1987), pp. 730–49.

113. Oberdorfer, *The Turn*, pp. 184–85 for quote; Garthoff, *Great Transition*, pp. 280–81.

114. Gates, *From the Shadows*, p. 365 for quote; Garthoff, *Great Transition*, pp. 281–82; Oberdorfer, *The Turn*, pp. 174–75.

115. Shultz, *Turmoil and Triumph*, pp. 728–29.
116. Ibid., p. 730.
117. *WSJ*, 9/9/86.
118. Ibid.; Shultz, *Turmoil and Triumph*, pp. 729–30; Garthoff, *Great Transition*, p. 282; Gates, *From the Shadows*, p. 367.

Reagan wrote Gorbachev that Daniloff was not a spy based on assurances from the CIA; when Gorbachev refused to take his word, he sent a stiff, angry message on the hot line. It was the first time the hot line had ever been used in this way.

119. *WP*, 9/18/86.
120. *WP*, 9/16/86; Reagan, *American Life*, p. 668.
121. Gates, *From the Shadows*, pp. 361–62.

The same month, unbeknownst to U.S. officials, the Soviets recruited a career CIA Soviet analyst, Aldrich Ames.

122. Ibid.; Garthoff, *Great Transition*, p. 224.
123. Gates, *From the Shadows*, pp. 362–65; Garthoff, *Great Transition*, pp. 224–25.

Yurchenko tipped off the CIA to Edward Lee Howard, a CIA Soviet-operations officer, who had been fired for drug use and heavy drinking. Howard, however, gave the FBI the slip, fled the country and later turned up in Moscow. Yurchenko also fingered William Pelton, a former National Security Agency employee, who had given the Soviets information on some of America's most sensitive technical intelligence information.

124. Gates, *From the Shadows*, pp. 359–61; Garthoff, *Great Transition*, pp. 268–69.

The State Department put off the announcement until after the Geneva summit, and then until after the party congress, but at that point it could no longer hold up the order.

125. Garthoff, *Great Transition*, p. 281; Oberdorfer, *The Turn*, p. 176; Walter Pincus and David Ottoway in *WP*, 9/14/86.

Pincus and Ottoway made the connection between the arrest of Zakharov and the previous spy embarrassments. By their account, Zakharov had no classified information except the three documents the FBI had provided.

David Hoffman in *WP*, 9/22/86, quotes officials saying that the Zakharov arrest was "part of a larger strategy to crack down on Soviet spying at the UN."

Because the attempt to crack down on Soviet spying at the UN had been highly politicized, the FBI may have felt itself under pressure to make an arrest. The administration officials who approved the arrest apparently did not understand just how the rules had been broken.

126. Shultz, *Turmoil and Triumph*, p. 733; Oberdorfer, *The Turn*, p. 177; Gates, *From the Shadows*, p. 366.
127. Gates, *From the Shadows*, pp. 366–67; Oberdorfer, *The Turn*, p. 177; Garthoff, *Great Transition*, p. 283, Shultz, *Turmoil and Triumph*, pp. 731–34.

In addition, Shultz was told by David Gergen of *U.S. News & World Report* that Daniloff had obtained some Soviet documents marked "secret" and sent them back to the magazine.

The KGB later videotaped Daniloff taking the packet of materials on Soviet military activities in Afghanistan from his informant (Garthoff, *Great Transition*, p. 283).

128. Shultz, *Turmoil and Triumph*, pp. 734–35, 737–39; Gates, *From the Shadows*, p. 367.

On September 17 Reagan wrote in his diary: "The press is obsessed with the Daniloff affair and determined to paint all of us as caving in to the Soviets which they of course say is the worst way to deal with them. The simple truth is we've offered no deal and are playing hardball all the way. . . ." This was hardly the case, though perhaps Poindexter presented it in this way (Ronald Reagan, *An American Life*, p. 668).

129. Shultz, *Turmoil and Triumph*, pp. 742–47.
130. Cannon in *WP*, 9/30/86, for White House statements; Shultz, *Turmoil and Triumph*, pp. 739, 745–46, 748.

Their achievement was particularly remarkable in that while he and Shultz negotiated the administration went forward with naval maneuvers off the Soviet coast in the Sea of Okhotsk—another provocative incursion into Soviet waters.

Also, there was a last-minute hitch which almost derailed the whole exchange. On September 29 the U.S. attorneys prosecuting the case in New York refused to release Zakharov: they had a confession and were seeking a life sentence. The problem was not resolved until the following morning, when, at Shultz's request, Attorney General Meese stepped in.

131. Garthoff, *Great Transition*, pp. 280–81; Oberdorder, *The Turn*, pp. 184–85; Michael Mandelbaum and Strobe Talbott, "Reykjavik and Beyond," *Foreign Affairs*, vol. 65, no. 3 (Winter 1986–87), p. 219, for expert meetings and Gorbachev quote; *WP*, 9/6/86; *WSJ*, 9/9/86; Cannon in *WP*, 9/16/86; Krauthammer in *WP*, 9/19/96.
132. Adelman, *Great Universal Embrace*, pp. 25–26; Cannon, *President Reagan*, p. 763; Reagan, *American Life*, pp. 669–72, for text of Gorbachev letter.

The letter did include some INF concessions: it withdrew the demand that the British and French INF forces be frozen, and agreed to an "interim option" of token deployments in Europe, as the U.S. negotiators now wanted.

Reagan's immediate acceptance was particularly interesting, since, according to Shultz, it was not until September 20 that Regan, Poindexter and the President began to understand that the Soviets had a strong case against Daniloff because of the CIA's mistakes. (Shultz, *Turmoil and Triumph*, pp. 734, 738, 744.)

133. Cannon in *WP*, 9/30/86; *WSJ*, 9/30/86.
134. Philip Geylin in *WP*, 10/5/86; Charles Krauthammer in *WP*, 10/3/86. Regan, *For the Record*, p. 342.

135. *WP,* 9/16/86, 9/30/86, 10/1/86.

Secretary Weinberger had said that the Soviets "have a rather strange set of priorities. They seem to have concluded that [the Daniloff arrest] would justify putting at risk, and indeed endangering, negotiations that could lead to a significant reduction in armaments" (*WP,* 9/6/86).

136. *WP,* 10/3/86; Hoffman in *WP,* 9/22/86; Cannon, *President Reagan,* p. 763.
137. *WSJ,* 10/1/86.
138. U.S. House of Representatives, *The Reykjavik Process: Preparation for and Conduct of the Iceland Summit and Its Implications for Arms Control Policy: Report of the Defense Policy Panel of the Committee on Armed Services,* 99th Cong., 2nd sess., January 1987 [hereafter *Reykjavik Process*], p. 7.
139. Talbott, *Master of the Game,* pp. 325, 314, for first two quotes; Cannon in *WP,* 10/7/86; Gelb in *NYT,* 10/12/86.
140. Larry Speakes with Robert Pack, *Speaking Out: The Reagan Presidency from Inside the White House* (New York: Scribner, 1988), p. 144, on numbers.
141. Shultz, *Turmoil and Triumph,* pp. 757, 767.
142. Ibid., p. 147; Talbott, *Master of the Game,* p. 325; Gwertzman in *NYT,* 10/13/86; Hoffman in *WP,* 10/13/86.
143. Text of Reagan's remarks in Gelb and Gwertzman articles in *NYT,* 10/13/86; Hoffman in *WP,* 10/12/86; House of Representatives, *Reykjavik and American Security: Report of the Defense Policy Panel, Committee on Armed Services,* 99th Cong., 2nd sess., February 1987. Gorbachev also proposed strict verification measures for INF and the elimination of short-range INF weapons.
144. *NYT,* 10/12/86; *WP,* 10/13/86.

The cover of *Time* magazine proclaimed, "No Deal: Star Wars Sinks the Summit" (Cannon, *President Reagan,* p. 770).

145. Text of speech in *WP,* 10/14/86.
146. Gelb in *NYT,* 10/25/86.
147. Hoffman in *WP,* 10/14/86; *WP,* 10/18/86.
148. Prial in *NYT,* 10/14/86; Gelb in *NYT,* 10/16/86; *NYT,* 10/15/86; U.S. House of Representatives, *Process and Implications of the Iceland Summit: Hearings Before the Defense Policy Panel, Committee on Armed Services,* 99th Cong., 2nd sess., November–December 1986 [hereafter *Process and Implications*], transcript of Perle's briefing at the DOD, October 14, 1986, p. 131; Gordon in *NYT,* 10/14/86.
149. Speakes, *Speaking Out,* p. 149.
150. Ibid., pp. 148–49.
151. Ibid., for quote; Mayer and McManus, *Landslide,* p. 284, for number of interviews.
152. *NYT,* 10/16/86; *WP,* 10/14/86; *NYT,* 10/18/86; Regan, *For the Record,* p. 355.
153. Weinraub in *NYT,* 10/15/86; see also Speakes, *Speaking Out,* pp. 148–49; Mayer and McManus, *Landslide,* p. 283.

Patrick Buchanan later called it "the most extensive and intensive communications plan" he'd ever been associated with at the White House.

154. Cannon, *President Reagan,* p. 770, Wirthlin polls.

The percentage of Americans who thought Reykjavik a success went from 48 percent on October 13 to 55 percent on October 17. (But this was nowhere near the 80 percent who thought Geneva a success.) Similarly, the percentage who thought it unsuccessful or a failure declined from 44 to 39. But there was an increase in the number of people who thought the U.S. was responsible for the failure: 26 to 31 percent. The percentage of those who approved Reagan's handling of U.S.-Soviet relations rose from 67 to 69. After the summit, 78 percent said that Reykjavik was not a major setback but part of a larger process that would lead to meaningful reductions. Forty-one percent thought the U.S. had gained the most from the summit; 19 percent thought the Soviet Union had gained the most; 25 percent said neither.

For the first time, a majority believed that a Reagan-Gorbachev meeting would lead to arms control. A *NYT*-CBS poll after Reykjavik showed this, and showed an eleven-point jump in approval of how Reagan was handling U.S.-Soviet relations (to 72 percent), and for the first time a majority of Americans believed that meetings between Reagan and Gorbachev would lead to nuclear arms control agreements (Cannon, *President Reagan,* p. 770).

On October 17, 73 percent were for SDI research on the grounds that it would help deter a nuclear attack, increase the chance of reaching an arms agreement and reduce the risk of war. By November 8, the percentage had gone down to 68; by December 18, it was 64.

155. Quoted in James Schlesinger, "Reykjavik and Revelations: A Turn of the Tide?," *Foreign Affairs,* vol. 65, no. 2 (1986).
156. Wirthlin polls; interview with Richard Wirthlin, April 4, 1995.

Ronald H. Hinckley, *People, Polls and Policy-Makers: American Public Opinion and National Security* (New York: Lexington Books, 1992), pp. 72–78. One poll Hinckley cites shows that 74 percent found that the most credible argument for SDI with the public was the fact that the Soviets believed it would work; 53 percent saw it as a threat to the Soviet Union. (The Wirthlin polls corroborate this.) According to Hinckley, Americans would strongly support SDI coupled with arms reductions.

157. Hoffman in *WP,* 10/13/86, 10/19/86.
158. Hoffman in *WP,* 10/19/86; Michael Gordon in *NYT,* 10/15/86.
159. Gelb in *NYT,* 10/16/86.
160. Senator Sam Nunn, "The Reykjavik Summit: What Did We Really Agree To?," floor speech, *Congressional Record,* October 17, 1986, pp. 150–53.

161. *NYT,* 10/13/86. Shultz's statement appeared in the transcript published by the *New York Times,* but the *Times* reporters, along with all the other journalists present, had neglected to mention it in their stories, because the three arms-control experts who gave the detailed briefings had spoken merely of the elimination of ballistic missiles.
162. Ibid.
163. *NYT,* 10/18/86.
164. *NYT,* 10/23/86.
165. *NYT,* 10/24/86; Gelb in *NYT,* 10/25/86.

A more detailed press-guidance document stated that, after Gorbachev made his proposal for the elimination of strategic weapons, the President "indicated that the elimination of nuclear weapons had always been his goal."

166. *NYT,* 10/26/86.
167. *NYT,* 10/28/86.
168. Bob Schieffer and Gary Paul Gates, *The Acting President* (New York: E. P. Dutton, 1989), p. 282 for Nunn quote; Schlesinger, "Reykjavik and Revelations," p. 429 for second quote.
169. *WP,* 11/18/86.
170. Smith, *Reagan and Thatcher,* p. 214.
171. Schlesinger, "Reykjavik and Revelations," p. 431.
172. *WP,* 11/18/86 for Kissinger article; Schlesinger, "Reykjavik and Revelations," p. 429. See also Senator Nunn's speech cited above; Brent Scowcroft, John Deutch and R. James Woolsey, "A Way Out of Reykjavik," *NYT Magazine,* January 1, 1987, pp. 40 ff; U.S. House of Representatives, *Reykjavik and American Security;* U.S. House of Representatives, *Reaction to the Reykjavik Proposals: Hearing Before the Subcommittee on Arms Control, International Security and Science of the Committee on Foreign Affairs,* 100th Cong., 1st sess., January 29, 1987.
173. Schlesinger, "Reykjavik and Revelations," p. 433; Fascell, "Congress and Arms Control," p. 743.
174. Schlesinger, "Reykjavik and Revelations," pp. 433–34; see also *Process and Implications,* Schlesinger testimony, p. 158.
175. *Process and Implications,* p. 99.
176. Oberdorfer in *WP,* 2/16/87.
177. *PPP* RR, vol. 2 (1986), p. 1571.

He went on to say, "These are the destabilizing weapons, these are the weapons that people in their mind can picture someone pushes a button and lots of places blow up," as if he were talking about ballistic missiles.

178. *Process and Implications,* p 44.
179. Ibid., p. 93.
180. *Reykjavik Process,* pp. 19, 20.
181. Oberdorfer, *The Turn,* pp. 185–86.
182. Kaiser and Pincus in *WP,* 10/13/86.
183. Ibid., pp. 185–87; Nitze, *From Hiroshima to Glasnost,* p. 429.

The Soviets had also, it became evident, decided not to make them all at once but to roll them out in a tempting fashion as the talks proceeded. There was only one leak: an Indian official quoted Dobrynin as saying that Gorbachev was planning to come to Reykjavik with major new proposals and then trap the U.S. into refusing to meet him halfway. This was a day or two before the meeting, and Nitze was one of the few in Washington who paid any attention to the report.

184. *Reykjavik Process,* p. 6.

The U.S. position on INF was now a global limit of two hundred long-range INF weapons (LRINF), one hundred in Europe and one hundred in Soviet Asia and the United States, along with collateral constraints of short-range missiles (SRINF).

185. Reagan, *American Life,* pp. 670–72, for text

The letter read, "They will lead nowhere unless you and I intervene personally. I am convinced that we shall be able to find solutions, and I am prepared to discuss with you in a substantive way all possible approaches to them and identify such steps as would make it possible—after prompt follow-up by appropriate government agencies—to make my visit to the United States a really productive and fruitful one."

According to Gates, CIA officials made the point that SDI would be Gorbachev's key issue at the various interagency meetings on arms control before the summit (Gates, *From the Shadows,* p. 409).

186. *Reykjavik Process,* p. 6.
187. *Process and Implications,* p. 118.
188. Shultz, *Turmoil and Triumph,* pp. 757–60; Oberdorfer, *The Turn,* pp. 190–91; *Reykjavik Process,* p. 8; Mikhail Gorbachev, *Reykjavik: Results and Lessons* (Madison, CT: Sphinx Press, 1987), pp. 47–49; Adelman, *Great Universal Embrace,* p. 47.

Reagan and Gorbachev spent the first half-hour of the session alone. Reagan spoke about human rights, regional issues and their mutual objective of eliminating all nuclear weapons. Gorbachev only wanted to talk about arms control. Shultz and Shevardnadze then joined them, and Gorbachev pulled out a thick stack of briefing papers, causing Reagan later on to ask mildly why the Soviet leader had more papers than he did.

According to Gorbachev, Shultz pressed for the "interim" INF proposal. Shultz says nothing about this, but he cannot have done otherwise.

189. Shultz, *Turmoil and Triumph,* p. 760.
190. Ibid., pp. 760–61, for Nitze quote; Adelman, *Great Universal Embrace,* p. 47; Oberdorfer, *The Turn,* p. 191; Talbott, *Master of the Game,* pp. 316–17, for Reagan quote; *Reykjavik Process,* p. 8.

    According to the House Armed Services Committee, Reagan's advisers discussed the fact that the Soviet position on SDI hadn't changed. Perle to the contrary, it did not change during the course of the negotiations.

    At this meeting Shultz proposed that working groups meet in the evening to review the progress made during the day, and Reagan agreed.

    The accounts of the meetings in the memoirs and histories differ somewhat, but—except in the case of the Reagan and Regan memoirs—there is no essential conflict between them. After all, there were minutes of the meetings, and the arms-control officials involved had access to them. Reports of what was said in the hallways are not so reliable, but they are of interest.
191. Adelman,*Great Universal Embrace,* p. 47; Shultz, *Turmoil and Triumph,* p. 761; Oberdorfer, *The Turn,* p. 193; Gorbachev, *Reykjavik: Results and Lessons,* pp. 50–51.
192. Text of October 14 speech, in Gorbachev, *Reykjavik: Results and Lessons,* p. 50.
193. Gorbachev, *Reykjavik: Results and Lessons,* pp. 50, 53–54; Shultz, *Turmoil and Triumph,* p. 761; Adelman, *Great Universal Embrace,* p. 48; Talbott, *Master of the Game,* p. 317.

    The working parties were Shultz's idea, and according to Shultz the purpose of them was to review what had been accomplished and to prepare some agreed statements.
194. Adelman,*Great Universal Embrace,* p. 50.
195. Talbott, *Master of the Game,* p. 319; Nitze, *From Hiroshima to Glasnost,* pp. 430–31; Shultz, *Turmoil and Triumph,* pp. 763–64.

    Nitze says he and Linhard went alone to wake up Shultz; Shultz remembers many people crowding themselves into his small sitting room, including Perle.
196. Talbott, *Master of the Game,* p. 321; Nitze, *From Hiroshima to Glasnost,* p. 431.
197. *Reykjavik Process,* p. 9; Nitze, *From Hiroshima to Glasnost,* pp. 423–27; Talbott, *Master of the Game,* p. 319, for quotes.

    The Soviets also agreed to freeze their SRINF weapons in Europe and Asia and, in principle, to verification procedures, including on-site inspections.
198. U.S. House of Representatives, *The Reykjavik Talks—Promise or Peril: Report of the Subcommittee on Arms Control, International Security and Science of the Committee on Foreign Affairs,* 100th Cong., 1st sess., January 1987, p. 20; Shultz, *Turmoil and Triumph,* p. 772; *NYT,* 10/15/86, 10/16/86; *Reykjavik Process,* n. 3 on p. 21.

    Shultz refused to discuss the ABM Treaty interpretation just after the summit; Poindexter also refused to discuss it.
199. Adelman,*Great Universal Embrace,* p. 70.
200. Shultz, *Turmoil and Triumph,* p. 764.
201. Gorbachev, *Reykjavik: Results and Lessons,* p. 50.
202. Adelman, *Great Universal Embrace,* p. 55.
203. Ibid., p. 60; Gorbachev, *Reykjavik: Results and Lessons,* pp. 48, 51, 54; Shultz, *Turmoil and Triumph,* pp. 762, 765–66; *Reykjavik Process,* p. 10.

    Shultz does not tell us in his memoir about the "interim proposal," but that was the U.S. position as of September 1986. According to Adelman, he may have backed off it by mistake: Shultz, on coming out of the meeting, said that the agreement was that the two sides would come down to one hundred INF weapons in Europe and one hundred in Asia. The American note-taker, however, said that Gorbachev had talked about no warheads in Europe and one hundred in Asia, and that's what Shultz and the President had agreed to. "Well then, that's it," Shultz said. One member of the delegation thought that they shouldn't accept the zero in Europe, because the Allies objected it would decouple the U.S. from European security, but others pointed out zero had been the U.S. position for five years, so there was no retreating from it: the U.S. had to take "yes" for an answer. The Europeans were notified immediately (Adelman, *Great Universal Embrace,* pp. 60–61).

    According to Shultz, Reagan told Gorbachev he would agree to these limits as an interim step but would continue to press for the elimination of all INF weapons in Asia (Shultz, *Turmoil and Triumph,* pp. 765–66).
204. Oberdorfer, *The Turn,* pp. 195–96, for quotes; Gorbachev, *Reykjavik: Results and Lessons,* pp. 55–57; Gorbachev's post-summit press conference in *NYT,* 10/13/86; Shultz, *Turmoil and Triumph,* pp. 767–68; *Reykjavik Process,* pp. 10–11.

    Shultz mentions the disagreement over the ABM Treaty, but Adelman does not, nor does the House Armed Services Committee report, because U.S. officials at the time passed over this point—but clearly it was what drove the two sides to agree to an overtime.
205. Shultz, *Turmoil and Triumph,* p. 768; Oberdorfer, *The Turn,* pp. 197–98, for quotes.
206. Talbott, *Master of the Game,* p. 323; Oberdorfer, *The Turn,* pp. 197–98; Shultz, *Turmoil and Triumph,* p. 769, for quote and text of statement.
207. Oberdorfer, *The Turn,* p. 197; Shultz, *Turmoil and Triumph,* p. 768; Nitze, *From Hiroshima to Glasnost,* p. 433n.
208. Oberdorfer, *The Turn,* p. 197.
209. Shultz, *Turmoil and Triumph,* p. 769; Oberdorfer, *The Turn,* p. 199.
210. Talbott, *Master of the Game,* p. 324.

    According to Talbott's source, Reagan said—referring to Gorbachev—"He gets his precious ABM treaty, and we get all his ballistic missiles. And after that we can deploy SDI in space. Then it's a whole new ball game."

211. Oberdorfer, *The Turn,* pp. 199–200.
212. *NYT,* 10/14/86.
213. Shultz, *Turmoil and Triumph,* p. 769; Gorbachev, *Reykjavik: Results and Lessons,* p. 58.
   Gorbachev gave the full text of the proposal in his October 14 speech.
214. Adelman, *Great Universal Embrace,* p. 74.
215. Shultz, *Turmoil and Triumph,* p. 769.
216. Talbott, *Master of the Game,* p. 325.
217. Oberdorfer, *The Turn,* p. 200.
218. Shultz, *Turmoil and Triumph,* p. 772; Gorbachev, *Reykjavik: Results and Lessons,* p. 64.
219. Shultz, *Turmoil and Triumph,* p. 770; Adelman, *Great Universal Embrace,* p. 72.
220. Oberdorfer, *The Turn,* p. 201; Regan, *For the Record,* p. 349, for quote.
221. *Reykjavik Process,* p. 12.
222. *NYT,* 10/26/86, for quote.
   Shultz says that there was much back-and-forth about "strategic" versus "ballistic" weapons and that he kept redrafting the American proposal, "trying to find the language of acceptance." (Shultz, *Turmoil and Triumph,* p. 771.)
   In the six memoirs by administration officials who attended the summit—Adelman, Nitze, Speakes, Shultz, Regan and Reagan—there are various accounts of what was said, but no specific denial that Reagan agreed to eliminate all strategic weapons and all nuclear arms.
   Shultz has Reagan agreeing only in the most general terms to the elimination of nuclear weapons. "It would be fine with me if we eliminated all nuclear weapons," he quotes Reagan as saying. But he does not tell us that this was all Reagan said on the subject. Curiously, Shultz does not even mention that he and the President told the congressional leadership something quite different two days after the event. (Shultz, *Turmoil and Triumph,* pp. 769–72.)
   Reagan's account is at variance with Shultz's. According to his memoir, he and Gorbachev agreed that, "in addition to nuclear missiles, . . . we would try to reduce and eventually eliminate other nuclear weapons as well, including bombers," and that Gorbachev volunteered drastic reductions in Soviet conventional forces in exchange for the elimination of "tactical battlefield nuclear weapons in Europe" (Reagan, *American Life,* pp. 676–77).
   But Reagan's memoir cannot be entirely trusted, for it also tells us that Gorbachev accepted the American proposal of July 25 on the first day of the Reykjavik summit—and that the U.S. made the new proposal for eliminating ballistic missiles that same day (Reagan, *American Life,* pp. 675–79).
   Donald Regan has everything confused. He tells us that the U.S.—not the Soviet Union—presented the written proposal for the elimination of strategic weapons. He claims that the "speediest possible elimination of strategic nuclear forces" was the President's "ultimate objective" before the summit began, and that is what the U.S. proposed on Sunday morning. He then presents us with a series of perfect non-sequiturs. The Soviet response, he writes, was discouraging because they wanted to keep their tactical nuclear weapons, so on Sunday afternoon the President presented a proposal "carpentered on the spot" for "eliminating all ballistic missiles by 1996." In the last session, according to Regan, the President asked Gorbachev what he meant by the "elimination of all strategic forces" and Gorbachev said it meant he favored eliminating "all nuclear weapons," so the President heartily agreed with the idea. (Regan, *For the Record,* pp. 343–50.)
223. Oberdorfer, *The Turn,* pp. 202–3; Shultz, *Turmoil and Triumph,* p. 772.
   Shultz has Gorbachev's reply about eliminating ballistic missiles.
   The last remark in the text sounds much more like Reagan than the translated and retranslated Soviet version in which Reagan says: "If we agree that by the end of the 10-year period, all nuclear arms are to be eliminated, we can refer this to our delegations in Geneva to prepare an agreement that you could sign during your visit to the United States" (Bessmertnykh press conference in *NYT,* 10/26/86).
   Regan has a slightly different version of this *(For the Record,* p. 350); Shultz in his memoir reports the first two exchanges but not Reagan's response to Gorbachev's "Let's eliminate them."
224. Reagan, *American Life,* p. 679, for first quote; Cannon, *President Reagan,* p. 769, for second and third quote; Speakes, *Speaking Out,* pp. 146–47.
   There are many versions of these last exchanges, but in all of them Gorbachev is trying to mend fences and Reagan is having none of it.
225. Reagan, *American Life,* p. 679; see also Regan, *For the Record,* pp. 351–52.
226. Speakes, *Speaking Out,* p. 145.
227. Adelman, *Great Universal Embrace,* pp. 77–78.
228. Gorbachev, *Reykjavik: Lessons and Results,* pp. 69–70, 77–80.
229. Hoffman in *WP,* 11/30/86.
   Reagan's only other issue was the promise of an anti-drug campaign. The public was for it, but it did not cut much ice politically.
230. Schieffer and Gates, *Acting President,* p. 280, for quote; Mayer and McManus, *Landslide,* p. 283.
   When the October 14 Reagan-Shultz briefing for the congressional leadership broke up, Senator Nunn said to Poindexter, "John, do you realize they're talking about doing away with all strategic weapons—bombers, submarines, cruise missiles as well as ballistics?"

Poindexter, who, according to another official at the meeting, looked pale and shaken, replied, "Well, we have some tidying up to do." (Schieffer and Gates, *Acting President,* p. 280.)

231. Admiral William J. Crowe, Jr., *The Line of Fire* (New York: Simon & Schuster, 1993), p. 266.
232. Ibid., pp. 267–68.
233. Adelman, *Great Universal Embrace,* p. 86. Adelman's account of the discussion—indeed, the entire meeting—is somewhat different from Crowe's.
234. Crowe, *Line of Fire,* p. 269.
235. *Reykjavik Process,* p. 14.
236. U.S. House of Representatives, *Reykjavik Talks,* p. 20.
237. *Reykjavik Process,* p. 15.
238. Nitze, *From Hiroshima to Glasnost,* pp. 436–37; see also Garthoff, *Great Transition,* p. 292.
239. Smith, *Reagan and Thatcher,* pp. 218–21.
240. Ibid., pp. 221–24.
241. *WP,* 11/18/86, 11/19/86; Adelman, *Great Universal Embrace,* pp. 82–83.
242. *Process and Implications,* p. 159.
243. Ibid., p. 60.

Aspin's committee report remarked, "The . . . impression is that the Reagan administration was focused solely on the political implications of the arms control deals they were discussing, ignoring the military and strategic ramifications." *(Reykjavik Process,* p. 18.)

Administration officials testifying before the committee disagreed on what U.S. policy was in the wake of the summit. Perle said the zero-ballistic-missile proposal remained on the table, whereas Adelman said it was "being deemphasized." Perle and Adelman said the U.S. would never negotiate away the nuclear forces of other countries, even though Shultz had told the *Washington Post* that the U.S. and the Soviet Union would not disarm unless the British, French and Chinese went along. Shultz had also said that the Chinese had assured him "on the highest authority" that, if the U.S. and the Soviet nuclear forces were substantially reduced, they would be ready to join in such an effort.

"Boy, I would like to see the cables on that," Aspin remarked. "I would love to see the back-up which says that."

Admiral Crowe told the committee that the Chiefs were studying the zero-ballistic-missile proposal but not the President's plan to share SDI technology with the Soviet Union. "I do think it a little premature," he said, "to study in isolation just a transfer of technology without knowing what we are talking about." *(Process and Implications,* pp. 38–40, 83, 100, 132.)

NINE: Falling Stars

1. Interview with James T. Bruce III, 6/26/90.
2. Michael K. Deaver, *Behind the Scenes* (New York: William Morrow, 1987), pp. 35, 106.
3. Douglas C. Waller, James T. Bruce III and Douglas M. Cook, *The Strategic Defense Initiative: Progress and Challenges* (Claremont, Calif.: Regina Books, 1987) [hereafter Waller et al.], p. 12.

   The Fletcher Commission had spoken of a 99-percent-effective defense, but this was presumably for heuristic purposes, because it was virtually impossible to achieve. Certainly administration officials never said it was the goal of SDI.
4. Janne E. Nolan, *Guardians of the Arsenal: The Politics of Nuclear Strategy* (New York: Basic Books, 1989), p. 198.
5. Ibid., pp. 177, 182–83; Robert Scheer in *LAT,* 9/22/85.
6. Waller et al., p. 29.

   The authors say that the estimate for a "technology-driven" research effort was thirty-two billion dollars. I have not seen this figure anywhere else.
7. Douglas Waller, James Bruce and Douglas Cook, "SDI: Progress and Challenges," staff report submitted to Senator William Proxmire, Senator J. Bennett Johnston and Senator Lawton Chiles, March 17, 1986 [hereafter Proxmire, Johnston and Chiles '86], pp. 14–15, fig. 3 on p. 11.

   Waller et al. normally give only the Defense Department budget. Of the two billion dollars, $1.78 billion was for Defense, the rest for the Department of Energy.
8. Waller et al., p. 14; Arms Control Association, ed., *Star Wars Quotes* (Washington, D.C.: Arms Control Association, 1986), p. 41.

   In January, George Keyworth, still Reagan's science adviser, gave an even more optimistic report. Speaking of "monumental breakthroughs" in research, he claimed that the U.S. would be able to make not just a development decision but a decision on the deployment of strategic defenses in the early 1990s.
9. Waller et al., p. 15; William J. Broad, *Teller's War* (New York: Simon & Schuster, 1992), pp. 185–86; Philip M. Boffey, William J. Broad, Leslie H. Gelb, Charles Mohr and Holcomb B. Noble, *Claiming the Heavens: The New York Times Complete Guide to the Star Wars Debate* (New York: Times Books, 1988), p. 88.
10. *NYT,* 12/15/85.

    Aspin thought the administration's real goal had to be the protection of strategic forces.
11. Nolan, *Guardians,* p. 219.
12. Ibid., pp. 219–20; Proxmire, Johnston and Chiles '86, p. 6.
13. Nolan, *Guardians,* p. 220; Waller et al., p. 41.
14. Waller et al., p. 41; *WP,* 7/24/86.

Library of Congress and General Accounting Office studies followed in 1986—the first at Johnston's request—and both concluded that the SDIO would probably have insufficient information to make a development decision in the early 1990s.

15. Broad, *Teller's War*, p. 205.
16. Ibid., pp. 182–99; *NYT*, 12/16/85, 12/20/85.

The SDIO continued to increase the budget for the X-ray laser. The funding went up to $349 million in fiscal year 1987 before coming down.

17. Proxmire, Johnston and Chiles '86, p. 44.
18. *WP*, 5/12/85, 1/18/87.

In January 1987 officials at the Army's Ballistic Missile Defense Command called directed-energy weapons "too Buck Rogers" and too much "in the 'if' stage" to be counted upon.

In April 1987 a panel of the American Physical Society delivered a 424-page report on SDI's directed-energy weapons program based on an eighteen-month study of the classified SDIO data. The panel and its review board, which included some of the world's leading authorities on lasers and particle beams, reported that, in spite of the progress made over two decades, there remained "significant gaps" in the scientific and technical understanding of how to turn directed-energy technologies into weapons, and concluded that even under the best of circumstances it would take "a decade or more of intensive research" to come to any decision about the effectiveness and survivability of exotic strategic defenses. In other words, there had been no breakthroughs in the field since the SDI program began. In presenting their report, members of the panel added that the survival of any space-based system seemed highly questionable and that an early deployment could not be justified on the grounds that directed-energy weapons would come along at a later phase. "If one relied primarily on scientific and engineering criteria, one would not make a decision for early deployment," the co-chair of the panel said.

The report also said that the "most crucial elements required for a [directed-energy weapons] system need improvements of several orders of magnitude." It added that SDI designs that "address the responsive threat are still in their infancy." And it said that the X-ray laser was of "uncertain" potential as an ABM weapon but potentially a "serious threat" to space-based satellites.

The report was completed in September 1986, but its release was repeatedly delayed by Pentagon civilians, who complained that it revealed too much about the SDI program. (R. Jeffrey Smith in *WP*, 4/23/87, 4/24/87; Boffey et al., *Claiming the Heavens*, p. 245.)

19. Waller et al., p. 39.

It weighed a ton and cost ten million dollars—whereas by SDIO projections the ERIS interceptor should weigh a hundred pounds and cost one million dollars. In 1985 the SDIO had said it should weigh seven to eight pounds (*WP*, 5/12/85).

20. Waller et al., p. 46.
21. Ibid., p. 39.
22. Proxmire, Johnston and Chiles '86, pp. 10–11, 49.
23. Waller et al., pp. 66–73.

In January 1986 the Challenger space shuttle blew up. It was a blow to Star Wars enthusiasts—and it left the U.S. with only three space shuttles.

24. Waller et al., p. 53; Matthew Bunn, "Early SDI: Deploying a Disaster," *Arms Control Today*, March 1987, p. 22, for DIA estimate; Strobe Talbott, *Deadly Gambits: The Reagan Administration and the Stalemate in Nuclear Arms Control* (New York: Alfred A. Knopf, 1984), pp. 316–17. The Soviet SS–13 was a solid-fuel rocket.
25. Waller et al., pp. 49–56, 59–60.
26. Ibid., pp. 25, 28–29, 98.

My figures include Department of Energy costs.

27. Ibid., p. 98; *WP*, 6/20/86; Joseph S. Nye, Jr., "Farewell to Arms Control?," *Foreign Affairs*, vol. 65, no. 1 (Fall 1986), p. 16.
28. *WP*, 6/20/86; *WSJ*, 7/22/86; Nolan, *Guardians*, pp. 221–23; Waller et al., p. 100.

A floor amendment sponsored by Johnston, Proxmire and Evans (Republican of Washington) to give SDI $3.2 billion, or a 3-percent increase, failed by only one vote.

29. Waller et al., pp. 99–100; *WP*, 6/28/86; Douglas C. Waller and James T. Bruce, "SDI: Progress and Challenges, Part Two," staff report submitted to Senator William Proxmire and Senator J. Bennett Johnston, March 19, 1987 [hereafter Proxmire and Johnston '87], pp. 5–6.
30. Nolan, *Guardians*, p. 217.
31. *WP*, 8/7/86.
32. Angelo Codevilla, *While Others Build* (New York: Free Press, 1988), p. 214; Evans and Novak in *WP*, 8/8/86.
33. Waller et al., p. 102, for quote; *WP*, 8/7/87, 8/9/87.
34. *NYT*, 8/12/86.
35. *WSJ*, 7/22/87.

A *WSJ*-NBC poll taken in July showed that 58 percent of those surveyed thought it would be a good idea to build an SDI system if it would protect people and cities, and 30 percent disagreed. On the other hand, 44 percent said it would be a good idea if the most SDI could do was to protect U.S. nuclear weapons—and 42 percent disagreed.

36. *WSJ*, 5/19/86.

Anderson overestimated the capability of one hundred ERIS deployment and put the cost very low. He said the deployment would be ABM Treaty–compliant.

37. *WSJ,* 7/22/86.
38. Talbott, *Master of the Game,* pp. 233–36, for all quotes except the last one; *WSJ,* 7/22/86, for last quote.
    Perle in the first instance was speaking to a conference sponsored by *Time* magazine.
39. Nolan, *Guardians,* pp. 216–19.
40. *WP,* 6/20/86; *NYT,* 9/6/86.
    "Terminal defense—that is, defense solely of our military assets, sites or missile silos—is not and never has been the goal of SDI," Weinberger said in July 1986 (Talbott, *Master of the Game,* p. 237).
41. Caspar Weinberger, *Fighting for Peace* (New York: Warner Books, 1990), p. 323.
42. Ibid., pp. 323–24.
43. *WP,* 8/7/86.
44. Codevilla, *While Others Build,* p. 215; *Arms Control Today,* March 1987, p. 5, for Gates; Waller et al., pp. 101–2.
45. Waller et al., p. 6; *WP,* 1/18/87.
    Lockheed engineers used this figure in classified briefings.
46. Jane Mayer and Doyle McManus, *Landslide* (Boston: Houghton Mifflin, 1988), p. 274.
47. U.S. Congress, *Report of the Congressional Committee's Investigation of the Iran-Contra Affair: Report to Senate Select Committee on Secret Military Assistance to Iran and the Nicaraguan Opposition, House of Representatives Select Committee to Investigate Covert Arms Transactions with Iran,* 100th Cong., 1st sess., S. Report No. 100–216, H. Report No. 100–433, November 1987 [hereafter *Select Committees*], p. 288.
48. Mayer and McManus, *Landslide,* p. 91.
49. *Select Committees,* p. 166, for quotes; George Shultz, *Turmoil and Triumph* (New York: Scribner, 1993), p. 656.
    This statement came in the wake of the hijacking of TWA flight 847 by Shiite militiamen. One American was killed and thirty-nine others were taken hostage for the release of Shiite prisoners in Israel and Kuwait. According to Shultz's account, Reagan wanted a deal but Shultz held off, not wanting an incident like this repeated. A deal was eventually made: the American hostages were released, and the Israeli government released its prisoners. Reagan's statement came after the Americans had been returned.
50. *Select Committees,* p. 293.
51. Ibid., p. 296.
52. Mayer and McManus, *Landslide,* p. 303.
    A *Los Angeles Times* poll taken a few days later showed that only 14 percent of Americans believed that Reagan was telling the truth (Shultz, *Turmoil and Triumph,* p. 824).
53. Shultz, *Turmoil and Triumph,* pp. 819–20.
54. *Select Committees,* p. 298.
55. Ibid.
56. Mayer and McManus, *Landslide,* p. 321; Shultz, *Turmoil and Triumph,* p. 832.
57. Lawrence Walsh, Independent Counsel, "Final Report of the Independent Counsel for Iran/Contra Matters," submitted to the U.S. Court of Appeals for the District of Columbia Circuit, August 4, 1993 [hereafter Walsh, "Final Report"), vol. II, pp. 325–74, 405–42.
    In the wake of the congressional investigations the following year, it was generally assumed that McFarlane, Poindexter and North had conducted these extraordinary operations in such secrecy that only they and a few CIA officials knew anything about it. In the hearings Shultz and Weinberger testified that, apart from the discussions with the President and his NSC advisers about the wisdom of the initiative in 1985 and January 1986, they were largely kept in the dark. Weinberger testified that he knew nothing about the 1985 shipments while they were going on and believed at the time that the arguments he and Shultz had made against the initiative had prevailed; Shultz for his part said that he had learned of two shipments but was not informed that they were consummated. In addition, both secretaries said they had only very sporadic and incomplete reports about the transfers in 1986. In his meticulous book on the Iran-contra affair published in 1991, the historian Theodore Draper wrote that the questions which arose most forcefully from the affair were: "How could a handful of little-known officials take virtually complete control of American foreign policy in areas of major concern? How could they operate in total disregard of Congress, outside the purview of the two departments most concerned, State and Defense, and indeed of almost the entire structure of the government?"
    In fact, as the independent counsel later discovered, both Shultz and Weinberger, along with their senior staff members, had monitored the entire Iran operation from start to finish. Weinberger, so his own notes showed, knew in advance that Reagan had decided to send arms to Iran through Israel in the summer of 1985 and had detailed contemporary knowledge of the arms transaction in November. Not only did McFarlane keep him informed, but he had reliable intelligence reports in the form of satellite intercepts about the progress of the initiative. In 1986 he had two briefings from Casey, numerous briefings from Poindexter and a steady stream of intelligence reports from January through November. Shultz for his part not only knew about the 1985 transactions but, contrary to his testimony, knew a good deal about the arms transfers in 1986. Casey had briefed him on the February transaction, Weinberger had informed him about McFarlane's disastrous trip to Teheran in late May and, according to the notes made by his assistant Charles Hill, his senior staff members kept him informed about the arms-for-hostages negotiations throughout the spring and summer.
    Shultz and Weinberger did not testify to having brought up the subject of the arms transactions in their private meetings with the President. Possibly they did, but were unable to convince him to stop the operation. If they did not, the question is why not.
    (See Theodore Draper, *A Very Thin Line* [New York: Hill and Wang, 1991], p. 558; Walsh, "Final Report," vol. I, pp. 325–74; vol. II, pp. 693–704.)

58. *Select Committees,* pp. 305–13; Shultz, *Turmoil and Triumph,* pp. 834–39.
59. Shultz, *Turmoil and Triumph,* pp. 839–44.
60. Mayer and MacManus, *Landslide,* p. 358.
61. Walsh, "Final Report," vol. II, pp. 714–15.

    Over the weekend of the 21st, the *Washington Post,* the *New York Times* and CBS carried reports that Mrs. Reagan, the President's California friends and Ed Meese wanted Shultz and Regan to go (Shultz, *Turmoil and Triumph,* p. 836).
62. Shultz, *Turmoil and Triumph,* pp. 835–37.

    During his "investigation," Meese strongly suggested to Shultz that he not talk about the President's knowledge of the legally fraught arms transaction. At the press conference in which he announced the diversion of funds, he said, when asked if Shultz should be fired, "I think that anyone who is a member of the President's staff or the President's Cabinet has an obligation either to support the policy decisions of the President or get out." (Shultz, *Turmoil and Triumph; WP,* 11/26/86, for quote.)
63. Walsh, "Final Report," vol. II, pp. 714, 718.

    Though officially asked to provide his records, Weinberger never gave his extensive notes to the Iran-contra committees of the Congress or to the independent prosecutor, and General Colin Powell, his aide in 1985, did not reveal that he kept a daily record of his activities. The notes were eventually found in the Library of Congress, where Weinberger put them for posterity, misfiled in the unclassified archives. Weinberger was indicted for lying to Congress but was never tried: on December 24, 1992, George Bush, in one of the last acts of his presidency, pardoned him along with Robert McFarlane, Elliott Abrams and three CIA officials, two of whom had also not yet been tried.
64. *WP,* 1/31/93.

    "Is the Vice-President in the Loop? You make the Call." (Excerpts from George Bush's Iran-contra Diary, p. C7.)

    The independent counsel had requested that the vice-president supply any documents in his possession in February 1987. The diary was finally supplied in December 1992, just before Bush left office as President of the United States. The Bush White House released portions to the public on January 15, 1993.
65. Mayer and McManus, *Landslide,* p. 356; Cannon, *President Reagan,* p. 703, for quotes; Schieffer and Gates, *Acting President,* p. 291.

    Reagan also called North, told him he considered him a national hero and said, "This is going to make a great movie one day."
66. Shultz, *Turmoil and Triumph,* pp. 854–58; Mayer and MacManus, *Landslide,* pp. 368–70.

    Donald Regan was partly responsible for this, for he passed Casey's message on to the President without objecting to it.

    The negotiations had come to involve not only U.S. arms but U.S. military information and the release of a group of terrorists jailed in Kuwait. As soon as it became clear that the U.S. would no longer trade arms for hostages, the Iranians quit the talks.
67. Walsh, "Final Report," vol. II, p. 719.
68. Ibid., pp. 720–21.
69. *WP,* 1/31/86, p. C6.
70. Mayer and McManus, *Landslide,* p. 358.
71. *WP,* 1/31/86, p. C6.
72. Walsh, "Final Report," vol. I, pp. 466–67, contains twelve of Reagan's diary entries between July 17, 1985, and January 17, 1986, including this one dated December 5, 1985: "NSC Briefing—probably Buds last—subject our undercover effort to free our last 5 hostages—complex undertaking with only a few in on it—won't even write in this diary what we were up to."
73. Ibid., vol. II, p. 686, for quote; *Select Committees,* p. 198; Draper, *Very Thin Line,* p. 229.

    McFarlane had the same impression of Reagan's remarks.
74. Donald Regan, *For the Record* (New York: Harcourt Brace Jovanovich, 1988), pp. 67–68; Shultz, *Turmoil and Triumph,* p. 870.

    According to Shultz, Carlucci was attempting to convince the President to put the NSC staff into an operational role in terms of U.S.-Soviet negotiations. Shultz would have none of this.
75. Talbott, *Master of the Game,* pp. 329–30; Evans and Novak in *WP,* 1/14/87; R. Jeffrey Smith in *WP,* 1/18/87.

    Evans and Novak report that Admiral Crowe was at the meeting, but he was not. See R. Jeffrey Smith article.
76. *WP,* 1/18/87.
77. Proxmire and Johnston '87, p. 6.
78. Ibid., pp. 6, 8–9.
79. Ibid., p. 10; R. Jeffrey Smith in *WP,* 1/18/87; Evans and Novak in *WP,* 1/14/87; George C. Wilson in *WP,* 1/14/87.
80. *NYT,* 1/16/87; *WP,* 1/18/87; Proxmire and Johnston '87, p. 7; Bunn, "Early SDI," p. 21; Simon P. Worden, "What Can We Do? When Can We Do It?," *National Review,* December 31, 1986, p. 40.
81. Proxmire and Johnston '87, p. 6.
82. *WP,* 1/18/87.
83. *NYT,* 1/16/87.
84. *WP,* 1/14/87, 1/18/87; *NYT,* 1/16/87.

85. *WP,* 1/18/87, for Abrahamson and Marquet quotes; *WP,* 1/13/87, for Crowe quote; see also Proxmire and Johnston '87, p. 7.

Later, in a letter to Congress, Crowe said that a decision on early deployment would be "premature" (Bunn, "Early SDI," pp. 13, 17).

86. *WP,* 2/3/87.
87. Smith and Oberdorfer in *WP,* 2/4/87.
88. Smith in *WP,* 2/5/87.
89. *Washington Times,* 2/6/87.
90. *WP,* 2/7/87; Nunn letter to the President, 2/6/87.
91. Smith and Doder in *WP,* 2/9/87.
92. *WP,* 2/11/87, 2/12/87 for quote, 2/14/87.
93. Smith in *WP,* 2/11/87.
94. The President may have thought that he was making a decision on deployment since Senate Minority Leader Robert Dole came out of the congressional briefing and told the press, "I think the president supports deployment in an early phase." Dole's staff retracted his statement after Shultz's briefing to the press. *(WP,* 2/4/87; *San Diego Union-Tribune,* 2/6/87.)
95. Smith in *WP,* 2/10/87, 2/17/87; Shultz, *Turmoil and Triumph,* p. 872.

In his memoir Shultz quotes from a memorandum he wrote to the President on February 6: "We have stated that a broad interpretation is warranted by an examination of the negotiating record—but we have designed the program within the framework of the narrow interpretation."

96. Smith in *WP,* 2/17/87.
97. Smith in *WP,* 2/22/87.
98. Weinberger's "Report to Congress on the Anti-Ballistic Missile Treaty," submitted on May 19, 1987, read: "The broad interpretation of the ABM Treaty would allow the United States to retain the option to deploy strategic defenses in the mid-1990s. Even under ideal conditions, the restrictive interpretation would delay deployment until the late 1990s." (James T. Bruce, Bruce W. MacDonald, and Ronald L. Tammen, "Star Wars at the Crossroads: The Strategic Defense Initiative After Five Years," staff report submitted to Senator J. Bennett Johnston, Senator Dale Bumpers and Senator William Proxmire, June 12, 1988 [hereafter Johnston, Bumpers, Proxmire, '88], pp. 39–40.)
99. Smith in *WP,* 4/2/87; quotes from *WP,* 2/10/87, 2/12/87.

In 1977 Paul Nitze had written, in a letter to Donald Brennan, "It was our clear intention that Article V of the ABM Treaty bar engineering development of a BAMBI-type ABM system." (*WP,* 4/2/87.)

In 1986 Dr. Louis Marquet, Abrahamson's deputy, wrote, "A pitcher throwing a baseball is an example of kinetic energy," and "Of course, machine guns are another kinetic energy weapon" (Louis Marquet, "The Strategic Defense Initiative: A Technical Overview," in James C. Haug, ed., *The Strategic Defense Initiative in Perspective* [Boulder, Colo.: Social Science Monographs, 1987], pp. 23, 25.

100. Raymond Garthoff, *Policy Versus the Law: The Reinterpretation of the ABM Treaty* (Washington, D.C.: Brookings Institution, 1987), p. 12.

Weinberger enlisted Patrick Buchanan to get a call for deployment included in the State of the Union address. Carlucci, however, argued that the administration had not made a deployment decision yet.

101. Shultz, *Turmoil and Triumph,* pp. 871–72; Robert M. Gates, *From the Shadows* (New York: Simon & Schuster, 1996), p. 354.

Robert Gates tells us that on April 7, 1986, Reagan went to the opening game of the baseball season in Baltimore and visited the Orioles' dugout. When Rick Dempsey, the catcher for the Orioles, suggested how Qaddafi might be taken care of, Reagan said, "You know what I'd do if Qaddafi was sitting here right now? I'd nail his balls to this bench and then push him over backwards."

Peggy Noonan tells the following story.

After the defeat of the Bork nomination, presumably in the fall of 1987, when the conservatives were in an uproar over numerous issues, Howard Baker let in a group of them, including Robert Jastrow, to talk to Reagan about the contras, the RENAMO rebels in Mozambique and SDI. Weinberger attended the meeting.

> On SDI, a participant said, Mr. President, you ought to announce that you are going for the immediate deployment of SDI. If JFK had said, "We're going to research going to the moon," he would never have gotten the funding or the support. You ought to say we're going to have a defensive shield that will stop incoming missiles before this decade is out.
>
> The President shook his head. Again, he said, I have to note that we just lack support for SDI.
>
> Jastrow leaned forward: *No one goes to the barricades for research funding!* Tell the people over and over what SDI can do, how it can protect us, and tell them we're going to deploy at least some parts of it before the decade is out.
>
> The secretary of defense turned to the President. "There is, of course, the argument that the Soviets are simply trying to slow us down long enough to get their SDI in place. I don't mean to suggest that they're doing it consciously, but by holding up strategic defense the Democrats are doing the work of the Soviet Union for them. I don't mean to say they're doing it consciously, but—"
>
> "Well, I will," Reagan said. Everyone laughed.

Noonan wondered why Reagan was so cautious in his strategy and so incautious in his remarks. (Peggy Noonan, *What I Saw at the Revolution* [New York: Random House, 1990], pp. 246–47.)

102. Talbott, *Master of the Game,* p. 332; Paul Nitze, with Ann M. Smith and Steven L. Rearden, *From Hiroshima to Glasnost: At the Center of Decision—a Memoir* (New York: Grove Weidenfeld, 1989), p. 446.
103. *ABMTC,* pp. 121, 131, 156.
104. Nitze, *From Hiroshima to Glasnost,* pp. 444–45.

Actually, Nitze tells us that the proposal was to proceed with testing "beyond that which was permitted by the broad interpretation of the ABM Treaty."

On the issue of the treaty interpretation, he tells us in contradictory fashion (a) that the Soviet Union "is not bound by the understandings of the Senate during the ratification process" and (b) that the ratification record and the record of subsequent practice "have a bearing, in international law, on the interpretation of a treaty where the text is ambiguous."

In an annex of his memoir, Nitze provides his own interpretation of the ABM Treaty in which he argues (a) that the "broad" interpretation is fully justified and (b) that it isn't.

105. *WP,* 2/5/87, 2/12/87.
106. Garthoff, *Policy Versus the Law,* p. 12; *WP,* 2/14/87.
107. *WP,* 2/12/87; Talbott, *Master of the Game,* p. 334; Nitze, *From Hiroshima to Glasnost,* p. 445; *WP,* 3/15/87.
108. Talbott, *Master of the Game,* pp. 334–35; *WP,* 3/15/87.
109. Nolan, *Guardians,* p. 226; interview with Robert Bell, June 28, 1990.
110. U.S. Senate, *Strategic Defense Initiative: Hearings Before the Subcommittee on Strategic and Theater Nuclear Forces of the Armed Services Committee,* 99th Cong., 1st sess., November 21, 1986 [hereafter SASC], p. 188; *ABMTC,* pp. 139–40; *Congressional Record,* March 11, 1987, p. S2974 for Nunn speech.
111. *ABMTIR,* p. 28.
112. Interview with Bell, June 28, 1990; *ABMTIR,* p. 28.
113. *Congressional Record,* March 12, 1987, p. S3095.

Sofaer presented the memorandum to the Senate Armed Services Committee.

Sofaer told the House the same thing on October 27, 1985, concerning the ratification record *(ABMTC,* pp. 122, 131, 156).

For Sofaer's *Harvard Law Review* article of June 1986, see *ABMTC,* pp. 536–38; see also *ABMTIR,* p. 33.

Sofaer maintained that nearly all the explanations of the treaty that Nixon-administration officials had given the Congress during the ratification proceedings were consistent with the "broad" interpretation. He had also maintained that U.S. statements about the treaty after ratification were mixed, but that the earlier ones—those before the SDI program was announced—tended to support the "broad" interpretation.

114. *Congressional Record,* March 12, 1987, p. S3095; *WP,* 2/6/87.

Levin wrote that Judge Sofaer "too often shaded the facts and frequently distorted the record." He concluded that Sofaer's analysis was "fatally flawed."

115. *Congressional Record,* March 12, 1987, p. S3095.

Shultz called Sofaer's work "a thorough and balanced analysis of the issues, more objective and complete than any prior study of the subject."

Levin had further correspondence on the subject with an assistant secretary of state and got the same response.

116. Ibid., March 11, 1987, p. S2985; March 12, p. S3095.

In his letter Sofaer also said that his classified study provided to the Senate in August 1986 "still fails to cover the subject in full depth" and "did not include various statements in the ratification record which I acknowledged supported the restrictive interpretation."

Three days later Sofaer went to Senator Levin and made the same confession, this time adding that the faulty document had been prepared by "young lawyers" on his staff.

117. *WP,* 3/17/87.
118. *Congressional Record,* March 11, 12, 13, 1987, pp. S2967–86; 3090–95; 3171–73 for Nunn's three speeches.
119. Ibid., p. S3172.
120. Ibid., pp. S2971–72.
121. *WP,* 3/15/87.
122. *WP,* 3/18/87.
123. *WP,* 4/13/87.
124. Nitze, *From Hiroshima to Glasnost,* p. 438.
125. Smith in *WP,* 1/18/87.

The old budget had shown a 12-percent cut for KEWs. Asking Congress for a $110-million supplement to the SDI appropriations bill, the SDIO budgeted $33 million more for space-based kinetic-energy weapons for fiscal 1987, plus $10 million more after the December meeting with Reagan. An extra $177 million was budgeted for fiscal 1988, thereby tripling the existing budget for these weapons.

126. Proxmire and Johnston '87, pp. 19–21, 26–28; *WP,* 4/19/87.

In the annual report to Congress for fiscal 1987, SDIO officials omitted the detailed budget data that they had previously included.

127. Proxmire and Johnston '87, pp. 30–34.

The SDIO was proposing a tenfold increase in expenditures for space transport (between the original, fiscal-1987 budget and the new, fiscal-1988 budget).

128. Ibid., pp. ii–iv, 34–39.
129. Ibid., p. 35.
130. Admiral William J. Crowe, Jr., *The Line of Fire* (New York: Simon & Schuster, 1993), pp. 301–3, 307.

131. Ibid., pp. 307–8.
132. Ibid., pp. 308–9.
According to Crowe, NSPG members lived in fear of meetings in which a politically fraught issue, such as SDI, would come up and give rise to a roaring argument in front of the President. On such occasions no decision would be taken, and the members would walk out wondering if they had been on the winning or losing side and certain that their adversaries would get in to see the President and bring him to a decision before they could.
133. Ibid., pp. 302, 305.
134. Ibid., pp. 304–5.
135. Smith in *WP*, 6/28/87.
136. WP, 6/28/87.
137. *WP*, 6/28/87, 7/9/87, 7/10/87; Joseph Romm, "Pseudo-Science and SDI," *Arms Control Today*, vol. 19, no. 8 (October 1989), p. 18.
138. *WP*, 7/9/87, 7/10/87.
139. Johnston, Bumpers and Proxmire '88, p. 10; Weinberger's Op Ed piece in *NYT*, 8/21/87.
140. *WP*, 6/28/87; Johnston, Bumpers and Proxmire '88, pp. 67–69.
Their sources said the SDIO had reached the last cost estimate in June 1987. Abrahamson did not reveal it publicly until February 1988. Apparently he had decided to phase in the high estimate slowly.
The SDIO itself estimated that the costs of simply getting to a development decision, or "Milestone Two," would be about forty billion dollars by 1992.
According to Crowe, the Chiefs believed that a full "Phase One" would cost hundreds of billions of dollars (Crowe, *Line of Fire*, p. 304).
141. Johnston, Bumpers and Proxmire '88, p. 70.
142. Weinberger does not mention the BAMBI-style concept in his book. He makes it sound as if the first concept were "brilliant pebbles."
143. Crowe, *Line of Fire*, p. 305.
144. Wirthlin's polls of October 25 and November 28, 1987, demonstrated this.
145. Anatoly Dobrynin, *In Confidence: Moscow's Ambassador to America's Six Cold War Presidents (1962–1986)* (New York: Times Books, 1995), p. 620.
Marshal Akhromeyev told more than one American visitor that his real concern was not an effective shield but weapons in space that could help to create a first-strike capability plus spillovers from SDI research that would create technical breakthroughs in strategic and conventional weaponry (Kaiser and Pincus in *WP*, 10/13/86).
146. Raymond L. Garthoff, *The Great Transition* (Washington, D.C.: Brookings Institution, 1994), pp. 516–17; AP, 4/15/97.
According to Garthoff, at least some in the KGB thought that Star Wars was a disinformation scheme. (Interview with Raymond Garthoff, 9/27/99.)
147. Shultz, *Turmoil and Triumph*, p. 874.
In discussing the February 3 NSPG meeting, Shultz tells us that Weinberger's call for deployment was a bad idea but had its diplomatic uses, in that it "was likely to make our offer at Reykjavik of a ten year period of no deployment all the more attractive to the Soviets."
148. *Seattle Times, St. Petersburg Times*, and *LAT*, 12/29/86; Lars Eric Nelson in *WP*, 1/2/87.
149. Andrei Sakharov, *Moscow and Beyond* (New York: Alfred A. Knopf, 1991), pp. 21–24. See also Talbott, *Master of the Game*, p. 360.
In his memoir Sakharov writes that, if the U.S. did decide to deploy an SDI defense while the Soviets were destroying their missiles as a part of a START treaty, the Soviet side could bring disarmament to a halt and build "new, powerful missiles with invulnerable launchers as well as weapons that could destroy and eliminate SDI."
150. Sakharov, *Moscow and Beyond*, p. 24; Talbott, *Master of the Game*, pp. 338–9.
151. *The Reagan Legacy*, Discovery Channel documentary, produced by Nick Gold, pt. II, "Star Wars," premiered on November 4, 1996, with Garrick Utley.
152. *WP*, 2/6/87; Talbott, *Master of the Game*, p. 360, has interview with Sagdeyev of 7/2/87. To Talbott, Sagdeyev and others acknowledged that Sakharov's argument had force.
153. David Remnick, *Lenin's Tomb* (New York: Vintage Books, 1994), pp. 164–65.

TEN: Reagan and Gorbachev

1. Donald Regan, *For the Record* (New York: Harcourt Brace Jovanovich, 1988), p. 97 for quotes, pp. 89–96, 367–68.
2. *Tower Commission Report* (New York: Bantam/Times Books, 1987), p. 81.
3. Regan. *For the Record*, pp. 368–74.
4. Lou Cannon, *President Reagan: The Role of a Lifetime* (New York: Simon & Schuster, 1991), p. 730.
5. *Tower Report*, pp. xii–xiii.
6. Regan, *For the Record*, p. 83, for first quote; Bob Schieffer and Gary Paul Gates, *The Acting President* (New York: E. P. Dutton, 1989), p. 302, for second quote.
7. Schieffer and Gates, *Acting President*, p. 308.

8. Gallup polls, late February 1987.
9. Colin Powell, with Joseph E. Persico, *My American Journey* (New York: Random House, 1995), p. 336 for quote. See also Cannon, *President Reagan,* pp. 733–37.
   To the disappointment of Weinberger and Shultz, the speech did not counter the Tower Board's criticism of them, because White House officials thought this would dilute the message.
10. Ibid., pp. 734–35; Regan, *For the Record,* p. 371.
11. Powell, *American Journey* , p. 374.
   Powell writes that the President would have gone for another hostage-freeing scheme if they had not dissuaded him. There were now nine hostages in Lebanon.
12. Cannon, *President Reagan,* p. 738.
   According to Gallup, the jump was eight points.
13. Gallup polls, late February 1987.
14. Schieffer and Gates, *Acting President,* p. 309, for congressional vote. John E. Rielly, ed., *American Public Opinion and U.S. Foreign Policy, 1987* (Chicago: Chicago Council on Foreign Relations, 1987), pp. 31, 35–38.
   Interestingly, only 27 percent of administration officials thought Europe more important than Asia, whereas 49 percent of other leaders did. And only 8 percent of the public thought the U.S. should support the South African government, though this was more or less administration policy. (Rielly, *American Public Opinion,* p. 27.)
15. George Shultz, *Turmoil and Triumph* (New York: Scribner, 1993), p. 875.
16. Kenneth Adelman, *The Great Universal Embrace: Arms Summitry, a Skeptic's Account* (New York: Simon & Schuster, 1989), pp. 316–19.
17. Don Oberdorfer, *The Turn: From the Cold War to the New Era: The United States and the Soviet Union 1983–1990* (New York: Poseidon Press, 1991), p. 217; Shultz, *Turmoil and Triumph,* p. 876.
18. *WP,* 3/13/87.
19. Shultz, *Turmoil and Triumph,* pp. 880–85; Oberdorfer, *The Turn,* pp. 217–19.
20. Adelman, *Great Universal Embrace,* pp. 203–4.
21. Shultz, *Turmoil and Triumph,* p. 900; Oberdorfer, *The Turn,* pp. 219–20.
   Some Soviet officials saw the charges of a KGB penetration of the embassy as one more sinister effort to disrupt U.S.-Soviet relations.
22. R. Jeffrey Smith in *WP,* 4/10/87, 4/11/87; Shultz, *Turmoil and Triumph,* p. 884; Adelman, *Great Universal Embrace,* pp. 203–4.
23. Shultz, *Turmoil and Triumph,* pp. 890–91; Oberdorfer, *The Turn,* pp. 222–25. *LAT,* 4/27/87.
   Both Gorbachev and Shevardnadze assured Shultz that there had been no physical penetration of the U.S. Embassy.
24. Adelman, *Great Universal Embrace,* pp. 207–9, 240–41; Shultz, *Turmoil and Triumph,* pp. 898–99; Oberdorfer, *The Turn,* p. 244.
   According to Adelman, the talk of eliminating nuclear weapons made life difficult for Kohl and Thatcher, because it fed into the rhetoric of the Social Democrats in Germany and the Labour Party in England.
25. Shultz, *Turmoil and Triumph,* p. 984; Strobe Talbott, *Master of the Game: Paul Nitze and the Nuclear Peace* (New York: Knopf, 1988), p. 339; Adelman, *Great Universal Embrace,* pp. 240–42.
26. *LAT,* 3/8/87.
27. *WP,* 4/26/87.
28. Shultz, *Turmoil and Triumph,* pp. 899–900.
29. Admiral William J. Crowe, Jr., *The Line of Fire* (New York: Simon & Schuster, 1993), p. 264; Nitze in *WP,* 3/30/87; Shultz, *Turmoil and Triumph,* p. 898.
   The figures Nitze gave at the time were thirteen hundred Soviet warheads, two hundred U.S. warheads—this in LRINFs alone. But see note 51 below.
30. Shultz, *Turmoil and Triumph,* p. 898; Crowe, *Line of Fire,* p. 264.
31. Shultz, *Turmoil and Triumph,* pp. 905, 984, 988.
   The issue of the Pershing Ia's came up belatedly because the U.S. claimed they were German and the Soviets claimed they were American. The Soviets wanted them eliminated; the administration deferred to Kohl.
   In April, Gorbachev called for the convening of a session of the Conference on Security and Cooperation in Europe "to open broad discussions aimed at radical reductions in the levels of tactical nuclear weapons, military forces and conventional armaments in Europe" (Milan Svec, "Removing Gorbachev's Edge," *Foreign Policy,* vol. 69 [Winter 1987–88], pp. 150–51).
32. Crowe, *Line of Fire,* pp. 263–64; Adelman, *Great Universal Embrace,* pp. 243–44.
   Two of the Chiefs were also reluctant to give up the Pershings.
33. Paul Nitze, with Ann M. Smith and Steven L. Rearden, *From Hiroshima to Glasnost: At the Center of Decision—A Memoir* (New York: Grove Weidenfeld, 1989), pp. 441–43; Raymond Garthoff, *The Great Transition: American-Soviet Relations and the End of the Cold War* (Washington, D.C.: The Brookings Institution, 1994), p. 327; Oberdorfer, *The Turn,* pp. 232–33; John Newhouse, *War and Peace in the Nuclear Age* (New York: Knopf, 1989), pp. 400–401.
   According to Oberdorfer, Gorbachev had asked his aides at the Geneva summit what they thought of Reagan's proposal of opening laboratories doing space-defense research. In the discussion someone made the point that the Soviet side needed such inspections more than the U.S. did, and Gorbachev said that,

since the U.S. was ahead of the Soviet Union in many aspects of military technology, extensive inspections would be more dangerous for the U.S. than for Moscow. The Soviet military finally accepted this radical piece of common sense.

34. Shultz, *Turmoil and Triumph,* p. 987.
35. Oberdorfer, *The Turn,* pp. 234–43.
36. Shultz, *Turmoil and Triumph,* p. 987.
37. Talbott, *Master of the Game,* pp. 346–47.
38. Garthoff, *Great Transition,* p. 319; Ronald Reagan, *An American Life* (New York: Simon & Schuster, 1990), p. 687.
39. Garthoff, *Great Transition,* pp. 314–15.
40. Ibid., p. 321.
41. See discussion in Dusko Doder and Louise Branscom, *Gorbachev* (New York: Viking, 1990), pp. 174–280.
42. Shultz, *Turmoil and Triumph,* pp. 995–1001; Oberdorfer, *The Turn,* pp. 248–54.
43. Shultz, *Turmoil and Triumph,* pp. 1001–2; Garthoff, pp. 323–24; Doder and Branscom, *Gorbachev,* pp. 274–77.
44. Shultz, *Turmoil and Triumph,* pp. 904, 983.
45. Reagan, *American Life,* p. 715.
46. Shultz, *Turmoil and Triumph,* p. 983.
47. *ABMTIR,* p. 66.
48. Sidney Blumenthal, *Pledging Allegiance* (New York: HarperCollins, 1990), pp. 38–39.
49. Joel Brinkley in *NYT,* 12/20/87.
50. Reagan, *American Life,* p. 697; Shultz, *Turmoil and Triumph,* p. 1005. Shultz says he had more trouble with his own delegation than with the Soviets.
51. Shultz, *Turmoil and Triumph,* pp. 1006–7; Garthoff, *Great Transition,* pp. 326–28; R. Jeffrey Smith in *WP,* 10/12/87; Smith and Oberdorfer in *WP,* 12/6/87.

    Shultz tells us in his memoir that the Soviets would be eliminating fifteen hundred deployed warheads and the U.S. 350. This is what he said at the time, but a secret appendix to the INF treaty, later declassified, showed that the Soviets had 15 percent fewer deployed INF missiles than the U.S. had previously stated: they had retired some of their older SS-4s, and they had 36 fewer SS-20s than estimated. The U.S., by contrast, had deployed more than officials had stated: it had 120, instead of 108, Pershing II's and 329 ground-launched cruise missiles deployed.

    By the terms of the treaty, the two sides also destroyed INF weapons in storage.
52. Powell, *American Journey,* p. 348; Nitze, *From Hiroshima to Glasnost,* pp. 439–40; Shultz, *Turmoil and Triumph,* p. 990.
53. Shultz, *Turmoil and Triumph,* p. 991, for quote; *NYT,* 11/4/87, on Adelman.

    Perle's designated successor, Frank Gaffney, another member of the hard right, had so irritated the Senate Armed Services Committee that his confirmation became impossible, and when Carlucci took over the Defense Department, he was forced to resign.
54. Shultz, *Turmoil and Triumph,* p. 1003, for Gates's assessment of November 6, 1987; Gallup poll, September 1987; Oberdorfer, *The Turn,* p. 257.

    Gorbachev's visit was only the third by a Soviet leader to Washington. Gorbachev declined Reagan's offer of a trip around the United States or to Camp David. There were security issues, and he did not know how he would be received.
55. Schieffer and Gates, *Acting President,* p. 331; Robert M. Gates, *From the Shadows* (New York: Simon & Schuster, 1996), p. 423, for Gates quote.
56. David Hoffman and Don Oberdorfer in *WP,* 12/13/87; Blumenthal, *Pledging Allegiance,* pp. 47–48, for quotes.
57. Schieffer and Gates, *Acting President,* p. 330.
58. Garthoff, p. 325.
59. Cannon, *President Reagan,* p. 775, for first exchange; Shultz, *Turmoil and Triumph,* p. 1010, for second exchange.
60. Shales in *WP,* 12/11/87.
61. Powell, *American Journey,* p. 361. Powell later found this out from Ken Duberstein, who had been delegated to deal with the First Lady.
62. Ibid., pp. 360, 362; Cannon, *President Reagan,* p. 775n.
63. Reagan, *American Life,* p. 698.
64. Marlin Fitzwater, *Call the Briefing!* (New York: Times Books, 1995), p. 146; Shultz, *Turmoil and Triumph,* p. 1010.
65. Powell, *American Journey,* p. 362.
66. Shultz, *Turmoil and Triumph,* pp. 1010–11.
67. Powell, *American Journey,* pp. 362–63, for Reagan quotes; Cannon, *President Reagan,* p. 776, for Powell quote; see also Fitzwater, *Call the Briefing!,* pp. 146–47; Shultz, *Turmoil and Triumph,* p. 1011.
68. Powell, *American Journey,* p. 363, for first quote; Fitzwater, *Call the Briefing!,* pp. 147–48, for last quote; Shultz, *Turmoil and Triumph,* p. 1011.
69. Powell, *American Journey,* p. 363, for first two quotes; Shultz, *Turmoil and Triumph,* p. 1011, for Shultz quotes; Fitzwater, *Call the Briefing!,* p. 148, for last Reagan quote; see also Cannon, *President Reagan,* p. 776.
70. Powell, *American Journey,* pp. 364–65.
71. Ibid., p. 365.
72. Garthoff, *Great Transition,* pp. 330–31.

73. Shultz, *Turmoil and Triumph*, p. 1013, speaks of a ballistic-missile ceiling, but he means warheads. See Talbott, *Master of the Game*, pp. 365–66, among other sources.
74. Hoffman and Oberdorfer in *WP*, 12/13/87; Powell, *American Journey*, p. 366; Fitzwater, *Call the Briefing!*, pp. 150–52, for quotes.
75. Reagan, *American Life*, p. 701.
76. Shultz, *Turmoil and Triumph*, p. 1003.
77. Garthoff, *Great Transition*, p. 335.
78. Shultz, *Turmoil and Triumph*, pp. 1087–88; Gates, *From the Shadows*, pp. 431–32; Oberdorfer, *The Turn*, p. 274.

    At the end of December 1987 Gates bet Assistant Secretary of State Michael Armacost twenty-five dollars that the Soviets would not be out of Afghanistan before the end of the administration, and Fritz Ermarth, the CIA national intelligence officer for the Soviet Union, bet Armacost fifty dollars.
79. Garthoff, *Great Transition*, pp. 330–31; Shultz, *Turmoil and Triumph*, pp. 1087–88.
80. Roy Gutman, *Banana Diplomacy: The Making of American Policy in Nicaragua, 1981–1987* (New York: Simon & Schuster, 1988), pp. 339–57.
81. Hoffman and Oberdorfer in *WP*, 12/13/87; Garthoff, pp. 330–31.

    There were follow-up discussions in which the Soviets made clear that their position was that both sides would stop supplying arms to the Nicaraguans.
82. Garthoff, *Great Transition*, pp. 275–330, 596; Svec, "Gorbachev's Edge," pp. 150–51.

    Both sides had called for a ban on chemical weapons at the Geneva summit, but it was largely pro forma. Conventional-force reductions had been under discussion for some years in the narrowly focused mutual-and-balanced-force reduction (MBFR) talks, but had gotten nowhere. Talks between NATO and Warsaw Pact countries on a new mandate for negotiations on conventional arms had begun on February 17, 1987, and were proceeding slowly.
83. Hoffman and Oberdorfer in *WP*, 12/13/87.
84. Adelman, *Great Universal Embrace*, pp. 226–27.
85. Talbott, *Master of the Game*, p. 365; *NYT*, 3/1/93, for Carlucci quote.
86. Talbott, *Master of the Game*, p. 365; Hoffman and Oberdorfer in *WP*, 12/13/87.
87. Talbott, *Master of the Game*, pp. 363–64; see also Oberdorfer, *The Turn*, p. 267.
88. Talbott, *Master of the Game*, p. 364.
89. Oberdorfer, *The Turn*, p. 267.
90. Talbott, *Master of the Game*, pp. 365–66; Powell, *American Journey*, pp. 365–66.

    Powell tells us that the last discussion was about the START sub-ceiling, but, like Shultz, he writes erroneously that it concerned ballistic missiles, as opposed to ballistic-missile warheads. He says nothing about the joint communiqué on SDI.
91. Nitze, *From Hiroshima to Glasnost*, p. 450; Joint U.S.-Soviet Summit Statement, December 10, 1987, the White House, Washington, D.C.
92. *WP*, 12/11/87; Talbott, *Master of the Game*, pp. 365, 367; Garthoff, *Great Transition*, p. 329.

    The Soviet spokesman, Gennadi Gerasimov, said at the time that the two sides had agreed to postpone their disagreements.
93. *WP*, 12/11/87.
94. Garthoff, *Great Transition*, p. 333.
95. Oberdorfer, *The Turn*, pp. 270–71.

    Gorbachev recognized this, for he later spoke of his impression, which he said had been confirmed by his visit, that "there is a growing desire in American society for improved Soviet-American relations." He also said that what had been accomplished during the meeting "will, with time, help considerably to improve the atmosphere in the world at large, and in America itself, in terms of its more correct and tolerant perception of my country, the Soviet Union." As to the substance of the meeting, he said, "There is still much work to be done, and we must get down to it without delay."
96. Cannon, *President Reagan*, p. 778, for Weyrich quote; Blumenthal, *Pledging Allegiance*, p. 45, for "useful idiot" and "Regachev"; Garthoff, *Great Transition*, p. 334; for "appearing pragmatists"; Peggy Noonan, *What I Saw at the Revolution* (New York: Random House, 1990), pp. 245–47.
97. Blumenthal, *Pledging Allegiance*, p. 47; Schieffer and Gates, *Acting President*, p. 337.
98. *PPP* RR, vol. 1 (1988), pp. 164–66.
99. Gutman, *Banana Diplomacy*, p. 359 for quotes; Michael Beschloss and Strobe Talbott, *At the Highest Levels* (Boston: Little, Brown, 1993), p. 59.
100. Shultz, *Turmoil and Triumph*, pp. 1086–92; Oberdorfer, *The Turn*, pp. 274–82; Garthoff, *Great Transition*, pp. 735–83.

    Shevardnadze later told Shultz that the Soviets would remove half of their troops in the first ninety days and shorten the withdrawal period by a month. This they did.

    The U.S. insistence on continuing military aid to the mujahedin left Pakistan in the position of having to violate the agreement it had signed with Afghanistan.

    Gates told Shultz positively that the Kabul regime would fall if the Soviets withdrew.
101. Oberdorfer, *The Turn*, p. 269.
102. Shultz, *Turmoil and Triumph*, p. 1085.
103. Helen Dewar in *WP*, 2/24/88.
104. Shultz, *Turmoil and Triumph*, p. 1083; *WP*, 2/6/88, 2/7/88, 2/9/88, 2/10/88, 2/11/88, 2/17/88, 6/11/88.

In an attempt to preclude any Senate action of this sort, Shultz gave the Senate the whole INF negotiating record. The Democrats then threatened to read it—and to hold up the vote until they finished.

Shultz later agreed to the Biden Condition with some reservations about the language, but no sooner was a compromise formula found than the chief White House lawyer sent Senate Republicans a letter which appeared to retract the concessions the secretary had made (*WP*, 5/1/88).

105. Shultz, *Turmoil and Triumph*, p. 1084; Talbott, *Master of the Game*, p. 374; Helen Dewar in *WP*, 4/20/88; R. Jeffrey Smith in *WP*, 5/1/88.

But it was not done very well, for a hastily written and improperly translated letter from Shevardnadze spoke of banning all INF missiles, nuclear and non-nuclear. This raised the question of whether the treaty might ban a missile equipped with something other than a weapon, and as it turned out there was no definition of "weapon" in the treaty.

106. Crowe, *Line of Fire*, pp. 310–13.
107. Nitze in *WP*, 6/21/88, for discussion of START; Talbott, *Master of the Game*, p. 371, for quote.

In addition, the negotiations had identified the remaining areas of disagreement at some level of technical detail.

108. Talbott, *Master of the Game*, p. 376.
109. Crowe, *Line of Fire*, p. 311; *WP*, 4/23/88.
110. Newhouse, *War and Peace*, p. 408.
111. Ibid., p. 407; *WP*, 4/19/88, 5/20/88; Talbott, *Master of the Game*, pp. 378–81.
112. Talbott, *Master of the Game*, pp. 381–82; *WP*, 5/31/88, 9/21/88.

According to Talbott, Nitze was unhappy with this petty overreaching. An interagency battle ensued, and by the time of the summit the Pentagon came up with a compromise: the counting rule should be ten missiles per plane. The Soviets were then asking for a counting rule of twelve.

113. Smith in *WP*, 3/21/88; *WP*, 3/30/88, 5/20/88, 5/31/88.

Interviewed by *Washington Post* reporters on April 20, Colonel General Nikolai Chervov, the chief spokesman on arms control for the Soviet Defense Ministry, recalling that the U.S. had been for mobile land-based missiles in the early 1980s and had turned against them when the MX became silo-bound, qualified the U.S. position as "market oriented." He nonetheless welcomed the move.

114. Talbott, *Master of the Game*, p. 382; Newhouse, *War and Peace*, p. 405.
115. See Newhouse, *War and Peace*, pp. 405–8, for quote; see Kissinger in *WP*, 4/24/88, and Nitze in *WP*, 6/21/88, for discussions.
116. Talbott, *Master of the Game*, p. 283.
117. Smith in *WP*, 1/16/88, 1/22/88; Oberdorfer in *WP*, 1/30/88; Talbott, *Master of the Game*, p. 373.

The Soviets proposed to do away with the defense-and-space treaty and deal with the matter in a special protocol attached to START, using the same ambiguous language.

118. Background Briefing by Senior Administration Official, Office of the Press Secretary, the White House, December 9, 5:05 P.M.
119. Talbott, *Master of the Game*, pp. 372–73; *WP*, 1/22/88.
120. Smith in *WP*, 1/22/88.
121. Smith in *WP*, 3/3/88.

The previous month the Space Command had tentatively been assigned responsibility for operating a potential space defense.

122. R. Jeffrey Smith in *WP*, 1/22/88; *WP*, 1/23/88, 1/30/88.

The title of the draft defense-and-space treaty the U.S. presented in Geneva on January 22 was "Treaty Between the United States of America and the Union of Soviet Socialist Republics on Certain Measures to Facilitate the Cooperative Transition to the Deployment of Future Strategic Ballistic Missile Defenses."

On a visit to Washington at the end of the month a senior Soviet official, Georgi M. Kornienko, charged that the U.S. had reneged on the understanding reached at the Washington summit and complained that, rather than leave the "conceptual dispute" to be resolved "at some later time," the U.S. delegation to the Geneva talks was again trying "to convince the Soviet delegation that it would be good to move forward to deployment of outer-space ABM systems." The proposal, he said, would make it impossible for the two sides to resolve their differences over the meaning of the ABM Treaty by the time of the Moscow summit, because the Soviet side would not under any circumstances accept the administration's reinterpretation of the ABM Treaty.

123. Talbott, *Master of the Game*, p. 390; *WP*, 5/5/88.

The administration's purpose in insisting on the "broad" interpretation was not the same as it had been the year before. In February, Defense Secretary Carlucci cut back the administration's previous SDI budget request for fiscal year 1989 and told the Senate Armed Services Committee that there would be no tests of SDI in space in the coming year, and that the tests scheduled for 1990 and 1991 would "probably not raise the treaty compliance issue" either. (Smith in *WP*, 2/20/88.)

In April, just after the House once again voted to prohibit spending for SDI tests that violated the traditional interpretation of the ABM Treaty, Les Aspin remarked, "All of us know we are kicking the can down the road" [until the next administration takes office] (*WP*, 4/28/88).

124. Garthoff, *Great Transition*, p. 342; Oberdorfer in *WP*, 5/29/88.
125. R. Jeffrey Smith in *WP*, 9/9/87, 9/10/87, 8/9/88.

The American team that visited the radar included experts from the National Resources Defense Council and Anthony Battista from the House Armed Services Committee, an electronics expert much respected by Republicans as well as Democrats on the committee. The radar was judged to have little value as a battle-management facility, because it was of such shoddy construction that it could not withstand the effects of a nuclear blast. The group judged that it was designed to track missiles and would be a technical violation of the ABM Treaty, if deployed, because by the terms of the ABM Treaty early-warning radars were to be located on the periphery of each nation, not inland. The Americans surmised that the Soviet military had built it inland because building it on the periphery of Siberia would have been much more difficult.

126. Oberdorfer, *The Turn,* pp. 287–88; Shultz, *Turmoil and Triumph,* p. 1098; Garthoff, *Great Transition,* pp. 341–44, 595–96.

In March, Shevardnadze said of the discussions of conventional-force reductions, "Let me say, in all honesty, we were amazed at the response of our American partners. They have shown, to put it mildly, no great enthusiasm to discuss the issue."

American officials did not think the Soviets were ready to make the necessary disclosure of data and to make larger reductions, so Shultz had referred him to the tedious NATO–Warsaw Pact negotiations to create a new forum on conventional arms.

127. *WP,* 4/23/88, for first quote; Oberdorfer, *The Turn,* op. cit., pp. 287–88, for second quote.

128. Jack Matlock, *Autopsy on an Empire* (New York: Random House, 1995), p. 121.

129. Garthoff, *Great Transition,* p. 347; Doder and Branscom, *Gorbachev,* pp. 307–8, for quote.

130. Garthoff, pp. 347–49; Doder and Branscom, *Gorbachev,* pp. 308–10; Archie Brown, *The Gorbachev Factor* (Oxford: Oxford University Press, 1996), pp. 172–74.

In the Politburo only Shevardnadze and Yakovlev condemned the Andreyeva letter outright.

131. Brown, *Gorbachev Factor,* pp. 179–86; Matlock, *Autopsy,* p. 122.

132. Brown, *Gorbachev Factor,* pp. 157, 123, 260; Doder and Branscom, *Gorbachev,* p. 312; J. G. Whelan, *Soviet Diplomacy and Negotiating Behavior: 1988–90,* Special Studies on Foreign Affairs Issues, vol. III (Washington, D.C.: Government Printing Office, 1991), p. 74.

133. Blumenthal, *Pledging Allegiance,* pp. 250–51; Talbott, *Master of the Game,* pp. 387–88; Kissinger in *WP,* 4/24/88.

134. Speech to the Dallas Council on World Affairs, excerpted in *Washington Times,* February 2, 1988, quoted in Garthoff, *Great Transition,* pp. 339–40.

135. *PPP* RR, vol. 1 (1988), pp. 488–93.

Reagan did note that U.S.-Soviet relations had taken "a dramatic turn towards realistic engagement."

136. Mikhail Gorbachev, *Memoirs* (New York: Doubleday, 1995), p. 452; Powell, *American Journey,* pp. 373–74.

According to Oberdorfer, Soviet conservatives had strong doubts about Reagan's commitment to the new relationship and there was some controversy in Party circles about inviting him to Moscow (Oberdorfer, *The Turn,* p. 285.)

137. Powell, *American Journey,* pp. 373–75; Shultz, *Turmoil and Triumph,* p. 1097.

Shultz does not mention this last part of the conversation. Nor does he say that Gorbachev explicitly told him that Reagan should not bring such rhetoric to Moscow, but he gathered that that was the message.

138. *WP,* 5/5/88; Cannon and Oberdorfer in *WP,* 5/25/88.

139. Cannon and Oberdorfer in *WP,* 5/25/88, 6/9/88; Cannon, *President Reagan,* pp. 784–85; Whelan, *Soviet Diplomacy,* pp. 83–84.

The focus group favored the President's efforts to improve superpower relations and liked Gorbachev, but they remained suspicious of Soviet intentions. People-to-people contacts were thus featured in the agreements and in the President's performance.

140. Carl Levin in *WP,* 5/22/88, for charges against Meese; George Lardner in *WP,* 5/30/88, for political impact; Whelan, *Soviet Diplomacy,* pp. 18–19; Cannon and Oberdorfer, "Reagan Off Today for Summit That Could Refurbish Presidency," *WP,* 5/25/88.

141. Whelan, *Soviet Diplomacy,* p. 6; *NYT,* 5/27/88, for quote; Talbott, *Master of the Game,* p. 390; Cannon and Oberdorfer, *WP,* 5/21/88.

At a White House briefing, senior administration officials, including Max Kampelman, expressed optimism about completing START before Reagan's term was up.

142. *WP,* 5/27/88; Shultz, *Turmoil and Triumph,* p. 1085.

Four out of the five votes against the INF treaty came from Republicans.

143. Cannon and Oberdorfer, *WP,* 6/9/88; Cannon, *President Reagan,* p. 785.

144. Steven V. Roberts in *NYT,* 5/15/88.

145. Matlock, *Autopsy,* pp. 121–22; *WP,* 5/26/88.

Shultz does not mention the "theses" in his memoir.

At a preparatory meeting of the Central Committee—one at which, according to Powell, the CIA Soviet specialists predicted that Gorbachev would have his head handed to him—Gorbachev gained the committee's approval for a somewhat modified version of his blueprint. The Central Committee did not agree that the conference could make major changes in its own membership. (Powell, *American Journey,* pp. 375–76; Brown, *Gorbachev Factor,* pp. 175–77.)

146. Gary Lee in *WP,* 6/2/88; Oberdorfer in *WP,* 6/2/88; Garthoff, *Great Transition,* p. 354; Gorbachev, *Memoirs,* p. 456; Cannon, *President Reagan,* p. 787.

147. Reagan, *American Life,* pp. 705–7; Whelan, *Soviet Diplomacy,* p. 25.

148. Gorbachev press conference transcript in *WP,* 6/2/88; Cannon and Oberdorfer in *WP,* 6/3/88; Shultz, *Turmoil and Triumph,* p. 1105, for Gorbachev quote; Powell, *American Journey,* pp. 378–80; Fitzwater, *Call the Briefing!,* pp. 153–57; Gorbachev, *Memoirs,* p. 458; Oberdorfer, *The Turn,* pp. 301–4.

149. Whelan, *Soviet Diplomacy*, p. 29.
   Shultz had laid plans for the Reagans to visit Yuri and Tatyana Zieman, a couple who had long been refused exit visas, but he called the visit off when, at the last moment, the Soviets sent a message to Helsinki saying they were confident that the visas could be obtained if the issue was not forced. Instead, the Reagans, at the behest of their advance team but against the wishes of the Secret Service, took a quasi-impromptu walk on the Arbat. The KGB was not alerted in time, and the police roughed up some members of the American press in an attempt to hold back the crowd. (Shultz, *Turmoil and Triumph*, p. 1102; Fitzwater, *Call the Briefing!*, pp. 157–61; Cannon and Oberdorfer in *WP*, 6/3/88.)
150. Shultz, *Turmoil and Triumph*, p. 1104, for quotes; *NYT*, 6/1/88; Cannon, *President Reagan*, p. 784; Whelan, *Soviet Diplomacy*, p. 42.
151. Whelan, *Soviet Diplomacy*, p. 36; Oberdorfer, *The Turn*, pp. 298–99, for quotes; Matlock, *Autopsy*, p. 123.
   Reagan had not much of an answer to Gorbachev's proposal on space cooperation: he said the experts were looking into it.
   Matlock writes that Gorbachev got Reagan's endorsement but that the price was the speeches on human rights and democratization.
152. Cannon, *President Reagan*, p. 787; Schieffer and Gates, *Acting President*, p. 334; Talbott, *Master of the Game*, p. 390.
153. *NYT*, 6/1/88, for House of Writers quote; Doder and Branscom, *Gorbachev*, p. 318, for quote to Sidey; see also Cannon, *President Reagan*, p. 785.
154. Doder and Branscom, *Gorbachev*, p. 318.
155. Kaiser in *WP*, 6/3/88; Cannon in *WP*, 6/2/88.
   During the summit Gorbachev and his aides fretted about Reagan's insistence on Soviet human-rights violations, maintaining that the Americans knew nothing about the realities, and in any case had no right to interfere in internal Soviet affairs. In June, Gorbachev further liberalized the regulations on emigration and travel abroad, with the result that most of those refuseniks whom Reagan had met at the ambassador's residence emigrated later that year. Jack Matlock later maintained that he did this because of Reagan's visit (*Autopsy*, p. 149). But Gorbachev had begun to liberalize these regulations in 1987, and that year over eight thousand Soviet Jews emigrated—the highest total since 1981. Between January and November 1988 the total rose to over fifteen thousand (Whelan, *Soviet Diplomacy*, p. 9), and Gorbachev continued to cut away at the restrictions long after Reagan left office. So, in a sense, Reagan may have been right that "the bureaucracy" was at fault.
156. Oberdorfer, *The Turn*, p. 307; Lee in *WP*, 6/3/88.
157. Lee in *WP*, 6/2/88, 6/3/88; Garthoff, *The Great Transition*, p. 357.
158. *WP*, 5/31/88 (which also states that about 90 percent of the verification issues on mobile missiles were settled at the summit); Oberdorfer in *WP*, 6/2/88; Hoagland in *WP*, 6/2/88; Garthoff, *The Great Transition*, p. 353, for the other small agreements signed.
159. McCartney in *WP*, 6/3/88, for Shultz quote; Havemann in *WP*, 6/4/88, for Powell.
160. Cannon in *WP*, 6/4/88; Havemann in *WP*, 6/4/88.
161. Cannon, *President Reagan*, p. 785.

ELEVEN: The End of the Cold War

1. Bob Schieffer and Gary Paul Gates, *The Acting President* (New York: E. P. Dutton, 1989), p. 336, and Gallup for Reagan polls; Archie Brown, *The Gorbachev Factor* (Oxford: Oxford University Press, 1996), p. 239, for Harris poll on Gorbachev.
2. Editorial cited in Cannon, *President Reagan: The Role of a Lifetime* (New York: Simon & Schuster, 1991), p. 783; see also J. G. Whelan, *Soviet Diplomacy and Negotiation Behavior: 1988–90*, Special Studies on Foreign Affairs Issues, vol. III (Washington, D.C.: Government Printing Office, 1991), p. 83; Cannon and Oberdorfer in *WP*, 6/9/88, for results of focus group.
3. *WP*, 6/2/88.
4. Sidney Blumenthal, *Pledging Allegiance* (New York: HarperCollins, 1990), pp. 249–51.
5. Don Oberdorfer, *The Turn: From the Cold War to the New Era: The United States and the Soviet Union 1938–1990* (New York: Poseidon Press, 1991), p. 329, for quote; see also Chalmers Roberts in *WP*, 9/11/88; Blumenthal, *Pledging Allegiance*, p. 254. Bush repeated this several times in speeches in June and July.
6. Hoffman in *WP*, 6/8/88.
   In a previous interview he expressed disagreement with Reagan's statement that "the bureaucracy" was responsible for emigration policies (*WP*, 6/3/88).
7. Michael Beschloss and Strobe Talbott, *At the Highest Levels* (Boston: Little, Brown, 1993), p. 9, for first quote; Blumenthal, *Pledging Allegiance*, p. 254, for second quote.
8. Smith in *WP*, 7/16/88; *WP*, 8/9/88, 9/16/88, 9/21/88.
   The timing was curious. The administration had been complaining about the radar since 1983, but had never made any attempt to negotiate it out of existence via some face-saving formula, as Nitze had repeatedly urged. The radar was just too valuable as a complaint. Yet recently the Soviets had taken the initiative to solve the problem themselves. In 1987 Shevardnadze had acknowledged to Shultz that the radar was a violation of the treaty. Construction on the radar complex was halted, and a U.S. congressional delegation permitted to visit it. Nonetheless, the senators' proposal found a good deal of support in the administration.

Frank Carlucci argued for it, maintaining that the U.S. should not actually withdraw from the ABM Treaty but simply threaten to do so until the radar was dismantled. He found allies in Edward Rowney, Edwin Meese, James Baker and William Webster, the director of central intelligence. At the two White House meetings called to discuss it, Baker and others argued that the formal charge should be made, to prevent the U.S. from appearing weak. General Robert Herres, the vice-chairman of the Joint Chiefs, however, made the familiar point that, if anyone benefited from an abrogation of the ABM Treaty, it would be the Soviets, since they could deploy an ABM system faster than the U.S. Nitze argued that taking a step with such serious legal implications was not necessary in order to make progress on the radar issue. Eventually Shultz and the Chiefs prevailed, and the negotiations continued.

In August the Soviets proposed to allow the U.S. to monitor the radar on a permanent basis; they also proposed to dismantle it when a defense-and-space agreement was reached: that is, when the U.S. ceased to insist on the "broad" interpretation of the ABM Treaty.

In September, Gorbachev offered to turn the radar into an international center for tracking objects in outer space. The U.S., however, continued to insist that the radar be dismantled at vast expense, and eventually the Soviets agreed to tear it down.

9. *WP,* 9/24/88.
10. Smith in *WP,* 11/17/88.
11. Whelan, *Soviet Diplomacy,* p. 74; Brown, *Gorbachev Factor,* pp. 179–86, and Jack Matlock, *Autopsy on an Empire* (New York: Random House, 1995), pp. 130–34, for structural reforms; see also Gorbachev's UN speech in *WP,* 12/8/88.

    Soviet officials, commentators and foreign-policy specialists spoke respectfully of the President and hailed the summit as a landmark event, though for reasons they described rather vaguely as the "deepening of the political dialogue" or the establishment of "a constructive basis for the long-term development of U.S.-Soviet relations." In addition, the polls—a new institution in the Soviet Union—showed that 52 percent of the Soviet public thought better of Reagan after the summit than before—and only 4 percent thought worse of him. (Haynes Johnson in *WP,* 6/3/88.)
12. Brown, *Gorbachev Factor,* p. 225, for first quote; Raymond Garthoff, *The Great Transition: American-Soviet Relations and the End of the Cold War* (Washington, D.C.: The Brookings Institution, 1994), pp. 362, 588 for second quote, 656; Matlock, *Autopsy,* pp. 142–47.
13. Shultz, *Turmoil and Triumph* (New York: Scribner, 1993), p. 1106; Colin Powell, with Joseph E. Persico, *My American Journey* (New York: Random House, 1995), p. 390; Oberdorfer, *The Turn,* p. 315.
14. Excerpts of text in *WP,* 12/8/88, see also Robert Kaiser's article in *WP,* 12/8/88.

    The *New York Times* editorial the next day read: "Perhaps not since Woodrow Wilson presented his Fourteen Points in 1918 or since Franklin Roosevelt and Winston Churchill promulgated the Atlantic Charter in 1941 has a world figure demonstrated the vision Mikhail Gorbachev displayed yesterday at the United Nations." *Newsweek* opined that Gorbachev's military cutback "was surely a move forced by his economic woes, but it was also a brilliant way to play a losing hand." (Oberdorfer, *The Turn,* pp. 318–19.)
15. Powell, *American Journey,* p. 391.
16. Ronald Reagan, *An American Life* (New York: Simon & Schuster, 1990), p. 720.
17. Powell, *American Journey,* p. 392; Shultz, *Turmoil and Triumph,* p. 1108, for quotes; Beschloss and Talbott, *At the Highest Levels,* pp. 10–11.
18. Oberdorfer, *The Turn,* pp. 320–21.
19. Brown, *Gorbachev Factor,* pp. 188–89, 247–51; Garthoff, *Great Transition,* pp. 400, 600–601.
20. Robert M. Gates, *From the Shadows* (New York: Simon & Schuster, 1996), pp. 447, 450.
21. Beschloss and Talbott, *At the Highest Levels,* pp. 47–48; speech at AAAS in *WP,* 10/15/88; Hoffman in *WP,* 5/14/89.

    In testimony to Congress later in December, Douglas MacEachin, the chief of SOVA, said that the CIA "never really looked at the Soviet Union as a political entity in which there were factors building which could lead to at least the initiation of political transformation." He added, "We never would have been able to publish it anyway, quite frankly. And had we done so, people would have been calling for my head. In all honesty, had we said a week ago that Gorbachev might come to the U.N. and offer a unilateral cut of 500,000 in the military, we would have been told we were crazy." (*Boston Globe,* 11/19/99.)
22. Robert L. Hutchings, *American Diplomacy and the End of the Cold War* (Washington, D.C./Baltimore, Md.: Woodrow Wilson Center Press/Johns Hopkins University Press, 1997), pp. 17–18.

    Polls taken in West Germany, Italy and the U.K. showed that only 24 percent or so of their publics considered the Soviet Union a threat (Oberdorfer, *The Turn,* p. 323). Before the Geneva summit, the percentages were reversed.
23. *NYT,* 12/29/88, for scholars; *NYT,* 1/19/89, for press-conference text.
24. CBS-*NYT* poll in *NYT,* 1/18/89.
25. *NYT,* 1/12/89; *Newsweek,* 1/9/89.

    During the Reagan administration, federal-government spending grew at a rate of 3.3 percent a year, and there were 150,000 more federal workers at the end than at the beginning.
26. Blumenthal, *Pledging Allegiance,* p. 323 for Reagan quote, and see p. 327; Beschloss and Talbott, *At the Highest Levels,* pp. 17–18, for Scowcroft quote.
27. Blumenthal, *Pledging Allegiance,* p. 324.
28. Ibid., pp. 322–23.

29. Matlock, *Autopsy*, p. 185; Shultz, *Turmoil and Triumph*, pp. 1137–38; Powell, *American Journey*, p. 389, on Carlucci; Beschloss and Talbott, *At the Highest Levels*, pp. 26–28.

Once in office, Baker told aides, "Remember, this is *not* a friendly take-over." (Beschloss and Talbott.)

Whatever was going through the minds of Bush and his advisers, it seemed to be the same thing that was going through the mind of Henry Kissinger. In April 1988 Kissinger had called for conventional-force reductions to accompany a START treaty—and Bush had followed suit. In late December, Kissinger admitted that Gorbachev's UN speech had pulled the teeth from the argument. Yet, in reflecting on Gorbachev's announcement of unilateral conventional-force reductions, Kissinger could not decide what it meant. Gorbachev's speech, he wrote, "will be significant either because it was a stage in disarming the West or as the opening move in a complex negotiation." In possibly the least coherent piece of his career, Kissinger wrote that NATO needed to strengthen its conventional forces; it was unlikely to do that, but if it did, Gorbachev could always stop his withdrawals and blame the West for rejecting his initiative, thus generating a storm of protest against Western governments. Either way, Gorbachev would win—unless his policy, combined with perestroika, dissolved the Warsaw Pact first—in which case there would be "a classic East European blow-up of the type that produced World War I." What the West needed was a well-thought-out long-term strategy. The Bush administration, he wrote, "must not let itself be stampeded but must define its own agenda and timetable." (*WP*, 12/20/88.)

30. James A. Baker III, *The Politics of Diplomacy* (New York: G. P. Putnam's Sons, 1995), p. 29.
31. Beschloss and Talbott, *At the Highest Levels*, pp. 24–25.
32. Ibid., p. 45.
33. Ibid., pp. 3–4.

Driving with Gorbachev to the airport after the Washington summit, Bush said that for seven years he had had to conceal his moderate views, since Reagan was surrounded by "marginal intellectual thugs," who would be delighted to seize on any evidence that the vice-president was a closet liberal.

34. David Hoffman in *WP*, 5/14/89.
35. Hutchings, *American Diplomacy*, p. 28.
36. *WP*, 4/24/88.
37. Hutchings, *American Diplomacy*, pp. 27–28.

Writing almost a decade after the fact, Hutchings does not question this dedication to nuclear deterrence, and, interestingly, he says virtually nothing about what Bush and his advisers thought was going on in the Soviet Union, as though the Soviet Union were somehow irrelevant to U.S. defense planning—as perhaps it was.

38. Cited in Frances FitzGerald, "The American Millennium," in *Estrangement*, ed. Sanford J. Ungar (New York: Oxford University Press, 1985), p. 259.
39. Blumenthal, *Pledging Allegiance*, pp. 252–53.

Bush said, "The liberal elite do not understand—they never understood—the common sense behind the consensus." This was not good history—as he certainly knew, given his references to Kennedy and Vietnam. He was simply reading the liberals out of his future consensus—and though the political exigencies of his situation forbade it, he surely meant to read out the troublesome right wing as well.

40. Beschloss and Talbott, *At the Highest Levels*, pp. 72–73.
41. Cannon in *WP*, 5/6/89.
42. *WP*, 5/9/89.
43. Beschloss and Talbott, *At the Highest Levels*, p. 135; Hoffman in *WP*, 12/5/89.

Two years later Bessmertnykh said, "If it were not for Malta, the Soviet Union would never have so smoothly surrendered its control of Eastern Europe or the Baltics." (Beschloss and Talbott, *At the Highest Levels*, p. 165.)

44. Dusko Doder and Louise Branscom, *Gorbachev* (New York: Viking, 1990), p. 371.

In December 1989, when the first Soviet opinion polls were taken, Reagan proved to be more popular than Boris Yeltsin or George Bush. Only Gorbachev and Sakharov drew more votes for Man of the Year. (Matlock, *Autopsy*, p. 125.)

45. Oberdorfer, *The Turn*, p. 327.
46. Doder and Branscom, *Gorbachev*, p. 370.
47. Hutchings, *American Diplomacy*, p. 327.
48. Beschloss and Talbott, *At the Highest Levels*, p. 14.
49. Caspar Weinberger, *Fighting for Peace* (New York: Warner Books, 1990), pp. 347–48, 351–52.
50. Daniel Deudney and G. John Ikenberry, "Who Won the Cold War?," *Foreign Policy*, vol. 87 (Summer 1992).

The authors give an account of the conservative arguments—and then argue that Reagan's nuclear abolitionism catalyzed the accommodations that brought the Cold War to an end.

51. Garthoff, *Great Transition*, pp. 516–17; AP, 4/15/97.

Soviet ABM work consisted of the following:

1. A modernization of the old Galosh ABM system around Moscow, which began in the early 1970s and was completed in the late 1980s. (This was the major expense, along with the maintenance of their air defenses.)

2. A program known as "Kaskad," begun in 1976 and given a funding boost by Andropov in 1983. It included a concept for space-based battle stations that would carry either interceptor missiles or lasers. Apart from drawings of the modules, which appeared in open literature, the most visible result of the program

was the launch of a mock-up of a battle station as a payload on the maiden flight of the Energya heavy space launcher in 1987. The module (which did not carry any lasers or interceptors) malfunctioned and did not reach orbit. The program produced no hardware (AP, 4/15/97; communication from Pavel Podvig, 8/31/99).

At a 1993 U.S.-Soviet conference, Bessmertnykh, Shevardnadze's deputy foreign minister, said that the Soviet military wanted better missiles to defend against Star Wars and those who wanted to end the Cold War wanted arms control (*NYT*, 3/1/93). From all other evidence the Soviets were going to rely on a proliferation of ICBMs to defeat any Star Wars deployment; they canceled their ASAT testing program in 1983, just after Reagan's SDI speech, because it was not succeeding.

After the break-up of the Soviet Union, when Russians looked most favorably upon the United States and hoped for American help, many Russians told Americans informally that SDI had accelerated the collapse (see Robert McFarlane in *NYT*, 8/24/93). But they offered no proof. To argue the case, they would have had to argue the untenable proposition that Gorbachev would not have made his reforms in the absence of SDI (see note 55 below).

Sakharov, Velikhov, and Sagdeyev were not among those who made such claims. After the nationalist reaction in Russia, this talk ended.

52. Garthoff, *Great Transition*, p. 506 n; *WP*, 3/31/86; Firth and Noren, *Soviet Defense Spending*, pp. 99–102.

According to Firth and Noren, p. 108, the spending hike in 1985–87 was led by strategic defenses. The Soviets were modernizing their Galosh system and adding SAMs (see notes 51 and 53).

53. Garthoff, *Great Transition*, pp. 538–39; Arms Control Association Background Paper, June 1990, for figures.

Spending for strategic offensive forces declined by 5.2 percent per annum in the years 1988–90 (Firth and Noren, *Soviet Defense Spending*, p. 108).

54. Stephen H. Meyer in *WP*, 10/19/86. See also Firth and Noren, *Soviet Defense Spending*, p. 112.

The U.S. spent a somewhat larger proportion of its military budget on strategic weapons because it bought very expensive high-tech systems, such as the B-1 and B-2 bombers.

55. Douglas J. MacEachin, "CIA Assessments of the Soviet Union: The Record Versus the Charges," *Studies in Intelligence*, vol. 1, no. 1 (1997). Firth and Noren, *Soviet Defense Spending*, p. 130.

MacEachin, a chief of SOVA in the 1980s, argues that the CIA was not oblivious to the deteriorating economic and social conditions that set the stage for the breakup of the Soviet Union. In the article and in the documents in appendix A (some of which are retrospective), there is much evidence for the proposition that in the 1980s the Soviet economy was in decline but not in a crisis. MacEachin adds that the breakup of the Soviet Union in 1991 was not inevitable, for there was no economic collapse. Rather, it was precipitated and shaped by decisions made by Gorbachev. Had Chernenko not died when he did, MacEachin writes, "how much longer would the Soviet Union have muddled along?"

In 1986 CIA analysts were forecasting that the economic decline, if not reversed, would eventually affect defense outlays, but that Gorbachev could postpone the issue, given the military-industrial infrastructure already in place.

At the time and in retrospect, CIA analysts saw Gorbachev's reforms as a response to Soviet domestic problems. So did Shultz.

After a meeting with Gromyko in Vienna in May 1985, at the height of the excitement about SDI in the U.S. and the Soviet Union, Shultz reported: "My impression was that the Soviets were preoccupied with their domestic problems, and this was forcing them to alter—for the better—the way they dealt with us." (Shultz, *Turmoil and Triumph*, pp. 715–16, 564.)

According to Firth and Noren (p. 112), the military share of the Soviet GDP rose from its historic level of about 15 percent to 17–18 percent in the mid-1980s—though for reasons that are not completely clear. Firth and Norman maintain that the burden of defense spending on the Soviet economy was so difficult to calculate that the CIA figures were never authoritative.

56. "The Reagans," *60 Minutes*, 1/15/89, CBS News transcript.

Reagan here spoke of "the beach house," as opposed to the pool house. In the two accounts below, he spoke of "the boat house."

57. Interview with Morton Janklow, 6/2/99.
58. Michael Korda, "Prompting the President," *The New Yorker*, October 6, 1997, pp. 88–95.

Michael Korda first published his account of the meeting with Reagan in *The New Yorker*, whose editors did not catch the fact that there was no arms agreement signed at the Geneva summit, and no talk of verification.

Korda ends the piece with another Reagan story from the summit. The President was staying at the Aga Khan's villa. Informed that one of the goldfish in his host's aquarium had died, he, feeling responsible, sent the Secret Service out for a replacement, and put the dead goldfish in his pocket in a matchbox. He then forgot to discard it, so that during his initial meeting with Gorbachev—one of the meetings on which hung the fate of the world—he was carrying a dead goldfish in his pocket.

Unfortunately, this story seems to be no more true than the one about Gorbachev. What happened, apparently, was that Reagan promised the Aga Khan's son, Hussain, that he would take good care of his aquarium, but while he was in residence someone, possibly a Secret Service man, accidentally disconnected the aquarium, killing a multitude of fancy tropical fish. Someone in Reagan's entourage replaced the fish. (Conversation with Prince Amyn Aga Khan, October 25, 1997.)

Reagan's memoir begins with a factually accurate account of the Geneva meeting between Reagan and Gorbachev. It presents Reagan as a Cold War hero.

AFTERWORD: NATIONAL MISSILE DEFENSES, 1989–99

1. *NYT,* 1/21/99.
2. Bruce W. MacDonald, "SDI—Lost in Space," *Arms Control Today,* September 1989 [hereafter MacDonald, 1989], p. 25, for Scowcroft; Fred Barnes, "Pebbles Go Bam-Bam," *New Republic,* April 17, 1989, pp. 12–15; William J. Broad, *Teller's War* (New York: Simon & Schuster, 1992), p. 260.

   In a debate with Jack Kemp in February 1988 Bush said, "Premature deployment of something that isn't totally effective would do nothing but cause the Soviets to break out of the ABM treaty and overwhelm what we've got." Yet in Chicago on August 22 he declared, "I am committed to the deployment of SDI as soon as feasible, and will determine the exact architecture of the system in my first term. . . . As president, I will not leave America defenseless against ballistic missiles." In an interview with a *New York Times* reporter three days later he pulled back from this statement somewhat, saying that full deployment would be very expensive and any decision would depend on further research. However, he said, "There are new technologies being looked at that would make it quite economical to deploy a major SDI." (Fred Barnes, "Pebbles Go Bam-Bam," p. 14.)
3. *NYT,* 1/27/89.
4. Michael Beschloss and Strobe Talbott, *At the Highest Levels* (Boston: Little, Brown, 1993), pp. 117–18, for Bush statement; MacDonald, 1989, for Cheney; *LAT,* 9/7/89.

   Vice-President Quayle said that Reagan "talked about this impenetrable shield that was going to be completely leak-proof" but that was "political jargon"—acceptable as such, but unrealistic in terms of the capability of a strategic-defense system.
5. MacDonald, 1989, pp. 25–26; *NYT,* 4/25/89.
6. *NYT,* 4/19/89, 6/1/89; *WP,* 9/7/89; MacDonald, 1989, p. 23

   In February 1990 Crowe, then retired, recommended funding of three billion dollars for fiscal 1991.
7. *NYT,* 4/24/89; *WP,* 7/19/90.
8. Lieutenant General James A. Abrahamson, Memorandum for the Deputy Secretary of Defense, "End of Tour" Report, February 9, 1989.

   Abrahamson's memo was declassified and distributed to the press by the Center for Peace and Freedom, a pro-SDI group associated with the Heritage Foundation *(WP,* 3/18/89).
9. Broad, *Teller's War,* pp. 251–55.
10. Ibid., p. 266; *WP,* 4/26/89.

    Brilliant Pebbles received eighteen million dollars in fiscal 1988; the funding was increased to forty-six million in fiscal 1989—but even that sum made it a relatively low-priority project.
11. Barnes, "Pebbles Go Bam-Bam," pp. 14–15.
12. *WP,* 4/26/89; Broad, *Teller's War,* p. 262; MacDonald 1989, pp. 24–25.
13. Bruce W. MacDonald, "Falling Star: SDI's Troubled Seventh Year," *Arms Control Today,* September 1990 [hereafter MacDonald, 1990], pp. 9–10; Broad, *Teller's War,* p. 266.

    The funding request for Brilliant Pebbles went from $175 million in 1990 to $392 million in 1991.
14. R. Jeffrey Smith in *WP,* 2/18/90.

    In 1989 the Defense Science Board and JASON, a group of independent scientists regularly consulted by the Pentagon, reviewed the Brilliant Pebbles design. The SDIO portrayed both studies as unqualified endorsements, when in fact the DSB had called the design incomplete and recommended against replacing the older interceptor concept, and JASON concluded that Brilliant Pebbles could not be assembled with off-the-shelf technology and expressed no confidence that the technical problems could be overcome.
15. In September 1989 Shevardnadze formally uncoupled START from any agreement on defense and space provided both sides continued to comply with the ABM Treaty. Shevardnadze wanted an explicit provision in START permitting either side to withdraw from it if the other side violated or withdrew from the ABM Treaty, but the Bush administration opposed the provision.
16. *WP,* 2/8/90.
17. R. Jeffrey Smith in *WP,* 2/18/90.
18. MacDonald, 1990, pp. 7–8.
19. Ibid.

    Robert Gates, now CIA director, repeatedly told Congress that U.S. intelligence experts "do not believe there is a concern about any unauthorized launch of any of the Soviet strategic or tactical systems" and that no additional countries would be able to threaten the U.S. with ballistic missiles "for at least a decade." (Gerard C. Smith, "Two Decades Later: The ABM Treaty in a Changed World, *Arms Control Today,* May 1992, p. 4.)
20. *WSJ,* 8/6/90; *NYT,* 8/5/90; *WP,* 8/5/90, 8/6/90; *NYT,* 10/23/90.

    The Democrats cut the funding back to $2.9 billion for fiscal 1991.
21. *WP,* 1/13/91.

    In addition, Cooper budgeted some funds for work on defenses against short- and medium-range missiles.
22. *WP,* 1/31/91, 2/15/91; Seymour Hersh, "Missile Wars," *New Yorker,* September 26,1994, p. 88.
23. Jeffrey Denny, "Star Struck," *Common Cause Magazine,* March–April 1991 for quotes; see also *WSJ,* 1/23/91, for editorial and piece by Oliver North; *Newsweek,* February 4,1991, for piece by Kenneth Adelman.

24. *WP,* 1/31/91, for Bush quotes; Denny, "Star Struck"; *USA Today,* February 28, 1991, for last quote.
25. Helen Dewar in *WP,* 3/14/91, 3/15/91.

The amended resolution stated that, if the Soviets would not agree to space-based systems in two years, the President should immediately determine whether the United States should continue to adhere to the treaty.

On behalf of the President, Scowcroft wrote Warner, "I believe it [the resolution] will send an unmistakable signal of our determination to proceed with ballistic missile defenses that enhance our national security." *(WP,* 3/14/91.)
26. *NYT,* 7/18/91; Mary McGrory in *WP,* 7/23/91.
27. Harold Brown in *WP,* 3/27/91; Gelb in *NYT,* 1/27/91; Charles E. Bennett in *WP,* 2/3/91; see also *WP,* 2/21/91.
28. Leslie Gelb in *NYT,* 1/27/91, for Army quote.

The day after Bush's State of the Union speech, the White House press secretary, Marlin Fitzwater, said, "The Patriot is a piece of technology that emerged from the SDI program in the sense that—well, some of the research that went into it was, and some of the concepts . . . emerged from that program." The difficulty Fitzwater had with this sentence said a great deal. (Smith in *WP,* 1/31/91.)

A few days after the speech, the *New York Times* ran an editorial headed, "Patriots Work, Star Wars Won't" (2/3/91).
29. The exceptions included George Will, who, contradicting Sam Donaldson, opined, "When you see a Patriot shooting down an incoming missile, you are seeing strategic defense, and you are seeing Star Wars technology" (Denny, "Star Struck"). Kenneth Adelman wrote in *Newsweek,* "The Patriot is a sort of SDI Jr., based on the principles of the larger model" (2/4/91).
30. Colin Powell with Joseph E. Persico, *My American Journey* (New York: Random House, 1995), p. 498; Fred Barnes, "Brilliant Pebble," *New Republic,* April 1, 1991; *WP,* 12/7/90, 12/16/90.

All but ten Democratic senators voted nay.
31. Mary McGrory in *WP,* 7/23/91; *WP,* 3/15/91.

Nunn's defeat of the Warner resolution was treated by journalists as a political comeback for the chair of the Armed Services Committee, and Nunn did not deny it.
32. START I was signed at the summit, July 30–31; it brought the warhead totals down to where they were when the START negotiations began in 1982. (Raymond L. Garthoff, *The Great Transition: American–Soviet Relations at the End of the Cold War* [Washington, D.C.: The Brookings Institution, 1994], p. 466.)

The Soviets specified abrogation or a "material breach" of the treaty (Matthew Bunn, "The ABM Talks: The More Things Change. . . ," *Arms Control Today,* September 1992).
33. *NYT,* 8/4/91; *Statesman Journal,* January 19, 1992; *NYT,* 11/18/91.
34. *NYT,* 5/28/92.
35. *WSJ* editorial, 1/23/91; George Melleon in *WSJ,* 2/10/92; *WP,* 4/25/91; *WP,* 3/11/92.
36. *NYT,* 6/4/92, 6/6/92; *NYT,* 1/30/91, for ERIS test description.
37. *NYT,* 6/2/92, for ERIS test; *NYT,* 6/4/92, 4/10/92, 6/6/92, 5/21/92, 6/2/92.

In April, Cooper said that deployment by 1996 would mean the engineers would have to manufacture several parts of the system before prototype models were fully tested. Still, he said, "Early deployment is not a big risk." On May 20 he acknowledged that there might be delays and cost overruns, but said the risk of fielding the system by 1997 was "acceptable" given "the urgency related to our uncertainty in predicting when we might actually be threatened with ballistic missile attack." The sentence required some parsing (*NYT,* 4/10/92, 5/21/92).
38. *NYT,* 6/2/92.
39. *NYT,* 6/6/92, 11/26/92.

Atwood said that he and Cooper had discussed the matter and agreed that the development process had to square with the Pentagon's rules for acquisitions (*NYT,* 6/6/92).
40. R. Jeffrey Smith in *WP,* 9/16/92; William Broad in *NYT,* 5/24/99; Dr. George N. Lewis, "Chronology of Missile Defense Tests," unpublished paper for Security Studies Program, MIT, Cambridge, Mass.

In the ERIS test two decoys were tethered to each side of the dummy warhead and the interceptor's computer had been programmed to pick out the target in the middle. About one second before impact the kill vehicle deployed an inflatable octagonal kill-enhancement device. The second ERIS test was aborted, and in the third one ERIS failed to hit its target.
41. *NYT,* 8/18/93, 7/23/94.
42. *NYT,* 4/10/92.
43. *WP,* 9/30/92; Seymour Hersh, "Missile Wars," *New Yorker,* September 26, 1994, pp. 86–99.

According to the GAO, the 158 Patriot missiles fired hit no more than four of the forty-five Scuds they were aimed at. There was therefore some evidence to support the position of the chief American critic of the program, Theodore Postol, that the Patriots had done more harm than good because they added to the number of missiles that fell on Israel.
44. *Oregonian,* 8/4/92.

Daniel O. Graham thought Teller and Wood had an excellent idea. "What Brilliant Pebbles would give you," he said, "is control of access to space."
45. *NYT,* 1/15/93.
46. *NYT,* 12/30/92.
47. *WP,* 5/14/93.

"I don't see an awful lot of change," Daniel O. Graham said. "They hope to camouflage this mismanaged mishmash with a new name," John Conyers charged *(WP,* 5/14/93).

Senator Malcolm Wallop said the reorganization seemed a good idea, and he hoped it meant a transition from research to acquisitions *(NYT,* 5/14/93, and see AP, 5/16/93).

48. *WP,* 9/5/95.

Fifteen Third World countries had ballistic missiles, but very few of them could be characterized as "rogue states."

49. John Pike, "Theatre Missile Defense Programs: Status and Prospects," *Arms Control Today,* May 1992, p. 13; *Bulletin of the Atomic Scientists,* Sept.–Oct. 1995, p. 50.
50. Spurgeon M. Keeny, Jr., "The Theater Missile Defense Threat to U.S. Security," *Arms Control Today,* September, 1994, pp. 5–6.

The agreement when the ABM Treaty was signed was that the treaty banned the testing of (fixed land-based) interceptors against reentry vehicles traveling more than two kilometers per second or at altitudes above forty kilometers.

In 1993 the U.S. proposed that interceptors be permitted provided that they did not have a "demonstrated" or tested capability against a reentry vehicle traveling at more than five kilometers a second.

The Clinton administration initially planned to submit the proposed modification to the Standing Consultative Commission, the body created to deal with ABM Treaty disputes, and treat it as a technical change. Clinton was later persuaded to treat it as a substantive change that would require the approval of the Senate.

Russian negotiators initially accepted a U.S. proposal to increase the acceptable target speed for testing anti-missile systems to five kilometers—provided that the interceptor's velocity be limited to three kilometers a second. They did not accept the U.S. proposal to distinguish between theater and strategic ABMs on the basis of the "demonstrated" capability of a system because it would prevent them from challenging those systems that had an inherent capability to counter strategic missiles but had not been tested against them. (Ibid.)

51. Pike, "Missile Defense Programs"; Mandelsohn and Rhinelander, "Shooting Down."

The Communist deputies argued, among other things, that the U.S. would take advantage of further strategic nuclear cutbacks to end the ABM Treaty and build an effective ABM system.

52. *WSJ,* 4/4/96.
53. *WP,* 5/9/95, 9/5/95, 9/7/95; *NYT,* 8/4/95, 12/29/95.
54. Senator J. James Exon in *Omaha World Herald,* 8/6/96, for partial text of bill; Scripps-Howard News Service, 8/4/96; AP, 6/6/96; *WP,* 6/5/96.
55. *WP,* 5/3/96, 7/28/96.
56. *WP,* 7/28/96.
57. *WP,* 9/5/95.

Clinton took the position that the Republican plan would waste billions and violate the ABM Treaty, but he did not have to spend much time on the issue.

58. *WP,* 7/28/96; Holgar Jensen in *Rocky Mountain News,* 12/3/96.

Dole's polls told him that three in ten Americans supported his Defend America Act. But doubtless the pollsters had to explain what this was.

59. Bradley Graham in *WP,* 4/27/98.
60. *NYT,* 9/27/97; Lisbeth Gronlund, "ABM: Just Kicking the Can," *Bulletin of the Atomic Scientists,* January/February 1988.

The accord permitted interceptors having a velocity of less than three kilometers per second as long as they were not tested against targets that had speeds of more than five kilometers. This was essentially the Russian going-in position.

The accord included a statement on higher-speed systems. It did not specify what systems are permitted or prohibited but merely noted that any permitted high-speed system must adhere to the same testing restriction as low-speed systems.

The accord also laid down three principles in regard to deployment: the interceptors may not be deployed for use against other treaty partners, they may not pose "a realistic threat to the strategic nuclear force" of a treaty partner, and the scale of the deployment must be consistent in number and geographic scope with the theater missile threat.

In addition the accord specified that Russia, Ukraine, Belarus and Kazakhstan would succeed the Soviet Union as parties to the treaty.

61. Ibid.; *NYT,* 3/7/97; Tim Weiner in *NYT,* 5/18/97.

In May 1997 Paul Kaminski, the undersecretary of defense in charge of weapons procurements, told Congress the Pentagon's efforts to create a hit-to-kill system had failed in 70 percent of the tests.

62. *NYT,* 7/16/98; *Seattle Times,* 5/1/98.

The CIA had cast doubt on its own ability to forecast missile technologies.

63. *WP,* 1/21/99; *LAT,* 1/21/99.
64. *NYT,* 9/10/98.
65. William Broad in *NYT,* 5/24/99.
66. *LAT,* 1/21/99, for quote; *WP,* 1/21/99; *NYT,* 1/21/99; Dow Jones News Service, 1/20/99; *WSJ,* 1/21/99; Walter Pincus in *WP,* 1/22/99; U.S. Department of Defense, Annual Report by the Director: Operational Testing and Evaluation, FY 1998.

According to Cohen and the Director of OT&E, the schedule of deployment in 2005 was still so compressed that there was a risk of failure.

67. *WSJ,* 1/21/99.
68. Robert L. Park, Op Ed, in *NYT,* 2/15/99.
69. *NYT,* 3/17/99, 3/18/99, 3/19/99, 5/21/99. In May the House passed the same bill as the Senate, 345 to 71.
70. *NYT,* 1/22/99, 1/25/99; editorial, in *WSJ,* 3/19/99.
71. *WP,* 6/22/99; *NYT,* 10/17/99, 10/21/99 for quotes.

    Russian officials said they had begun to consult with China about possible political and military cooperation in the event the U.S. withdrew from the ABM Treaty.
72. Walter Pincus in *WP,* 1/22/99; *NYT,* 10/21/99.

    Allowing the Soviets to MIRV their launchers was discussed in the Pentagon. (Walter Pincus in *WP,* 1/22/99.)

    Many Republicans in Congress opposed a START III treaty.
73. Editorial, in *WSJ,* 3/19/99; *NYT,* 3/24/99.
74. *NYT,* 10/17/99, 11/25/99.
75. *NYT,* 10/21/99, 11/20/99.

    In early November, Russia sponsored a UN resolution opposing any missile defense system that would undermine the ABM Treaty. The resolution passed by a committee vote of 54 to 7, with all of the members of the European Union either voting with Russia or abstaining (*NYT,* 11/6/99).
76. Lewis, "Chronology"; *NYT,* 10/4/99.
77. *NYT,* 5/18/97; George N. Lewis, Theodore A. Postol and John Pike, "Why National Missile Defense Won't Work," *Scientific American,* August 1999.

    "We can make a bullet hit a bullet," Paul Kaminsky, the undersecretary of defense in charge of weapons procurements said in 1997. "We can demonstrate that under ideal conditions. The next step is to move from hitting, not occasionally, but to hit routinely under stressful operating conditions" (*NYT,* 5/18/97).

    John Pike, director of the Space Policy Project of the Federation of American Scientists, said, "The odds are pretty slim that they're going to be able to consistently and reliably hit every missile, and that's what's required when you are defending against a nuclear-armed missile. There is no margin for error, so if even the smallest thing goes wrong, it fails" (*NYT,* 3/30/99).
78. Lewis et al., "Why National Missile Defense Won't Work," p. 39.
79. Ibid., p. 40.

    ABM proponents often dismissed counter-measures on the grounds that states such as North Korea were not technically sophisticated enough to mount them. Critics, however, argued that there were numerous counter-measures, some of them quite simple, that would defeat the current interceptor. According to Richard Garwin and others, one of them was wrapping a warhead in a Mylar balloon and releasing a lot of similar balloons along with it *(WSJ,* 3/19/99).
80. *Milwaukee Journal Sentinel,* 3/28/99 (for Pike quote); *WSJ,* 3/19/99 (for Cirincione quote). See also *NYT,* 3/18/99.
81. *WSJ,* 11/2/99.
82. James Lindsay and Michael O'Hanlon in *NYT,* 11/26/99.
83. *NYT,* 9/4/99. By December the Clinton administration had persuaded North Korea not to carry out a second test of its long-range missile (*NYT,* 12/8/99).
84. Heritage Foundation "Backgrounder" No. 1166.

    Similarly, the House vote in March 1999 had made no mention of technical feasibility.
85. *WSJ,* 3/19/99; Peter Maass, "Get Ready, Here Comes the Exoatmospheric Kill Vehicle," *NYT Magazine,* September 26, 1999, p. 81.

    Later that year Representative Weldon said, "Space is going to become a more critical part [of the NMD program]. Space-based sensing, space-based queing and space-based assets. It is a fact that we are going to have to deal with. We might as well be honest about that. In the end, the most capable response will come from outer space." (Ibid.)

Bibliography

BOOKS

Acheson, Dean. *Present at the Creation.* New York: W.W. Norton, 1969.

Adelman, Kenneth. *The Great Universal Embrace: Arms Summitry—A Skeptic's Account.* New York: Simon & Schuster, 1989.

Adler, Selig. *The Isolationist Impulse: Its Twentieth-Century Reaction.* New York: Free Press, 1966.

Anderson, Martin. *Revolution.* New York: Harcourt Brace Jovanovich, 1988.

Arms Control Association, ed. *Star Wars Quotes.* Washington, D.C.: The Arms Control Association, July 1986.

Au, William A. *The Cross, the Flag and the Bomb.* Contributions to the Study of Religion, no. 12. Westport, CT: Greenwood Press, 1985.

Baker, James A., III. *The Politics of Diplomacy.* New York: G.P. Putnam's Sons, 1995.

Baucom, Donald R. *The Origins of SDI, 1944–1983.* Lawrence, KS: University Press of Kansas, 1992.

Beschloss, Michael, and Strobe Talbott. *At the Highest Levels: The Inside Story of the End of the Cold War.* Boston: Little, Brown, 1993.

Bjork, Rebecca S. *The Strategic Defense Initiative: Symbolic Containment of the Nuclear Threat.* Albany, NY: State University of New York Press, 1992.

Blumenthal, Sidney. *Pledging Allegiance.* New York: HarperCollins, 1990.

———. *The Rise of the Counter-Establishment.* New York: Times Books, 1986.

Blumenthal, Sidney, and Thomas Byrne Edsall, eds. *The Reagan Legacy.* New York: Pantheon Books, 1988.

Boffey, Philip M., William J. Broad, Leslie H. Gelb, Charles Mohr, and Holcomb B. Noble. *Claiming the Heavens: The New York Times Complete Guide to the Star Wars Debate.* New York: Times Books, 1988.

Boyarsky, Bill. *The Rise of Ronald Reagan.* New York: Random House, 1968.

Boyer, Paul, ed. *Reagan as President.* Chicago: Ivan R. Dee, 1990.

Broad, William J. *Star Warriors.* New York: Simon & Schuster, 1985.

———. *Teller's War.* New York: Simon & Schuster, 1992.

Brown, Archie. *The Gorbachev Factor.* Oxford, England: Oxford University Press, 1996.

Brownstein, Ronald, and Nina Easton. *Reagan's Ruling Class.* New York: Pantheon Books, 1983.

Broyles, J. Allen. *The John Birch Society: Anatomy of a Protest.* Boston: Beacon Press, 1964.

Bruce-Biggs, B. *The Shield of Faith: The Hidden Struggle for Strategic Defense.* New York: Simon & Schuster, 1988.

Bundy, McGeorge. *Danger and Survival: Choices About the Bomb in the First Fifty Years.* New York: Random House, 1988.

Bundy, William. *A Tangled Web: The Making of Foreign Policy in the Nixon Administration.* New York: Hill and Wang, 1998.

Bundy, William P., ed. *The Nuclear Controversy: A Foreign Affairs Reader.* New York: New American Library, 1985.

Callahan, David. *Dangerous Capabilities: Paul Nitze and the Cold War.* New York: HarperCollins, 1990.

Cannon, Lou. *President Reagan: The Role of a Lifetime.* New York: Simon & Schuster, 1991.

———. *Reagan.* New York: Putnam, 1982.

Carlton, David, and Carlo Schaerf, eds. *The Arms Race in the Era of Star Wars.* New York: St. Martin's Press, 1988.

Cimbala, Stephen J. *The Reagan Defense Program: An Interim Assessment.* Wilmington, DE: Scholarly Resources, 1984.

Codevilla, Angelo. *While Others Build: A Commonsense Approach to the Strategic Defense Initiative.* New York: Free Press, 1988.

Committee on the Present Danger. *Alerting America: The Papers of the Committee on the Present Danger.* Charles Tyroler II, ed. Washington, D.C.: Pergamon-Brassey's, 1984.

Crowe, Admiral William J., Jr. *The Line of Fire: From Washington to the Gulf, the Politics and Battles of the New Military.* New York: Simon & Schuster, 1993.

Dallmayer, Dorinda G., ed., in association with Daniel S. Papp. *The Strategic Defense Initiative: New Perspectives on Deterrence.* Boulder, CO: Westview Press, 1986.

Darman, Richard G. *Who's In Control? Polar Politics and the Sensible Center.* New York: Simon & Schuster, 1996.

Davis, Vincent. "The Reagan Defense Program: Decision Making, Decision Makers and Some of the Results." In *The Reagan Defense Program: An Interim Assessment,* edited by Stephen J. Cimbala. Wilmington, DE: Scholarly Resources, 1984.

Deaver, Michael K. *Behind the Scenes.* New York: William Morrow, 1987.

Dobrynin, Anatoly. *In Confidence: Moscow's Ambassador to America's Six Cold War Presidents (1962–1986).* New York: Times Books, 1995.

Doder, Dusko, and Louise Branscom. *Gorbachev.* New York: Viking Press, 1990.

Draper, Theodore. *Present History: On Nuclear War, Detente and Other Controversies.* New York: Random House, 1985.

———. *A Very Thin Line: The Iran-Contra Affairs.* New York: Hill and Wang, 1991.

Drell, Sidney D., Philip J. Farley, and David Holloway. *The Reagan Strategic Defense Initiative: A Technical, Political and Arms Control Assessment.* Cambridge, MA: Ballinger Publishing, 1985.

Drew, Elizabeth. *Portrait of an Election: The 1980 Presidential Campaign.* New York: Simon & Schuster, 1981.

Dugger, Ronnie. *On Reagan: The Man and His Presidency.* New York: McGraw-Hill, 1983.

Duignan, Peter, ed. *The United States in the 1980s.* Palo Alto, CA: Hoover Institution, Stanford University, 1980.

Edwards, Anne. *Early Reagan.* New York: Morrow, 1987.

Erickson, Paul D. *Reagan Speaks: The Making of an American Myth.* New York: New York University Press, 1985.

Evans, Rowland, and Robert Novak. *The Reagan Revolution.* New York: E.P. Dutton, 1981.

Faber, Harold, ed. *The Road to the White House: The Story of the 1964 Election.* By the Staff of the *New York Times.* New York: McGraw-Hill, 1965.

Felsenthal, Carol. *The Sweetheart of the Silent Majority: A Biography of Phyllis Schlafly.* New York: Doubleday, 1981.

Firth, Noel E., and James H. Noren. *Soviet Defense Spending: A History of CIA Estimates, 1950–1990.* Texas: Texas A&M Press, 1998.

FitzGerald, Frances. "The American Millennium." In *Estrangement,* edited by Sanford J. Ungar. New York: Oxford University Press, 1985.

Fitzwater, Marlin. *Call the Briefing! Reagan and Bush, Sam and Helen: A Decade with Presidents and the Press.* New York: Times Books, 1995.

Freedman, Lawrence. *The Evolution of Nuclear Strategy.* New York: St. Martin's Press, 1989.

———. *The Price of Peace: Living with the Nuclear Dilemma.* New York: Henry Holt, 1986.

Gallup, George, Jr. *The Gallup Poll.* Vols. 1980–88. Wilmington, DE: Scholarly Resources.

Garthoff, Raymond L. *The Great Transition: American-Soviet Relations and the End of the Cold War.* Washington, D.C.: The Brookings Institution, 1994.

———. *Policy versus the Law: The Reinterpretation of the ABM Treaty.* Washington, D.C.: The Brookings Institution, 1987.

Gates, Robert M. *From the Shadows: The Ultimate Insider's Story of Five Presidents and How They Won the Cold War.* New York: Simon & Schuster, 1996.

Gelb, Leslie H. "Domestic Change and National Security Policy." In *The Next Phase in Foreign Policy,* edited by Henry Owen. Washington, D.C.: The Brookings Institution, 1973.

Germond, Jack W., and Jules Witcover. *Blue Smoke and Mirrors: How Reagan Won and Why Carter Lost the Election of 1980.* New York: Viking Press, 1981.

Glass, Matthew. *Citizens Against the MX: Public Languages in the Nuclear Age.* Chicago: University of Illinois Press, 1993.

Goldwater, Barry M. *The Conscience of a Conservative.* Shepherdsville, KY: Victor Publishing, 1960.

———. *Why Not Victory? A Fresh Look at American Foreign Policy.* New York: McGraw-Hill, 1962.

Gorbachev, Mikhail. *The Challenges of Our Time.* New York: International Publishers, 1986.

———. *Memoirs.* New York: Doubleday, 1995.

———. *Reykjavik: Results and Lessons.* Madison, CT: Sphinx Press, 1987.

———. *Socialism, Peace and Democracy.* Atlantic Highlands, NJ: Zwan Publications, 1987.

Graham, Lt. Gen. Daniel O. *High Frontier: A New National Strategy.* Washington, D.C.: High Frontier, 1982.

Graham, Lt. Gen. Daniel O., and Gregory A. Fossedal. *A Defense that Defends.* Old Greenwich, CT: Devin-Adair Publishers, 1983.

Green, Mark, and Gail MacColl. *Reagan's Reign of Error.* New York: Pantheon Books, 1987.

Gutman, Roy. *Banana Diplomacy: The Making of American Policy in Nicaragua, 1981–1987.* New York: Simon & Schuster, 1988.

Haig, Alexander. *Caveat: Realism, Reagan and Foreign Policy.* New York: Macmillan, 1984.

Haldeman, H. R. *The Haldeman Diaries: Inside the Nixon White House.* New York: G.P. Putnam and Sons, 1994.

Haley, P. Edward, and Jack Merrit, eds. *The Strategic Defense Initiative: Folly or Future?* Boulder, CO: Westview Press, 1986.

Hammond, Paul Y. "NSC-68: Prologue to Rearmament." In *Strategy, Politics and Defense Budgets,* by Warner R. Schilling, Paul Y. Hammond and Glenn Snyder. New York: Columbia University Press, 1962.

Hannaford, Peter. *The Reagans: A Political Portrait.* New York: Coward-McCann, 1983.

Hartmann, Frederick H. *Naval Renaissance: The U.S. Navy in the 1980s.* Annapolis, MD: Naval Institute Press, 1990.

Haug, James C., ed. *The Strategic Defense Initiative in Perspective.* Boulder, CO: Social Science Monographs, 1987.

Herken, Gregg. *Cardinal Choices: Presidential Science Advising from the Atomic Bomb to SDI.* New York: Oxford University Press, 1992.

Hertsgaard, Mark. *On Bended Knee: The Press and the Reagan Presidency.* New York: Farrar, Straus, and Giroux, 1988.

Hinckley, Ronald H. *People, Polls and Policy-makers: American Public Opinion and National Security.* New York: Lexington Books, 1992.

Hobbs, Charles D. *Reagan's Call to Action.* Nashville, TN: T. Nelson, 1976.

Hofstadter, Richard. *The Paranoid Style in American Politics and Other Essays.* New York: Vintage Books, 1967.

Hutchings, Robert L. *American Diplomacy and the End of the Cold War.* Washington, D.C.: Woodrow Wilson Center Press; Baltimore, MD: Johns Hopkins University Press, 1997.

Hyland, William. *Mortal Rivals: Superpower Relations from Nixon to Reagan.* New York: Random House, 1987.

Ignatius, David. "Reagan's Foreign Policy and the Rejection of Diplomacy." In *The Reagan Legacy,* edited by Sidney Blumenthal and Thomas Byrne Edsall. New York: Pantheon Books, 1988.

Johnson, Haynes. *Sleepwalking Through History: America in the Reagan Years.* New York: W.W. Norton, 1991.

Jones, Joseph M. *The Fifteen Weeks.* New York: Viking Press, 1955.

Kelly, Kitty. *Nancy Reagan: The Unauthorized Biography.* New York: Simon & Schuster, 1991.

Kissinger, Henry. *Diplomacy.* New York: Simon & Schuster, 1994.

Kornbluh, Peter, and Malcolm Byrne, eds. *The Iran-Contra Scandal: The Declassified History.* New York: New Press, 1993.

Kwitney, Jonathan. *The Man of the Century: The Life and Times of Pope John Paul II.* New York: Henry Holt, 1997.

Lees, John D., and Michael Turner, eds. *Reagan's First Four Years.* Manchester, England: Manchester University Press, 1988.

Lehman, John. *Command of the Seas.* New York: Charles Scribner and Sons, 1988.

LeMay, Curtis. *America Is in Danger.* New York: Funk and Wagnalls, 1968.

Lewis, Joseph. *What Makes Reagan Run? A Political Profile.* New York: McGraw-Hill, 1968.

Lieb, Michael. *The Children of Ezekiel.* Durham, NC: Duke University Press, 1998.

Linenthal, Edward Tabor. *Symbolic Defense: The Cultural Significance of the Strategic Defense Initiative.* Urbana, IL: University of Illinois Press, 1989.

Matlock, Jack. *Autopsy on an Empire: The American Ambassador's Account of the Collapse of the Soviet Union.* New York: Random House, 1995.

May, Ernest R. *American Cold War Strategy: Interpreting NSC-68.* New York: St. Martin's Press, 1993.

Mayer, Jane, and Doyle McManus. *Landslide: The Unmaking of the President, 1984–1988.* Boston: Houghton Mifflin, 1988.

McFarlane, Robert C., with Zofia Smardz. *Special Trust.* New York: Cadell and Davies, 1994.

Menges, Constantine C. *Inside the National Security Council: The True Story of the Making and Unmaking of Reagan's Foreign Policy.* New York: Simon & Schuster, 1988.

Miles, Michael M. *The Odyssey of the American Right.* New York: Oxford University Press, 1980.

Miller, Steven E., and Stephen Van Evera, eds. *The Star Wars Controversy.* Princeton, NJ: Princeton University Press, 1986.

Newhouse, John. *War and Peace in the Nuclear Age.* New York: Alfred A. Knopf, 1989.

Nitze, Paul, with Ann M. Smith and Steven L. Rearden. *From Hiroshima to Glasnost: At the Center of Decision—a Memoir.* New York: Grove Weidenfeld, 1989.

Nolan, Janne E. *Guardians of the Arsenal: The Politics of Nuclear Strategy.* New York: Basic Books, 1989.

Noonan, Peggy. *What I Saw at the Revolution: Political Life in the Reagan Era.* New York: Random House, 1990.

Oberdorfer, Don. *The Turn: From the Cold War to a New Era: The United States and the Soviet Union, 1983–1990.* New York: Poseidon Press, 1991.

Oliver, James K., and James A. Nathan, "The Reagan Defense Program: Concepts, Continuity and Change." In *The Reagan Defense Program: An Interim Assessment,* edited by Stephen J. Cimbala. Wilmington, DE: Scholarly Resources, 1984.

Olivier, Laurence. *On Acting.* New York: Simon & Schuster, 1986.

O'Neill, Tip, with William Novak. *Man of the House: The Life and Times of Speaker Tip O'Neill.* New York: Random House, 1987.

Owen, Henry, ed. *The Next Phase in Foreign Policy.* Washington, D.C.: The Brookings Institution, 1973.

Oye, Kenneth A., Robert J. Lieber, and Donald Rothschild, eds. *Eagle Resurgent?* Boston: Little, Brown, 1987.

Parmet, Herbert. *George Bush: The Life of a Lone Star Yankee.* New York: Scribner, 1997.

Patterson, James T. *Mr. Republican: A Biography of Robert A. Taft.* Boston: Houghton Mifflin, 1972.

Pemberton, William E. *Exit with Honor: The Life and Presidency of Ronald Reagan.* Armonk, NY: M.E. Sharpe, 1997.

Pierard, Richard V., and Robert D. Linder. *Civil Religion and the Presidency.* Grand Rapids, MI: Academie Books, 1988.

Powell, Colin, with Joseph E. Persico. *My American Journey.* New York: Random House, 1995.

Pratt, Erik K. *Selling Strategic Defense: Interests, Ideologies and the Arms Race.* Boulder, CO: Lynne Rienner Publishers, 1990.

Pressler, Larry. *Star Wars: The Strategic Defense Initiative Debates in Congress.* New York: Praeger, 1986.

Pringle, Peter. *SIOP.* New York: Norton, 1983.

Reagan, Maureen. *First Father, First Daughter.* Boston: Little, Brown, 1989.

Reagan, Michael. *On the Outside Looking In.* New York: Kensington Publishing, 1988.

Reagan, Nancy, with William Novak. *My Turn.* New York: Random House, 1989.

Reagan, Ronald. *An American Life.* New York: Simon & Schuster, 1990.

———. *Speaking My Mind.* New York: Simon & Schuster, 1989.

Reagan, Ronald, with Richard G. Hubler. *Where's the Rest of Me?* New York: Duell, Sloan and Pearce, 1965.

Rearden, Steven L. *The Evolution of American Strategic Doctrine: Paul H. Nitze and the Soviet Challenge.* Boulder, CO: Westview Press; [Washington, D.C.] Foreign Policy Institute, SAIS, Johns Hopkins University, 1984.

Regan, Donald. *For the Record.* New York: Harcourt Brace Jovanovich, 1988.

Remnick, David. *Lenin's Tomb: The Last Days of the Soviet Empire.* New York: Vintage Books, 1994.

Rielly, John E., ed. *American Public Opinion and U.S. Foreign Policy, 1987.* Chicago: Chicago Council on Foreign Relations, 1987.

Rollins, Ed. *Bare Knuckles and Back Rooms.* New York: Broadway Books, 1996.

Romm, Joseph J. "The Problems with the Strategic Defense Initiative." In *The Arms Race in the Era of Star Wars,* edited by David Carlton and Carlo Schaerf. New York: St. Martin's Press, 1988.

Sakharov, Andrei. *Moscow and Beyond.* New York: Alfred A. Knopf, 1991.

Sanders, Jerry W. *Peddlers of Crisis: The Committee on the Present Danger and the Politics of Containment.* Boston: South End Press, 1983.

Scheer, Robert. *With Enough Shovels: Reagan, Bush and Nuclear War.* New York: Random House, 1982.

Schell, Jonathan. *The Fate of the Earth.* New York: Alfred A. Knopf, 1982.

Schieffer, Bob, and Gary Paul Gates. *The Acting President.* New York: E.P. Dutton, 1989.

Schilling, Warner R., Paul Y. Hammond and Glenn Snyder. *Strategy, Politics and Defense Budgets.* New York: Columbia University Press, 1962.

Schlafly, Phyllis. *A Choice Not an Echo.* Alton, IL: Pere Marquette Press, 1964.

Schlafly, Phyllis, and Chester Ward. *Ambush at Vladivostock.* Alton, IL: Pere Marquette Press, 1976.

———. *The Betrayers.* Alton, IL: Pere Marquette Press, 1968.

———. *The Gravediggers.* Alton, IL: Pere Marquette Press, 1964.

———. *Kissinger on the Couch.* New Rochelle, NY: Arlington House Publishers, 1975.

———. *Strike from Space.* Alton, IL: Pere Marquette Press, 1965.

Scoville, Herbert, Jr. *MX: Prescription for Disaster.* Cambridge, MA: MIT Press, 1981.

Shevardnadze, Eduard. *The Future Belongs to Freedom.* New York: Free Press, 1991.

Shultz, George. *Turmoil and Triumph.* New York: Charles Scribner's Sons, 1993.

Smith, Geoffrey. *Reagan and Thatcher.* New York: W.W. Norton, 1991.

Smith, Hedrick. *The Power Game: How Washington Works.* New York: Random House, 1988.

Smith, Hedrick, Adam Clymer, Leonard Silk, Robert Lindsey, and Richard Burt. *Reagan, the Man, the President.* New York: Macmillan, 1980.

Snow, Donald. "Ballistic Missile Defense: The Strategic Defense Initiative." In *The Reagan Defense Program: An Interim Assessment,* edited by Stephen J. Cimbala. Wilmington, DE: Scholarly Resources, 1984.

Speakes, Larry, with Robert Pack. *Speaking Out: The Reagan Presidency from Inside the White House.* New York: Scribners, 1988.

Steinberg, Gerald M., ed. *Lost in Space.* Lexington, MA: Lexington Books, 1988.

Stockman, David. *The Triumph of Politics: How the Reagan Revolution Failed.* New York: Harper and Row, 1986.

Strober, Deborah Hart, and Gerald S. Strober. *Reagan: The Man and His Presidency.* Boston: Houghton Mifflin, 1998.

Taft, Robert A. *A Foreign Policy for Americans.* Garden City, NY: Doubleday, 1951.

Talbott, Strobe. *Deadly Gambits: The Reagan Administration and the Stalemate in Nuclear Arms Control.* New York: Knopf, 1984.

———. *Master of the Game: Paul Nitze and the Nuclear Peace.* New York: Knopf, 1988.

———. *The Russians and Reagan.* New York: Vintage Books, 1984.

Teller, Edward. *Better a Shield than a Sword: Perspectives on Defense and Technology.* New York: Free Press, 1987.

———. *The Legacy of Hiroshima.* Garden City, NY: Doubleday, 1962.

———. "Technology: The Imbalance of Power." In *The United States in the 1980s,* edited by Peter Duigan. Palo Alto, CA: Hoover Institution, Stanford University, 1980.

Thompson, Kenneth W., ed. *Leadership in the Reagan Presidency.* New York: Madison Books, 1992.

———. *Foreign Policy in the Reagan Presidency: Nine Intimate Perspectives.* Charlottesville, VA: University Press of America, 1993.

Timberg, Robert. *The Nightingale's Song.* New York: Simon & Schuster, 1995.

Tirman, John, ed. *Empty Promise: The Growing Case Against Star Wars.* The Union of Concerned Scientists. Boston: Beacon Press, 1986.

Tower Commission Report. New York: Bantam Books and Times Books, February 1987.

Ungar, Sanford J., ed. *Estrangement.* New York: Oxford University Press, 1985.

Van Cleave, William R., and W. Scott Thompson. *Strategic Options for the Early Eighties: What Can Be Done?* New York: National Strategic Information Center, 1978.

Viguerie, Richard A. *The New Right: We're Ready to Lead.* Falls Church, VA: Viguerie, 1981.

Von Damm, Helene. *At Reagan's Side.* New York: Doubleday, 1989.

Waller, Douglas C. *Congress and the Nuclear Freeze.* Amherst, MA: University of Massachusetts Press, 1987.

Waller, Douglas C., James T. Bruce III, and Douglas M. Cook. *The Strategic Defense Initiative: Progress and Challenges.* Claremont, CA: Regina Books, 1987.

Weinberger, Caspar. *Fighting for Peace: Seven Critical Years in the Pentagon.* New York: Warner Books, 1990.

Whelan, Joseph G. *Soviet Diplomacy and Negotiating Behavior: 1988–90.* Special Studies on Foreign Affairs Issues, vol. III. Washington, D.C.: Committee on Foreign Affairs, House of Representatives, April 1991.
Wills, Garry. *Reagan's America: Innocents at Home.* New York: Doubleday, 1987.
Witcover, Jules. *Marathon: The Pursuit of the Presidency, 1972–1976.* New York: Viking Press, 1977.
Woodward, Bob. *Veil: The Secret Wars of the CIA, 1981–1987.* New York: Simon & Schuster, 1987.
Wymbs, Norman E. *Ronald Reagan's Crusade.* Boca Raton, FL: Skyline Publications, 1997.

ARTICLES

Allen, Richard V. "The Man Who Changed the Game Plan." *The National Interest* 44, (summer 1996): 60–65.
Ball, George W. "The War for Star Wars." *The New York Review of Books,* April 11, 1985.
Barnes, Fred. "Brilliant Pebble." *The New Republic,* April 1, 1991.
———. "Pebbles Go Bam-Bam." *The New Republic,* April 17, 1989.
Brower, Brock. "Semper Fi." *The New York Times Magazine,* January 22, 1989.
Brzezinski, Zbigniew, Robert Jastrow, and Max Kampelman. "Defense in Space Is Not Star Wars." *The New York Times Magazine,* January 27, 1985.
Bundy, McGeorge, George Kennan, Robert S. McNamara, and Gerard Smith. "The President's Choice: Star Wars or Arms Control." *Foreign Affairs,* 63, no. 2 (winter 1984–85).
Bunn, Matthew. "The ABM Talks: The More Things Change . . ." *Arms Control Today,* September 1992.
———. "Early SDI: Deploying a Disaster." *Arms Control Today,* March 1987.
Denny, Jeffrey. "Star Struck." *Common Cause Magazine,* March/April 1991.
Deudney, Daniel, and G. John Ikenberry. "Who Won the Cold War?" *Foreign Policy* 87 (summer 1992).
Draper, Theodore. "Dear Mr. Weinberger." *The New York Review of Books,* November 4, 1982.
"Early Dismantlement of the ABM Treaty." *Arms Control Today,* March 1987.
Fascell, Dante B. "Congress and Arms Control." *Foreign Affairs* 65, no. 4 (spring 1987).
FitzGerald, Frances. "Annals of Justice: Iran-contra." *The New Yorker,* October 16, 1989.
———. "Death of a Salesman." *Rolling Stone,* February 25, 1988.
———. "Memoirs of the Reagan Era." *The New Yorker,* January 16, 1989.
Gaddis, John Lewis, and Paul H. Nitze. "NSC-68 and the Soviet Threat Reconsidered." *International Security* 4, no. 4 (spring 1980).
Gelb, Leslie H. "The Mind of the President." *The New York Times Magazine,* October 6, 1985.
Graham, Lt. Gen. Daniel O. "Toward a New U.S. Strategy: Bold Strokes Rather than Increments." *Strategic Review,* spring 1981.
Gronlund, Lisbeth. "ABM: Just Kicking the Can." *Bulletin of the Atomic Scientists,* January/February 1988.
Gronlund, Lisbeth, George Lewis, Theodore Postol, and David Wright. "Highly Capable Theater Missile Defense and the ABM Treaty." *Arms Control Today,* April 1994.
Harak, Simon G. "One Nation Under God: The Soteriology of SDI." *Journal of the American Academy of Religion* LVI/3 (fall 1988).
Herken, Gregg. "The Earthly Origins of Star Wars." *Bulletin of the Atomic Scientists,* October 1987.
Hersh, Seymour. "Missile Wars." *The New Yorker,* September 26, 1994.
Johnson, Robert H. "Periods of Peril." *Foreign Affairs* 61 (spring 1983).
Keeny, Spurgeon M., Jr. "The Theater Missile Defense Threat to U.S. Security." *Arms Control Today,* September 1994.
Korda, Michael. "Prompting the President." *The New Yorker,* October 6, 1997.
Larabee, F. Stephen, and Allen Lynch. "Gorbachev: The Road to Reykjavik." *Foreign Policy* 65 (winter 1986–87).
Lemann, Nicholas. "The Peacetime War." *The Atlantic Monthly,* October 1984.
Lewis, George N., Theodore A. Postol, and John Pike. "Why National Missile Defenses Won't Work." *Scientific American,* August 1999.
Maass, Peter. "Get Ready, Here Comes the Exoatmospheric Kill Vehicle." *The New York Times Magazine,* September 26, 1999.
MacDonald, Bruce W. "Falling Star: SDI's Troubled Seventh Year." *Arms Control Today,* September 1990.
———. "SDI—Lost in Space." *Arms Control Today,* September 1989.
MacEachin, Douglas J. "CIA Assessments of the Soviet Union: The Record Versus the Charges." *Studies in Intelligence* 1, no. 1 (1997).
McFarlane, Robert C. "Effective Strategic Policy." *Foreign Affairs* 67, no. 1 (fall 1988).
Mandelbaum, Michael, and Strobe Talbott. "Reykjavik and Beyond." *Foreign Affairs* 65, no. 3 (winter 1986–87).
Mendelsohn, Jack, and John B. Rhinelander. "Shooting Down the ABM Treaty." *Arms Control Today,* September 1994.
"A New Threat to the ABM Treaty: The Administration's TMD Proposal." A symposium in *Arms Control Today,* January/February 1994.
Newhouse, John. "The Abolitionist." *The New Yorker,* January 2, 1989.
———. "The Abolitionist II." *The New Yorker,* January 9, 1989.
———. "A Reporter in Washington." *The New Yorker,* December 9, 1985.
Nitze, Paul H. "Assuring Strategic Stability in an Era of Detente." *Foreign Affairs* 54, no. 2 (January 1976).
———. "Deterring Our Deterrent." *Foreign Policy* 25 (winter 1976–77).
Nye, Joseph S., Jr. "Farewell to Arms Control?" *Foreign Affairs* 65, no. 1 (fall 1986).

Pike, John. "Theater Missile Defense Programs: Status and Prospects." *Arms Control Today,* September 1992.
Pipes, Richard. "Team B, the Reality Behind the Myth." *Commentary,* October 1986.
———. "Why the Soviets Think They Can Fight and Win a Nuclear War." *Commentary,* July 1977.
Reeves, Richard. "America's Choice: What It Means." *The New York Times Magazine,* November 4, 1984.
Rielly, John E. "America's State of Mind." *Foreign Policy* 66 (spring 1987).
Romm, Joseph J. "Pseudo-Science and SDI." *Arms Control Today* 19, no. 8 (October 1989).
Rosenberg, Tina. "The Authorized Version." *The Atlantic Monthly,* February 1986.
Schlesinger, James. "Reykjavik and Revelations: A Turn of the Tide?" *Foreign Affairs* 65, no. 2: *America and the World* (1986).
Scowcroft, Brent, John Deutch, and R. James Woolsey. "A Way Out of Reykjavik." *The New York Times Magazine,* January 25, 1987.
Smith, Gerard C. "Two Decades Later: The ABM Treaty in a Changed World." *Arms Control Today,* May 1992.
Smith, Hedrick. "How Many Billions for Defense?" *The New York Times Magazine,* November 1, 1981.
Svec, Milan. "Removing Gorbachev's Edge." *Foreign Policy* 69 (winter 1987–88).
Tammen, Ronald, James T. Bruce, and Bruce MacDonald. "Star Wars After Five Years: The Decisive Point." *Arms Control Today,* July/August 1988.
Wallop, Malcolm. "Opportunities and Imperatives of Ballistic Missile Defense." *Strategic Review,* fall 1979.
Warnke, Paul. "Apes on a Treadmill." *Foreign Policy* 18 (spring 1975).
Wells, Samuel F. "Sounding the Tocsin: NSC-68 and the Soviet Threat." *International Security* 4, no. 2 (fall 1979).
White, Theodore H. "Weinberger on the Ramparts." *The New York Times Magazine,* February 6, 1983.
Woolsey, R. James. "The Politics of Vulnerability: 1980–1983." In *The Nuclear Controversy,* edited by William P. Bundy. New York: New American Library, 1985.
Worden, Simon P. "What Can We Do? When Can We Do It?" *The National Review,* December 31, 1986.
Worden, Simon P., and Bruce P. Jackson. "Space, Power and Strategy." *The National Interest,* fall 1987.

FILM

"Reagan," in *The American Experience* series, produced by Adriana Bosch, narrated by David McCullough. WNET, February 23 and 24, 1998.
"The Reagan Legacy" Part II: "Star Wars." Produced by Nick Gold, narrated by Garrick Utley. The Discovery Channel, premiered November 4, 1996.
"The Reagans." *60 Minutes.* January 15, 1989. CBS News transcript.

DISSERTATION

Graham, Thomas Wallace. "The Politics of Failure: Strategic Nuclear Arms Control, Public Opinion and Domestic Politics in the United States—1945–1980." Ph.D. diss., Massachusetts Institute of Technology, June 1989.

U.S. CONGRESSIONAL DOCUMENTS

Congressional Digest. "The President's Strategic Defense Initiative." March 1985, pp. 70–71.
Congressional Quarterly Weekly Report, 38, no. 29, July 19, 1980, p. 2049.
Congressional Quarterly Weekly Report, October 27, 1984, pp. 2828–38.
Congressional Record. "The Reykjavik Summit: What Did We Really Agree To?" Floor speech by Senator Nunn. 99th Cong., 2d sess., October 17, 1986.
Congressional Record. 100th Cong., 1st sess., March 11, 12 and 13, 1987.
U.S. Congress. *Iran-Contra Investigation: Joint Hearings Before the House Select Committee to Investigate Covert Arms Transfers with Iran and the Senate Select Committee on Secret Military Assistance to Iran and the Nicaraguan Opposition.* Testimony of Donald T. Regan and Caspar Weinberger. 100th Cong., 1st sess., July 30, 31 and August 3, 1987.
U.S. Congress. *Report of the Congressional Committees Investigation of the Iran-Contra Affair. Report to Senate Select Committee on Secret Military Assistance to Iran and the Nicaraguan Opposition, House of Representatives Select Committee to Investigate Covert Arms Transactions with Iran.* 100th Cong., 1st sess., November 1987. S. Report No. 100–216, H. Report No. 100–433.
U.S. Congress. *Restructuring of the Strategic Defense Initiative (SDI) Program: Joint Hearing Before the Senate Committee on Armed Services and the House Committee on Armed Services.* 100th Cong., 2d sess., October 6, 1988.
U.S. House of Representatives. *Process and Implications of the Iceland Summit: Hearings Before the Defense Policy Panel, Committee on Armed Services.* 99th Cong., 2d sess., November/December 1986.
U.S. House of Representatives. *Reaction to the Reykjavik Proposals: Hearing Before the Subcommittee on Arms Control, International Security and Science of the Committee on Foreign Affairs.* 100th Cong., 1st sess., January 29, 1987.
U.S. House of Representatives. *Reykjavik and American Security. Report of the Defense Policy Panel, Committee on Armed Services.* 99th Cong., 2d sess., February 1987.
U.S. House of Representatives. *The Reykjavik Process: Preparation for and Conduct of the Iceland Summit and Its Implica-*

tions for Arms Control Policy. Report of the Defense Policy Panel of the Committee on Armed Services. 99th Cong., 2d sess., January 1987.

U.S. House of Representatives. *The Reykjavik Talks: Promise or Peril. Report of the Subcommittee on Arms Control, International Security and Science of the Committee on Foreign Affairs.* 100th Cong., 1st sess., January 1987.

U.S. House of Representatives Committee on Foreign Affairs. *The ABM Treaty Interpretation Dispute: Hearings Before the Subcommittee on Arms Control, International Security and Science.* 99th Cong., 1st sess., October 22, 1985.

U.S. Senate. *The ABM Treaty and the Constitution: Joint Hearings Before the Committee on Foreign Relations and the Committee on the Judiciary.* 100th Cong., 1st sess., March 11, 26 and April 29, 1987.

U.S. Senate. *The ABM Treaty Interpretation Resolution. Report of the Committee on Foreign Relations.* 100th Cong., 1st sess., 1987.

U.S. Senate. *Nomination of Robert M. Gates to Be Director of Central Intelligence. Report of the Select Committee on Intelligence.* 102d Cong., 1st sess., October 24, 1991.

U.S. Senate. *Strategic Defense Initiative: Hearings Before the Subcommittee on Strategic and Theater Nuclear Forces of the Armed Services Committee,* 99th Cong., 1st sess., November 21, 1986.

U.S. Senate Committee on the Armed Services. *Department of Defense Authorization for Appropriations for Fiscal Year 1985. Part 6, Strategic Defense Initiative.* 98th Cong., 2d sess., March 8 and 22; April 24, 1984.

U.S. Senate Committee on the Armed Services. *Department of Defense Authorization for Appropriations for Fiscal Year 1986. Strategic and Theater Nuclear Forces.* 99th Cong., 1st sess., February–March 1985.

U.S. Senate Foreign Relations Committee. *Strategic Defense and Anti-Satellite Weapons.* 98th Cong., 2d sess., April 25, 1984.

STAFF REPORTS TO SENATOR J. BENNETT JOHNSTON ET. AL. ON SDI (UNPUBLISHED). COURTESY OF THE OFFICE OF SENATOR JOHNSTON

Bruce, James T., Bruce W. MacDonald and Ronald L. Tammen. "Star Wars at the Crossroads: The Strategic Defense Initiative After Five Years." Staff report submitted to Senator J. Bennett Johnston, Senator Dale Bumpers and Senator William Proxmire, June 12, 1988.

Waller, Douglas C., James T. Bruce and Douglas Cook. "SDI: Progress and Challenges." Staff report submitted to Senator William Proxmire, Senator J. Bennett Johnston and Senator Lawton Chiles, March 17, 1986.

Waller, Douglas C., and James T. Bruce. "SDI: Progress and Challenges, Part Two." Staff report submitted to Senator William Proxmire and Senator J. Bennett Johnston, March 19, 1987.

OTHER U.S. GOVERNMENT DOCUMENTS

Abrahamson, Lt. Gen. James A. "End of Tour." Memorandum for the Deputy Secretary of Defense. February 9, 1989. (unpublished)

Carter, Jimmy. *Public Papers of the Presidents of the United States: Jimmy Carter, 1979.* Vol. 2. Washington, D.C.: GPO.

Graham, Daniel O. Letter to Alexander Haig, Jr. July 21, 1981. Courtesy of the office of Senator J. Bennett Johnston.

Graham, Daniel O. Letters to Caspar Weinberger. February 11, March 17, March 31, April 13, April 14, November 5, 1982. Courtesy of the office of Senator J. Bennett Johnston.

Keyworth, George. Draft of insert to Ronald Reagan's March 23, 1983, speech with Reagan's handwritten changes. Courtesy of Martin Anderson.

Reagan, Ronald. *Public Papers of the Presidents of the United States: Ronald Reagan, 1980–88.* Washington, D.C.: GPO.

Reynolds, Herbert. "Point Paper on Global Ballistic Missile Defense." Office of the Under Secretary of Defense. September 28, 1981. (unpublished) Courtesy of the office of Senator J. Bennett Johnston.

U.S. Department of the Air Force. "Technical Evaluation, Unsolicited Proposal, SRI No. ESU 81-171, Global Ballistic Missile Defense Examination." January 1982. (unpublished) Courtesy of the office of Senator J. Bennett Johnston.

U.S. Department of Defense. *Operational Testing and Evaluation.* Annual report by the Director. February 1998. (unpublished)

Walsh, Lawrence M. "Final Report of the Independent Counsel for Iran/Contra Matters." Vols. I and II. Submitted to the U.S. Court of Appeals for the District of Columbia Circuit. August 4, 1993.

Weinberger, Caspar. Letter to Daniel O. Graham. November 24, 1982. Courtesy of the office of Senator J. Bennett Johnston.

MISCELLANEOUS

Anderson, Martin. "Policy Memorandum No. 3: Foreign Policy and National Security." Reagan for President Campaign. Los Angeles, August 1979. (unpublished)

Lewis, George N. "Chronology of Missile Defense Tests." (unpublished) Security Studies Program, Massachusetts Institute of Technology.

Wirthlin, Richard. Selected polls by Decision/Making/Information of the Wirthlin Group.

AUTHOR'S INTERVIEWS

Amyn Aga Khan, 10/25/97
Morton Abromowitz, 7/11/96
Kenneth Adelman, 6/22/90
Richard V. Allen, 6/4/98; 6/5/98
Martin Anderson, 5/4/92
Les Aspin, 5/23/93, 4/95
Robert G. Bell, 6/28/90
Captain Linton Brooks, 6/30/98
Harold Brown, 11/5/90
James T. Bruce III, 6/26/90
Zbigniew Brzezinski, 8/24/93; 8/27/98
Angelo Codevilla, 5/4/92
Richard G. Darman, 4/6/95
Michael K. Deaver, 12/5/95
Thomas S. Foley, 4/3/95
Raymond L. Garthoff, 9/27/99
Robert S. Gates, 7/16/96
Leslie H. Gelb, 7/2/90; 6/28/93; 11/11/94
Daniel O. Graham, 6/29/90
Frank Gaffney, 6/27/90
Fred Iklé, 6/28/90
Bruce P. Jackson, 10/23/90
Morton Janklow, 6/2/99
Henry Kissinger, 2/12/97
Robert C. McFarlane, 6/20/90; 6/26/90
Rodney B. McDaniel, 4/5/95
Edwin Meese III, 10/25/90
Paul H. Nitze, 6/21/90; 8/14/90
Richard Perle, 10/22/90; 10/23/90
Pavel Podvig, 8/31/99
Theodore Postol, 6/30/98
Walter Raymond, 4/4/95
Thomas C. Reed, 6/23/98; 10/14/98
James Schlesinger, 2/15/91
John Sears, 10/25/90
James Timby, 4/5/95
Paul Warnke, 6/27/90
James D. Watkins, 4/6/95
Caspar Weinberger, 9/11/90
Richard Wirthlin, 4/4/95
Simon P. Wordon, 10/23/90

Acknowledgments

WHILE I WAS WRITING this book, my thanks have continually gone to the Washington journalists who had to make sense out of Reagan administration policies on a daily deadline. It's impossible to name all of those whose reporting has contributed to this book, but some stand out. One of them is R. Jeffrey Smith of the *Washington Post,* who understood the issues, many of them buried under layers of official deception, surrounding the reinterpretation of the ABM Treaty and the uses made of the SDI program. The others are better known to readers as they have also written the first histories of the period: Lou Cannon of the *Washington Post,* who followed Reagan since the time of his governorship in California; Robert Scheer of the *Los Angeles Times,* who provided the first insights into the strategic policies of the Reagan administration; William Broad of the *New York Times,* who reported on the SDI program from its inception; and Don Oberdorfer of the *Washington Post,* who wrote on U.S.-Soviet relations at the end of the Cold War.

My education in the arms control policies of the Reagan administration came largely from the work of two other reporters: John Newhouse, then of *The New Yorker,* and Strobe Talbott, then of *Time,* whose books *Deadly Gambits* and *Master of the Game* were my constant companions and reference sources.

My lifeline in terms of U.S.-Soviet relations during the Reagan administration was Raymond Garthoff's book *The Great Transition.*

Those who helped me in understanding the interplay between politics, psychology and nuclear weapons policies include Lawrence Freedman, Janne Nolan and Leslie Gelb.

I am grateful to Michael and Alice Arlen, Mark Danner, Erhard Dortmund, Raymond Garthoff, Susan Harding, Michael Janeway, Robert Lescher, Ronald Steel, Jim Sterba and David Wright for reading all, or parts, of my manuscript and giving me the benefit of their wisdom.

Michael Train, who in the latter stages of this enterprise became my researcher, deserves credit, along with my thanks, for his careful checking of my sources and quotes.

My enormous gratitude goes to Alice Mayhew, Roger Labrie and the many others at Simon & Schuster who worked on this book. Alice is justly famous for her ability to turn a wandering piece of prose into a compelling narrative. To the extent that my narrative holds the reader, it is her doing. Roger, for reasons that may have to do with the stars, has a background in arms control, so he was able to help me not only with good editorial advice but with the technicalities of the subject.

Needless to say, any mistakes of fact or interpretation are my own.

Finally, I thank my husband, Jim Sterba, who not only provided emotional and intellectual support but forced me into the electronic age. I could not have done this book without him. How can I count the ways?

INDEX